Contents

*The original year of publication and page numbers are shown
for each full paper.

Selections from
Human Factors
and Ergonomics
Society
Annual
Meetings
1980-1993

HUMAN FACTORS PERSPECTIVES ON
WARNINGS

Edited by
Kenneth R. Laughery, Sr.
Michael S. Wogalter
and
Stephen L. Young

Published by
the Human Factors
and Ergonomics
Society

The HFES annual meeting proceedings are indexed or abstracted in the following publications or services: Applied Mechanics Reviews, Engineering Index Annual, EI Monthly, EI Bio-engineering Abstracts, EI Energy Abstracts, Ergonomics Abstracts, ISI Index to Scientific & Technical Proceedings, and International Aerospace Abstracts. This publication is also available on microfilm from University Microfilms International, 300 N. Zeeb Rd., Department P.R., Ann Arbor, MI 48106; 18 Bedford Row, Department P.R., London WC1R 4EJ, England.

To obtain copies of papers not included in this book, readers may:
   1. purchase back volumes (see page 283 for ordering information),
   2. access documents available through the above-listed indexing/abstracting services,
   3. obtain a microfilm/microfiche copy through UMI (see above), or
   4. order photocopies from HFES at the cost of $7.50 per paper ($17.50/paper for rush orders).

Additional copies of this book may be obtained from the Human Factors and Ergonomics Society at $35.00 per copy for HFES members and $50.00 for nonmembers. Add $7.00 per copy for shipping and handling; California sales tax if applicable. Discounts apply on purchases of 5 or more copies; contact the Society at the address given above for more information.

Library of Congress Cataloging-in-Publication Data

Human factors perspectives on warnings : selections from Human Factors and Ergonomics
    Society Annual Meetings, 1980–1993 / edited by Kenneth R. Laughery, Sr., Michael S.
    Wogalter, and Stephen L. Young.
        p.   cm.
    Includes bibliographical references and index.
    ISBN 0-945289-02-2 : $50.00
    1. Risk communication--Congresses. 2. Warnings--Congresses. 3. Product safety--
Congresses. I. Laughery, Kenneth R., 1935-   . II. Wogalter, Michael S., 1955-   .
III. Young, Stephen L., 1967-   . IV. Human Factors and Ergonomics Society. Meeting.
T10.68.H86   1994
620.8'6--dc20   94-22254
                                                                                CIP

Abstracts

Preface

Three factors contributed to the genesis of this book. First, our aim is to encourage wider distribution of the many outstanding warnings research and application papers that are presented at Human Factors and Ergonomics Society annual meetings. Although attendance at these meetings now exceeds 1500, there is a broad community to which these important findings have not been disseminated. Professionals working in the areas of communications, safety engineering, health care, marketing, and other fields in which safety is emphasized will find a great deal of useful information here.

Second, the increasing number of requests for papers on warnings that HFES receives from members of the legal community led us to investigate the feasibility of compiling the most useful papers from past years into a single volume. *Human Factors Perspectives on Warnings* contains many of the papers that are in highest demand in legal matters involving warnings.

Finally, individuals who have attended HFES annual meetings, and those who have purchased past proceedings volumes, can enjoy the benefits of easier access to this important body of literature.

The Contents

This collection consists of 55 papers that are reprinted in their entirety, 36 that are represented by an abstract, and 132 that are listed in a bibliography. Obviously, decisions had to be made about which papers to include. Our primary criterion was how well the papers dealt with the issues concerning the perception and understanding of hazards and risks, and the design and effectiveness of warnings. Empirical work or theoretical analysis was also given priority.

To include every paper published in HFES proceedings related to the topic of warnings would be a huge undertaking and probably not a very useful one. Instead, rather than reprinting some papers—for example, those on auditory displays in aircraft, labeling for controls, and highway signs—we elected to include only their abstracts. Although research on these topics is important and often has implications for warnings as conceptualized in this book, it is not the main focus of the collection. These papers, which have potential implications for warnings and risk perception, are listed as bibliographical references.

We tried to minimize our own biases in selecting the articles. The purpose of this collection is to make the research more easily accessible, not to impose an editorial evaluation on it.

How To Use This Book

There are three ways to locate information in this collection. Full papers appear first, in alphabetical order by primary author. Abstracts follow that section and are also presented in alphabetical order by first author. The author and subject indexes identify all authors and the major concepts addressed in the papers and abstracts. The bibliographic entries are listed alphabetically by primary author and are not indexed.

For those who wish to cite any of the papers or abstracts in their original citation format, the year of publication and page numbers are provided following the title of each article in the contents (for full papers) and following each abstract. The titles of the proceedings covered in this book are listed separately following the bibliography.

We hope that *Human Factors Perspectives on Warnings* will occupy an important place in your safety library for many years to come.

WHAT IS A WARNING AND WHEN WILL IT WORK?

Thomas J. Ayres, Madeleine M. Gross, Christine T. Wood, Donald P. Horst, Roman R. Beyer, and J. Neil Robinson
Failure Analysis Associates, Inc.

The term warning is applied to a variety of stimuli. From a safety standpoint, the most appropriate definition of warning ties it to any information that has the potential to change behavior and prevent accidents. The results of an extensive literature review suggest that warnings are unlikely to be effective unless a series of conditions are met. The failure of many intended warnings, including most on-product warning labels, to reduce accidents reflects the difficulty of overcoming the problems inherent in their use.

INTRODUCTION

This paper addresses two questions: "What do we mean by a *warning*?" and "When will a warning work to prevent accidents?" Although, as we will show, the overall picture of when warnings do *vs.* do not work is clear, the literature has generated a considerable amount of confusion. We believe this has occurred largely because the term "warning" is used to apply to a broad, complex, and somewhat amorphous concept.

The solution is not, we believe, to try to reach a consensus on a single, narrow definition of a "*warning*," but rather to develop a clear understanding of the many variations that this concept encompasses; to understand the potential impacts of different forms of warnings on different people in different contexts; and to avoid simplistic answers to the question "When do warnings work?"

WHAT IS A WARNING?

Definitions

Generic definition. We define a warning generically as information about a possible negative consequence -- a message that something undesirable may occur to someone or something as a result of taking (or failing to take) some action.

Multiple definitions. Communication theory, which addresses the transmission and use of information, provides a critical distinction for defining a warning. From this perspective, communication involves a sender (or source, or stimulus), a message (and a channel for transmission), and a receiver (and response) (Driver, 1987; McGuire, 1981). Each component can provide a possible definition of a warning:

> Sender: A warning is any message intended by the sender to provide information about possible negative consequences of an action (or inaction).

> Message/Channel: A warning is any message about possible negative consequences of an action (or inaction) that meets some criteria of message content and/or form.

> Receiver: A warning is any message interpreted by the receiver as providing information about possible negative consequences of an action (or inaction).

Given that our concern is the prevention of accidents, only the definition of a warning from the perspective of the receiver is relevant. That is, no matter what the intentions of the sender and no matter how closely the message conforms to some guideline or standard, the important question is what, if anything, did the receiver get out of the message.

"Effective" Warnings. By an effective warning, we mean one that changes behavior in a way that results in a net reduction in the relevant negative consequences. The question of when people understand and remember warnings is considered here only insofar as it is relevant to understanding the potential effects of warnings on behavior and accident reduction.

Inappropriate Distinctions

Safety warnings versus other warnings. A distinction is often made between messages about possible injury or death (safety warnings) and messages about other negative consequences such as property damage, social disapproval, loss of time or money, or penalties imposed by police, employers, parents, or other authorities. The rationale is that concern about physical injury is uniquely motivating to people in that no one would willingly risk physical injury or death. However, both common experience and formal research provide abundant evidence that this rationale is false. The threat of physical injury or death is of little concern unless the likelihood of injury or death is perceived as quite high. For example, few people worry about the very real, but low-probability, threat of death when traveling in a car, but many avoid using a pay phone that says "out of order," even though the negative consequence, if true, is only the loss of a few cents (Godfrey, et.al., 1985). Thus, it is important to keep in mind that, for purposes of understanding when warnings work, the distinction between the remote chance of personal injury and other negative consequences is generally unimportant.

Instructions versus warnings. Instructions are sometimes distinguished from warnings on the grounds that they are not intended or designed to alert a user to the possibility of negative consequences. With respect to the impact on the receiver, however, the distinction may be irrelevant. On the one hand, warnings often include instructions, at least by implication, on how to avoid the negative consequences. On the other, instructions often convey, at least implicitly, some information about negative consequences if the instructions are not followed. Whether or not a safety message acts as a warning depends more on the person and the situation than on message content.

Rules versus warnings. A final distinction to consider concerns the difference between rules and warnings. This is an important practical distinction, because a sign saying simply "Do Not Do X," with the implication that it is a rule of someone with authority, may have more impact on behavior than a sign that says "Doing X May Cause Injury. To Avoid Any Risk of Injury, Do Not Do X."

As we have defined warnings, however, a rule is simply a warning involving a special category of negative consequences. Instead of (or in addition to) possible injury, the consequences stated or implied by the "rule" may include offending the relevant authority and/or a possibility of various penalties. Thus, rules might be viewed as a variation of warnings in which some of the negative consequences derive from displeasing or disobeying the rule makers.

WHEN WILL IT WORK?

The research bearing on the effectiveness of on-product warning labels was reviewed by McCarthy et.al., (1984a), who found no demonstrated impact of on-product warning labels on behavior or accidents. Studies reported subsequently showed that certain forms of warnings, predominantly other than on-product warning labels, had at least some impact on human behavior in the laboratory (e.g., Godfrey, et.al., 1985), although no actual reduction in accidents or injuries was demonstrated.

In 1986, two reviews of the warnings research literature incorporated the new results and addressed the general question of when warnings of various kinds might work and when they will not (Lehto and Miller, 1986; Horst, et.al., 1986). Since 1986, additional studies of warning effectiveness, many of which are referenced below, have been published. These studies, taken in the context of the large bodies of research in the broader fields of human communication and behavior, provide an increasingly clear and consistent picture of the effects, if any, of warnings on human behavior.

In order for a warning to prevent an accident, a complex chain of events must occur . To simplify considerably, the person who is the target of the message must process the message, and the information that is extracted, when added to knowledge acquired over a lifetime of experience plus additional information extracted from the immediate environment, must motivate the person to change behavior in some way that will prevent an accident (see also Lehto and Miller, 1986). These events, together with some conditions that affect whether the events take place or not, are summarized in Figure 1 and discussed below.

Organization and data. Many of the conditions are well established through common experience and a wealth of research in the behavioral sciences. In most cases, we have also cited relevant studies that have addressed warnings directly, with special emphasis on studies published from 1986 to present. References are restricted primarily to studies showing impacts of warnings on behavior, rather than studies where only subjects' opinions are reported, because opinions have proven to be poor predictors of warning effectiveness (McCarthy, et.al, 1987; Wogalter et.al., 1987).

Limitations. It is important to emphasize two limitations of the list of factors presented in Figure 1. First, aside from highway safety research, most of the actual behavioral tests of the effectiveness of safety messages have involved laboratory experiments (in which the participants knew that they were being observed). Any generalization of findings to the real world must be made cautiously when social behavior such as

Figure 1. Conditions for possible safety impact of warnings.

WHEN MIGHT A WARNING WORK?	
A WARNING (SIGN OR LABEL) MIGHT CHANGE BEHAVIOR IF A PERSON:	
1. Reads and understands the warning, and	2. Is motivated and able to change behavior.

Person:
Is alert and sober, and
Is seeking information, and
    Feels need for information, based on past experience
    Hazards suspected, but not observable
Doesn't filter out the warning
    Not overloaded with information
    Not previously exposed to excessive, unnecessary warnings
 	
Sign or label:
Is present (only) when and where needed, and
Includes (only) the information needed, and
Is in an appropriate format
    Noticeable, at person's level of information seeking
    Brief, legible and understandable
	Person:
	Would not know there was a hazard without the warning, and
	Believes the warning, and
	    Warning information is consistent with past experience
	    Conduct of others is consistent with warning
	    Source is credible
	Does not accept the risk, and
	    Consequences seen as highly likely [or severe and
	      moderately likely]
	    Does not believe hazard is under his/her control
	    Risk outweighs the attraction of the activity
	    Risk outweighs the social pressure to take risk
	    Risk outweighs the cost/effort of avoidance
	Is capable of making an appropriate change, and
	Remembers to change.

CHANGES IN BEHAVIOR MAY IMPROVE SAFETY IF:	
1. The right people change, and	2. The changes reduce accidents.

response to persuasive or instructional messages is involved (e.g., Cronbach, 1975), and it should be noted that on-product warning labels have been much more successful in laboratory experiments than in the field.

Second, the research literature suggests that there may be other important factors that have not yet been explicitly discussed and tested with respect to warnings. For example, in some situations people may resent and deliberately disobey threatening messages (Pennebaker & Sanders, 1976), and people sometimes respond to the form of social communication without considering its content (Langer et.al., 1978). These phenomena may place further limits on the ability of a warning to promote safe behavior.

PROCESSING THE MESSAGE

In order for a warning to have any chance of influencing behavior, key information from the warning must be processed by the receiver. This in turn depends heavily on the attitude and actions of the person who is involved, on the context within which it is encountered, and on the message itself. Within broad limits, the format and exact wording of the message may play little or no role in affecting behavior.

Person

Alertness. Warnings may have little or no effect on a tired, distracted, or intoxicated audience. There is abundant evidence of decrements in cognitive, perceptual, and motor performance under those conditions.

Information seeking. Results of recent warnings studies are consistent with the communication theory principle that people who not are looking for a particular type of information (be it instructions or warnings) are unlikely to notice and use that information if they encounter it (deTurck & Goldhaber, 1988; Dorris & Purswell, 1977; Friedmann, 1988; Strawbridge, 1986; Wright, 1979).

Filtering. Safety messages in familiar situations on familiar products are likely to be filtered out. Reading (self-reported and actual) and complying with safety information has consistently been found lower for familiar or recently-used products (Nikmorad, 1985; Otsubo, 1988; Purswell et.al., 1986). Constant exposure to excessive, unnecessary warnings can be expected to produce habituation. Warnings may be filtered out even in unfamiliar situations, especially in a context of information overload, or under stress when the amount of information or the number of response alternatives considered is reduced (Keinan, 1987). Widespread use of warnings probably reduces their potential effectiveness by decreasing their prominence, similar to the effect of embedding important information in surrounding text (Strawbridge, 1986).

Sign or Label

Time and place. The message must be available at an appropriate time and place, generally where behavior needs to change. People learn to filter out stimuli that are not consistently relevant to their behavior, making it difficult for an ever-present safety message to have any impact, even as a reminder. Even a dynamic warning, such as the audible backing-up alarm on a mining vehicle, can lose its value through habituation simply because it is presented so frequently (Duchon & Laage, 1986).

Content. Often, much of the required safety information is included in the preexisting knowledge of the reader, so a warning need include only enough information to trigger the appropriate response. In unfamiliar laboratory tasks, subjects were unlikely to use available protective equipment unless instructed or warned to do so (Otsubo, 1988; Wogalter et.al., 1987). However, addition of warning elements (signal word, hazard and consequence statements) to explicit instructions may not produce significantly greater behavior change than do instructions alone (Strawbridge, 1986), and may be outweighed by a loss of clarity in the instructions (McCarthy et.al., 1987). If the remedy or appropriate behavior is obvious, then explicit instructions are unnecessary and may in fact be unwise, because they are likely to produce increased filtering of warnings in general.

Format. Obviously, a warning sign or label must be sufficiently conspicuous, legible, understandable, and brief for the audience to process and retain the key information. These minimal requirements have been extensively documented in the general experimental and safety literature. In recent laboratory studies, where subjects were actively seeking information but were confronted with a relatively heavy information load, more prominent instructions or warnings have had greater impacts on behavior in some situations (Desaulniers, 1987; Strawbridge, 1986; Wogalter et.al., 1987; Zlotnik, 1982). Even a very conspicuous label can be completely ignored, however, (Dorris & Purswell, 1977; Gill et.al., 1987), and an attractive label on a "toxic" container can have the undesired effect of increasing contact by small children (Schneider, 1977; Culver-Dickinson et.al., 1982).

MOTIVATION AND ABILITY TO CHANGE

Receiving the information from a warning sign or label is only a preliminary link in the chain of events required for a warning to affect behavior. If the information is to change a person's behavior, it must add something substantial to what the person already knew (i.e., not available from past experience or the present context). The information perceived as new must then motivate the person to change, and the person must be able to act as recommended and remember to do so.

Non-redundant information. We start with the assumption that the target of a warning sign or label would be doing something if the warning were not there and may be highly motivated to proceed. If the person perceives nothing substantially new in the information extracted from a sign or label, there is no reason to change.

Credibility. Communications research shows that when a message conflicts with experience, it is the message, rather than the person's experience, that is discredited, unless the message comes from a highly credible source (Aronson, et.al., 1963; Hovland & Weiss, 1951).

Consequences. People accept some risk in all activities (Slovic et.al., 1980), and are unlikely to heed a warning unless the perceived risks of noncompliance are excessive. Laboratory subjects who complied with warnings on chemicals perceived the products as more hazardous than did non-compliers (Friedmann, 1988). Compliance appears to depend primarily on perceived likelihood of injury (Friedmann, 1988; Godfrey, 1985), rather than on expected severity of injury, for which mixed results have appeared (Otsubo, 1988; Stern et.al., 1975).

Control. The issue of perceived control is complex. Someone who feels helpless in the face of a threat will not take any avoidance action (Stern et.al., 1975). On the other hand, a person who feels that the situation is already under control does not feel any need to comply with the recommendations of a warning (Friedmann, 1988; Weinstein, 1984). Unless the recommended remedy is perceived as being both necessary (mere caution is not enough) and sufficient (able to protect), compliance with the warning is apt to be low (Laner & Sell, 1960; Otsubo, 1988).

Attractive risk. A potentially hazardous activity may be attractive, either in its own right (enjoyable, addictive) or for its very riskiness (exciting). Several studies have found low compliance with warnings associated with higher scores on a risk-taking questionnaire (Nikmorad, 1985; Purswell et.al., 1986). Other evidence for risk attraction includes the observation that adolescent males, who have the highest scores on sensation-seeking scales (Zuckerman et.al., 1978), are more likely than older or female respondents to drink and are less likely to wear seat belts while driving (Bradstock et.al., 1987).

Conformity. Social example or pressure is known to play a major role in attitude change and behavior. Complying with a safety message in the presence of complying peers could afford perceived social approval, whereas complying in the presence of non-complying peers could yield social disapproval. Experimental results are consistent with this view (Wogalter et.al., 1989).

Cost. Compliance with recommendations decreases with greater perceived cost (discomfort or effort) of the remedy (Wogalter et.al., 1987; Wogalter et.al., 1989). It is likely that people implicitly compare the cost with the perceived risk of not using the remedy (Stern et.al., 1975). However, even a trivial "cost" (e.g., fastening a seat belt) may outweigh the remote possibility of serious injury or death for many people.

Ability to Change. A person who wants to change behavior must be able to do so. This is probably not a major factor in most situations involving warning signs and labels, but may become important when complex skills or physical strength are involved, or when recommended equipment is unavailable.

Memory. Research on memory for warnings has concentrated on the ability of subjects to recall the content of a warning when later asked to do so. Although a recall or recognition measure may be useful to ascertain that the message was processed and stored, the more crucial issue is whether the message is recalled at the time it is needed. Studies of absent-mindedness (Reason & Mycielska, 1982) and of response to warnings (Strawbridge, 1988) reveal the frequent failure of such timely recall.

ACCIDENT REDUCTION

There are at least two ways that a warning can fail to have a positive impact on safety despite measurably changing behavior.

Inappropriate Target Audiences. If the people who are most likely to be involved in accidents do not change their behavior, then a warning can have little effect. Some campaigns to encourage wearing of seat belts appear to produce no noticeable decrease in highway accident fatality rates, apparently because those drivers most likely to be involved in traffic accidents are least likely to wear seat belts (vonBuseck et.al., 1980; McCarthy et.al., 1984b).

Inappropriate Changes. A warning sign could produce a change in behavior which increases or leaves unchanged the frequency or severity of accidents, either because the recommended course of action is not the one actually adopted, or because it turns out to be inappropriate. For example, male adolescents reported greater likelihood of diving in a pool where a no-diving sign was posted (Goldhaber & deTurck), and installation of stop signs can increase accident rates (as described below).

APPLICATION TO EXAMPLES OF WARNINGS

Relating these principles to two familiar categories of warnings -- on-product warning labels and stop signs -- illustrates why some warnings have some impact and others have none.

On-Product Warning Labels

The user of a consumer product is unlikely to be seeking information, and is likely to filter out a warning label. If the user does read and understand a warning, it is unlikely to be informative, since such products generally have few non-obvious hazards. Unexpected hazards are often so unlikely that the typical person is willing to accept whatever risks are represented. If the warning conflicts with previous experience or the examples set by others, it may not be believed; manufacturers may have little or no credibility, given the clutter of continuously-present warning labels, many prompted by litigation.

An example of a possible (though unproven) exception is a product container, such as for medicine, paint, or a cleaner. A person unfamiliar with the contents of a container may in some instances be seeking instructions and respond to information an a label, whether or not it is presented in a warning format. However, where a person believes he or she is familiar with the product, it is unlikely that anything beyond the product name will affect behavior.

Stop Signs

Often cited inappropriately to demonstrate that warning signs in general are effective in modifying behavior, stop signs indicate situations with highly likely negative consequences, including social disapproval and potential penalties. People are trained to look for and respond to stop signs, and the information-seeking process becomes almost automatic. These signs also illustrate that it is not necessary to meet format standards (eg., signal words, hazard and consequence identification, detailed instructions) in order for a warning sign to affect behavior, even though proposed standards for warning signs and labels require all of these features (ANSI Z535).

Stop signs also illustrate that behavioral changes may not produce the desired outcome. Field research has shown that most drivers do not come to a full stop at stop signs (Stockton et.al., 1981), and that upgrading intersections from yield to stop signs can increase the number of accidents (Polus, 1985).

SUMMARY AND RECOMMENDATIONS

The potential effectiveness of a warning for changing behavior depends on diverse factors. Some of the influences have been specifically studied in a warnings context; others can be extrapolated from research and theory in related areas of human behavior. An important direction for future research will be to develop more realistic laboratory studies and to accumulate an increasing body of real world data. In the meantime, results of laboratory experiments, field studies, and accident analyses continue to demonstrate the difficulty of enhancing safety through warnings. On-product warnings and other common safety messages typically fail to meet minimal requirements for effectiveness due to limitations inherent in their use.

REFERENCES

ANSI Z535.4 Product Safety Signs and Labels. American National Standards Institute, Draft January 1987.

Aronson, E., Turner, J. A. & Carlsmith, J. M. (1963). Communicator credibility and communication discrepancy as determinants of opinion change. Journal of Abnormal and Social Psychology, 67 (1), 31-36.

Bradstock, M. K., Marks, J. S., Forman, M. R., Gentry, E. M., Hogelin, G. C. Binkin, N. J. & Trowbridge, F. L. (1987). Drinking-driving and health lifestyle in the United States: Behavioral risk factors surveys. Journal of Studies on Alcohol, 48 (2), 147-152.

Cronbach, L. J. (1975). Beyond the two disciplines of scientific psychology. American Psychologist, 30, 116-127.

Culver-Dickinson, P., Vernberg, D. D. & Spyker, D. A. (1982). The deterrent value of "Mr. Yuk" stickers. International Congress of Clinical Toxicology.

Desaulniers, D. R. (1987). Layout, organization, and the effectiveness of consumer product warnings. Proceedings of the Human Factors Society, 56-60.

deTurck, M. A. & Goldhaber, G. M. (1988). Consumers' information processing objectives and effects of product warnings. Proceedings of the Human Factors Society, 445-449.

Dorris, A. L. & Purswell, J. L. (1977). Warnings and human behavior: Implications for the design of product warnings. Journal of Products Liability, 1, 255-264.

Driver, R. W. (1987). A communication model for determining the appropriateness of on-product warnings. IEEE Transactions on Professional Communication, PC 30 (3), 157-163.

Duchon, J. C. & Laage, L. W. (1986). The consideration of human factors in the design of a backing-up warning system. Proceedings of the Human Factors Society, 261-264.

Friedmann, K. (1988). The effect of adding symbols to written warning labels on user behavior and recall. Human Factors, 30 (4), 507-515.

Gill, R. T., Barbera, C. & Precht, T. (1987). A comparative evaluation of warning label design. Proceedings of the Human Factors Society, 476-478.

Godfrey, S. S., Rothstein, P. R. & Laughery, K. P. (1985). Warnings: Do they make a difference? Proceedings of the Human Factors Society, 669-673.

Goldhaber, G. M. & deTurck, M. A. Effectiveness of warning signs: Gender and familiarity effects. Manuscript.

Horst, D. P, McCarthy, G. E., Robinson, J. N., McCarthy, R. L. & Krumm-Scott, S. (1986). Safety information presentation: Factors influencing the potential for changing behavior. Proceedings of the Human Factors Society, 111-115.

Hovland, C. I. & Weiss, W. (1951). The influence of source credibility on communication effectiveness. Public Opinion Quarterly, 15, 635-650.

Keinan, G. (1987). Decision making under stress: Scanning of alternatives under controllable and uncontrollable threats. Journal of Personality and Social Psychology, 52 (3), 639-644.

Laner, S., & Sell, R. G. (1960). An experiment on the effect of specially designed safety posters. Occupational Psychology, 34(3), 153-169.

Langer, E., Blank, A. & Chanowitz, B. (1978). The mindlessness of ostensibly thoughtful action: The role of "placebic" information in interpersonal interaction. Journal of Personality and Social Psychology, 36 (6), 635-642.

Lehto, M. R. & Miller, J. M. (1986). Warnings Volume 1. Fundamentals, Design, and Evaluation Methodologies. Ann Arbor, MI: Fuller Technical Publications.

McCarthy, R. L., Finnegan, J. P., Krumm-Scott, S. & McCarthy, G. E. (1984a). Product information presentation, user behavior, and safety. Proceedings of the Human Factors Society, 81-85.

McCarthy, R. L., Taylor, R. K., Sanford, S. B. & Lange, R. C. (1984b). Seat belts: Effectiveness of mandatory use requirements. SAE Technical Paper Series, No. 840329.

McCarthy, G. E., Horst, D. P., Beyer, R. R., Robinson, J. N. & McCarthy, R. L. (1987). Measured impact of a mandated warning on user behavior. Proceedings of the Human Factors Society, 479-483.

McGuire, W. J. (1981). Theoretical foundations of campaigns. In R. E. Rice & W. J. Paisley (Eds.), Public Communication Campaigns. Beverly Hills: Sage Publications.

Nikmorad, H. (1985). A study of behavioral responses in regard to the warning labels on consumer products. Unpublished master thesis, University of Oklahoma.

Otsubo, S. M. (1988). A behavioral study of warning labels for consumer products: Perceived danger and use of pictographs. Proceedings of the Human Factors Society, 536-540.

Pennebaker, J. W. & Sanders, D. Y. (1976). American graffiti: Effects of authority and reactance arousal. Personality and Social Psychology Bulletin, 2 (3), 264-267.

Polus, A. (1985). Driver behavior and accident records at unsignalized urban intersections. Accident Analysis and Prevention, 17 (1), 25-32.

Purswell, J. L., Schlegel, R. E. & Kejriwal, S. K. (1986). A prediction model for consumer behavior regarding product safety. Proceedings of the Human Factors Society, 1202-1205.

Reason, J. & Mycielska, K. (1982). Absent-Minded? The Psychology of Mental Lapses and Everyday Errors. New York: Prentice-Hall.

Schneider, K. C. (1977). Prevention of accidental poisoning through package and label design. Journal of Consumer Research, 4, 67-74.

Slovic, P., Fischoff, B. & Lichtenstein, S. (1980). Facts and fears: Understanding perceived risk. In R. C. Schwing & W. A. Albers, Societal Risk Assessment: How Safe is Safe Enough?. New York: Plenum Press.

Stern, G. S., Blyth, D. P., Kreye, M. W. & Coons, C. E. (1975). Perceived aversiveness of recommended solution and locus of control as determinants of response to danger. Journal of Research in Personality, 9, 37-47.

Stockton, W. R., Brackett, R. Q. & Mounce, J. M. (1981). Stop, Yield, and No Control at Intersections. Federal Highway Administration, Report No. FHWA-RD-81/084.

Strawbridge, J. A. (1986). The influence of position, highlighting, and imbedding on warning effectiveness. Proceedings of the Human Factors Society, 716-720.

von Buseck, C., Evans, L., Schmidt, D. & Wasielewski, P. (1980). Seat belt usage and risk taking in driving behavior. Presented at the Society of Automotive Engineers Congress.

Weinstein, N. D. (1984). Why it won't happen to me: Perceptions of risk factors and susceptibility. Health Psychology, 3 (5), 431-457.

Wogalter, M. S., Godfrey, S. S., Fontenelle, G. A., Desaulniers, D. R., Rothstein, P. R. & Laughery, K. R. (1987). Human Factors, 29 (5), 599-612.

Wogalter, M. S., Allison, S. T. & McKenna, N. A. (1989). Effects of cost and social influence on warning compliance. Human Factors, 31 (2), 133-140.

Wright, P. (1979). Concrete action plans in TV messages to increase reading of drug warnings. Journal of Consumer Research, 6, 256-269.

Zlotnik, M. A. (1982). The effects of warning message highlighting on novel assembly task performance. Proceedings of the Human Factors Society, 93-97.

Zuckerman, M., Eysenck, S. & Eysenck, H. J. (1978). Sensation seeking in England and America: Cross-cultural, age, and sex comparisons. Journal of Consulting and Clinical Psychology, 46 (1), 139-149.

Alcohol Beverage Warnings in Print Advertisements

Todd Barlow
Monterey Technologies, Inc.
Cary, NC

Michael S. Wogalter
Department of Psychology
Rensselaer Polytechnic Institute
Troy, NY 12180

ABSTRACT

This experiment investigated the impact of warnings in alcoholic beverage advertising by embedding warnings in print (magazine) advertisements. Warning conspicuity (size and contrast) and shape (plain rectangle, rectangle with signal icon, and circle/arrow) were manipulated. Under the assumption that the research was a marketing study concerned with print media, participants paged through a simulated magazine and evaluated each page on its visual appeal. Later they were given an unexpected memory test on the content, location, and configuration of the warnings. The results showed that information in highly conspicuous (larger, higher contrast) warnings was remembered better than in less conspicuous warnings, and that warning advertisements can communicate information about the hazards of alcohol consumption. Implications of the results are discussed, including their applicability to warnings for other kinds of consumer products advertised in the print medium.

INTRODUCTION

The cost of alcohol abuse and alcoholism in the United States is estimated to be approximately 136 billion dollars annually (National Institute on Alcohol Abuse and Alcoholism, 1989). Almost 18 million Americans experience medical, social, or personal problems directly related to the consumption of alcoholic beverages. The staggering cost to society due to alcohol-related problems and the rising rate of alcohol-related fatalities suggest that either people are not aware of the risks associated with alcohol consumption, or public awareness campaigns have not had the intended effect on people's knowledge, attitudes, beliefs, and behavior. The magnitude of the problem associated with alcohol consumption resulted in legislation passed in the United States Congress mandating that a warning appear on the labels of all containers of alcoholic beverages after November 18, 1989 (Federal Register, 1989).

Since the enactment of this law, additional legislative measures have been proposed that would require warnings in alcoholic beverage advertisements (e.g., Kennedy, 1990). Although these bills specify certain aspects of the warnings, there is virtually no empirical basis for most of the proposed design features. In addition, the bills do not specify other aspects of the warnings, leaving their characteristics to the discretion of manufacturers. Failure to stipulate the critical features might allow methods of presenting warnings that diminish their potential effectiveness. The purpose of the present research is to identify the factors that might influence the utility of warnings in alcoholic beverage advertisements and their ability to communicate alcohol-related hazards.

In the context of magazine advertisements, warnings must compete with other images for attention. Inconspicuous warnings would seem to stand little chance of capturing a reader's attention. Young and Wogalter (1990) found that conspicuous print warnings in an owners manual were remembered better than plain print warnings. Viscusi, Magat, and Huber (1986) found that subjects reported that they would take greater precautionary behavior as the size of a warning on labels for liquid bleach and liquid drain opener increased. In the current study, warning conspicuity of the alcohol beverage warnings in magazine advertisement was manipulated. Highly conspicuous warnings were defined as larger, bolder print warnings with high foreground-background contrast relative to the less conspicuous

warnings. It was expected that highly conspicuous warnings would be noticed more often, and therefore, the messages that they contain would be more likely read and remembered compared to less conspicuous warnings.

The shape of the warning may also affect noticeability (Bhalla & Lastovicka, 1984; Myers, Iscoe, Jennings, Lenox, Minsky, & Sacks, 1981; Riley, Cochran, & Ballard, 1982). For example, Myers et al. (1981) found that, of nine shapes tested, an octagon and an arrow pointing into a circle were more likely to be noticed and were most appropriate for warnings. Bhalla and Lastovicka (1984) found that when used as the shapes for the Surgeon General's warning in cigarette advertisements, both an elongated rectangle and the arrow pointing into a circle increased memory for the warning. Though warning shape appears to be important in these studies, as well as in an earlier study by Riley, Cochran, and Ballard (1982), not all research research has shown an effect. A recent study by Jaynes and Boles (1990) found no influence of shape on warning compliance. In the current study two basic shapes enclosing the warning were compared (a rectangle and an arrow pointing into a circle).

In addition, because many guidelines on warning design (e.g., American National Standards Institute, 1988; FMC Corporation, 1985; Westinghouse Printing Division, 1981) suggest that a signal icon be included in warnings to help gain attention and communicate the existence of a hazard, a third shape condition, a rectangle with a signal icon, was included in the study. It was expected that the circle/arrow shape and the rectangle with signal icon would be noticed, read and remembered more often than the plain rectangle.

Thus, in the current study, the effects of warning conspicuity and shape were investigated in the context of print advertising for alcoholic beverages. Their effects were examined with respect to memory and knowledge of the warnings' content, their location in the advertisements, and awareness of the warning configuration (the combination of conspicuity and shape).

METHOD

Design

The experimental design was a 2 (conspicuity) x 3 (shape) between-groups design. The highly conspicuous warnings were defined as 11-point bold black (sans serif) print on a white background with a total warning surface area of 23 cm^2. The less conspicuous warnings were defined as plain black print on the advertisement background with a surface area that was 60% of the highly conspicuous warnings.

The text for the warnings was contained in: (a) a plain rectangle, (b) an identical rectangle with a triangle/exclamation point signal icon within its borders to the left of the text, or (c) an arrow pointing into a circle. Within each conspicuity level, the three warning shapes were constructed to displace the same surface area and contained the same size print. Examples of the combinations of conspicuity and shape are shown in Figure 1. A seventh condition, in which no warnings appeared, served as a control.

Participants

One-hundred-five undergraduate students from the introductory psychology courses at the University of Houston,

FIGURE 1. *Warning Configurations examples. The gray areas represent the advertisement background.*

Plain Rectangle

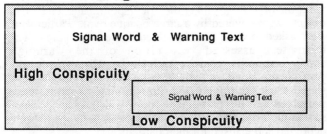

Rectangle with Signal Icon

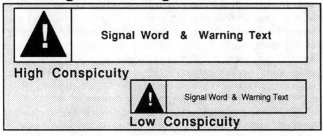

Circle and Arrow

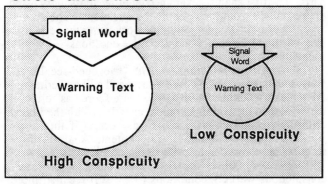

Rice University, and Rensselaer Polytechnic Institute were assigned randomly to one of the seven conditions in equal proportions by school. Fifty-five percent of the participants were male.

Materials and stimuli

Alcoholic beverage advertisements were presented in a simulated, realistic-appearing magazine format which also included articles and advertisements for other (nonalcoholic) products and services. All pages were high quality color photocopies in a double-sided format that were held in laminate enclosures inside a hard-cover three-ring binder.

A preliminary study, involving participants from Rensselaer Polytechnic Institute, assessed common knowledge of alcohol facts and hazard. Based on the results of this study, 10 warnings were constructed containing two to four lesser-known facts related to the hazards of alcohol consumption. The reason for using less well known information was to maximize differences in knowledge between participants who did or did not read the warnings in the advertisements. The warnings are shown in Table 1.

In another preliminary study, 12 participants from Rensselaer Polytechnic Institute rated 65 full-page, color, alcoholic beverage advertisements on attractiveness, appeal, and the relative amount of text and pictures. Each dimension was based on a 9-point Likert-type scale. The scales were

TABLE 1

Warnings in the Alcohol Beverage Advertisements

WARNING: Drinking alcohol during pregnancy may cause the baby to have behavior problems, mental retardation, or deformities.

WARNING: Daily drinking of alcohol increases the risk of throat, stomach, and prostate cancer and diseases of the liver and heart.

WARNING: Beverage alcohol (also called ethyl alcohol or ethanol) is an addictive drug. Children of alcoholics have 4 times the risk of being alcoholics.

WARNING: Drinking alcohol and taking sleeping pills or pain killers can be deadly. Antibiotics, when combined with alcohol, may not work.

WARNING: Drinking coffee, taking a cold shower or vigorous activity does NOT help to sober up. The body needs 2 hours to get rid of the alcohol from 1 drink.

WARNING: Carbonated alcohol is absorbed faster than noncarbonated alcohol. Within 2 minutes alcohol is absorbed by the stomach and carried by the blood to the brain.

WARNING: Acts of violence are more likely after drinking alcohol, including sexual abuse, rape, child beatings, and murders.

WARNING: In many states, the minimum penalty for driving legally drunk is 6 months suspension of driver's license, 15 days in jail, and a $1500 fine.

WARNING: 55% of traffic deaths are alcohol related. With alcohol, people are overconfident and have slower responses.

WARNING: Drunk driving is the number-one killer of children and young adults. There is an alcohol-related death every 22 minutes.

anchored by 0 and 8 at the low and high ends, respectively. In addition, the location of the focal point, as defined as the most "eye-grabbing" or "attention-getting" part of each advertisement, was assessed by asking the participants to point to the area that attracted their attention the most. Focal point data were recorded using a coordinate system that was superimposed on the advertisement.

From the original set of 65 advertisements, ten were chosen according to the following criteria.

(1) Advertisements with predominantly black or white backgrounds were eliminated because: (a) with a black background, it would be impossible to see the warnings in the low conspicuity conditions, and (b) with the white background, the conspicuity manipulation would be confounded with advertisement background.

(2) Advertisements with the highest appeal ratings were included (mean ratings of 4.0 or less were eliminated).

(3) Advertisements with the highest attention-gettingness ratings were included (mean ratings of 4.0 or less were eliminated).

(4) Of the remaining advertisements, advertisements with the least variable focal points were included (i.e., the ads that showed the least agreement were eliminated).

(5) Finally, multiple advertisements for the same brand were eliminated.

The purpose of the second and third criteria was to increase the probability that participants would look at the advertisement. The purpose of the fourth criterion was to informally examine the relationship between memory of the warning and the distance of the warning from the focal point. It was expected that warnings more distant from the focal point would less likely be noticed and remembered.

The 10 warnings were randomly assigned to each of the remaining advertisements. Warnings were placed in the largest uncluttered area of the advertisement.

Advertisements for nonalcoholic products and services were selected based on an analysis by Jacoby and Hoyer (1987) of the most frequently advertised products in the top 18 nationally published magazines. The nonalcoholic beverage advertisements were from categories represented by 2% or greater in the analysis. Forty-three advertisements for apparel, business, cosmetics, food, cigarettes, retail, furniture, building materials, and automobiles were included in the magazine.

Article content was taken from *Capital* magazine, a monthly publication about people and events in the Albany, NY area. Two major articles were chosen for their probable interest to participants. One article described 50 different entertainment activities available in the surrounding area. The other article was about a local woman convicted of killing seven of her eight children. Article content accounted for ten pages of the magazine.

Procedure

Participants were told that *Capital* magazine was a very successful magazine and that a local publishing company would like to know whether the graphic layout of the magazine is responsible for its success. The purpose of the cover story was to prevent subjects from determining the true nature of the study and to allow a test of incidental memory of the warnings. Participants were given the magazine and response sheets and asked to rate each page on the question: "If you were turning through the magazine, how willing would you be to stop and look at the page?" Participants responded on a 9-point Likert-type scale with the following verbal labels on the odd-numbered anchors: (1) not at all willing to stop and look, (3) somewhat willing to stop and look, (5) moderately willing to stop and look, (7) willing to stop and look, and (9) very willing to stop and look. As practice, participants first rated the magazine's cover page, and the experimenter answered any questions. For the remainder of the magazine, they were given 30 s to rate each two-page spread. These intervals were signaled by a tone, and upon hearing each tone, the participants turned the page and rated each of the next two pages. After the participants rated all of the pages, the magazine was removed and three memory tests were administered.

The first test was a 24-item questionnaire assessing recall and recognition of the warning content (seven open-ended, four multiple choice, and 13 true/false). The second test assessed memory of the warning's location. In this test, three areas of each alcoholic beverage advertisement (the location of the warning, the focal point, and one other object) were covered by a large opaque oval. Participants were asked to write what appeared in the hidden area. The third test assessed recognition of the warning's configuration. Representations of all six warning configurations (i.e., combinations of the two sizes and three shapes) and the option of a "no warning" response were presented and the participant chose which, if any, he/she saw in the magazine. After the third test, participants were debriefed and thanked for their participation.

RESULTS

Data were analyzed using a series of 2 (conspicuity) x 3 (shape) between-subjects analyses of variance (ANOVAs). For all tests, each correct answer was given one-point. Then the data were converted to proportions by dividing the participants' scores by the total possible points. For all tests, contrasts were also made between the warning conditions and the no warning control condition.

Warning content

The first test on warning content was analyzed in two parts. The first analysis examined cued-recall memory using the responses from the open-ended questions. The second analysis examined recognition memory using the responses from the multiple-choice and true-false questions.

Cued-recall of warning content. The cued-recall responses were scored using both a strict and a liberal criterion. With the strict criterion, responses were scored as correct if they matched the warning content exactly. With the liberal criterion, responses were scored as correct if they were similar in meaning to the warning content. Analysis of the strict scores showed a main effect of conspicuity, $F(1,84) = 8.28$, $MSe = .008$, $p < .01$. Participants in the highly conspicuous warning conditions ($M = .23$) recalled more warning content than participants in the less conspicuous warning conditions ($M = .17$). There was no significant main effect of shape or interaction (*ps* > .05). Contrasts between the warning conditions and the no warning condition were not significant (*ps* > .05). No significant effects were found using the liberal scores (*ps* > .05).

Recognition of warning content. Analysis of the content recognition scores showed a significant main effect of conspicuity, $F(1, 84) = 6.07$, $MSe = .012$, $p < .05$. Exposure to the highly conspicuous warnings increased recognition of warning content ($M = .56$) compared to the less conspicuous warnings ($M = .50$). There was no significant main effect of shape or interaction (*ps* > .05). The contrast between the condition with the highly conspicuous-signal icon/rectangle warning ($M = .58$) and the no warning condition ($M = .49$) was significant ($p < .05$). No other contrasts were significant (*ps* > .05).

Warning location

Participants were asked to recall the content of three areas in the advertisement, one of which was the warning's location. The answers were scored as correct in two ways: (1) an indication that a warning was present under any one of the ovals in the advertisement (liberal), and (2) an indication that a warning appeared at the correct location (strict). Analysis of the liberal data showed a significant main effect of conspicuity, $F(1, 84) = 77.37$, $MSe = .103$, $p < .0001$. Participants in the highly conspicuous warning conditions ($M = .75$) recalled that a warning appeared in the advertisements more often than participants in the less conspicuous warning conditions ($M = .15$). There was no significant main effect of shape or interaction (*ps* > .05). Contrasts showed that participants in all of the warning conditions more often recalled that warnings appeared in the alcoholic beverage advertisements than participants in the no warning control condition ($M = .00$), *ps* < .05. However, there were two exceptions. The less conspicuous-plain rectangle ($M = .13$) and the less conspicuous circle/arrow ($M = .10$) conditions did not differ from the control condition (*ps* > .05).

Analysis of the strict data showed a significant main effect of conspicuity, $F(1, 84) = 77.54$, $MSe = .064$, $p < .0001$. Participants in the highly conspicuous warning conditions ($M = .58$) were more accurate in recalling the location of the warnings than participants in the less conspicuous warning conditions ($M = .11$). There was no significant main effect of shape or interaction (*ps* > .05). Contrasts showed that participants in all three highly conspicuous warning conditions correctly recalled the warning locations more often than participants in the no warning control condition ($M = .00$), *ps* < .05. None of the less conspicuous warning conditions differed from the control (*ps* > .05).

Configuration recognition

Analysis of the configuration recognition scores showed a significant main effect of conspicuity, $F(1, 84) = 26.84$, $MSe = .183$, $p < .0001$. Participants in the highly conspicuous warning conditions ($M = .82$) recognized the appropriate configuration more often than participants in the less conspicuous warning conditions ($M = .36$). There was no significant main effect of shape or interaction (*ps* > .05). Contrasts showed that participants in the less conspicuous rectangle with signal icon ($M = .20$) and the less conspicuous circle/arrow shape ($M = .33$) had significantly lower

configuration recognition than the control participants whose correct answer was that no warning was present ($M = .67$), *ps* < .05. The control participants had significantly lower configuration recognition than participants in the highly conspicuous circle/arrow warning condition ($M = 1.00$), $p < .05$. No other contrasts were significant (*ps* > .05).

Reliability

The reliability of the cued-recall data of the first test was examined by having 20% of the data scored by another judge. This judge was unaware of the participant's experimental condition. The Pearson product-moment correlation coefficient between the two scorers was $r = .83$ ($p < .0001$).

Focal point-warning location

To determine if the distance of the warning from the focal point was related to noticing the warning, two analyses were performed. First, Pearson product-moment correlations were calculated between the warning location test scores and the distance of the warning from the focal point for each of the six warning conditions. The only significant correlation was a positive relation involving the conspicuous plain rectangle ($p < .05$). Second, the correlations for each participant were transformed into Fisher's z-prime scores and these data were analyzed using a 2 (conspicuity) X 3 (shape) ANOVA. No significant effects were found (*ps* > .05)

DISCUSSION

Conspicuity and shape of warnings in magazine alcoholic beverage advertisements were examined to determine their effects on knowledge and memory. Several measures showed a significant increase in performance for the warning conditions compared to the no warning control condition. This indicates that the warnings in alcoholic beverage advertisements in the print medium have the potential to communicate information on the hazards related to alcohol.

In addition, for virtually every measure, participants viewing highly conspicuous warnings knew more about the warnings than participants viewing the less conspicuous warnings. Highly conspicuous warnings present the warning in a way that makes them more salient and isolates the information from visual noise. These warnings do not blend in with surrounding pictures and text, and are more likely to attract and hold the reader's attention. The results concur with the findings of Young and Wogalter (1990) that participants noticed and retained more information from the highly conspicuous warnings compared to the less conspicuous warnings.

Although it was expected that the presence of a signal icon in the rectangle and the novel shape of the circle/arrow would produce positive effects on knowledge and memory, no effect for warning shape was found. These results fail to support several earlier studies showing shape to be an important factor for warnings (Bhalla & Lastovicka, 1984; Myers et al., 1981; Riley et al., 1982). However, the failure to find an effect of shape concurs with Jaynes and Boles (1990) who also found no effect for this variable. While no shape effect was found, these results should not be used to rule out the possibility that shape influences exist. In the present experiment, it is clear that conspicuity was the more important of the two independent variables. Perhaps the large effect of conspicuity obscured any possible differences attributable to shape. The results suggest that participants did not see (or at least did not often see) the warnings in the low conspicuity conditions, but did see them in the high conspicuity conditions--regardless of shape. Once noticed, the warnings, due to their uniqueness, were looked at and remembered (Hunt & Smith, 1989; Pezdek, Whetstone, Reynolds, Askari, & Dougherty, 1989). Possibly, at intermediate levels of conspicuity, shape might be a more important factor.

An informal analysis of warning recall and distance between the warning and advertisement focal point was performed. It was expected that the greater the distance, the less likely the warning would be noticed and remembered. Support for this expectation was not found as only one significant relationship was noted and it was in the opposite direction. However, this assessment should be considered tentative because (1) these data are correlational (focal-point distance was not manipulated), and (2) only ten distance-recall pairs were analyzed. Further research specifically designed to test the effect of focal point distance could provide more conclusive statements on the noticeability of warnings placed far from the most attention-getting aspects of a printed advertisement.

In addition, further research should address other means of increasing salience, for example, the use of color and alternative configurations. It might be expected that regardless of a warning's salience (conspicuity or shape), a constant warning format will no longer attract and hold a person's attention. Several formats may be necessary (e.g., via intermittent rotation) to prevent people from, over time, habituating to the warning (cf. Bhalla & Lastovicka, 1984; Wogalter & Silver, 1990).

Though alcoholic beverage advertisements were used in the present study as the vehicle to present warnings in print advertisements, these results may be applicable to warnings in print advertisements for other kinds of consumer products (e.g., drugs and recreational vehicles). The relative lack of empirical literature on this topic suggests that additional research is needed to determine the important variables that influence the communication of product hazards. For a warning to be useful in advertisements, it must be designed to compete with other visual stimuli that are purposely made to be attention-getting and appealing, making the development of effective warnings in this context a challenge.

ACKNOWLEDGMENTS

The authors would like to thank Kent P. Vaubel and John W. Brelsford for their help in this research.

REFERENCES

American National Standards Institute. (1988). *American national standard on product safety signs: Z535.4-Draft.* New York: Author.

Bhalla, G., & Lastovicka, J. L. (1984). The impact of changing cigarette warning message content and format. *Advances in Consumer Research, 11,* 305-310.

Federal Register. (1989). *Implementation of the Alcoholic Beverage Labeling Act of 1988* (Pub. L. 100-690, 27 CFR Parts 4, 5, 7, & 16), Vol. 54, pp. 7160-7164. Washington DC: U.S. Department of Treasury.

FMC Corporation. (1985). *Product safety sign and label system.* Santa Clara, CA: Author.

Hunt, J. M., & Smith, M. E. (1989). Processing effects of expectancy discrepant persuasive messages. *Psychological Reports, 65,* 1359-1376.

Jacoby, J., & Hoyer, W. D. (1987). *The comprehension and miscomprehension of print communications: An investigation of mass media magazines.* East Sussex, UK: Lawrence Erlbaum.

Jaynes, L. S., & Boles, D. B. (1990). The effects of symbols on warning compliance. In *Proceedings of the Human Factors Society 34th Annual Meeting* (pp. 984-987). Santa Monica, CA: Human Factors Society.

Kennedy, J. (1990). *Sensible Advertising and Family Education Act.* 102nd United States Congress HR 4493.

Myers, M. L., Iscoe, C., Jennings, C., Lenox, W., Minsky, E., & Sacks, A. (1981). *Staff report on the cigarette advertising investigation.* Washington DC: Federal Trade Commission.

National Institute on Alcohol Abuse and Alcoholism. (1989). *Measuring the impact of alcohol warning labels.* (DHHS Pub. No. AA-89-06) Washington DC: Government Printing Office.

Pezdek, K., Whetstone, T., Reynolds, K., Askari, N., & Dougherty, T. (1989). Memory for real-world scenes: the role of consistency with schema expectation. *Journal of Experimental Psychology: Learning, Memory, and Cognition, 15,* 587-595.

Riley, M. W., Cochran, D. J., & Ballard, J. L. (1982). An investigation of preferred shapes for warning labels. *Human Factors, 24,* 737-742.

Viscusi, W. K., Magat, W. A., & Huber, J. (1986). Informational regulation of consumer health risks: An empirical evaluation of hazard warnings. *Rand Journal of Economics, 17,* 351-365.

Westinghouse Printing Division. (1981). *Westinghouse product safety label handbook.* Trafford, PA: Author.

Wogalter, M. S., & Silver, N. C. (1990). Arousal strength of signal words. *Forensic Reports, 3,* 407-420.

Young, S. L., & Wogalter, M. S. (1990). Comprehension and memory of instruction manual warnings: Conspicuous print and pictorial icons. *Human Factors, 32,* 637-649.

EFFECTS OF AN AVERSIVE VICARIOUS EXPERIENCE AND MODELLING ON PERCEIVED RISK AND SELF-PROTECTIVE BEHAVIOR

Evangeline A. Chy-Dejoras
Xerox Corporation
El Segundo, California

A 2 x 3 between-subjects design was used to determine the effects of modelling and aversiveness of a vicarious experience on perceived risk and self-protective behavior. Modelling and aversiveness of experience were manipulated using an instructional videotape. Unprotected model and protected model conditions were compared. Benign, slightly aversive, and highly aversive conditions were compared. The dependent variables were self-protective behavior and perceptions regarding the hazardousness of the product, severity of injury, likelihood of injury, likelihood of an accident, and familiarity with the product.

More subjects in the protected model group exhibited self-protective behavior compared to the control group. There was no difference in levels of perceived risk between the two groups. Aversiveness had an effect on self-protective behavior. The slightly aversive group showed an incidence of self-protective behavior significantly greater than that of the control group and the highly aversive group. Examination of the nature of manipulation used in the slightly aversive condition suggests that an ambiguous portrayal of the consequences of a hazard while implying its potential to inflict harm causes people to behave cautiously. The incidence of self-protective behavior in the highly aversive group did not differ significantly from that of the control group despite a significant difference in perceived levels of hazardousness. This is explained as a manifestation of the so-called "self-protective attribution of responsibility." Perceived hazardousness was found to be the primary predictor of self-protective behavior. Perceived severity and likelihood of injury were found to be the primary predictors of perceived hazardousness. A strong association was found between self-protective behavior and perceived personal susceptibility to injury.

Introduction

A number of studies have shown that people tend to base their decisions to protect themselves upon the degree of perceived risk. Wogalter et al. (1987) reported that perceived hazardousness correlated highly with the degree of precaution reported by subjects when using a product. It is generally believed that safe behaviors become more likely to the extent that the product is perceived as being dangerous, or conversely, become less likely if a product is perceived as being safe.

Perceptions of risk seem to be determined by perceived severity and probability of accidents associated with an activity (Slovic et al., 1980). Perceived severity of injury has been found to be the best single predictor of perceived risk so far. Probability of injury provided a small but significant increment in the prediction of perceived risk (Wogalter et al.,1987).

Perceived risk may be influenced by a benign or an aversive experience. Based on research in the field of people's responses to natural disasters, Dorris and Purswell concluded that the extent to which a product is perceived to be hazardous is influenced by past experience with the product (1977). If a warning is presented without an incident taking place, the likelihood of responding to subsequent warnings is lessened. Meltsner (1978) supports this contention by proposing that one's exposure to a specific dangerous condition reinforces indifference toward that condition, unless

serious personal damage is incurred. Prior personal experience with an injury may increase the likelihood of warning compliance. It appears that the extent to which a hazard-specific experience is benign may be negatively related to the degree of perceived risk.

There is some evidence that the effect of a benign or aversive experience on people's responses to warnings involving natural disasters also holds true for people's responses to product warnings. A study by Karnes, Leonard, and Rachwal (1986) on perceived risk as a function of experience with all-terrain vehicles and types of warnings reported no significant difference in risk perceived between those who had not been in accidents and those who had been in non-injury accidents. They reported higher levels of perceived risk among those who experienced injury accidents compared to those who experienced non-injury accidents.

The behavior of other people has also been found to have a very strong influence on warning compliance. A study conducted by Wogalter et al. (1988) reported 100% compliance by subjects when a confederate complied with a warning. Whether or not the high degree of compliance was mediated by increased risk perceptions due to other people's safe behavior is unknown. Given that the level of aversiveness of an experience affects risk perception and warning compliance, what the nature of this relationship would be in the presence of a model who does or does not exhibit protective behavior warrants investigation.

Most of the above findings were based on observations, hypothetical responses and expressed intentions, thereby allowing only the determination of correlations and associations rather than causal relationships. The present study was designed to fill that gap by employing direct manipulation of variables relevant to risk perception and observation of actual self-protective behavior. The first objective of the study was to empirically determine the effects of an aversive vicarious experience and modelling of a protective behavior on perceptions of product hazardousness and actual self-protective behavior. The second objective was to empirically determine the factors that best predict overall risk perceived and actual self-protective behavior.

Method

Two independent variables were tested: (1) aversiveness of a vicarious experience, and (2) modelled behavior. Aversiveness of experience had three levels: (1) benign (no accident), (2) slightly aversive (non-injury accident), and (3) highly aversive (injury accident). Modelled behavior had two levels: (1) a model not using protective gloves, and (b) two models, one not using protective gloves and the other using protective gloves.

The independent variables were introduced using 6-minute instructional videotapes for tiling floors with a model showing the process step-by-step. All six versions of the videotape were identical, with the exception of a segment showing an incident involving the use of an adhesive remover. Each incident depicted one of six possible combinations of levels of the independent variables. A benign experience was depicted by the correct and successful application of the adhesive remover. The slightly aversive experience was depicted by the model spilling the adhesive remover and verbally expressing pain. The highly aversive experience was depicted by the model spilling the adhesive remover followed by a shot of a severely burned hand. As the incidents were shown, a statement was narrated cautioning the viewer to have a bucket of water and first-aid kit handy in the event of an accident. The intent was to portray the incident as part of the instructional scheme.

The dependent variables were: 1) perceived hazardousness of the product, (2) perceived severity of injury, (3) perceived likelihood of an injury, (4) perceived likelihood of an accident, (5) familiarity with the product, and (6) self-protective behavior. The first five dependent variables were measured on a seven-point scale. Self-protective behavior was measured based on whether or not the subjects wore protective gloves while performing the experimental task.

Each condition had ten subjects. The control group had sixteen subjects. Students from the California State University at Northridge participated in the experiment and received credits to satisfy partial requirements of an introductory psychology class.

The experimental manipulation was embedded by presenting the study as a marketing survey. Subjects answered a questionnaire pertaining to three consumer products (adhesive remover, drain opener, and mildew remover). Embedded in the survey were pre-test measures pertaining to familiarity, frequency and recency of use, perceived hazardousness, perceived probability of accidents, perceived probability and severity of injury, and types of injury associated with the product. The videotape was then shown. Subjects answered a questionnaire to test their understanding of the content of the videotape, a task designed to further embed the purpose of the experiment.

Subjects were then given a mini-tiling project. They were asked to first remove the hardened adhesive from mock old flooring using an adhesive remover and scraper. A pair of gloves was provided among a set of materials normally used in tiling projects. No sharp objects or tools were provided. The adhesive remover had a warning which was 3/4" x 3" in size and was located in the middle section of the back label. It contained the text "DANGER: Contains highly active chemicals. To avoid severe burns, put on protective gloves before opening." and a pictograph of a hand coming in contact with liquid matter. No instructions were given to instigate the subjects to read the back label.

When subjects began to pour the adhesive remover or dip the brush into the container, the experiment was stopped. Subjects' risk perceptions were again measured using a questionnaire. Probe questions were asked, followed by a debriefing session.

Results

Table 1 shows the percentages of self-protective behavior based on marginal frequencies. A three-way frequency analysis showed a significant association between self-protective behavior and modelled behavior, partial $\chi^2(1, N = 76) = 7.59$, $p < .01$. Self-protective

Table 1
Percentages of Self-Protective Behavior
Based on Marginal Frequencies

INDEPENDENT VARIABLES	DEPENDENT VARIABLE: SELF-PROTECTIVE BEHAVIOR		
MODELLED BEHAVIOR	GLOVES	NO GLOVES	TOTAL
UNPROTECTED	57%	43%	100%
PROTECTED	87%	13%	100%
AVERSIVENESS	GLOVES	NO GLOVES	TOTAL
BENIGN	65%	35%	100%
SLIGHT	90%	10%	100%
HIGH	60%	40%	100%
CONTROL	50%	50%	100%

behavior and aversiveness of experience were significantly associated, partial $\chi^2(2, N = 76) = 6.38$, p< .05. No significant three-way interaction was found between self-protective behavior, aversiveness and modelled behavior. *A priori* contrasts showed significant differences in the incidence of protective behavior between the control and slightly aversive groups, z=2.41, p<.05, between the slightly aversive and the highly aversive groups, z=2.00, p<.05, and between the control and protected model groups, z=2.52, p<.05. The percentage of subjects who wore gloves increased significantly from 50% in the control group to 90% in the slightly aversive condition. This dropped significantly to 60% in the highly aversive condition. The percentage of subjects who wore gloves increased significantly from 50% in the control group to 87% in the protected model group.

Table 2 shows the mean ratings for the five continuous dependent variables. A 2 x 3 multivariate analysis of covariance revealed no interaction between modelled behavior and aversiveness on the combined dependent variables, after adjusting for the pre-test measures. Results of a one-way MANCOVA (including the control group), univariate, and stepdown analyses showed that aversiveness had an effect on perceived hazardousness of the product, stepdown $F(3, 65) = 7.06$, p<.001, and on perceived likelihood of injury, stepdown $F(3, 63) = 3.79$, p<.05. *A priori* contrasts showed a significant difference in perceived hazardousness of the product between the control and benign groups, t(65) = -3.70, p< .001, and between the control and slightly aversive groups, t(65) = -3.62, p<.001. Perceived hazardousness in the highly aversive group was found to be significantly higher than the control group in a post-hoc comparison, t(65) = 4.58, p<.001. Levels of aversiveness did not differ from each other in terms of perceived hazardousness. *A priori* contrasts of perceived likelihood of injury revealed that the highly aversive group perceived a greater likelihood of injury compared to the slightly aversive group, t(63) = -2.89, p<.01. The same series of statistical tests were employed to determine the effect of modelled behavior on the combined dependent variables and revealed no significant effects.

Using a hierarchical multiple regression analysis, perceived hazardousness was found to be the primary predictor of subjects' protective behavior, F(1, 74) = 10.00, p<.01, accounting for 12% of the variance. Those who wore gloves rated the product more hazardous (M = 4.29) than those who did not wear gloves (M = 3.16). A hierarchical multiple regression also revealed perceived severity of injury to be the best predictor of perceived hazardousness, F(1, 74) = 47.11, p<.001, accounting for 39% of the variance. Perceived likelihood of injury added to the prediction of perceived hazardousness by perceived severity of injury, F(2, 73) = 25.54, p<.001, accounting for 16% of the variance.

Responses to the post-experimental questionnaire were examined. It was observed that 80% of the subjects who wore the gloves reported

feeling personally susceptible to injury (i.e., responded "Yes" to the question "Did you feel any threat of being injured while doing the task?"), such as skin irritations or burns. Ninety-six per cent of the subjects who did not wear the gloves reported not feeling any personal threat of being injured. Table 3 shows the incidence of self-protective behavior and perceived personal susceptibility to injury. A frequency analysis showed a highly significant two-way association between perceived personal susceptibility to injury and self-protective behavior, partial $\chi^2(1, N = 76) = 25.15$, p <.001. A z-value of 4.52 was obtained which is significant at p<.001, indicating a very strong association between perceived personal susceptibility to injury and self-protective behavior. Perceived personal susceptibility to injury accounted for 48% of the variance in self-protective behavior. Perceived personal susceptibility to injury was not significantly associated with aversiveness nor with modelled behavior.

Discussion

Presenting a model of safe behavior increased the subjects' self-protective behavior. This is consistent with the strong effect of social influence on

Table 2
Mean Ratings for Dependent Variables

INDEPENDENT VARIABLES	DEPENDENT VARIABLES				
MODELLED BEHAVIOR	FAMILIARITY	HAZARD	LIKEACC	LIKEINJ	SEVINJ
UNPROTECTED	2.37	4.17	3.53	3.37	4.40
PROTECTED	2.70	4.30	3.93	3.90	4.03
AVERSIVENESS	FAMILIARITY	HAZARD	LIKEACC	LIKEINJ	SEVINJ
BENIGN	2.95	4.10	3.60	3.55	4.25
SLIGHT	2.55	4.15	3.20	3.05	3.90
HIGH	2.10	4.45	4.40	4.30	4.50
CONTROL	2.38	3.06	3.06	2.81	3.81

Table 3
Incidence of Perceived Personal Susceptibility to Injury and Self-Protective Behavior

	GLOVES	NO GLOVES	TOTAL
PERCEIVED PERSONAL SUSCEPTIBILITY TO INJURY	53%	1%	54%
PERCEIVED NO PERSONAL SUSCEPTIBILITY TO INJURY	14%	32%	46%
TOTAL	67%	33%	100%

13

warning compliance found in past research (Wogalter et al., 1988). This result has some interesting practical implications. For example, in a hazardous workplace where no hazard-prevention practices are in place, merely seeing other people's protective behavior, even without the benefit of a warning advising the desirability of this behavior, may provide enough motivation for other people to protect themselves. Thus, modelling a safe action is helpful in getting people to act safely, even without the benefit of hazard information (for example, warnings). This can only be generalized to situations where the observer does the same kind of work as the model, as was the case in the experiment. The protective device must also be accessible for imitation of protective behavior to take place. Many subjects indicated that they would go ahead and do the task without the gloves if these were not available.

Viewing a model who exhibited non-protective behavior did not decrease the subjects' self-protective behavior, possibly because no behavioral standards to ensure appropriate task performance and avoidance of harm were set for the subjects. Subjects did not perceive that "not" wearing gloves was "non-protective" because they didn't see gloves being worn as a standard to compare with.

Modelling protective and non-protective behaviors did not affect perceived risk. It seems that the modelled behavior was simply used as a guide for appropriate action in subsequent task performance.

All levels of aversiveness produced higher degrees of perceived hazardousness than shown by the control group. The videotape seems to have given the subjects, who initially were only slightly familiar with the product, a better awareness of the nature of the product, and hence, ideas of what the hazards might be. There were, however, no significant differences in degrees of perceived hazardousness between levels of aversiveness. It seems that this is due to failure of the accident scenarios to create varying levels of perceived severity of injury, a measure that accounts for 39% of the variance in perceived hazardousness. Interestingly, despite the absence of differences in perceived hazardousness, a difference in self-protective behavior was found between the slightly aversive group and the highly aversive group. The slightly aversive group, which was shown a non-injury accident, showed a very high incidence of self-protective behavior, a level that is much higher than predicted compared to the control group, and contrary to prediction, significantly higher than that of the highly aversive group, which was shown an injury accident. The highly aversive group, which was expected to show the highest degree of self-protective behavior, did not differ significantly

from the control group in this regard. This led to the possibility that some other factor was at play that caused the difference in incidence of self-protective behavior between the three levels.

The fact that the incidence of self-protective behavior in the slightly aversive group was much higher than predicted compared to the control group could be attributed to the ambiguity of the accident scenario portrayed in this condition. The scenario was such that an accident was shown and a slight injury was implied verbally, but not visually. What seems to have occurred was that the ambiguously hazardous situation led to a feeling of uncertainty about the product's potential to inflict harm, and caused an increase in perceived hazardousness and self-protective behavior. This "uncertainty" seems to be characterized by a lack of knowledge of the nature of the hazard that befell the model, and, perhaps, a lack of knowledge of the probability of it occurring, and the severity of its consequences. This suggests that if people see a seemingly injurious accident and have a vague notion of what type of harm had befallen a person, if at all, then they may tend to be more careful and protective of themselves, when put in the same situation as the other person.

In order to identify possible reasons for the unexpectedly low incidence of self-protective behavior in the highly aversive group, the incidence of feeling personally susceptible to injury, a factor which showed the strongest association with self-protective behavior, was examined. There was no significant difference in the number of people who perceived personal susceptibility to injury between the slightly and highly aversive groups. However, in the slightly aversive group, 67% of those who did not perceive personal susceptibility to injury wore the gloves for various reasons. On the contrary, in the highly aversive group, none of those who perceived personal susceptibility to injury wore the gloves. This difference may be explained by "self-protective attribution of responsibility" proposed by Shaver in 1970. According to Shaw and McMartin (1977), "self-protective attribution of responsibility" is such that when the outcome of an accident is inconsequential, an observer may attribute the victim's plight to chance. However, the observer is likely to hold the victim of an accident responsible if he or she finds the outcome of the accident considerably serious and if there is a similarity between the victim's and his or her situation. The observer allocates the blame to the other person, and thinks that he or she is unlike the victim and, by doing so, dissociates himself or herself from a possible, similar tragedy. Since the injury shown in the highly aversive group was more serious, subjects may have allocated the blame on the model and manifested this perceived personal insusceptibility by not wearing the protective device provided. This is evidenced by comments such as "It can't happen to me," "I am careful enough," and "The actor was careless." Hence, while an aversive vicarious experience may cause an increase in people's perception of a product's hazardousness, it will not necessarily elicit self-protective behavior but may instead instigate non-protective behavior.

It has been suggested that the consequences must be explicitly conveyed when potential hazards are severe to increase cautious intent, particularly because people's perceptions of severity do not correlate with actual accident frequencies (Laughery, et al., 1991). In this experiment, the explicit portrayal of the consequence did not cause an increase in actual self-protective behavior. People's intentions will not necessarily translate into the intended behavior. There may be other factors we ought to explore that determine the user's final actions. One of them may be the phenomenon called "self-protective attribution of responsibility."

The present study also pointed out that the commonly measured "perceived likelihood of injury" may refer to a large extent to perceived likelihood of injury to others, rather than to likelihood of injury to self. While the slightly aversive group perceived the likelihood of injury to be significantly lower compared to the highly aversive group, the number of subjects who personally felt that they could get injured while doing the task did not differ significantly. Based on the strong association between perceived personal susceptibility to injury and self-protective behavior, it is recommended that future research measure this factor instead of "perceived likelihood of injury" which has little value in the prediction of perceived hazardousness.

Conclusions

The results of this experiment suggest that showing a model who exhibits protective behavior can effectively increase people's self-protective behavior even without the perception of a written warning. This increase in self-protective behavior is not associated with an increase in perceived level of risk. The results also suggest that people, when placed in a situation where the potential for a hazard is perceived but the hazard itself is not known, would tend to behave in a more self-protective manner. On the other hand, viewing a model experiencing severe injury while using a product will not necessarily increase self-protective behavior, perhaps because subjects may blame the model for the injury and perceive themselves as being unlike the model. The results also point to the relevance of perceived personal susceptibility to injury in predicting actual self-protective behavior.

Acknowledgements

This research was conducted to partially satisfy the requirements for the degree of Master of Arts in Human Factors/Applied Experimental Psychology, at California State University, Northridge. I would like to express my sincere thanks to Dr. Mark S. Sanders for his help throughout this research endeavor, and to Xerox Corporation for its support.

References

Dorris, A.L. & Purswell, J.L. (1977). Warnings and human behavior: implications for the design of product warnings. Journal of Products Liability, 1, 207-220.

Karnes, E.W., David Leonard, S., & Rachwal, G. (1986). Effects of benign experiences on perceptions of risk. Proceedings of the Human Factors Society - 30th Annual Meeting, 121-125.

Laughery, K.R., et al. (1991). Effects of explicitness in conveying severity information in product warnings. Proceedings of the Human Factors Society - 35th Annual Meeting, 481 - 485.

Melstner, A.J. (1978). Public support for seismic safety: where is it in California? Mass Emergencies, 3, 167-184.

Shaver, K.G. (1970). Defensive attribution: Effects of severity and relevance on the responsibility assigned for an accident. Journal of Personality and Social Psychology, 14, 101-113.

Shaw, J.I. & McMartin, J.A. (1977). Personal and situational determinants of attribution of responsibility for an accident. Human Relations, 30, 95-107.

Slovic, P., Fischhoff, B., & Lichtenstein, S. (1980). Facts and fears: understanding perceived risk. In Schwing, R.C., & Albers, W.A. Jr. (eds.). Societal Risk Assessment. New York: Plenum Press.

Wogalter, M.S., Desaulniers, D.R., & Brelsford Jr., J.W. (1987). Consumer products: how are the hazards perceived? Proceedings of the Human Factors Society - 31st Annual Meeting, 615-619.

Wogalter, M.S., McKenna, N.A., & Allison, S.T. (1988). Behavioral effects of cost and consensus. Proceedings of the Human Factors Society - 32nd Annual Meeting, 901-904.

Consumer Product Warnings: Review and Analysis
of Effectiveness Research

David M. DeJoy
Department of Health Promotion and Behavior
University of Georgia
Athens, GA 30602

ABSTRACT

This paper provides a critical review of recent research (1984-1988) on the effectiveness of consumer product warnings. The majority of available data come from laboratory studies of college students, and wide variations in effectiveness have been reported. The perceived hazardousness of the product, its familiarity, and the ease of complying with the warning all appear to be important factors. Some preliminary trends have emerged concerning the contribution of various message attributes; however, these factors do not appear to be as important as the user's product-related expectations. The implications and limitations of these findings are discussed.

INTRODUCTION

The purpose of this paper is to provide a critical review of recent research on the effectiveness of consumer product warnings. In an earlier review, McCarthy and colleagues (McCarthy, Finnegan, Krum-Scott, & McCarthy, 1984) concluded that product warnings are not effective; however, this conclusion was based more on an absence of data than on the existence of non-supportive data. Since 1984, a number of additional studies have been conducted and it is now appropriate to revisit the effectiveness question. The importance of this issue is underscored by the frequency with which warnings are at issue in product liability litigation (Interagency Task Force on Products Liability, 1977). Inherent in deciding whether a given product contained an adequate warning is the assumption that warnings are, or can be, effective.

SCOPE AND METHODS OF REVIEW

The present review focuses on research published between 1984 and 1988 and is limited to data-based studies of warning effectiveness; no attention is given to articles or reports addressing design standards, presentation guidelines, social or legal implications, or other similar issues. A multi-stage search procedure was followed to identify pertinent studies. First, computerized searches were conducted using standard behavioral, social, and life science data bases. This was followed by manual searches of relevant journals and proceedings. Finally, the reference section of each identified article was reviewed as a possible source of additional studies. The search was limited to peer-reviewed publications in the open literature.

A total of 38 articles were identified. Articles which upon inspection did not involve data collection (e.g., reviews) or that made only indirect reference to data were eliminated from further consideration; this reduced the total to 30 articles. A number of articles contained the results of two or more studies and, for review purposes, each study was treated separately. There was some double counting of studies, in that, the results of a particular study might be contained in a conference proceedings and also published in a journal; in all, 40 separate studies were identified.

GENERAL CHARACTERISTICS OF THE LITERATURE

The majority of available findings are derived from laboratory studies of college students. There have been relatively few field studies or attempts to replicate laboratory findings in field settings, and population-based studies of in-use warnings are conspicuously absent. Existing studies represent a wide variety of consumer products, experimental tasks, instructional sets, and subject ploys or deceptions. Fifteen studies employed some type of behavioral compliance measure. Other effectiveness-related measures have included: ratings of perceived effectiveness, perceived risk and compliance likelihood; warning detection, reading time/rate and recall; and warning need/expectation and accident scenario generation.

BEHAVIORAL COMPLIANCE

Behavioral compliance has usually been assessed in terms of whether subjects took some precautionary action in using a particular product. Compliance rates have varied between zero and 100 percent; specific products and warning configurations have yielded compliance rates of around 40 percent in several instances. Not surprisingly, many people who notice a warning do not read it, and of those who read it, many fail to take the recommended precautions (see Table 1).

The question of whether the presence of a warning improves compliance relative to its absence depends on the type of control condition employed. Many studies have factorially combined various product and warning characteristics without including any type of control condition. Certain warnings may be more effective than others, but such designs do not answer the question of whether including a warning is superior to no warning. In studies with control groups, control subjects have been either provided with no warning information at all or the warning information was integrated within instructions or other materials.

Table 1. Percentages of Subjects who Noticed, Read, and Complied with Warnings in Three Studies.

Study	Noticed	Read	Complied
Friedmann (1988)	88%	46%	27%
Otubso (1988)	64.3	38.8	25.5
Strawbridge (1986)	91	77	37

Based on fairly limited data, it appears that including a warning is better than not providing warning information at all. For example, Wogalter, Godfrey, et al. (1987, Exp. 1) reported that 10% of subjects used available safety equipment when no warning information was present while 50-90% used the equipment when various warnings were provided. Otubso (1988) found 0% compliance in the absence of warnings and 12.5% to 50% compliance for various warning combinations. Related research suggests that warnings may, at least, sensitize users to safety hazards (Orr & Hughes, 1988; Rothstein, 1985). These effects, however, have not been particularly robust or entirely consistent (Goldhaber & deTurck, 1988a).

Thus far, research has failed to show the clear superiority of separate warnings. Strawbridge (1986) placed warning information in the directions section of a product label and reported a 33% compliance rate for these subjects versus 37% for those receiving various types of separate warnings. Placing the warning information within the directions actually increased the percentage of subjects who read this information. McCarthy et al. (1987) examined safety-related installation errors for automobile child restraint devices and found no differences between those receiving safety information in instruction versus warning formats; in fact, warning subjects committed slightly more errors.

PRODUCT HAZARDOUSNESS AND FAMILIARITY

Strong and consistent data exist to show that warning effectiveness increases with the perceived hazardousness of the product. Familiarity tends to decrease effectiveness, but familiarity may not be as important as perceived

hazardousness (Wogalter et al., 1986). Perceived hazardousness appears to be related to injury severity and/or injury probability (e.g., Friedmann, 1988; Otsubo, 1988; Wogalter, Desaulniers & Brelsford, 1987). Table 2 contains a summary of relevant findings.

COSTS OF COMPLIANCE

The costs of complying with warnings have been examined in two studies. In one field study, building users were confronted with an exit door that appeared to contain damaged glass (Wogalter, Godfrey et al., 1987). A warning sign directed the subjects to one of three other exits. Distance to this other exit provided the manipulation of cost. Compliance rates for the high, medium, and low cost options were 0%, 5.9%, and 93.3%, respectively. A laboratory study using a chemistry experiment paradigm (Wogalter et al., 1988) found that personal protective equipment was more likely to be used when compliance costs were low (73%) versus high (17%). While the amount of data on costs of compliance is quite limited, the findings are consistent with those in the more extensive medical compliance literature (Masur, 1981).

WARNING MESSAGE ATTRIBUTES

Studies have examined the value of adding symbols/icons and other enhancements to warnings, the relative importance of the four standard warning components, the arrangement and formatting of warning content, and the location of warnings on products and within instructions. Some preliminary trends have emerged, but the amount and consistency of research is not sufficient to permit definitive conclusions.

As seen in Table 3, the addition of symbols or icons failed to yield consistent effects; only Wogalter's work shows positive effects. Limited results have also been found for various conspicuity measures such as adding color, varying the type face and size, and highlighting. Gill et al. (1987) found that using an interactive label increased detection but not compliance.

Three studies suggest that the particular signal word used in the warning may not be very important to effectiveness (Leonard et al., 1987; Ursic, 1984; Wogalter, Godfrey et al., 1987). Karnes and Leonard (1986) varied signal word along with other aspects; some effects were noted, but their design did not permit separating out the effects of signal word per se. Other research (Wogalter, Godfrey et al., 1987) suggests that the signal word may be the most redundant element of the warning message. These same data also suggest that the hazard and instruction statements may be the least redundant. Leonard et al. (1986) found that providing a consequences statement led to increased risk perception and compliance likelihood.

Table 2. Summary of Product Hazardousness and Familiarity Findings.

Study	Principal Effects
Donner & Belsford (1988)	Hazardousness increased accident scenarios, degree of precaution, and likelihood of reading warning
Friedmann (1988)	Hazardousness increased warning reading, recall, and compliance
Godfrey & Laughery (1984)	Familiarity decreased likelihood of noticing warnings
Goldhaber & deTurck (1988a)	Familiarity decreased detection and compliance likelihood
Goldhaber & deTurck (1988b)	Familiarity decreased perceived risk and compliance likelihood
Karnes et al. (1986)	Familiarity decreased perceived risk
LaRue & Cohen (1987)	Hazardousness increased/familiarity decreased willingness to read and need for warnings
Leonard et al. (1986)	Hazardousness increased compliance likelihood and need for warnings
Otubso (1988)	Hazardousness increased/familiarity decreased warning reading and compliance
Wogalter et al. (1986)	Hazardousness increased/familiarity decreased willingness to read warnings and warning need and expectation
Wogalter, Desaulniers, & Brelsford (1987)	Hazardousness increased likelihood of user precautions
Wogalter, Godfrey et al. (1987)	Hazardousness increased perceived effectiveness of warnings

Table 3. Summary of Warning Enhancement Findings

Study	Attribute	Effects
Friedmann (1988)	symbols	No effects on compliance
Gill et al. (1987)	color/interactive design	Increased warning detection but not compliance
Leonard et al. (1986)	size/color of signal word	No effects perceived risk or warning effectiveness
Otubso (1988)	pictographs	No effects on warning detection, reading time, recall, or compliance
Strawbridge (1986)	highlighting	No effects on warning detection, recall, or compliance; improved reading of warning
Ursic (1984)	lettering/pictographs	No effects on perceived safety or warning recall
Wogalter, Godfrey, et al. (1987)	size/pictorials/ color	Combination of enhancements increased compliance
Young & Wogalter (1988)	print/icons	Each factor increased warning recall

The general organization of the warning content may influence effectiveness; Desaulniers (1987) found that warnings in outline format (as compared to paragraph) and organized according to type of hazard were rated as having greater appeal, ease of processing, and effectiveness. Two follow-up experiments involving the format variable showed the outline format to be superior on measures of reading time and compliance. Rothstein (1985), failed to find recall differences between paragraph and list formats. Karnes and Leonard (1986) found that fairly minor rearrangements of warning information improved understanding of risks and precautionary actions and Strawbridge (1986) found that the imbedding of "critical" warning information within the warning section reduced compliance.

The location of the warning has also been studied. Strawbridge (1986) tested three positions (top/middle/bottom of label) and reported no effects for compliance and minor effects for recall. Wogalter, Godfrey et al. (1987) reported that compliance was improved by placing the warning at the beginning of the instructions. Users are likely to expect warnings on products that they perceive to be dangerous (LaRue & Cohen, 1987; Wogalter et al., 1986); other data suggest that previous experience with a type of product tends to decrease warning detection (Godfrey & Laughery, 1985); Goldhaber & deTurck, 1988a).

DISCUSSION AND CONCLUSIONS

Warnings can influence user perceptions and behavior, at least as indicated by tests of statistical significance applied within laboratory or field simulations. Further, the perceived hazardousness of the product, its familiarity, and the ease of complying with the warning all appear to be important factors. Some preliminary guidance is also available concerning the relative importance of various warning attributes. However, care should be exercised in generalizing from this literature given the limited amount of field data and the heavy reliance on college student subjects. In addition, variations in instructional sets and experimental ploys may account for some results. For example, telling subjects that will be asked to operate a piece of equipment or be tested on a set of instructions tends to improve warning compliance/recall. In contrast, providing non-specific instructions or making the reading of instructions incidental to task performance often depresses warning effectiveness. Many studies used ploys to conceal the true purpose of the study; some appear to be more plausible than others. Human subjects guidelines also appear to limit the realism of experimental simulations.

Concluding that a warning can influence user behavior is not the same as saying that it is effective. If 30% of users follow a set of precautions when a warning is present while only 10% do so when it is absent, can we conclude that the warning was effective? What is an acceptable level of compliance? For many widely used products a 20% increase in self-protective behavior would produce important reductions in injury outcomes. But what about the 70% of people who still fail to take necessary precautions? Do we conclude that the warning was inadequate? Do we judge the adequacy of the warning on a case by case basis?

It is probably unreasonable to expect high levels of effectiveness from product warnings. Injury control measures are often arrayed on the passive-active continuum (e.g., Wilson & Baker, 1987). Passive measures involve little or no conscious effort by the user; at the other extreme, fully active measures require modification of behavior on repeated occasions. Warnings typically call for one or more conscious actions each time the product is used. Indeed, with many product warnings, people are asked to take persistent measures to prevent relatively rare events. Warnings can be useful; however, they are not as likely to be as effective as measures which do not depend on modifying user behavior.

Perhaps the most striking aspect of the warnings literature is the importance of perceived hazardousness and familiarity. These findings are consistent with the value-expectancy models which have guided research on health behavior for the past twenty years (Cleary, 1987). Such models are based on the premise that people estimate the seriousness of risks, evaluate the costs and benefits of various actions, and then choose a course of action that will maximize the expected outcome. Accordingly, users who believe that they are personally susceptible to serious injury while using a particular product should be more likely to look for, attend to, and comply with warning information. The perceived effectiveness of the indicated precautions and the costs associated with compliance are also likely to be important. Warning results are essentially consistent with these predictions.

The user's product-related perceptions may over-ride the best designed warning message. The overall magnitude and consistency of the warning attribute findings suggests that the configuration of the warning may not be as important as the expectations that the user brings to the situation. While warnings may sensitize users to hazards, the ability of a well-designed warning to alter the expectations of experienced or "confident" users remains to be determined. This point notwithstanding, poorly designed warnings benefit no one.

At this point, there is a need for additional systematic research on warning effectiveness. Laboratory research has progressed to the point where certain effects need to be replicated and extended, and methodological improvements can be identified which should improve the usefulness of future laboratory simulations. Field replications of findings are also needed; however, the potential of field testing is limited by both logistics and ethical considerations. Since large numbers of people currently use products that contain warnings, opportunities exist for conducting population-based studies of effectiveness. Greater use might also be made of available injury databases for this purpose and for conducting retrospective analyses of why warnings were not heeded. Such studies would also provide needed data on morbidity/mortality outcomes.

REFERENCES CITED

Cleary, P.D. (1987). Why people take precautions against health risks. In N.D. Weinstein (Ed.), Taking Care: Understanding and encouraging self-protective behavior. New York: Cambridge University Press.

Desaulniers, D.R. (1987). Layout, organization, and the effectiveness of consumer product warnings. Proceedings of the 31st Meeting of the Human Factors Society (pp. 56-60). Santa Monica, CA: Human Factors Society.

Donner, K.A., & Brelsford, J.W. (1988). Cueing hazard information for consumer products. Proceedings of the 32nd Meeting of the Human Factors Society (pp. 532-535). Santa

Monica, CA: Human Factors Society.

Friedmann, K. (1988). The effect of adding symbols to written warning labels on user behavior and recall. Human Factors, 30, 507-515.

Gill, R.T., Barbera, C., & Precht, T. (1987). A comparative evaluation of warning label designs. Proceedings of the 31st Meeting of the Human Factors Society (pp. 476-478). Santa Monica, CA: Human Factors Society.

Godfrey, S.S., & Laughery, K.R. (1984). The biasing effects of product familiarity on consumers' awareness of hazard. Proceedings of the 28th Meeting of the Human Factors Society (pp. 483-486). Santa Monica, CA: Human Factors Society.

Goldhaber, G.M., & deTurck, M.A. (1988a). Effects of consumer's familiarity with a product on attention and compliance with warnings. Journal of Products Liability, 11, 29-37.

Goldhaber, G.M., & deTurck, M.A. (1988b). Effectiveness of warning signs: Gender and familiarity effects. Journal of Products Liability, 11, 271-284.

Interagency Task Force on Products Liability (1977). Final Report II-54. Washington, D.C.: Department of Commerce.

Karnes, E.W., & Leonard, S.D. (1986). Consumer product warnings: Reception and understanding of warning information by final users. Trends in Ergonomics/Human Factors III (pp. 995-1003).

Karnes, E.W., Leonard, S.D. & Rachwal, G.(1986). Effects of benign experiences on the perception of risk. Proceedings of the 30th Meeting of the Human Factors Society (pp. 121-125). Santa Monica, CA: Human Factors Society.

LaRue, C., & Cohen, H.H. (1987). Factors affecting consumers' perceptions of product warnings: An examination of the differences between male and female consumers. Proceedings of the 31st Meeting of the Human Factors Society (pp. 610-614). Santa Monica, CA: Human Factors Society.

Leonard, S.D., Matthews,D. & Karnes, E.W.(1986). How does the population interpret warning signals? Proceedings of the 30th Meeting of the Human Factors Society (pp. 116-120). Santa Monica, CA: Human Factors Society.

Masur, F.T. (1981). Adherence to health care regimens. In C.K. Prokop & L.A. Bradley (Eds.), Medical psychology: Contributions to behavioral medicine. New York: Academic Press.

McCarthy, R.L., Finnegan, J.P., Krumm-Scott, S. & McCarthy, G.E. (1984). Product information presentation, user behavior, and safety. Proceedings of the 28th Meeting of the Human Factors Society (pp. 81-85). Santa Monica, CA: Human Factors Society.

McCarthy, G.E., Horst, D.P., Beyer, R.R., Robinson, J.N. & McCarthy, R.L. (1987). Measured impact of a mandated warning on user behavior. Proceedings of the 31st Meeting of the Human Factors Society (pp. 479-483). Santa Monica, CA: Human Factors Society.

Orr, M., & Hughes, S.T. (1988). Effectiveness of product safety warnings over time, and the generalization of warning signs. Proceedings of the 32nd Meeting of the Human Factors Society (pp. 897-900). Santa Monica, CA: Human Factors Society.

Otsubo, S.M. (1988). A behavioral study of warning labels for consumer products: Perceived danger and use of pictographs. Proceedings of the 32nd Meeting of the Human Factors Society (pp. 536-540). Santa Monica, CA: Human Factors Society.

Rothstein, P.R. (1985). Designing warnings to be read and remembered. Proceedings of the 29th Meeting of the Human Factors Society (pp. 684-688). Santa Monica, CA: Human Factors Society.

Strawbridge, J.A. (1986). The influence of position, highlighting, and imbedding on warning effectiveness. Proceedings of the 30th Meeting of the Human Factors Society (pp. 716-720). Santa Monica, CA: Human Factors Society.

Ursic, M. (1984). The impact of safety warnings on perception and memory. Human Factors, 26, 677-682.

Wilson, M., & Baker, S. (1987). Structural approach to injury control. Journal of Social Issues. 43, 73-86.

Wogalter, M.S., Desaulniers, D.R. & Brelsford, J.W., Jr. (1986). Perceptions of consumer products: Hazardousness and warning expectations. Proceedings of the 30th Meeting of the Human Factors Society (pp. 1197-1201). Santa Monica, CA: Human Factors Society.

Wogalter, M.S., Desaulniers, D.R. & Brelsford, J.W., Jr. (1987). Consumer products: How are the hazards perceived? Proceedings of the 31st Meeting of the Human Factors Society (pp. 615-619). Santa Monica, CA: Human Factors Society.

Wogalter, M.S., Godfrey, S.S., Fontenelle, G.A., Desaulniers, D.R., Rothstein, P.R. & Laughery, K.R. (1987). Effectiveness of warnings. Human Factors, 29, 599-612.

Wogalter, M.S., McKenna, N.A. & Allison, S.T. (1988). Warning compliance: behavioral effects of cost and consensus. Proceedings of the 32nd Meeting of the Human Factors Society (pp. 901-904). Santa Monica, CA: Human Factors Society.

Young, S.L., & Wogalter, M.S. (1988). Memory of instruction manual warnings: Effects of pictorial and conspicuous print. Proceedings of the 32nd Meeting of the Human Factors Society (pp. 905-909). Santa Monica, CA: Human Factors Society.

A Revised Model of the Warnings Process Derived from Value-Expectancy Theory

David M. DeJoy
Department of Health Promotion and Behavior
University of Georgia
Athens, GA 30602
U.S.A.

Recent research indicates that product-related perceptions and expectations account for a major portion of the variance in user self-protective behavior. The present paper examines value-expectancy theory and research and proposes a replacement for the information processing model of the warnings process. The revised model focuses on the risk appraisal activities of the user and attempts to capture the dynamic nature of precautionary behavior.

INTRODUCTION

Research suggests that product-related perceptions and expectations play an important role in determining whether users will comply with consumer product warnings (DeJoy, 1989a). Indeed, these factors may account for the major portion of variance in user self-protective behavior. In view of this situation, the prevailing information processing model of the warnings process (e.g., Lehto & Miller, 1988; Ramsey, 1985) may need to be revised to improve its ability to guide research and practice in this area.

This paper examines value-expectancy theory and research in terms of how this work might further our understanding of consumer product warnings. Value-expectancy theory has been an important theoretical framework for research on health behavior during the past twenty years (Cleary, 1987), and within this perspective, major emphasis is given to attitude-belief factors. The present paper had three distinct purposes:

1) To assess the extent to which warning findings are consistent with the predictions offered by value-expectancy theories or models.

2) To identify the attitude and belief factors that may be important to warning compliance behavior.

3) To propose a revised model of the warnings process that more accurately reflects the importance of attitude/belief factors.

VALUE-EXPECTANCY THEORY

Value-expectancy theory is based on the premise that people estimate the seriousness of risks, evaluate the costs and benefits of various actions, and then choose a course of action that will maximize the expected outcome. This general perspective has taken a variety of forms, for example, the health belief model (Becker, 1974), the theory of reasoned action (Ajzen and Fishbein, 1980), and protection motivation theory (Rogers, 1983). Considerable empirical support can be found for this general cost-benefit, decision-making perspective (e.g., Cleary, 1987; Janz & Becker, 1984).

While the various value-expectancy formulations are each different to some extent, they all emphasize the individual's threat-related beliefs or perceptions. Of principal importance are perceptions related to: susceptibility, severity, the perceived effectiveness of the preventive behavior, and the perceived costs or barriers associated with the preventive action. The theory of reasoned action is somewhat less narrowly focused on the threat in that it attempts to include all salient outcomes, not just those directly related to the preventive action (Weinstein, 1988). For example, peer group disapproval may be an important factor in the adolescent driver's decision to use a seat belt.

WARNINGS RESEARCH

While all of the major elements of value-expectancy theory have not been investigated in the context of product warnings, findings to date are largely consistent with the predictions of this theoretical perspective (see DeJoy, 1989a). In particular, a number of studies have examined the effects of perceived product hazardousness and familiarity, and data are quite convincing in showing that warning effectiveness increases with perceived hazardousness and decreases with familiarity. Although less thoroughly studied, evidence also indicates that warning effectiveness decreases as the costs of compliance increase (Wogalter, Allison, & McKenna, 1989). In contrast, results are much less consistent regarding the value of various warning attributes or enhancements (DeJoy, 1989a). Studies in this category have addressed the value of adding symbols/icons and other enhancements, the relative importance of various warning components, the arranging and formatting of the warning, and the location of warnings on products and within instructions. Some preliminary trends and guidance can be extracted from these data, but there is little to suggest that even the best designed warning will override the beliefs and expectations that the individual brings to the product use situation.

Looking at the four categories of threat-related perceptions identified in the preceding section, some of these can be matched with warnings-related findings. Perceived hazardousness is an important factor with respect to warning effectiveness, and perceived hazardousness appears to be closely related to injury severity (Wogalter, Desaulniers, & Brelsford, 1987). Products thought to be capable of inflicting serious injuries are perceived as more hazardousness than those associated with minor injuries. Injury probability may also be involved here to some extent (Friedmann, 1988). Evidence can also be found showing that warning effectiveness decreases as the costs of compliance increase (Wogalter et al., 1989). Perceived susceptibility has been less directly examined within the warnings literature, however, the familiarity of the product may be important with respect to this variable. Perceived susceptibility is likely to be lower for products which are familiar or when the user has had considerable benign experience with the product or class of product. The susceptibility question is complicated by the well-documented optimism bias (DeJoy, 1989b; Weinstein, 1987); people tend to be unrealistically optimistic or confident when judging their personal susceptibility to a wide variety of negative events. Finally, little attention has been given to examining how perceptions concerning the effectiveness of recommended precautions will impact warnings-related behavior.

RELEVANT ATTITUDE AND BELIEF FACTORS

The various value-expectancy models and their associated literatures suggest a number of factors or variables that may be important to warnings-related behavior. The most prominent candidates are organized into four categories and summarized in Table 1. Among those not already discussed, self-efficacy refers to perceptions of mastery or control (Bandura, 1977). Individuals will be more likely to follow recommended precautions when they believe that they are capable of performing the required behaviors. As such, lengthy and/or complicated instructions may be ignored if users conclude that they could never figure them out. Enabling factors include any characteristic of the environment that facilitates preventive behavior and any skill or resource required to attain the behavior. The final category includes subjective norms and cues to action. Subjective norms reflect the idea that what others think

might very well influence whether we will take indicated precautions. Cues to action refer to events that might provide additional motivation. For example, an injury to a friend might sensitize an individual to the risks of all-terrain vehicles.

Table 1. Summary of value-expectancy factors

Threat-Related Perceptions	Action-Related Perceptions
susceptibility severity	effectiveness costs/barriers self-efficacy
Enabling Factors	Motivational Factors
demographic structural psychosocial	subjective norms cues to action

CURRENT MODEL OF THE WARNINGS PROCESS

Borrowing from models of human information processing, the warnings process is typically portrayed as a linear sequence of steps or stages beginning with attention/perception, proceeding through comprehension and decision-making, and ending with response selection and execution (e.g., Lehto & Miller, 1988; Ramsey, 1985). A generalized schematic of the information processing model is presented in Figure 1. The model's form suggests that the effectiveness of a warning is determined by the success at each stage of the model. If, for example, a warning is not attended to, it will not be processed any further.

Within this model, the attitudes and beliefs of the user are either not explicitly considered or they are included somewhere between the comprehension and decision-making steps. Attitudes and beliefs enter into the process principally in terms of how the warning impacts their acquisition or change. This portrayal is simply not consistent with the growing body of research which suggests that product-related perceptions and expectations broadly determine how the user approaches the product and its related materials such as warning and instructions.

REVISING THE MODEL

At a minimum, it is important to acknowledge that warnings are devices for communicating risk, and that risk communication is an interactive process (National Research Council, 1989). Adopting an interactive perspective requires that greater importance be attached to what the user brings to the

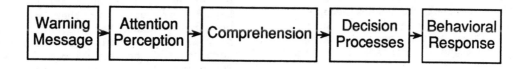

Figure 1. Information processing model

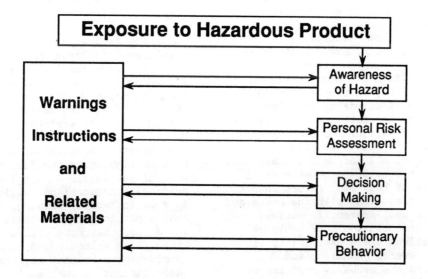

Figure 2. Revised model of the warnings process

situation and to how the user interacts with warnings and other product materials. Obviously, one aspect of revising the warnings model is to assign greater importance to the user's threat-related beliefs and to the weighing of personal cost and benefits.

However, the traditional value-expectancy approach is not without limitations. A major shortcoming is that these models tend to ignore the dynamic and changing nature of precautionary behavior. Put another way, they ignore the fact that the importance of specific beliefs and types of information varies depending on where the individual is in the change process (Janis & Mann, 1977; Prochaska & DiClemente, 1986; Weinstein, 1988). Weinstein summarized the problem quite effectively: value-expectancy models "...assume that the relative probability of action is an algebraic function of the individual's beliefs. Relying on a single predictive equation, however, implies that nothing changes during the entire precaution adoption process except the values of variables in the equation. Which variables are involved,

the weights they receive, and the ways they interact are presumed to remain constant from the moment when the person first learns of the threat to the time when action begins." (p. 357)

The model portrayed below assigns central importance to the individual's risk appraisal activities and attempts to capture the dynamic nature of precautionary behavior (see Figure 2). Following exposure to the hazardous product, self-protective behavior progresses through four stages: 1) awareness of the hazard, 2) personal risk assessment, 3) decision-making, and 4) precautionary behavior. At each stage, there is a bi-directional link to the product warning, or for that matter to instructions, inserts, or other product materials.

An important aspect of this model is that is that the type of information needed to move people closer to self-protective behavior varies as a function of the stage involved. For example, for the user who is unaware of the hazard, the warning must sensitize him or her to the presence of some type of hazard. On the other hand, the user who is already aware of the hazard will look to the warning for information related to the nature and significance of personal risk. The user who acknowledges personal risk will seek information on how to minimize that risk. At the decision-making stage, the user weighs the costs and benefits of compliance.

Major determinants of hazard awareness are likely to include product familiarity/experience and communications received from various sources, including product materials, the media, friends and family members, and co-workers. Personal risk assessment is assumed to occur only after the user is aware of the hazard. Threat-related perceptions, especially susceptibility and severity, are likely to be key factors during this second stage. Sources of information identified as important in the first stage may also play a role in personal risk assessment. Decision-making involves the weighing of costs and benefits, and in this stage, action-related perceptions play an important role. As the model is structured, decision-making occurs only after the individual perceives himself or herself to be at risk of injury. The nature of this risk enters into the decision-making process along with the costs and benefits of various self-protective actions. For example, greater costs would probably be tolerated in situations where user injury is both probable and severe. Enabling and motivational factors are probably most important during decision-making, but they may enter the model during other stages. Returning to the ATV illustration used earlier, an injury to a friend may impact decision-making but it may also trigger hazard awareness or perceptions of personal susceptibility and injury severity.

The basic architecture of the model suggests that people move sequentially through the stages - that the model is cumulative. However, movement in both directions is certainly possible. Most people who use a standard household hammer ignore the warning and fail to wear eye protection (Dorris & Purswell, 1978). Presumably, these users have decided that such protection is not necessary. This notwithstanding, a personal injury, a near-miss, or even a newspaper article may return them to the personal risk assessment or decision-making stages. Similarly, benign experience with a product may cause someone to discontinue recommended precautions.

CONCLUSIONS

The ideal warning must meet the needs of users who are at different stages and who bring different perceptions and expectations to the product use situation. The proposed model emphasizes the individual's risk appraisal

activities and presents a dynamic model of the warnings process. At each stage in the model, different combination of attitude/belief factors become important. Together, existing research on warnings and other preventive behaviors provides considerable guidance for the design of warnings and the formation of a research agenda. The proposed model suggests a number of hypotheses about the contribution of various attitude/belief factors to warnings-related behavior, and these hypotheses need to be tested. Data are also needed on the relative importance of various message attributes and design features at each stage in the adoption process.

How typical users "think" about a product should be considered during product development and during initial evaluation of all safeguards, including warnings. Knowledge of this type can lead to improved decision-making with respect to the type of warning selected, its design and content, and the various enhancement and conspicuity devices employed in the warning. The present reformulation of the warnings process highlights the fact that we ask a great deal of warnings. Warnings must serve two critical functions: persuasion and education. In some instances, warnings must persuade people that a particular product is dangerous; in other instances, they must tell us how to avoid or minimize an acknowledged hazard. These are formidable tasks that require a full understanding of the user' product-related perceptions, beliefs, and experiences.

REFERENCES

Ajzen, I., & Fishbein, M. (1980). Understanding attitudes and predicting behavior. Englewood Cliffs, NJ: Prentice-Hall.

Bandura, A. (1977). Self-efficacy: Toward a unifying theory of behavioral change. Psychological Review, 84, 191-215.

Becker, M.H. (Ed.) (1974). The health belief model and personal health behavior. Health Education Monographs, 2(4).

Cleary, P. (1987). Why people take precautions against health risks. In N.D. Weinstein (Ed.), Taking care: Understanding and encouraging self-protective behavior (pp. 119-149). New York: Cambridge University Press.

DeJoy, D.M. (1989a). Consumer products warnings: Review and analysis of effectiveness research. Proceedings of the 33rd Meeting of the Human Factors Society (pp. 936-940). Santa Monica, CA: Human Factors Society.

DeJoy, D.M. (1989b). The optimism bias and traffic accident risk perception. Accident Analysis and Prevention, 21, 333-340.

Dorris, A.L., & Purswell, J.L. (1978). Human Factors in the design of effective product warnings. Proceedings of the 22nd Meeting of the Human Factors Society (pp. 343-346). Santa Monica, CA: Human Factors Society.

Friedmann, K. (1988). The effect of adding symbols to written warning labels on user behavior and recall. Human Factors, 30, 507-515.

Janis, I.L. & Mann, L. (1977). Decision-making: A psychological analysis of conflict, choice, and commitment. New York: Free Press.

Janz, N.K., & Becker, M.H. (1984). The health belief model: A decade later. Health Education Quarterly, 11(1), 1-47.

Lehto, M.R., & Miller, J.M. (1988). The effectiveness of warning labels. Journal of Products Liability, 11, 225-270.

National Research Council (1989). Improving risk communication. Washington, DC: National Academy Press.

Prochaska, J.O., & DiClemente, C. (1986). Toward a comprehensive model of change. In W.E. Miller & N. Healther (Eds.), Treating addictive behaviors: Processes of change. New York: Plenum.

Ramsey, J.D. (1985). Ergonomic factors in task analysis for consumer product safety. Journal of Occupational Accidents, 7, 113-123.

Rogers, R.W. (1983). Cognitive and psychological processes in fear appeals and attitude change: A revised theory of protection motivation. In J.T. Cacioppo & R.E. Petty (Eds.), Social psychophysiology (pp. 153-176). New York: Guilford.

Weinstein, N.D. (1987). Unrealistic optimism about illness susceptibility: Conclusions from a community-wide sample. Journal of Behavioral Medicine, 10, 481-500.

Weinstein, N.D. (1988). The precaution adoption process. Health Psychology, 7, 355-386.

Wogalter, M.S., Allison, S.T., & McKenna, N.A. (1989). Effects of cost and social influence on warning compliance. Human Factors, 31, 133-140.

Wogalter, M.S., Desaulniers, D.R., & Brelsford, J.W., Jr. (1987). Consumer products: How are the hazards perceived? Proceedings of the 31st Meeting of the Human Factors Society (pp. 615-619). Santa Monica, CA: Human Factors Society.

LAYOUT, ORGANIZATION, AND THE EFFECTIVENESS
OF CONSUMER PRODUCT WARNINGS

David R. Desaulniers
Rice University

ABSTRACT

Three experiments are presented examining the effects of warning layout (spatial structure) and organization (semantic structure) on the readability and memorability of warning information. In Experiment 1 these factors were tested in a 2 (levels of layout) x 3 (levels of organization) factorial design. The two levels of layout were the typical paragraph format and an experimental version having the appearance of an outline. Warning content was organized according to hazard, type of statement, or randomly. Warnings were ranked according to three criteria; eye appeal, ease of processing, and effectiveness. In general, warnings in outline layout and type of hazard organization were ranked as having greater eye appeal, easier to process, and more effective than alternative organization-layout conditions. In Experiments 2 and 3, only warning layout was manipulated and a cover story was used to elicit reading and compliance behaviors likely to occur in the home. Experiment 2 results indicate that, when asked to read the warnings, subjects spent less time reading warnings in paragraph layout than warnings in outline layout. In Experiment 3, the decision to read the warning was at the discretion of the subjects. Results indicated that warnings in outline layout were read and complied with by a larger proportion of subjects than warnings in paragraph layout. Implications for warning design and future research are discussed.

INTRODUCTION

Why would a person see the word "WARNING" and fail to read the message which follows? A potential explanation is that the warning may have an overwhelming appearance, too difficult or long to read. In essence, one might judge the effort to read the warning greater than the benefit of understanding the hazard.

Unfortunately, there is a paucity of warnings research addressing such issues. Factors which influence the comprehensibility, legibility, and readability of written communications have received considerable attention in other research domains. The results of these studies have guided the development of numerous guidelines (e.g. specific font characteristics), many applied widely in warning design. Surprisingly, two text characteristics, layout and organization, have received very little consideration in the warnings context. Layout, the spatial structure of the warning, and organization, the semantic structure off the warning, are two features likely to influence an individual's propensity to read and ability to remember warning information. Such factors can be expected to ultimately influence the effectiveness of a warning.

A review of research on text layout suggests that reading and comprehension are facilitated when spacing is used to parse the information into predictable and easily encoded units (e.g. Frase and Schwartz, 1979; Hartley, 1981). Additionally, Carver (1970) found evidence of a preference for vertical layouts. It has also been suggested that some degree of white space might act as an attentional or motivational factor eliciting higher levels of reading behavior (Goldfarb, 1982; Saunders, 1982; Schoff and Robinson, 1984).

Research on text organization has shown that higher levels of comprehension and recall can be obtained if information is organized hierarchically (Frase and Schwartz, 1979), and the reader is aware (or made aware) of the organization (Frase, 1969).

Present guidelines for warning design recommend that warnings be composed of four components: a signal word, statement of the hazard, statement of the consequences, and instructions (FMC, 1980). When a warning addresses a single hazard they typically appear in this order. In consumer product warnings, multiple hazards must often be addressed. However, little is known about how to optimally organize these components. Furthermore, little is known about the effectiveness of alternative methods of conveying information about the nature of the organization of the warning to the reader.

In the present research, principles of organization and layout, discussed above, were applied and tested. Warnings were developed according to a 2 (levels of layout) x 3 (levels of organization) factorial design and several aspects of the warning communications process were assessed.

The three levels of organization were organization by hazard, by type of warning statement, and random. Warnings organized by hazard, possess the hierarchical organization suggested by research on text organization. Such warnings begin with a hazard statement, followed by a statement of a consequences associated with that hazard, followed by the safety instructions specific to avoiding that consequence. If the hazard presents multiple consequences, the remaining pairs of consequences and instructions are presented. The order is then repeated for the remaining hazards addressed in the warning.

Warnings organized by type of statement present all hazard statements first, then all consequence statements, and finally the instructions statements. This organization is a reasonable alternative against which hierarchical organization might be assessed. It has the advantage of presenting all the critical hazard information at the beginning of the warning and provides a framework within which all the precautionary instructions can be found in one section.

The third organization presented warning statements in a random order.

Layout was manipulated such that warnings were presented in outline or paragraph layout. Outline layout provides the reader with spatial cues as to the organization of the text. Levels of indentation are used to indicate transitions from hazard information, to consequence information, to instruction statements. This format incorporates more white space than text in paragraph format. Thus it is likely to increase the attention getting and motivational characteristics of the warning. The predictability of the beginning of idea units is increased, as each new topic is signaled by indentation and each sentence is intiated on a new line. This format also has the effect of increasing the vertical orientation of the warning.

Experiment 1: Eye Appeal, Ease of Processing, and Effectiveness.

Warning stimuli were ranked according to three criteria, assessing perceptions likely to influence one's willingness to read a warning. Independent subject groups ranked the eye appeal, ease with which they could process, and the perceived effectiveness of the warnings.

Method

Materials and Design. Warnings from six consumer products were selected according to the primary criterion that they present at least two or more hazards. For example, bug spray is not only toxic but also flammable. The six products selected were bug spray, fabric protector, pool shock, a steam iron, an electric rechargeable drill, and a blow dryer. Six versions of each product warning were developed according to a 2 (levels of layout) x 3 (levels of organization) factorial. The two levels of layout were paragraph layout and outline layout. The three levels of organization were type of hazard, type of statement, and random organization. Warnings were presented in 12-point Geneva font, on white, 8 1/2 x 11 inch sheets of paper.

Subjects and Procedure. Fifty-four Rice University undergraduates participated. Subjects were evenly divided between the three ranking tasks such that each ranking task was completed by eighteen subjects.

Subjects completing the eye appeal rankings were asked to rank order the warnings according to their immediate visual impression of the warning. In order to preclude any effects of content which might influence this ranking, all warning information was replaced with X's for this task. All capitalization and punctuation was retained, thus the stimuli were content free yet reflected the shape of the warning. Subjects in the ease of processing task, were instructed to rank the six versions of each warning according to the ease with which they could read, understand, and remember the warning. Subjects in the third group were asked to rank the warnings according to how effective they expected each version to be.

Each subject completed six trials. A trial consisted of sorting the six versions of a product warning according to the criterion stated by the experimenter. Thus each subject ranked the six versions of the warnings for each of the six products.

Results and Discussion

The rank ordered versions of each warning were scored from 1 to 6, corresponding to the rankings of best to worst on the given criterion. Rankings were collapsed across subjects and products to provide a mean ranking for each combination of layout and organization.

These mean rankings are provided in Table 1. Examination of the first two rows reveals that the warnings in outline layout were perceived as having greater eye apppeal than those in paragraph layout, $F (1,17)=9.31$, p <.01. These rankings also reflect an effect of organization, $F (2, 34)=19.16$, p <.0001. Warnings organized by type of hazard were ranked as having greatest eye appeal while warnings with random organization were perceived as having the least. The interaction of these two factors approached, but did not reach, traditional levels of statistical significance $F (2,34)=2.90$, $p =.07$.

Table 1
Mean Rankings as a Function of Criterion, Layout, and Organization.

| Criterion | Organization | | |
Layout	Type of Hazard	Type of Statement	Random
Eye Appeal			
Outline	2.27	2.70	3.51
Paragragh	4.01	3.63	4.92
Ease of Processing			
Outline	1.77	3.29	4.52
Paragraph	2.82	3.77	4.84
Effectiveness			
Outline	1.64	2.60	4.56
Paragragh	3.52	3.43	5.23

The mean ease of processing rankings are presented in rows three and four of Table 1. The pattern of results is similar to that obtained in the eye appeal rankings. Warnings in outline layout are consistently ranked as easier to process than those in paragraph layout while warnings in type of hazard organization are ranked as easier to process than both type of statement and randomly organized warnings. A two analysis of variance indicates that the main effect of organization is significant, $F (2,34)=33.54$, p <.0001, while the main effect of layout approaches significance, $F (1,17)=4.09$, $p =.06$. The effect of layout was consistent across the three conditions of organization. However, the effect was considerably larger in the hierarchical organization condition, contributing to the significant organization by layout interaction, $F (2,34)=3.81$, $p =.03$.

The mean perceived effectiveness ranking are provided in the bottom two rows of Table 1. Once again a similar pattern of results can be observed. Warnings in outline layout are ranked as more effective than warnings in paragragh layout, $F (1,17)=16.36$, $p=.0008$. There was also a significant effect of organization, $F (2,34)=48.40$, *p* <.0001. However, there was a significant layout by organization interaction, F (2,34)=10.22, *p* <.003. Although the hierarchical organization was ranked as most effective in outline layout, it is ranked somewhat less effective than the type of statement organization in the paragraph condition.

In general, the layout and organization manipulations sizeably and reliably influenced assessments of the warnings on all three criteria. The results suggest that the principles of organization and layout, drawn from the general research literature, have the potential for useful application in the warnings domain. Experiment 2 is an attempt to extend these findings by examing behavioral responses to warnings as a function of warning layout.

Experiment 2: Reading Rates, and Warning Compliance.

Experiment 2 examines the influence of warning layout on the reading rate, recall, and warning compliance of subjects asked to read a warning as a task incidental to the primary experimental objective. Subjects were led to believe that their primary task was to test the ergonomic design of a fabric protector dispenser. This was to be done by applying the product in a simulation of home usage. Thus the task of reading the product's warning was incidental to the task of testing the dispenser design.

Method

Materials and Design. The product dispenser to be tested was an opaque, white, 10 ounce capacity pump spray dispenser. The container was filled with water and one ounce of mint mouthwash to provide scent to the bogus fabric protector. The warning for this product was printed on an 8 1/2 by 11 inch piece of paper and presented as part of a packet of information. In addition to the warning, the packet contained a bogus information release form, included to enhance the cover story, and the instructions on how to use the product.

The warning primarily addressed the hazards associated with the toxicity of the product. Specifically, the warning indicated that the product is harmful and potentially fatal if used in a small and/or unventilated room. The warning also indicated that if the product was to be used indoors, windows and doors should be opened and fans should be used to increase ventilation.

The experiment was conducted in a 6 x 8 foot experimental cubicle. The room was without windows and the door was closed. In the room were a small table and chair at which the subject was seated, an upholtered chair which was to be treated with fabric protector, and a small box fan.

Subjects and Procedure. The experimenter first obtained several hand measurements in order to reinforce the cover story (i.e. that the experiment concerned the ergonomic design of the pump dispenser). Subjects were led to an experimental cubicle, shown the chair they were to treat with the fabric protector, and provided the information packet. They were instructed to read the contents of the information packet and then knock on the one-way mirror before applying the product. The experimenter, said to be completing paperwork in the next room, would then come to the window to take notes on the manner in which they used the product. These instructions were used to explain the presence of the one-way mirror but lead subjects to believe that they were not being observed while they were reading.

In actuality, the experimenter observed all reading behavior and recorded the total time devoted to reading the instructions page and the warning page. The reading time for the instructions page served as a baseline measure. The experimenter also recorded four measures of warning compliance; opening the cubicle door, use of the fan, leaving the cubicle to apply the product, and questioning the safety of the procedure.

Forty-eight Rice University undergraduates participated, divided equally into paragraph and outline layout conditions.

Results and Discussion

Each subject's instruction and warning reading times were converted into separate reading rates. Reading rate calculations were based upon the assumption that the entire passages were read. This is an assumption which will subsequently come into question.

The instructions page, identical for the two groups, was read at an average rate of 186 wpm by the group receiving the warning in paragraph layout, while subjects receiving the warning in outline layout read the instructions at an average rate of 188 wpm. Reading rates for both groups approximated normal distributions. This baseline measure indicated that the treatment groups differed little in terms of average reading rate.

In general, the average reading rate for the warnings was considerably higher than the average reading rate for the instructions. Warnings in paragraph layout were read at 291 wpm, an 86% increase over the instructions reading rate. In contrast, the average reading rate for warnings in outline layout only increased by 28%, to 244 wpm.

Examination of the reading rate distributions reveal that the outline and paragraph warnings elicited similar median reading rates, 230 and 244 wpm respectively. However, while readings rates for outline warnings approximated a normal distribution, reading rates for paragraph warnings were positively skewed. Reading rates for eight of the twenty-four subjects exceeded 350 wpm. One must ask if these subjects were skimming the warning rather than reading it for full comprehension. The skewed distribution of reading rates suggests that the paragraph layout increases the variability in reading behaviors, and the tendency to skim, rather than simply facilitate an increased reading rate.

Behavioral measures of warning compliance suggest that the two layouts are comparable in eliciting compliance behaviors. Of the twenty-four subjects in each condition, 11 (46%) complied with the warning in outline layout and 10 (42%) complied with the warning in paragraph layout. The distribution of compliance behaviors is provided in Table 2. Twelve compliance behaviors were recorded for subjects in the outline condition and 15 compliance behaviors for subjects in the paragraph condition.

Table 2
Frequency of Compliance Behaviors as a Function of Warning Layout

	Behavior			
Layout	Used Fan	Opened Door	Left Room	Questioned Safety
Outline	2	7	1	2
Paragraph	6	8	0	1

Note. One subject in the outline condition and five subjects in the paragragh condition opened the <u>door</u> and used the <u>fan</u>.

The frequency of specific behaviors differed only slightly across the two conditions. Chi square tests revealed that these differences were not reliable, p>.20. One might suspect that warnings in outline layout, which were read for a longer period of time, will be more effective. However the compliance data do not support such expectations.

The reading rate distributions obtained in Experiment 2 suggest that warnings presented in paragraph layout are more likely to be skimmed than warnings in outline layout. Although the layout manipulation did not elicit differential levels of warning compliance, this result may have been dictated by the experimental methodology. Warning layouts are likely to influence warning compliance via their effect on someone's willingness to read the warning. In the present experiment subjects were explicitly asked to read the warning. Thus the effect of layout on the tendency to read a warning, and consequent warning compliance, may have been constrained by these instructions. In Experiment 3 this problem is eliminated by leaving the decision to read the warning at the discretion of the subject.

Experiment 3: Tendency to Read and Warning Compliance.

This experiment examines the effect of warning layout on the likelihood of the warning being read. The methodology employed in Experiment 3 is nearly identical to that of Experiment 2. Consequently only departures from Experiment 2 methodolgy will be noted.

Method

Materials and Design. Warnings in this experiment were presented as a plastic laminated label on the product container. In order for the instructions and warning to be presented on the label, the font size was reduced. The letter height was 1/16 inch, representative of the size used in labels of many similar products.

Prior to the last sentence of the warning, the following sentence was inserted, "Do not use if you have read this far." The warning was recorded as having been "read completely" if the subject read to this point. The warning was recorded as having been "read partially" if the subject failed to read this statement, but was able to recall specific warning content in a subsequent test of free recall. The free recall test was administered immediately after the subject finished reading the warning. Free recall was

scored according to a pre-determined listing of idea units considered essential to safe use of the product. The time each subject devoted to reading the label was also recorded.

Subjects and Procedure. Fifty Rice University undergraduates participated, evenly and randomly divided into outline and paragraph conditions.

When displaying the bottle of fabric protector, the experimenter briefly turned the bottle to reveal the label and told subjects, "So that you will have the same information the consumer will ultimately receive, the information concerning how to apply the fabric protector is provided on the label".

Results

Tendency to Read Warnings. Of the twenty-five subjects in the outline condition, 17 partially or completely read the warning, while 8 did not read the warning at all. In the paragraph condition, only 10 subjects read at least part of the warning, and 15 did not read the warning at all. A Chi square test of the difference in these proportions indicates that it is statistically reliable, $\chi 2(1, n=50)=3.94$, $p<.05$.

Warning Compliance. In the outline condition, 12 subjects read the warning completely and did not use the product. The other 13 subjects did not read the entire warning, thus using the product in what were depicted as potentially lethal conditions. In comparison, only 4 subjects read the entire warning in paragraph layout, the remaining 21 subjects applied the fabric protector in direct contradiction of the precautions stated in the warning. A Chi square test of the difference in these proportions indicates that the difference is statistically significant, $\chi 2(1, n=50)=4.50$, $p<.05$.

Examination of reading rates for those subjects who at least partially read the warning reveals that the two layouts elicited highly similar reading rates. The median reading rates were 200 and 202 wpm for outline and paragraph layouts respectively. These data indicate that the paragraph and outline warning layouts elicit similar reading rates. Thus, as previously suggested, the difference in reading rates observed in Experiment 2 is likely due to a higher proportion of subjects skimming the warning in paragraph layout.

A comparison of mean recall scores reveals that subjects in the outline condition scored somewhat higher in free recall (M=3.04) than subjects in the paragraph warning condition (M=1.88). However, the difference was not statistically significant, $t(48)=1.4, p>.10$.

SUMMARY

At the outset of this paper it was suggested that one reason a user may fail to read a product warning is that the warning may have an overwhelming appearance. In essence, an informal utility analysis might be made in which the benefit of reading the warning is weighed against the perceived effort to read the warning. A review of document design, typographic, and educational research literature, suggests that two factors, layout and organization, should receive further consideration in warning design.

Appropriate manipulation of these features of the warning may reduce the actual and perceived effort to read the warning, thereby increasing one's willingnes to read it.

Principles of organization and layout were derived from the literature reviewed. The research indicated that warnings might be most effective if hierarchically organized, particularly if the reader was made aware of the organization. The layout of the warning was seen as a potential means of conveying this information. Levels of indentation were used to indicate transitions between conceptual groups of information, in a fashion similar to methods used to present the outline of a text. Thus the layout not only provided information about the warning's organization, but also parsed the information into smaller groups of ideas.

In Experiment 1, the effect of these manipulations were tested on three perceptions likely to influence one's tendency to read a warning. The results of this study indicated that these manipulations have the potential to influence one's immediate visual impression of a warning, perceptions of how difficult the warning is to process, and expectations about the effectiveness of the warning. These effects are consistent with the behavioral measures obtained in prior research. In particular, hierarchically organized warnings in outline layout were ranked as having the greatest eye appeal, easiest to process, and were perceived to be the most effective.

In Experiment 2, calculation of reading rates for the two layouts was based upon the assumption that the entire warning was read. However, in light of the normal distribution of reading rates obtained on the baseline measure, the skewed distribution of reading rates for the warning in paragraph format suggests that this may been an incorrect assumption. Many subjects dramatically increased their reading rates for the warning in paragraph format, indicating they may have skimmed the warning, rather than reading it for detail and full comprehension.

Although the compliance data of Experiment 2 suggested that the warning was equally effective in either layout, it was suggested this may have been dictated by methodological constraints. Data collected in Experiment 3 clearly demonstrates that the two warning layouts differed considerably in terms of the number of subjects who voluntarily read the warning. While 68% of the subjects read at least part of the warning in outline layout, only 40% of the subjects read at least part of the paragraph format warning. Perhaps more striking, three times as many subjects complied with the warning in outline layout (48%), in comparison to the proprortion of subjects who complied with the warning in paragraph layout, only 16%.

The results of these three experiments have important implications for warning design. These data sugggest that decisions concerning how to organize and layout a warning are likely to be as important as decisions of what information to provide and how to express it. Furthermore, these techniques are sufficiently general to be applied to a wide variety of product warnings. However, one should note that the effectiveness of these manipulations in other product environments is yet to be established. This should be the focus of continued research.

Future studies should be conducted which also assess the effects of alternative organizations on behavioral responses to warnings. With respect to layout, the effectiveness of outline layout for depicting alternative organizations should be examined. Finally, the methodolgy employed in Experiments 2 and 3 represents a useful tool for the study of warning design in a laboratory setting. It allowed for the creation of a believable scenario in a well controlled experimental setting.

REFERENCES

Carver, R. P. (1970) Effect of "chunked" typography on reading rate and comprehension. Journal Of Applied Psychology, 54, 288-296.

FMC. (1980) Product Signs and Safety System, (3rd ed.). FMC: Santa Clara, CA: Author.

Frase, L.T. (1969) Paragraph organization of written materials: the influence of conceptual; clustering upon the level and organization of recall. Journal of Educational Psychology, 60, 394-401.

Frase, L. T., & Schwartz, B. J. (1979) Typographical cues that facilitate comprehension. Journal of Educational Psychology, 71, 197-206.

Goldfarb, S. M. (1982) Writing policies and procedures manuals. IEEE Transactions on Professional Communications, Vol. PC-25, No.1., 14-15.

Hartley, J. (1981) Eighty ways of improving instructional text. IEEE Transactions on Professional Communications Vol. PC-24, No.1, 17-27.

Saunders, A. (1982) Writing effective assembly procedures. IEEE Transactions on Professional Communications, Vol. PC-25, No. 1, 20-21.

Schoff, G. H., & Robinson, P. A. (1984) . Format and mechanics. In G. F. Schoff and P. A. Robinson (Eds.) Writing and designing operator manuals (pp. 62-69). California: Lifetime Learning Publications.

A MOST CRITICAL WARNING VARIABLE:
TWO DEMONSTRATIONS OF THE POWERFUL EFFECTS OF
COST ON WARNING COMPLIANCE

Thomas A. Dingus   Jill A. Hathaway   Bruce P. Hunn

University of Idaho
Moscow, Idaho

The effects of cost on warning compliance have been demonstrated in several previous studies. These studies have shown that cost reduction can dramatically increase compliance with a warning label's intent. The current paper describes two studies which support these previous findings under situations of household consumer product and recreational protective equipment use. In addition, these studies demonstrate that cost reduction can positively influence behavior under circumstances known to be detrimental to warning effectiveness. Such circumstances include low risk perception, familiar products, and inadequate warning labels/signs. These studies also show that increasing the cost associated with warning compliance, even a seemingly minor amount, can have devastating effects on compliance rates. These results indicate that the greatest effort possible should be taken to reduce compliance cost in hazardous situations when warnings are relied upon for hazard control.

INTRODUCTION

Previous research (e.g. Wogalter, Godfrey, Fontenelle, Desaulniers, Rothstein and Laughery, 1987; Wogalter, McKenna and Allison, 1988) has demonstrated the effects of cost on warning compliance. This research has shown that reduction in cost can dramatically increase compliance with a warning's intent. When these results are considered in the general context of warning research, it is apparent that cost reduction may be one of very few options available to a practitioner to increase warning compliance rates.

Despite the demonstrated importance of low cost on warning compliance, a number of research issues remain. One important issue for the practitioner is a determination of circumstances and situations for which cost reduction can be effective, and to what degree. "Cost" defined in the broadest sense can refer to many types of hindrances to appropriate and safe behavior. Such hindrances can include such widely varying circumstances as: increased task time required to take a safer route, discomfort associated with wearing hearing protection, or the perception of one's looks while wearing a respirator.

In addition to the widely varying circumstances that can result in high cost, situations of hazard controlled by warnings also vary greatly. A number of factors involved in such situations have, in addition to cost, been shown to influence perception and/or behavior. These include: situation familiarity, warning label design and perceived risk, just to name a few.

The objective of the current paper is to describe selected results of two field studies that give insight into the potential effectiveness of warning compliance cost reduction and the problems associated with circumstances of high cost.

METHOD - STUDY 1

The first study involved the manipulation of several warning variables in a racquetball test domain where compliance was the wearing of protective eyewear. The experimental design chosen was a 2 x 3 x 3 complete factorial between subjects design conducted at two large racquetball centers (The University of Idaho and Washington State University). Nine-hundred-twenty racquetball players were unobtrusively observed and subsequently filled out a post-test questionnaire as part of the experimental procedure. None of the subjects were aware of the observation or the purpose of the study (as determined by a post-test question probe).

The three factors investigated as part of this study were warning salience, cost of compliance and warning information content. The manipulation of each of these factors is described below:

Warning Location/Salience

The location of the warning signs was varied between the two locations used for this study. In one location, the warning sign(s) were placed on the door to the racquetball court. The sign(s) were developed in accordance with ANSI standards (American National Standards Institute, 1987) and measured 14" by 8". In the second location, the sign(s) were placed inside the racquetball court on the front wall. The purpose of placing the signs in this location was to provided a constant reminder to the racquetball players and to make the warning information as salient as possible. The signs were constructed of heavy clear plastic material of a thickness that would not alter the normal path or velocity of a racquetball if struck. These signs measured 42" by 24" with large lettering to account for the worst case of readability in a standard size racquetball court.

Cost of Compliance

Compliance cost was manipulated in this study by varying the amount of effort required on the part of the subject to obtain eyewear. Subjects who already had their own eyewear were not considered as part of the study. That is, only the "target population" of racquetball players who did not go to the trouble and expense to buy eyewear were included. For the target population of interest, subjects were exposed to one of three experimental conditions. In the high cost condition, no eyewear was provided on-site for the subjects to wear. Therefore, if the subject wanted to comply with the warning information, they either had to refrain from playing or leave the building to obtain eyewear. The middle cost condition required the subjects to walk 60 feet to a checkout booth (which they all passed on the way to the courts) to check out eyewear. For the low cost condition, eyewear was provided in a box just outside the door to every court. No sign drawing attention to the presence of eyewear was included as part of the low cost (eyewear provided by the court door) condition.

Warning Information Content

Three levels of warning information content were provided as part of this study. One level consisted of no warning or information signs posted in the area and served as a baseline condition. A second level consisted of a warning sign, developed in accordance with ANSI standards (ANSI, 1987), posted in the area. The third level consisted of the ANSI warning with the addition of a "specific consequence" information sign. The signs used in the study are illustrated in Figure 1.

The information signs were posted in each of the two testing locations under the following scheme: baseline condition first, ANSI warning second and ANSI plus specific consequence third. This scheme was utilized so as to minimize subject sensitization to previous conditions. Subjects who had seen previous signs or had participated in a previous condition were not re-used.

RESULTS - STUDY 1

Several results of this first study are of interest for the current paper. These results are summarized below:

- When cost was lowest (eyewear provided just outside the courts), compliance rates for players who did not have their own eyewear were as high as 60%. However, for the middle level of cost (eyewear 60 feet away) and the high level of cost, compliance rates were 0% for all conditions.

- For the lowest cost of compliance condition (eyewear provided outside the courts), the compliance rates for players who did not have their own eyewear was 18% overall when no signs were present. The ANSI and ANSI plus specific consequence information signs significantly increased compliance for the low cost conditions. For the middle and high cost conditions, the signs had no effect on compliance or perceived risk.

- A sign location by cost interaction was marginally significant (chi-squared = 3.30, p=0.069). When the warning sign was posted on the door of the court, compliance under the low-cost condition was greater than when a much larger sign was posted inside the court. One possible explanation for this difference is cost. The sign located inside the court actually resulted in a slightly higher compliance cost than the sign on the court door since a player had to leave the court upon reading the sign inside the court to obtain the eyewear.

METHOD - STUDY 2

The second study involved the use of a "new formulation" consumer cleaning product. Compliance for this study was the use of protective gloves. The experimental design used for this study was a 2 X 3 X 2 between subjects factorial design. The factors explored for this study were: warning information content (standard generic instruction label and ANSI label plus specific consequence information, shown in Figure 2), required physical interaction with the warning label (1. standard label; 2. one-time required interaction where the label was "spot-glued" to the spray bottle nozzle requiring removal for use; and, 3. continuous required interaction where the label was attached to a "trigger guard" requiring manipulation for product use on each occasion), and cost (operationally defined as gloves provided or not provided as part of the packaging).

Three-hundred-eighteen subjects participated in this research in a field setting. Products were distributed to students at the University of Idaho under the guise of a "product quality and marketing" study. Subjects were told that they were to take home a package containing a new consumer

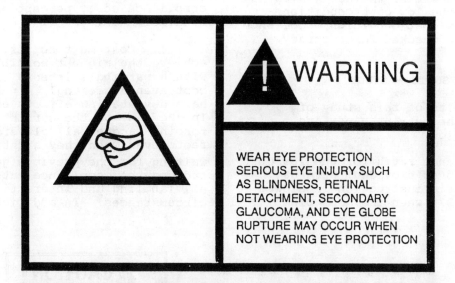

WARNING

WEAR EYE PROTECTION SERIOUS EYE INJURY SUCH AS BLINDNESS, RETINAL DETACHMENT, SECONDARY GLAUCOMA, AND EYE GLOBE RUPTURE MAY OCCUR WHEN NOT WEARING EYE PROTECTION

RACQUETBALL FACTS

1. Wearing appropriate eyewear while playing racquetball can prevent 99% of all eye injuries.
2. There are 70,000 eye injuries per year, 40% of which occur while playing racquet sports.
3. Odds for obtaining an eye injury while playing racquetball is one in four.
4. Racquet balls can penetrate open eyeguards.
5. Eye glasses and contact lenses offer no protection from racquetball eye injuries. They can shatter and be lodged in the eye.

Figure 1. ANSI and Specific Consequence Warning Signs Used in Study 1.

product and use it for a period of one week. At the end of the week the subjects were to return the product in the original package and fill out a questionnaire. The questionnaire contained a number of distracter questions relating to marketing and product quality, as well as questions regarding product use, behavior while using the product, and risk perception. In addition to the above information, a question probe assessing the subject's perception of the purpose of the study was asked as part of the questionnaire. Any subject who indicated that the study purpose was to test warnings or glove use was eliminated from the study (four subjects were eliminated for this reason).

Due to the type of supplied gloves used and their configuration as part of the packaging, it was possible to objectively determine whether gloves had been worn in the low cost condition. Therefore, low-cost condition compliance estimates were checked for accuracy.

RESULTS - STUDY 2

The results of this study of interest to the current paper are summarized below:

- Compliance rates for the low cost condition (gloves provided) were 88% when the generic instruction label was provided and 87% when the ANSI plus

specific consequence information label was provided. Compliance when the gloves were not provided was 25% overall and did not significantly vary with label type or interactivity.

- The perceived risk of using the product was relatively low (3.13 overall on a five point "safe" to "dangerous" scale). In addition, 83% of the subjects indicated that the product was as safe or safer than their normal brand. Yet even subjects who responded that the product was not dangerous and was similar to brands that they commonly used wore gloves, when provided, a large percentage of the time.

DISCUSSION

The results of the two studies described above illustrate several important points regarding warning compliance cost, perception and behavior.

1. Cost must be very low to achieve the highest possible compliance with a warning's intent. Increasing the cost even a seemingly minor amount can have devastating effects on compliance. In the case of the current studies, forcing racquetball players to walk 60 feet (even when they had time while waiting for the previous game to finish) reduced the compliance rate to zero for all labeling and interactivity circumstances. In addition, the minor

Instructions: Always wear gloves. Avoid contact with skin and eyes. Spray on cleaner and wipe off with clean paper towel. Do not use on wood surfaces.

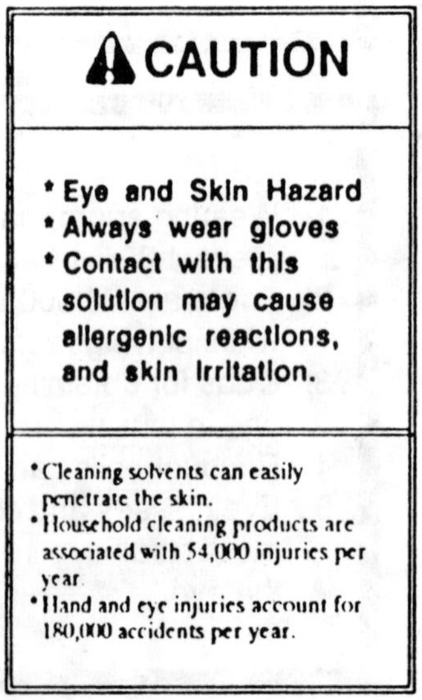

⚠ CAUTION

* Eye and Skin Hazard
* Always wear gloves
* Contact with this solution may cause allergenic reactions, and skin irritation.

* Cleaning solvents can easily penetrate the skin.
* Household cleaning products are associated with 54,000 injuries per year.
* Hand and eye injuries account for 180,000 accidents per year.

Figure 2. Generic Instructions and ANSI plus Specific Consequence Warning Sign Used in Study 2.

cost increase associated with having to walk just outside the court to obtain eyewear upon entering and reading warning information sign(s) apparently reduced compliance to some extent.

The findings described above, along with previous research (e.g. Wogalter et al., 1987) illustrate that the relationship between cost and compliance is very sensitive. That is, increasing cost can drive compliance rates to zero very quickly.

2. When cost is very low the resulting behavioral effects can partially or totally eclipse the inadequacy of a warning label or sign. Obviously warnings should be optimized; however, the results showed that even in a situation of an inadequate generic instruction label (in the consumer product case) or no warning at all (in the racquetball case) compliance can be positively and drastically affected by cost minimization.

3. In circumstances shown to be undesirable for warning compliance, behavior can be altered in a significantly positive way by reducing cost. In the consumer product scenario, the perceived product danger was quite mild and many subjects stated that the product was not stronger than their normal brand of household cleaner. Yet, even given this lack of perceived danger, a large percentage of the subjects still wore the gloves provided. A number of previous studies (e.g. Rogers, 1987) have shown that risk or danger perception can effect compliance. However, this finding indicates that there are circumstances where compliance can be quite high when the perception of danger is relatively low.

In addition to the danger rating results, many subjects rated the product similar to their normal brand. In such circumstances of product familiarity, previous research (e.g. Rogers, 1987) has shown that compliance can be adversely affected. However, when gloves were provided, subjects wore gloves a large percentage of the time despite this familiarity.

There is little doubt that warning label compliance is a very complex multivariate problem. It is clear from these findings, however, that compliance cost, operationally defined for these studies as the availability of protective equipment, is an extremely important determinant of behavior. These studies indicate that cost may be the most critical determinant of compliance behavior in comparison to other known influencing factors. This is not to say that other factors are not important to maximize warning compliance; but in many circumstances of high cost, the practitioner may have few options to increase compliance much above zero.

ACKNOWLEDGEMENTS

The authors would like to thank Richard Gill for his ideas in conceptualizing the design of these two studies and Paul Costanza, Jacki Miller and Steve Adolph for their assistance in running subjects.

REFERENCES

American National Standards Institute, Accredited Standards Committee. (1987). Safety Signs and Colors, National Bureau of Standards. Gaithersburg, Maryland.

Rogers, G.O. (1987). Public recognition of hazard. In V.T. Covello et al. (Eds.), Uncertainty in Risk Assessment, Risk Management and Decision Making (pp. 103 - 106). New York: Plenum.

Wogalter, M.S., Godfrey, S.S, Fontenelle, G.A., Desaulniers, D.R., Rothstein, P.R. and Laughery, K.R. (1987). Effectiveness of warnings. Human Factors, 29(5), 599-612.

Wogalter, M.S., McKenna, N.A. and Allison, S.T. (1988). Warning compliance: Behavioral effects of cost and consensus. Proceedings of the Human Factors Society, 32nd Annual Meeting, 2, 901-904.

TWO REASONS FOR PROVIDING PROTECTIVE EQUIPMENT
AS PART OF HAZARDOUS CONSUMER PRODUCT PACKAGING

by

Thomas A. Dingus   Bruce P. Hunn   Steven S. Wreggit

University of Idaho
Moscow, Idaho

In a few instances, appropriate personal protective devices are included in the packaging of hazardous consumer products (e.g. gloves in hair coloring kits). The inclusion of such devices serves to decrease the cost of complying to warnings specifying their use. It has been shown in several studies that decreasing cost can substantially increase compliance with warnings. A second, previously undocumented advantage of providing protective devices is that their mere presence can increase the perception of danger associated with using the product. In two field studies utilizing consumer cleaning products it was found that the inclusion of protective devices significantly increased the perceived danger of using the products. The inclusion of protective equipment also (for reasons of reduced cost and increased perceived danger) resulted in highly significant and substantial increases in warning compliance. These results indicate that providing personal protective devices as part of product packaging can be a powerful method for substantially increasing warning compliance in at least some circumstances.

INTRODUCTION

Providing protective equipment as part of hazardous consumer product packaging will, in many circumstances, serve to lower the cost to the user associated with wearing the equipment. The reason for this cost reduction is a simple circumstance of effort required to exhibit safe behavior. It is apparent that if the effort is reduced, the tendency for greater compliance will be present. Previous research has shown that cost reduction can have a dramatic influence on safe behavior. (See Dingus, Hathaway and Hunn, 1991 in this Proceedings). When these results are considered in the context of persuasion injury control in general, and warning compliance research specifically, it is apparent that cost reduction may be one of very few options available to effectively alter behavior.

Two studies were conducted with the objective of exploring the effects of compliance cost in conjunction with other factors, including warning label content and required user/label physical interaction, on the perception of risk and behavior associated with product use. These three variables were selected for two reasons:

1. Previous research has shown that these variables have singularly shown success at modifying risk perception or behavior in similar circumstances.

2. All three variables can be practically implemented as part of consumer product packaging under many circumstances.

A different "product" was tested for each of the two field studies. The products were actually site manufactured to ensure non-toxic mixtures. Both products were successfully pre-tested for adequate cleaning performance. For the first study, a common household consumer cleaning product was used. The second study utilized an "industrial strength tile-descaler" as the product under test. A pre-test questionnaire revealed that subjects perceived the label used for the household consumer cleaner as "slightly dangerous" and the tile de-scaler as "dangerous" on average (statistically significant at the $p < 0.01$ level).

The focus of the current paper is a previously undocumented and common finding of the two studies: The inclusion of protective equipment not only served to reduce compliance cost (as was expected) but also served to increase the perceived danger associated with the use of the products.

METHOD - STUDY 1

Three-hundred-eighteen subjects were given a "new formulation" consumer cleaning product to take home and use at their discretion over a period of one week. The products were distributed in sealed packages under the guise of a consumer product quality study. The packages were distributed with the following variations:

1. Two types of warning information (a generic instruction label and a warning label constructed to ANSI specifications and including additional specific consequence information).

2. Three levels of required physical interactivity. The levels consisted of a standard spray bottle; a "billboard" configuration (consisting of a label mounted on cardboard and glued to the spray nozzle) requiring one-time interaction to tear off the cardboard label; and a "trigger guard" (consisting of the warning mounted on a plastic flap covering the trigger of the spray bottle) requiring continuous interaction to use the product.

3. Two levels of compliance cost, manipulated by the inclusion of gloves as part of one-half of the spray bottle packages.

At the end of the one week test period, the package and its contents were returned by the subjects and a questionnaire completed. The questionnaire contained questions regarding the study purpose, the perceived risk associated with the product's use, the perceived strength and familiarity of the product, as well as a number of distractor questions regarding product quality and buying behavior.

The subjects were required to return all of the package contents at the end of the one-week period. This allowed inspection of all of the bottles and gloves that were provided. The bottles were each outfitted with an unobtrusive spot of latex paint on the threads of the nozzle. This allowed determination of whether the nozzle had been opened by the subject, thus giving a check of actual product use. By inspecting the gloves that were returned, it could be determined whether or not they were actually worn. The gloves, which came pressed flat in a box, exhibited rounding of the fingertips when worn, giving an objective check on compliance. Data for 38 subjects (approximately 12%) were discarded for reasons of suspicion regarding the study objectives, apparent cheating or misplaced bottles/gloves.

RESULTS - STUDY 1

The results of the study of interest to the current paper include two findings regarding the inclusion of the gloves as part of the product packaging. The first finding was that including the gloves significantly affected compliance. The presence of the gloves resulted in a significant (chi-squared = 187.29. $p<0.0001$) and meaningful (from 25% to 88%) increase in compliance. This finding supports previous findings (e.g. Wogalter, Godfrey, Fontenelle, Desaulniers, Rothstein and Laughery, 1987) that decreasing cost can increase compliance. No other interactions involving the cost variable were significant at the $p< 0.05$ level.

The second result of interest to the current paper was the finding that the presence of the gloves in the product packaging increased the perception of danger of product use across all other labeling and interactivity conditions. The responses to the Likert scale question "How dangerous do you think this product is to skin and eyes?" (1=safe, 5=dangerous), showed a significant difference depending on whether gloves were present or not [$F(1,302) = 7.59$, $p=0.0062$]. The mean response for the low cost (gloves provided) condition was 3.34; the mean response for the high cost (gloves not provided) was 2.94. No other main effect or interaction approached significance for this question.

METHOD - STUDY 2

As previously mentioned, a major difference between Studies 1 and 2 involved the products used by the consumers. This study utilized an "industrial strength tile de-scaler" to test various alternative warning techniques and their effectiveness in persuading the consumer to comply with warnings. In addition, subjects were given both a filter mask and protective gloves as part of the product packaging.

Experimental manipulations similar to those utilized in Study 1 were utilized for this study (see Method - Study 1 for a more detailed description). The experimental design was a 2 x 3 x 3 between subjects factorial with two cells which were not tested. Two levels of cost of compliance (high cost, no gloves or mask provided; and low cost, gloves and mask provided), three levels of warning label physical interactivity (standard spray bottle, no physical interactivity; "billboard", one time interactivity; and "trigger guard", continuous physical interactivity), and three warning label formats (conventional product instructions, ANSI warning, and ANSI plus specific consequence warning) were used to test their affect on consumer compliance to warnings.

Four out of the 18 cells described by the factorial above were not tested due to: (1) a desire to limit the resources required for the study, and (2) a low probability for success for several configurations. The configurations that were not tested included the billboard and trigger guard configurations used in conjunction with standard product labeling for both the low and high cost conditions (four cells total). It was felt that these configurations provided the least useful information and would not provide the optimal level of compliance. This was felt to be the case since the physical interactivity served to highlight only the somewhat inadequate warning information found on the standard information labels.

Participants for Study 2 consisted of 224 volunteer subjects from the Moscow, Idaho area. A booth was set up in a local mall where subjects volunteered to participate in the study. A drawing for $250.00 dollars was offered to the volunteers as incentive to participate in the study.

The consumer product which was used in the study, although labeled as an "industrial strength descaling", was, as previously discussed, a non-toxic, non-harmful cleaning solution. A descaling agent was used because: (1) Hard water stains are widespread in the Moscow, Idaho area. Therefore, consumers were receptive to the product and participated in the experiment readily; and, (2) De-scaling products were rated as more hazardous than several other common products on a pre-study questionnaire including the cleaning product described in Study 1.

For this study, a station was set up in the Palouse Empire Mall, Moscow, Idaho, under the guise of testing public opinion regarding the "quality" of a new cleaning product. This deception was used to conceal the fact that the study was being conducted to examine methods of increasing safe behavior. Subjects were informed that the study purpose was to test a newly developed cleaning product so that its cleaning effectiveness and consumer appeal could be reviewed before it was put on the market.

The distribution of the products for the conditions described above was accomplished by having the subjects take home a sealed, opaque package containing various items. Items given to the participating subjects included a spray bottle configured with one of three types of labeling and one of the three levels of interactivity. The consumers in the low cost of compliance group were also issued protective gear (gloves and mask) which was advised on the product instructions and/or warnings. The consumers were informed that they would have to bring all the contents of the package back to the same location in the mall after approximately one week had passed. A convenient time for the subject was noted and a majority of the subjects did return to the mall. If a subject could not return to the mall at the specified time an alternate time was scheduled or the researcher arranged a time to pick up materials at the person's place of residence. Upon return of the materials, participants filled out a post-test questionnaire.

Two categories of questions were asked on the post-test questionnaire. One type of question pertained to the subject's satisfaction with the product. For example, "How well did the product work?"; "Would you buy this product instead of other similar products on the market?", etc. The above questions were used as distractors which contributed to the guise that a new product was being tested. Mixed within the consumer satisfaction questions were questions concerning the subject's perception of risk and behavior in dealing with the product.

The methods utilized to determine subject suspicion, objective glove and mask use, and cheating by subjects in Study 1 were also utilized in Study 2.

RESULTS – STUDY 2

The Study 2 results that are within the scope of the current paper are summarized below:

As with Study 1, the inclusion of protective devices as part of the product packaging resulted in dramatic effects. Cost of compliance was significant with respect to both glove and mask use. The inclusion of masks and gloves as part of the product packaging resulted in substantial increases in compliance rates (e.g. 0% to 30% for the high cost cells and 50% to 100% for the low cost cells). In addition, both mask and glove compliance were statistically significant at $p < 0.0001$ for cost. There were no interactive effects between cost and any other factor.

The increase in danger perception due to the inclusion of protective equipment present in Study 1 was also present in Study 2. The mean responses to the product danger question were 2.83 for the low-cost condition and 2.43 for the high-cost condition on a 1 = not at all dangerous, 3 = dangerous and 5 = extremely dangerous scale. The mean values were significantly different for these groups as well [$F(1,220) = 4.74$, $p = 0.0306$].

CONCLUSIONS

These results indicate that the inclusion of protective equipment as part of the product packaging in these studies served two purposes which ultimately contributed to an increase in compliance. First, the presence of the equipment resulted in a reduction in compliance cost since the gloves and masks were conveniently located. Second, the inclusion of the protective equipment increased the subjects' perception of the danger associated with using the products. In contrast, the presence of several different configurations of warnings developed in accordance with ANSI standards did not affect danger perception in either study when compared to standard "generic" instruction labels.

It is clear from the results of these studies that operationally defining the inclusion of protective equipment as a compliance cost reduction is not entirely correct. Although cost probably had a major impact on the compliance rates reported here, it is unknown to what degree perception of danger affected the results. Further research is needed to separate the positive contributions of these effects, as well as the moderating effects of adaptation to such techniques over time. Further research is also needed to determine if these results will generalize to other (e.g. occupational) domains.

The results of these studies highlight two reasons supporting the inclusion of personal protective devices with hazardous consumer product packaging. Such devices, including gloves, dust masks, eyewear and hearing protection, can often be added to packaging at low cost relative to the total product cost. These results indicate that inclusion of such devices may be an extremely effective method to increase compliance in some circumstances.

ACKNOWLEDGEMENTS

The authors would like to thank Rhonda Kinghorn and Paul Costanza for their assistance with data collection.

Much of this research was made possible through funding provided by The Idaho Research Council.

REFERENCES

Dingus, T.A., Hathaway, J.A. and Hunn, B.P. (1991). A most important warning variable: Two demonstrations of the powerful effects of cost on warning compliance. <u>Proceedings of the Human Factors Society, 35th Annual Meeting</u>.

The Effectiveness of an Interactive Warning in a Realistic Product-Use Situation

Richard R. Duffy
Department of Psychology
Rensselaer Polytechnic Institute
Troy, New York 12180

Michael J. Kalsher
Department of Psychology
Rensselaer Polytechnic Institute
Troy, New York 12180

Michael S. Wogalter
Department of Psychology
North Carolina State University
Raleigh, North Carolina 27695

ABSTRACT

Warning labels are widely used to convey information about the safe use of products. In an attempt to design better warnings, researchers are exploring factors that influence their effectiveness. One design factor that appears promising is an interactive label that requires manipulation by the consumer using the product. In the present research, the effectiveness of two interactive warning labels (with and without a color component) were compared to a standard label in the context of a realistic product-use task. Additionally, task load was manipulated (low vs. higher). The results showed that the interactive labels were noticed, recalled and complied to more often than the standard on-product label. No effect of increasing task load and adding color to the interactive label was observed. The results indicate that the interactive label is a viable means of facilitating warning effectiveness.

INTRODUCTION

Although warnings are an important means of providing information concerning the safe use of a product, their presence does not necessarily ensure that consumers will use products safely (DeJoy, 1989). As a result, researchers have begun to systematically examine the factors that may influence warning effectiveness. Measures of effectiveness include changes in hazard perception, knowledge, and behavioral compliance. The majority of warnings research has focused on the physical design of warnings. Warning design factors include the attributes of the warning itself (e.g., increasing the size of the warning, adding color and pictorials) and extra-warning characteristics (e.g., proximal location and lack of contextual clutter). However, it is not always the case that changes in intra- and extra-warning characteristics result in increased effectiveness (e.g., DeJoy, 1989).

In order to increase the likelihood that a user will read a warning, and ultimately comply with it, it must first be noticed. One design that has shown promise in increasing noticeability is the interactive warning label, initially examined by Gill, Barbera and Precht (1987). This type of warning requires manipulation prior to (or while) using a product. Research has shown that the interactive label is more noticeable than a conventional on-product label (Frantz and Rhoades, in press; Gill et al., 1987; Hunn and Dingus, 1992; Wogalter, Barlow, and Murphy, 1992).

One explanation for the ability of the interactive label to draw attention (as compared to a non-interactive label) may be related to cognitive theories of mental models (Johnson-Laird, 1983), schemas (Bozinoff, 1981; Brewer and Treyens, 1981), and scripts (Schank and Abelson, 1977). Script theory suggests that after experience in a particular domain, people tend to use behaviors based on that experience in future encounters. With repeated experience, these sets of behavioral sequences become well-learned and become connected into larger sequences of behavior, and are theorized to occur automatically without much conscious thought. Therefore, if a person is familiar with a product, most behaviors associated with that product will be driven by scripted sequences of actions. In order to "break" these script-driven processes, some sort of non-scripted component needs to be introduced into the situation. Because the physical manipulation of an interactive label is a novel behavior, it may serve to break into or interrupt the individual's script, making it more likely that the individual will notice, read, and comply with the warning than without the interruption.

Although research has shown that interactive warnings can be effective in drawing attention to (i.e., noticing) warning information, research on its potential to produce behavioral compliance is less clear cut. For example, both Gill et al. (1987) and Hunn and Dingus (1992) found no advantage for an interactive warning in promoting compliance, whereas, two recent studies (e.g., Frantz and Rhoades, in press; Wogalter et al., 1992) have shown a beneficial effect of interactive labels on compliance. Closer inspection of these studies, however, shows that variations in experimental procedures may, at least in part, account for the observed differences in behavioral compliance. The procedures differed with respect to whether the task mirrored realistic product-use conditions, and the degree of familiarity the participants were likely to be with the products and tasks. While it is difficult to disentangle the specific reasons for the differing results between studies, particularly when numerous variables differed between experiments, it is important to re-test the concept of label interactivity because it holds potential promise for increasing warning effectiveness. The most appropriate follow-up test would employ an interactive warning label in conjunction with a familiar consumer product in a realistic product-use situation. In addition, an incidental exposure paradigm should be used in which the experimental situation does not draw explicit attention to the product and warning to assure external validity. Therefore, one purpose of the present study was to examine the effectiveness of two kinds of warnings (conventional tag vs. interactive) on a familiar product (an electrical extension cord) under incidental exposure conditions within a set of tasks that consumers might perform in the home or at work (i.e., realistic product-use conditions).

A second purpose of the study was to examine the effect of task load on warning noticeability and compliance. Task load refers to the number of tasks an individual is carrying out at any given time. Several theories of human information processing posit that an increased level of task load can negatively impact performance (Wickens, 1989). A similar decrement might be expected for warning-related behaviors. Specifically, if an individual is carrying out several tasks at once (e.g., reading instructions, assembling parts, or talking on the phone), increased task load may result in a failure to notice, read, and comply with a warning.

Before the present study was performed, a pilot study was used to make an initial examination of the potential effect of task load on noticing, reading, and complying with a warning. Participants were asked to plug the electrical cord of various products such as a TV and videocassette recorder (VCR) into outlets using a set of extension cords. The cords contained safety information about their proper use. Under the increased task load condition, participants had to insert a videotape into a VCR, rewind the tape, and then cue it to a specified position. It had been expected that participants in the increased task load condition would be thinking about the secondary task (i.e., cueing the tape) as they were plugging in the products (i.e., primary task), which would decrease the likelihood that they would see, read, and comply with the warning. Nevertheless, the task load manipulation failed to show any effect. One potential explanation for this null finding is that the two tasks occurred in serial order, and not simultaneously. Thus, the extra task might have had no effect during the time participants were using the extension cords. In the present study, another task load manipulation was developed in which the additional (secondary) task was expected to be performed simultaneously with the primary task.

Another issue was examined in the present study - the possible influence of color in a warning. The presence of color might enhance the noticeability of a warning. Most studies concerned with color in the warning literature have measured people's preference and the level of connoted hazard of various colors, but surprisingly, color has received very little systematic investigation in behavioral compliance research. One study by Wogalter, Godfrey, Fontenelle, Desaulniers, Rothstein, and Laughery (1987) showed that a sign with color on a water fountain (that warned of contaminants) was more effective in dissuading drinking than a sign without color. However, color was only one of several enhancements made to the color-present sign; the size of the warning was increased and a pictorial was added as well. Therefore, it is difficult to determine from the Wogalter et al. (1987) study whether and how much influence color had in facilitating compliance. Thus, a third purpose of the present study was to isolate a potential effect of color by comparing an interactive warning label with color (bright safety orange background) to the same label without color (white background) on warning effectiveness measures.

In summary, three variables were manipulated in the present experiment: label type, task load and color. Three dependent measures were used to assess warning effectiveness: (1) noticing, (2) reading, and (3) complying. It was hypothesized that an interactive colored warning label under lower task load conditions would be most effective.

METHOD

Participants

One hundred twenty undergraduates at Rensselaer Polytechnic Institute participated in the study. They received credit toward an introductory psychology course in which they were enrolled. Participants were randomly assigned, in equal proportions, to one of eight experimental conditions.

Design

A 2 Task Load (Low, Increased) x 4 Label Type (No Label Control, Tag, Interactive with Color-Absent, Interactive with Color-Present) between-subjects factorial design was used. Three dependent variables were examined: noticing the warning label, recall of the warning content (as an indicant of reading), and behavioral compliance. Noticing and recall were assessed by items on a post-task questionnaire. Compliance was assessed by observing whether the participants' performed the safety behaviors directed by the warning.

Materials

Four sets of white extension cords were used. Each cord had a removable outlet cover which was permanently attached near the female receptacle of an extension cord. The cover was designed to fit into the female receptacle to prevent shock when the female receptable of the cord was not in use. The original manufacturers warning was located on the plastic outlet cover, molded in raised white text on a white background. The original manufacturers warning was removed due to its low visibility and readability (i.e., small raised white letters on a white background).

The four pairs of extension cords differed only in terms of the presence, location, and color of the warning. In the No-Label (Control) condition, there was no warning information provided anywhere on the cords. In the Tag condition, the warning label was permanently attached to the extension cord five cm above the female receptacle. In the two interactive conditions, the warning label was affixed to the outlet cover on the female receptacle. The two interactive labels were identical except for the use of color. The redesigned warning contained information about potential fire and electrical hazards associated with plugging too many products into the extension cords. Figure 1 shows the label used in the three warnings-present conditions.

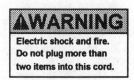

Figure 1. Warning Label used in the Three Warning-Present Conditions. The Gray Shading Represents Orange Color used in the Tag and Interactive Color-Present Conditions. In the Interactive Color-Absent Condition, the Background was White.

The text on all of the warning labels occupied a space of 3.8 cm x 2.2 cm. The font used for the signal word and warning instructions was 18-point sans serif and 8-point sans serif, respectively. The signal word (WARNING) was printed in black text on a white background (Color-Absent condition) and in black text on a bright, highly saturated safety orange background (Tag and Color-Present conditions). In addition, a signal icon (i.e., exclamation point surrounded by a triangle) was located to the left of the signal word.

Procedure

Participants were initally told they would be evaluating instructional media. Each participant was led into a room in which a TV, VCR, and videotape rewinder were set up on a small table. The lights in the room were turned off and the equipment was intentionally left unplugged to make the room appear as if it was not properly set up for the experiment. Upon entering the room, the experimenter turned on the lights and gave the participant an informed consent form to complete. The experimenter then left the room for a few seconds and returned with a pair of extension cords (all conditions) and a small battery operated tape player (Increased Task Load condition only) and casually placed the extension cords on a chair about 1 m from the video equipment and the tape player on a table in front of the participant.

Upon examining the equipment, the experimenter remarked that he had left the videotape in another room and would have to retrieve it. The experimenter then explained what the participant would be asked to do. Participants in the Low Task Load condition were told that they would be watching an instructional videotape about job training and then would complete two questionnaires. Participants in the Increased Task Load group were told that they would be listening to an audiotaped lecture (concerning industrial control rooms), then would watch an instructional videotape, and would later complete two questionnaires.

In the Increased Task Load condition, the experimenter started the audiotape and told the participant that he would return shortly with the videotape. The Low Task Load condition lacked the audio tape and all procedures associated with it. Before exiting the room, the experimenter asked each participant (regardless of condition) if he or she would mind "helping out" by plugging in the television, VCR and videotape rewinder. For those participants in the Increased Task Load condition, this task was to be carried out while they listened to the audiotape. The experimenter then left the room, and after approximately four min had elapsed, the experimenter returned to the room with the videotape.

Finally, participants were taken into another room to complete two post-task questionnaires. The first questionnaire requested various demographic data (e.g., age, gender) and ratings of 18 consumer products including electrical extension cords. The rating questions evaluated three dimensions: perceived hazard, severity of injury and product familiarity. Responses were based on 9-point Likert-type scales anchored with "0" denoting absence of quantity to "8" indicating maximum quantity. The specific questions and numerical and verbal anchors were:

(a) "How hazardous is the product?" with the anchors: (0) not at all hazardous, (2) slightly hazardous, (4) hazardous, (6) very hazardous, and (8) extremely hazardous.
(b) "How severely might you be injured with this product?" with the anchors: (0) not at all severe, (2) slightly severe, (4) severe, (6) very severe, and (8) extremely severe.
(c) "How familiar is the product?" with the anchors: (0) not at all familiar, (2) slightly familiar, (4) familiar, (6) very familiar, and (8) extremely familiar.

For each of the above questions, the products were arranged into three random orders.

The second questionnaire asked participants whether they saw a warning label, and if so, specifically what did it say. Participants in the Increased Task Load condition were also asked to recall the content of the audiotaped lecture.

After completing the questionnaires, participants were debriefed, thanked for their participation, and dismissed. The experimenter then examined the two extension cords to determine how they were connected by the participant. Correct performance (compliance) was operationally defined as plugging in two of the three products into one extension cord and one product into the other extension cord.

RESULTS

Two raters independently scored the open-ended items on the questionnaires. Inter-rater agreement was computed using the formula: agreements/(agreements + disagreements) x 100. Inter-rater agreement for each item ranged from 96% to 100% with a mean of 97% across all items.

A 2 Task Load (Low, Increased) x 4 Label Type (No-Label Control, Tag, Interactive with Color Absent, Interactive with Color Present) between-subjects Multivariate Analysis of Variance (MANOVA) was performed on three dependent variables: noticing, recall, and compliance. Multivariate tests of significance using Hotelling's criterion indicated a main effect of Label Type, $F(9, 326) = 17.48$, $p < .001$, but not Task Load, $F(3, 110) < 1.0$, nor their interaction, $F(9, 326) < 1.0$.

Separate univariate one-way analyses of variance (ANOVAs) were performed on each dependent variable for the significant main effect shown in the MANOVA. Post-hoc tests (i.e., Newman-Keuls Multiple Range Test at an α of .05) were used to compare conditions. The following three sections describe the results of these analyses.

Noticeability of the Warning

There was a significant effect of Label Type on noticing the warning label, $F(3, 116) = 49.67$, $p < .001$. Participants reported seeing both interactive labels ($M = 76.7\%$ and $M = 86.7\%$ for the color absent and present conditions, respectively) significantly more often than the tag label ($M = 16.7\%$) and when no label was present ($M = 0.0\%$). There was no significant difference between the Interactive Color-Absent and Interactive Color-Present conditions, nor between the Tag condition and the No-Label Control condition.

Recall of the Warning Content

There was also a significant effect of Label Type on recall of the warning content, $F(3, 116) = 29.00$, $p < .001$. Participants recalled the content of both interactive labels ($M = 53.3\%$ and $M = 73.3\%$ for the color absent and present conditions, respectively) significantly more often than the tag label ($M = 10.0\%$) and when no label was present ($M = 0.0\%$). There was no significant difference between the Interactive Color-Absent and Interactive Color-Present conditions, nor between the Tag condition and the No-Label Control condition.

Compliance to the Warning

There was a significant effect of Label Type on behavioral

compliance, $F(3, 116) = 14.57$, $p < .001$. Participants complied with both interactive labels ($M = 53.3\%$ and $M = 43.3\%$ for the color absent and present conditions, respectively) significantly more often than the tag label ($M = 6.7\%$) and when no label was present ($M = 0.0\%$). There was no significant difference between the Interactive Color-Absent and Interactive Color-Present conditions, nor between the Tag condition and the No-Label Control condition.

Analysis of Ratings

The results confirmed that participants were highly familiar with the product. Participants gave electrical extension cords a mean familiarity rating of 6.79 (just below the midpoint of the verbal anchors of "very familiar" and "extremely familiar" on the scale). They also assigned extension cords a mean hazard rating of 3.05 (midway between the verbal anchors of "slightly hazardous" and "hazardous" on the scale), and a mean severity of injury rating of 3.08 (between the verbal anchors of "slightly severe" and "severe" on the scale). None of the groups differed with respect to familiarity, hazard or severity of injury ($ps > .05$).

Compliance Contingencies

Of the 54 participants who reported seeing the warning, 43 (80%) were able to recall its contents ($\Phi = .62$, p < .0001) and 31 (57%) complied with it ($\Phi = .59$, p < .0001). Of the participants who recalled the warning, 72% complied with it ($\Phi = .76$, p < .0001). All of the participants who complied with the warning reported seeing it and could correctly recall its content.

DISCUSSION

The results of this study showed that the interactive label was noticed, read (as measured by recall), and complied with more often than a conventional on-product (tag) label. These findings are consistent with those of Frantz and Rhoades (in press) and Wogalter et al. (1992), who also showed a positive effect of interactive warnings. However, this study only partially confirmed the results of Gill et al. (1987) and Hunn and Dingus (1992). Their findings showing increased noticeability were confirmed, but not their findings of no effect on compliance.

While positive effects were found for the interactive label, none was found for the tag relative to the no-label control. Research by Wogalter and Young (in press) has shown another kind of tag label (attached to a small bottle container) to benefit compliance. However, the two kinds of tags were very different. Wogalter and Young's (in press) label, unlike the one used in the present study, required more interaction by the user while using the product.

This study failed to demonstrate an influence of task load on warning compliance. Possibly, the high task load condition (i.e., attending to the audiotape) did not actually produce an increase in cognitive effort at the point in time expected. Post-task questioning indicated that 78% of the participants in this condition reported hearing the contents of the audiotape, but it is not clear whether they were listening to the tape at the precise moment they were plugging in the electrical equipment. As task load has been found to influence performance in a variety of other tasks, additional research on its effect on warning compliance is needed. Some other potential task load manipulations might include having participants simultaneously attend to an important telephone conversation concurrent with the warning-related task or constructing a situation where performance speed is emphasized. If task load is found to have an impact on warning effectiveness, steps should be taken to design warnings that will attract a user's undivided attention and persuade them that compliance is a most important primary task.

The presence of color did not significantly enhance the interactive warning's effectiveness. However, there was a (non-significant) trend favoring color for noticeability and recall, but not for compliance. One possible explanation for this is that the strong effect of the interactive label might have mitigated any additional effect of color. As was noted in the Introduction, research showing effects of color on compliance has been sparse. Additional research is needed to determine not only the effect of color (its presence versus absence), but also the effects of different hues, brightness and saturation on measures of warning effectiveness.

This and other research indicates that interactive warnings are useful in conveying safety information. However, an important question that remains is whether consumers would accept and purchase products with interactive warning labels. By its very nature, the interactive design is intrusive, by purpose interrupting task performance. According to script theory this interruption is necessary to break into people's highly familiar sequence of actions. Thus, a balance probably needs to be maintained between too much intrusiveness and not enough. How such a balance could be determined and achieved is an important topic of future research.

REFERENCES

Bosinoff, L. (1981). A script theoretic approach to information processing: An energy conservation application, *Advances in consumer research*, 9, 481-486. St. Louis, MO: Association for Consumer Research.

Brewer, W. G., and Treyens, J. C. (1981). Role of schemata in memory for places. *Cognitive Psychology*, 13, 207-230.

DeJoy, D. M. (1989). Consumer product warnings: Review and analysis of effectiveness research. In *Proceedings of the Human Factors Society 33rd Annual Meeting* (pp. 936-940). Santa Monica, CA: Human Factors Society.

Frantz, J. P., and Rhoades, T. P. (in press). A task analytic approach to the temporal placement of product warnings. *Human Factors*.

Gill, R. T., Barbera, C., and Precht, T. (1987). A comparative evaluation of warning label designs. In *Proceedings of the Human Factors Society 31st Annual Meeting* (pp. 476-478). Santa Monica, CA: Human Factors Society.

Hunn, B. P., and Dingus, T. A. (1992). Interactivity, information and compliance cost in a consumer product warning scenario. *Accident Analysis and Prevention*, 24, 497-505.

Johnson-Laird, P. N. (1983). *Mental models*. Cambridge, UK: Cambridge University Press.

Lehto, M. R. (1991). A proposed conceptual model of human behavior and its implication for design of warnings. *Perceptual and Motor Skills*, 73, 595-611.

Lehto, M. R., and Miller, J. M. (1988). The effectiveness of warning labels. *Journal of Products Liability 11*, 225-270.

Miller, J. M., Lehto, M. R., and Frantz, J. P. (1990). *Instructions and Warnings: The Annotated Bibliography*. Ann Arbor, MI: Fuller Technical Publications.

Schank, R. C., and Abelson, R. (1977). *Scripts, plans, goals, and understanding*. Hillsdale, NJ: Erlbaum.

Wickens, C. D. (1989). Attention and skilled performance. In D. Holding (ed.), *Human skills* (2nd ed., pp. 71-105). New York: Wiley.

Wogalter, M. S., Barlow, T., and Murphy, S. A. (1992). *Accessory safety directives on electronic equipment increases compliance to safety warnings in an owner's manual*. Poster presented at the Human Factors Society 36th Annual Meeting, Atlanta, October.

Wogalter, M. S., Godfrey, S. S., Fontenelle, G. A., Desaulniers, D. R., Rothstein, P. R., and Laughery, K. R. (1987). Effectiveness of warnings. *Human Factors, 29*, 599-612.

Wogalter, M. S., and Young, S. L. (in press). Enhancing warning compliance through alternative product label designs. *Applied Ergonomics*.

Young, S. L. (1991). Increasing the noticeability of warnings: Effects of pictorial, color, signal icon and border. In *Proceedings of the Human Factors Society 35th Annual Meeting* (pp. 580-584). Santa Monica, CA: Human Factors Society.

THE ABILITY OF TWO LAY GROUPS TO JUDGE PRODUCT WARNING EFFECTIVENESS

J. Paul Frantz
Miller Engineering
Ann Arbor, Michigan

James M. Miller
University of Michigan
Ann Arbor, Michigan

Bruce W. Main
Miller Engineering
Ann Arbor, Michigan

How well can lay people assess the effectiveness or "adequacy" of product warnings without assistance from expert testimony? To begin to answer this question, two studies were conducted to determine the extent to which law students and engineering students could assess the relative effectiveness of two drain opener warning label designs. In the first experiment, only 18 of the 38 engineering students (47%) correctly identified the warning label design that had, in a previous study, been shown to be significantly more effective with similar subjects who actually used the product. In addition, these subjects did not accurately predict the likelihood that their peers would read and comply with the precautions. In the second experiment, only 14 of the 42 law students (33%) correctly identified the more effective of two label designs. This research contradicts several legal authors who postulate that juries are capable of determining the effectiveness of a warning unaided by well-founded expert testimony. More specifically, these studies do not support the assertion that the "knowledge of ordinary people" is sufficient to 1) distinguish between warnings that differ in their behavioral effectiveness and 2) accurately predict the likelihood that people such as themselves will read and heed safety instructions when using a product.

INTRODUCTION

During trials involving failure-to-warn allegations, individuals with no specific training, education, or experience in the design of product warnings are asked to make judgments regarding warning "adequacy" or effectiveness. In such cases, human factors professionals are often called upon to provide expert testimony with respect to warnings issues. From a human factors perspective, expert assistance regarding warnings is quite reasonable considering the body of empirical and theoretical warnings research that has emanated from the human factors community and the growing recognition that applying this research to the design of warnings can yield more effective warnings (cf. Dingus, Hathaway, Hunn, Lewis, and Wreggit, in press; Frantz and Rhoades, in press; Frantz, 1993; Lehto, 1992; Miller, Frantz, and Rhoades, 1991; Miller, Lehto, and Frantz, 1990; Wogalter, Barlow, and Murphy, 1992; Wogalter and Young, 1992). Despite these developments, certain attorneys question the view that juries can be assisted by warnings experts (Hardie, 1991; Houser and Clark, 1993). Hardie, for example, proposes that:

> The defendant should try to exclude all opinion evidence on warnings, leaving the evaluation of the warnings to the jury and lawyer's arguments. . . . The legal principles applicable to liability for failure to warn were developed by courts without the benefit of communication theorists. These legal principles are based on common sense, fairness, and the knowledge of ordinary people. In this spirit, juries are not well served by witnesses who are nothing more than professional advocates (Hardie, 1991, pp. 14, 21).

Clearly, this viewpoint postulates that juries are capable of accurately judging the adequacy or effectiveness of a warning without assistance from a warnings expert. To begin to test this assertion it is important to answer the question, "How well can lay people assess the effects of product warnings which are directed toward their peers?" This paper describes two studies primarily aimed at answering that question. The specific objectives of the research were to determine the ability of lay people to: 1) Assess the relative effectiveness of two product warning label designs and 2) Predict the likelihood that their peers would read and follow precautions presented in different forms. It should be noted that, in the context of this research, "lay people" refers to individuals who do not have special knowledge or training in hazard communication.

STUDY #1

Method

Subjects. For the purposes of both experiments, it was necessary to have a group of people predict the effectiveness of warning labels for a specific product and then to compare these responses to observed and reported behaviors of a similar group of people who actually used the product. The latter group of subjects was obtained from a recently completed study of drain opener warnings (Frantz, 1993). In that study, a group of undergraduate students from a large midwestern university, serving as subjects, used a drain opener product to unclog a sink. In the present experiment, we sought similar subjects who could assess the effectiveness of the labels that were empirically tested in the previous experiment. The result was a group of thirty-eight students in two industrial engineering classes who participated in the study on a voluntary basis. There were 16 females and 22 males. It is important to note that, although these subjects would not constitute a typical jury, they were certainly peers of the individuals who actually used the product in the earlier experiment.

<u>Procedure</u>. With a can of crystal drain opener in hand, the experimenter read a statement explaining the hazardous nature of the product when it reacts with water and other substances in a drain. The introductory information also noted that at least 21 people have been seriously injured while using the product and that the manufacturer wished to inform users that it is essential that they wear rubber gloves and protective goggles. Subjects were further instructed that the manufacturer had narrowed the location of these safety instructions to one of two places on the label -- either in the Precautions Section or in the Directions for Use Section.

A color transparency of the drain opener label was then displayed via an overhead projector. The size of the projected image was such that the subjects could see the sections of the label, but the printing within the sections of the label was not large enough to be legible.

Following the introduction, subjects were asked: "In your opinion, which of the two potential locations will produce the more effective label [the Precautions Section or the Directions for Use Section]?" Subjects recorded their answers in response booklets.

Subjects were then asked to assume that college students such as themselves were using the drain opener to unclog the drain of a kitchen sink. Given this assumption, they were asked to estimate: 1) What percentage of users would read at least one of the two key messages if the messages appeared in the Precautions Section, 2) What percentage of users would wear rubber gloves if the gloves were available next to the drain opener in the cabinet under the sink, and 3) What percentage of users would wear protective goggles if the goggles were available next to the drain opener in a cabinet under the sink. The subjects were then told to assume that the manufacturer had instead decided to include the instructions to wear gloves and goggles in the Directions for Use Section rather than the Precautions Section. They were then asked to make the same three estimates.

Next, subjects were asked to indicate how much of each section of the back of the label they would read if they were actually using the product to unclog a drain. They were given a seven point scale with verbal anchors ranging from "None" to "All."

It should be noted that, when asked to estimate the percentage of college students that would wear gloves or goggles, the subjects were shown a transparency which illustrated the location of the gloves and goggles in the kitchen where subjects in the prior study actually used the product to unclog a sink.

<u>Results</u>

<u>Ability to Assess Relative Effectiveness of Warning Designs</u>. As previously mentioned, Frantz (1993) conducted an earlier experiment to measure the behavioral effect of placing safety instructions in the Precautions Section versus the Directions for Use Section of a drain opener label. The results of the experiment showed that placing the safety instructions in the Directions for Use Section dramatically increased the percentage of subjects who read and complied with the instructions. Specifically, moving the instruction to use protective eyewear from the Precautions Section to the Directions for Use Section increased the percentage of subjects reading the instruction from 30% to 90% and the percentage of subjects complying from 25% to 65%. For the instruction to wear rubber gloves, moving the instruction from the Precautions Section to the Directions for Use Section increased the percentage of subjects reading the instruction from 38% to 90% and the percentage of subjects complying from 45% to 80%. Clearly, the more effective label design was to present the safety instructions in the Directions for Use Section rather than in the Precautions Section. Thus, in the present experiment the ability of a person to judge the effectiveness of a label was measured by his/her response to the question: Which of the two potential locations will produce the more effective label [the Precautions Section or the Directions for Use Section]?

Only 18 of the 38 subjects (47%) correctly recognized that the more effective label design was the one with the safety instructions placed in the Directions for Use Section. That is, slightly more than half of the subjects (53%) incorrectly identified the more effective label as being the one with the safety instructions placed in the Precautions Section rather than the Directions for Use Section.

<u>Predicted Versus Measured Compliance with Precautions</u>. Table 1 shows the average predicted compliance rates from the present study and the observed compliance rates obtained from the previous experiment. This table illustrates that the *predicted* compliance rates were virtually identical regardless of the location of the safety instructions. Thus, subjects in this experiment apparently did not consider the location of the safety instructions to be an important factor in determining compliance with the safety instructions. In contrast, the *observed* compliance rates obtained from the previous study differed substantially from one another.

It is also noteworthy that, for both safety instructions, subjects reliably predicted a compliance rate that exceeded the observed compliance rate when the safety instructions appeared in the Precautions Section [$t(37) = 2.11$, $p < 0.05$ for wearing gloves; $t(37) = 2.29$, $p < 0.05$ for wearing eye protection]. On the other hand, when the safety instructions appeared in the Directions for Use Section, subjects reliably predicted a lower compliance rate than was actually observed [$t(37) = -5.54$, $p < 0.01$ for wearing gloves; $t(37) = -6.31$, $p < 0.01$ for wearing eye protection].

<u>Predicted Versus Measured Attention to Label Components</u>. Table 2 shows the average percentage of users that the subjects predicted would read at least one of the two safety instructions if the instructions were placed in the Precautions Section versus the Directions for Use Section. This table also shows the percentage of subjects in the previous experiment (Frantz, 1993) who reported reading each safety instruction (i.e., observed reading rate). These results are similar to the compliance data described above. The predicted percentage of people who would read at least one safety precaution did not differ significantly when the instructions were presented in the Precautions Section versus the Directions for Use Section [$t(37) = 0.56$,

Table 1

Observed and mean predicted rates of compliance with two drain opener safety instructions by location of instruction.

Safety Instruction	Location of Safety Instruction			
	Precautions Section		Directions for Use Section	
	Observed Compliance Rate *(from Frantz, 1993)*	Average Predicted Compliance Rate *(from present study)*	Observed Compliance Rate *(from Frantz, 1993)*	Average Predicted Compliance Rate *(from present study)*
Use protective eyewear	25% (n=40)	36% (n=38)	65% (n=40)	37% (n=38)
Wear rubber gloves	45% (n=40)	55% (n=38)	80% (n=40)	55% (n=38)

Table 2

Observed and mean predicted percentages of subjects reading at least one of the two safety instructions when the instructions appeared in the Precautions Section versus the Directions for Use Section.

	Location of Safety Instruction			
	Precautions Section		Directions for Use Section	
	Observed Reading Rate* *(from Frantz, 1993)*	Mean Predicted Reading Rate *(from present study)*	Observed Reading Rate* *(from Frantz, 1993)*	Mean Predicted Reading Rate *(from present study)*
Percentage of users reading at least one of the two safety instructions (wear gloves/goggles)	38% (n=40)	62% (n=38)	93% (n=40)	65% (n=38)

* Observed reading rates represent the proportion of subjects who reported reading these precautions during structured interviews immediately following the use of the product.

47

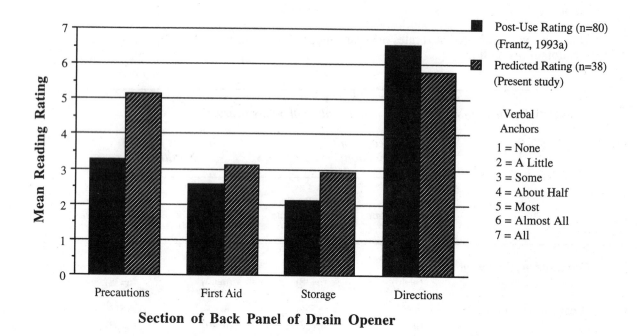

Figure 1. *Mean reading ratings for each section of the back of the drain opener label. Predicted reading ratings refer to those provided in the present study. Post-use reading ratings refer to those provided by subjects in an earlier experiment (Frantz, 1993).*

p > 0.10]. Again, this suggests that the location of safety instructions was not considered to be an important factor affecting the likelihood that people will read the safety instructions. However, in the earlier experiment, this factor was found to be extremely important. More specifically, placing the instructions in the Directions for Use Section rather than in the Precautions Section significantly increased the percentage of subjects who reported reading at least one of the instructions from 38% to 93%.

As with the compliance rate data, subjects reliably predicted a reading rate that exceeded the observed reading rate when the safety instructions appeared in the Precautions Section [t(37) = 6.08, p < 0.01]. When the safety instructions appeared in the Directions for Use Section, subjects reliably predicted a lower reading rate than was actually observed [t(37) = -7.36, p < 0.01].

Recall that subjects in the present experiment were also asked to rate the amount of each section of the label that they would read. Figure 1 shows a comparison between the average ratings provided by subjects in the present study and those obtained in the earlier experiment. In the earlier experiment, subjects were asked to report how much of each section of the label that they actually read during their use of the product.

The Mann-Whitney U test was used to analyze the difference between reading ratings provided by the subjects in the earlier study who had just used the drain opener and subjects in the present study who were predicting how much of each section they would read. For the Precautions Section, the predicted reading rating was significantly higher than the post-use rating (z = 4.2, p < 0.01). For the

First Aid Section, the reading ratings did not differ significantly (z = 1.9, p > 0.05). For the Storage and Disposal Section, the predicted reading rating was significantly higher than the post-use rating (z = 3.9, p < 0.01). Finally, for the Directions for Use Section, the predicted reading rating was significantly lower than the post-use rating (z = 5.4, p < 0.01). Thus, subjects predicted that they would read a greater proportion of the Precautions Section and of the Storage and Disposal Section than similar subjects who actually used the product. However, subjects predicted that they would read less of the Directions for Use Section than subjects who actually used the product.

STUDY #2

Method

Subjects. Forty-two first year law students from a large midwestern university participated on a voluntary basis. Again, although these subjects did not constitute a typical jury, they were considered members of the lay population with respect to the behavioral effectiveness of warnings.

Procedure. The procedure was the same as that described for Study #1 with the exception that the law students were not asked questions regarding the likelihood that people such as themselves would read and comply with the safety instructions.

Results

Only 14 of the 42 subjects (33%) recognized that the more effective label design was the one with the safety instructions placed in the Directions for Use Section. That is, two thirds of the subjects (66%) incorrectly identified the more effective label as being the one with the safety instructions placed in the Precautions Section rather than the Directions for Use Section.

GENERAL DISCUSSION AND CONCLUSIONS

Less than half of all the subjects indicated that placing the safety instructions in the Directions for Use Section would produce the more effective label. One explanation for this finding is that subjects in Study #1 predicted that they would read a large portion of both the Precautions Section and the Directions for Use Section. For example, on average, subjects reported that they would read most of the information in the Precautions Section. This assumption, coupled with the intuitive appeal of categorizing instructions to wear gloves and goggles as safety precautions, seems to provide a logical basis for incorrectly concluding that presenting the safety instructions in the Precautions Section would produce the more effective label. The flaw in this logic is the subject's inability to predict how much of the Precautions Section they would actually read. More specifically, relative to their peers who actually used the product, subjects in the present experiment overestimated the amount of the Precautions Section that they would read and underestimated the amount of the Directions for Use Section that they would read. Similarly, it is easy to see how a jury might also make such an error in judgment. Consequently, they could fall prey to the argument that if only an additional warning message had been added to the Precautions Section, the user would have noticed the warning and the accident would have been prevented.

The proportion of subjects indicating that including the safety instructions in the Precautions Section would produce a more effective label is not surprising in light of the prevalence of this design approach. A large proportion of consumer product labels separate safety precautions from the Directions for Use (e.g., pesticide/insecticide products regulated by the Environmental Protection Agency). The intuitive basis for this design strategy (and a potential explanation for the finding in this experiment) is that safety-critical information should not be buried in "mundane" Directions for Use, instead it should be set apart in order to increase its prominence and somehow enhance the user's awareness of the hazard.

This research contradicts Hardie's (1991) position that juries are capable of determining the effectiveness of a warning unaided by well-founded expert assistance. Specifically, this study does not support the assertion that the "knowledge of ordinary people" is sufficient to 1) distinguish between warnings that differ in their behavioral effectiveness and 2) predict accurately the likelihood that people such as themselves will read and comply with safety instructions when using a product.

In closing, consider the likely trial scenario in which the drain opener product used in this experiment is alleged to have a defective warning because the instructions to wear gloves and goggles appeared in the Directions for Use

Section and not in the Precautions Section. In such a situation, the "common sense, fairness, and the knowledge of ordinary people" upon which Hardie suggests relying would likely lead a jury to the incorrect conclusion that the warning was inadequate and that the safety instructions could have been and should have been made more prominent by placing them in the Precautions Section. In a broader sense, this example illustrates the utility of well-founded human factors testimony in the courtroom.

REFERENCES

Dingus, T.J., Hathaway, J.A., Hunn, B.P., Lewis, V.R., and Wreggit, S.S. (in press). Warning variables affecting personal protective equipment use. *Safety Science*.

Frantz, J.P. (1993). Effect of location and presentation format on attention to and compliance with product warnings and instructions. To appear in *Journal of Safety Research*.

Frantz, J.P. and Rhoades, T.P. (in press). A task analytic approach to the temporal and spatial placement of product warnings. *Human Factors*.

Hardie, W.H. (1991). Can experts evaluate the effectiveness of warnings? *For the Defense*, October, 14-21.

Houser, D.G. and Clark, R.J. (1993). Human factors testimony: Does the jury really need it? *For the Defense*, May, 13-19.

Lehto, M.R. (1992). Designing warning signs and warning labels: Scientific basis for initial guidelines. *International Journal of Industrial Ergonomics*, *10*, 115-138.

Miller, J.M., Frantz, J.P. and Rhoades, T.P. (1991). A model for developing product information. In *Proceedings of the Human Factors Society 35th Annual Meeting*, (pp. 1063-1067). Santa Monica, CA: Human Factors Society.

Miller, J.M., Lehto, M.R. and Frantz, J.P. (1990). *Instructions and warnings: The annotated bibliography*. Ann Arbor, MI: Fuller Technical Publications.

Wogalter, M.S., Barlow, S.T., and Murphy, S. (1992, October). *An accessory safety directive increases compliance to warnings in an owner's manual*. Poster session paper presented at the Human Factors Society 36th Annual Meeting.

Wogalter, M.S. and Young, S. L. (1992, October). *Enhancing warning compliance through alternative product label designs*. Poster session paper presented at the Human Factors Society 36th Annual Meeting.

A COMPARATIVE EVALUATION OF WARNING LABEL DESIGNS

Richard T. Gill
Mechanical Engineering Department
University of Idaho
Moscow, Idaho

Christine Barbera
Psychology Department
University of Idaho

Terrence Precht
Mechanical Engineering Department
University of Idaho

ABSTRACT

The objective of this research was to compare the effectiveness of different warning label designs. Three different warning label designs for a portable electric heater were tested: (1) a traditional non-human factored label; (2) a color-coded "ski pass" label attached near the male end of the electric cord; and (3) a color-coded "interactive" label that required the user to interact with the label in order to use the heater. Subjects were informed that they were participating in a problem-solving experiment. Their task was to devise a system, meeting various constraints, to melt a votive candle in a cup. Several potential heat sources were available including an unsafe heater and extension cord combination. The results showed that the interactive design was most effective in attracting the users' attention, but none of them were effective in mediating safe user behavior.

INTRODUCTION

The ultimate purpose of a warning label is to mediate safe user behavior. Intuitively, this task seems easily attainable. However, such is not the case.

Initially, research on warning label design focused on their format. These studies were concerned with identifying the factors, such as lettering and color, that would maximize legibility. The findings from such studies formed the basis of current standards (ANSI, 72). Other early works focused on the content of the warning label and were concerned with issues such as wording and subjective ratings of perceived effectiveness. Dorris and Purswell (1978) were among the first researchers to identify the importance of the behavioral aspects of warning labels. They noted that "the purpose of warnings is to induce a certain behavior. . ., yet the extent to which warnings modify behavior is discouraging." They concluded that the problem of designing effective warning labels was one that needs to be undertaken by human factors specialists.

Somewhat surprisingly, the human factors research community did not respond in a timely fashion. It wasn't until the now classic paper by McCarthy, Finnegan, Krumm-Scott, and McCarthy (1984) that the ability, or more accurately the inability, of warning labels to alter user behavior came under close scrutiny. McCarthy, et al., reviewed over 400 papers concerned with warning label design and concluded that there was no evidence to support the notion that warning labels were effective in mediating safe user behavior.

Since then, there has been considerable attention focused on the efficacy of warning labels in altering user behavior (Godfrey, Rothstein, and Laughery, 1985; Wogalter, Fontenelle, and Laughery, 1985). In short, the findings have been quite discouraging. McCarthy and colleagues (Horst, McCarthy, Robinson, McCarthy, and Krumm-Scott, 1986) have expanded their literature review to include, among others, these more recent studies and drew the same conclusion.

If a warning label is to be effective in mediating safe user behavior, then it must attract the users' attention and induce them to read its contents. Failure to do so guarantees the ineffectiveness of the warning label. The primary objective of this research was to assess the effectiveness of an interactive warning label on a typical consumer product. It was hypothesized that if the user was forced to interact with the warning label in order to use the product, they would be more likely to attend to its contents.

METHOD

Three different warning label designs and configurations for a 1350-watt portable, forced air, electric space heater were tested: (1) Traditional Design -- a one- by three-inch black and white tag, with written warnings only, affixed to the rear of the heater; (2) Ski Pass Design -- three- by five-inch tag with red color coding, pictographs, and written warnings affixed near the male end of the heater's electric cord; and (3) Interactive Design -- the ski pass warning label design affixed to a flexible, curved piece of plastic that was attached to the male end of the cord such that it had to be bent back in order to connect the cord to a power source.

Subjects

Eighty-three subjects were recruited from the community of Moscow, Idaho, and paid six dollars each for their participation. Both males and females over eighteen years of age were used. A between-subjects design was implemented with subjects being randomly assigned to one of three conditions: (1) traditional design; (2) ski pass design; or (3) interactive design.

Procedure

All subjects were initially told that they were participating in an experiment investigating the human ability to perform problem-solving tasks. The purpose of this deceit was to minimize the demand characteristics of the experiment. Each subject was required to solve three types of problems: (1) a visual problem-solving task; (2) an abstract problem-solving task; and (3) a verbal problem-solving task. It was stressed that there was no time limit for any of the tasks. Only the final solution was of interest.

After reading the instructions, subjects were asked to perform the visual problem-solving task. This task consisted of six problems from Raven's Progressive Matrices (Raven, 1956). The purpose of this task was to assure that the subjects were convinced that they were participating in a problem-solving experiment.

Once the visual task was completed, the subjects were given the abstract problem-solving task. They were required to melt a votive candle inside a metal cup without lighting it. The subjects were given a list of constraints (i.e., do not do anything destructive or dangerous, the cup must be elevated between five and ten inches off the surface of the table, etc.). This list of constraints was given to provide a reasonably challenging task and to emphasize the need for safety. Subjects were provided with numerous tools and miscellaneous hardware such as pliers, files, clamps, nails, bolts, and screwdrivers. These items were to be used to create a supporting structure to elevate the cup according to the constraints. The three different heat sources provided were: (1) the heater, (2) a flood lamp, and (3) a large candle with a lighter. Also provided was an undersized extension cord, whose use was warned against in all three warning label

designs. Neither the heater nor the flood lamp could reach the receptacle without the use of the extension cord.

After the subjects completed the abstract problem-solving task, they were given a complex verbal problem-solving task. The purpose of this task was to erase the subjects' working memory. After five minutes, the task was interrupted and subjects were given a questionnaire in which they were asked to identify the location and content of all warning labels on the heater, flood lamp, extension cord, and any other item available for use in the abstract problem-solving task.

RESULTS

For the traditional design, ten of thirty subjects solved the abstract task without the use of the heater. As revealed by the questionnaire, none of them chose the alternative heat source as a means of circumventing the use of the unsafe heater and extension cord combination. Of the twenty subjects that did use the heater and extension cord, five of them recalled seeing a warning label and could accurately describe the location. However, none of them could recall the information presented by the warning label.

For the ski pass design, nine of twenty-nine subjects solved the abstract task without the use of the heater. As evidenced by the questionnaire, none of them did so as a means of avoiding the use of the heater and extension cord. Of the twenty subjects who did use the heater, six of them recalled seeing a warning label and identified its location. Once again, none of the subjects could recall the content of the label.

For the interactive design, four of twenty-four subjects solved the abstract task without the use of the heater. Again, none did so in order to avoid using the heater and extension cord combination. Of the twenty subjects who did use the heater, ten of them recalled seeing a warning and identified its location, but none of the subjects could recall the content.

DISCUSSION

Clearly, none of the warning labels were effective in mediating safe user behavior. That is, for all three designs, not one subject balked at using the unsafe heater and extension cord combination even though they were specifically told not to do anything unsafe or dangerous.

With respect to their effectiveness at attracting the user's attention, the trend was in the expected direction. That is, ten of twenty subjects recalled observing the interactive warning label which was a significantly higher proportion than the six of twenty who recalled seeing the ski tag label ($z = 1.83$, $p < .05$) or the five of twenty who recalled seeing the traditional label ($z = 2.31$, $p < .02$). However, the difference between the ski tag and traditional labels was not significant ($z = .50$, $p > .1$).

CONCLUSIONS

The ultimate goal of a warning label is to mediate safe user behavior. Yet in this experiment, as is most typically the case, none of the warning labels had the desired effect. That is, none of the subjects heeded any of the warning labels.

Warning label effectiveness was compromised at two levels. First, most of the subjects (65% over all three conditions) could not recall having even seen a warning label. Secondly, of those that could recall having seen a warning label, none of them could identify the content. Based on experimenter observations and past hoc questioning, this was universally a consequence of the subjects' failure to read the warning label. This is not to say that no one ever reads warning labels, but it does suggest that there is a significant portion of the user population that does not. This problem seems to be more acute as product familiarity increases (Lichtenstrin, et al., 1978; Loewenthal and Riley, 1980). More research is needed to identify the parameters that will make warning labels more salient, more likely to be read, and ultimately alter the user's behavior.

So where does this leave the design engineer? Two important points should be made. It is unrealistic to expect warning labels to universally mediate safe behavior in the user population. Thus, every attempt should be made to either remove or guard against all potential hazards. If this is not physically possible (for example, a high pressure paint sprayer), then considerable attention should be paid to the design and placement of the warning label (for specific details, see Robinson, 86) in order to maximize its effectiveness.

REFERENCES

1. ANSI (1972). Specifications for accident prevention signs (ANSI Z35.1). New York, NY: American National Standards Institute.

2. Dorris, A. L., and Purswell, J. L. (1977). Warnings and human behavior: implications for the design of product warnings. *Journal of Products Liability*, 1, 255-264.

3. Godfrey, S. S., Rothstein, P. R., and Laughery, K. P. (1985). Warnings: do they make a difference? In R. W. Swezey, et al. (Eds.), *Proceedings of the Human Factors Society 29th Annual Meeting* (pp. 669-673).

Santa Monica, California: The Human Factors Society.

4. Horst, D. P., McCarthy, G. E., Robinson, J. N., McCarthy, R. L., and Krumm-Scott, S. (1986). Safety Information Presentation: Factors Influencing the Potential for Changing Behavior. *Proceedings of the Human Factors Society 30th Annual Meeting*.

5. Lichtenstrin, S., Slovic, P., Fischoff, B., Layman, M., Combs, B. (1978). Perceived frequency of low probability lethal events, *Decision Research Reports* (76-2), Decision Research: A Branch of Percepronics.

6. Loewenthal, A., and Riley, N. W. (1980). The effectiveness of warning labels. *Proceedings of the Human Factors Society 24th Annual Meeting* (pp. 389-391).

7. McCarthy, R. L., Finnegan, J. P., Krumm-Scott, S., and McCarthy, G. E. (1984). Product information presentation, user behavior, and safety. In J. J. Alluisi, S. de Groot, and E. A. Alluisi (Eds.) *Proceedings of the Human Factors Society 28th Annual Meeting* (pp. 81-85). Santa Monica, CA: The Human Factors Society.

8. Raven, J. C. (1956). *Raven Progressive Matrices*. New York: Psychological Association.

9. Robinson, G. H. (1986). Toward a Methodology for the Design of Warnings. *Proceedings of the Human Factors Society 30th Annual Meeting*.

10. Wogalter, M. S., Fontenelle, G. A., and Laughery, K. R. (1985). Behavioral effectiveness of warnings. In R. S. Swezey, et al. (Eds.), *Proceedings of the Human Factors Society 29th Annual Meeting* (pp. 679-683). Santa Monica, CA: The Human Factors Society.

WARNING MESSAGES: WILL THE CONSUMER BOTHER TO LOOK?

Sandra S. Godfrey and Laurel Allender
Rice University, Houston, Texas

Kenneth R. Laughery and Victoria L. Smith
University of Houston, Houston, Texas

ABSTRACT

One way to encourage the safe use of potentially hazardous household products is to provide a warning message on the label. But will the consumer bother to look at the message? In Experiment 1 subjects were asked to imagine themselves purchasing a number of household products. They then rated the products on skin-contact hazard, inhalation hazard, swallowing hazard and overall hazard. They also rated the likelihood that they would look for a warning and how familiar they were with the product. In Experiment 2 more detailed information about familiarity with products was collected along with hazard ratings. Together the results of the two experiments indicate that subjects do discriminate products on overall hazard. They also rate skin contact hazard lowest, inhalation hazard intermediate and swallowing hazard highest. The more hazardous they perceive a product, the more likely they will look for a warning. Further, females are more likely to look for warnings than males. Also, perceived hazard varies inversely with familiarity. The principal conclusion is that factors such as perceived hazard, familiarity and sex influence the consumer's decision to look for a warning message on the labels of potentially hazardous household products.

INTRODUCTION

The increasing complexity and rush of daily life has created a market for timesaving products to use when performing household chores. In some instances, timesaving means stronger, and perhaps more hazardous, chemical content. As a result, the problem of the safe use of these products arises. Also as a result, product liability laws have become increasingly stringent. Indeed, given the present state of the law, even if a product is unadulterated and as safe as present technology can render it, the manufacturer may still have the responsibility to the consumer for any dangerous consequences of its use. This responsibility takes the form of warning and instructing the consumer concerning the safe use of the product.

Warning and instructing are often carried out by means of a label on the product. Research by Easterby and Hakiel (1981), Wright (1981) and Wright, Creighton and Threlfall (1982) has shown that many factors can determine the effectiveness of the label. For example, physical factors such as the label's size, shape, color, location, and arrangement of information are important in perceiving the message. After the warning label is perceived, another set of factors-- language, vocabulary, clarity of expression, structure, organization, and the length of the message--are important for comprehension. Broadbent (1977) reports that in most instances simple, affirmative sentences are better understood than sentences containing passive or negative constructions. Wright (1981) points out that characteristics of the reader such as age, intelligence and training may influence the motivational effects the

message has.

In related research, Easterby and Hakiel (1981) investigated the comprehension of symbols. Of particular interest is the finding that comprehension differed with varying characteristics of the people surveyed. Those who indicated they had seen the symbol previously had better comprehension. Men's comprehension was higher than women's. The lowest comprehension was that of women who were not in the work force, possibly due to their lack of experience with the symbols. Also people over 55 years old did not comprehend as well as younger people. In another study Cahill (1975) tested mechanical engineering students' comprehension of heavy machinery control panel symbols. She found that even with such a highly technical group, those with prior experience demonstrated better comprehension than those with no prior experience.

Thus far, the studies reported have addressed the physical properties of the warning label as they affect perception, the language of the warning label as it affects comprehension, and the characteristics of the user as they affect comprehension and motivation. However, if we think about the entire sequence of events from purchase to use of a product, we realize that important decisions are made by the user even earlier than the perception process. Wright, Creighton and Threlfall (1982) found that when a product is judged more familiar, easier to use, safer, cheaper, and is used frequently, people are less likely to bother to read the instructions. Similarly, the two experiments reported here were designed to look at the effects of certain factors at early stages in the interaction between users and warnings.

EXPERIMENT 1

What factors affect whether a consumer will bother to look for a warning on a product label? Some of the factors may be the same ones that have been shown to influence comprehension of a label and how much of it will be read. How hazardous the consumer perceives the product to be, how familiar the consumer is with the product, and the sex of the consumer are the factors that were investigated. Also, the purchasing situation was included. It was hypothesized that when a person purchases a product on a weekly grocery store trip, he or she will be less likely to look for a warning label than when purchasing a product on a trip to a specialty store of some sort.

The products chosen are those used for chores involving the home and the car. The study was carried out in the laboratory using undergraduates as subjects. No actual products were present. Subjects were asked to imagine various situations in which they would be shopping for these products. They then rated the products on various hazard dimensions, and on their likelihood to look for, read, and heed a warning label. Certain demographic information was collected as well.

Method

Materials and Design. Eight generic household products meeting two criteria were selected for the experiment. One criterion was that all the products be available in a grocery store and a discount store. The other criterion was that two of the products be available at each of four types of specialty stores--a hardware store, an automotive store, a nursery, and a paint store. The eight generic products were dishwashing detergent and oven cleaner available at a hardware store; carburetor flush and antifreeze, automotive store; plant food and pesticide, nursery; and turpentine and mildew remover, paint store. Four different brand names of each generic product were used resulting in 32 different products altogether.

Four purchasing situations were used-- weekly trip to a grocery store, special trip to a grocery store, trip to a discount store, and trip to a specialty store. The weekly trip to a grocery store involved purchasing foodstuffs along with the product of interest; whereas the other three situations involved purchasing only the product of interest.

The design was completely within subjects. For a given subject, the four brand names of each generic product were assigned to a different purchasing situation. Thus, each situation was used eight times, once for each generic product. Across subjects, brand names and situations were appropriately counterbalanced.

The 32 products were arranged in a single random order and were presented in booklet form, one product per page. Note that whereas the order of presentation of the products was the same for all subjects, the assigned purchasing situation varied. At the top of each page was a brief statement giving the name of the product and where it was purchased. For example, "You made a special trip to the discount store and brought home the following item; Joy Dishwashing Detergent."

Following were seven 6-point rating scales. Four were hazard scales--inhalation, swallowing, skin irritation and overall; and three were likelihood scales--likelihood to look for a warning message on the label, likelihood to read it, and likelihood to heed it. The first three hazard scales were anchored with behavioral descriptions such as skin irritation, 1 = dry skin and 6 = 3rd degree burns. On the overall hazard scale, the anchors were 1 = not very hazardous and 6 = very hazardous; for the three likelihood scales, 1 = not very likely and 6 = very likely.

A separate sheet contained eight 6-point familiarity rating scales with one scale for each generic product. The anchors were 1 = not very familiar and 6 = very familiar. A demographic information sheet contained blanks for age, sex and type of residence (campus, parents, own).

Subjects and Procedure. Thirty-two Rice University undergraduates participated in the study for extra credit in psychology classes. Thirteen subjects were females and 19 were males. The mean age was 19.8 with a range of 17 to 24. Twenty-five lived on campus, two with their parents and five in their own residences.

The subjects participated alone or in groups of two to five. First they completed the demographic questionnaire. Next the experiment was described as a research project in consumer psychology. The subjects imagined themselves in various purchasing situations and circled the type of store to help focus their attention. After being presented with each situation, the subjects rated the product on the four hazard scales and the three likelihood scales. They were instructed to make full use of the rating scales and to proceed through the booklet without going back or changing any ratings.

Results and Discussion

All analyses involving the purchasing situation variable yielded nonsignificant results; therefore, purchasing situation will not be further discussed. As expected, subjects discriminated among the types of products as evidenced by the range of hazard ratings shown in Table 1. The differences were statistically significant, $F (7, 217) = 52.92$, $p < .001$.

Table 1

Mean Overall Hazard Ratings for the Eight Generic Products

Dishwashing detergent	1.91
Plant food	2.93
Antifreeze	3.75
Oven cleaner	4.24
Mildew remover	4.33
Turpentine	4.34
Carburetor flush	4.35
Pesticide	4.58

The overall hazard rating correlated significantly with the likelihood to look for a warning, $r = .53$, $p < .01$. The more hazardous a product was perceived to be, the more likely the subject was to look for a warning.

An ANOVA using the likelihood to look for a warning message as the dependent measure and product as the independent variable showed that females (3.84) are more likely to look for a warning message than males (3.18), $F (1,30) = 6.34$, $p < .02$. This difference was in turn a function of type of product, $F (7,210) = 2.26$, $p < .05$. The sexes differed most on antifreeze, mildew remover and turpentine and least on dishwashing detergent and plant food. Thus, females are more likely than males to look for a warning message on those products which are rated as more hazardous by both sexes. However, for the products rated less hazardous, both sexes are equally likely to look. Due to the high intercorrelation of likelihood to read and likelihood to heed with likelihood to look, no further analyses were performed using those two measures.

A comparison of the three subtypes of hazard ratings showed that they were consistently rated differently. Across all products the skin-contact hazard was rated the lowest (2.94), inhalation hazard intermediate (3.35) and swallowing hazard highest (4.71), $F (2.62) = 88.14$, $p < .001$. This ranking seems consistent with intuition.

The degree of familiarity with a product appears to be related to the likelihood to look for a warning message in a somewhat complex manner; the relationship varies with perceived hazard. When consumers encounter products rated highly hazardous (pesticide, turpentine and carburetor flush), degree of familiarity has no effect. However, with products rated less hazardous, greater familiarity results in lower likelihood to look. This result is illustrated by the significant negative correlation when the product is dishwashing detergent, $r = -.50$, $p < .003$.

The correlation between the familiarity ratings and the hazard ratings follow a similar pattern. They are not significant for the same three highly hazardous rated products, while for dishwashing detergent, $r = -.33$, $p < .07$.

EXPERIMENT 2

In Experiment 2, our concern is with how various aspects of familiarity relate to the perceived hazard of a product. How hazardous the consumer perceives the product was assessed along with four measures of familiarity--familiarity with the product, familiarity with a similar product, frequency of use, and recency of use. Undergraduate subjects saw actual products, read the labels, and answered questions about them.

Method

Materials and Design. Forty household products used in the experiment were chosen so that a variety of hazard levels were represented. Hazard level was defined by the signal word used in the warning message--danger, warning, caution or none. Examples of products chosen are Wylers bouillon cubes, Cragmont sugar-free cola, Aquanet hairspray, Sterno liquid fuel, Comet cleanser, Lysol spray disinfectant, Fast-flush carburetor cleaner, and Supertabs chlorine tablets.

Each subject saw 12 of the 40 products. Although the specific products varied across subjects, each subject saw three products from each hazard level.

Response sheets consisted of the following five questions and choices of answers:

(1) Have you ever used this product? (yes/no)
(2) Have you ever used another brand of the same type of product? (yes/no)
(3) How often have you used the product or one like it? (daily/weekly/monthly/yearly/never)
(4) When was the last time you used it? (within the last month/within the past 3-6 months/within the past year/never)
(5) How hazardous do you think use of the product is? (extreme/considerable/moderate/slight/none)

Questions (1) through (4) were designed to assess aspects of familiarity: 1 = familiarity, 2 = similiarity, 3 = frequency and 4 = recency. Question (5) was designed to assess perceived hazard.

Subjects and Procedure. Eighty-eight (49 male and 39 female) University of Houston students received extra credit in courses for participation in the experiment. The age range was 17 to 26. Thirteen lived on campus, 58 with their parents and 17 lived in their own residences.

The study was conducted in a manner similar to a biology lab exam. Twelve "stations", each

containing a different product and a stack of
response sheets, were set up on long tables.
The subjects participated in groups of up to 12.
After reporting demographic information, each
subject began at one of the 12 stations, read
the product label and completed the response
sheet for that product. Subjects proceeded from
station to station until all 12 had been vis-
ited. Approximately three minutes were spent
at each product station.

Results and Discussion

For the data analysis perceived hazard was
coded numerically; extreme = 4, considerable =
3, moderate = 2, slight = 1, and none = 0. The
mean perceived hazard ratings are shown in Table
2 and are tabulated separately for each of the
four questions--familiarity, similarity, frequency, and recency.

The data indicate that when a product is
reported to be familiar (question 1), its perceived hazard is less than when it is reported
to be unfamiliar. These two measures have a
statistically significant negative correlation,
$r = -.19$, $p < .001$. Likewise, when a similar
product is also reported to be unfamiliar (question 2), the target product's hazard is less
than when no similar product is familiar, $r =
-.33$, $p < .001$. Correlations of perceived ha-
ard with the frequency and recency responses
show similar patterns. The more frequently a
product is reported to be used, the less hazardous it is perceived to be, $r = -.33$, $p <
.001$; and the more recently a product is re-
ported to have been used, the less hazardous
it is perceived to be, $r = -.32$, $p < .001$. Thus
for all four aspects of familiarity, the same
relation is seen; increasing familiarity with
a product accompanies a perception of less
hazard.

Table 2

Mean Perceived Hazard Ratings for Familiarity,
Similarity, Frequency and Recency

Familiarity
No	Yes
2.24	1.75

Similarity
No	Yes
2.44	1.62

Frequency
Never	Yearly	Monthly	Weekly	Daily
2.54	1.84	2.06	1.76	1.41

Recency
Never	Yearly	3-6 Months	Month
2.53	1.99	1.66	1.65

CONCLUSIONS

The results of the study indicate that subjects discriminate among products as to how hazardous they are. In turn, their rating on how
likely they are to look for a warning message on
a product label is closely related to their hazard rating.

Females are more likely to look for a warning label on products perceived as hazardous
than males. Does this difference mean that men
have more accidents than women? By taking into
account the sex of the most likely user, manufacturers might be able to design more effective
warning labels.

The purchasing situation had no effect on
hazard ratings or ratings of likelihood to look
for a warning message. Possibly the design of
the experiment and/or the subject population was
inappropriate for detecting such an effect. Alternatively, it may be that the place of purchase simply does not matter.

The results obtained in Experiment 1 indicate that increased familiarity is related to
increased likelihood to look for a warning label
when perceived hazard is low but not when perceived hazard is high. While these relationships were fairly weak, the results concerning
familiarity in Experiment 2 were stronger.
The more familiar subjects were with a product,
the lower they rated the hazard. These results
are consistent with the findings of Wright,
Creighton and Threlfall (1982), wherein people
reported themselves to be less likely to read
the instructions on products used frequently.
Research from several areas indicates that repeated exposure to the same stimulus changes
the manner in which we respond to that stimulus. This principle may extend to our response
to warning labels on hazardous products.

If indeed familiarity does affect perceived hazard, what is the exact nature of the
relationship? The answer to this question could
well determine how one might attempt to deal
with familiarity effects in designing warning
labels. One possible familiarity effect could
be that the consumer overestimates the hazard
on initially encountering a product, but with
repeated use the hazard estimate becomes more
accurate. Alternatively, the initial hazard
estimate may be appropriate, but familiarity
leads to underestimates. There are other alternatives, but the point is that the different
situations might lead to different labeling
strategies.

REFERENCES

Broadbent, D. E. Language and ergonomics.
Applied Ergonomics, 1977, 8, 15-18.

Cahill, M. Interpretability of graphic symbols
as a function of context and experience
factors. *Journal of Applied Psychology*,

1975, 60, 376-380.

Easterby, R. S. and Hakiel, S. R. Field testing
    of consumer safety signs: The comprehen-
    sion of pictorially presented messages.
    Applied Ergonomics, 1981, 12, 143-152.

Wright, P. "The instructions clearly state..."
    Can't people read? Applied Ergonomics,
    1981, 12, 131-141.

Wright, P., Creighton, P. and Threlfall, S. M.
    Some factors determining when instructions
    will be read. Ergonomics, 1982, 25, 225-
    237.

THE BIASING EFFECTS OF PRODUCT FAMILIARITY
ON CONSUMERS' AWARENESS OF HAZARD

Sandra S. Godfrey and Kenneth R. Laughery
Rice University, Houston, Texas

ABSTRACT

Although toxic shock syndrome (TSS) and its connection to tampon use has been highly publicized, the extent of the average consumer's knowledge of the specific hazards involved is questionable. Women become familiar with this product and therefore may underrate its hazards and fail to notice warnings. A survey was conducted to determine women's awareness of the hazards of tampon use, their awareness of warnings about TSS, and their knowledge of the symptoms of TSS. They were not so likely to notice warnings on or in the tampon packages when they switched products as they were earlier. They were not well informed as to the symptoms of TSS, and many did not know that more absorbent tampons are more hazardous. The relationship of these results to the familiarity effect is discussed. Also, implementation by manufacturers of effective warnings on these products in order to enable women to use them safely is discussed and recommended.

INTRODUCTION

A recent study by Godfrey, Allender, Laughery and Smith (1983) indicated that increased familiarity with a product or with one similar to it results in a reduction of the perceived hazard of that product. Perhaps special attention should be paid to the design of warnings on hazardous products which are especially familiar to consumers. Tampons seem to be a likely candidate to produce the familiarity effect. Most women are aware that toxic shock syndrome (TSS) is related to the use of tampons. However, the nature of these products and their use give rise to the suspicion that women may not be sufficiently warned against the specific hazards involved. Tampon use becomes habitual and almost automatic and continues for many years. Thus in spite of the extensive publicity given to TSS, women may continue to use tampons without thinking seriously about the hazards or giving much attention to the warnings that are on and in the packages.

One characteristic of the product that makes it hazardous is the super absorbent fibers. If women are unaware of this fact, they may change to a more absorbent and more hazardous tampon without checking for warnings, because they are already familiar with the similar but less hazardous product. Therefore, even though some manufacturers use stronger warnings with the more absorbent products, these women will still not be warned of the hazard of greater absorbency.

Another aspect of the warning problem is that the hazard of TSS and its relation to tampon use was not identified until after the product had been in use for many years. Many women, probably including some who were stricken with TSS, had been using them for years with no problems, as had their acquaintances, friends and relatives. Indeed, changes or so-called improvements (i.e. the more absorbent fibers) in the product made it more hazardous probably without the knowledge of most users. This situation puts a special burden on manufacturers to warn in a manner such that the attention of consumers will be captured and focused on the hazard and the procedures to avoid it.

The foregoing discussion raises the possibility that extended tampon use causes women to underrate the hazard involved and thereby to overlook relevant warnings. In order to determine if the use of this product does indeed produce the familiarity effect, a survey was designed and administered. The questions assessed the history of use, storage practices, awareness of hazards connected with tampon use, awareness of warnings and knowledge of symptoms of toxic shock syndrome.

METHOD

Materials and Design

The survey consisted of 35 questions preceeded by a consent form, brief instructions and an explanation of the purpose of the study. The first group of questions asked for age and other demographic information. The next section assessed history of tampon use. The first question determined the brand and absorbency level used. Absorbency was coded on four different levels; super plus, super, regular and junior. Then subjects were asked at what age they began using tampons, if they ever switched brands or absorbency levels, where they store tampons, and who introduced them to the use of tampons.

The next questions were about knowledge of instructions and warnings on or in the package. Subjects were asked if they were aware of instructions on or in the package and what led to their noticing the instructions. The same question was asked about warnings. The question about instructions was included mainly to cause the subjects to differentiate between instructions and warnings in their answers. Then they were asked what the warning said, if they noticed warnings when <u>changing brands or absorbency levels</u>, what led them to notice that warning, and what it said.

The final questions were about the hazards of tampon use, their knowledge of TSS and their opinions about warnings. They were asked if tampon products differ in hazard and if so, what is the difference, what they know about TSS and its symptoms, how that knowledge has affected their tampon use if at all, how manufacturers can best warn against the dangers of TSS, where the warning should be, and what it should say.

Subjects and Procedure

One hundred ten women ranging in age from 16 to 43 participated in the survey. The mean age was 20.8. Most of the subjects were undergraduate and graduate students at Rice University. Seventeen were students at a local public high school, and some were not in college. Some of the undergraduates received extra credit in psychology courses for their participation. The remaining subjects were volunteers.

The survey was distributed by two graduate student experimenters, two undergraduate students and one high school student. Subjects were given unlimited time to answer the questions. Most finished in 20 to 30 minutes. The experimenters were available to answer questions. Participants were assured of their privacy and anonimity and urged to recall the requested information as carefully and accurately as possible.

RESULTS AND DISCUSSION

The following two questions about warnings were asked:

Question 1: Are you aware of any warning messages on or in the package of any of the brands of tampons that you use?

Question 2: Did you notice warnings when you changed brands or types of tampons?

Of the 96 women who reported using tampons, 71 (73%) said they noticed a warning on or in the package although 11 of them did not remember what it said. However, only 32 (42%) of the 76 women who reported switching from one tampon product to another noticed a warning on the new product.

Seventy-two women answered both questions. The number of responses in each of the four possible combinations of Yes and No answers are shown in Table 1.

Table 1

Answers to Questions 1 and 2 About Warnings

| | | Question 1 | | |
		Yes	No	Total
Question 2	Yes	22	31	53
	No	8	11	19
	Total	30	42	72

The Yes/Yes cell are women who notice warnings. The No/No cell are women who do not notice warnings. The fact that the former is larger than the latter is both interesting and reassuring. But more interesting and relevant to the issues addressed in this study is the relationship between the Yes/No and the No/Yes cells. The familiarity hypothesis holds that women become so familiar with the product that they underrate the hazard and fail to notice warnings. A prediction follows from the hypothesis. Most women will notice warnings when first using tampons but will not notice warnings later when switching to another brand or to a more absorbent product. The Yes/No cell (women who notice warnings at first but not when switching) is larger than the No/Yes cell (women who only notice when switching). This difference is significant, $z = 3.69$, $p < .001$; therefore, the hypothesis is supported.

The hypothesis is also supported by results related to age. Women ages 27 and older were less likely to have noticed a warning than the younger women. Only fifty percent of the older as opposed to 78% of the younger women noticed warnings. That difference is significant, $z = 2.31$, $p < .05$. This result could also have been predicted by the familiarity effect. Older women have probably been using the product longer. If so, they are more familiar with it and may be less likely to notice the arning on the package.

Of the 110 women surveyed, 37 did not correctly name any symptoms of TSS, 22 named one symptom, 46 named two symptoms, and only five women named all three of the most important symptoms. So even though women have heard of TSS and associate it with tampon use. over 50% do not have a very good chance of recognizing the disease if they come in contact with it. This lack of knowledge could have very serious consequences to some of them.

In the total sample 70 women (65%) did not

know that tampons differ in hazard because some are more absorbent. One reason for this fact may be that although manufacturers sometimes put a stronger warning on the more absorbent products none of the warnings explains the differences among products. An additional reason may be that because of the familiarity effect, women only look at one warning, if any, and never notice that the more absorbent products have stronger warnings.

Women who use the more absorbent, more hazardous tampons are no more likely to notice a warning than those who use the less absorbent, less hazardous product. In fact 71% of those who use the more absorbent noticed warnings while 75% of those who use the less absorbent noticed warnings. This result is opposite to the way it should be if warnings and the notice taken of them reflected the seriousness of the hazards involved in the various products. If manufacturers are trying to get the attention of women who use the more hazardous products by using stronger warnings, they are not succeeding.

Sixty-eight percent of the women who were introduced to the product by their mothers noticed warnings while 75% of the women introduced in other ways noticed them. This difference was expected because a woman might be less cautious with a product recommended by her mother. A mother's introduction might have the same effect as familiarity. However, the difference between the two percentages is not significant.

Three different brands were named by the subjects. Notice of warnings did not differ among the users of the different brands. This result indicates that the warnings on the different brands do not differ in effectiveness.

All respondents but one stated that they store tampons in the package. That practice reduces the chance that they will find and read any warnings that are written on an insert packed between the rows of tampons--a type of insert common to this product.

CONCLUSIONS

The results of the survey support the familiarity effect reported by Godfrey et al. (1983). Subjects were more likely to notice a warning the first time that they used this product than they were when they switched to a similar product. This finding implies that being familiar with the product or a similar product led to their perceiving the hazard as lower than they would have otherwise thereby causing them not to notice warnings.

This effect has very serious implications in this particular situation because the chances are fairly good that they were switching to a more hazardous product. It was probably more hazardous because women often switch to a more absorbent type of tampon as they mature. Also

the more hazardous types came on the market only recently--after the safer ones had been in use for many years. Thus consumers had become familiar with a relatively safe product. The result was that the more hazardous tampon was used with no more and maybe even less caution than the original, less hazardous product.

As previously mentioned, some manufacturers use stronger warnings on the more absorbent products. However many women may not notice these warnings because of the familiarity effect. One solution may be to warn of the greater hazard of increased absorbency on all products no matter what the absorbency level. Another solution is to improve the quality of the warnings that are used. Even the stronger warnings often do not follow accepted guidelines for good warnings. One questionable practice is the previously mentioned one of placing an insert with a warning between the rows of tampons. Other manufacturers wrap the insert around the end of the row so that it must be removed. In the latter location it is more likely to be noticed.

Women are not well informed as to the hazard of greater absorbency or as to the symptoms of TSS. This fact implies that the warnings used are not effective. An examination of the warnings on the packages shows that they do not follow guidelines either for attracting attention or for imparting hazard information clearly. For instance, one of the more absorbent products of the brand named second most often by the respondents does not display the warning with either contrasting background color or print. "Attention" is the signal word that is used instead of the standard danger, warning, or caution. Among the references containing guidelines for warnings are McCormick and Sanders (1982) and Product Safety Sign and Label System (1980).

Another problem with that particular package is that it displays two different messages. One is less important because it does not mention TSS--only some very vague symptoms. Yet its signal word is "caution" which is more important than "attention" which is on the other message. One respondent in a pilot study failed to notice the more important message because she was distracted by the less important one. Failure to impart this important information may cost some women their lives. The course of the disease is very rapid, and recognizing symptoms early may make the difference.

The majority of the women in this sample are from an above average intelligence population of graduate and undergraduate students. Yet the results show that even these women are not satisfactorily informed about the hazards of tampon use. Being familiar with a similar product and having used the product frequently are factors that may make them less cautious. Thus they would not be informed because they had not

noticed the warnings. If these college women
are lacking in caution, how do others treat these
products? Are women who are illiterate or of
relatively low intelligence informed about these
hazards? One suspects they are not. Manufacturers have a responsibility to improve this
situation with more effective warnings.

REFERENCES

Godfrey, S. S., Allender, L., Laughery, K. R., &
Smith, V. L. (1983). Warning messages: Will
the consumer bother to look? In A. T. Pope
and L. D. Haugh (Eds.). Proceedings of the
Human Factors Society 27th Annual Meeting (pp.
950-954). Santa Monica, California: The
Human Factors Society.

McCormick, E. J., & Sanders, M. S. (1982). Human
factors in engineering and design. New York:
McGraw-Hill.

Product safety sign and label system. (1980).
Santa Clara, California: FMC Corporation.

THE NEW ALCOHOL WARNING LABELS: HOW NOTICEABLE ARE THEY?

Sandra S. Godfrey, Kenneth R. Laughery, Stephen L. Young, Kent P. Vaubel,
John W. Brelsford, Keith A. Laughery, and Elizabeth Horn

Rice University
Houston, Texas 77251

An experiment was conducted to assess the effect of various existing warning design factors on the noticeability of warnings on alcoholic beverage containers. One-hundred containers, 50 with warnings and 50 without, were used as stimuli and the time required to determine whether or not a warning was present was recorded. The results indicate that warnings on the front label were found more quickly than warnings appearing in any other location. Also, warnings printed horizontally were found more quickly than warning printed vertically. A regression analysis found that features of the signal word/phrase ("Government Warning"), as well as the amount of "noise" or clutter on the surrounding label, significantly influenced warning detection times. Thus, some of the design features currently used were shown to have an effect on noticeability of warning information. It is suggested that proper manipulation of these features could make the mandated warning more noticeable.

INTRODUCTION

Health related warnings are mandated for several types of consumer products (*e.g.*, cigarettes, saccharin, prescription and non-prescription drugs). These warnings take various forms such as on-product labels, detailed product inserts, etc. However, evaluating the impact of such warnings is difficult because of the inability to control for potentially confounding variables (*e.g.*, public education programs which begin simultaneously with the onset of the warning's appearance). Reliability issues notwithstanding, cases have been documented in which mandated health warnings have influenced behavior. Among the more successful examples are those reviewed by Richardson (1987) which include warnings on beverages containing saccharin (Schucker, Stokes, Stewart & Henderson, 1983), patient package inserts in prescription drugs (Morris, Mazis & Gordon, 1977) and cigarette warnings (Swedish National Smoking and Health Association Study, 1978).

As a result of growing concern for safety and health problems associated with alcohol consumption, Congress mandated that the following warning must appear on all alcohol beverage containers marketed in the United States as of November, 1989:

GOVERNMENT WARNING: (1) ACCORDING TO THE SURGEON GENERAL, WOMEN SHOULD NOT DRINK ALCOHOLIC BEVERAGES DURING PREGNANCY BECAUSE OF THE RISK OF BIRTH DEFECTS. (2) CONSUMPTION OF ALCOHOLIC BEVERAGES IMPAIRS YOUR ABILITY TO DRIVE A CAR OR OPERATE MACHINERY, AND MAY CAUSE HEALTH PROBLEMS.

Since the effectiveness of any warning depends initially on whether it is noticed, design features of warnings are often manipulated to ensure that they will be seen (or not seen). In this study, actual alcohol containers (some of which contained a warning) were used as stimuli, and the time necessary to determine the presence or absence of a warning was recorded. Thus, the goal of the present research was to identify currently employed design factors which affect the noticeability of the mandated warning.

METHOD

Subjects

Sixty subjects were recruited from two local community centers and from the University of Houston. They were distributed across ethnic group (Blacks, n=20; Hispanics, n=23; Whites, n=17) and gender (Males, n=31; Females, n=29). Eighty-five percent of subjects drank alcoholic beverages on some regular basis.

Materials and Apparatus

Roughly 250 different alcohol beverage containers (beer, wine, and liquor) were collected before and after the mandated warning appeared on the labels. Of these, 100 containers (50 with the warning and 50 without) were chosen which varied according to size, type (*e.g.*, aluminum can versus bottle) and label dimensions. Furthermore, containers were selected so that the different dimensions of warning salience currently used would be represented. Such dimensions included the location of the warning on the container, legibility and orientation of the warning print, as well as contrast between the warning and its background.

A code number (ID) located on the bottom of each container was used for identification purposes. A MacIntosh computer was used to record and store subject's data. For each trial, the computer's timer was started by a key-press (from the experimenter) and stopped by a voice-activated relay. This relay was used so that subjects could respond verbally when they found the warning, while still being able to pick up and rotate the containers with both hands. The relay also eliminated some additional "noise" in the dependent measure by excluding the motor-response time which would normally exist with a button press or some other physical response. A barrier held by the experimenter concealed the container from subjects until the timer was started.

Procedure

After completing a questionnaire, subjects were seated at a table facing the experimenter and informed as to the nature of the task. They were then provided with an example of the warning. Subjects were instructed that each trial would be timed and that they should respond as quickly as possible. However, they were cautioned that it was very important to be accurate in their responses.

After entering the ID number in the computer, the experimenter placed the container behind a barrier so that the subject could not see it. The container was positioned toward the subject such that the warning was facing the subject directly (0°), was to the left (90°) or right (270°), or was facing opposite the subject (180°). One of these four orientations was chosen randomly by the computer for each trial. The experimenter then started the timer (by pressing a key) and, at the same time, removed the barrier to reveal the container. The subject's task was to examine each container as it was presented and respond with a "Yes" if the warning was present and a "No" if it was not. The subject's verbal response triggered the voice-activated relay and the timer stopped. Ten practice trials were used to familiarize the subjects with the task and to adjust the sensitivity of the relay's microphone.

RESULTS

Individual Trial Data

The first set of analyses examined the raw data from subjects' individual trials (*i.e.*, not collapsed across subjects or containers). These analyses examined some facets of the experimental procedure, rather than the nature of the warnings on the containers.

Warning Orientation. The orientation of the warning relative to the subject had a significant effect on time to find the warning, $F (3, 2990) = 21.9, p < .001$. As expected, if the warning was presented facing the subjects, they found it more quickly ($m = 3052$ ms) than when the warning was placed at 90° ($m = 3253$ ms), 180° ($m = 3957$ ms) or 270° ($m = 3705$ ms) to subjects' view (p's < .05).

Misses. A miss was defined as subjects giving a "No" response when the warning was present. Subjects were more likely to miss a warning when it was printed on the neck of a container ($m = 15\%$ missed) than when it appeared on either the front ($m = 6.8\%$ missed) or the back ($m = 7.6\%$ missed) of the container, $F (2, 2574) = 17.3, p < .001$. Also, warnings printed vertically were more likely to be missed ($m = 10.7\%$) than were warnings printed horizontally ($m = 7.9\%$), $F (1, 2547) = 5.89, p < .02$.

Scores for all remaining analyses were collapsed across subjects to obtain a mean response time for each container. Analyses using these collapsed scores were carried out in order to determine which container and warning features best predict time to find the warning.

Analyses of Covariance

The first analysis with collapsed scores examined detection time as a function of the different qualitative variables associated with the warnings such as the location of the warning on the container (front, left, right or back side) and the direction of print (horizontal or vertical). Containers displaying vertically printed warnings were further categorized as to whether they "read up" or "read down". Since these manipulations were not independent of other features of the warnings, the effect of the eight objective measurements (described below, see Table 1 - items 1 through 8) were covaried out of the analysis. This helped insure that possible confounds with location would be held constant. Warnings were initially coded by their position on the container in 90° zones. The "front zone" included the center of the main brand label and 45° to either side of the center (cans were excluded from this analysis). The right, left and back zones were determined relative to the front. It was found that warnings printed on the front of the container were found significantly faster ($m = 2650$ ms, n = 6) than were warnings on the left ($m = 3932$ ms, n = 9), the back ($m = 3585$ ms, n = 19) or the right side of the container ($m = 3527$ ms, n = 9), $F (3, 31) = 3.71, p < .03$ (see Figure 1).

With the effect of the eight objective measures held constant, warnings printed horizontally produced significantly faster times ($m = 3296$ ms) than warnings printed vertically ($m = 3673$ ms), $F (1, 40) = 14.0, p < .001$. Of the warnings that were printed vertically, the warnings which "read up" were found significantly faster ($m = 3407$ ms) than warnings which "read down"($m = 4071$ ms), $F (1,15) = 9.75, p < .01$. There were no interactions between these variables.

Regression Analyses

Physical measurements of the warnings on the containers were used as predictor variables in the regression analysis. These variables are listed as items one through eight in Table 1. Although a description accompanies each variable, the rationale behind two of them warrants mention here. Initially, it was our impression that many of the warnings were difficult to read because the text was compressed. Previous research has shown that there are optimum sizes (usually expressed in height-to-strokewidth ratio) for printed text and that print legibility suffers as type size decreases below this point (*e.g.*, Hodge, 1962; Hind, Tritt & Hoffmann, 1976). Thus, an attempt was made to quantify the extent to which individual characters of text were compressed within the alcohol warnings. Two variables were used as measures of compression: *Government Warning Density* and *Characters per Centimeter*. The former was assessed in addition to the latter because the type for "Government Warning" differs from that of the remaining text, in that it is usually larger and always in boldface print. Therefore, this phrase might not be subject to as much compression as the rest of the warning text. These two measures allowed us to evaluate the effect of text compression on noticeability of the warning.

In addition to these objective warning measures, it was reasoned that a classification scheme based on more holistic (albeit subjective) criteria might prove useful. Toward this, four subjective dimensions of the warnings were evaluated: 1) *Label Clutter*, 2) *Noticeability of the Warning*, 3) *Noticeability of the Government Warning* and 4) *Reading Difficulty*. Descriptions of these dimensions are presented in

Table 1. Classification variables for the containers

Variable	Description
Physical Measurements	
1. Number of Labels	Total number of independent labels (aluminum cans excluded)
2. Number of Lines	Number of lines used to print the entire warning
3. Letters per Line	Number of letters in the line immediately below the line containing the words "Government Warning"
4. Line Length	Length (in cm) of the line immediately below the line containing the words "Government Warning"
5. Government Warning Length	Length (in cm) of the words "Government Warning"
6. Characters per Centimeter	Characters per centimeter in the line just below the line containing the words "Government Warning"
7. Government Warning Density	Characters per centimeter in the words "Government Warning"
8. Warning Area	The rectangular area (in cm^2) of the entire warning
Ratings	
9. Label Clutter	Subjective rating of the "business" or clutter of the container's labels
10. Noticeability of the Warning	Subjective rating of the overall noticeability of the entire warning - How well did the warning "stand out" from the background?
11. Noticeability of the Government Warning	Subjective rating of the overall noticeability of the word "Government Warning"
12. Reading Difficulty	Subjective rating of how difficult it was to read the warning, given that it was already located

Table 1 (items nine through twelve). Members of the research team rated each container on 7-point Likert-type scales for each of these measures, with 1 representing a low or poor value (*e.g.,* not at all noticeable) and 7 representing a high or positive value (*e.g.,* extremely noticeable). The means of the ratings served as the score for a given container on that dimension. While it is likely that these subjective criteria account for some of the same information provided by the objective measures, it was believed that they would provide additional explainable variance not accounted for by the objective measures alone.

The twelve predictors listed in Table 1 were regressed on subjects' response times. Combined, they accounted for 66% of the total variance of detection time. An effort was then made to select a subset of these predictors (using stepwise regression) which would maximize the amount of the explainable variance. This analysis selected three variables (*Noticeability of the Warning, Label Clutter, Noticeability of the Government Warning*, see Table 2), which accounted for 53% of the total variance in subjects' response latencies. Examination of the regression coefficients in Table 2 demonstrates that higher salience ratings for the phrase "Government Warning" were associated with faster response times. A similar relationship was also found with regard to the rated noticeability of the entire warning. Finally, a positive relationship was observed between subjects' perceptions of label clutter and the time necessary to locate the warning. Specifically, increases in perceived label clutter were associated with longer response times.

It can be seen that only the subjective ratings were selected by this stepwise regression. Earlier it was suggested that these subjective measures shared variance with the

objective measures and in fact, this is the case. Table 3 shows the intercorrelations between the twelve predictors. This table demonstrates that the subjective ratings were significantly correlated with many of the physical measurements. In order to determine the relative importance of each of the objective predictors on the subjective ratings selected in the overall regression, separate regression analyses were performed for *Noticeability of the Warning*, *Label Clutter* and *Noticeability of the Government Warning*, with the objective measures as regressors.

The eight objective predictors accounted for 48% of the variance of *Noticeability of the Warning*. A stepwise regression showed that *Government Warning Length* (b = .458, standardized regression coefficient) and *Letters per Line* (b = -.373) predicted a significant amount of this variance by themselves (accounting for 41% of the variance of *Noticeability of the Warning*). A similar analysis was done for *Label Clutter*, in which the eight predictors accounted for 55% of the total variance. A stepwise regression revealed that *Number of Labels* (b = .529), *Government Warning Length* (b = .697) and *Warning Area* (b = -.456) predicted a significant amount of variance (48%). Finally, a regression of the objective predictors on *Noticeability of the Government Warning* showed that these measurements accounted for 45% of the variance of this variable. A stepwise regression showed that *Number of Lines* (b = .432) and *Government Warning Length* (b = .334) accounted for a significant amount of variance (39%).

DISCUSSION

The results of this experiment show that various warning design parameters of actual alcohol containers influence the noticeability of the mandated warning. The variables which

Table 2. Regression scores of the three predictors on detection time

Predictor	Cumulative R^2	Regression Coefficient	Standardized Regression Coefficient
Noticeability of the Warning	.259	-230.26	-.3029
Label Clutter	.470	468.72	.5047
Noticeability of the Government Warning	.532	-284.49	-.3893

exerted the greatest influence on noticeability were all rating measures: *Noticeability of the Warning*, *Noticeability of the Government Warning* and *Label Clutter*. It should be recognized that, while these three variables were subjective in nature, they were not entirely independent of the physical or objective dimensions of the warnings. This contention is clearly supported by the regression of the objective criteria on these rating measures.

The results also indicate that the location of the warning is important to its noticeability. Warnings printed on the front were more noticeable than if they were printed in any other location. This finding was independent of the orientation of the warning at the time of presentation and of the other salience features of the warning. The results concerning location are not entirely surprising, given that the majority of relevant container information is usually found on the front label. Moreover, the results show that warnings were more noticeable and were less likely to be missed when printed horizontally, rather than vertically.

Government Warning Length was an important variable in this study by virtue of the fact that it loaded on all three of the subjective measures selected in the stepwise regression. "Government Warning" is the signal "word" or phrase used in this warning and one of its purposes is to attract attention. However, it should be kept in mind that the task in this experiment required subjects to simply determine whether a warning was present or absent. In effect, the signal word or phrase was the only part of the warning that *had* to be detected in order to make a correct response. The results of the regression analyses suggest that subjects used features of the signal word (*i.e.*, length) to help them locate the warning. Moreover, responses in a post-session interview indicated the most common method of search was to look for this signal phrase. Thus, it is not surprising that the attributes of the words "Government Warning" significantly affected detection time in this study.

What are the implications for warnings on alcohol beverage containers, assuming one of the goals of the warning design is to attract the consumer's attention? First it must be noted that suggestions based on the current research are constrained by the fact that the stimuli employed were actual containers from the marketplace. The number of warning design parameters, as well as the range of values for each parameter, were limited to what was available on these containers. For example, proper contrast and color, large print, good location and highlighting features (*i.e.*, borders) were the exception and not the rule. The selection of *Label*

Clutter in the overall stepwise regression suggests that this is the case, since it is not a direct manipulation of the warnings itself. The more noticeable warnings were associated with less surrounding "noise". This *suggests* that the warnings did not necessarily "stand out" from their background, as much as they were simply not obscured by neighboring information when the labels were uncluttered. Nevertheless, it seems clear that some of the design factors currently used can influence noticeability of warnings. Location, orientation, context (clutter) and size of the signal word/phrase are parameters which, if properly manipulated, can affect the noticeability of warnings.

ACKNOWLEDGEMENT

This research was supported by National Institute on Alcohol Abuse and Alcoholism Grant SRCA (32) 1 R01 AA08538-01 to Kenneth R. Laughery.

REFERENCES

Hind, P. R., Tritt, B. H. & Hoffmann, E. R. (1976). Effects of level of illumination, strokewidth, visual angle and contrast on the legibility of numerals of various fonts. In *ARRB Proceedings*, *8*, 46-55.

Hodge, D. C. (1962). Legibility of a uniform-strokewidth alphabet: I. Relative legibility of upper and lower case letters. *Journal of Engineering Psychology*, *1*, 34-46.

Figure 1. Response time as a function of location of warning on the container

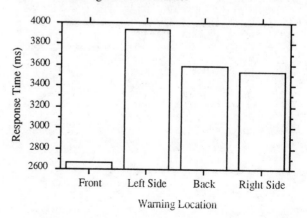

Table 3. Intercorrelations of predictors used in the regression

	Variables										
	1	2	3	4	5	6	7	8	9	10	11
2	.206										
3	-.311*	-.925*									
4	-.318*	-.709*	.781*								
5	-.050	.311*	-.177	.342*							
6	.090	-.155	.119	-.482*	-.878*						
7	.072	-.164	.075	-.447*	-.941*	.929*					
8	-.166	.222	-.057	.420*	.850*	-.806*	-.794*				
9	.570*	.208	-.222	-.040	.283*	-.194	-.211	.048			
10	.238	.493*	-.454*	-.154	.524*	-.438*	-.481*	.469*	.178		
11	.211	.536*	-.483*	-.257	.468*	-.292*	-.350*	.366*	.230	.760*	
12	.173	.338*	-.293*	.179	.793*	-.747*	-.773*	.675*	.352*	.796*	.606*

Note: Column and row numbers refer to variables listed in Table 1.
* $p < .05$

Morris, L.A., Mazis, M.B., & Gordon, E. (1977) A survey of the effects of oral contraceptive patient information. *Journal of the American Medical Association, 238(23)*, 2504-2508.

Richardson, P., Reinhart, G., Rosenthal, A., Hayes, C., & Silver, R. (1987). *Review of the research literature on the effects of health warning labels.* (Contract No. ADM 281-86-0003). Washington, DC: National Institute on Alcohol Abuse and Alcoholism.

Schucker, R.E., Stokes, R.C., Stewart, M.L., & Henderson, D. P. The impact of the saccharin warning label on sales of diet soft drinks in supermarkets. *Journal of Public Policy and Marketing, 2*, 46-56.

Swedish National Smoking and Health Association Study of Sweden's rotational label system (1978). Unpublished. Contact Dr. Lars Ramstrom, Director General of the National Smoking and Health Association.

WARNINGS: DO THEY MAKE A DIFFERENCE?

Sandra S. Godfrey, Pamela R. Rothstein, Kenneth R. Laughery

Rice University
Houston, Texas

ABSTRACT

Four experiments were conducted in order to determine whether warnings are effective and to identify factors that influence their effectiveness. Warnings were posted on a copy machine, a public telephone, a water fountain, and two sets of doors. The first two warnings were effective in that most people did not use the copy machine and the telephone when they had the warnings on them. The warning on the water fountain was not effective when a single, small warning was used. When that warning plus a larger, more forceful warning was used, most people did not drink from the fountain. The warnings on the doors were not obeyed when a convenient alternative exit was not available. However, when the warning directed people to a nearby, convenient exit, most of them obeyed it. Warning with a low cost of compliance are apparently more effective. The results indicate that warnings can be effective, but not unless they are well designed in appearance and content.

INTRODUCTION

An important question regarding warnings is whether they actually influence people's behavior. Existing research does not provide a satisfactory answer to this question. The purpose of the work reported here was to conduct a systematic investigation of the effectiveness of warnings in a field setting, and to begin to identify the attributes of warnings that influence their effectiveness.

Recent reports (McCarthy, Finnegan, Krumm-Scott, & McCarthy, 1984) have cast doubt on the effectiveness of warnings in general because of the lack of research to indicate otherwise. But this lack of evidence should not give rise to the conclusion that all warnings are ineffective in all circumstances. Before warnings are abandoned as a strategy for protecting people from hazards, their potential usefulness should be further examined.   Experiments 1 and 2 are simple, straightforward demonstrations of effective warnings.

EXPERIMENT 1

This study was conducted in a copy room in the library of a large medical center. The room contains two copy machines. It was determined by asking staff members that the machines are kept fairly busy at all hours of the day.

Method

Data was collected during sessions at mid morning on three separate weekdays. The purpose of the first and third sessions was to collect base line data. One machine was kept busy by the experimenters. The number of people who used the other machine during a one hour period was recorded.

The second session was the experimental session. Again the first machine was kept busy by the experimenters. A three by five inch warning sign was placed on the second machine. The message was as follows:

CAUTION
MACHINE DOES NOT WORK
MAY CAUSE DELAY
USE ANOTHER MACHINE

The number of people who used the machine during a one hour period was again recorded. Also recorded was the number of people who entered the room carrying written material, approached the machine, appeared to be intending to use it, looked at the sign, and left without using it.

Results and Discussion

The results are illustrated in Table 1. Six people used the second machine during the first session, and eight during the third session. The first row, second column number is the average of the first and third sessions (base line data). During these base line data collection sessions, no one with the apparent intent to use the machine left without using it.

During the second (experimental) session, four people used the machine, and 11 people approached the machine but did not use it. The two variables (Warning/No Warning and Did Use/Did Not Use Machine) represented in Table 1 are significantly correlated , $X^2 = 7.54$, $p < .01$. The warning sign was effective in that most of the people who apparently intended to did not use the machine when the warning was posted.

Table 1

Number of Users of Copy Machine With and Without Posted Warning

	Warning	No Warning	Σ
Used machine	4	7	11
Did not use machine	11	0	11
Σ	15	7	22

Note. X^2 = 7.54, p<.01.

EXPERIMENT 2

This study is similar to Experiment 1. It was conducted in the lobby of a large medical office building. Three pay telephones are located on the wall in the lobby near a sitting area. Data was collected at mid afternoon on three separate weekdays.

Method

As before, the middle session was experimental, and the first and third were for the purpose of collecting base line data. The experimenters kept two telephones busy during the 45 minute sessions. During the base line data collection sessions, the number of people who used the third telephone was recorded. During the experimental session, a three by five inch warning sign was placed on the receiver of the middle telephone. The message was as follows:

CAUTION
TELEPHONE IS OUT OF ORDER
MONEY WILL BE LOST
USE OTHER TELEPHONE

The number of people who approached this telephone obviously intending to use it, looked at the sign, and walked away without using it was recorded.

Results and Discussion

Eight people used the free telephone during the first session, and five during the third session. As before these two baseline observations were averaged, and the mean is in the first row, second column of Table 2. During these base line sessions, no one approached the telephone with the apparent intent to use it and left without using it. During the second, experimental session, seven people approached the telephone with the warning sign on it, looked at the sign, and walked away without using it.

The relationship between the two variables (Warning/No Warning and Did Use/Did Not Use

Telephone) represented in Table 2 is significant, X^2 = 9.79, p<.01. The warning sign was effective because none of the people who apparently intended to used the telephone when the warning was posted. In the baseline data collection session when no warning was posted, everyone who approached the telephone used it. Therefore behavior was changed by the presence of the sign.

Table 2

Number of Users of Telephone With and Without Posted Warning

	Warning	No Warning	Σ
Used telephone	0.0	6.5	6.5
Did not use telephone	7.0	0.0	7.0
Σ	7.0	6.5	13.5

Note. X^2 = 9.79, p<.01.

EXPERIMENT 3

The previous two studies were conducted to demonstrate that warnings are effective under some circumstances. Obviously the next step is to determine specifically what those circumstances are. Any research scientist knows that human behavior is complex, and there is no reason to believe that people's responses to warning messages are any exception. Experiment 3 was undertaken in order to begin to tease out the variables that influence behavior related to warnings. The first variable tested was an obvious one. The hypothesis was simply that the more noticeable a warning is, the more effective it will be. The study was conducted at a water fountain in the gymnasium on a college campus.

Method

The fountain was first observed during the early evening on a weekday for a thirty minute period. The number of people who drank from the fountain was recorded. Two days later at the same time of day the first experimental session was conducted. A sign was placed on the wall behind the water fountain that read as follows:

WARNING
WATER CONTAMINATED
DO NOT DRINK

The sign was unobscured and at about eye level. It was about five by nine inches with one/half inch print. Again the fountain was observed for a 30 minute period, and the number of people who approached and/or drank from it was recorded. The second experimental session took place one week after the baseline data was collected (again at the same time of day). Two warning signs were posted at the same water fountain. The message on the first sign was as follows:

WARNING
BAD FILTER CAUSED
WATER CONTAMINATION
DO NOT DRINK WATER

This sign was posted behind the fountain in the same location as the sign in the first experimental session. The attention-getting characteristics for this sign were enhanced. It was about nine by 14 inches. "Warning" was printed in one inch black letters on an orange background across the top. It also contained a pictorial message. The drawing was the head and torso of a person in profile with the mouth open and the digestive tract revealed (Product Safety Sign and Label System, 1980). The remainder of the message was under the figure in one/half inch letters. The second sign was placed on top of the fountain itself (though not blocking the water). It was the same sign used in the first experimental session. The number of people who approached the fountain and/or drank from it during a 30 minute period was recorded.

Results and Discussion

As can be seen in Table 3, the behavioral effect of the first sign was not statistically significant. Twenty-two people drank from the fountain during the 30 minute baseline data collection session. During the first experimental session when the first, unenhanced warning was posted, 30 people drank from the fountain. Four people walked toward the fountain, touched it, or otherwise indicated that they wanted to drink, but never did.

Table 3

Number of Users of Water Fountain With and Without Posted Unenhanced Warning

	Unenhanced Warning	No Warning	Σ
Used fountain	30	22	52
Did not use fountain	4	0	4
Σ	34	22	56

Note. The correlation between the two variables (Unenhanced Warning/No Warning and Did Use/Did Not Use Water Fountain) is not significant, $\chi^2 = 1.30$, $p \sim .25$.

During the second experimental session when the enhanced warning was posted, only five people drank from the fountain. Ten people stopped at the fountain, bent over it, or touched it, but never drank the water. As Table 4 illustrates the presence of the enhanced warning caused a

significant change in behavior at the water fountain, $\chi^2 = 20.10$, $p < .001$. The experimenter observed that many people simply did not seem to notice the sign during the first experimental session. This finding illustrates and emphasizes the importance of designing warnings that are highly visible, noticeable, and persuasive.

Table 4

Number of Users of Water Fountain With and Without Posted Enhanced Warning

	Enhanced Warning	No Warning	Σ
Used fountain	5	22	27
Did not use fountain	10	0	10
Σ	15	22	37

Note. The relationship between the two variables (Enhanced Warning/No Warning and Did use/Did Not Use Water Fountain) is significant, $\chi^2 = 20.10$, $p < .001$.

EXPERIMENT 4

The next variable that was investigated was cost of compliance. It was predicted that warnings that do not require very much time or trouble for compliance will be effective and that warnings which require considerably more time and trouble will not be effective. The study was conducted on the campus of a large university. Two sessions took place in the lobby of a classroom building. The lobby has two sets of double doors on the same wall about 50 feet apart. The third session was conducted in another building used for classes and offices. The exit used is at the end of a hallway leading from the lobby. The closest exits to the exit used are located in the lobby about 200 feet away.

Method

The first session was the high cost of compliance condition. It was conducted using one of the sets of double doors in the classroom building. The doors were first observed during the early afternoon for the purpose of collecting baseline data. The number of people exiting the building through each of the single doors in the double door set was recorded. Two days later, at the same time of day, a warning was placed on the door on the left at about eye level. The message of the warning for this session was as follows:

WARNING
BROKEN DOOR
COULD INJURE
USE ANOTHER EXIT
←

This warning directed users to the other set of double doors which were about 50 feet away. Also below the sign in the lower right corner of the door a piece of brown paper approximately two feet square was taped to the door to make it appear broken. The number of people who exited through each of the doors while the sign was posted was recorded. Baseline data collection and experimental observation each lasted for a period of one hour.

The isolated set of doors in the other building was used for the second session. This session was a variation of the high cost of compliance condition and was conducted at the same time as the low cost of compliance condition to be described later. The procedure was the same as that of the first session. The warning was the same except there was no arrow since the nearest exit was back down the hall and across the lobby--about 200 feet. Thus cost of compliance in this session was even higher than that of the first session. The doors were observed for 40 minutes during this session for both the baseline and experimental data collection.

The third session was the low cost of compliance condition. The same procedure was followed as for the first session, and the same door was used. Therefore one high cost condition was conducted at the same door as the low cost, and the other was conducted at the same time. The warning message was as follows:

WARNING
BROKEN DOOR
COULD INJURE
USE OTHER DOOR

This warning directed users to the door on the right which was immediately adjacent. Thus the cost of compliance was relatively low. The number of people who exited through each of the doors was recorded while the sign was posted for a period of one hour.

Results and Discussion

As can been seen in Table 5, only three people obeyed the high cost of compliance warning that was posted during the first session. Forty-eight people ignored the warning and exited through the doors instead of using the other exit 50 feet away as the warning directed. When no warning was posted, 88 people exited through the doors. Thus the effect of this warning was not statistically significant.

The warning used in the second session that exacted an even higher cost for compliance received no compliance at all as illustrated in Table 6. Twenty people people exited through the door while the warning was posted. No one obeyed

the sign by turning around and returning to the lobby to another exit. Twenty-five people exited through the door when no sign was posted.

Table 5

Number of Users of Door With and Without Posted High Cost of Compliance Warning

	Warning	No Warning	Σ
Used door	48	88	136
Did not use door	3	0	3
Σ	51	88	139

Note. The relationship between the two variables (Warning/No Warning and Did Use/Did Not Use Door) is not significant, $x^2 = 2.87$, p~.1.

Table 6

Number of Users of Double Door With and Without Posted Higher Cost of Compliance Warning

	Warning	No Warning	Σ
Used door	20	25	45
Did not use door	0	0	0
Σ	20	25	45

Note. The relationship between the two variables (Warning/No Warning and Did Use/Did Not Use Door) is not significant, $x^2 = 0$, p>.99.

During the third session when the cost of complying with the warning was relatively low, 60 people obeyed the sign as indicated in Table 7. Only four people used the door on the left instead of the door on the right as the warning instructed. When no warning was posted 25 people used the door on the left, and 20 people used the door on the right. When the cost of compliance was low, the warning was effective.

The baseline data in the second column of Table 7 indicates that people do not have a tendency to use either the left or right door in this set of doors. (The baseline data in Table 5 replicates that pattern. Of the 88 people who exited the door in that session, 42 used the left door and 46 used the right door.) This pattern contrasts with behavior in the experimental condition shown in the first column of Table 7 in which almost every one used the right door as directed by the warning message. Therefore the low cost of compliance warning was effective in that it produced a change in behavior. The high cost of compliance warnings did not produce any such significant change.

Table 7

Number of Users of Door With and Without Posted
Low Cost of Compliance Warning

	Warning on door on left	No Warning	Σ
Used door on left	4	25	29
Used other door	60	20	80
Σ	64	45	109

Note.   The relationship between the two variables
(Warning/No Warning and Used Door on Left/ Used
Other Door) is significant, $\chi^2 = 32.90$, $p < .001$.

CONCLUSIONS

Warning effectiveness has been demonstrated in
four diverse situations. The populations sampled
varied from the wide variety of people waiting in the
lobby of the physicians' office building to college
students to physicians and staff in the medical
library. Most of these people were influenced in
their behavior by one of the warnings used in this
study. Therefore warnings can be used, at least in

A number of explanations could be given for the
increase in effectiveness shown by using the second
warning sign on the water fountain. Appropriate
use of color to highlight the background of the
signal word could have been a factor. The pictorial
could have increased the impact of the message by
making it more vivid and salient. The larger size
of the sign may have made it more noticeable. The
changes that were made were undertaken to
improve the attention-getting qualities of the sign.
Whatever the explanation, the important point is
that the enhanced warning was effective whereas
the unenhanced warning was not.

The same fact is true of the warning on the
doors. The high cost of compliance warnings were
not effective; whereas the low cost of compliance
warning was. The changes that were made in the
warnings in this study could be tried with other
ineffective warnings. If a warning is not being
heeded, it should be evaluated. Does it attract
attention? Does it exact a high cost for compliance?
Cost of compliance could be reduced in many ways.
For instance, if a warning on a product calls for the
use of rubber gloves, the gloves should be
provided. Such a provision would decrease the cost
of compliance.

Only two factors that possibly mediate the
effectiveness of warnings have been addressed in
this study. Of course there are many other
possible explanations for lack of compliance.
Some of these were discussed in recommendations
for warnings on tampon products in an earlier study

(Godfrey & Laughery, 1984). Wogalter,
Desaulniers, & Godfrey (in press) have investigated
the effect of redundancy in a warning on perceived
effectiveness. The further identification and
analysis of these variables will establish a much
needed data base for the design and evaluation of
warnings.

References

Product Safety Sign and Label System. (1980).
Santa Clara, California: FMC Corporation.

Godfrey, S. S., & Laughery, K. R. (1984). The
biasing effects of familiarity on consumers'
awareness of hazard. In M. J. Alluisi, S. de
Groot, & E. A. Alluisi (Eds.). Proceedings
of the Human Factors Society 28th Annual
Meeting (pp. 483 - 486). Santa Monica,
California: The Human Factors Society.

McCarthy, R. L., Finnegan, J. P, Krumm-Scott,
Susan, & McCarthy, G. E. (1984). Product
information presentation, user behavior, and
safety. In M. J. Alluisi, S. de Groot, & E. A.
Alluisi (Eds.). Proceedings of the Human
Factors Society 28th Annual Meeting (pp. 81 -
85). Santa Monica, California: The Human
Factors Society.

Wogalter, M. S., Desaulniers, D. R., & Godfrey,
S. S. (in press). Perceived effectiveness of
environmental warnings. Proceedings of the
Human Factors Society 29th Annual
Meeting. Santa Monica, California: The
Human Factors Society.

A Developmental Analysis of Warning Signs:
The Case of Familiarity and Gender

Gerald M. Goldhber, Ph.D.
Department of Communication
State University of New York at Buffalo
Buffalo, New York 14260

and

Mark A. deTurck, Ph.D.
Department of Communication
State University of New York at Buffalo
Buffalo, New York 14260

ABSTRACT

Three NO DIVING signs were placed at one middle and one high school in suburban Buffalo and one middle and one high school served as controls (no signs). A total of 864 students participated in the study. It was found that males were more likely than females to notice the signs, but that males tended to perceive less danger associated with shallow water diving than females. High school males were much more likely than females to dive into the shallow end of their school's pool, especially when the NO DIVING signs were present. In addition, students with a history of diving into the shallow end of their school's pool were much more likely to notice the NO DIVING signs than students who never dove into the shallow end of the pool. Moreover, compared to students who never dove into the shallow end of their school's pool, students with a history of diving into the shallow end of their school's pool tended to perceive less danger and were more likely to dive into the shallow end of the pool again. It appears that warning signs are less effective with high school students than with middle school students.

Students of product safety have devoted considerable research energy toward identifying the factors in warning signs that affect consumers' uncertainty about product safety. Although studies have examined the effectiveness of warning signs using different age groups, there is little empirical evidence regarding the effects of warning signs with adolescents. Adolescents constitute a respectable consumer force with unique socioemotional characteristics that make them vulnerable to personal injury from products due to risk-taking.

A principle goal of this study is to test the effectiveness of warning signs in their naturally occurring environment. Toward this end, the effectiveness of NO DIVING signs posted by school pools was examined. An overriding concern of the current study is to determine if NO DIVING signs are more or less effective with younger or older adolescents. More specifically, the goals of the current study are twofold; first, to compare the effectiveness of NO DIVING signs for males and females at two different stages of adolescence (middle school versus high school); and second, to compare the effectiveness of NO DIVING signs across these same two stages of adolescent development controlling for students' history of diving into the shallow end of their school's pool.

METHOD

Sample

Eight hundred and sixty-four students (1/2 male and 1/2 female) from two suburban Buffalo middle schools and two suburban Buffalo high schools participated in the current study.

Procedures

A NO DIVING sign was professionally designed and produced and permanently affixed at eye level in three conspicuous locations on 3 walls by the shallow end of one high school's pool and one middle school's pool (Figure 1). The NO DIVING sign contained all four "essential" elements of a warning as outlined by others: signal word (DANGER), statement of hazard (Shallow Water), consequences of ignoring of hazard (You Can Be Paralyzed), and how to avoid hazard (NO DIVING) (ANSI Z535, 1-4, 1987; FMC, 1980; Westinghouse, 1981; Wogalter, Godfrey, Fontenelle, Desaulniers & Rothstein, 1987). The signal word DANGER was printed in white letters (1") on a red oval background with a white boundary on a black rectangular background (2.25"). The remainder of the text was printed in black letters (.75"). The pictograph was in black with the international symbol for wheelchair handicaps in blue. The slash configuration was in red. The background for the warning sign was white. The dimensions of the entire sign were 10" x 15".

FIGURE 1

The warning signs remained by the pool for a period of four weeks. After the four-week period, students responded to a questionnaire that measured their awareness and understanding of the sign, their perceived risk and likelihood of diving into the pool, and their history of diving into this and similar pools.

RESULTS

Overall Summary

In the schools with the NO DIVING signs, 34% of the students indicated they saw the signs, 33% indicated they did not see the signs, and 33% said they were not sure; whereas in the schools without the NO DIVING signs, 8% indicated they saw the signs, 48% indicated they did not see the signs, and 44% said they were not sure, Chi-square (2) = 68.07, p < .0001.

There was virtually no difference in terms of the level of danger associated with diving into the shallow end of the pools between the schools with the NO DIVING signs (M= 6.58), and the schools without the NO DIVING signs (M=6.53), F(1,846) < 1. Similarly, there was no difference in the likelihood that students would dive into the shallow end of the pools in the schools where the NO DIVING signs were present (M=3.85) and the schools without the NO DIVING signs (M=3.86), F(1,846) < 1.

Awareness of No Diving Signs

As predicted, students in the middle school were more aware of the NO DIVING signs than students in the high school, Chi-square (6) = 249.42, p < .0001. The pattern of awareness (Table 1) indicates that almost twice as many students in the middle school compared to high school students were aware of the NO DIVING signs when they were present (41% versus 24%). Moreover, when the signs were absent, middle school students were about 4.5 times more accurate than high school students in reporting that there were no signs (69% versus 15%). It is apparent that high school students were less likely to notice the NO DIVING signs and were more unsure if the signs were present than middle school students. That no more than 41% of the middle school or high school students were aware that there were NO DIVING signs is consistent with previous research on awareness of warning signs (cf. Goldhaber & deTurck, 1988a, 1988c, 1988d).

TABLE 1
Percentage of Students Who Were Aware of NO DIVING Signs as a Function of Schools

Aware of Signs	Middle Sch.		High Sch.	
	Sign	No Sign	Sign	No Sign
Yes	41%	6%	24%	11%
No	35	69	28	15
Note Sure	24	25	48	74

Effects of Gender. It is apparent from the pattern of awareness that males were more likely than females to notice the NO DIVING signs, but that the difference between males and females was especially noticeable for high school students (Table 2).

Although levels of awareness dropped off for both males and females from the middle school students to the high school students, the drop in awareness was particularly large for females (34% versus 8%). To isolate the exact effects of gender and developmental stage on awareness, separate Chi-square analyses were conducted for each school by gender.

TABLE 2
Percentage of Male and Female Students Who Were Aware of NO DIVING Signs as a Function of Schools

Aware of Signs	Middle Schools				High Schools			
	Sign		No Sign		Sign		No Sign	
	M	F	M	F	M	F	M	F
Yes	49%	34%	7%	5%	37%	8%	14%	8%
No	35	36	75	62	41	12	20	8
Not Sure	16	30	18	33	22	80	66	84

In the middle school with the NO DIVING signs, males were more likely than females to be aware of the signs and females were more unsure than males if there were NO DIVING signs present, Chi-square (2) = 8.51, p < .05.

In the middle school without the NO DIVING signs, males were more accurate than females in reporting no signs were present and females were more uncertain than males if signs were present, Chi-square (2) = 8.11, p < .05.

In the high school with the NO DIVING signs, males were much more likely than females to notice the NO DIVING signs whereas females were much more uncertain than males if there were signs present, Chi-square (2) = 58.87, p < .0001. In the high school without the NO DIVING signs, males also were more accurate than females in reporting no signs were present while females were more uncertain than males if there were signs present, Chi-square (2) = 6.13, p < .05.

History of diving into shallow end of pool. Overall, students who dove into the shallow end of the pool in the past were more aware (24%) of the NO DIVING signs than students who never dove into the shallow end of the pool (18%). A separate analysis of each school revealed that students' history of diving into the shallow end of the pool only affected awareness significantly among high school students (Table 3).

TABLE 3
Effects of History of Diving Into Shallow End of Pool on Awareness of NO DIVING Signs as a Function of Schools

Aware of Signs	Middle Schools				High Schools			
	Sign		No Sign		Sign		No Sign	
	M	F	M	F	M	F	M	F
Yes	41%	39%	6%	6%	32%	15%	13%	10%
No	39	29	70	64	37	18	28	2
Not Sure	20	32	24	30	31	68	59	88

In the high school with the NO DIVING signs, students with a history of diving were more than twice as aware of the signs as students who never dove in the shallow end (32% versus 15%) and students who never dove in the shallow end were more than twice as uncertain about the presence of the signs than students with a history of diving into the shallow end of the school's pool (68% versus 31%), Chi-square (2) 22.33, p < .0001.

In the high school without the signs, students with a history of diving into the shallow end of the pool were more than twice as likely as students who never dove into the shallow end to report accurately that NO DIVING signs were not present, and students without a history of diving into the shallow end of the pool were much more uncertain about the presence of the signs than students with a history of shallow water diving, Chi-square (2) = 21.95, p < .0001.

There was very little difference

between the middle school students' levels of awareness as a function of their history of diving into the shallow end of the pool whether the NO DIVING signs were present [Chi-square (2) = 4.93, p < .09] or absent [Chi-square (2) = 2.76, p < .43].

Effects of NO DIVING Signs on Likelihood of Compliance and Perceived Danger

Gender. As predicted, high school males were more likely to dive into the shallow end of the pool than middle school males, especially when the NO DIVING signs were present; by contrast, high school females were much less likely to dive than middle school females when the NO DIVING signs were present F(3,844) = 2.73, p < .05 (Table 4). It should be noted that this effect was not mediated by whether the sign was noticed. There was a significant main effect for gender; males (M=4.34) were more likely to dive into the shallow end of the pool than females (M=3.48), F(1,850) = 10.09, p < .005.

TABLE 4
Likelihood of Diving Into Shallow End of Pool as a Function of Gender and Schools

	Middle Sch.		High Sch.	
	Sign	No Sign	Sign	No Sign
Male	4.36	4.63	4.49	3.68
Female	3.82	3.67	2.22	3.78

High school males perceived less danger from diving into the shallow end of the pool than middle school males when the NO DIVING signs were present, whereas high school females perceived more danger associated with shallow water diving than middle school females when the NO DIVING signs were present; however, this trend was not significant F(3,844) = 1.23, p < .30 (Table 5).

TABLE 5
Perceived Danger of Diving Into Shallow End of Pool as a Function of Gender and Schools

	Middle Sch.		High Sch.	
	Sign	No Sign	Sign	No Sign
Male	6.39	6.99	6.13	5.94
Female	6.58	6.81	7.21	6.82

History of diving into shallow end of pool. As predicted, the likelihood students would dive into the shallow end of the school's pool was jointly influenced by their history of diving into the shallow end and their developmental stage (middle school versus high school) F(3,847) = 2.70, p < .05. It is apparent from the pattern of means (Table 6) that students with a history of diving into the shallow end of the pool were more likely to dive into the shallow water, but this effect was more pronounced in the schools where the NO DIVING signs were present. The main effect of students' history of diving into the shallow end of the pool was highly significant, F(1,847) = 265.58, p < .0001.

TABLE 6
Likelihood of Diving Into Shallow End of Pool as a Function of Students' History of Diving Into Shallow End and School

Ever Dive in Shallow End Before	Middle Sch.		High Sch.	
	Sign	No Sign	Sign	No Sign
Yes	5.43	5.28	5.16	4.83
No	1.40	2.05	1.55	2.61

The interaction between presence of signs and history of diving into the shallow end of the pool on perceived danger from diving was not significant, F(3,847) = 1.49, p <.22. However, there was a very large main effect for students' history of diving into the shallow end of the pool, F(1,847) = 51.24, p < .0001. Students with a history of diving into the shallow end were much more likely to dive into the shallow end again than students who never did so (Table 7).

TABLE 7
Perceived Danger From Diving Into Shallow End of Pool as a Function of Students' History of Diving Into Shallow End and School

Ever Dive in Shallow End Before	Middle Sch.		High Sch.	
	Sign	No Sign	Sign	No Sign
Yes	6.00	5.87	5.64	5.16
No	7.45	8.80	7.70	7.51

DISCUSSION

Findings from the current study indicate that the majority of adolescents were unaware of the NO DIVING signs placed around their school's pools. Moreover, the highest levels of awareness were among the teenagers most likely to dive into the shallow end of their pool -- males and students with a history of diving into the shallow end of the pool. Compared to school's without the NO DIVING signs, it is apparent from the results that the NO DIVING signs did not reduce the likelihood that a substantial number of swimmers would dive into the shallow end of their school's pool. More specifically, the NO DIVING signs decreased the perceived danger of shallow water diving for older adolescent males and older teens with a history of diving into shallow water, and as a result, increased the likelihood that these same groups of swimmers would dive into the shallow end of the pool. In fact, these groups of swimmers were more likely to dive into the shallow water when the NO DIVING signs were present than when they were absent.

That the NO DIVING sign did not affect students' perception of diving into shallow water as dangerous, or their intentions to dive into the shallow water, supports previous research that indicates NO DIVING signs do not deter swimmers from intending to dive into shallow water (see for example, Goldhaber & deTurck, 1988a, 1988c, 1988d). A NO DIVING sign is only one piece of information affecting swimmers' decisions to dive into shallow water. If swimmers dove into shallow water in the past without injuring themselves, they may feel more certain and more confident that they know how to dive into shallow water without hurting themselves. In fact, the current results suggest that a NO DIVING sign may serve only to make people with a history of diving into shallow water feel that diving into shallow water is <u>not</u> as dangerous as people who never dove into shallow water, and as a result, may increase the likelihood that these people would dive into shallow water.

References

American National Standards Institute, (1987). American national standard specification for accident prevention signs. ANSI, Z535, draft.

deTurck, M.A. & Goldhaber, G.M. (1988). Consumers' Information Processing Objectives and Effects of Product Warnings. <u>Proceedings of the Human Factors Society</u>. 32, 445-449.

FMC, Inc. (1980). <u>Product safety sign and label system</u>. 3rd ed., Santa Clara, CA.: FMC Corporation.

Goldhaber, G.M., & deTurck, M.A. (1988a). Effects of consumers' familiarity with a product on attention to and compliance with warnings. <u>Journal of Products Liability</u>, 11, 29-37.

Goldhaber, G.M., & deTurck, M.A. (1988b). A dimensional analysis of signal words. <u>Forensic Reports</u>, 1, 201.

Goldhaber, G.M., & deTurck, M.A. (1988c). Effectiveness of warning signs: Gender and familiarity effects. <u>Journal of Products Liability</u>, 11, 271-284.

Goldhaber, G.M., & deTurck, M.A. (1988d). Effectiveness of warning signs: "Familiarity effects". <u>Forensic Reports</u>, 1, 281-301.

Goldhaber, G.M., & deTurck, M.A. (1988e). Effects of product warnings on adolescents in an educational setting. <u>Product Safety and Liability Report</u>, 16, 949-955.

Westinghouse Corporation (1981). <u>Westinghouse product safety handbook</u>. Trafford, Pa.: Westinghouse Printing Division.

Wogalter, M.S., Godfrey, S.S., Fontenelle, G.A., Desaulniers, D.R., Rothstein, P.R., & Laughery, K.R. (1987). Effectiveness of Warnings. <u>Human Factors</u>, 29, 599-612.

EVALUATING THE EFFECTIVENESS OF WARNINGS UNDER PREVAILING WORKING CONDITIONS

Frank E. Gomer
Behavioral Science Applications
Yellow Springs, Ohio 45387

ABSTRACT

Due to a lack of published test results from which to draw conclusions about the effectiveness of warnings under different working conditions, I conducted a field study as an aid in the formulation of expert opinion during the discovery phase of pending product-liability litigation. My intent was to measure the effectiveness of a label which warned of the risk of delayed lung disease. The design of the warning conformed to the existing requirements for the period of interest – the mid 1960s. To replicate the prevailing conditions in the plant at the time that exposure to the hazard occurred, appropriate engineering and administrative controls purposefully were omitted. The warnings failed to cause a significant reduction in the incidence of unsafe behavior.

INTRODUCTION

Human factors specialists are being called upon more frequently to provide expert consultation during product-liability litigation. The content and appearance of warnings, an issue in many cases, is an area in which human factors considerations have been applied extensively. In fact, it has been suggested that a human factors specialist should testify in every case involving the adequacy of warnings (Messina, 1984).

Certainly, warnings should be but one element of an integrated health and safety program for minimizing exposure to a hazard that cannot be effectively removed from the workplace through design changes. The other elements consist of engineering and administrative controls. Beginning with frequent monitoring, engineering controls serve to isolate the worker from the hazard and may include such methods as enclosure, guarding, exhaust ventilation, and proper job design. Administrative controls, on the other hand, include: (1) enforceable policies which limit the number of workers exposed and, as appropriate, require the wearing of personal protective equipment; (2) strict housekeeping practices; (3) periodic medical examinations; and (4) compulsory training and educational programs. Thus, the proper role of a warning is to reinforce what has been learned through compulsory education and carefully supervised training.

Despite many recent appeals that warnings be tested for effectiveness under representative working conditions (Christensen, 1983; Dorris and Purswell, 1977; Peters, 1984), such testing usually is limited to subjective evaluations of preference for or, perhaps, recall of competing warnings. Why should effectiveness testing under representative working conditions be an important consideration? Clearly, one reason is to minimize prospective liability, by documenting the comprehensiveness of the foreseeability analysis performed during the development of the warning. Second, if several formats and message contents seem applicable, then realistic effectiveness data can be factored into the design trade-offs. Third, due to a lack of published data from which to draw conclusions about the effectiveness of warnings under different working conditions, it may be necessary to conduct tests during the discovery phase of pending litigation, as an aid in the formulation of expert opinion.

BACKGROUND

Recently, I was asked to provide expert opinion in a case in which a failure to warn was alleged to be a contributing factor in the causation of occupational disease. The plaintiffs in the case had been exposed to asbestos fibers in the 1950s and 1960s at an asbestos insulation manufacturing plant. A review of the case exhibits and plant-related documents revealed that prescribed engineering and administrative controls were missing, and that warnings, had they been present on bags of raw asbestos entering the plant, would have been the principal method of controlling the hazard.

Besides their primary functions in minimizing exposure to a hazard, it seems evident that engineering and administrative controls also serve to heighten a worker's awareness of a hazard and the attendant risk. If these controls are indeed missing or deficient, might this not constitute a set of working conditions which could predispose an otherwise reasonable individual to devalue a warning that arguably was adequate in terms of basic design? And would this be especially true if the hazardous material had a delayed effect on the health of the individual? The functionally disabling, life-shortening nature of asbestos-related diseases now is well documented in the medical literature (Nicholson, Perkel, and Selikoff, 1982). However, case histories and epidemiological studies underscore the long latent period between initial exposure to asbestos fibers and the presence of definitive clinical symptomatology.

The question I attempted to answer empirically was what immediate impact would a well-designed warning have had, if "suddenly" presented under these prevailing conditions? In the design of this study, I focussed on unskilled laborers among the plaintiffs who had unloaded and stacked porous bags of asbestos on an irregular basis for varying periods of time. Many had been provided to the plant by temporary employment agencies, and many had handled bags of asbestos for only a few days or weeks. No exhaust ventilation or respirators had been provided by the plant, proper dust control and housekeeping had been nonexistent, and no educational and training programs had been made available to describe the risks and to teach proper work practices and safeguards. Moreover, although perceived by the workers as annoying and bothersome, the asbestos material itself was not considered to be hazardous.

Clearly, I could not expose individuals in a field study to asbestos fibers; therefore, I substituted granular limestone – a nontoxic material classified as producing nuisance dust. However, the warning was modeled after an appropriate asbestos-related warning for the early to mid 1960s, i.e., not after the asbestos-related warnings which began to appear at that time nor, for that matter, after the current OSHA-mandated warning. Since the late 1930s, there had been general agreement that workers in asbestos insulation plants were at risk to develop asbestosis. However, consensus within the medical community concerning a causal relationship between exposure to asbestos and the development of lung cancer and mesothelioma was not achieved until the late 1960s, following publication in December 1965 of the Proceedings of the New York Academy of Sciences International Meeting on the Biological Effects of Asbestos.

In designing the format and content of a label which warned of a hypothetical limestone-dust hazard, I consulted the open literature and trade journals of the period, 1945 to 1971 revisions of the Manufacturing Chemists Association Manual L-1 (entitled "Warning Labels: A Guide to the Preparation of Warning Labels for Hazardous Chemicals"), and the 1976 ANSI Standard for precautionary labeling of hazardous industrial chemicals. Table 1 presents a listing of current guidelines for developing warning labels. These guidelines have been extracted from consensus standards, federal regulations, industry handbooks, government recommendations, textbooks, and journal articles. It is noteworthy that, of the guidelines prescribed today, only hazard-specific color coding and the use of attention-directing symbols and pictographs were not recommended by the 1960s.

EXPERIMENT

Workplace

A government warehouse was selected as the test site, since a wide variety of packaged materials is received from vendors, unloaded from trucks, stored, and eventually reloaded for shipment to other government installations. Moreover, it is not uncommon for individual containers or bags to be removed from or placed within truck

Table 1. Current Guidelines for Warnings

I. Does the warning command attention?
   A. Is the warning conspicuous?
      1. Is the warning clearly visible?
      2. Have attention-directing symbols and pictographs been used?
      3. Has the appropriate signal word been used?
      4. Has appropriate color-coding been used?
      5. Is the size of the warning scaled to the dimensions of the product?
      6. Has a border been used to isolate the warning.

II. Does the text of the warning:
   A. Identify the hazard?
   B. Indicate the degree of risk and the consequences of exposure?
   C. List conditions under which the product is likely to be a hazard?
   D. List precautions and means of avoiding the hazard?
   E. Identify actions to be taken if exposure to the hazard occurs?
   F. Employ clearly understandable, familiar language?
   G. Provide a message that:
      1. Is accurate?
      2. Uses active voice?
      3. Is affirmative and avoids "fudge" words?
      4. Creates the appropriate concern for safety and perception of the risk by incorporating an urgency that is commensurate with the danger?
      5. Is concise?
   H. Take into account the persons to whom the warning is addressed?
   I. Conform to common standards, regulations, and practices?

III. Is the warning placed in reasonable proximity to the hazard?

IV. Is the text readable?
   A. Has a foreseeability analysis considered reading distance, illumination levels, and other factors?
   B. Have label life and degradation been considered?
   C. Have typographic features been considered?

trailers by hand, rather than be secured to pallets and transported by forklift.

Subjects

Seventeen men who were experienced in heavy loading and unloading were studied. Since it was important to eliminate the influence of administrative controls that were rigorously enforced by management, the men were not part of the work force assigned to this facility. Instead, they were employed by an agency routinely contacted by the warehouse when experienced workers were needed for loading and unloading shipments after normal duty hours.

Procedure

Nine of the workers reported to the warehouse from 4 to 8 p.m., and they were assigned to 2 un-loading crews of four and five persons, respec-tively. The other eight workers were told to report from 9 p.m. to 1 a.m., and they were assigned to 2 loading crews of four persons each.

The study was conducted on three consecutive days during the two time periods noted above. Again, unloading and loading tasks were performed at different times. Depending on the time period, the workers were told when first arriving that they would be unloading or loading shipments of limestone for the next three days. There was no discussion of a potential health hazard, nor was any safety-related training provided. The un-loading crews were instructed to remove individ-ual bags stacked in rows in the trailer and to place them on pallets positioned by the edge of the dock. The loading crews were instructed to lift individual bags from pallets also positioned by the edge of the dock and to stack them in rows in the trailer.

Individual bags of limestone weighed 22.7 kgs and were approximately 48 by 29 by 10 cm in dimension. During each time period, two trucks were either unloaded or loaded by separate crews at adjacent docks. The pallets were filled and emptied sequentially. Forklifts transported pallets to and from the docks. Each crew handled approximately 800 bags of limestone every day. Because the bags were perforated along the sides and at the top, and because there were no pro-visions for exhaust ventilation or portable dust collection, the dust was very visible and con-centrated in the air within the trucks and sur-rounding the docks. The clothing and exposed areas of all workers were literally covered with this dust during the unloading and loading tasks.

On the first day, the workers acclimated to the task requirements. Bags of limestone with-out warning labels were unloaded and loaded in accordance with the procedures described above. The second day consisted of data collection in the control condition; again, no warning labels were present on the bags. The third day was devoted to data collection in the experimental condition; warning labels (as depicted in Figure 1) were present and clearly visible on every bag handled by the workers. A within-subjects design was chosen to examine the veracity of claims by certain plaintiffs in the case, that they would have heeded warnings on bags of as-bestos even if such warnings appeared after they had begun working at the plant.

Recorded were: (a) the time required to fill and empty each pallet; (b) the number of workers requesting and wearing respirator masks; and (c) the number of workers reporting inadequate

CONTAINS LIMESTONE

| WARNING! | DUST IS CREATED WHEN LIMESTONE IS HANDLED. BREATHING LIMESTONE DUST CAUSES DELAYED LUNG DISEASE. SMOKING INCREASES THE RISK. |

- Do Not Breathe Limestone Dust.

- Handle Limestone Only in Areas Where There Is Exhaust Ventilation.

- Always Wear an Approved Protective Mask When Handling Limestone.

- If Limestone Dust Has Been Inhaled, Contact Plant Management.

Figure 1. Format and Content of Warning.

exhaust ventilation or exposure to hazardous dust. All data were collected unobtrusively. It was decided that undue psychological stress could not be caused by having any of the workers believe that they were at risk for days or weeks. Therefore, all workers were fully debriefed after work on the same day that the warnings were in-troduced.

Results

At the beginning of the second work day (i.e., prior to the appearance of the warnings), 3 of the 17 workers requested and then wore res-pirator masks for the remainder of the study. Because many of the workers had prior work experience in other dusty environments and since they did communicate with each other during the unloading and loading tasks, it is not surpris-ing that some workers, at least generally safety conscious, would seek protection after being exposed to the heavy dust on the first day. In fact, it supports the credibility of the test environment. However, a change from 0 to 3 in the number of workers wearing respirator masks is not statistically significant (Fisher exact probability test, $p > 0.10$). What is surpris-ing is the finding that when the warning labels were introduced, only 3 of the 14 workers who were not wearing respirator masks at the time requested and wore them. This does not repre-sent a statistically significant reduction in unsafe behavior (Fisher exact probability test, $p > 0.10$). If we adopt a legal criterion instead of a statistical criterion, an effective warn-ing is one that "more probably than not" will reduce the occurrence of unsafe behavior in the workplace. Clearly, the instruction to wear respirator masks was not heeded by a majority of workers. Moreover, none of the 17 workers re-ported the hazard or complained about a lack of exhaust ventilation.

If a worker does not explicitly follow the instructions in a warning, can it be assumed that he or she does not appreciate the risk. Perhaps real or perceived pressures from fellow workers or management can cause a worker to continue handling a substance without a respirator. Thus, it is possible that the warnings could have engendered the appropriate perception of risk even though unsafe behavior continued in the workplace. Since an abrupt change in the time required to complete a practiced task can be a sensitive measure of work-related stress, response time data were entered into a 2 X 2 X 20 repeated measures analysis of variance, representing task (unloading vs. loading), workday (control vs. experimental), and pallet number (1 through 20), respectively. Neither the main effect of workday nor any interaction involving this factor were significant; the time required to fill and empty pallets was not affected by the presence of warnings.

Although the work area was extremely dusty and they observed their co-workers wearing respirator masks, 11 workers still failed to comply with this precautionary measure after the warnings were introduced. All workers reported during the debriefing that they had seen the warnings. None stated that they had dismissed the warning as false or because it was insufficiently strong in wording. Rather, they believed that they could continue loading or unloading as they had the previous two days.

While the motivating factors which influence a person's decision to accept or reject risk are not well understood (Fischhoff, 1977), in times of high unemployment workers will take greater risks because they must remain on the job. Further, if exposure to the hazard is painless, albeit annoying, and the disease takes years to be manifest, then denial is a likely defense mechanism. In view of the special emphasis now being placed on warnings as a result of OSHA's new Hazard Communication Standard, hopefully even greater pressure can be exerted for effectiveness testing under a variety of representative working conditions.

CONCLUDING COMMENTS

Two additional points must be made. First, by the late 1960s, bags of asbestos handled in insulation manufacturing plants should have contained warnings specifically describing the risks of lung cancer and mesothelioma. Second, this paper should not be cited as proof that great care need not go into the design of warnings. Rather, in addition to training workers to interpret warnings, the findings of this study suggest that workers also should receive training to _act_ in accordance with the warning.

REFERENCES

Christensen, J. M. (1983). Human factors considerations in lawsuits. In G.A. Peters and D. B. Esau (Eds.), Safety law: A legal reference. Park Ridge, IL: American Society of Safety Engineers.

Dorris, A. L., & Purswell, J. L. (1977). Warnings and human behavior: Implications for the design of product warnings. Journal of Products Liability, 1, 255-264.

Fischhoff, B. (1977). Cognitive liabilities and product liability. Journal of Products Liability, 1, 207-219.

Messina, J. (1984). The human factors expert in torts litigation. Trial, 20, 38-42.

Nicholson, W. J., Perkel, G., & Selikoff, I. J. (1982). Occupational exposure to asbestos: Population at risk and projected mortality. American Journal of Industrial Medicine, 3, 259-311.

Peters, G. A. (1984). Fifteen cardinal principles to ensure effectiveness of a warning system. Occupational Health and Safety, May, 76-79.

CONSUMER ACCEPTANCE OF THREATENING WARNINGS IN THE RESIDENTIAL ENVIRONMENT

Jean E. Harris
Michael E. Wiklund
American Institutes for Research
Bedford, MA

ABSTRACT

In the course of designing warnings a manufacturer of residential swimming pools, American Institutes for Research (AIR) conducted several surveys of potential pool users to determine whether threatening (i.e. morbid, disturbing, or fear-arousing) or non-threatening warnings were more appropriate for the residential environment. This study focused on determining (1) how effective both types of warnings would be in preventing serious pool injuries and (2) the likelihood that a pool owner would post the warnings. The warnings addressed the two major swimming pool hazards, as determined by the U.S. Consumer Product Safety Commission's (CPSC) statistics: (1) diving accidents involving teenage males and (2) drowning accidents involving children under the age of 5 years. We conducted an initial survey of 15 potential pool users to assess the pool manufacturer's existing warnings. Then we surveyed 27 potential pool users to determine their preferences from several design alternatives. Finally, we validated comprehension of the pictographs with a survey of 135 subjects. During these surveys, a substantial proportion of the subjects indicated that people might have reservations about posting a threatening warning. The final warning designs reflect the conclusion that it is better to provide warnings that do not offend people's sensibilities. This increases the chance that pool owners will post the warnings in a residential environment.

INTRODUCTION

Designers and manufacturers of consumer products must take care to ensure that their products are safe to use. This involves designing a product that is safe when used for the intended uses and as well as for reasonably predictable unintended uses. Although it is perhaps impossible to guarantee a user's safety, there are precautions the manufacturers can take to provide clear instructions and adequate warnings of the hazards involved with their products. But despite a significant amount of research on warnings, there are still many unsolved issues surrounding warning design and use. These design issues include the optimum layout (Desaulniers, 1987), the use of pictographs (Young and Wogalter, 1988; Friedmann, 1988), and even the effectiveness of warnings in general (Otsubo, 1988).

On behalf of a pool manufacturer, we recently designed a series of warnings for residential swimming pools. Although pools are generally perceived as benign, fun products, thousands of people are injured or killed in pools every year. For example, about 600 children under the age of five are killed and about 3,000 are severely injured in drowning accidents annually (National Safety Council, 1988; CPSC, 1988). It was therefore important for us to design an effective warning.

A person must see a warning before he/she will comply with it. Therefore, the conspicuity of the warning is an important characteristic. For most consumer products, this can be accomplished by placing the warnings in a prominent location on the product so it can be read easily. However, the pool warnings we designed are contained in a packet of literature that arrives with a new pool.

It is up to the pool owners to post the warnings, for there are currently no laws (at least in Massachusetts) requiring them to do so. One goal of our design process was to increase the likelihood that the pool owners would post our warnings.

In designing our warnings, one of the first issues we faced was how threatening they should be. A threatening warning contains a pictograph or text that may be morbid, disturbing, or fear-arousing. After examining the available literature, there does not appear to be much research done in this area. However, some of the work that has been done suggests that a more threatening warning may not necessarily be more effective (Evans, et al. 1970). In addition, our preliminary work revealed that the people might have reservations about voluntarily posting a threatening warning in their backyards. This paper will discuss the results of our efforts to determine the optimum level of threat for warnings which are posted by the consumer in a residential environment.

PRELIMINARY RESEARCH

In 1988, AIR completed a study for the U.S. Consumer Product Safety Commission (CPSC) on the effectiveness of various swimming pool warning signs (Loring and Wiklund, 1988). We conducted a small set of interviews to assess several preliminary design ideas. Using the results, we suggested improved swimming pool warning designs to the CPSC. These tests revealed that determining the appropriate threat level was important in the design of warnings to be posted by the consumer.

In that study, we showed the subjects the following pictograph alternatives for a "Prevent Drowning" warning:

Figure 1
More Threatening

Figure 2
Threatening

Figure 3
Less threatening

Based on the results of the tests, Figure 1 was eliminated because of its excessive morbidity. The subjects, especially the parents, found the pictograph harsh and shocking. They were also concerned that it would frighten young children. Figures 2 and 3 were both considered possible candidates for a "Prevent Drowning" warning.

DESIGNING NEW WARNINGS

Our first step in developing the signs was to evaluate an existing sign from the manufacturer to determine what, if any, improvements should be made. The subjects for this test were 10 teenagers (8 male, 2 female) and 5 parents of young children (3 male, 2 female). These were the two target populations for the warnings. The test consisted of a structured interview and a questionnaire. We asked the subjects to comment on their interpretation of the existing warnings and to suggest improvements.

In general, the suggestions relating to the threat level of the warnings indicated that they should be more threatening.

Figure 4
"No Diving" Pictograph

PREVENT DROWNING

Look for swimmers in trouble.

Figure 5
Threatening

PREVENT DROWNING

Watch pool users at all times.

Figure 6
Less Threatening

For example, on the "No Diving" pictograph (Figure 4), two people suggested that the diver should look more seriously injured, and five people recommended that the impact lines (around the head) should be redrawn to suggest a more serious injury. The subjects felt that increasing the threat level of the warnings would increase their effectiveness. It is important to note here that we asked these subjects to comment on the effectiveness of the warnings without regard to the fact that the sign would have to be posted by consumers.

Based on these results, we determined that we should design new warnings. Therefore, we developed several alternatives for the components of the warnings to test. We designed and adapted text and pictograph alternatives in varying threat levels.

To test the alternatives, we interviewed 16 teenagers (14 male, 2 female) and 11 parents of young children (3 male, 8 female). During the tests, we asked the subjects to choose the most appropriate alternative for each component and to give their comments and criticisms.

The subjects had to choose an approach for the "Prevent Drowning" warning. We showed the subjects the alternatives in Figures 5 and 6. The pictograph in Figure 5 shows a child in distress, an image considered to be upsetting to people. Figure 6 shows an adult watching a child playing safely in the water, a less threatening image.

Overall, the subjects preferred the approach in Figure 6 (63% to 27%). Although some subjects felt that the child in distress would be more effective, they expressed a concern that people might not voluntarily post such a disturbing warning. Seventy-five percent of the teenagers we tested preferred the approach in Figure 6. Many of them, especially the younger ones, identified with the child in the pictograph and found the approach in Figure 5, as one teenager stated, "too gruesome." Although 55% of the parents preferred the approach in Figure 5, 45% preferred the less threatening warning. Therefore, almost half the subjects could have reservations about posting the more threatening warning.

During this test, none of our subjects stated outright, "No, I would not post a threatening warning." However, many voiced a concern, as shown in the following comments, that others might find the warning too threatening to post (or to view) in a residential environment:

> "There are people probably who wouldn't put it up."

> "[Figure 6] is a little more neutral; it has a more positive appearance."

> "I don't want to scare my friends from the pool."

Subjects also stated that people might be concerned about frightening small children or interfering with the aesthetics of their backyards. This led us to conclude that many pool owners would reject a threatening warning. In our testing situation, where the subjects knew the tests were about safety warnings, it is likely that the subjects were biased towards stating that they would do the "right" thing, that is, that they would post the signs (Purswell, Krenek, and Dorris, 1987). It is likely, given the testing situation, that this reaction is a manifestation of their own reservations about posting a threatening warning. In fact, one subject still has not posted the warnings which came with her pool almost a year ago.

We also performed a test to determine the best statement of consequence for our "No Diving" warning. For this test, we had 50 college students (40 male, 10 female) rate the following 9 statements for the likelihood of (1) catching their attention and (2) stopping them from diving:

1. You can be seriously injured or killed.
2. You can be paralyzed or killed.
3. You can be permanently injured or killed.
4. You can be crippled or killed.
5. You can be paralyzed.
6. You can be permanently injured.
7. You can be seriously injured.
8. You can be crippled.
9. You can break your neck.

The subjects used a scale of 1 (unlikely) to 10 (likely). The nine statements are intentionally quite similar. In fact, four of them have been repeated with the phrase "or killed" added at the end. We decided that the warning should address the reader – "You" – and should be in the active voice. Therefore, we were mainly concerned with the wording of the possible injury. Some of the phrases were adopted from existing signs.

After collecting the data, we averaged the ratings for each statement. Figure 7 shows a graph of the average ratings for each statement.

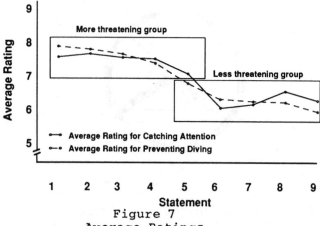

Figure 7
Average Ratings

We then performed t-tests comparing the average ratings for each statement and found that the statements with the phrase "or killed" were rated significantly higher than those without the phrase. There are 20 comparisons of a statement with the phrase "or killed" to one without for catching attention and for preventing diving. Out of these 40 comparisons, p<.01 for 35, p<.05 for 2, and p>.05 for 3. Those with the phrase "or killed" have therefore been placed into the "threatening" group, based on their average ratings. Those without the phrase have been placed into the "less threatening" group. The only exception is the phrase "You can be paralyzed" which is in the threatening group for catching attention.

Within each group (threatening or less threatening), the effectiveness of each statement does not differ significantly. We also did not find a significant difference between the ratings for catching attention and preventing diving (p>.05 for each statement).

Although this test indicates that the more threatening statements are perceived to be more effective, we again had to face the question, "Will the pool owners post a threatening sign near their pool?" We could have used a statement of consequence which included the phrase "or killed", potentially increasing the effectiveness of the warning, but we would have risked having pool owners not post the warning. We concluded that as long as the readers understand the message quickly and easily, the less threatening message would be more effective overall, because more pool owners would be likely to post the sign.

We also found that, in general, the subjects recommended that the "No Diving" warning be more morbid, while they preferred a less morbid "Prevent Drowning" warning. This may indicate that the seriousness of the injury described in the warning may not necessarily dictate the threat level. In designing future warnings, it will be necessary to ensure that the threat level is acceptable for that particular warning.

CONCLUSIONS

Our research showed the following results: (1) generally, a more threatening warning is perceived as more effective; but (2) people are uneasy about posting a threatening warning in their backyard; and therefore (3) it is better to make less threatening warnings which are more likely to get posted.

For our final warning solutions (Figures 8 and 9), we used what we believed to be an appropriate threat level.

Figure 8   Figure 9
"No Diving"   "Prevent Drowning"

The "No Diving" warning is somewhat threatening, showing a serious neck injury. The "Prevent Drowning" warning is less threatening, showing an adult watching a child play safely in the water.

It would be difficult to prove how much more likely someone is to post one warning over another, or how much more effective one warning is. Taking into account the threat level of the warnings will encourage more pool owners to post them. If

more people post the warnings, the message will get to more people; thus, the warnings will be more effective overall. It is possible to make a warning more appropriate for a residential environment without degrading its impact. These results can be applied to any warnings where the consumer is required to post warnings in a residential environment. There is a growing trend toward providing warnings with hazardous products. It is likely that soon, products such as insecticides, children's jungle gym sets, barbecues, and other outdoor equipment will come with warnings which are to be posted by the owner.

REFERENCES

Desaulniers, D., "Layout, Organization, and the Effectiveness of Consumer Product Warnings," *Proceedings of the Human Factors Society 31st Annual Meeting*, 1987, pp 56-60.

Evans, R.; Rozelle, R.; Lasater, T.; Dembroski, T.; and Allen, B., "Fear, Arousal, Persuasion, and Actual vs. Implied Behavioral Change," *Journal of Personality and Social Psychology*, 1970, 16(2), pp 220-227.

Friedmann, K., "The Effect of Adding Symbols to Written Warning Labels on User Behavior and Recall," *Human Factors*, 1988, 30(4), pp 507-515.

Loring, B. and Wiklund, M., "Effectiveness of Swimming Pool Warning Signs and Labels," American Institutes for Research, Prepared for: U.S. Consumer Product Safety Commission, 1988.

National Safety Council, *Accident Facts*, 1988.

Otsubo, S., "A Behavioral Study of Warning Labels for Consumer Products: Perceived Danger and Use of Pictographs," *Proceedings of the Human Factors Society 32nd Annual Meeting*, 1988, pp 536-540.

Purswell, Jerry, Krenek, Richard, and Dorris, Alan, "Warning Effectiveness: What Do We Need to Know?," *Proceedings of the Human Factors Society 31st Annual Meeting*, 1987, pp 1116-1120.

U.S. Consumer Product Safety Commission, National Electronic Injury Surveillance System (NEISS), 1988.

Young, S. and Wogalter, M., "Memory of Instruction Manual Warnings: Effects of Pictorial Icons and Conspicuous Print," *Proceedings of the Human Factors Society 32nd Annual Meeting*, 1988, pp 905-909.

SAFETY INFORMATION PRESENTATION:
FACTORS INFLUENCING THE POTENTIAL FOR CHANGING BEHAVIOR

D.P. Horst, G.E. McCarthy, J.N. Robinson, R.L. McCarthy, S. Krumm-Scott
Failure Analysis Associates
Palo Alto, California

ABSTRACT

Studies of several on-product warnings and product safety messages provide evidence that on-product warnings have not been effective in preventing injuries. However, there are examples of information presentations that, in conjunction with other factors, do modify human behavior. Some of these examples are safety-related. The authors examine the factors that influence the potential for changing human behavior and their implications for safety information about consumer products.

INTRODUCTION

The presentation of safety information is generally intended to change behavior so as to reduce the frequency of accidents and injuries. Studies have shown that in some cases safety information presentations do not lead to changes in behavior or reductions in the numbers of injuries. McCarthy, et al. (1984a) examined the effectiveness of on-product warning labels, summarized an extensive search of the literature, and concluded that all available quantitative studies showed the warnings under investigation to have no impact on safety. Experience with other information presentation media and results from other studies provide examples of messages, some safety-related, with greater success in modifying human behavior. Examples include highway stop signs, railroad crossing signals, and specially constructed laboratory tests.

We have attempted here to integrate the above-described observations, other studies identified since 1984 in our ongoing search of the literature, and experience from controlled research studies and numerous accident investigations. From the results of these studies and a general background provided by the fields of experimental psychology, communication theory, and human factors research, we have identified factors that influence the potential of safety information for changing behavior.

In this paper, we are primarily concerned with "safety information" about hazards that may lead to physical injuries, but in order to understand the effects of safety information on behavior, we extend the definition very broadly to include information about any negative consequence.

"Presentation" of safety information can be via warning signs or labels, and much of our interest has been focused on the effectiveness of information presented via these media. However, we also discuss other media used to present safety information, including instruction sheets and manuals, and audible and visual alarms.

REVIEW OF RESEARCH

Experimental Psychology and Communication Theory

Much of our understanding of the effects of safety information on behavior derives from research conducted in human learning, attention, and motivation. From research in these areas, we know that the individual is characterized by a limited attentional capacity, and that attention is controlled by complex mechanisms influenced by learning. In simple terms, we learn to filter out most of the information that bombards our senses and to attend to things that we have learned to view as important or interesting. Thus, much of the information that reaches our eyes and ears, including at least some safety information, is never processed at any conscious level, and may have virtually no effect on our behavior.

When safety information is not filtered out and is considered consciously, the effects upon behavior are determined by a complex combination of genetic inheritance, personal development, physical conditions, and experience. The information may be perceived as something that requires action or change in established behavior patterns. However, if the information is perceived as familiar or redundant, it may simply be dropped from short term memory, and have no further effect on behavior. Alternatively, if the information is perceived as inconsistent with existing knowledge and beliefs, it may be rejected as not credible. Even if the information is previously unknown and is accepted as true, the recipient may be insufficiently motivated to alter behavior.

The field of communication theory also provides insight. A key concept is that humans are not passive receivers who absorb all information directed toward them. On the contrary, unless a person is in an "information seeking" mode, the message may not be received at all. Communications theorists also emphasize the importance of the credibility of the source of a message. Unless the source is credible, the message may have no potential to achieve the intended effect.

Human Factors

Much research has focused on the formats for warning signs or labels and on the content categories to be included. Studies on formats for warning signs and labels go back many years, and include investigation of colors and lettering that will maximize legibility. Current standards incorporate many of the findings of this research (ANSI, 1972).

Some research has been done on the content of warning signs, but most consists of presenting different signs to subjects in a laboratory setting and asking for their opinions about which content is the most convincing. This type of research, supported by a substantial amount of arm-chair logic, appears to be responsible for the widely encountered guidelines that warnings should comprise four elements: a standard signal word, and statements of the hazard, the potential consequences, and how to avoid the hazard. An individual exposed to a hazard must have access to these kinds of information to be motivated and able to respond appropriately. However, it is erroneous to suggest that either (a) all of the information must be provided by a warning sign or label in order for the sign or label to affect behavior or (b) that inclusion of all of this information will guarantee effectiveness. In fact, much or all of the information about many hazards is supplied by a combination of situation cues and previous experience. Some of the most effective signs do not include any of the four items listed above.

Quantitative Research on Behavioral Effects

While the behavioral effects of safety information have received much less attention than have format and content, some informative studies have been conducted. In this section, we discuss examples of these studies and attempt to identify factors that influenced behavior. Limited space renders this list incomplete; for further discussion of this topic see McCarthy et al. (1984a).

Hammer warnings study: One hundred students used hammers in a laboratory study, and none even noticed the warning labels on the hammers (Dorris and Purswell, 1977). This illustrates that a warning label on a familiar product is not necessarily a salient item. It may be filtered out by the user's attentional mechanisms and never processed at a conscious level.

Road sign study: Drivers were stopped and interviewed after passing "curve" signs. Most did not remember the signs, especially when stopped during daylight hours. (Shinar and Drory, 1983). The study showed that such signs attracted little conscious attention. It is possible that the signs provided information that was utilized at a pre-attentive level as part of the total stimulus pattern for drivers approaching the curve. However, other cues provide adequate information to negotiate most curves safely, and the information provided by curve signs may be entirely redundant under conditions of normal visibility. Overuse of such signs may also have impaired their credibility.

Lawnmower safety campaign study: Lawnmower safety campaigns were carried out under various treatment and control conditions in different communities. Poster and media campaigns with distribution of danger spot stickers were scarcely noticed. An interpersonal communication campaign was noticed, but injuries at this site actually increased (Kerpelman, et al., 1978). It seems likely that the safety information provided in the campaign was redundant or irrelevant to the events leading to real accidents.

Label-reading study: Households where product instructions were read and kept had no fewer injuries than households where instructions were thrown away unread (Tokuhata, et al., 1976). This illustrated that lack of printed safety information is not necessarily the reason for unsafe behavior and that redundant information is unlikely to reduce accidents.

Poison storage study: Households that had experienced poisonings showed no safer patterns of poison storage than did randomly selected households (Baltimore and Meyer, 1969). This study also illustrated that lack of knowledge is not the reason for unsafe behavior and redundant information is unlikely to affect safety.

Warnings on cigarettes and on diet soft drinks containing saccharin: Failure Analysis Associates is currently undertaking research into these areas. In neither case does there appear to have been any detectable effectiveness of the on-product warning. Space does not allow detailed presentation of this material here. The authors intend to make these results available for publication at a future date.

Seatbelt studies: Studies show that many people will not make even the minor effort required to fasten a seat belt to reduce the risk of injury from a motor vehicle accident. Since serious accidents are comparatively infrequent, seatbelt warnings have, in effect, a high "false alarm" rate. Seatbelt campaigns and buzzer/light warning systems have had little effect on seatbelt usage, whereas legislation has lead to higher usage rates. This shows that a moderate threat of a ticket is more motivating than the low probability of serious injury. Research by McCarthy et al. (1984b) shows that an increase in safety-related behavior often does not result in a comparable reduction in injuries. Those at highest risk for accidents may be over represented in the population of non-belt users.

Instructions studies. A laboratory study by Zlotnik (1982) involved warnings at key points in a set of assembly instructions for an electric motor kit. Differences in the formats of the warnings had no significant effect, but for all formats that he tried, he found a reduction in errors and an improvement in assembly times over instructions with no warnings. These results appear to be directly related to circumstances in which the subjects were actively seeking information in an unfamiliar situation, and the use of a warning format increased the saliency of the key steps in the procedures. A somewhat similar study was undertaken by Wogalter, et al. (1985).

Information and warning sign studies. Godfrey et al. (1985) observed reactions of the public to "do not use" signs on a copy machine, public telephone, water fountain, and door. All had substantial effects on behavior except for a small sign not to drink from the fountain because of poisoned water (a larger sign had a greater effect), and a sign saying "Do not use this door" when no alternative was available. This study illustrates several points. First, signs on the copier and phone did not convey safety information, but the signs apparently had credibility, and many people obeyed them. The sign on the door was obeyed when an alternative door was adjacent, but when no convenient alternative was available, many ignored the sign.

Here it is significant that "do not use" signs on office or consumer equipment normally have very low false alarm rates. In this respect they differ very markedly from typical on-product warnings which have high false alarm rates in terms of injuries occurring from product use. Also significant is that, had the fountain actually been poisoned, the warning sign alone would have been woefully inadequate to the task since effectiveness was well below 100 percent; a measurable effect does not necessarily imply a satisfactory safety approach.

Effective Signs in Widespread Use

Stop signs. While relatively few real-world safety information signs have been the subject of formal research, some can be readily observed to have behavioral effects. An example is the stop sign. However, it has no standard danger signal word, no statements of the hazards or consequences, and only the most rudimentary explanation of how to avoid the consequences. The signs are effective because the negative consequences of failing to respond appropriately are universally familiar and highly probable. They include injury, property damage, police citations, and the wrath of other drivers.

Railroad crossing warnings. Many railroad crossings are guarded by warning signs plus flashing lights, bells, and/or barriers. The probability of an accident or police citation if such a warning is ignored is high, consequences are severe, the lights, bells, and barriers are highly salient and they are present when and where relevant. Compliance is obviously high, but it is important to note that it is far from perfect. Leibowitz (1985) reports that approximately 650 people are killed annually at such railroad crossings.

Restroom signs. These signs do not contain any of the four frequently recommended components, but they are very effective. The high probability of social embarrassment is clearly a much stronger motivator than the remote possibility of serious injury.

DISCUSSION

The logic behind the expectation that safety information will be effective seems, at first glance, to be simple and compelling:

o No one wants to be injured.

o If a person knew that a particular behavior could lead to injury, he or she would choose an alternative behavior.

o An appropriately designed warning will provide the person with the required information and lead to the desired, alternative behavior.

The evidence, as we have seen, indicates that this logic is inapplicable to many situations, and reflects the fallacy that people take risks because they lack information. Why do people take risks? Why do we behave in ways that lead to injury? The simple answer is that there is no way to avoid all risk, but it is possible to be more specific and identify motives for accepting risks that, strictly speaking, we could avoid. For example, we take risks to enjoy routine luxuries like electricity, stairs, and cars, to save time, to have a good time, because taking risks is itself exciting, because it takes effort to be careful, and sometimes because we do not know about a hazard. Most accidents are the result of very unlikely events, and we take many low-probability risks even with knowledge of the possible consequences. We would argue that this is rational behavior. A person who tried to follow every conceivable safety guideline might reduce his or her probability of a serious accident on a given day from "infinitesimal" to some fraction of infinitesimal, but the quality of life of such a person would surely be greatly affected, and the general public would see such a person as highly neurotic.

Other common fallacies include:

o Information about potential injury or death (i.e. a "warning") is uniquely effective in affecting behavior.

o Warning signs act as constant reminders to work or behave safety.

o Warnings can't hurt, so when in doubt warn.

Research described above shows that the first two of these points are generally not true. The third point is discussed in more detail below.

Factors Influencing the Effectiveness of Safety Information

For safety information to be effective in changing behavior, it must reach a person who does not already comply. That person must process the information, find that the information is non-redundant, pertinent, and credible, and be motivated to change behavior appropriately.

The behavior of the person who encounters a safety message is controlled by a wealth of other cues from the environment as well as knowledge and habits acquired over a lifetime of learning. The safety message may be a drop in the bucket when compared to the other information available and may have correspondingly little impact on behavior.

The research described above, coupled with experience from risk analyses and accident investigations, has lead us to identify a number of factors that influence the effectiveness of safety information (see Table 1). We expect to refine this list further as additional research

TABLE 1. FACTORS THAT INFLUENCE THE POTENTIAL OF SAFETY INFORMATION FOR CHANGING BEHAVIOR

FACTOR	Conditions Tending to Leave Behavior Unchanged	Conditions Tending to Change Behavior
PRODUCT/SITUATION	Familiar	Unfamiliar
HAZARD/ACCIDENT	Low Probability Usually mild consequences Under control of individual	High Probability Usually severe consequences Not under control of individual
PERSON	Not Seeking Information: - No hazards expected, or - Hazards clearly visible, or - Hazards well known Familiar with product/situation: - Hazard already known, and/or - Previous benign experience Fatigued, Intoxicated Motivated to take risk: - Risk attractive, and/or - Avoidance aversive	Information Seeking: - Hazards suspected, but not observable Unfamiliar with product/situation: - Safety information new, but consistent with experience Alert, Sober Not motivated to take risk: - Risk unattractive, and/or - Avoidance non-aversive
SAFETY INFORMATION	Location: - Not present at hazard, and/or - Present at irrelevant locations Timing: - Not present when relevant, or - Constantly present Presentation/Format: - Difficult to find - Difficult to read - Complex wording Source not credible Context: - Environment saturated with inappropriate, ineffective warnings and instructions	- Present at hazard, and - Not present elsewhere - Present when relevant, and - Not present other times - Salient - Legible - Easy to understand Source highly credible - Environment includes safety information only where essential to the safety of the typical individual

results become available. Presentation/format, which has received much attention, is only one of many factors; based on research discussed above it is often one of limited importance.

As noted in the seatbelt studies, even when the behavior of some persons is changed, there may not be a corresponding drop in injuries, because the persons who change their behavior may not be the ones who would have had accidents.

McCarthy et al. (1982) proposed that warnings should be restricted to higher risk events so that the impact of significant warnings would not be reduced by the diluting effect of numerous less significant messages. As Kantowitz and Sorkin (1983) state:

"From a human factors perspective, excessive warnings are as bad as insufficient warnings. People become accustomed to the warnings and tend to ignore them. Warnings should be reserved for high-probability events. Even then, it is difficult to get people to pay attention to them."

Results of research discussed in this paper imply that a second criterion for the use of warnings should be added. Warnings should also be restricted to those that have a reasonable potential for reducing the frequency of accidents.

SUMMARY AND CONCLUSIONS

Factors considered to influence the potential effectiveness of safety information were discussed in the context of research findings on human information processing and human behavior. Important factors include credibility of the presentation, familiarity and previous experience with the product or activity, the "false alarm" rate, whether the person is seeking information, and the ease or attractiveness of following safety instructions. Attention to the presentation and format of safety messages is not sufficient to change safety-related behavior.

The implications for on-product warnings for consumer products are that they are likely to be ineffective in preventing accidents because most consumer products are reasonably safe and familiar, and because on-product warnings often address hazards that do not manifest themselves during most of the time the product is being used. These characteristics, in themselves, probably undermine the credibility of on-product warnings as a class. Warnings should be used selectively to avoid further undermining their effectiveness.

REFERENCES

ANSI (1972). Specifications for accident prevention signs (ANSI Z35.1). New York, NY: American National Standards Institute

Baltimore, C., and Meyer, R.J. (1969). A study of storage, child behavioral traits, and mother's knowledge of toxicology in 52 poisoned families and 52 comparison families. *Pediatrics*, 44, 816-820.

Dorris, A.L., and Purswell, J.L. (1977). Warnings and human behavior: implications for the design of product warnings. *Journal of Products Liability*, 1, 255-264.

Godfrey, S.S., Rothstein, P.R., and Laughery, K.P. (1985). Warnings: do they make a difference? In R.W. Swezey, et al. (Eds.), *Proceedings of the Human Factors Society 29th Annual Meeting* (pp. 669-673). Santa Monica, California: The Human Factors Society.

Kantowitz, B.H., and Sorkin, R.D. (1983). Human factors: understanding people-system relationships. New York, NY: John Wiley & Sons, Inc.

Kerpelman, L.C. (1978, March). Evaluation of the effectiveness of outdoor power equipment information and education programs (AAI No. 78-27). Cambridge, MA: ABT Associates, Inc.

Leibowitz, H.W. Grade crossing accidents and human factors engineering (1985). *American Scientist*, 73, 558-562.

McCarthy, R.L., Finnegan, J.P. Krumm-Scott, S., and McCarthy, G.E. (1984a). Product information presentation, user behavior, and safety. In M.J. Alluisi, S. de Groot, & E.A. Alluisi (Eds.), *Proceedings of the Human Factors Society 28th Annual Meeting* (pp. 81-85). Santa Monica, CA: The Human Factors Society.

McCarthy, R.L., Robinson, J.N., Finnegan, J.P., and Taylor, R.K. (1982). Warnings on consumer products: objective criteria for their use. In R.E. Edwards and P. Tolin (Eds.), *Proceedings of the Human Factors Society 26th Annual Meeting* (pp. 98-102). Santa Monica, CA: The Human Factors Society.

McCarthy, R.L., Taylor, R.K. Sanford, S.B., and Lange, R.C. (1984b). Seat belts: effectiveness of mandatory use requirements (SAE 840329). Warrendale, PA: Society of Automotive Engineers, Inc. 161-171.

Shinar, D., and Drory, A. (1983). Sign registration in daytime and nighttime driving. *Human Factors*, 25(1), 117-122.

Tokuhata, G., Colflesh, V., Smith, M., Ramaswamy, K., and Digon, E. (1976). Consumer behavior and product injuries. *Journal of Safety Research*, 8(3), 116-125.

Wogalter, M.S., Fontenelle, G.A., and Laughery, K.R. (1985). Behavioral effectiveness of warnings. In R.W. Swezey, et al. (Eds.), *Proceedings of the Human Factors Society 29th Annual Meeting* (pp. 679-683). Santa Monica, CA: The Human Factors Society.

Zlotnik, M.A. (1982). The effects of warning message highlighting on novel assembly task performance. In R.E. Edwards and P. Tolin (Eds.), *Proceedings of the Human Factors Society 26th Annual Meeting* (pp. 93-97). Santa Monica, CA: The Human Factors Society.

THE EFFECT OF SYMBOLS ON WARNING COMPLIANCE

Linda S. Jaynes* and David B. Boles
Psychology Department, Rensselaer Polytechnic Institute
Troy, New York

ABSTRACT

The present study investigated whether different warning designs, specifically those with symbols, affect compliance rates. Five conditions were tested: a verbal warning, a pictographs warning with a circle enclosing each graphic, a pictographs warning with a triangle on its vertex enclosing each graphic, a warning with both words and pictographs (triangular enclosures), and a control (no warning). Participants performed a chemistry laboratory task using a set of instructions that contained one of the five conditions. The warnings instructed them to wear safety goggles, mask and gloves. All four warning conditions had significantly greater compliance than the no-warning condition. The highest rate of compliance occurred with the verbal plus pictographs condition, although it did not differ significantly from the verbal condition. A significant main effect was found for the "presence of pictographs" variable, suggesting that the addition of pictographs to a verbal warning will increase compliance rates. The unexpected finding that the pictographs warning with triangular enclosures had significantly lower compliance means than the verbal warning may be due to the different types of message modes or design criteria used. The enclosure shape made no difference in compliance rates, despite research that indicates that unstable shapes are preferred as warning enclosures. The results suggest the importance of conducting behavioral studies rather than relying on preference data.

INTRODUCTION

The use of symbols as a part of warnings has received little attention despite some literature suggesting that symbols may have a positive influence on warning effectiveness (Laner & Sell, 1960; Wogalter et al., 1987; Otsubo, 1988; Friedmann, 1988). Most of the research on warning symbols has investigated the effects of symbols on users noticing, comprehending, and recalling the warning, as well as users' preferences. Few warning symbol studies have measured whether warnings change behavior or reduce accidents.

Enclosure shape of warnings has not been investigated in a warning compliance study, despite research that the triangle on its vertex is the preferred warning surround (Riley, Cochran & Ballard, 1982). In the present study, the triangular enclosure on its vertex was contrasted with the circular enclosure which, although frequently used as a warning surround, was found by Riley et al. to be one of the least preferred warning shapes.

Another factor that had yet to be tested was whether a good graphic warning could stand alone and be as effective as a verbal warning. Research indicates that people recognize and recall pictures more quickly and accurately than words (Janda & Volk, 1934; Paivio, Rogers & Smythe, 1968; Standing, Conezio & Haber, 1970; and Ells & Dewar, 1979).

More recent research suggests that the optimal warning format in terms of retention and comprehension may be a combination of pictographs and words (Booher, 1975; Schmidt & Kysor, 1987; and Young & Wogalter, 1988). However, previous compliance studies have failed to show that warning symbols added to verbal warnings significantly affect compliance rates (Otsubo, 1988; Friedmann, 1988).

The present chemistry laboratory experiment investigated whether different warning designs, specifically those with symbols, affect compliance rates.

*Presently at Digital Equipment Corporation, 146 Main St. ML011-3/L12, Maynard, MA 01754-2571

METHOD

Subjects

Eighty volunteer students from a
technical institution were recruited from
summer classes or from campus
advertisements, and were paid for their
participation.

Materials

Chemistry equipment, such as a triple
beam balance, Erlenmeyer flasks and
measuring scoops, were used in the task.
Harmless solutions and substances were
disguised to help give the appearance that
subjects were mixing potentially hazardous
chemicals.

Subjects were given a printed set of
instructions for the chemistry task. The
warnings were placed in the middle of an
instruction sheet as this method (Wogalter,
Allison & McKenna, 1989) has worked well in
the past for avoiding ceiling or floor
effects in compliance rates.

The first paragraph of the instructions
told the subjects that they had a limited
amount of time to complete the task and
that the final product would be evaluated
for accuracy. Following the introduction,
one of four warning designs (verbal only,
pictographs with circular enclosures,
pictographs with triangular enclosures, or
verbal plus pictographs with triangular
enclosures) or the control appeared. The
control appeared as blank space on the page
following the first paragraph of
instructions. The verbal warning was:
"WARNING: Wear goggles, mask and gloves
while performing the task to avoid
irritating fumes and possible irritation of
skin." All the pictograph conditions used
the same three images: goggles, mask and
gloves. Figure 1 shows the pictographs with
triangular enclosures. These images were
evaluated for understandability by Collins,
Lerner and Pierman (1982) and they all met
the minimum criterion for ISO
recommendation. Under the warnings, the
chemical mixing instructions appeared
describing how to measure and mix certain
quantities of the substances and solutions.

Figure 1. Pictographs with triangular
enclosures

Procedure

Subjects were tested individually and
each was told that the study was to
investigate the role of human factors in
chemistry. The instructions and materials,
which included the safety gear, were on a
worktable in the lab room.

Compliance with the warning was scored
as a "0", "1", "2" or "3" depending on the
number of pieces of gear put on. Because
these precautionary measures should be
taken prior to mixing the chemicals, the
experiment was stopped after the subject
finished the first step of the chemical
mixing instructions.

A follow-up questionnaire was
administered to each subject immediately
following the task. The questionnaire
asked whether subjects noticed, read and
recalled the warnings.

RESULTS

Within the control group, no one was
observed using any of the protective gear.
Across the warning conditions, the overall
results showed 89% noticed the warning, 64%
correctly recalled all three precautionary
steps to take, yet only 43% put on all
three types of gear. Ninety-seven percent
of the subjects in the two verbal
conditions (verbal only and verbal plus
pictographs) stated that they read the
warning. Table 1 shows the percentages of
subjects who noticed, read, recalled and

Table 1

Percentages of Subjects Who Noticed, Read, Recalled and Complied
with the Warning as a Function of Warning Condition

	Noticed	Read	Recalled	Complied
No Warning	--	--	--	0%
Verbal	100%	100%	69%	63%
Pictographs w/ circ.	81%	--	69%	38%
Pictographs w/ triang.	81%	--	58%	31%
Verbal & pictographs w/ triang.	94%	94%	93%	81%

complied with the warning as a function of the warning condition.

Of those subjects who put equipment on, 10% put on one piece of gear, another 10% put on two of three pieces, and the rest (81%) put on all three pieces of gear. A chi-square analysis found that the number of protective gear put on was significantly different among the four warning designs, chi square $(9, \underline{n}=64)=16.82$, $p<.05$.

A one-way ANOVA was conducted to analyze the effects of the type of warning condition. The dependent variable was the number of pieces of gear put on ranging from 0 to 3. A significant difference was found between the type of warning condition and total gear compliance $(F(4,75)=12.26, p<.001)$. The compliance mean was lowest for the control and highest for the verbal plus pictographs condition.

Comparisons between the pairs of means were conducted using the least significant difference test. All of the warning designs were significantly different from the control condition $(p<.05)$. The pictograph with triangular enclosure had significantly lower compliance than the verbal condition and the verbal plus pictographs condition $(p<.05)$. The pictograph with the circular enclosure had significantly lower compliance than the verbal plus pictographs condition $(p<.05)$.

A two-way ANOVA was also conducted where "presence of pictographs" and "presence of words" were the independent variables. For example, the verbal condition was coded as: words present, pictographs not present. The pictographs with circular enclosure condition was not included in the analysis. The dependent variable was the number of pieces of safety gear put on ranging from 0 to 3. No significant interaction was found between "presence of pictographs" and

"presence of words" $(F(1,63)=.88, n.s)$. A significant main effect of "presence of pictographs" was found $(F(1,63)=14.06, p<.001)$. A significant main effect of "presence of words" was also found $F(1,63)=49.00, p<.001)$.

DISCUSSION

Among the warning designs, the compliance rates varied with the pictograph conditions having the lowest compliance and the verbal plus pictographs condition the highest compliance. Similar to Otsubo's results (1988), the verbal condition did not differ significantly from the verbal plus pictographs condition, though a trend toward greater compliance with the verbal plus pictographs condition existed.

Collapsing the "presence of words" variable, the two-way ANOVA found a significant main effect of the "presence of pictographs" variable. The results suggest that the addition of pictographs to a verbal warning will increase compliance rates. That is, since there was no interaction between the variables, one would expect the two main effects to be additive.

The pictograph warning with triangular enclosures was not as effective as the verbal warning. One explanation for the results is that the verbal condition contained more message modes (Hakiel & Easterby, 1984) or major design criteria (Wogalter et al., 1987) than the pictograph conditions. In the present study, the verbal warning contained both a prescriptive message, "Wear goggles, mask and gloves...", and a descriptive message, "...to avoid irritating fumes and possible irritation of skin." The pictographs condition contained only a prescriptive image; the graphics only instructed what protective gear to wear and did not describe the nature of the hazard. Future compliance studies should compare pictograph and verbal conditions that contain the same message modes or major design criteria.

The enclosure shape made no difference for compliance rates, despite Riley et al.'s study (1982) indicating that unstable shapes were preferred as warning enclosures. Thus the performance data failed to match the previous preference data. The results stress the importance of conducting behavioral studies rather than relying on preference data. However, it may be that Riley et al.'s results cannot be replicated or that shapes in the context of a pictograph may not show preference differences.

REFERENCES

Booher, H.R. (1975). Relative comprehensibility of pictorial information and printed words in proceduralized instructions. Human Factors, 17, 266-277.

Collins, B.L., Lerner, N.D. & Pierman, B.C. (1982). Symbols for industrial safety. (Report No. NBSIR82-2485). Washington, DC: National Institute of Occupational Safety and Health.

Ells, J.G. & Dewar, R.E. (1979). Rapid comprehension of verbal and symbolic traffic sign messages. Human Factors, 21, 161-168.

Friedmann, K. (1988). The effect of adding symbols to written warning labels on user behavior and recall. Human Factors, 30, 507-515.

Hakiel, S.R. & Easterby, R.S. (1984). Issues in the design of safety sign systems. In Easterby, R.S. & Zwaga, H.I. (Eds.), Information design: The design and evaluation of signs and printed materials, (pp. 419-448). Chichester: John Wiley and Sons.

Janda, H.F. & Volk, W.N. (1934). Effectiveness of various highway signs. Highway Research Board Proceedings, National Research Council, 14, 442-447.

Laner, S. & Sell, R.G. (1960). An experiment on the effect of specially designed safety posters. Occupational Psychology, 34, 153-169.

Otsubo, S.M. (1988). A behavioral study of warning labels for consumer products: Perceived danger and use of pictographs. Proceedings of the Human Factors Society, 32, 536-540.

Paivio, A., Rogers, T.B. & Smythe, P.C. (1968). Why are pictures easier to recall than words? Psychonomic Science, 11, 137-138.

Riley, M.W., Cochran, D.J. & Ballard, J.L. (1982). An investigation of preferred shapes for warning labels. Human Factors, 24, 737-742.

Schmidt, J.K. & Kysor, K.P. (1987). Designing airline passenger safety cards. Proceedings of the Human Factors Society, 31, 51-55.

Standing, L., Conezio, J. & Haber, R.N. (1970). Perception and memory for pictures: Single-trial learning of 2500 visual stimuli. Psychonomic Science, 19, 73-74.

Wogalter, M.S., Allison, S.T. & McKenna, N.A. (1989). Effects of cost and social influence on warning compliance. Human Factors, 31, 133-140.

Wogalter, M.S., Godfrey, S.S., Fontenelle, G.A., Desaulniers, D.R., Rothstein, P.R. & Laughery, K.R. (1987). Effectiveness of warnings. Human Factors, 29, 599-612.

Young, S.L. & Wogalter, M.S. (1988). Memory of instruction manual warnings: Effect of pictorial icons and conspicuous print. Proceedings of the Human Factors Society, 32, 905-909.

A WARNING LABEL FOR SCAFFOLD USERS

Daniel Johnson
Daniel Anthony Johnson, Inc.
Olympia, Washington

The purpose of this research project was to develop a warning label which would: a) alert scaffold workers to the potential of danger when working on scaffolds, and b) to increase the likelihood they would seek out and read the safety guidelines supplied with the scaffolds. A warning was developed and tested on 150 potential users. It significantly increased subjects' behavioral intentions to seek safety information before working on a scaffold they had not been on before. This was true for inexperienced and experienced scaffold workers. This effect was not found for scaffolds the subjects supposedly had been on before. Highly experienced workers were less likely to comply with the warning than less experienced workers. It was concluded that the warning would increase the use of safety guidelines by those working on a scaffold that was new to them. But a new warning on a scaffold a worker had already been on would have no effect on the reading of safety guidelines.

INTRODUCTION

Severe injuries and death can occur if workers do not follow safe procedures when erecting and using scaffolds. These procedures are presented in the form of detailed safety guidelines that should be consulted by workers. Scaffolds may be used by both experienced and inexperienced workers, and by those who are working under close supervision or none at all. Since it is often beyond the manufacturer's control that the scaffold be erected and used correctly, manufacturers are concerned that workers learn about and are persuaded to follow the safety guidelines. To achieve this end the research reported here was sponsored by, and done under contract to, The Scaffold Industry Association and The Scaffolding, Shoring & Forming Institute.

All the information needed for working safely on scaffolds is so extensive that it is impractical to present it on the scaffold itself. Instead, it was decided to develop a warning to workers that a danger did exist and to persuade them to review the safety information.

Safety information can be distinguished from warnings. A common definition of "warning" was provided by Dorris and Purswell who state that a warning is a "message intended to reduce the risk of personal or property damage by inducing certain patterns of behavior and discouraging or prohibiting certain other patterns of behavior." (Dorris and Purswell, 1978).

Lehto and Miller (1986) point out that there are various ways of changing these patterns of behavior. Some common approaches are to inform, persuade, instruct, and warn. "These concepts must be disentangled in order to scientifically evaluate warnings"

according to Lehto and Miller, who go on to state their definition of warning as a separate subset of safety instructions: "...(W)arnings are specific stimuli which alert a user to the presence of a hazard, thereby triggering the processing of additional information regarding the nature, probability, and magnitude of the hazard. This additional information may be within the user's memory or may be provided by other sources external to the user. Much of the current controversy regarding warnings is actually related to the need for this additional information" (Lehto and Miller, 1986, p.16).

This approach distinguishes between a warning of a hazard and everything a person must know to understand the consequences of certain actions or inactions associated with that hazard. This point is important when it comes to pieces of equipment, such as a scaffold, where there are many causes of injury or damage as well as many ways to avoid injury or damage.

Lehto and Miller acknowledge that some safety information may be within the user's memory, or located external to the individual. If it is external to the individual, then it follows that the safety information may be either attached to the equipment the user is attempting to use, or may be otherwise accessible to the user (Lehto and Miller, 1986, p.16).

It appeared to be impractical to attach all safety guidelines to each scaffold in a comprehensive, readable, and easily understandable format. The decision was made to produce a warning that would alert the user to the potential of possible injury and to instruct and persuade the user to review the safety guidelines.

METHOD

A prototype warning label was designed (see Figure 1) which incorporated several features: 1) a signal word, 2) a graphic illustration, and 3) instructions informing the reader that serious injury could occur and to review the safety guidelines.

Warning Design

Signal Word. Three signal words commonly used on warnings are Caution, Warning, and Danger. Which one to use depends on the potential risk for serious injury or damage. According to ANSI Z535.4-1991, entitled "Product Safety Signs and Labels", the signal words should be used in the following conditions:

"Danger" indicates an imminently hazardous situation which, if not avoided, will result in death or serious injury. This signal word is to be limited to the most extreme situations.

"Warning" indicates a potentially hazardous situation which, if not avoided, could result in death or serious injury.

"Caution" indicates a potentially hazardous situation which, if not avoided, may result in minor or moderate injury. It may also be used to alert against unsafe practices.

The signal word "Warning" was selected as most appropriate for the scaffold warning label. In addition, a triangle encompassing an exclamation point, was used in accordance with ANSI Z535.4-1991.

Graphic. The graphic depicting a person falling off of a scaffold was intended to gain the readers's attention and convey a message of concern for safety.

Text. The text instructs potential users to check with their boss as to the scaffold's safe use prior to using it since they could be killed or seriously injured. The text also was designed to persuade users with the following sentence: "There are many ways YOU CAN BE hurt or even KILLED using scaffolds." The capitalized words were printed in safety orange, as compared to the other words which were printed in small case and in white against the black background.

Type Size. The type size selected was 11 point; this means a rounded capital letter measures approxi-

mately 0.11 inches (.28 cm) from the top to bottom. ANSI Z535.4-1991 recommends a letter height of 0.09 inches (.23 cm) at a reading distance of 28 inches (71cm) under favorable reading conditions.

Readability. Sentence length and number of syllables per word were selected in such a way that they would be easily readable. A Flesch test for readability (Flesch, 1979) indicated the message should be easily understood by a person with a 6th grade education.

Layout. When the label was attached to the smallest diameter tubing used on scaffolds (outside

Figure 1. *The warning label measured 5.67" (14.4 cm) by 2.58" (6.55 cm). The shaded area, including the capital letters, were printed in orange. This artwork is copyrighted and cannot be used without permission.*

diameter = 1.5 inch (3.81 cm)) the words could be read without moving one's head.

Color. The label was printed in two colors: black and orange. In accordance with ANSI Z535.4-1991 the word "Warning" was printed in black letters on an orange background; the message panel was printed in white letters against a black background except for the capitalized words which were printed in safety orange. The pictorial panel was printed in black against a white background. The border was orange to increase its conspicuity.

Questionnaire Design

The behavioral intentions of the potential scaffold users before and after seeing the warning were measured. The relationship between behavioral intentions and behavior has been established over the past two decades (Ajzen, 1971; Ajzen and Fishbein, 1969, 1970, 1972, 1973; Brislin and Olmstead, 1973; Johnson, 1974). Appropriately designed interviews can elicit verbal responses highly correlated with actual behavior.

Subjects

Altogether, 150 subjects (36 women and 114 men) were tested individually. There were 93 experienced workers (10 women; 83 men) and 26 women and 31 men who had not been on a scaffold before.

The experienced subjects had been on scaffolds an average of 11.2 times. They had worked on scaffolds an average of 4.45 years, with a range of 1 to 28 years: 16 of them had worked on scaffolds for 10 years or more. The age of the experienced subjects ranged from 19 to 81, with an average of 37.8 years. The age of the inexperienced subjects ranged from 18 to 82, with an average of 38.7 years.

PROCEDURE

A trained interviewer went into the community around Olympia, Washington, to administer a questionnaire to individuals she encountered on the street, and in parks and other public places. Questions were first asked as to each subject's experience on scaffolds.

Then the subject was handed an illustration of a worker climbing up the side of a standing scaffold and asked the following question: "Say you were ready to

get on one that was already set up, like the one in the picture. This is the first time up on this scaffold, and you have not read the safety guidelines before. Would you review the safety guidelines with your boss to see if the scaffold was ready and safe to use before climbing up to go to work? Assume a sheet of safety guidelines was available." The subject then answered on a five-point scale, from "Definitely Not Review" to "Definitely Will Review."

The subject was then handed a section of scaffolding pipe 18 inches (45.7 cm) long and 1.5 inch (3.81 cm) in diameter to which the warning (shown in Figure 1) had been attached. The subject was asked: "Let's say you see this label on a scaffold you are about to work on for the first time. For you it is a NEW scaffold. Would you review the safety guidelines with your boss?" Answers were recorded on the same five-point scale.

The subject was then asked: "Let's say you see this label on a FAMILIAR scaffold, one you had been on before. Do you think you would review the safety guidelines with your boss?" The same scale was used.

RESULTS

The warning significantly increased the percent of people who indicated they would review the safety instructions prior to using a NEW scaffold, one they had not been on before. There was a statistically significant shift toward the "Definitely Will Review" end of the scale for both inexperienced as well as experienced subjects (see Figures 2 and 3).

Figures 2 and 3 show that the average response of subjects before the warning was between the "Might or Might Not Review" and the "Probably Will Review." After reading the warning, their average response shifted toward the "Definitely Will Review" anchor point. The differences were statistically significant for both inexperienced subjects (t = 5.015, 1 dF, N=57, p<.0005) and experienced subjects (t = 5.021, 1 dF, N=93, p<.0005).

The differences in absolute scores on the response scales for experienced and inexperienced was analyzed. There were relatively more women in the inexperienced group and this could have affected the difference between inexperienced and the experienced group scores. However, when experience was statistically controlled for, sex of the respondent was not related to warning effectiveness for either a NEW

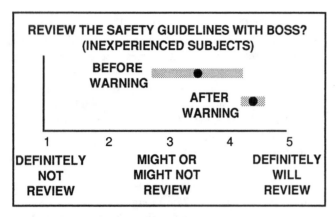

Figure 2. *Response means* ● *and standard deviations* ▓▓▓▓ *before and after seeing the warning for inexperienced subjects. The difference was significant: t = 5.015, 1 dF, N = 57, p <.0005.*

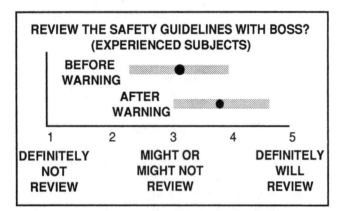

Figure 3. *Response means* ● *and standard deviations* ▓▓▓▓ *before and after seeing the warning for experienced subjects. The difference was significant: t = 5.021, 1 dF, N = 93, p <.0005.*

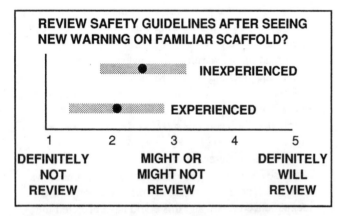

Figure 4. *Response means* ● *and standard deviations* ▓▓▓▓ *for experienced and inexperienced subjects. The difference in responses before seeing the warning and after was not significant for either men (t = .32) or women (t = 1.5, dF = 35, p>.1).*

scaffold (F = .15, dF = 1/147, p = .7) or a FAMILIAR scaffold (F = .35, dF = 1/147, p = .35).

Experience on scaffolds is the major factor associated with whether a person would or would not seek out safety information; the less experienced were more likely to state they would read the safety instructions even before seeing the warning. The number of times a person had been on scaffolds (in general) was negatively correlated with his or her willingness to read the safety instructions before seeing the warning: r = -.18, N = 150, p =.0245. And, if a person had been on a given scaffold he or she would be less likely to heed the warning prior to working on that scaffold compared to a person who had not been on that scaffold.

Furthermore, the more times a subject had been on a scaffold the less likely the warning to read the safety information would be heeded prior to working on a NEW scaffold; r = -25, N = 150, p = .002).

After having worked on a scaffold most people, even those inexperienced with scaffolds, said they would not review the safety guidelines if a new warning were to be placed on the FAMILIAR scaffold. There was virtually no shift toward reviewing the guidelines for men (t = .32) or women (t = 1.5, dF = 35, p>.1) as a result of the warning (see Figure 4).

Placement of Warning

The following guidelines for warning placement were provided to manufacturers and distributors to ensure the warnings could be seen and easily read:

1) For the warning text to be readable by both tall and short individuals the top of the label should be affixed 0 to 12 inches (0 to 30.5 cm) from the top of each vertical frame of the scaffold. (Frames usually stand between 3 and 6.5 feet (91 and 198 cm) high.) On shorter frames the label should be as close to the top as practical. On taller frames the top of the label should be about 8 to 12 inches (20 to 30.5 cm) below the top where practical. The 5 percentile standing male, looking up, would see the top of the text about 8 inches (20.3 cm) above his eye height;

2) The warning should be attached to the scaffold in such a manner that a person could read the entire text without having to move any portion of his body, other than his eyes;

3) The warning should be placed so that it would not be easily abraded during normal handling and storage, thereby becoming illegible; and

4) The warning label(s) should be placed on the scaffold so that a person approaching the scaffold with the intent to work on it would be able to see at least one label before starting to climb the scaffold.

CONCLUSIONS

The warning label caused a significant increase in the stated intentions of subjects to seek out safety information before working on a scaffold they had not been on before. This increase was noted for people who had never been on a scaffold as well as those with experience on scaffolds.

Subjects did not say they would read the safety instructions because they thought that was what the interviewer wanted them to say. When asked the same question about scaffolds they supposedly had worked on they said they would not. The reduced likelihood of reading and complying with warnings on familiar items has been found in other studies. DeJoy (1989) reviewed the literature on warnings and found 7 studies where familiarity decreased the likelihood of noticing, reading, or complying with warnings. Studies where familiarity had no effect were not reported.

Consequently, it is reasonable to expect the warning label will increase the seeking out of safety information by scaffold workers who are to work on a scaffold for the first time. Experienced workers will be less likely to comply with the warning than less experienced workers. A new warning on a scaffold the worker has already been on will have little effect.

An implication of this is that management must encourage workers, especially experienced ones, to read safety guidelines before working on scaffolds. And then, of course, safety guidelines -- to be effective -- must be easy to read and understand. They should be designed with the user's capabilities, limitations and information requirements in mind.

REFERENCES

Ajzen, I. (1971). Attitudinal vs. normative messages: An investigation of the differential effects of persuasive communication in behavior. *Sociometry, 34*, 263-416.

Ajzen, I. and Fishbein, M. (1969). The prediction of behavioral intentions in a choice situation. *Journal of Experimental Social Psychology*, 5, 400-416.

Ajzen, I. and Fishbein, M. (1970). The prediction of behavior from attitudinal and normative variables. *Journal of Experimental Social Psychology, 6,* 466-487.

Ajzen, I. and Fishbein, M. (1972). Attitudes and normative beliefs as factors influencing behavioral intentions. *Journal of Personality and Social Psychology, 21*, 1-9.

Ajzen, I. and Fishbein, M. (1973). Attitudinal and normative variables as predictors of specific behaviors. *Journal of Personality and Social Psychology, 27*, 41-57.

ANSI Z535.4-1991, (1991). *Product safety signs and labels*, published by the National Electrical Manufacturers Association, Washington, D.C., approved by American National Standards Institute.

Brislin, R. W. and Olmstead, K. H. (1973). An examination of two models designed to predict behavior from attitude and other verbal measures. *Proceeding of the 81st Annual Convention of the American Psychology Association*, 259-260.

DeJoy, D. M. (1989). Consumer product warnings: Review and analysis of effectiveness research, *Proceedings of the Human Factors Society 33rd Annual Meeting*, 936-940.

Dorris, A. L. and Purswell, J. L. (1978). Human factors in the design of effective product warnings, *Proceeding of the Human Factors Society, 22nd Annual Meeting*, 343-346.

Flesch, R. (1979). *How to write plain English: A book for lawyers and consumers*. Harper and Row.

Johnson, D. A. (1974). *Attitude-behavior consistency in racial discrimination*. Ph.D. dissertation, Claremont Graduate School, Claremont, CA.

Lehto, M. R. and Miller, J. M. (1986.) *Warnings*. Fuller Technical Publications, Ann Arbor, MI.

Posted Warning Placard: Effects on College Students Knowledge of Alcohol Facts and Hazards

Michael J. Kalsher, Steven W. Clarke, and Michael S. Wogalter

Department of Psychology
Rensselaer Polytechnic Institute
Troy, NY 12180

ABSTRACT

Federal legislation requires a warning label on all alcoholic beverage containers sold in the U.S. However, this method of communicating the hazards of alcohol consumption is lacking because (a) it is not designed to reach the underage population, (b) the warning label is small and contains limited information, and (c) the information is not communicated when alcoholic beverages are not served in their original container (e.g., by the glass). The present study was conducted to determine if a posted placard would effectively convey alcohol-related information to college students. A warning sign containing this information was field-tested in eight fraternities assigned to conditions of a Solomon four-group (pre-post) design. In the warning intervention conditions, signs were posted at various locations in fraternity houses. A questionnaire was distributed that assessed knowledge of five categories of hazards associated with alcohol consumption. Results indicated that, in general, students were knowledgeable about alcohol consumption facts and hazards, but that knowledge of alcohol-related information significantly increased as a result of exposure to the warning.

INTRODUCTION

Alcohol abuse and alcoholism are among the most serious public health problems affecting our nation. The costs associated with the use of alcohol account for nearly 20% of this nation's $427 billion annual health care expenditures (Kinney, 1991). Although the overall consumption of alcohol in the U.S. has decreased during the last decade, national surveys suggest that alcohol consumption among college students has remained constant during the same period. Between 70 and 96% of U.S. college students drink alcohol, and as many as one fourth of them are heavy drinkers (Kivilan, Coppel, Fromme, Williams, & Marlatt, 1989). Moreover, most college students are between the ages of 16 and 24 years which also places them at increased risk with regard to alcohol consumption since driving while intoxicated (DWI) is the leading cause of death for individuals in this age group.

These and other problems of alcohol abuse led to the mandate by Congress for the following alcohol warning label on all beverage alcohol containers sold in the U.S.:

GOVERNMENT WARNING: (1) ACCORDING TO THE SURGEON GENERAL, WOMEN SHOULD NOT DRINK ALCOHOLIC BEVERAGES DURING PREGNANCY BECAUSE OF THE RISK OF BIRTH DEFECTS. (2) CONSUMPTION OF ALCOHOLIC BEVERAGES IMPAIRS YOUR ABILITY TO DRIVE A CAR OR OPERATE MACHINERY, AND MAY CAUSE HEALTH PROBLEMS.

This warning on labels of beverage alcohol containers is not optimal, and may be ineffective for several reasons. First, due to its small size, drinkers of alcohol may be unable to read or even see the warning message, especially as drinkers become increasingly intoxicated. Second, the current alcohol warning message is often indistinguishable from other information (e.g., ingredients) on the label. Third, certain portions of the warning are not specific, and thus, may not convey intended information effectively. For example, the label warning states that alcohol may cause health problems, but it does not specify the type or severity of these problems. Fourth, the warning is only found on beverage alcohol containers, and therefore the message is not always available at the time beverage alcohol is consumed. Thus, if an alcoholic beverage is served outside the original container (e.g., via cup, glass, mug) or served from a keg or other bulk service method, the drinker misses the opportunity to view the warning message. Finally, the warning lacks important information relevant to high risk groups other than pregnant women (e.g., college students), including: (1) the danger of consuming alcohol with other drugs, (2) the potential legal liabilities of drinking and driving, (3) the effects of alcohol on performance, and (4) the effects of alcohol on the body.

A poster (large placard) might be an efficient means for disseminating alcohol-related information to college students because it: (1) is more conspicuous than the current warning labels and is more likely to attract attention, (2) can be constructed to compliment and/or extend the information contained in the current warning label, (3) allows individuals to view the warning message when alcohol is served from kegs or other bulk service method, (4) describes important information too numerous for a beverage alcohol container label, (5) does not require that a person consume alcohol to learn about alcohol hazards, and (6) allows placement at tactical locales that would promote it being read (e.g., bathroom stalls, elevators).

Although the use of posters to convey safety information is not a new concept, there are only a few published demonstrations of their effectiveness (Sell, 1977). Laner and Sell (1960) and Saarela (1989) showed that posters are effective in decreasing unsafe behavior in field settings. In addition, Saarela (1989) showed that a poster campaign increased workers' knowledge of job-related hazards. The present research assessed the effectiveness of a poster to convey information to college students. Specifically, a poster containing alcohol-related information considered relevant for persons in this age-group was constructed and displayed in high-traffic areas of social fraternities.

METHOD

Participants and setting

The participants were 134 undergraduate and graduate students at Rensselaer Polytechnic Institute. Their ages ranged from 18 to 25 years. Fifty were under 21 years of age, the legal drinking age in New York State. The study was conducted at eight campus social fraternities.

Stimulus materials

Warning poster. A 30.5 x 45.7 cm (12 x 18 in) three-color poster containing alcohol-related information considered relevant to college-age students was developed (see Figure 1). The entire poster was covered with plastic lamination to increase its durability. Alcohol-related information was presented in five knowledge categories: (1) death and injury, (2) legal liability and penalties, (3) performance while under the influence of alcohol, (4) physiological effects, and (5) use of a BAC nomogram. The signal word CAUTION and an accompanying triangle/exclamation point icon were placed at the top of the poster.

Development of pictorials. A yellow and black colored pictorial depicting a potential hazard for each category was placed to the left of each heading and accompanying text. The purpose of the pictorials was twofold: (1) to capture the attention of the participants, and (2) to communicate the hazards associated with a particular category quickly. The pictorials that were included on the poster were selected on the basis of a preliminary study in which artists initially drew several possible pictorials for each category. Later, 10 individuals were tested by giving them verbal descriptions of each category and then asking them to choose which among a number of pictorials best represented the category. The pictorials chosen most often were used on the poster.

Verbal content. The verbal content of the poster consisted of less commonly known facts based on information obtained from published research articles, New York State and Federal Government technical reports and manuals, National Safety Council's *Accident Facts* (1989) and a training manual for servers of alcohol (Health Education Foundation, 1985).

Dependent Measures

A 36-item Alcohol Knowledge Survey was developed to assess participants' knowledge of information contained on the warning poster. Twelve fill-in-the-blank items were designed to measure knowledge of current New York State Laws concerning the minimum and maximum penalties for DWAI and DWI. Twenty-three multiple choice items were used to assess knowledge of information presented in the five knowledge categories. Finally, a problem-solving question was included to determine participants' ability to use the BAC nomogram to estimate alcohol-impairment.

Design

The experiment was a Solomon Four-Group Design (Rosenthal & Rosnow, 1984; Solomon, 1949). This design not only enables examination of the effect of intervention, but also (a) possible sensitization to or contamination of the intervention and/or posttest because of exposure to the pretest, and (b) the difference between the pretest and posttest attributable to the time of testing. Each fraternity was randomly assigned to one of the following conditions: (1) pretest, no intervention, posttest (PNP); (2) pretest, intervention, posttest (PIP); (3) intervention, posttest (NIP); or (4) posttest only (NNP). Individual participants were not tracked over time in order to preserve their anonymity. Consequently, between-subjects statistical tests were utilized for all analyses.

Procedure

Participants in the pretest conditions completed the Alcohol Knowledge Survey at their weekly fraternity meeting. Then, four warning posters were placed in each fraternity house assigned to the intervention groups (PIP and NIP). Posters were placed in high traffic areas (e.g., meeting rooms, general bulletin boards, kitchens, and bathrooms). No warning signs were placed in the fraternity houses assigned to the no intervention groups (PNP and NNP). The warning materials remained in place for two weeks and were then removed. One week later, all participants completed the Alcohol Knowledge Survey at their weekly fraternity meeting.

RESULTS

Several analyses are required to describe the results of the Solomon design. The first set of analyses examined posttest differences between groups, and in particular focused on whether the poster intervention increased knowledge of alcohol consumption facts and hazards. The second set of analyses focused on the equivalence of test scores for conditions with or without intervention.

Survey items that were answered correctly received a score of 1, whereas items answered incorrectly received a score of 0. The total for each participant was divided by the total number of items to yield overall knowledge scores (proportion correct). The proportion scores were also computed for each of the five knowledge categories when the overall knowledge analysis was significant. The overall knowledge means are shown in Table 1.

2 X 2 analysis of poster intervention on posttest scores

Overall knowledge. The first analysis examined the *posttest* scores of the four groups. A 2 Poster Intervention (presence vs. absence) X 2 Pretesting (presence vs. absence of a pretest) between-subjects analysis of variance (ANOVA) was performed. Results indicated a main effect of Poster, $F(1, 130) = 16.64$, $p < .0001$. Participants in groups exposed to the poster (PIP and NIP) had significantly higher overall knowledge scores ($M = .70$) than participants in groups not exposed to the poster (PNP and NNP; $M = .60$). There was no significant effect of Pretesting, nor was the interaction significant ($Fs < 1.0$).

Similar 2 X 2 ANOVAs were performed on each of the five knowledge categories. These analyses are described below.

Death and injury. The ANOVA showed a significant main effect of intervention, $F(1, 130) = 8.74$, $p < .01$. Participants in groups exposed to the poster had significantly higher scores on the death and injury items ($M = .48$) than

TABLE 1

Overall Test Proportion Means for Conditions in Solomon Four-Group Design.

Group	Pretest	Intervention	Posttest
PNP	.568	-	.603
PIP	.632	Poster	.681
NIP	-	Poster	.709
NNP	-	-	.590

⚠CAUTION

Death & Injury

- o 14,000 people age 16 to 24 are killed and hundreds of thousands are seriously injured in preventable traffic crashes each year.
- o Drivers 24 and under represent 16% of the driving population, but are involved in over 44% of the alcohol-related traffic crashes.
- o Over 50% of all traffic deaths are caused by alcohol.
- o As many as 90% of all the fatally injured drinking drivers are male.
- o The majority of alcohol-related traffic crashes are caused by individuals who have **not** been identified as problem drinkers.

Liability

In addition to financial law suits brought against you, your parents, your fraternity, and your university, did you know that in New York State:

- o The MINIMUM penalties for 1st offenders convicted of driving while alcohol impaired (DWAI) or driving while intoxicated (DWI) are:
    DWAI (BAC ≥ .05): 90-day suspension of driver's license, 15 days in jail, and $250 fine.
    DWI (BAC ≥ .10): 6-month revocation of driver's license, 1 year in jail, and $350 fine.
- o The MAXIMUM penalties for repeat convictions of these offenses are:
    DWAI: 6-month revocation of driver's license, $1500 fine and 90 days in jail.
    DWI: 1-year revocation of driver's license, $5000 fine and 4 years in prison.
- o Chemical test refusal will result in a 6-month revocation of driver's license and $100 fine.
- o Minors who refuse chemical tests will lose their license for 1 year or until they reach 21 years of age, whichever is the greater penalty.
- o Insurance costs increase dramatically following conviction of DWAI <u>or</u> DWI.

Performance

- o Response time and overconfidence in one's driving performance increases with each additional drink.
- o Drugs and medicines, when combined with alcohol, dramatically affects driving response times and overconfidence.

Alcohol Consumption Facts

- o In general, the major factor determining individual differences in blood alcohol concentration (BAC) is overall body weight.
- o Individuals with a high percentage of body fat will attain a greater BAC than same-weight, low body fat individuals if both drink at a similar rate.
- o Regardless of hot coffee, cold showers, or vigorous activity, **your body processes alcohol at a constant rate of approximately .25 oz. of alcohol per hour.**
- o The following measured amounts of beverage contain approximately **0.5 oz.** of alcohol:
    - 12 oz. can of regular beer (4.2% alcohol)
    - 4 oz. glass of wine (12% alcohol)
    - 1 oz. "shot" of 100 proof spirits (50% alcohol)
    - 1.25 oz. "shot" of 80 proof spirits (40% alcohol)
- o Eating food before and during alcohol consumption slows the rate at which alcohol is absorbed.
- o Carbonated beverage alcohol (beer, champagne) will increase the rate at which alcohol is absorbed.
- o Because every person's metabolism is different,
    Don't Feel Compelled to Keep Up With Anyone Else's Drinking.

Do You Know Where You Stand? Know Your Own Limits

Instructions: Count up all the drinks you've had. Then, subtract 1 drink for every 2 hours that have elapsed since you began drinking. Now, locate your approximate BAC on the chart below. Remember, this is only an estimate and does not take into account other important factors like those mentioned above.

					Number of Drinks							
		DWAI			DWI							
Body Weight	1	2	3	4	5	6	7	8	9	10	11	12
100	.038	.075	.113	.150	.188	.225	.263	.300	.338	.375	.413	.450
120	.031	.063	.094	.125	.156	.188	.219	.250	.281	.313	.344	.375
140	.027	.054	.080	.107	.134	.161	.188	.214	.241	.268	.295	.321
160	.023	.047	.070	.094	.117	.141	.164	.188	.211	.234	.258	.281
180	.021	.042	.063	.083	.104	.125	.146	.167	.188	.208	.229	.250
200	.019	.038	.056	.075	.094	.113	.131	.150	.169	.188	.206	.225
220	.017	.034	.051	.068	.085	.102	.119	.136	.153	.170	.188	.205
240	.016	.031	.047	.063	.078	.094	.109	.125	.141	.156	.172	.188

Figure 1. Alcohol Warning Poster. Actual Dimensions were 30.5 x 45.7 cm (12 x 18 in). The areas around the signal word and pictorials were in bright fluorescent yellow.

participants in groups not exposed to the poster (*M* = .37). There was no significant effect of pretesting (*F* < 1.0), nor was the interaction significant, *F*(1, 130) = 1.05, *p* > .05.

Legal liability and penalties. The ANOVA showed a significant main effect of intervention, *F*(1, 130) = 5.62, *p* < .02. Participants in groups exposed to the poster had significantly higher scores on the legal items of the questionnaire (*M* = .69) than participants in groups not exposed to the poster (*M* = .59). There was no significant effect of pretesting or interaction (*F*s < 1.0).

Performance while under the influence of alcohol. The ANOVA for this knowledge category failed to show any significant effects (*F*s < 1.0).

Physiological effects. The ANOVA showed a significant main effect of intervention, *F*(1, 130) = 8.33, *p* < .01. Participants in groups exposed to the poster had significantly higher scores on the items concerning alcohol's physiological effects (*M* = .83) than participants in groups not exposed to the poster (*M* = .76). The ANOVA also showed a significant main effect of prior testing, *F*(1, 130) = 4.75, *p* < .05. Participants in groups having an earlier pretest scored significantly lower on the posttest (*M* = .77) for items of this category than participants in groups taking only the posttest (*M* = .82). The interaction was not significant (*F* < 1.0).

Use of a BAC nomogram. The ANOVA showed a significant main effect of intervention, *F*(1, 130) = 32.34, *p* < .0001. Participants in groups exposed to the poster had significantly higher scores on items concerning their ability to use a BAC chart correctly to assess personal levels of blood alcohol content (*M* = .54) than participants in groups not exposed to the poster (*M* = .12). There was no significant effect of pretesting (*F* < 1.0), nor was the interaction significant, *F*(1, 130) = 1.57, *p* > .05.

Knowledge of Pretest-Intervention-Posttest group

Analysis examined whether overall performance by the PIP group on the pretest and posttest differed. Because the experimental protocol prevented tracking of particular participants, it was not possible to match scores. The opportunity to pair scores of individual participants would have allowed the use of a more powerful repeated-measures analysis. Instead, a more conservative between-subjects analysis was used. This test showed a marginal, but nonsignificant, increase in overall test scores from the pretest to the posttest, *t* (54) = 1.77, *p* = .08. Similar analyses were performed between the pretest and posttest of the PIP group for each of the five knowledge categories. In all instances the means showed improvement on the posttest compared to the pretest, however, none were significant at the .05 probability level.

Equivalence of conditions

A one-way between-subjects ANOVA was performed using overall test scores for participants in three groups who were not exposed to the poster intervention: (1) the *pretest* of the PNP group, (2) the *pretest* of the PIP group, and (3) the *posttest* of the NNP. The ANOVA showed no significant difference among the means, *F*(2, 92) = 1.28, *p* > .05. An analysis showed no significant difference between the *posttests* of the two no intervention groups (PNP and NNP), *t*(63) = 0.33, *p* > .05. Another analysis showed no

significant difference between the *posttest* scores of the two groups receiving intervention (PIP and NIP), *t*(67) = 1.00, *p* > .05. Finally, an analysis showed no significant difference between the *pretest* and *posttest* scores of the PNP group, *t*(54) = 0.85, *p* > .05.

DISCUSSION

The results of this study show that the warning poster significantly increased participants' knowledge of alcohol-related information. Groups exposed to the warning poster received a mean posttest score of .70, whereas groups not exposed to the poster received a mean posttest score of .60, an increase of 17%. Moreover, comparison of these groups' posttest scores for each of the five knowledge categories revealed that groups exposed to the warning poster had significantly higher posttest scores in all but one category. These findings are consistent with the results of earlier studies showing that posters can be an effective means of conveying safety-related information (Laner & Sell, 1960; Saarela, 1989). Additionally, the use of the Solomon design ruled out any possibility of sensitization or contamination due to the pretest or passage of time.

Although these results are encouraging, several caveats deserve mention. The failure to detect a significant pretest-posttest difference for the PIP group was puzzling. Although the overall and the five individual category means showed improvement, none were significant. There are several possible explanations for the modest increase in knowledge for this group. First, because university policy requires complete anonymity for study participants, especially when issues of alcohol are involved, it was impossible to match participants' pretest and posttest scores. Therefore it was necessary to use a between-subjects design. Had it been possible to match participants' pretest and posttest scores, it is likely that a more powerful within-subjects design would have yielded significant results, given that the obtained difference in overall knowledge for this group was, in fact, marginally significant. Second, although each fraternity was randomly assigned to conditions of the Solomon design, by chance the group scoring highest on the pretest was assigned to the PIP condition. This assignment may have indirectly produced a type of ceiling effect. A third possibility is related to the content of the warning poster. It was presumed that information included on the poster was not common knowledge. However, the results of the pretest (overall and by individual category) suggest that students already knew most of the information prior to implementation of the warning poster. Thus, future efforts in this area should pretest poster content beforehand to ensure that less well known information is presented for a given target audience.

Another aspect of the study that deserves mention is the "passive" nature of the intervention. Specifically, nothing other than the posted warnings was used to disseminate alcohol-related information. However, some "active" communication might have occurred, given that fraternities are social groups in which considerable communication occurs between members. Thus, it is possible that only a few parti-cipants in the intervention groups actually read the poster. These individuals may have then communicated this information to other fraternity members. Future studies should capitalize on this possibility by arranging focus groups or other kinds of interactive sessions to discuss the rationale for providing information through this medium. Such an approach may enhance the effectiveness of alcohol warning posters.

Perhaps the most important contribution of this study is the finding of a cost-effective means for communicating alcohol facts and hazards to specific target audiences. It is noteworthy that the sixteen posters used in this study cost less than $100 to make (excluding the time required to construct them). Further research in this area could extend the present findings by creating warning posters that target other high-risk groups, such as Native Americans or women of child-bearing age. Warning posters designed for particular high-risk target audiences appear to be an efficient means of enhancing knowledge of alcohol facts and hazards in ways the current container label can not.

REFERENCES

Health Education Foundation. (1985). *Trainer manual: Training for intervention procedures by servers of alcohol*. Washington DC: Health Communications, Inc.

Kinney, J. (1991). *Clinical manual of substance abuse*. St. Louis, MO: Mosby-Year Book, Inc.

Kivilan, D. R., Coppel, D. B., Fromme, K., Williams, E., & Marlatt, G. A. (1989). Secondary prevention of alcohol-related problems in young adults at risk. In K.D. Craig & S. M. Weiss (Eds.), *Prevention and early intervention: Biobehavioral perspectives*. New York: Springer.

Laner, S., & Sell, R. G. (1960). An experiment on the effect of specially designed safety posters. *Occupational Psychology, 34*, 153-169.

McGuire, F. L. (1982). Treatment of the drinking driver. *Health Psychology, 1*, 137-152.

National Safety Council. (1989). *Accident Facts*. Chicago: Author.

Rosenthal, R. & Rosnow, R. L. (1984). *Essentials of behavioral research: Methods and data analysis*. New York: McGraw-Hill.

Solomon, R. L. (1949). An extension of control group design. *Psychological Bulletin, 46*, 137-150.

Saarela, K. L. (1989). A poster campaign for improving safety on shipyard scaffolds. *Journal of Safety Research, 20*, 177-185.

EFFECTS OF BENIGN EXPERIENCES ON THE PERCEPTION OF RISK

Edward W. Karnes
Metropolitan State College
Denver, Colorado

S. David Leonard
University of Georgia
Athens, Georgia

Glen Rachwal
Metropolitan State College
Denver, Colorado

ABSTRACT

In accordance with simple reinforcement theory it is assumed that experiences with potentially dangerous events that do not result in harm to an individual will tend to extinguish the individual's perception of the risk associated with those events. The purpose of the experiment described here is to evaluate the extent to which experiences that have not resulted in injury or concern for injury may affect the perception of risk associated with warnings. In line with theory, those persons having had experience with all terrain vehicles (ATVs) showed less perception of risk than those without such experience. Further, the efficacy of warnings against use with passengers varied as a function of prior passenger experience.

INTRODUCTION

The purpose of the experiment described here was to evaluate the extent to which experiences that have not resulted in injury or concern for injury affect the perception of risk associated with warnings. The design of warning signs has several components that concern human factors workers. The basic purpose of warnings is to affect behavior. Dorris and Purswell (1977) listed three criteria for warnings: "1) the warning message must be received; 2) the message must be understood; 3) the individual must act in accordance with the message." (p. 256). This report is concerned with the latter two criteria.

Dorris and Purswell (1977) noted that people often fail to obey warnings. And McCarthy, Finnegan, Krumm-Scott, and McCarthy (1984) concluded that there was no evidence of effectiveness of warning signs. Lerner (1985) has noted the difficulty in making warnings realistic, in that individuals' "benign" experiences may rebut warnings. McCarthy, Robinson, Finnegan, and Taylor (1982) suggested that a plethora of warnings might be counterproductive, because they would compete with one another for attention.

Other investigators have given evidence that warnings may be at least attended to, perhaps as a function of the perceived risk of the situation. Subjective impressions of whether instructions might be read were obtained by Wright, Creighton, and Threlfall (1982), who found that more complex items and items assumed to be dangerous produced greater subjective likelihood that the instructions would be read. Further, Godfrey, Allender, Laughery, and Smith, (1983) suggest that the tendency to look for warning messages on labels of potentially dangerous household products may vary with perceived hazard of the product. It is more difficult to determine experimentally that the warnings have an effect.

Some evidence for the effectiveness of warnings was obtained by Godfrey, Rothstein, and Laughery (1985) in naturalistic settings. They found that compliance with warnings on a copy machine, a telephone, a water fountain, and a door was fairly good, but compliance decreased when the cost was high. This result is in accord with the explanation given by Slovic, Fischoff, and Lichtenstein (1978) who suggested that heeding warnings was controlled by reinforcement experiences. In effect, this view is that failure to be punished for potentially dangerous responses (or lack thereof) extinguishes the inhibition (or actions) associated with the warnings. Thus, the more frequently a response (or no response) is made without either direct or vicarious reinforcement the greater the extinction of that response. The findings of Godfrey, et al. (1985) seem to follow, if strength of response is measured by effort expended.

Data obtained in a previous experiment (Karnes and Leonard, 1986) suggest, in line with theory, that persons having had experience with all terrain vehicles (ATVs) perceive less risk than those without such experience. This experiment was devised to examine the trend associated with amount of riding experience.

The data presented here include unpublished data from the experiment performed by Karnes and Leonard, 1986) which for convenience will be called Experiment 1. Because of the results of this experiment, more complete information was sought.

EXPERIMENT 1

ATVs look like big toys with large balloon tires that suggest great stability and correspondingly safe operation. Unfortunately, not only is the appearance of stability deceiving, but some ATVs have a very long seat that beckons for a passenger. A passenger on such an ATV is at great risk, because there are no handholds or foot restraints. Thus, if the ATV is actually used in rough terrain, there is a high probability of being thrown off. Two adults might not use an ATV in rough terrain, because the extra weight robs it of power, but two early teenagers might readily try such use. This experiment was designed to test the effect of different warnings on the perception of the risk of riding double.

Method

Subjects. College, high school, and junior high students were sampled in the Denver area. Undergraduate psychology classes from a state supported commuter college provided 105 female and 52 male subjects, while 81 female and 67 male subjects were drawn from a middle to upper-middle class suburban high school, and 83 females and 59 males were obtained from a junior high school in the same suburb.

Apparatus and Procedure. Videotapes were made of several scenes showing one or two persons riding a four-wheeled ATV. Nine of these scenes were presented (in the same order) to all subjects. Each scene was followed by 10 s of blank screen to allow time for responses. Three scenes displayed rather hazardous events such as "wheelies," and the other six scenes were devised so that the same set of three different scenes were shown once with a single rider and once with a passenger.

Type of warning was manipulated by showing a close-up view by the videotape of the ATV in one of four states. The control condition displayed the ATV basically as it came from the manufacturer. Although a warning sign is attached to the ATV under the handlebars on the left side, it was so small that it was not legible on the screen. Each of the other close-up shots included a view of a sign 10 x 7 in. (25.40 x 17.78 cm) attached to the left rear fender. The signs' contents determined the experimental conditions. Three levels of warning were given. The simplest sign merely said "Warning, do not carry passengers" (Warning Only condition). A more complex sign included the phrase "Severe injury possible," and showed a pictograph of a driver and passenger with the slash (Warning with Consequences condition). The third experimental condition used the word 'Danger' on the sign as well as indicating that a severe injury could result (Danger condition). A more complete description of the signs is presented in Karnes and Leonard, 1986.

Subjects were run in intact classes with the condition for each class chosen randomly except where groups were run to equalize numbers of subjects in a condition. First, a brief questionnaire was given that included items such as age, sex, and whether they had ridden an ATV as either driver or passenger. They were then instructed to use a risk-of-personal-injury rating scale with one as very low risk and seven as the highest risk and asked to rate three practice items (sky-diving, football, and ping-pong) on the scale. Following the practice ratings, the task of rating the scenes on the videotape was described. Subjects were asked to rate the risk involved in each scene and also to write comments about what was dangerous

in each scene. Because intact classes were used, the sample sizes per condition within age groups varied from 23 to 49, but across all age groups the range per condition was from 107 to 120. Because of the disparity of group sizes all analyses used the unweighted means procedure.

Results and Discussion

In all analyses, age groups and signal conditions were between subjects comparisons and type of ride (single versus double) was a within subjects comparison. General findings as reported by Karnes and Leonard (1986) were no differences among conditions for single-rider ratings, but for double-rider ratings, significance was found. Comparisons among the signal groups for double-riding sequences showed all warning groups significantly higher than the control, and the danger and warning with consequences conditions (which did not differ) were significantly higher than the warning condition. Except for the control group, double ridership was rated as significantly riskier than single. Analyses within the subgroups produced similar results. No significant differences occurred as a function of sex of respondents.

It was noted that some of the results were not as strong in the junior high age group. This group also had the largest proportion of subjects that had experience as a driver or a passenger. Therefore, it seemed worthwhile to examine the effect of ridership on perception of risk more closely. (It should be noted that most subjects who said they had been drivers also indicated they had been passengers, although many who had been passengers had not driven the vehicle. In these analyses both drivers and passengers only were combined.)

Because the proportion of riders varied markedly by age group, a total analysis was first done to equate experience level as proportionately as possible. Data from 176 riders and 260 nonriders were included in the analysis. A two-factor unweighted means ANOVA with prior experience as a between subjects factor and scene type as a within subjects factor was performed on the summed ratings for the single-rider and double-rider scenes. Experienced subjects rated the scenes significantly less risky than nonriders did, and double-rider scenes were rated significantly higher in risk than single-rider scenes. The interaction was not significant.

For both the single- and double-rider scenes, 2 x 2 ANOVAS were conducted with experience versus no experience and control versus the combined experimental groups as the factors. For the single-rider scenes the experience factor was significant with the riders' ratings lower, but there was no effect of signs, and no significant interaction. The double-rider scenes produced significant effects for both experience and the signs with riders and control condition producing lower risk ratings. The interaction was not reliable. The means for the groups are presented in Table 1.

Table 1

Mean Ratings of Risk as a Function of Riding Experience, Scene Type, and Exposure to Warning Signs

| | Single | | Double | |
	Control	Signs	Control	Signs
Riders	3.77 (n=39)	3.58 (n=54)	3.79	4.68
Nonriders	4.03 (n=137)	3.89 (n=206)	4.24	5.05

These results are consonant with the view that experiences of avoiding unfavorable consequences may, indeed, extinguish feelings of fear and risk.

EXPERIMENT 2

The results obtained in Experiment 1 were suggestive of an attenuating effect on the perception of risk of benign experiences. Other interpretations could also be given for the results. In particular, the relationship observed might have been simply a coincidence, and the statistical significance merely followed the observed cases. If there is, indeed, an extinction of the fear that might be associated with a known sort of danger, it would seem reasonable that the greater the number of trials, the greater the amount of extinction. Further, interpretation of the results was dependent on the assumption that the experiences were truly benign. Thus, it was decided to replicate the essential features of Experiment 1 and to evaluate the character of the experiences also.

Method

Subjects. A total of 198 subjects were examined in undergraduate psychology courses. Of these subjects 50 stated they had been both driver and passenger, 26 had been driver only, and 122 indicated they had no experience with ATVs.

Apparatus and procedure. The basic procedure was the same as in Experiment 1. The same videotaped scenes were presented, but to simplify the analysis only the control condition and danger sign condition were presented. The questionnaire that subjects completed was modified slightly to include questions about how frequently they had ridden ATVs, whether they had ever been involved in an accident while using an ATV, and whether they had been injured as the result of an accident using an ATV.

Results and Discussion

Because the numbers of cases in the various groups were not equally distributed, unweighted means analyses were used in all cases.

Analyses of subjects in the control condition and in the danger condition were performed separately, because it was presumed that subjects with no experience would have no a priori reason to consider many of the scenes to be hazardous. A 3x3 ANOVA was performed on the ratings of the control subjects with previous type of participation (driver and passenger, driver only, or no experience) as a between subjects factor and type of scene (hazardous, double rider, or single rider) as a within subjects factor. The main effect of type of scene was significant, $F(4,196) = 16.25$, $p<.01$, but neither the experience effect nor the interaction was significant. The hazardous scenes were rated as significantly risker than either the double-riding or single-riding scenes which were not reliably different. The means for these groups as well as those in the danger condition are displayed in Table 2.

Table 2

Mean Ratings of Risk as a Function of Riding Experience, Scene Type, and Signal Condition

		Scene Type		
	n	Hazardous Acts	Double Rider	Single Rider
Control				
Driver/passenger	28	3.68	3.50	3.70
Driver only	15	3.69	3.33	3.02
No experience	58	3.79	3.21	3.38
Danger				
Driver/passenger	22	3.95	4.03	3.33
Driver only	11	3.85	5.09	3.52
No experience	64	4.48	5.08	3.69

A similar analysis was performed for the data from the danger group. In this analysis the Experience X Scene Type interaction was significant, $F(4,88) = 8.08$, $p<.01$; thus, analyses of experience effects were performed at each level of scene type. Differences among the experience groups were not significant for the hazardous scenes or for the single-riding scenes, but were significant for the double-riding scenes. This might be expected, because the indication of danger was explicitly directed toward riding double. In line with the notion that experience has an effect, in the danger sign condition the group with the experience of being both driver and passenger showed significantly less perception of risk than the other two. Also, the danger sign reliably increased perceptions of risk for riding double among subjects having either no experience

107

or driver only experience. The danger sign did not, however, create a reliably higher perception of ride for those subjects having both driver and passenger experience.

A further indication of the effect of the danger sign may be seen in the comparisons among the scene types at the different levels of experience. For all experience levels, the scenes presenting hazardous activities were rated significantly riskier than the single riding scenes. Further, in the no-experience group and the rider-only group, the double riding scenes were judged significantly riskier than the scenes involving hazards. But in the group with both types of experience, there was no reliable difference between the double-riding scenes and the hazardous scenes. This provides some suggestion that extinction of the feeling of being at risk is related to the amount of experience one has had.

Another test of the effects of amount of experience was provided by correlations of estimated frequency of riding ATVs with overall risk perception for subjects having ATV experience. These correlations included all subjects whatever their type of riding was. The correlation in the control group was $r = -.18$, and the correlation in the danger group was $r = -.14$. Neither correlation was reliable.

Although these correlations do not support the hypothesis of greater effects of greater amounts of benign experience, the relatively small sample sizes and the possibility that learning to ignore riskiness is not linearly related to frequency of riding leaves the question of whether there is a relationship still open.

One of the human factors problems with many safety devices is the failure of people to use them consistently. Clearly, one needs the seat belt securely fastened in one's automobile only when there is an accident. From accident statistics we may infer that many people never have accidents. Although one may presume that accidents with ATVs aren't common there are no reliable data on the frequency of such accidents. Thus, to get an idea of just how benign our subjects' experiences were, we asked them whether or not they had ever had an accident. Of our sample of 76 riders a total of 24 had been involved in an accident and 4 had sustained injuries. Thus, although most of our sample had, indeed, experienced no mishaps on an ATV, the percentage of accidents (32%) is, however, rather high.

Comparison of perception of risk between those who had been in accidents and those who had not been in accidents produced no significant difference. In some ways this might be expected, in that one's feeling of safety might be enhanced by experiencing no problems from having an accident. A rather interesting sidelight to this is seen in the comparison among accident victims who had suffered injury and those who had not. As shown in Table 3, the perceptions of risk are a good bit higher for those who suffered injury. Although the number of cases is too small for these results to be dependable, clearly it is a finding worthy of further investigation.

Table 3

Mean Ratings of Risk as a Function of Accident and Injury Experience, Scene Type and Signal Condition

| | | Scene Type | | |
	n	Hazardous Acts	Double Rider	Single Rider
Control				
Accident only	12	3.97	3.64	3.50
Accident/injury	3	4.78	4.44	4.00
Danger				
Accident only	8	3.67	4.33	3.21
Accident/injury	1	4.67	5.33	3.33

GENERAL DISCUSSION

The data from these experiments support the notion that experience of a benign sort may produce some extinction of the perception of risk, at least, for ATVs. In both experiments the perception of risk in dangerous situations was lower for individuals who had experience with the vehicles. An especially important finding in experiment 2 was that while the danger sign was effective in creating a reliably increased perception of risk of double-riding for subjects who had no previous passenger experience, it was not reliably effective for subjects who had ridden as passengers.

Some failure to support the position occurred in the lack of a significant correlation between stated amount of experience and ratings of risk; however, this might simply be related to nonlinearity of the learning curve to ignore risk. Again, the number of cases is too small for determining the shape of that curve. This is particularly the case in this study, as failure to recall correctly and a certain amount of padding are to be expected in self-reports of this sort. Thus, error variance is greater than in the case where direct observation is made.

Experience with the aversive circumstances may be as important (or more so) in increasing one's perception of risk as the sort of extinction that might come from benign experiences. The data available are too skimpy to judge clearly, but they are suggestive and should be followed up.

Although we would like to think that these data are generalizable to other situations, some cautions are in order. The division of subjects into riders and nonriders is clearly a form of self-selection. It is influenced to some extent by economic factors in that one must either have a certain amount of disposable income or have enough desire for the sort of experience to sacrifice other things for it. In both situations there may be correlated personality factors that could affect one's perception of risk. It should be noted, however, that in the control group there was little difference between riders and nonriders.

One of the ways in which it may be possible to neutralize the potential personality factors is through manipulation of various types of (vicarious) experiences that may give the subjects evidence of the actual dangers. In this way, it might also be possible to produce training procedures that would be more effective in creating safe behavior.

REFERENCES

Dorris, A.L., and Purswell, J.L. (1977) Warnings and human behavior: Implications for the design of product warnings, Journal of Products Liability, 1, 255-263.

Godfrey, S.S., Allender, L., Laughery, K. R., & Smith, V.L. (1983) Warning messages: Will the consumer bother to look. In Proceedings of the 27th Annual Meeting of the Human Factors Society, Human Factors Society, Santa Monica, CA, 950-954.

Godfrey, S.S., Rothstein, P.R., and Laughery, K.R. (1985) Warnings: Do they make a difference? In Proceedings of the 29th Annual Meeting of the Human Factors Society, Human Factors Society, Santa Monica, CA, 669-673.

Karnes, E.W., & Leonard, S.D. (1985)Consumer product warnings: Reception and understanding of warning information by final users. In W. Karwowski (Ed.) Trends in Ergonomics/ Human Factors, III, New York: Elsevier Science Publishing Inc., 995-1003.

Lerner, N.D. (1985). Slope safety warnings for riding type lawn mowers. In Proceedings of the 29th Annual Meeting of the Human Factors Society, Santa Monica, CA: Human Factors Society, 674-678.

Martin, G.L., and Heimstra, N.W. (1973). The perception of hazard in children. Journal of Safety Research. 5, 238-246.

McCarthy, R.L., Roginson, J.N., Finnegan, J.P., and Taylor, R.K. (1982). Warnings on consumer products: Objective criteria for their use. In Proceedings of the 26th Annual Meeting of the Human Factors Society, Santa Monica, CA: Human Factors Society, 98-102.

McCarthy, R. L., Finnegan, J.P., Krumm-Scott, S., and McCarthy, G.E. (1984). Product information presentation, user behavior, and safety. In Proceedings of the 28th Annual Meeting of th Human Factors Society, Santa Monica CA: Human Factors Society, 81-83.

Slovic, P., Fischoff, B., and Lichtenstein, S. (1978). Accident probabilities and seat belt usage: A psychological perspective. Accident Analysis and Prevention, 10, 281-285.

Ursic, M. (1984). The impact of safety warnings on perception and memory. Human Factors, 26(6), 677-682.

Wogalter, M.S., Fontenelle, G.A., and Laughery, K.R. (1985). Behavioral effectiveness of warnings. In Proceedings of the 29th Annual Meeting of the Human Factors Society, Santa Monica, CA: Human Factors Society, 679-683.

Wright, P., Creighton, P., and Threlfall, S.M. (1982). Some factors determining when instructions will be read, Ergonomics, 25, 225-237.

KNOWLEDGE OF WARNING LABELS ON ALCOHOLIC BEVERAGE CONTAINERS

by Lee Kaskutas and Tom Greenfield
Alcohol Research Group
2000 Hearst Avenue
Berkeley, CA 94709-2176

ABSTRACT. Health warning labels are now required on alcohol beverage containers in the United States. This study addresses who has seen these labels and changes in relevant knowledge. Random national samples of adults were interviewed by telephone six months prior to and six months after the enactment in November 1989 of the warning label law (N=2006 and 2000, respectively). Six months after introduction of warning labels, over one fifth of the respondents reported having seen the labels. Greater proportions of key target groups, such as young men at risk for drunk driving and heavy drinkers, reported seeing the warnings. Strength of belief in the truth of included label content increased significantly but very slightly, while for several non-included potential warnings it declined somewhat. The findings suggest that the current warning labels are being noticed by many of those at risk of hazards discussed in the labels. Health information on alternative messages was initially less well known and knowledge levels declined, suggesting these also be considered as suitable warning messages.

INTRODUCTION

After twenty years of debate, warning labels are now required on alcoholic beverage containers. Responding to a perceived need to inform the American public of health hazards that may result from the consumption or abuse of alcohol beverages, Congress envisioned the warning labels as providing a "clear, nonconfusing reminder of such hazards" (Public Law 100-690, 1988). Yet controversy surrounding this seemingly innocuous policy has continued (Engs, 1989), fueled by concerns, including those expressed by alcohol industry representatives, that warning labels are not an effective medium for conveying the complexities of alcohol health hazards; that the American public is already aware of such hazards as those proposed for the warning label messages; that the labels may not be implemented in a manner that maximizes their effectiveness; and that increases in knowledge may not necessarily bring about desired changes in alcohol-related attitudes and behavior (U.S. Department of Treasury, 1980; Richardson, 1987; Committee on Commerce, Science, and Transportation, 1988; Jacobs, 1989).

The question of effectiveness of a policy intervention such as this is complex. Viewed simply as a reminder, or as an instrumental step towards the long range public health goals, the warning label law may be considered effective simply if people are found to have noticed the labels' presence on beverage containers. A more rigorous vision of efficacy would require a significant increase in knowledge of the health hazards stressed in the warning labels attributable to noticing them. Even more stringent interpretations would argue that attendant changes in attitudes and behavior regarding alcohol use and misuse also must be evidenced (after controlling for confounding influences) if success is to be claimed. Using data collected six months before and six months after the advent of the warning labels (from the first two of a three-wave National Alcohol Warning Label Survey), this paper addresses the question of the current label's initial effectiveness as a reminder of alcohol-related hazards. It considers also the potential of alternative warning messages that might be used in the future to inform the American drinking public of several less well-known hazards.

Conclusions regarding the efficacy of the warning labels must be tempered by careful consideration of the confounders that are present during the period of study, making it problematic to attribute changes that may be found in knowledge to the warning labels per se. Confounders include a secular decrease in alcohol consumption levels (Williams, 1991), a drift towards conservatism in public attitudes about the role of alcohol in American society (Hilton and Kaskutas, forthcoming), public service messages on network television about the hazards of drunk driving (Rothenberg, 1988), the presence of other warnings at points of outlet, and a purported surge in health awareness and concern among Americans during this period (Crawford, 1980; *Prevention* Magazine, 1988).

The current warning label, which was required on all alcohol beverage containers manufactured, imported, or bottled for sale or distribution in the United States after November 1989, reads as follows:

GOVERNMENT WARNING: (1) ACCORDING TO THE SURGEON GENERAL, WOMEN SHOULD NOT DRINK ALCOHOLIC BEVERAGES DURING PREGNANCY BECAUSE OF THE RISK OF BIRTH DEFECTS. (2) CONSUMPTION OF ALCOHOLIC BEVERAGES IMPAIRS YOUR ABILITY TO DRIVE A CAR OR OPERATE MACHINERY, AND MAY CAUSE HEALTH PROBLEMS.

The four hazards included in the warning label were culled from an initially proposed series of nine which in addition covered the danger of mixing alcohol with other drugs, the fact that alcohol is a drug and may be addictive, and the alcohol-related risks of developing hypertension, liver disease, and cancer (Committee on Commerce, Science, and Transportation, 1988). Two of the warnings included may be considered partially targeted at specific groups--women of childbearing age (Committee on Commerce, Science, and Transportation, 1988) and young men who are at elevated risk for drunk driving (Buchanan and Lev, 1989), while the other seven are applicable to the general population of drinkers (although heavier drinkers might arguably be targeted for the three alcohol-related health problems).

SAMPLE AND METHODOLOGY

This paper reports on the first and second in a series of three annual waves of telephone interview data collection designed to assess the effects of alcoholic beverage warning labels in the general U.S. population. The initial pre-intervention survey focused on respondents' knowledge, attitudes, and behavior regarding alcohol and alcohol-related problems, and on prevention measures. The first of two planned post-intervention data collection efforts was undertaken during the summer of 1990, six months after the enactment of the warning label law, to assess short-term changes in relevant knowledge, attitudes and behavior. A second post-intervention wave will be repeated in the summer of 1991, to investigate changes that may be attributable to the warning label law after 18 months.

Data were collected in June and July 1989 from a nationwide telephone survey of 2,006 adults. A second, similar telephone survey of 2,000 adults was conducted during June, July and early August 1990. The fieldwork for this project was done by Survey Design and Analysis, Inc. of Ann Arbor, Michigan. Details of the data collection procedure not given in these brief paragraphs can be found in the technical reports for the project (Survey Design and Analysis, 1989 and 1990; see also Hilton and Kaskutas, forthcoming).

Random digit dialing (RDD) techniques were employed to sample adult respondents in the 48 contiguous states. Adults aged 18 and older were eligible for interview, with respondents chosen randomly within households by the most-recent-birthday technique. Calculated over a base of all eligible respondents, the response rate in 1989 was 65%, and in 1990 was 64% (Survey Design and Analysis, 1989 and 1990). These rates are comparable to recent experience with such surveys (Frey, 1989).

To achieve population-based results, the data were statistically weighted, adjusting independently for (1) number of eligible adults per contacted household and (2) number of distinct telephone numbers within households, and then for (3) age and sex combinations. Percentages and statistical analyses reported here are based on the weighted data, while the N's reported are unweighted.

We believe the design effects for this study to be modest. Loss in precision due to our samping design arises primarily from the unequal probabilities of selection caused by more than one telephone number and/or more than one adult in a household. We estimate an increase in sample variance of approximately 23% each year due to unequal telephone numbers, unequal numbers of adults in a household (Technical Reports, 1989 and 1990), and weighting, resulting in a design effect of 1.23 for each year. For the purpose of calculating confidence limits, the effective sample size at each time is approximately 1,626 for 1989, and 1,621 for 1990.

Measures

Amount of drinking was assessed using what has been described as a "graduated frequencies" approach (Hilton, 1989). Respondents were asked, during the last 12 months, how often they drank twelve or more drinks per day, eight to eleven drinks, five to seven drinks, three or four drinks, and one or two drinks. To create a Volume measure, the reported frequencies were then multiplied by category midpoints and summed across the question set to arrive at an estimate of the number of self-reported drinks consumed per month. For tabular display of results distinguishing responses of heavy drinkers and abstainers compared to others, a second, categorical measure of alcohol consumption pattern was derived. We define "heavy drinkers" as those who reported drinking five or more drinks at least once a week, "other drinkers" as all other drinkers (within the past year), and "abstainers" as those who had not consumed in the prior 12 month period.

The questionnaire asked respondents whether they saw the warning labels ("Now, thinking about the last 12 months, have you seen any warning labels on bottles or cans of beer, wine, or liquor?"), continuing with a series of eight questions about what the warning labels said ("Did the warning labels say anything about ...?") In this manner, respondents at each time were asked about three of the four actual warning label messages (birth defects, drunk driving, and operating machinery) and five additional ones not included on the warning labels (cancer, drinking when taking other drugs, arthritis (added as an unobtrusive validity check on acquiescence), sulfites, and addiction to alcohol). Given that noticing the label was self-reported, as a validity check on true noticing we operationally defined a "true noticing" indicator as follows: respondents are considered to have "probably" seen a warning label on an alcohol beverage container if they (1) reported seeing it, (2) affirmed that the label included one of the three assessed messages actually on the label, and (3) responded correctly to one other question in the series (by accurately recalling whether a message is or is not on the label). Respondents not meeting this criterion are classified either as having seen only the sulfite labels on wine bottles, or as "probably" not having seen any labels at all. Below (see Results, "Seeing Warning Labels") we contrast the rate of self-report for having seen the warning labels with the results including application of the "true noticing" variable developed to increase validity. In principle, any change found in the aggregate level of noticing labels as measured before and after the law took effect could be corrected by subtracting the pre-law noticing level (i.e., the false positive rate). This approach has been used in other warning label studies which have reported false positive rates ranging from 9% (Mayer, Smith and Scammon, 1991) to 23% (Mazis, Morris, and Swasy, 1990). The approach taken here--of establishing an individual-case-level criterion, based on some correct recall of content--was preferred for the subgroups and associational analyses. But it should be noted that each approach "purifies" results to a similar degree.

In addition to questions about messages on the warning labels, the questionnaire contained questions related to respondents' knowledge of nine alcohol-related health hazards. The hazards discussed in this series of questions include the four messages on the current labels and five additional risks not currently incorporated on the warning label on alcohol beverage containers. Answer categories were offered which allowed respondents to indicate the degree of certainty of their knowledge (definitely true, probably true, probably false, definitely false). For ease of reporting and statistical comparisons of knowledge "certainties", the false answer categories were collapsed into one category, since the cell sizes in the two false categories tended to be small.

RESULTS

Seeing Warning Labels

Overall, over a quarter of the respondents (27%) responded affirmatively to having seen warning labels on alcohol beverage containers in the 12 months prior to the June 1990 survey, with more men reporting that they had seen them than women (31% versus 23%). When subjected to the validity criterion (based on an accurate recollection of some of the label's contents---see

Measures), fewer respondents were judged to actually have seen the label on a beverage container (21%), again with more men than women likely to have seen the labels (25% versus 18%). The difference in noticing between the men and the women was significant for both variables (p<.01). The six percent difference between reported seeing and "true seeing" is approximately equivalent to the percentage of "false positives" in 1989 who reported seeing the labels (8%) in June, 1989 prior to their adoption. So the validity criterion appears to have been "set" at approximately the correct level of severity. Hereafter we shall only use the "true seeing" measure when refering to respondents having seen the labels.

In 1990, when assessed across age categories, having seen the label decreased with age. About a third of the younger respondents aged 18 to 29 saw the labels; 28% of those aged 30 to 39, 17% of those aged 40-59, and only 7% of the respondents 60 years of age and older, had seen the labels. The differences across age categories were substantive and highly significant (Chi-square=94.7, p<.00001).

The strongest difference found with regard to personal characteristics was across drinker categories. Thirty-nine percent of the heavy drinkers, compared to 23% of the other drinkers, saw the labels in 1990; curiously, a notable portion of abstainers (8%) also saw the warning label on alcohol beverage containers. The differences in the percentages of respondents in the drinking categories that had seen the labels on alcohol beverage containers were statistically highly significant (Chi-square=112.8, p<.00001).

Among those targeted by the warning label messages, young male drivers (deemed at risk for drunk driving) were among the more frequent respondents to have seen the warning label on alcohol beverage containers: over a third (36%) of the male respondents ages 18-29 were judged as having seen the warning label on a beverage container, compared to 20% for all others (Chi-square=22.2, p<.00001). This is not surprising, since young males tended to be heavy drinkers and thus would have been frequently exposed to the labels; however, we found that a large portion of the other drinkers in this group also had seen the warning labels. Among the young males in our sample, forty percent were heavy drinkers and over 40% were "other" drinkers; nearly half (46%) of the heavy drinkers and over a third (35%) of the "other" drinkers saw the warning labels on alcohol beverage containers (Chi-square=9.7, p<.01).

Over one fourth (27%) of the women of childbearing age also saw the warning labels compared to 11% for all others (Chi-square=33.5, p<.00001), with the heavy drinkers in this group, again, the most likely to have seen the labels (almost 40%) as compared to the "other" drinkers (28%) (Chi-square=17.3, p<.0001).

Only 18% of the black and hispanic respondents saw the warning labels, but among the heavy drinkers in this group, one third (33%) saw the labels (Chi-square=13.7, p<.001).

Knowledge

We did not find a significant statistical association between respondents' having probably seen the warning label and their knowledge of the health hazards. However, in the sample the knowledge levels were lower in 1989 (six months before the labels appeared on alcohol beverage containers) than in 1990 (six months after they appeared) for all of the four health messages on the labels (Table 1); the implied increases were modest (1%-2%) yet two were statistically significant (p<.05) and two almost so (p<.07).

Note that initial knowledge levels in 1989 were already very high for the four messages included on the labels, with over 95% responding that each of the four statements of hazards were "probably true" or "definitely true". In 1990, this figure attained nearly 97%, and for two of the messages (drinking and driving, and drinking during pregnancy) the respondents' belief in the hazards also appeared to have strengthened (i.e., more responded "definitely true"). Thus, in 1990 as compared to 1989, fewer respondents did not believe the statements about hazards which appear on the warning labels, and more respondents were definite in their beliefs that drinking and driving, and drinking during pregnancy, are hazards.

This pattern did not hold for the other two warning label messages, where among those believing the warning, there was a trend (not statistically significant) towards a lessening in the strength of respondents' belief that drinking may cause health problems and that drinking impairs one's ability to operate machinery.

A very different picture emerged for the five specific health hazards not included on the alcohol warning label. On the average, the initial knowledge levels in 1989 were not as high for these hazards when compared to the four chosen for inclusion on the warning label. Further, the overall knowledge of not-included hazards declined in 1990, with more respondents not believing the statements and fewer respondents indicating "definitely true". The most striking example is for the health statement that "Drinking alcohol can increase the risk of developing cancer", with nearly a 5% increase in the "false" attribution from 1989 to 1990 (from 25.3% to 30.0%, p=.005). For all five statements of hazards not included on the warning label, we found consistent reductions in the strength of belief, and for all but two (the statements about liver disease and about alcohol in combination with drugs) respondents also became more likely to disbelieve the statements.

We examined changes in knowledge for respondents with different consumption patterns. Fewer abstainers in 1990 than 1989 disbelieved the statement "Drinking alcoholic beverages may cause health problems" (p=.02). No statistically significant changes in knowledge were found among the heaviest drinker group. Among the "other" drinkers, knowledge levels declined in 1990 for one of the risks included on the warning labels (impairment to operate machinery; p=.02) and three alcohol-related risks not included on the warning labels: blood pressure (p=.003), liver disease and cancer (p=.02). There was a lessening in the strength of belief in these risks among the "other" drinkers, and the proportion who did not believe the statements about the alcohol-related risks of high blood pressure and cancer increased slightly in 1991 (3% and 4%, respectively).

Table 1
Changes in Knowledge
1989 vs. 1990

Percentage of Respondents
Answering:

	Definitely or Probably False	Probably True	Definitely True	X^2	P
Information Currently on Labels					
Drinking impairs driving				6.26	.04
1989	2.5	8.8	88.6		
1990	1.4	9.6	89.0		
Pregnant women should not drink				6.05	.05
1989	2.6	10.7	86.7		
1990	1.5	11.5	87.1		
Drinking may cause health problems				5.51	.06
1989	4.4	26.6	69.0		
1990	3.1	28.9	68.0		
Drinking impairs ability to operate machinery				5.40	.07
1989	1.2	8.6	90.1		
1990	.8	10.7	88.5		
Alternative Messages for Warning Labels					
Drinking increases risk of cancer				10.79	.01
1989	25.3	55.0	19.7		
1990	30.0	53.6	16.4		
Drinking increases risk of high blood pressure				11.11	.01
1989	5.6	46.6	47.9		
1990	7.2	50.6	42.2		
Drinking increases risk of liver disease				6.01	.05
1989	1.3	18.6	80.1		
1990	1.1	22.0	76.8		
Alcohol plus drugs is hazardous				3.97	.14
1989	1.1	10.1	88.7		
1990	.7	11.8	87.5		
Alcohol may be addictive				2.38	.30
1989	3.0	14.8	82.2		
1990	3.1	16.7	80.1		

DISCUSSION

It would not have been surprising to find that the warning labels had not been noticed during the brief, 6-month, experience with warning labels: the labels are often relatively inconspicuous and their print tiny, and drinkers have no reason to pay much mind to the writing on the containers (beyond perhaps noticing the brand and price). Yet we find that 21% of the respondents probably <u>have</u> seen the labels and remembered at least some of the message content. While there is surely some confounding from other health warnings on restaurant signs, posters, and television, these preliminary data nonetheless indicate that the labels on beverage containers are being noticed, read, and recalled by some consumers.

Among those specifically targeted by the health messages, results are more impressive: the labels have "probably" been seen by 39% of the heavy drinkers, 39% of the women of childbearing age who are heavy drinkers, 46% of the young men who are most at risk for drunk driving, and a third of the black and hispanic heavy drinkers. That they are seen so much more often by the heavy drinkers lends some validity to our measure of noticing the labels, since more alcohol beverage containers presumably pass through the hands of the heavy drinkers and before their eyes. This is an important finding because the health messages are especially salient to these groups, precisely because they do drink more, on the average, than other groups, are being intensely targeted by alcohol producers, and are at risk for specific hazards covered.

In terms of overall knowledge of the health hazards associated with alcohol consumption, the messages chosen for inclusion do not represent areas where consumer knowledge is low. Thus it is not surprising that only a slight trend toward improvement in knowledge was found for the messages on the current warning labels. However, the declines in knowledge levels for the hazards **not** included on the labels (such as the increased risk of cancer, high blood pressure, and liver disease) were unexpected. While trends found from these preliminary data are certainly not conclusive and must await confirmation from the third survey in June 1991, they may indicate that consumers are thinking as though "if a message is not on the warning label, it must not be a hazard." Should this finding be substantiated, it would serve as a strong argument in favor of a system of rotating health messages on alcohol beverage containers. Another interpretation, unverified but consistent with the results, is that there is a general slippage in health knowledge related to alcohol (as indicated by the 5% decline in knowledge of non-included hazards such as the risk of cancer), partially offset by knowledge of the included warnings among those exposed to the labels.

A possible policy implication of our preliminary findings relates to the charter of the warning labels as a vehicle to inform and remind the public of the health hazards associated with the consumption of alcohol. In light of the relatively low levels of knowledge for those health hazards not included on the warning labels (when compared to those that were chosen for inclusion on the labels), a warning label policy that would increase consumer knowledge of health hazards might experience greater success if the less widely known dangers associated with alcohol consumption were instead selected. It is certainly plausible (and consistent with these early findings) that rotating messages so as to keep them "fresh", while increasing exposure to lesser known facts, would be a useful strategy. It is one our data indicates should be tested.

ACKNOWLEDGMENTS

This research was supported by a National Institute on Alcohol Abuse and Alcoholism Grant (AA08557-01) to the Alcohol Research Group, Institute of Epidemiology and Behavioral Medicine, Medical Research Institute of San Francisco.

REFERENCES

Buchanan, D.R. and Lev, J. Beer and Fast Cars: How brewers target blue-collar youth through motor sports sponsorships. Washington, D.C.: AAA Foundation for Traffic Safety. 1989.

Committee on Commerce, Science, and Transportation. U.S. Senate, 100th Congress, 2nd session. Alcohol Warning Labels Hearing before the Subcommittee on the Consumer...to Require a Health Warning Label on All Alcoholic Beverage Containers. Washington, D.C.: U.S. Government Printing Office. August 10, 1988.

Crawford, R. "Healthism and the Medicalization of Everyday Life." International Journal of Health Services, 1980, 10 (3), 365-388.

Engs, R.C. "Do Warning Labels on Alcoholic Beverages Deter Alcohol Abuse?" Journal of School Health, 1989, 59 (3), 116-118.

Frey, J.H. Survey Research By Telephone. Newbury Park, CA: Sage Publications, Inc. 1989.

Hilton, M. and Kaskutas, L. "Public Support for Warning Labels on Alcoholic Beverage Containers." British Journal of Addictions. (forthcoming).

Jacobs, M.C. "The Alcohol Beverage Labeling Act of 1988: A Critical Analysis." Syracuse Law Review, 1989, 40, 1223-1254.

Mayer, R.N., Smith, K.R., and Scammon, D.L. "Evaluating the Impact of Alcohol Warning Labels". Advances in Consumer Research, 1991, 18.

Mazis, M.B., Morris, L.A., and Swasy, J.L. "An Evaluation of the Alcohol Warning Labels: Initial Survey Results." Journal of Public Policy and Marketing, 1990, 10 (1), in press.

Prevention Magazine. The Prevention Index. A Report Card on the Nation's Health. Emmaus, PA: Rodale Press. 1988.

Public Law no. 100-690, 100th Congress, 2nd session. "Alcoholic Beverage Labeling Act of 1988." November 18, 1988.

Richardson, P., et al. Review of the Research Literature on the Effects of Health Warning Labels: A Report to the United States Congress. Silver Springs, MD: Macro Systems, Inc. 1987.

Rothenberg, R. "TV Industry to Fight Against Drinking and Driving." New York Times, August 31, 1988, C1.

Survey Design and Analysis, Inc. Alcohol Warning Label Study: Technical Report. Ann Arbor, MI: Survey Design and Analysis, Inc. 1989.

Survey Design and Analysis, Inc. Alcohol Warning Label Study: Technical Report. Ann Arbor, MI: Survey Design and Analysis, Inc. 1990.

U.S. Department of the Treasury and U.S. Department of Health and Human Services. Report to the President and the Congress on Health Hazards Associated with Alcohol and Methods to Inform the General Public of these Hazards. Washington, D.C.: U.S. Government Printing Office. November 1980.

Williams, G.D., et al., Apparent Per Capita Alcohol Consumption: National, State and Regional Trends: 1977-1988: Surveillance Report #16. Washington, D.C.: Alcohol Epidemiologic Data System. February 1991.

FUZZY SETS: AN APPLICATION TO WARNINGS AND INSTRUCTIONS

John C. Kreifeldt, Ph.D.
Kodali V. N. Rao, M.S.
Department of Engineering Design
Tufts University
Medford, MA 02155

ABSTRACT

Instructions and Warnings while often requiring the reader to make fairly precise sensory judgements or physical actions, yet convey these requests in the qualitative terms of common discourse, such as the phrase "fairly precise" in this sentence, or the instruction "press firmly". The consequences of "not following instructions" can range from less than satisfactory product performance (e.g., "poor shine") to broken equipment or even serious personal injury. The writer of instructions and warnings must know (1) how such qualitative or "fuzzy" terms will be quantitatively translated into action and (2) how to design terms (e.g. "press firmly but not hard") to produce the desired user action. This paper describes initial work undertaken to apply fuzzy set theory to these problems and comparison of empirical definitions of a membership function.

INTRODUCTION

Consider the following instructions adapted from an actual product.

"Press the knob down (firmly) with your fingers. It should move down (about) an inch. ...The unit must be replaced if you can (easily) push the knob down more than one inch."

The words "firmly", "about", "easily", are called fuzzy linguistic variables after Zadeh[1]. One problem for writers of instructions/warnings is to communicate to the reader via simple words with the intention of producing physical or sensory actions and/or judgements usually having definite desired limits or values. In effect, the writer must treat the reader as an instrument or controller which can be made to respond quantitatively to "fuzzy terms."

The instruction/warnings writer must know: (1) how fuzzy terms will be quantitatively translated into action, and (2) how to design phrases (e.g. "press firmly but not hard") in order to produce the desired quantitative user action. Although there is a large literature addressed to writing warnings and instructions, such as books,[2] guidelines,[3] and general research,[4,5]. There is apparently very little[6,7] addressed to the two critical problem areas just addressed.

Fuzzy set theory[8] would seem to offer a methodological framework and approach to these problems not just for the "tech writer" but also for the product designer. Maiers & Sherif[9] (1985) for example offers a bibliography of other applications of fuzzy set theory to human factors issues as well as a brief description of it. A more extensive description can be found in ref. 8.

A membership function is a basic construction of fuzzy set theory. For example, every value of a lifted weight can be considered to be "HEAVY" but some more so than others. That

is, every weight "w" has some value [0,1] of membership (e.g. 0.4) in the fuzzy set "HEAVY" and has (usually) other values of membership in the fuzzy sets "LIGHT", "MEDIUM", etc. Mathematically, the fuzzy set "HEAVY" is defined as

$$0 \leq \mu(w) \leq 1$$

w is any value of weight.

One of the characteristics distinguishing fuzzy set theory from probability theory is that the same value (w) can belong to an arbitrary number of membership functions and its membership values in each need not sum to any particular value.

The calculus of fuzzy sets permits certain operations such as "dilation" and "intensification" on fuzzy sets which modify their shapes in predictable ways. For example, if it can be imagined that just the membership functions "LIGHT" and "HEAVY" have been determined over all values of weight, then, e.g. the membership function "VERY LIGHT", is theoretically derivable from the primitive function "LIGHT".

A very basic and practical problem, however, is the determination of a membership function. That is, how exactly should values [0,1] be assigned to every weight spanned by the descriptor "HEAVY"?

Accordingly our research has two objectives:

(1) explore various empirical derivations of a membership function
(2) begin the determination of membership functions for common fuzzy terms

PROBLEM STATEMENT

As preparation for our study, we reviewed instructions/warnings for numerous products and found the following list of fuzzy words and phrases as shown in Figure 1.

AWAY	HOT	REDUCE
ADEQUATE	HIGH	REPEATEDLY
AS LITTLE AS	HEAVY	RIGOROUSLY
ABOUT	HARD	
		SMALL
BLURRED	LONG	SUFFICIENT
	LIGHT(LY)	SHORT
CAREFULLY	LESS	STEADY
CONFINED	LOOSE(LY)	SPARINGLY
	LITTLE	STRONG
DARK	LARGE	SOFT
DRY		SMOOTHLY
	NECESSARY	SLIGHTLY
EVEN(LY)	NEAR	SLOWLY
EXCESSIVE		SEVERAL
FIRM(LY)	OUT OF	
FREE(LY)	OCCASIONALLY	TIGHTLY
FREQUENT(LY)		THOROUGHLY
FULLY	PROLONGED	
FLAT	PLENTY	UNIFORMLY
	PERIODICALLY	VIROROUSLY
GENTLE(LY)		
	QUIET(LY)	WELL
	QUICK(LY)	WARM

Figure 1 Fuzzy Words Commonly Found In
Product Instructions For Use.

In order to focus our research, we imagined
an instruction writer who must complete the
instructions for a simplified version of a
product as shown in Figure 2.

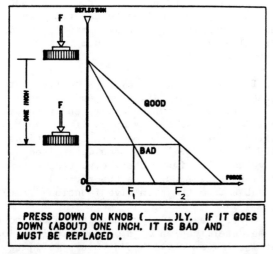

PRESS DOWN ON KNOB (_____)LY. IF IT GOES
DOWN (ABOUT) ONE INCH. IT IS BAD AND
MUST BE REPLACED .

Figure 2   A Prototypical Problem For Writing
Instructions

For present purposes, it can be imagined
that the product regulates the flow of gas to
a home waterheater and that the unit has a
knob which can be pushed down as part of its
operation. Because of certain design/manufact-
uring/quality control problems, some of the
several million units in homes are BAD while
others are GOOD. The BAD type has a spring
characteristic such that it can be pushed all
the way down by hand "too easily" thus
defeating an internal safety mechanism. The
GOOD type poses no safety problem if the

knob is pressed down with "normal" forces.
Written materials will be sent to the several
millions of homes asking the occupants to
check their own units to see if they are GOOD
or BAD.

The design engineers know the specific
forces and quantitative tests required to
distinguish GOOD from BAD valves and must
communicate this information qualitatively to
the instruction reader who will perform the
tests without benefit of instrumentation. The
instruction writer might say "press (gently)"
or "(firmly)", etc. with the expectation that a
variable force will result among the population
of readers. The goal of the instruction writer is
to distinguish BAD from GOOD valves without
missing too many BAD ones (a definite personal
and property safety hazard) or falsely
identifying too many GOOD ones as BAD (a
definite excessive replacement cost and
unnecessary service problem). For the sample
problem it is desired that readers confine their
pressing force f so that $F_1 \leq f < F_2$ (if they can
accurately judge "one inch").

If the writer had a lexicon equating fuzzy
words with their physical resultants (like
anthropometry tables), statistical analysis
of the presumed results could be made to determine
e.g. the expected number of misses (BAD units
wrongly identified by users as GOOD because the
phrase did not cause them to push hard enough
(i.e. $f < F_1$)) and the expected number of FALSE
ALARMS (GOOD units falsely identified as BAD
because $f < F_2$).

This introduces the second problem for
instruction writers in that none of the fuzzy
words in the lexicon may be statistically suitable, i.e. they may all produce too many MISSES
and/or FALSE ALARMS. For example, if the only
words in the lexicon are "GENTLE", "FIRM",
"HARD", none of which is statistically suitable
then phrases such as "press (very firmly but
not hard)" should be constructable from the
three primitives and should have predictable
results just as mixing males & females in any
proportion produces a predictable statistical
height distribution. The calculus of fuzzy
sets purportedly can operate on membership
functions modifying their shapes in predictable
ways. Thus the instruction writer should be
able to design phrases to produce statistically
predictable results.

However, two theoretical/empirical problems
must be solved before "phrase crafting" can
occur:

1. How to define (determine) a membership
   function empirically for practical use,
2. The relationship (if any) between
   fuzzy sets and probability/statistics.

Although the calculus of fuzzy sets requires membership functions (as statistical theory requires distributions), very little work is reported on how to derive (as opposed to postulate them, and we were unable to find any discussion of the relationship between membership functions and statistical distributions - the basic entries needed for the lexicon.

RESEARCH

Our research concentrated on the fuzzy phrases: ("about)one inch", "squeeze (gently)" "squeeze (firmly)", and "squeeze (hard)", mostly because of the availability of a hand dynamometer and existing data for the common maximum hand strength instruction. However, the research procedures are applicable to the "push" phrases originally set out.

"(ABOUT ONE INCH)"

We used the three techniques of Estimation, Production and Rating to derive and contrast the membership function "(about) one inch" produced in each case.

Estimation - 43 subjects were given prepared sheets of 26 different, randomly oriented bars ranging from 0.3 to 1.5 inches and asked to checkmark each length they accepted as "about one inch". The membership function (Figure 4) was derived by normalizing the largest frequency to unity.

Rating - In this method, 26 subjects were given prepared sheets containing 13 randomly oriented bars and asked to rate each on a scale of 0-10 as to how strongly they felt it could be called "about one inch" in length, where 10 signified "perfectly comfortable". Values for each length were averaged and again normalized to unity to define a membership function (Figure 4).

Production - In the production method subjects were asked to "draw (some) lines about one inch long". Each subject drew different numbers ("some") of lines although the standard deviations were proportionally small. Figure 3a shows the distributions of average lengths drawn and the individual standard deviation.

Figure 3b shows the cumulative distribution of the number of lines drawn in response to the fuzzy word "SOME".

As Figure 4 shows, the three different methods produce somewhat different membership functions with the Estimation and Production methods showing a bias towards underestimation while the rating method is apparently unbiased and would accept lines longer than 1.5 inches as describable by "about one inch".

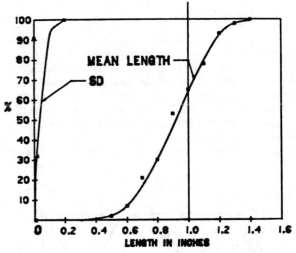

Figure 3a Cumulative Plots of the Means and Standard Deviations of Lines Drawn "About One Inch"

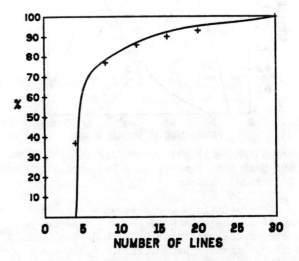

Figure 3b Cumulative Distribution of the Number of Lines Drawn In Response to "SOME".

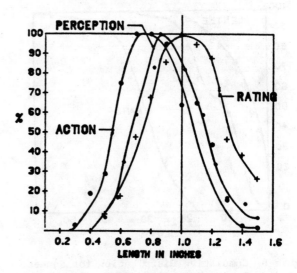

Figure 4 The Membership Functions for "About One Inch" Produced by Three Different Methods

GENTLE, FIRM, HARD

In this set of experiments, subjects were asked to squeeze a hand dynamometer to bring the needle indicator to one of a predefined randomized set of 6 values between 5 and 30 kg inclusive. Subjects then described the squeeze as "Gentle", "Firm", or "Hard". Each subject's maximum squeeze force was also determined to serve as a percentage normalizing value. The three membership functions are shown in Fig. 5

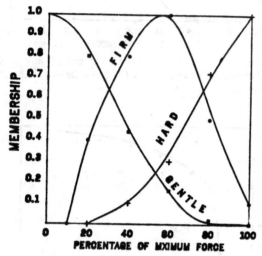

Figure 5 Membership Function for GENTLE, FIRM, and HARD Hand Squeeze as a Percentage of the Individual Maximum.

For statistical comparison, a different group of 57 subjects was asked to produce squeeze forces according to each of the words "gentle", "firm", "hard". Figure 6 shows the cumulative results.

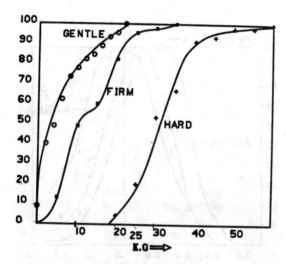

Figure 6 Cumulative Distribution for Squeeze Forces Produced in Response to the Request:

DISCUSSION

At this point we have produced the initial constructs needed to continue our work on applying fuzzy set theory to instructions and warnings. It is clear that fuzzy phrases produce definite statistical distribution and membership functions and that the membership function is somewhat dependent upon the method of acquiring the experimental data. It is also evident that membership functions are most likely context dependent in that the additions of the phrase "squeeze (as hard as you can)" would probably modify the existing curves of Figure 5 to make HARD look more like the FIRM curve while "AS HARD AS YOU CAN" would probably look like HARD. This same phrase addition would simply shift the cumulative curves of Figure 6 to the left perhaps without serious shape modification.

Context dependency is a familiar problem even in anthropometry when "sitting height" can be defined and measured as "normal" (slumped) or "rigidly erect", etc. Fuzzy set theory will need to acknowledge this context dependency as well.

It is also clear that instructions containing fuzzy phrases or words should be experimentally evaluated to determine the results they produce so that proper evaluation of the consequences can be made.

FUTURE WORK

Our next work will use the present results to test predictions made by the calculus of fuzzy sets as to modifying the shapes of the primitive functions. For example, membership function for VERY GENTLY is theoretically derivable from the GENTLE function. Such predictions will be experimentally tested. To the extent the theoretical predictions are experimentally verified, the instruction writer may proceed with some confidence in designing compound phrases based on the primitive entries.

Additional work is directed toward establishing a means of relating membership functions to statistical distributions. This is a necessity if statistical predictions based on fuzzy phrases are to be made.

REFERENCES

1. Zadeh, L.A., (1973) Outline of a new approach to the analysis of complex systems and decision processes. *IEEE Transactions on Systems, Man and Cybernetics*, Vol. SMC-3

2. Schoff, G. A., Robinson, P.A., (1984) WRITING AND DESIGNING OPERATORS MANUALS. Lifetime Learning Publications, Belmont, CA

3. Johnson, D. (1980) The Design of Effective Study Information Displays. <u>Proc. Human Factors and Industrial Design in Consumer Products</u>, Tufts University, Medford, MA 314-328

4. Rothstein, P.R. (1985) Designing Warnings To Be Read and Remembered. <u>Proc. Human Factors Society 29th Annual Meeting</u> 684-688

5. Wogalter, M., Fontenelle, G. Laughery, K. Behavioral Effectiveness of Warnings, <u>Proc. Human Factors Society 29th Annual Meeting</u> 679-683

6. Hammerton, M. (1976) How Much Is A Large Part? <u>Applied Ergonomics</u> 7.2, 10-12

7. Goodwin, A. R., Thomas, S., Hartley, J., (1977) Are Some Parts Larger Than Others? Qualifying Hammerton's Quantifiers. <u>Applied Ergonomics</u>, 8.2 93-95

8. Dubois, D., Prade, (1980) FUZZY SETS AND SYSTEMS: THEORY AND APPLICATIONS. Academic Press, N. Y.

9. Maiers, J., Sherif, Y.S. (1985) Applications of Fuzzy Set Theory. <u>IEEE Transactions on Systems, Man, and Cybernetics</u>, SMC-15 No.1.

RECEIVER CHARACTERISTICS IN SAFETY COMMUNICATIONS

Kenneth R. Laughery and John W. Brelsford
Rice University
Houston, Texas

ABSTRACT

Safety instructions and warnings are communications. It is important that characteristics of receivers, the target audience, be taken into account in designing such communications. Four categories of receiver characteristics that are important for warnings are demographic (gender and age), familiarity and experience with the product or situation, competence (technical knowledge, language and reading ability), and the perception of hazardousness. Research and experience indicate that variability in these receiver dimensions has important implications for the design and effectiveness of warnings. Even when the warning designer has attempted to take into account these target audience factors, there is a final step that generally should be included in the design process. This step is to "test" the warning on a target audience sample.

INTRODUCTION

Safety instructions and warnings are properly viewed as communications. A standard communications model is shown in Figure 1. Several components are commonly identified in such models, including the sender, the message, the medium and the receiver.

The sender, or source, represents the origin or originator of the communication. The message, of course, is the hazard, consequences and instructional information to be communicated. The medium refers to the channels or routes through which information moves from the source to the receiver. Media for warnings include on-product labels, package inserts, signs, verbal instructions, and so forth. The receiver refers to any and all people to whom the warning is directed. Characteristics or parameters of each of these components may and often do play a critical role in the effectiveness of the warning.

Figure 1 might be viewed as representing the elements of a communication system where the manufacturer of a product is warning the end user of the product. However, circumstances in which safety information and warnings need to be communicated may be much more complex. For example, Figure 2 could represent the elements of a warning communication system for a product that is being used in an industrial setting. Here the product might be marketed through a distributor (or a series of distributors) to an employer (the

business) who in turn communicates in various ways with the end user (employee). These indirect communications from the manufacturer to the end user through various intermediaries may be accompanied by direct communications to the end user such as labels on the product. The media through which the information gets communicated may be quite varied. Feedback between various components may be involved such as an employer notifying the manufacturer about a safety problem associated with the use of the product. More complex systems such as depicted in Figure 2 would have several receivers of the warning information, including distributors, employers and end users. Further, these receivers might differ markedly in their characteristics. For example, an industrial toxicologist who serves as the employer's receiver will probably have a great deal more technical knowledge than the laborer working in the plant who is the end user of the product, and this knowledge difference may have implications for the warning system accompanying the product. A parallel example in a very different context would be the differences between the prescribing physician and the patient who are both receivers of safety/warning information about medications manufactured by a drug company.

Whether the circumstances are simple or complex as characterized by the above examples, the success of a warning communication system is dependent on taking into account the properties of the various components of the system. In this paper we focus on one of these components — the receiver. We pose the questions: What are the characteristics of receivers that must be taken into account in formulating safety instructions and warnings? and, How do receiver characteristics influence the effectiveness of warnings to which they are exposed.

<u>Figure 1</u>. Standard Communication Model

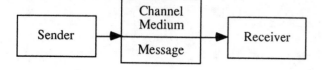

Figure 2. Complex Warning Communication System

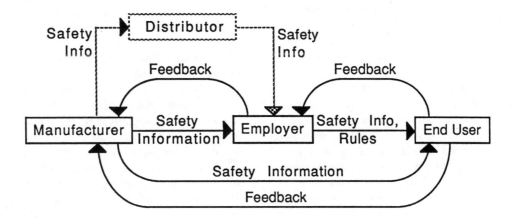

Recent years have witnessed the development of a body of research that addresses these questions. The purpose of this paper is twofold: (1) to review some of the findings regarding relevant receiver characteristics; and (2) to examine some implications of these factors for designing effective warnings. The analysis is organized into four categories: demographic variables, familiarity and experience, competence, and hazard and risk perception factors. Finally, we will offer a few principles for warnings design that take into account receiver characteristics.

DEMOGRAPHIC VARIABLES

In this section two demographic variables will be addressed, gender and age.

Gender. While research results are not entirely consistent regarding male-female similarities and differences, there are some reasonably clear trends that have implications for the design and effectiveness of warnings. Several studies have examined gender differences in the degree to which subjects will look for warnings on products and the likelihood they will read them; examples are Godfrey, et al. (1983), LaRue & Cohen (1987), and Young, et al. (1989). Generally the findings indicate women report a greater likelihood than men to look for and read warnings. Other research has examined gender differences in the reported likelihood of taking appropriate precautions in response to warnings; that is, behavioral intentions. Examples of such studies are Goldhaber & deTurck (1988b), Viscusi, et al. (1986), and Desaulniers (1991). It appears that women are more likely than men to comply with warnings.

Trends in research findings such as those reported above indicate that warnings are more likely to be

effective with women than with men. This conclusion may have special implications where hazards associated with products or environments are more likely to be encountered by one of the sexes. If one is attempting to influence the safety behavior of men, the task may be especially difficult.

Age. As with the studies cited above regarding gender effects, the effects of age in warnings research have not been completely consistent; however, trends do exist. Desaulniers (1991) has reported that older people, 40 and above, are more likely to take precautions in response to warnings as reflected in their behavioral intentions. Two studies (Collins & Lerner, 1982; Easterby & Hakiel, 1981) have found that older subjects exhibit lower levels of comprehension for safety signs involving pictorials. Results such as these suggest that older receivers are more influenced by warnings, but greater attention to issues of comprehension may be necessary.

FAMILIARITY AND EXPERIENCE

One of the issues that has received a good deal of research attention concerns the familiarity/experience that people have with products and how this familiarity influences the effectiveness of warnings. Familiarity has generally been defined in terms of frequency of use of a product or of similar products. Measures of effectiveness have included subject's reports of intent to look for a warning, to notice a warning, to read a warning, and to comply with a warning.

Numerous studies have explored the effects of familiarity on whether or not subjects will look for, notice and read a warning. Godfrey, et al. (1983), Godfrey & Laughery (1984), LaRue & Cohen (1987), Otsubo (1988) and Wogalter, et al. (in press) have reported results showing that people are less likely to look for, notice and read warnings on consumer products with which they are familiar than they are with unfamiliar products. Goldhaber and deTurck (1988a) have shown that people are less likely to notice swimming pool signs if they are familiar with pools.

While there has been less research on familiarity effects employing behavioral compliance measures, there are a few studies. Examples are the work of Goldhaber & deTurck (1988a, 1988b) on swimming pool warnings and Otsubo's (1988) study on circular saw and jigsaw warnings. Results showed that people more familiar with these products were less likely to comply with warnings.

Overall, the familiarity effect seems to be a consistent and robust finding. Why does familiarity decrease the likelihood that the receiver will be influenced by a warning? A possible answer lies in the fact that the more people use a product without experiencing a safety problem, the less hazardous they perceive the product to be. As will be discussed in a later section of this paper, perceived hazardousness has a substantial influence on warning effectiveness, and may, therefore, be the intervening mechanism for explaining the familiarity effect. In any case, it seems clear that products that are used repetitively pose special warning problems.

COMPETENCE

There are many dimensions of receiver competence that may be relevant to the design of warnings. For example, sensory deficits might be a factor in the ability of some special target audiences to be directly influenced by a warning. The blind person would not be able to receive a written warning, nor would the deaf receive an auditory warning. Opposite the sensory end of the sequence of events associated with warning effectiveness is output or behavior. If special equipment is required to comply with the warning, it must be available or obtainable. If special skills are required, they must be present in the receiver population. To some extent, these sensory and behavioral limitations of receiver populations are rather obvious; although we are constantly amazed at the number of warnings that violate such considerations — especially in the behavior domain where instructions are frequently given that are, at best, difficult to carry out.

In this section we address what might be regarded as more cognitive receiver characteristics; technical knowledge, language and reading ability. Our analyses of these aspects of warning target audiences is based primarily on personal observations of a variety of warning designs and some established principles of communications and displays.

Technical Knowledge. One of the issues in warning design concerns the level of technical information to be communicated. Comprehension of such information is generally a function of the relevant technical knowledge possessed by the receiver. Here we are referring to conceptual knowledge that includes both factual information and process understanding (the receiver's mental model). Some examples of familiar problem areas are: (1) hazards associated with medications where knowledge of physiology may be relevant; (2) chemical hazards where understanding chemical reactions may be involved (what not to mix with what); and (3) mechanical knowledge needed to understand hazards of handling materials, such as on a construction site. Clearly it is important to take into account the relevant technical knowledge of the receiver in formulating warnings that address such hazards. Further, the problem may be more complicated in the sense that warnings regarding a particular product hazard may be directed to multiple groups that differ with regard to relevant knowledge about factual information and process understanding. In addressing complex warning communication systems such as shown in Figure 2, we cited two examples that fit this multiple groups circumstance: (1) physicians and patients who are receivers of warnings about medications; and, (2) industrial toxicologists and laborers who are concerned with safety in the use of industrial chemicals.

The point to be emphasized here is not that variability in knowledge about facts and process exists within the target audience for a particular product warning. Rather, the point is that the level or levels of knowledge and understanding must be understood and taken into account. There may be various approaches to addressing these concerns. One approach, of course, is to construct warnings that may be understood at the lowest knowledge levels represented in the target audience. Alternatively, multiple warnings may be developed that specifically target different subgroups that vary in technical knowledge.

Language. The issue here is straightforward, but it is also increasingly important. We are referring not only to subgroups in our own society that speak and read languages other than English, such as Spanish. As trade becomes more international, requirements for warnings to be directed to non English readers increase. Ways of dealing with this problem include warnings stated in multiple languages (note the instruction booklets that accompany various electronic products such as watches and calculators) and the use of pictorials.

Reading Ability. Time and again we have encountered warnings on products used by the general population that require high reading levels. A grade 12 level is not uncommon. The usual recommendation for general target audiences is that the reading level be in the grade 4-6 range. Obviously, if comprehension of a warning is to be achieved, reading levels must be consistent with reading abilities of receivers. A discussion of reading level measures and their application to the design of instructions and warnings can be found in Duffy (1985).

One additional problem associated with reading level should be noted. We have seen a variety of estimates on literacy in the American adult population. One estimate is that there are 16 million functionally illiterate adults; thus, the problem may require more than simply keeping reading levels to a minimum. We offer no simple solutions to this problem, but certainly pictorials, verbal warnings, special training programs, etc. may be important ingredients of warning systems for such populations.

HAZARD AND RISK PERCEPTION

The phrase "hazard and risk perception" in the present context refers to people's notions or understanding about the safety problems associated with some product or set of circumstances. This understanding may involve what can happen, the likelihood it will happen, and the severity of the consequences. Recent research has addressed various interactions between hazard and risk perception and warnings. The issues presented here include how the effects of warnings are influenced by people's perceptions as well as how warnings influence hazard perceptions.

A consistent finding in warning research is that people's perception of the hazardousness associated with a product or situation is an important determiner of warning effectiveness. As stated above, hazard perception may include notions about likelihood of an accident as well as the severity of a potential injury. Generally, research has indicated that perceived severity of consequences has a strong influence on behavioral intentions. Numerous studies have shown the greater the a priori perception of hazardousness, the more likely people will look for and read a warning, and the more likely they will comply by taking safety precautions (Donner & Brelsford, 1988; Godfrey et al., 1983; Friedmann, 1988; LaRue & Cohen, 1987; Leonard et al., 1986; Otsubo, 1988; and Wogalter et al., in press).

Since perception of hazardousness appears to be an important factor in the safety precautions people take, the influence of warnings on such perceptions is of interest. Two studies (Laughery & Stanush, 1989; Sherer & Rogers, 1984) have shown that the explicitness with which the severity of injury consequences is expressed is an important determiner of perceived hazardousness and of recall of warning information. As expected, the more explicit the consequence information the greater the perceived hazard and the more information recalled.

From the above results it is clear that warnings designers need to be aware of people's perceptions of hazards and risks. This understanding would be particularly important where such perceptions lead to an underestimation of safety problems, as might be the case with familiar products.

CONCLUSIONS AND RECOMMENDATIONS

In this paper we have focussed on characteristics of receivers that are important in the design of warnings. There are several principles or guidelines that appear warranted on the basis of the analyses presented.

Principle #1 - Know thy receiver. This statement may seem trivial and obvious; yet, as noted earlier, warnings are constantly encountered that appear to have been designed with little or no regard for characteristics of the people to whom they are directed. Statements written at a grade 12 or higher reading level that are intended for a general audience, and statements containing technical terminology unfamiliar to the receivers are examples of such warnings. Gathering knowledge and data about relevant characteristics of target audiences may require time, effort and money. Analyzing existing data such as demographic information or collecting new data by conducting surveys may be necessary. Without such information, however, the warning designer and ultimately the receiver will be at a serious disadvantage.

Principle #2 - When variability exists in the target audience, design for the low-end extreme. Whether the variability exists in competence, technical knowledge, familiarity, perception of hazardousness or other receiver characteristics, it is important that warnings not be designed for the average.

Principle #3 - When the target audience consists of subgroups that differ in relevant characteristics, consider employing a warning system that includes different components for the different subgroups. A corollary to this principle is do not try to accomplish too much with a single warning. An example of where this corollary may be violated is the current OSHA guidelines regarding the variety of subgroups in the target audience for material safety data sheets (MSDS's). These subgroups include toxicologists, safety engineers, managers, physicians and end users (such as the laborer using the stuff). If the warning system does not include communication media, in addition to the MSDS, it is probably destined to fail.

Principle #4 - Market test the warning system. Despite the designer's knowledge of receiver characteristics and efforts to apply that knowledge, warnings should be market tested. Such tests may consist of "trying it out" on a target audience sample to assess comprehension and behavioral intentions. Our experience indicates that such minimal efforts are seldom part of the warning design process.

To conclude, it is important that warnings be viewed as communications and that the characteristics of the intended receivers be taken into account in their design. The analyses of relevant characteristics presented in this paper was not intended to be exhaustive; others may be added. The essential point is that our experience with warning systems indicates that this type of receiver information is often not taken into account in warning design, at least not adequately. If increased warning effectiveness is to be achieved, such considerations must be addressed.

REFERENCES

Collins, B.L. and Lerner, N.D. (1982). Assessment of fire-safety symbols. Human Factors, 24, 75-84.

Desaulniers, D.R. (1991). An examination of consequence probability as a determinant of precautionary intent. Unpublished doctoral dissertation, Rice University, Houston.

Donner, K.A. & Brelsford, J.W. (1988). Cueing hazard information for consumer products. In Proceedings of the Human Factors Society 32nd Annual Meeting, Human Factors Society, Santa Monica, CA, 532-535.

Duffy, T.M. (1985). "Chapter 6: Readability formulas: What's the use?" In Designing Usable Texts, T.M. Duffy and R. Waller (Eds.), Academic Press, Inc., Orlando, 113-140.

Easterby, R.S. & Hakiel, S.R. (1981). The comprehension of pictorially presented messages. Applied Ergonomics, 12, 143-152.

Friedmann, K. (1988) The effect of adding symbols to perceptions. In Proceedings of Interface 89, Human Factors Society, Santa Monica, CA, 73-78.

Godfrey, S.S., Allender, L., Laughery, K.R. & Smith, V.L. (1983). Warning messages: Will the consumer bother to look? In Proceedings of the Human Factors Society 27th Annual Meeting, Human Factors Society, Santa Monica, CA, 950-954.

Godfrey, S.S. & Laughery, K.R. (1984). The biasing effect of familiarity on consumer's awareness of hazard. In Proceedings of the Human Factors Society 28th Annual Meeting, Human Factors Society, Santa Monica, CA, 483-486.

Goldhaber, G.M. & deTurck, M.A. (1988a). Effects of consumer's familiarity with a product on attention and compliance with warnings. Journal of Products Liability, 11, 29-37.

Goldhaber, G.M. & deTurck, M.A. (1988b). Effectiveness of warning signs: Gender and familiarity effects. Journal of Products Liability, 11, 271-284.

LaRue, C. & Cohen, H. (1987). Factors influencing consumers' perceptions of warning: An examination of the differences between male and female consumers. In Proceedings of the Human Factors Society 31st Annual Meeting, Human Factors Society, Santa Monica, CA, 610-614.

Laughery, K.R. & Stanush, J.A. (1989). Effects of warning explicitness on product perceptions. In Proceedings of the Human Factors Society 31st Annual Meeting, Human Factors Society, Santa Monica, CA, 431-435.

Leonard, S.D., Matthews, D. & Karnes, E.W. (1986). How does the population interpret warning signals? In Proceedings of the Human Factors Society 30th Annual Meeting, Human Factors Society, Santa Monica, CA, 116-120.

Otsubo, S.M. (1988). A behavioral study of warning labels for consumer products: Perceived danger and use of pictographs. In Proceedings of the Human Factors Society 32nd Annual Meeting, Human Factors Society, Santa Monica, CA, 536-540.

Sherer, M. & Rogers, R.W. (1984). The role of vivid information in fear appeals and attitude change. Journal of Research in Personality, 18, 321-334.

Viscusi, W.K., Magat, W.A. & Huber, J. (1986), Informational regulation of consumer health risks: An empirical evaluation of hazard warnings. Rand Journal of Economics, 17, 351-365.

Wogalter, M.S., Desaulniers, D.R., Brelsford, J.W. & Laughery, K.R. (in press). Consumer product warnings: The role of hazard perception. Journal of Safety Research.

Young, S.L., Martin, E.G. & Wogalter, M.S. (1989). Gender differences in consumer product hazard perceptions. In Proceedings of Interface 89, Human Factors Society, Santa Monica, CA, 73-78.

EFFECTS OF WARNING EXPLICITNESS ON PRODUCT PERCEPTIONS

Kenneth R. Laughery and Julie A. Stanush
Rice University
Houston, Texas

ABSTRACT

A common assumption of manufacturers is that explicit warning labels will deter consumers from purchasing products. This study explored people's reactions to explicit and nonexplicit warning labels, where explicitness refers to how specifically the potential injury consequences were described. 108 subjects completed a 12-item questionnaire for each of nine familiar consumer products. The questions covered the severity of potential injury, product familiarity, product hazards and dangerousness, manufacturer's concerns, and potential purchasing decisions. Results suggest that products are perceived as more dangerous and related injuries as more severe when warnings are explicit. Also, with explicit warnings subjects report that they better understand the hazards, that they are being provided with all the necessary safety information, and that manufacturers are more concerned about safety. There was no clear indication that more explicit warnings either deter people from purchasing a product or increase the likelihood of a purchase.

INTRODUCTION

The design of warning labels on consumer products is an important issue to manufacturers. A common assumption is that if the warning label describing product hazards is too strong, consumers will be influenced either not to buy the product or to purchase an alternative with a milder warning. Thus, manufacturers are often hesitant to fully, or perhaps even adequately, warn consumers of the dangers associated with the use of their products.

Little research has been done that addresses this issue. One study by Schwartz, dePontbriand and Laughery (1983) compared the relative influence of product hazard level, cost and effectiveness on anticipated purchase decisions. Their results showed that hazard level, defined as probability of an injury, was a factor in anticipated decisions. Another study by Ursic (1984) explored the effects of the presence or absence of a warning as well as several warning design parameters on people's perception of product effectiveness and safety. He reported that the presence of a warning had a positive effect on the perception of both effectiveness and safety.

The above studies are suggestive regarding the issue of whether or not the strength of a warning will affect purchase decisions. The Schwartz et al. (1983) results indicate hazard information may be relevant to such decisions. The Ursic (1984) findings suggest that warnings may actually increase the likelihood of purchase. Obviously, such conclusions are vastly overgeneralized at this point. Nevertheless, the issue is important, because labeling decisions are being made based on oversimplified and possibly incorrect assumptions about warning effects on purchase decisions.

Why would a stronger warning potentially lead to a greater likelihood that the product would be preferred? Ursic (1984) suggested that buyers may infer that the manufacturer is more careful in producing and marketing the product. In short, the manufacturer is perceived to be more concerned about consumer safety. He further notes that the reason may be because people will wonder about the dangers of a similar product that does not have a safety warning. This latter point is similar to an analysis found in the marketing literature on consumer risk taking. Bauer (1960) has conceptualized various kinds of potential losses, including physical, a consumer faces when making a purchase. These losses form the perceived risk. When a buying decision among alternatives is made, perceived risk can be minimized by decreasing the level of uncertainty about the alternatives. Thus, stronger or more explicit warnings may serve to reduce uncertainty about safety.

This paper presents the results of a study that explored people's reactions and perceptions after exposure to warnings on nine common consumer products. Warnings varied in "explicitness"; that is, how specifically the potential injury consequences were described. The methodology involved showing subjects product warnings and then having them answer a series of questions about the product, the label, the manufacturer, and their potential buying decisions. The purpose was to shed light on the issue of whether or not warning explicitness influences buying decisions and if so, why?

METHOD

Materials and Design

Warning labels were prepared for nine products. The nine products were aluminum ladder, antihistamine, drain cleaner, hair dryer, motorcycle helmet, nausea medicine, oven cleaner, pesticide, and sunlamp. The products were chosen because they vary on type and seriousness of hazard, and all are generally familiar to the consumer. One product, the motorcycle helmet, differed from the others, because it is a safety equipment item and its warning did not address wrongful use. Rather, the label warned about injuries that could occur even if the product was being used correctly.

The warning labels for each product were developed by studying actual warning labels found in stores. Each product had two warning labels that differed on the variable explicitness. An explicit warning contained more specific and detailed information about the consequences associated with use or misuse, as compared with the nonexplicit warning. For the two labels associated with a given product, only explicitness varied. Other design factors, including content, were kept as constant as possible.

Figure 1 presents the explicit (top) and nonexplicit (bottom) warnings for one of the products, nausea medicine.

A 12-item questionnaire was used to obtain subjects' responses. The questions are listed below. Each question was followed by a 7-point rating scale, except for question 10, which required a Yes/No response, and question 11, which asked for a written response. Following each question below, in parentheses, are the verbal labels used to anchor the scales. The first label was associated with the value of 1 on the scale and the second label with 7.

1. If you had an injury or illness as a result of using this product, how severe do you think it would be? (not at all severe -- very severe)
2. Do you think the manufacturer is concerned with your safety or following government labeling rules? (following government labeling rules -- concerned with your safety)

WARNING

- Do not exceed recommended dosages because nervousness, dizziness, or sleeplessness may occur.
- Do not drive while using this product.
- If symptoms do not improve within 7 days or are accompanied by a high fever, discontinue use and call a physician.

WARNING

- Do not exceed recommended dosages because undesirable effects may occur.
- Do not drive while using this product.
- If symptoms do not improve within 7 days or are accompanied by a high fever, discontinue use and call a physician.

Figure 1: Explicit (Top) and Nonexplicit (Bottom) Warnings for Nausea Medicine.

3. After reading the warning label on this product, will you look for an alternative product or will you still buy this product? (buy this product -- look for alternative product)

4. How concerned would you feel if a close friend were to use it? (not at all concerned -- very concerned)

5. How confident are you that you understand the hazards associated with this product? (not at all confident -- very confident)

6. Do you feel that this warning label gives all the information necessary to insure your safety during the product's use? (gives no information -- gives all the information)

7. How likely is it that the injury or illness would be your fault? (not at all likely -- very likely)

8. Do you think that the warning label on this product exaggerates the dangerousness of this product? (not at all exaggerates -- greatly exaggerates)

9. How often have you used this kind of product? (never -- many times a day)

10. Have you or someone you have known had an injury or illness as a result of using this kind of product? (yes -- no)

11. Describe injuries and/or illnesses that could occur while using this product.

12. How dangerous do you think this product is? (not at all dangerous -- very dangerous)

A packet given to the subject consisted of each of the nine product warning labels with the same 12-item questionnaire immediately following each product's label. The products were in a random order within the packet, and any given product was randomly assigned either the explicit or the nonexplicit condition within the constraint that each subject got five of one and four of the other - this assignment was balanced across subjects. Consequently, explicitness was a between-subjects variable with 54 sets of responses for the explicit warning label for each product, and 54 sets of responses for the nonexplicit label.

Subjects and Procedures

Subjects were 108 University of Houston students who were currently enrolled in an introductory psychology class. A page of instructions was stapled to the front of each packet. In the instructions, subjects were told that they would be shown typical warning labels from nine different consumer products. They were instructed to read each warning label and answer the 12 questions that followed it. The subject was to base his/her answers on the information in the warning label. Unlimited time was allowed to complete the questionnaires.

RESULTS

Mean ratings for a given product and for each question were determined by collapsing the scores across subjects. Responses to question 11 were open-ended and will not be presented here.

The data were analyzed by coding the explicitness value of the warning as 0 (explicit) or 1 (nonexplicit) and computing correlation coefficients between this variable and responses to the questions. It should be noted that this procedure is equivalent to computing t-tests, where the statistical significance of the correlation is the same as the significance level of the explicitness treatment difference in the t-test.

Two of the questions, 9 and 10, asked about consumers' experiences with the product. Since subjects were randomly assigned the explicit and nonexplicit warnings, significant correlations were not expected, as such results would indicate some sort of sampling bias in the subject population. None of the correlations for any product approached significance on either question.

The results of questions 4 (concern for a close friend using the product) and 7 (injury your fault) showed no correlations that were statistically significant. On question 8 (dangerousness exaggerated) a significant correlation for drain cleaner, $r = -.23$, $p < .02$, indicated subjects felt the explicit warning exaggerated the danger level of this product. No other correlations on question 8 approached significance.

Of most interest to this study were the questions related to perceptions of the product (1, 5 and 12), the label (6), the manufacturer (2), and purchase decisions (3). Of 54 possible effects related to product explicitness (9 products and 6 questions), 14 were significant at a $p < .05$ level. The correlations for each of these questions and each product are shown in Table 1. It should be noted that given the coding of the explicitness variable and the labeling of the rating scales, negative correlations are consistent with expected outcomes; that is, more explicit warnings would be associated with ratings of more severe injures, greater manufacturer concern, better understanding of hazards, more safety information, and greater dangerousness. Also, negative correlations for question 3 would indicate a greater likelihood to look for alternative products.

For question 1, which dealt with injury severity , three of the nine products showed significant effects (drain cleaner, hair dryer and nausea medicine). All but two of the products had correlations in the expected negative direction. Eight products had negative correlations for question 5, understanding the hazard, although only one

was significant (antihistamine). Question 12, dangerousness, showed one significant negative correlation (aluminum ladder) and four others that were negative. While these results are not overly strong, they are certainly suggestive given that all significant correlations and most of those that did not reach statistical significance were in the expected direction. They suggest that more explicit warnings are associated with perceiving a product as more dangerous and leading to more severe injuries, as well as a sense of better understanding the hazards.

Question 2, manufacturer's concern, showed significant effects with three products (antihistamine, hair dryer and motorcycle helmet). All but two of the products had negative correlations, which suggests that explicit warning labels are related to the belief that manufacturers are showing greater concern for consumers' safety.

For question 6, adequacy of information, seven of the nine products had negative correlations; four were significant (antihistamine, drain

Table 1: Correlations Between Questionnaire Responses and Warning Explicitness.

Product	Question Number					
	1	2	3	5	6	12
Aluminum Ladder	-.01	-.17	-.01	-.07	-.09	-.28*
Antihistamine	.01	-.21*	-.13	-.19*	-.20*	-.04
Drain Cleaner	-.23*	-.04	-.20*	-.15	-.23*	-.06
Hair Dryer	-.20*	-.20*	-.10	-.01	.04	-.09
Motorcycle Helmet	-.11	-.19*	.31*	-.11	-.21*	.13
Nausea Medicine	-.29*	-.07	.00	-.09	-.17	-.08
Oven Cleaner	-.12	.02	-.02	.03	.00	-.06
Pesticide	-.07	-.03	.03	-.07	-.27*	.00
Sunlamp	.08	.11	.02	-.03	-.14	.08

*$p<.05$

cleaner, motorcycle helmet and pesticide). These responses suggest that consumers believe they are being provided more safety information when given explicit warnings than when given nonexplicit warnings.

Question 3 addressed the issue of purchase decisions. Two of the nine products had significant correlations, but in opposite directions (drain cleaner was negative and motorcycle helmet was positive.) Of the remaining 7 products, four had negative correlations while three were positive. Thus, these results do not show any clear effects of warning explicitness on possible buying decisions.

To further examine the relationships between perception of manufacturer's concern and buying decisions and between degree of hazard understanding and buying decisions, correlations were computed between responses to questions 2 and 3 and questions 5 and 3. The correlation between perceived manufacturer's concern and buying decisions was significant, $r = -.20$, $p < .04$ for the antihistamine product. The same correlation was close to statistical significance, $r = -.17$, $p < .07$, for the motorcycle helmet. No other correlations were significant. These two results suggest that greater perceived understanding of hazards may be associated with higher likelihood to purchase.

CONCLUSIONS

The results indicate that the explicitness of potential injury severity in warning labels has some effect on the perceptions of products. Explicit warning labels generally make subjects think that the product is more dangerous and that more severe injuries are possible. Subjects also report that they better understand the hazards associated with the product and are being provided with the necessary safety information when explicit warnings are used. The latter result can only be interpreted as a perception of understanding, however, since hazard understanding or knowledge was not directly assessed. One possible implication of these

outcomes is that when warnings are nonexplicit, people may underestimate hazardousness and potential consequences.

Of central interest here are the responses to questions 2 and 3 and 5. Ursic's (1984) notion that warnings may be interpreted as reflecting the manufacturer's concern for consumer safety receives some support. The results of question 2 show that stronger warnings were associated with perceived greater concern by manufacturers. The findings however, failed to show any clear-cut effects of perceived manufacturer's concern on potential buying decisions. There is some indication in the correlations between questions 5 and 3 that greater hazard understanding, reduction of uncertainty in Bauer's (1960) terms, may lead to a greater likelihood to purchase. Overall, other than for drain cleaner, this study does not support the assumption that strong, more explicit warnings are a deterrent to purchasing a product.

REFERENCES

Bauer, R.A. (1960). Consumer behavior as risk taking. In R.S. Hancock (Ed.) *Dynamic Marketing for a Changing World* (pp. 389-398). Chicago: American Marketing Association.

Schwartz, D.R., dePontbriand, R.J. & Laughery, K.R. (1983). The impact of product hazard information on consumer buying decisions: A policy capturing approach. In *Proceedings of the Human Factors Society 27th Annual Meeting* (pp. 955-957). Santa Monica, CA: Human Factors Society.

Ursic, M. (1984). The impact of safety warnings on perception and memory. *Human Factors*, *26*, 677-682.

AN EYE SCAN ANALYSIS OF ACCESSING PRODUCT WARNING INFORMATION

Kenneth R. Laughery, Sr. and Stephen L. Young

Rice University
Houston, Texas 77251

Eye tracking procedures were employed to study eye scan patterns of subjects searching for warning messages in product labels. Thirty-eight alcoholic beverage labels were constructed, 24 of which contained a warning. For each label, subjects indicated whether or not it contained a warning. Salience of the warning was manipulated by the presence or absence of four features which appeared individually or in combination. The features were a pictorial, an icon, color and a border. Of particular interest was the ability to decompose the total time it takes to find the warning in two components: *location time* and *decision time*. Location refers to the time it takes to find the area where the warning is, and decision refers to the time it takes to determine if the given information is a warning, as well as the time to make an overt response. The results show that the singular addition of a pictorial, an icon, color or a border did not produce a significant improvement in total time or in location time relative to a warning with no salient features (the baseline warning). The addition of a pictorial did improve decision time compared to the baseline warning. The combination of a pictorial, color and an icon produced a significant decrease in total time, location time and decision time. These results show that salience manipulations affect time to find a warning, as well as time to determine if given information is a warning.

INTRODUCTION

Research on design and effectiveness of product warnings has frequently employed as a dependent measure whether or not people notice and/or read warnings (DeJoy, 1989). Generally, measures have included subjects' reports of whether or not they notice and/or read a warning (e.g., Strawbridge, 1986) and memory tests (recognition or recall) for information contained in the warning (e.g., Young & Wogalter, 1990).

In a somewhat different approach to exploring the effects of warning design parameters on noticeability, Young (in press) employed a response time measure. Specifically, he measured the time between the onset of computer-presented alcohol beverage container labels and subjects' responses regarding the presence or absence of a warning statement in the label. The appearance of the warnings was orthogonally manipulated by attention-enhancement features: pictorials, icons, color or borders. Young reported that the presence of pictorials, icons and color substantially decreased response times. The presence of a border had little or no effect on this measure of noticeability.

The research reported here represents a more direct approach to assessing what information people access in product labels, with particular interest directed to warning information. Specifically, eye scan equipment has been employed to record scanning patterns of people who are looking for warning information in the labels used by Young (in press).

We have found very little reported research involving the application of eye scan analysis to the study of warnings. One such study (Fisher et al., 1989) analyzed eye scans of subjects viewing cigarette ads that contained warnings. It was found that in 43.6% of cases, the warning was not viewed at all.

One of the purposes of this study was to explore warning design factors that might influence noticeability of warnings. As noted, Young's (in press) experiment showed that three design factors substantially decreased the amount of time required to locate and report a warning in labels. Eye movement data will permit response times regarding the presence or absence of a warning to be divided into two components. The first component is the time from the onset of the label display to the subject's eyes arriving at the warning. This measure will be referred to as the *location time*. The second component is the time from the eyes arriving at the warning to the subject's response (pushing a button) indicating the presence of the warning. This component will be referred to as the *decision time*. We recognize that decision time includes the output portion of the actual decision (the button press). However, we assume that this portion is constant across subjects and labels. Thus, differences in this measure should reflect variations in decision time to determine if the warning is present or not.

Several predictions can be made about the following research. First, we predict that location time will be shortened by the presence of a pictorial, an icon, color and a border, compared to warnings with no salience features. These four features should be attention directing or orienting, thus enabling the warning to be located more quickly. Second, we predict that pictorials and icons will lead to shorter decision times, since these features contain content/warning information which is partially redundant with the warning text. This redundancy should decrease decision times. Because color and borders are not redundant with warning information (other label information may also be in color or surrounded by a border), these two features are not expected to result in shorter decision times. A third hypothesis regards the border manipulation alone. Although Young (in press) found no effect of border on total time, it

Figure 1a. Example warning in Zone 4 with no salience features

This special beer is designed and produced by the Iron City Brewing Co., Detroit, MI and is brewed under a special agreement with Spoetzl Brewery, Chicago, Illinois

Grand Prix Lager

12 Fluid Ounces

GOVERNMENT WARNING: (1) ACCORDING TO THE SURGEON GENERAL, WOMEN SHOULD NOT DRINK ALCOHOLIC BEVERAGES DURING PREGNANCY BECAUSE OF THE RISK OF BIRTH DEFECTS. (2) CONSUMPTION OF ALCOHOLIC BEVERAGES IMPAIRS YOUR ABILITY TO DRIVE A CAR OR OPERATE MACHINERY, AND MAY CAUSE HEALTH PROBLEMS

Beer Certificate
Based on an average analysis,
contains: Calories..98
Carbohydrates..3.5 grams
Fat..0.0 grams
Protein..0.8 grams

Figure 1b. Eye scan path for the label in Figure 1a.

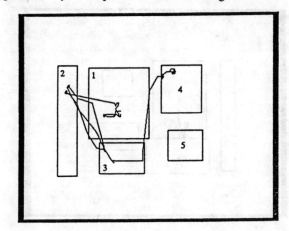

Figure 1c. Time line of the eye scan for Figure 1b.

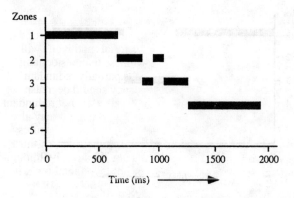

was suggested in his paper that (in certain cases) borders can interfere with discrimination of the warning text. It was suggested that borders draw attention like other salience manipulations, but that they interfere with discrimination of the information and increase decision time. This hypothesis can be tested in the present study. We expect that a border will produce shortened location times, but longer decision times.

METHOD

Subjects. Five students from Rice University were paid for participation.

Materials and Equipment. Thirty-eight simulated "alcohol labels" were selected from a pool of 96 labels for fictitious beer, wine and liquor products. Twenty-four labels contained a warning and fourteen did not. Their selection was based on findings from earlier research using these same labels as stimuli (Young, in press; Laughery & Young, in press). Each label was partitioned into 5 "zones", which were general areas that could contain information (see Figures 1a and 2a). Zone identification numbers are shown in Figures 1b and 2b. Zone 1 always contained the brand logo, and Zone 2 was always printed vertically from top to bottom. Only Zones 2, 3 and 4 could contain the warning. Non-warning information included material on the ingredients used, the importer, the brewery, nutritional content, and bar codes. Figure 1a shows an example label with the warning in Zone 4. Figure 2a shows an example warning in Zone 3. While the verbal content of the warnings was held constant, the warnings were manipulated with regard to four salience features. Eight different conditions were employed: 1) plain (no salience feature), 2) pictorial,

Figure 2a. Example warning in zone 3 with all four salience features (color not shown)

3) color (red), 4) icon, 5) border, 6) pictorial-color, 7) pictorial-color-icon, and 8) pictorial-color-icon-border. Each manipulation occurred 3 times, once in each of the three locations. Figure 1a contains a warning with no salience features and Figure 2a has all four salience features with the warning (the red color of the warning is not shown). In order to provide appropriate control conditions, labels that did not contain warnings did include color and borders, as well as non-warning pictorials and icons.

The labels were presented with SuperCard (Silicon Beach Software) on an Apple MacIntosh IIcx, with an Apple 12" RGB color monitor. A Panasonic WV-1400 TV camera collected stimulus scene information (the area of the subject's view). An RCA color video camera with a HOYA 58mm infrared lens collected pupil positions. An ISCAN RK-416 Pupil Tracking system and an ISCAN RK-520 Autocalibration system, connected to a PC computer, were used to record and analyze data from these cameras.

Procedure. Subjects were seated in front of the computer monitor and their relative pupil position was calibrated with the stimulus scene. Subjects viewed the labels one at a time, and indicated whether the warning was on the label by pressing a button labeled "Yes" (warning present) or a different button labeled "No" (warning absent). After pressing either button, the PC stopped recording eye fixation data and the stimulus screen turned white for 4 seconds. After 4 seconds, an "X" appeared in the center of the stimulus screen, alerting the subject that the next label would appear within one second. Subjects were instructed to focus on the "X" until the subsequent label appeared and then to start searching for the warning. Thus, each fixation sequence began in Zone 1 (the center of the label).

Figure 2b. Eye scan path for the label in Figure 2a.

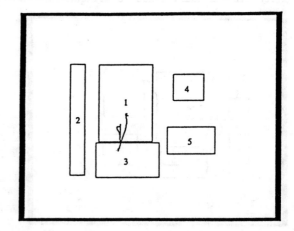

Figure 2c. Time line of the eye scan for Figure 2b.

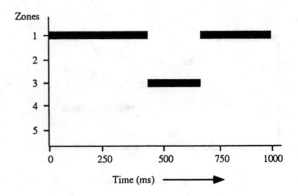

132

RESULTS

The basic data which was automatically recorded consisted of a time sequencing of the subjects eye fixations. This data included which zone the subject was looking at and the time for the beginning of that fixation. Figures 1b and 2b show the scan paths for one subject searching the two labels for the warning information. Figures 1c and 2c are time-lines showing the scan chronology of the same two searches.

In this section the results employing three dependent measure will be presented. These measures are total time, location time and decision time. Total time, of course, is the sum of the location and decision times. Figure 3 presents the mean times for these three measures for each of the warning design conditions.

Total Time. A one-way analysis of variance (ANOVA), treating each of the eight design combinations as a separate condition, showed a significant main effect of the design variable, $F(7,110) = 6.28$, $p < .0001$. Specific comparisons between the single enhancement features (pictorial, color, icon or border) and the baseline (the warning with "none" of the salience items) indicated that, while response times were shortened by the addition of these features, none of them resulted in a statistically significant improvement. A *post hoc* test of the manipulations showed that combinations of the features (represented by the three bars on the right of Figure 3) did result in total response times that were shorter by an amount that was statistically significant ($p < .05$).

Location Time. A similar one-way ANOVA on location time showed a significant main effect of the design variable, $F(7,110) = 2.65$, $p < .02$. Specific comparisons between the single feature conditions (pictorial, color, icon or border) and the "none" condition indicated that, while response times were shortened by the addition of these features, none of

them alone resulted in a statistically significant effect. Again, a *post hoc* test showed that the combinations of features did have a statistically significant effect ($p < .05$), as represented by the two bars on the right of Figure 3.

Decision Time. A one-way ANOVA on decision time showed a significant main effect of the design variable, $F(7,110) = 4.68$, $p < .0001$. Specific comparisons between the pictorial and the "none" conditions and between the icon and the "non" conditions indicated that response times were shortened when a pictorial was included, $p < .02$. The effect of icon was in the expected direction, but was not significant ($p > .05$). Combinations of the features (the last two bars in Figure 3) did show a statistically significant improvement in decision times ($p < .05$).

Scanning Sequences. In addition to the time analyses listed above, subjects' scanning sequences of the five different label zones were examined. The present analysis was limited to scans of labels with no enhancement features, which included three labels with warnings and three with no warnings. The reason for limiting the analysis to these stimuli was to focus on subject scanning strategies independent of the attracting effect of the design features. As noted earlier, subjects' scanning sequences began with Zone 1, the zone in the center of the screen containing product brand information. Thus, Zone 1 was always the first stop in the scanning sequence. Analysis of the two zones that subjects looked at after leaving Zone 1 showed no discernable pattern across subjects.

DISCUSSION

The results of the total time analysis are generally consistent with findings reported by Young (in press). Responses regarding the presence of a warning were faster when the warning included combinations of the attention-enhancing features. Further, the magnitude of these effects

Figure 3. Total response times for each warning condition divided into location time (shaded region) and decision time (unshaded region).

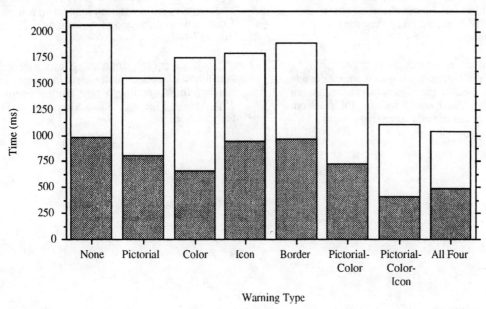

133

were substantial. From Figure 3, the mean total response time when the warning contained no enhancement features (2064 ms) was reduced by 50% (to 1038 ms) when all four features were present and by 47% (to 1109 ms) with the pictorial, icon and color features. Individually, these manipulations did not result in statistically shorter response times, although all of these times were in the direction of being shorter.

Results of the location and decision time analyses provide a more detailed picture of where and how the enhancement features influence the noticeability of warnings. Clearly, both the process of finding or noticing the warning and the process of deciding if the information in a zone is a warning is enhanced by combinations of the features. Again, the magnitudes of these effects are substantial, on the order of 50% improvement for both measures.

Our predictions included differential effects of the various enhancement features on the location and decision phases of the response times. For location time, the effects of the individual features did not produce statistically significant improvements at the usual $p < .05$ level, although in a few cases they were close. For example, the location time was 32% shorter when the warning included color ($p = .088$). Regardless of the statistical significance, all of the outcomes were in the expected direction. For decision times, it was predicted that the presence of a pictorial or an icon would show an improvement because they contain warning-redundant information. This hypothesis could not be supported for icon, but was supported for pictorial, which produced a 29% improvement in decision times ($p < .05$). Regarding the third prediction, there were no differential effects of border on location or decision times.

Overall the results of this study are consistent with the notion that enhancement features, such as pictorials, color, and, to a lesser extent, icons and borders, can result in warnings being more noticeable or attention orienting. This conclusion is especially true when the features are used in combination. Also, pictorials allow information to be recognized as a warning more quickly. Combined with the location findings, it seems that designers of warnings should give consideration to pictorials when designing warnings. It should also be kept in mind that the beneficial effects of pictorials are substantially increased when they are paired with other salience features.

A final point here concerns the use of eye movement procedures in studying the effects of various warning design factors. This study focussed on the effects of various design parameters on noticing and interpreting warning information. While these measures are not directly assessing people's

behavioral responses to a warning, they do represent critical phases in the sequence of steps that determine if a warning will be effective. Miller and Lehto (1986) have applied an information processing model to warning effectiveness that notes a sequence of steps that must be successfully completed if a warning is to accomplish its purpose. These steps include noticing (attending), reading (processing), understanding, forming appropriate intentions, and carrying out the appropriate behavior. Eye movement data can be particularly useful in developing a better understanding of the earlier stages in this model. The results reported here are examples of such data applied to the first stage.

REFERENCES

DeJoy, D. M. (1989). Consumer product warnings: Review and analysis of effectiveness research. In <u>Proceedings of the Human Factors Society 33rd Annual Meeting</u>. Santa Monica, CA: The Human Factors Society. pp.936-940.

Fischer, P. M., Richards, J. W., Berman, E. J. & Krugman, D. M. (1989). Recall and eye tracking study of adolescents viewing tobacco advertisements. <u>The Journal of the American Medical Association</u>, <u>261</u>, 84-89.

Laughery, K. R. & Young, S. L. (in press). Consumer product warnings: Design factors that influence noticeability. In <u>Proceedings of the 11th Congress International Ergonomics Association</u>. Paris.

Miller, J. M. & Lehto, M. (1986). <u>Warnings: Volume I: Fundamentals, Design, and Evaluation Methodologies</u>. Ann Arbor, MI: Fuller Technical Publications.

Strawbridge, J. A. (1986). The influence of position, highlighting, and imbedding on warning effectiveness. In <u>Proceedings of the Human Factors Society - 30th Annual Meeting</u>. Santa Monica: The Human Factors Society, 716-720.

Young, S. L. & Wogalter, M. S. (1990). Comprehension and memory of instruction manual warnings: Conspicuous print and pictorial icons. <u>Human Factors</u>, <u>32</u>, 637-649.

Young, S.L. (in press). Increasing the noticeability of warnings: Effects of pictorial, color, signal icon and border. In <u>Proceedings of the Human Factors Society 35th Annual Meeting</u>. Santa Monica, CA: The Human Factors Society.

PEST-CONTROL PRODUCTS: READING WARNINGS AND PURCHASING INTENTIONS

David C. Leonard
Psychology Department
University of Richmond
Richmond, VA 23173

Kathryn A. Ponsi
Psychology Department
University of Richmond
Richmond, VA 23173

N. Clayton Silver
Psychology Department
Appalachian State University
Boone, NC 28608

Michael S. Wogalter
Psychology Department
Rensselaer Polytechnic Institute
Troy, NY 12180

ABSTRACT

This research is part of a large study examining people's perceptions of household pest-control products. Described in this report are the variables associated with peoples' willingness to read warnings on these products and the variables associated with likelihood to purchase. Two subject samples, comprised of 70 undergraduates and 20 adults, examined 22 pest-control products and responded to a questionnaire assessing perceptions of the products, the packaging, and the warnings. Results showed that product hazardousness, warning understandability, and warning attractiveness strongly related to subjects willingness to read the warnings. Unexpectedly, readability analyses indicated subjects would more likely read warnings with more sentences/statements and written at higher grade levels. A different set of variables was related to purchasing intentions. Subjects reported greater willingness to purchase products that were more familiar and which had more attractive packaging. Regression analyses were also performed to obtain models predictive of reading warnings and purchasing intentions. The results are discussed in terms of manufacturers' concerns of sales and consumer safety. The relative independence of subjects' purchasing intentions and the variables related to reading warnings suggests that manufacturers can place appropriate and effective warnings on pest-control products without the fear of reduced buying intentions.

INTRODUCTION

Based on a sample of representative hospitals in the U.S., the National Electronic Injury Surveillance System (NEISS) estimates that in 1988, 14,736 people were admitted to emergency rooms for pesticide product-related injury (U.S. Consumer Product Safety Commission, 1988). Of these injuries, 88.3% were released following medical treatment, while 11.7% resulted in hospitalization. Most pest-control products contain warnings and instructions, many of which are required by the Federal Insecticide, Fungicide, Rodenticide Act (McKenna, Conner, & Cuneo, 1987) for the purpose of warning consumers against misuse and accidents. Despite the presence of warnings and the extensive publicity in the media, people are apparently not adequately aware of the potential misuse of pesticides as evidenced by the number of injuries.

The purpose of the present research was to examine people's perceptions of one category of consumer pesticides, household pest-control products. One focus of the present report was to investige the variables predictive of reading warnings on these products.

Prior research has examined variables related to reading instructions and warnings for a wide range of various product categories. Using a list of 60 products, Wright, Creighton, and Threlfall (1982) found that subjects were less likely to read instructions for products used frequently and simple to operate. However, other attitudes, including product safety, did not relate to willingness to read instructions. Godfrey and Laughery (1984) surveyed women on their awareness of the hazards of tampon use, knowledge of the symptoms of toxic shock syndrome, and awareness of warnings. They found that females who were more familiar with tampon products were less likely to notice warnings when they subsequently switched brands.

Using eight generic names of common consumer products (including plant food, oven cleaner, and pesticide)

as stimuli, Godfrey, Allender, Laughery, and Smith (1983) found that subjects would be more likely to look for warnings on less familiar and more hazardous products. However, for products that were most hazardous (e.g., pesticide), subjects' degree of familiarity did not matter: Subjects still reported they would look for and read warnings.

Wogalter et al. (1986) also examined the relationship between willingness to read warnings and perceptions of hazardousness and familiarity. Ratings of 72 consumer products indicated that while perceptions of hazardousness and familiarity are both highly related to willingness to read warnings, perception of hazardousness was the most important determinant of people's reported willingness to read warnings.

Thus, prior research suggests that reading warnings can be predicted from perceptions of hazardousness, and to some extent, familiarity. However, subjects in these studies rated a wide range of consumer goods and were exposed to generic product names--not to actual products. Thus, it is not clear whether perceptions of hazardousness and familiarity are useful predictors of reading warnings when subjects are exposed to actual products and when products within a class (pest-control products) are considered rather than a range of consumer products. Would the results found in earlier research be confirmed? In particular, would willingness to read warnings be predicted by product hazardousness and familiarity?

Also examined was whether warning understandability/comprehensibility is a useful predictor of reading warnings. The importance of warning comprehensibility is self evident: Warnings need to be understood to be effective. Warning comprehensibility was assessed in two ways: (1) Subjects rated the warnings on understandability, and (2) the warning text was analyzed by two standard readability formulae.

Would these measures be related to willingness to read warnings?

Another purpose of the present report was to examine whether purchasing intentions can be accounted for by the same variables predictive of reading warnings, and if not, to determine the types of variables related to likelihood of purchasing pest-control products. There are two reasons why this relationship was of interest. The first is the often heard claim offered by manufacturers in litigation cases for not including strong (and perhaps, more effective) warnings on their products: It will scare consumers and decrease sales. The second reason comes from an intriguing finding of Ursic (1984). Ursic presented subjects with display boards containing information on three hypothetical brands of bug killers and hair dryers in which warnings were manipulated. Ursic found that people perceive products with warnings to be safer and more effective. However, variations in the warnings' format had no effect. The present research asked: Would people's purchase decisions be influenced by warning-related variables?

METHOD

Subjects

Seventy University of Richmond freshmen participated for class credit in their introductory psychology courses. A second group, consisting of 20 adults (M = 36.95, SD = 7.70), were paid for their participation.

Four pesticide experts were asked to evaluate the products' hazardousness. One was employed by the Virginia Department of Health's Toxic Substance Information Department, one with the Virginia Department of Agriculture and Consumer Services' Office of Pesticide Regulation, and two were administrators with different professional pest-control organizations.

Materials and Procedure

Twenty-six household pest-control products that are available over-the-counter in hardware, drug, and grocery

Table 1. Pest-Control Products Categorized by Type.

Fumigators		
	Hobbs	Raid
Foggers		
	Black flag	d-Con
	Hot Shot	No-Roach
	Raid	Real Kill
	Rid-A-Bug	TNT
Sprays		
	Black Flag	Combat
	d-Con	Hot Shot
	No-roach	Raid
	Real Kill	TAT
Controller Systems		
	Black Flag	Combat
	d-Con	Raid

stores were purchased. All of the products were claimed to control roach problems. Flying-insect sprays and agricultural pesticide products were not included. Product brands were selected for inclusion based on their being sold in at least three chain stores in the Richmond, Virginia area. Of the original set, four were roach traps which did not contain warnings on the packaging. Because the primary interest of this report was to examine the variables related to reading warnings, analyses of the trap data will not be discussed here. The 22 included products are shown in Table 1 categorized by product type.

A product perception questionnaire was used to assess subjects' perceptions of the products' packaging, labeling, and warnings. Responses were recorded using 8-point Likert-type scales anchored with 0 denoting absence of quantity to 8 indicating maximum quantity. Items from the questionnaire are shown in Table 2.

Table 2. Product Perception Questionnaire.

1. "*How hazardous* do you think the product is?" with the anchors: (0) not at all hazardous, (2) somewhat hazardous, (4) hazardous, (6) very hazardous, and (8) extremely hazardous.
2. "*How familiar* are you with this product?" with the anchors: (0) not at all familiar, (2) somewhat familiar, (4) familiar, (6) very familiar, and (8) extremely familiar.
3. "*How likely* is it that you would *read* the warning on the *back* (or side) panel of the package?" with the anchors: (0) never, (2) unlikely, (4) likely, (6) very likely, and (8) extremely likely.
4. "*How understandable* is the warning on the *back* (or side) panel of the package?" with the anchors: (0) not at all, (2) somewhat understandable, (4) understandable, (6) very understandable, and (8) extremely understandable.
5. "*How attractive* (appealing) is the warning label on the *back* (or side) panel of the package?" with the anchors: (0) not at all attractive, (2) somewhat attractive, (4) attractive, (6) very attractive, and (8) extremely attractive.
6. "*How attractive* (appealing) is the packaging of this product in general?" with the anchors: (0) not at all attractive, (2) somewhat attractive, (4) attractive, (6) very attractive, and (8) extremely attractive.
7. "*How strong* (potent) do you think the product is?" with the anchors: (0) not at all strong, (2) somewhat strong, (4) attractive, (6) very strong, and (8) extremely strong.
8. "*How careful* would you be when using this product?" with the anchors: (0) not at all careful, (2) somewhat careful, (4) careful, (6) very careful, and (8) extremely careful.
9. "*How likely* are you to be injured in any way while using this product?" with the anchors: (0) never, (2) unlikely, (4) likely, (6) very likely, and (8) extremely likely.
10. "*How difficult* would it be to use this product?" with the anchors: (0) not at all difficult, (2) somewhat difficult, (4) difficult, (6) very difficult, and (8) extremely difficult.
11. "*How likely* are you to *purchase* this product?" with the anchors: (0) never, (2) unlikely, (4) likely, (6) very likely, and (8) extremely likely.

All 22 products contained the same basic three-line front-panel warning:

KEEP OUT OF REACH OF CHILDREN
CAUTION
See back (side) panel for additional precautionary statements

This front-panel warning is required by the Federal Insecticide, Fungicide, and Rodenticide Act (McKenna, Conner, & Cuneo, 1987). Because the front-panel warning was nearly identical for all products, the items of the questionnaire assessing its perception will not be reported here. Rather, the present report focusses on perceptions of the longer back- (or side) panel warnings

The large study also included collection of subject demographics and other product-related data. The demographic information included sex, age, place of residence, prior pest-control problems, and previous use of pest-control products. Products were coded for objective characteristics such as chemical contents (e.g., active and inert ingredients and percentages), duration of effectiveness, pests effective against, packaging characteristics, characteristics of the warnings (e.g., location on package, text formatting, size, and color). The content of the warnings were also categorized and coded including mention of symptoms, antidote, danger to pets, note to physician, and poison hot-line information. Analyses of the demographic and the objective product characteristics data will not be discussed in this report.

Product Perception Procedure. Subjects were run in groups of three to eight. The pest-control products were placed on tables in a large room each next to a numbered identification. After completing a demographics question-naire, subjects were given the product perception questionnaire and a booklet of randomly-ordered response forms. They were told that each response form was numbered to correspond to one of the products in the room, that they were to examine each of the products in the order indicated by his or her own response form packet, and to complete the questionnaire for each product before moving to the next one. For safety reasons, subjects were allowed to handle the products but not to operate them in any way.

Readability. Measures of readability of the back-(or side) panel warning text were obtained. Because many statements on the containers lacked punctuation, prior to the readability assessments, punctuation was added where appropriate to avoid erroneous sentence length scores. Each label was analyzed for the number of words, number of sentences/statements, and two measures of reading grade level: the Flesch index (1948) as modified by Gray (1975), and the Coleman and Liau (1975) index. Because it was difficult to distinguish between warnings and instructions on the labels, a warning was thus defined as all text containing signal words, directions/instructions for preparation, proper use, and storage/disposal, and text that described physical, chemical and environmental hazards.

RESULTS

Subject ratings for each product and question were collapsed producing 22 product means for each of the rated questions and these scores (pest-control products) were used as the random variable in the analyses. The expert ratings of the products' hazardousness validated the students', $r = .931$, $p < .001$, and adults' $r = .609$, $p < .001$, perceptions of the pest-control products' hazardousness.

Likelihood of Reading Warnings

Student Perceptions. Initial analyses of the student data sought to determine the variables related to subjects' likelihood of reading warnings. Table 3 shows that willingness to read warnings was significantly and positively related to product hazardousness, judged understandability of the warning, attractiveness of the warning, carefulness when using the product, and likelihood of being injured while using the product.

Adult Perceptions. Table 3 also shows the correlations for the adult subjects. In general, the relationships were smaller for the adults than the were for the students but they demonstrate a similar pattern. Like the student subjects, willingness to read warnings was significantly and positively related to product hazardousness, judged understandability of the warnings, and attractiveness of the warnings. In addition, strength/potency and difficulty in using the product was positively related to willingness to read the warnings. The positive relationships of willingness to read warnings with carefulness and injury likelihood that were seen with the student data were not shown.

Likelihood of Purchasing

Student Perceptions. For the most part, a different set of variables was related to likelihood of purchasing the products. Likelihood of purchasing was positively related to product familiarity, packaging attractiveness, and product strength/potency, and was negatively related to product hazardousness, likelihood of being injured, and difficulty of using the product. Thus, only two variables in the set, hazardousness and likelihood of injury, were significantly related with both willingness to read the warning and likelihood to purchase; however, the relationships were relatively small and in opposite directions. The simple

Table 3. Correlations of Willingness to Read and Likelihood to Purchase Pest-Control Products with Perception Variables of Student and Adult Subjects.

	Students		Adults	
	Read Warning	Likely to Purchase	Read Warning	Likely to Purchase
Hazardousness	.643**	-.429*	.498*	.059
Familiar Product	-.036	.951**	.189	.858**
Understand Warning	.931**	.029	.893**	.287
Attractive Warning	.892**	.118	.685**	.370
Attractive Package	-.098	.777**	.255	.772**
Strong/Potent	.350	.760**	.518*	.462*
Careful Using	.510*	-.404	.239	-.238
Injury Likelihood	.449*	-.476*	.294	-.087
Difficult to Use	.233	-.461*	.449*	-.184

* $p < .05$
** $p < .01$

correlation between willingness to read the warning and likelihood of purchasing the product was not significant ($r = .038$, $p > .05$).

Adult Perceptions. For likelihood to purchase, the adults, like the students, showed positive relationships with product familiarity, packaging attractiveness, and product strength/potency, but unlike the students, the adults showed no relationship with injury likelihood and difficulty of using the product. The simple correlation between willingness to read the warning and likelihood of purchasing the product was not significant ($r = .259$, $p > .05$).

Readability

Judgments of warning understandability was strongly and positively related to willingness to read warnings. An additional set of analyses examined whether readability of the warnings as assessed by two readability formulae would relate to willingness to read warnings. Table 4 shows for both the students and the adults, willingness to read the warnings was positively related to the number of sentence/statements and to both reading grade-level indices.

Table 4. *Correlations of Willingness to Read with Readability Variables for Student and Adult Subjects.*

| | Willingness to Read Warnings | |
	Students	Adults
Number of Words	.401	.342
Number of Sentences	.614**	.444*
Flesch Index	.552**	.456*
Coleman-Liau Index	.446*	.492*

   * $p < .05$
  ** $p < .01$

Prediction of Reading Warnings

Multiple regression analyses were used to determine the variables that contribute to the prediction of willingness to read warnings. Because previous research (Godfrey, et al., 1983; Godfrey & Laughery, 1984; Wogalter, et al., 1986) suggests that hazardousness and familiarity might be important factors used by people in judging whether to read warnings, regression models including these factors were considered first.

Student Data. Alone, hazardousness accounted for 41.3% of the variance, $F(1, 20) = 16.06$, $p < .002$. With the inclusion of familiarity, the increment of 4.2% was not significant, $F(1, 19) = 1.47$, $p > .05$. Additional regression analyses showed that warning understandability and warning attractiveness each added significant unique variance to the model containing hazardousness (p's $< .0001$). When all three predictors were included the variance accounted for was substantial (96.1%), $F(3, 18) = 148.47$, $p < .0001$. No other variables (including the readability measures) significantly improved this prediction model.

Adult Data. The hazardousness variable accounted for 24.8% of the variance of willingness to read the warnings, $F(1, 20) = 6.58$, $p < .02$. The addition of product familiarity did not significantly enhance prediction (by .6%), $F(1, 19) < 1.0$. The addition of warning attractiveness to the model including hazardousness incremented the prediction of reading warnings (by 33.1%), $F(1, 19) = 14.96$, $p < .001$. The further addition of understandability significantly enhanced the model (by 24.0%), $F(1, 18) = 23.92$, $p < .0001$. No other individual variable added to the prediction of willingness to read. The regression model with hazardousness, warning attractiveness, and warning understandability accounted for 81.9% of the variance of willingness to read, $F(3, 18) = 27.19$, $p < .0001$.

Prediction of Purchase Intentions

Multiple regression analyses were also used to determine the variables that predict likelihood to purchase the products.

Student Data. Alone, product familiarity accounted for 90.5% of the variance of purchase intentions, $F(1, 20) = 191.21$, $p < .0001$. Product attractiveness added a small but significant increment of variance accounted for (by 2.0%), $F(1, 19) = 4.96$, $p < .04$. Adding a third predictor, difficulty of using the product, further enhanced the prediction (by 2.2%), $F(1, 18) = 7.55$, $p < .02$. No other individual variable added significant variance to the model. The regression model with familiarity, product attractiveness, and difficulty of use accounted for 94.7% of the variance of willingness to purchase, $F(3, 18) = 107.45$, $p < .0001$.

Adult Data. Product familiarity accounted for 73.6% of the variance of purchase intentions, $F(1, 20) = 55.65$, $p < .0001$. Product attractiveness added significant variance to the prediction (by 6.2%), $F(1, 19) = 5.86$, $p < .03$. No other individual variable added significantly to the model. The regression model with familiarity and product attractiveness accounted for 79.8% of the variance of willingness to purchase, $F(2, 19) = 37.52$, $p < .0001$.

DISCUSSION

Earlier research (e.g., Wright et. al, 1982; Godfrey & Laughery, 1984) suggested that product familiarity was related to reading warnings and instructions. The present results failed to find this relationship. The results, however, do indicate that perceived hazardousness is an important determinant of willingness to read warnings. That hazard perception is more important than perceptions of familiarity with regard to willingness to read warnings on dangerous products supports the basic conclusions of Godfrey et. al (1983) and Wogalter et. al (1986). For example, Godfrey et. al's (1983) found that familiarity was negatively related to looking for warnings on low hazard products, but for products like pesticide, hazardousness predicted reading warnings and the degree of familiarity did not.

Two other variables, the perceived understandability and attractiveness of the warnings, were shown by correlational and multiple regression analyses to be related to reading warnings. These results suggest that the appearance of the warning enhances people's willingness to read warnings. Apparently, good warning design can be a means of motivating people to seek out hazard information.

Another measure of understandability, readability, was also assessed. It had been expected that people would be more willing to read shorter, lower grade-level warnings, since most warning guidelines recommend that good warnings be concise and written for the lowest denominator of the reading public. However, the present results did not find this. Indeed, the results were significant in the opposite direction. Correlational results showed that subjects were more willing to read warnings on products that had text with containing more sentences/statements and more difficult material. On average, both readability formulae indicated that the warnings were written at approximately at the tenth-grade level. Given that our subjects were taken from populations having higher reading levels than the general population, this finding becomes less surprising. Our subjects might have preferred reading material closer to their reading level than material at lower levels. Subjects may have been willing to read longer warnings based on the assumption that they contained information that they did not know, and needed to know. More hazardous products would more likely have longer warnings in order to convey the dangers and necessary precautionary information. Because this is relational data, it is difficult to determine the direction of cause and effect: It might be that warnings with more information and having more difficult material cause perceptions of hazardousness.

Variables related to likelihood of purchasing the pest-control products were also examined. Of particular interest was to determine whether purchasing intentions could be accounted for by the same variables predictive of reading warnings. The results showed no evidence of a relationship between buying intentions and reading warnings. Familiarity and packaging attractiveness appeared to be the primary predictors of likelihood to purchase and these variables held no relationship to reading warnings. Thus, the present results suggest that in order to increase consumers' purchase intentions, manufacturers should take steps to increase consumers' familiarity with their product e.g., via advertising), and should make their product more appealing to the eye (to increase packaging attractiveness). Enhancement of these variables are apparently more likely to affect sales than variables related to the warnings.

Increasing perceptions of hazardousness, warning understandability, and warning attractiveness may facilitate that warnings will be read. The relative independence of buying intentions for these products and willingness to read warnings suggests that manufacturers can place appropriate and effective warnings on pest-control products and not be concerned with lowered consumer buying intentions. That is, better warnings should have the positive effect of reducing accidental injury, but at the same time not effecting consumer buying intentions. This finding should eliminate

manufacturers' fears that warnings that effectively convey hazard information will consequently reduce sales. Instead, manufacturers should concern themselves with the high rate of pesticide product-related accidents due to misuse, which hopefully can be reduced with effective warning labels.

Finally, it should be noted that these conclusions might be limited to the set of products used in the present research. Whether the relative independence of the warning-related variables and purchasing decisions holds for other consumer other than pest-control products is an empircal question that needs further investigation; however, recent results by Stanush and Laughery (1989) suggests that the present finding might be generalizable to other classes of products as well.

REFERENCES

Coleman, M., & Liau, T. L. (1975). A computer readability formula designed for machine scoring. *Journal of Applied Psychology, 60,* 283-284.

Flesch, R. F. (1948). A new readability yardstick. *Journal of Applied Psychology, 32,* 384-390.

Godfrey, S. S., Allender, L., Laughery, K. R., & Smith, V. L. (1983). Warning messages: Will the consumer bother to look? In *Proceedings of the Human Factors Society 27th Annual Meeting* (pp. 950-954). Santa Monica, CA: The Human Factors Society.

Godfrey, S. S. & Laughery, K. R. (1984). The biasing effects of product familiarity on consumers' awareness of hazard. In *Proceedings of the Human Factors Society 28th Annual Meeting.* Santa Monica, CA: The Human Factors Society.

Gray, W. B. (1975). *How to measure readability.* Philadelphia: Dorrance and Co.

McKenna, Conner, & Cuneo. (1987). *Pesticide Regulation Handbook, Revised.* Washington, D.C.: Executive Enterprises Publications Co., Inc.

Stanush, J. A., & Laughery, K. R. (1989). Effects of warning explicitness on product perceptions. In *Proceedings of the Human Factors Society 33rd Annual Meeting.* Santa Monica, CA: The Human Factors Society.

U.S. Consumer Product Safety Commission (1988). *Preliminary NEISS Estimates of National Injuries,* Washington D.C.

Ursic, M., (1984). The impact of safety warnings on perception and memory. *Human Factors, 26,* 677-682.

Wogalter, M. S., Desaulniers, D. R., & Brelsford, J. W. (1986). Perceptions of consumer products: Hazardous- ness and warning expectations. In *Proceedings of the Human Factors Society 30th Annual Meeting* (pp. 1197-1201). Santa Monica, CA: The Human Factors Society.

Wright, P., Creighton, P., & Threlfall, S. M. (1982). Some factors determining when instructions will be read. *Applied Ergonomics, 25,* 225-237.

Wright, P. (1981). "The instructions clearly state..." Can't people read? In *Applied Ergonomics, 12,* 131-141.

How Does the Population Interpret Warning Signals?

S. David Leonard and David Matthews
University of Georgia

Edward W. Karnes
Metropolitan State College

ABSTRACT

The experiment concerns the problem of responding appropriately to warnings. Some organizations, such as the military and the American National Standards Institute have adopted particular meanings for certain signal words. The population at large is not trained in these respects. Therefore, it is not known how they interpret different signal words. In keeping with the assumption that the stronger the warning, the more likely it will be heeded, an effort was made to determine how the population in general differentiates levels of warnings. The study examined population stereotypes for various signal words. Contrary to some studies (cf. Karnes and Leonard, 1986), no differences were found in ratings of perception of risk to different signal words. Further, size of the signal word and color of the signal word had no effect on perception of risk. Statements of consequences of disregarding the warnings and type of risk situation did affect rated perception of risk. Also, circumstances in which the subjects might be placed affected ratings of likelihood of disregarding warnings. These results were discussed in terms of an adaptation level of information for perception of risk.

INTRODUCTION

The experiment described here relates to the problem of what effects signal words have on how people respond to warnings. It seems reasonable that the stronger the warning, the more likely it will be heeded, yet little research information is available on how the general population differentiates levels of warnings. Some organizations, such as the military and the American National Standards Institute (ANSI) have adopted particular meanings for certain signal words. One might presume that organizations that use these standards would offer training, at least to some of their members, in the meanings given to these signal words. But the population at large is not trained in these meanings. Thus, we wanted to obtain information about the population stereotypes for these terms.

Theoretical Background

Several aspects of warning signs concern human factors workers. One of the most important concerns is how warnings affect the behavior of individuals. In essence, the basic assumption for the use of warnings is that they will affect behavior. Dorris and Purswell (1977) listed these criteria for warnings:

1) the warning message must be received; 2) the message must be understood; 3) the individual must act in accordance with the message. (p. 256).

Although recognizing the need to develop standards of visibility and legibility, our concern in the experiment reported here is with the last two of these criteria.

Dorris and Purswell (1977) found that people often do not follow warnings. The conclusion of McCarthy, Finnegan, Krumm-Scott, and McCarthy

(1984) from an extensive review of the literature was that there was no evidence of effectiveness of warning signs. Lerner (1985) has noted the difficulty in making warnings realistic, in that individuals' "benign" experiences may contradict warnings. Further, McCarthy, Robinson, Finnegan, and Taylor (1982) stated that excessive warnings might become counterproductive by competing with one another for attention.

Despite these caveats, some evidence exists that warnings may at least elicit some attention. Wright, Creighton, and Threlfall (1982) obtained subjective impressions of whether or not instructions might be read and found that more complex items and items assumed to be dangerous produced greater subjective likelihood that the instructions would be read. Further, Godfrey, et al. (1983) suggest that the tendency to look for warning messages on labels of potentially dangerous household products may vary with perceived hazard of the product. Although warnings may be read, it is more to determine experimentally that the warnings have an effect. As Peters (1985) points out: Moral, ethical, and legal considerations legislate against experimentation in some situations.

Godfrey, Rothstein, and Laughery (1985) presented evidence for the effectiveness of warnings in naturalistic settings. They found that compliance with warnings on a copy machine, a telephone, a water fountain, and a door was fairly good, but compliance decreased when the cost (in time or effort) was high. Attitudes toward products that carry warnings was evaluated by Ursic (1984), who concluded that the presence of a warning had a positive impact on individuals' perceptions of the effectiveness and safety of a brand.

Factors that influence the perception of risk are not immediately apparent; however, it would seem that some higher-order conditioning of fear responses might occur as various words are used in conjunction with words or situations having previously developed aversive properties. Thus, if the word 'danger' is associated with death on numerous occasions, it might acquire a stronger connotation of risk than a word such as 'notice' that had been more commonly associated with less serious circumstances. If this is the case, warnings accompanied by some signal words should produce a greater perception of risk than when accompanied by other signal words. To test this hypothesis the words caution, warning, and danger were used in conjunction with a number of sources of injury or other harmful effects and subjects were asked to rate their perception of the risks involved.

METHOD

Subjects. A total of 368 subjects were drawn from psychology courses at the University of Georgia (UGA), a largely residential institution in a small city that draws undergraduates who are in the main just out of high school, and Metropolitan State College (MSC), a commuter school drawing many nontraditional students from a metropolitan area with a population of 1.5 million or more. At UGA 142 females and 123 males who received credit for participating in a large group session where several questionnaires were filled out completed usable data sheets. MSC subjects participated in class, and 56 females and 47 males elected to complete the form.

Materials and Procedure.

Questionnaires were devised to vary size of warning signal, color of sign, and presence or absence of a statement of consequences. These factors were combined with each of three signal words (Caution, Warning, and Danger). The questionnaires were produced by simulating 12 signs that described 12 different hazards, for example, electric shock. Each of these signs were made in a form with each of the signal words.

The signs were produced by using Helvetica Medium dry transfer lettering. All signs were made in a form with each signal word, (caution, warning or danger). On some signs the signal word was twice the height of the remainder of the words on the sign, while on others the signal word was the same size as all others. On some signs the signal word was first produced in 48-point type. (Large Condition) and on the others it was produced in 24-point type (Small Condition). All signs had a brief description, in 24-point type, of the hazard and a recommended action, for example, explosives, keep away. On some of the signs no other information was given (No Consequence Condition), and on the others a brief statement in 24-point type of what might happen (you could be destroyed) if the sign were disregarded (Consequence condition). The signs were then reduced by 35 per cent and printed four signs to the page on the left hand half of the page for No Consequences items. The final heights of the letters were 8 mm for the large letters and 4 mm for the small letters. A rectangular border 3 mm thick surrounded each sign. These signs were reproduced in red and in

black on white paper. Finally, a statement was typed (in black elite type) for each sign to fit the right hand side of the page indicating where the sign might be located, for example, on the side of a portable shed. Booklets of three pages with four signs to a page were compiled. The signs were presented in the same order with respect to content in each booklet, but each booklet contained one page with the caution condition, one page with the warning condition, and one page with the danger condition. The order of the signal words was counterbalanced in a Latin square design. Thus, signal word was a within subject factor for the No Consequence condition.

The same set of descriptions was used in the Consequences condition, but no red signs were used in this condition. In addition, because of print size, the booklets were compiled with four pages of three signs to a page. A further difference was that for the Consequences condition all signs in a booklet had the same signal word. This allowed for a between subjects test of this condition. All booklets had the same cover sheet instructing the subjects to rate the amount of risk on a scale from one, almost no risk or danger of personal injury, to seven, extremely high risk or danger of personal injury.

The extent to which signs might produce compliance by the subjects was also examined. An additional booklet was prepared with two sets of 12 situations that were paired with the 12 signs. These described possible scenarios involving the individual and the objects of the signs. For example, referring to the sign involving explosives in a portable shed the scenarios were as follows:

1. Someone tosses a Frisbee from a car, and it lands on top of the shed. You are asked to climb on top of the shed to retrieve the Frisbee.

2. A gust of wind takes the term paper that you must turn in within an hour or get an F, and it lands on top of the shed. You must climb up on the shed to get it.

Subjects were instructed to rate each situation on a seven-point scale as to whether they would obey or disregard the sign in this particular situation. Subjects were also instructed not to change any of their previously made ratings of risk during the compliance rating phase of the experiment. Most subjects complied with this request, but data from two subjects were dropped because they failed to do so.

Subjects were run in groups, and the various forms were distributed in a haphazard fashion with an effort being made to get approximately equal numbers of each form distributed within each group. Because the Consequences forms were not available when the MSC group was sampled, they were used only with the UGA subjects. In addition, some of the forms with red signs were discovered to be printed incorrectly, and data based on them were discarded, resulting in an imbalance in numbers between the red and the black conditions.

Table 1

Means of Ratings of Perception of Risk and
Likelihood of Disregarding Warning Signs

Hazard	No con- sequences	Conse- quences	No con- sequences	Conse- quences	No con- sequences	Conse- quences
Radiation hazard	5.51	5.59	3.43	3.42	3.89	4.16
Power saw	4.64	4.38	3.70	3.47	4.01	3.70
Explosives	4.76	5.45*	3.02	2.79	4.86	4.68
Electric shock	5.15	6.06*	2.16	1.96	3.51	3.23
Shallow water	3.58	3.93	2.47	2.75	4.06	3.98
Amusement park ride	3.66	3.71	3.25	3.16	3.34	3.05
Gymnastic equipment	3.26	3.79*	4.36	3.84*	3.47	3.17
Car battery	2.75	4.01*	3.50	3.13	3.53	3.01
Pressurized can	2.01	3.06*	4.71	4.16*	4.87	4.32
Toxic cleaner	4.35	4.72*	2.32	2.34	2.97	2.78
Contaminated water	5.28	5.56	1.89	2.09	4.97	4.48
Over-counter pills	3.99	4.34	3.64	3.34	4.16	3.68

NOTE. No consequence group included only black signs. Situation 2 produced no significant interaction, but overall effects were significant.

*$p < .05$

RESULTS

Because of the unequal sample sizes obtained in using intact groups, the data were first examined to determine whether or not differences existed between the male and female respondents by testing each of the subsets with t-tests. Of the twelve comparisons made, six showed higher ratings by males and six by females. Only one test reached statistical significance. Thus, it was concluded that no differences existed as a function of sex, and the male and female subjects were combined in further analyses. An ANOVA performed on the data from the black forms with groups as a between subject factor and signal order as a within subjects factor showed no effect of group membership, signal order, or their interaction. In all cases the **F**-values were less than 1. Thus, UGA and MSC subjects were pooled for further analyses.

The analyses of concern for the differences among signal words were comparisons of the sets of items having the same hazards described but different signal words. Totals on each set of four items were computed for each subject and comparisons

were made for the different sets. Comparisons were made within the orders for the No Consequence condition sets and for the parallel sets in the Consequences condition. Although the Consequences condition was between subjects, the overall ratings of the sets varied and it was assumed that a greater effect of signal word would be associated with situations that would evoke lesser perceptions of risk. Contrary to expectations, no effects of signal words were found in any of the analyses of either perceived risk or compliance whether in the Consequences or No Consequences conditions. Most **F**-values were less than 1, and none suggested a reliable effect. In all cases, however, there were significant differences among the sets within the same order indicating differences in perceptions of risk for different hazards. Similar analyses for the effects of the different motivational situations on likelihood of disregarding the signs were performed, and the same type of results were obtained. Generally, more noncompliance was associated with lesser hazards.

Analyses of the effect of the size of the signal words were performed in both the red and black sign conditions and in the consequences conditions, separately, and no significant effects of signal word size or of the interaction with the subset condition were found.

One other set of analyses compared the overall red, black, and consequences conditions for the ratings of perception of risk and also for the separate motivational conditions. As with size and signal words no effect of color differences were obtained, but in the test of risk perception and in the test of the second set of compliance conditions the Consequences condition was significantly different from both the red and black No Consequence conditions. There were no significant differences among these groups in the first compliance condition. The overall mean risk perception for the Consequences group was 54.60, and the means for the red and black sign groups were 47.87 and 48.94. Consonant with this, the ratings of likelihood of disregarding the signs were 44.18 for the Consequences group and 47.45 and 47.64 for the red sign and black sign groups. Thus, although color of sign had no effect, a statement of the consequences that might result from failure to obey the sign did affect both risk perceptions and ratings of expected behavior.

Because of the effect of the consequences an analysis was performed with Consequence condition versus black No Consequence condition as a between subject variable and specific items as a within subjects variable. In this analysis a significant interaction was found. Thus, comparisons were made among the means for each item separately. The means are displayed in Table 1. Similar analyses were performed for the two motivational conditions, and a significant interaction was also found for the set of items comprising the first set of situations, but not the second set, although the overall difference between the signal conditions was significant. Means of ratings of likelihood of disregarding the signs are also presented in Table 1.

Correlations were computed between the scale values for risk perception and likelihood of disregarding the signs. As might be expected, these correlations were negative and fairly high and significant for Situation 1, being -.64 for the no consequences condition and -.71 for the consequences condition. In addition, the correlation between the ratings of risk for the two conditions was .91. However, correlations with Situation 2 were uniformly low at .08 for the no consequence condition and .23 for the consequences condition. This suggests that perception of risk is heavily mediated by the cost of compliance to the individual.

DISCUSSION

The population from which the participants in this study were drawn is not the same as the general population. Although this limits generalization to some extent, this subpopulation is at an age where the amount of experience with signals of hazards is such that their concepts of the meanings of the signal words should be well developed. Further

the MSC population includes a substantial number of older working individuals, and the responses of the MSC group were not different from those of the UGA group.

The finding of no difference among the signal words was somewhat surprising. At least, it contradicted the subjective impressions of the experimenters. Perhaps a different sort of procedure, such as a semantic differential scaling task, would produce different results. Further, the lack of a difference between large and small signal words and between red and black signs is of interest. This should not be construed as indicating that size and color are not useful in directing attention to hazards, but it does seem to indicate that the perception of risk is predicated on the information content of the sign.

One possible explanation of these results is that prior experience has generated a certain level of perception of risk, based on personal experiences and, perhaps, on vicarious experiences through the communications media. These perceptions would be information based (whether correctly or incorrectly), and changes would be related to the disparity between information on the sign and previously held views. Although a signal word might have some modest effect, it would add little information to the previous store regarding radiation hazards or electric shock. The prior experience, in a fashion analogous to Helson's (1964) adaptation level, would absorb the effect without showing a difference. Clearly, color and size would add little to the information already at hand, even though there is knowledge that red is associated with danger. However, information about the consequences of becoming involved with an object or event, if it were sufficiently different from one's prior perception could raise the average perception of risk. The differential effects of the consequences condition is in accord with this assumption in that the three hazards perceived least risky in the No Consequences condition were all perceived to be significantly more risky in the Consequences condition.

It is also worthy to note that possible effects of signs on behavior seem to be highly related to the costs, as illustrated by the differences in correlations between the ratings of risk and the likelihood of compliance in different situations. Although not all individuals may heed warning signs, the efficacy of signs is probably not just a function of the signs themselves. Thus, it seems useful to present as much warning information as may be feasible, in order that any individual may make an informed choice.

ACKNOWLEDGEMENTS

The authors wish to thank Kathy L. Overstreet for assistance in producing stimulus material, and Dr. Morey Kitzman for an insightful review of the manuscript.

REFERENCES

Dorris, A.L., and Purswell, J.L. (1977) Warnings and human behavior: Implications for the design of product warnings, Journal of Products Liability, 1, 255-263.

Godfrey, S.S., Allender, L., Laughery, K.R., & Smith, V.L. (1983) Warning messages: Will the consumer bother to look. In Proceedings of the 27th Annual Meeting of the Human Factors Society, Human Factors Society, Santa Monica, CA, 950-954.

Godfrey, S.S., Rothstein, P.R., and Laughery, K.R. (1985) Warnings: Do they make a difference? In Proceedings of the 29th Annual Meeting of the Human Factors Society, Human Factors Society, Santa Monica, CA, 669-673.

Helson, H. (1964). Adaptation level theory. New York: Harper & Row.

Karnes, E.W., & Leonard, S.D. (1985)Consumer product warnings: Reception and understanding of warning information by final users. In W. Karwowski (Ed.) Trends in Ergonomics/ Human Factors, III, New York: Elsevier Science Publishing Inc., 995-1003.

Lerner, N.D. (1985). Slope safety warnings for riding type lawn mowers. In Proceedings of the 29th Annual Meeting of the Human Factors Society, Santa Monica, CA: Human Factors Society, 674-678.

McCarthy, R.L., Roginson, J.N., Finnegan, J.P., and Taylor, R.K. (1982). Warnings on consumer products: Objective criteria for their use. In Proceedings of the 26th Annual Meeting of the Human Factors Society, Santa Monica, CA: Human Factors Society, 98-102.

McCarthy, R. L., Finnegan, J.P., Krumm-Scott, S., and McCarthy, G.E. (1984). Product information presentation, user behavior, and safety. In Proceedings of the 28th Annual Meeting of the Human Factors Society, Santa Monica CA: Human Factors Society, 81-83.

Ursic, M. (1984). The impact of safety warnings on perception and memory. Human Factors, 26(6), 677-682.

Wright, P., Creighton, P., and Threlfall, S.M. (1982). Some factors determining when instructions will be read, Ergonomics, 25, 225-237.

EVALUATION OF SYMBOLS FOR FIRE SAFETY

Neil D. Lerner and Belinda L. Collins

Environmental Design Research Division
National Bureau of Standards
Washington, D.C. 20234

ABSTRACT

Twenty-five symbols for fire-alerting, of which 22 were proposed by the International Organization for Standardization, were evaluated for 91 U.S. subjects. The purpose of the experiment was two-fold: 1) to determine the understandability of each symbol; and 2) to assess the effects of variations in both presentation and response methods upon the measurement of understandability. There was no significant effect of the mode of stimulus presentation: slides, placards, or booklets. The two response methods--providing a definition or selecting among choice alternatives (and providing confidence ratings for answers)--led to generally similar conclusions. Some serious problems in understandability and several dangerous confusions in meaning were identified for symbols proposed for international standardization.

INTRODUCTION

Pictorial signs may have a number of potential advantages over written signs, in addition to the obvious advantages of communication with the illiterate or foreign-speaking (Green and Pew, 1978; Modley, 1976; Collins and Pierman, 1979). Some of these advantages may be especially important in fire emergencies: visibility, intelligibility despite visual interference or degradation, and perceptibility under conditions of distraction or stress. Because of the confusing proliferation of symbols for some ideas, and the lack of effective pictograms for other messages, national and international standards groups have become concerned with standardizing symbols for fire situations (Pierman and Lerner, 1980). While some of these efforts have included testing in the development or evaluation of the symbol set, standardization often proceeds without regard to objective testing with user populations. Easterby (1970) and others have emphasized the need for objective evaluation.

This paper describes research and issues in the development of fire safety symbols. These symbols are intended for pictographic signs to visually alert building occupants to aspects of egress, fire alarm, fire fighting, and fire safety. Special interest is focused on the symbol set (ISO/TC21/SC1, 1978) proposed (though not yet adopted) for international use by the Committee on Equipment for Fire Protection and Fire Fighting of the International Organization for Standardization (ISO).

Understandability is an important criterion for evaluating any set of symbols, but it is critical where unambiguous safety information must be conveyed to the general public during possible emergency conditions. For such applications, the need for training and familiarization should be minimal. As a result, we conducted an experiment utilizing 91 U.S. participants that assessed the understandability of selected fire-safety symbols. The purpose of the experiment was two-fold: 1) to determine for a group of potential users the understandability of 25 fire safety symbols, including 22 proposed by ISO; and 2) to assess the effects of certain methodological variables upon the assessment of understandability.

METHOD

The experiment consisted of two general portions--one on symbol meaningfulness and the other on symbol production. The meaningfulness portion evaluated how well a set of fire-safety symbols conveyed the intended messages. The production portion determined the kinds of images produced by subjects for a given message.

The procedure of the symbol meaningfulness portion defined a two-factor, independent groups experimental design. One factor was the mode of symbol presentation: placards, slide projections, or booklets. The other factor was the type of response required of the subject: providing a short definition of the meaning of each symbol, or selecting the correct meaning from among four multiple choice alternatives. Thus the understandability portion of the experiment was a 3 x 2 design (3 modes of stimulus presentation, 2 types of responses), with six independent groups of subjects.

Although there are numerous ways in which experimenters have attempted to measure symbol understandability, each method has limitations. Requiring subjects to provide a definition has been widely used, but suffers from problems of scoring criteria, rater reliability, differences in terminology, illegibility, and time and expense involved in scoring (especially when multiple raters are used for reliability). Consequently, a multiple choice procedure designed to avoid these problems while minimizing problems inherent in multiple choice was included for comparison with the usual definition method. The multiple choice procedure utilized as alternative choices those definitions frequently provided by subjects in an earlier experiment using a similar symbol set (Collins and Pierman, 1979). Since the alternatives cover the general types of answers given by most of these earlier subjects using a definition procedure, it is likely that one of the alternatives will be similar to that which the subject would provide in a definition procedure, thus minimizing constraints on answers. The multiple choice procedure also required subjects to rate their confidence in the correctness of each alternative. This allowed guessing to be identified. It has the further advantage of providing more than simple binary information (correct or incorrect) about a given answer. Because this multiple choice method is based on obtaining alternatives from a prior group of definition subjects, the methodological comparisons here were really directed at their appropriateness for programs of large scale and expense.

RESULTS AND DISCUSSION

The mode of symbol presentation had no discernible effect on performance, nor did it interact significantly with other factors. Each of these presentation modes--slides, placards, and booklets--has distinct advantages for particular applications. Slides are useful for presentation to large groups. Placards present the symbols in a form which may most closely approximate real signs as seen in buildings. Booklets are efficient in that subjects are self-paced, independent, and do not require the presence of an experimenter (in fact, subjects could be reached by mail or through intermediary organizations). From a methodological viewpoint, booklets have the further advantage of allowing a different random order of symbols for each subject, thus minimizing the possibility of sequential effects in the group data. Because the present experiment suggested that presentation method does not differentially affect symbol meaningfulness, it appears that the most convenient method may be selected for a particular application.

Scoring problems were indeed a significant concern for the definition method. Answers for each symbol were scored by 3 independent judges according to both strict and lenient criteria. Although the rank-order correlation for these criteria was good (rho = 0.96), the mean difference in the percentage correct for lenient and strict scoring of individual symbols was about 11 percent, and the discrepancy ranged up to 40 percent. While agreement among the individual scorers was good, it was due to part to adopting quite strict criteria for "correct" scoring and quite lenient criteria for "partially correct" scoring. Thus the agreement was sometimes achieved at the cost of increasing the size of the ambiguous "partially

correct" category; this category accounted for 20 percent or more of the responses for about one-fourth of the symbols. This indicates a need for caution in interpreting the results of experiments where only a single "percent correct" is given.

The results of the multiple choice method were in generally good agreement with the definition method (r = 0.87). Table 1 lists the percentage of correct answers for each of the 25 symbols. It includes both strict and lenient scoring of the definition responses, as well as the multiple choice responses. Since agreement was generally poorest for symbols that scored poorly with both methods, the two response procedures agree very closely in discriminating the performance of more reasonable symbols. Where discrepancies did occur, the confidence ratings were useful in elucidating the reasons. Both methods also agreed in identifying common confusions and misinterpretations. Thus the multiple choice (with confidence ratings) procedure appears to warrant consideration. Both methods have advantages and disadvantages, so that the particular application should determine the selection. The multiple choice method appears most suited for large-scale testing of specific symbol sets.

The production data, in which subjects drew whatever image they felt conveyed a given message, also provided valuable insight into the effectiveness of a particular image for a given referent. A selected image is most likely to be optimal if it is both accurately recognized on the understandability task and commonly drawn on the production task. Similarly if images, such as those proposed for egress, do poorly in both tasks, this suggests that the image concept is more difficult to portray graphically, and that graphic redesign and user education are needed. Finally, of course, the production data suggest alternative ways of portraying a particular concept that should be assessed further.

In some cases the most frequently produced image agreed with the ISO proposed image (e.g., fire extinguisher, no smoking, do not lock). In other cases there was not agreement, particularly for those referent messages for which the ISO symbol was not well understood. The concept of "exit" proved especially difficult for subjects to symbolize. Some subjects did not produce any image, while about one-third of the participants used the word "EXIT" despite explicit instructions (generally well followed) not to use words. Other than incorporating an arrow as part or all of the symbol, there was little agreement among subjects on an image for exit. Despite its critical nature, there does not appear to be a good image stereotype for "exit."

Table 1. Percentage of Correct Answers for Each Symbol

Symbol		Percent Correct		
#	Meaning	Multiple Choice	Definition (Lenient)	Definition (Strict)
1.	Fire Extinguisher	100.0	97.8	97.8
2.	Hose & Reel	95.7	91.1	77.8
3.	Fire Ladder	19.6	53.3	24.4
4.	Fire Bucket	95.7	80.0	60.0
5.	Fire Fighter's Equipment	0	2.2	0
6.	Direction to Equipment	22.2	6.7	2.2
7.	Break Glass For Access	28.3	15.6	11.1
8.	Slide Doors To Right	56.5	15.6	4.4
9.	Do Not Use Water	76.1	91.1	88.9
10.	Do Not Lock	89.1	84.4	68.9
11.	No Smoking	100.0	95.6	95.6
12.	No Open Flame	87.0	88.9	75.6
13.	Do Not Block	2.2	20.0	0
14.	Keep Fire Door Shut	18.5	35.6	28.9
15.	Emergency Phone	93.5	93.3	71.1
16.	General Phone	87.0	95.6	82.2
17.	Fire Alarm Horn	77.8	22.2	22.2
18.	Fire Alarm Call Point	32.6	15.6	13.3
19.	Fire Exit - (Yannone, 1979)	95.7	91.1	86.7
20.	Emergency Exit ISO Original	57.8	62.2	22.0
21.	Emergency Exit ISO Proposed	69.6	86.7	68.9
22.	No Exit ISO Proposed	69.6	53.3	33.3
23.	No Exit ISO Original	30.4	11.1	6.7
24.	U.S. EXIT-Green	93.5	97.8	93.3
25.	U.S. EXIT-Red	91.3	97.8	97.8

The overall data on understandability indicated an extreme range (0 to 100% correct) in the performance of the various symbols. Of special concern was the relatively poor performance of symbols proposed for the critical concepts of "EXIT" and "NOT AN EXIT." Furthermore, some dangerous confusions were revealed even among proposed ISO standard symbols. To mention a few, a sign indicating firefighting equipment was often interpreted as indicating shelter; a fire-fighting ladder symbol often suggested fire-escape; and perhaps most seriously, a "not an exit" symbol was frequently interpreted as exit. These data emphasize the need for testing with potential users, rather than relying solely on "expert judgment."

There is also a need to test fire safety symbols for special user groups. This experiment has agreed with other research in identifying significantly reduced understanding among older persons. This group warrants special attention since they are grossly over-represented in fire fatality rates. Other groups may also require special concern in public firesafety alerting. These include children, visually and developmentally handicapped, and drug or alcohol users (who are especially over-represented in fatality rates, based on data from home fires; see Berl and Halpin, 1979). Symbols may have potentially great advantage over word signs for communicating with these special user groups, but these advantages may not be realized unless specific attention is paid to them.

Despite its primacy, understandability is not the only criterion for effective fire-safety symbols. Among others, visibility under emergency conditions such as darkness and smoke may be important for some symbols (e.g., exit, no exit, alarm call point). Research currently in progress has already indicated a wide range of performance among suggested symbols in this regard. Interestingly, new ISO symbols designed to improve understandability may have led to reduced visibility. Such problems emphasize the need to incorporate testing as an integral part of the symbol development process.

REFERENCES

Berl, W. G., and Halpin, B. M. Human Fatalities from Unwanted Fires, *Fire Journal*, 1979, 73(5), pp. 105-115.

Collins, B. L., and Pierman, B. C., Evaluation of Safety Symbols, National Bureau of Standards (U.S.), NBSIR 79-1760, 30 pages, (June 1979).

Easterby, R. S. The Perception of Symbols for Machine Display, *Ergonomics*, 1970, 13, pp. 149-158.

Green, P., and Pew, R. W. Evaluating Pictographic Symbols: An Automotive Application, *Human Factors*, 1978, 20(1), pp. 103-114.

ISO/TC 21/SC 1, Equipment for Fire Protection and Firefighting - Safety Signs, Draft Proposal 6309, Geneva: International Organization for Standardization, 1978.

Modley, R. Speaking of Sign Language, *Industrial Design*, 1976, 23, pp. 60-63.

Pierman, B. P. and Lerner, N. D. Testing Symbols for Fire Situations, *Fire Command*, 1980, 47, pp. 12-13.

Yannone, A. G. "Fire Exit" Symbol, Copyright 1979. Available from International Safety Signs, Inc., 33 West Elm Street, Brockton, MA 02501.

IMPROVING SWIMMING POOL WARNING SIGNS

Beth A. Loring
Michael E. Wiklund

American Institutes for Research
Bedford, MA 01730

ABSTRACT

The U.S. Consumer Product Safety Commission sponsored us to perform a human factors evaluation of existing swimming pool warning signs. Our study covered warnings which convey the messages "NO DIVING" and "WATCH CHILDREN". These warnings are particularly intended to reduce the incidence of diving accidents involving teenage boys and drowning accidents involving children under five; population groups that are over-represented in accident statistics. Our evaluation of twenty-two existing signs uncovered deviations from warning sign design principles and identified opportunities to improve each of the signs. Following the evaluation, we developed improved signs and tested them using teenage boys and mothers of young children as subjects. We then made final recommendations to the CPSC for improved signs.

INTRODUCTION

Accident statistics collected by the U.S. Consumer Product Safety Commission (CPSC) show that teenage boys and children under five are at highest risk, compared to other population segments, of being injured or killed in swimming pools. Drowning is one of the leading causes of death for children under five, because they are not accomplished swimmers and can escape adult supervision. Teenage boys are most likely to have diving accidents resulting in head or neck injury because they may not perceive the risks and consequences of diving into shallow water, may use pools while intoxicated, and are prone to be risk-takers.

To mitigate these problems, numerous warning signs for pools have been developed by the swimming pool industry and by safety groups. The signs vary widely in format, message content, and use of pictorials (illustrations). The majority of the signs could be improved through the application of human factors research and warning sign design principles.

The CPSC wanted to evaluate existing swimming pool warning signs and develop recommendations for signs that people would likely post, voluntarily, at their own pools. In response, we designed new signs based on human factors principles, design criteria provided in ANSI standards, and subject testing. In the process, we recognized the debate over whether warning signs will actually reduce accidents (McCarthy, et al., 1984). Yet, we felt that the signs that are posted should be optimally designed and sufficiently tested.

PROBLEMS WITH EXISTING POOL WARNING SIGNS

We collected existing pool warning signs from the CPSC, safety groups, independent consultants, and the pool industry. Although it appeared that considerable effort was applied to develop good signs, each of the twenty-two that we examined was found to have one or more design deficiencies.

Many signs incorporated messages that were too long. Several had multiple paragraphs of instructions. We considered it unlikely that people would take the time to read such long messages. Also, some of the signs had poor sentence structure or messages that were too complicated, with vocabulary aimed at an audience with an advanced education level. For example, one sign said "Never trust flotation devices. Inflatable water toys can deflate." The complexity of the words "flotation" and "deflate" was a problem because the reading levels of pool users can be low.

Several signs had messages written in character fonts that were difficult to read, and some used all uppercase letters and centered lines of text. Human factors research has determined that the text style that is best for rapid, continuous reading is left-justified with a ragged right margin, using mixed upper and lowercase characters (Tinker, 1963). We also found that some of the pictorials included on the existing pool signs were not easily recognized or could be misinterpreted.

Finally, some of the existing signs omitted one of the three key elements for good warning signs specified in the American National Standard ANSI Z535.2-Draft-1987: signal word, text message, and pictorial. While pictorials are not deemed mandatory by the standard, their use is recommended because pictorials communicate to people who do not read English or who are illiterate (FMC Corp., 1985; Westinghouse, 1981; Fasbinder, 1987).

WHAT MAKES A GOOD WARNING SIGN?

We reviewed warning sign design literature covering diverse applications including traffic safety, industrial safety and consumer product safety. Seeking to create a coherent compilation of design recommendations, we assessed the applicability of a variety of recommendations to swimming pool warning signs and created a final checklist for our evaluations and subsequent redesign efforts.

We determined that a good swimming pool warning sign should have (1) a signal word such as DANGER, WARNING, or CAUTION, (2) a text message, and (3) a pictorial. The format, or overall layout, of the sign should follow one of the formats given in ANSI Z535.2-Draft-1987. The signal word should be chosen using the criteria in that standard as well. The text message should describe the hazard, its consequences, and tell the reader how to avoid the hazard. The message should be worded simply so that people with a low reading level can understand it. The sentences should be short and concise, with no unnecessary information. The lettering style should be large and bold enough to be read from the expected viewing distance. References such as the Human Factors Design Handbook (Woodson, 1982) are an appropriate source of guidelines for character heights at varying distances. The lettering should be left justified with a ragged right margin, in a sans serif style.

If a pictorial is included, it should be large enough to convey its meaning at the expected viewing distance. It should be simple, without unnecessary details that could confuse or add visual clutter. It should not be so abstract that the viewer needs to

study it at length in order to understand it.

HOW WE DEVELOPED OUR IMPROVED SIGN CANDIDATES

Since we found at least minor deficiencies in all of the existing warning signs we examined, we were left with the task of developing more effective ones. This task was complicated by the fact that the signal word, text message, and pictorial elements of a warning sign are inter-related, working together to convey a complete warning. Our goal was to develop the best integrated warning sign, as opposed to just optimizing each of the elements. We knew, for instance, that a pictorial judged best on a stand-alone basis might not produce the best warning when combined with a text message. However, we chose first to determine the most promising options for the three discrete elements of the warning signs, and then test them in combination.

To determine the most promising elements, we conducted an in-house evaluation. Twenty-two adults were asked to rank order alternative messages and pictorials for "NO DIVING" and "WATCH CHILDREN" signs. The alternatives were selected based on the results of our critique of the existing signs and our judgment. For the text message alternatives, we added new options to the most promising existing messages to provide a wider range of phrasings. For the pictorials, we added one "NO DIVING" option created by following the FMC guidelines (FMC Corp., 1985), and we added several original "WATCH CHILDREN" options.

From the results of the effective-ness survey, we settled on a set of preferred warning sign elements that could be combined to form complete warning sign candidates. The signal word "DANGER" was treated as a constant based on the scenarios in question and our understanding of the hazard level as described in the ANSI standard.

Figures 1 and 2 show alternative warning signs for the categories "NO DIVING" and "WATCH CHILDREN." When we prepared complete warning signs from the best alternative elements, we used the horizontal format prescribed by ANSI Z535.2-Draft-1987. We used a Helvetica Bold font because it was plain and maxi-mized readability from a distance. The signs included black text on a white background, except for the signal word, which used white letters on a red background.

HOW WE DECIDED ON OUR FINAL RECOMMENDATIONS

Instead of deciding for ourselves which messages and pictorials worked best together, we conducted a small-scale test. We produced a set of alternative warning sign designs with varied combinations of texts and pictorials. When the warning sign design effort was complete, we prepared mockups of each sign.

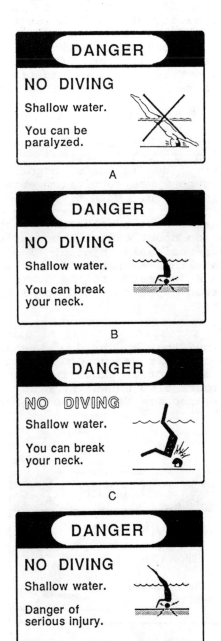

Figure 1: Alternative NO DIVING Signs

Figure 2: Alternative WATCH CHILDREN Signs

Our test had to be limited to nine subjects, a requirement for federally sponsored surveys conducted without Office of Management and Budget clearance. Because accident statistics indicated that teenage boys were the high risk group for diving accidents and children under five years of age were the high risk group for drowning accidents, our sample included five teenage boys who participated in swimming programs, and four mothers of young children. Although the teenage boys were the principal target of the "NO DIVING" signs and the mothers were the principal target of the "WATCH CHILDREN" signs, each group provided feedback on all of the signs.

The subjects preferred the messages "You can be paralyzed" and "You can break your neck" to "Danger of serious injury." One teenager said, "'Serious injury' is just no big deal. I wouldn't listen to that." The teenage boys told us that the signs with the most "gruesome" pictorials would be most effective to them. One subject

151

cautioned us that teenage boys would look at the pictorial and possibly read the words "NO DIVING," but would not take the time to read any more of the message. Although the subjects generally preferred the pictorial that was the most human looking (A in Figure 1), they could not see it very well from a distance, reportedly because it was an outlined rather than solid figure.

The mothers of young children were disturbed by the "WATCH CHILDREN" pictorials. One brought her hands to her face and said, "I hate it! This is awful!" The subjects overall preferred the pictorial that showed a struggling child, rather than one at the bottom of the pool, because the child was still alive. The mothers pointed out that they would not post a sign with an excessively morbid pictorial.

Although our subjects had varying preferences among the alternative warning sign elements, we were able to identify the preferred warning sign designs.

OUR IMPROVED "NO DIVING" SIGNS

We committed to the text message "NO DIVING" after the effectiveness study because it was shorter and was considered more effective than the message "DO NOT DIVE." The message is written in all capital letters to highlight it as the most important part of the total text. We tested the effectiveness of writing "NO DIVING" in red during our pilot test. Although some people felt that the red color drew greater attention to the message, most people did not feel the color coding was necessary. Though either alternative would fit ANSI guidelines, we concluded that black lettering would be slightly more legible when read from a distance or in low lighting conditions and would not detract from the visibility of the signal word. We added an exclamation point after the phrase "NO DIVING" because a large number of people in the effectiveness survey and pilot test suggested it would add emphasis.

The messages "You can break your neck" and "You can be paralyzed" were considered most effective among the alternative phrasings. Mothers generally preferred "You can break your neck" because they felt that the word "paralyzed" might not be understood by younger children due to their limited vocabulary. The teenagers thought that the phrasing "You can be paralyzed" was best because it was dramatic, threat-

ening and attention-getting. We believe that both phrasings could be effective. However, since some people might not understand the word "paralyzed" while virtually everybody would understand the threat "You can break your neck," we recommended the latter. Another alternative phrasing, "Danger of serious injury," was considered too vague by both subject groups.

The alternative pictorials varied in terms of their level of human likeness and the symbol used to indicate an impact or injury. Subjects generally preferred the more human looking symbol shown in A of Figure 1, while they liked the visibility of the silhouetted human likenesses shown in B, C, and D. The less human-looking symbols were described as "fish" and "folding chairs." This feedback suggested that we use a realistic human silhouette.

Subjects felt that it was best to show the human in a distressed condition, rather than a healthy condition (though surrounded by impact symbols). The dislocated head shown in C of Figure 1 was considered effective for this reason. Both of the impact/injury symbols shown in B and C of Figure 1 were considered effective, leaving no doubt that the person's neck had been seriously injured. The straight lines emanating from the head in sign A suggested to the subjects that the person might only end up with a headache.

As a result of these findings, we determined that a hybrid of the alternative pictorials was needed and we developed the pictorial shown in Figure 3. This figure also shows the other features we recommended for an improved "NO DIVING" sign.

Figure 3: Recommended NO DIVING Sign

Figure 5: Recommended WATCH CHILDREN
Sign (Alternative 2)

OUR IMPROVED "WATCH CHILDREN" SIGNS

Based on the results of our earlier effectiveness study, we concluded that the text message "Prevent child drownings. Watch children at all times." was optimal. There was nearly complete agreement among subjects that the pictorial showing a struggling child was best because it indicated a child in distress, and was not excessively morbid. The pictorial showing a child at the bottom of the pool was considered too harsh for the residential environment and was criticized because it showed death, as opposed to distress. The pictorial that included a mother (C in Figure 2) was understood by subjects to illustrate the precise message; a positive scene showing an adult watching a child playing in the water. However, the subjects thought the two threatening pictorials were more effective.

Our final recommendation was complicated by the fact that most people felt that they or their parents would not post a sign showing a drowning child; that they would be more inclined to post the more positive sign. Therefore, we recommended that the warning sign designs shown in Figures 4 and 5 be considered for implementation and that the CPSC collect more information regarding the likelihood that either sign would be posted by consumers.

REFERENCES

American National Standards Institute. (1987) ANSI Z535.2-Draft-1987: *American National Standard for Environmental and Facility Safety Signs*, New York.

Fasbinder, J. (1987) Attorney pushes for pictograms illustrating dangers of diving. *Pool & Spa News*, Los Angeles, CA.

FMC Corporation. (1985) *Product Safety Sign and.Label System*. Santa Clara, CA.

McCarthy, R.L., Finnegan, J.P. and Krumm-Scott, S. (1984) Product information, user behavior, and safety. *Proceedings of the Human Factors Society 28th Annual Meeting*, 81-85.

Tinker, M.A. (1963) *Legibility of Print*. The Iowa State University Press, Ames, IA.

Westinghouse Electric Corporation. (1981) *Product Safety Label Handbook*. Westinghouse Printing Division, Trafford, PA.

Woodson, W.E. (1982) *Human Factors Design Handbook*. McGraw-Hill, Washington, D.C.

Figure 4: Recommended WATCH CHILDREN
Sign (Alternative 1)

EFFECTS OF PROCESSING DEPTH ON MEMORY
FOR THE ALCOHOL WARNING LABEL

David P. MacKinnon[1], Alan W. Stacy[2], Liva Nohre[1], and R. Edward Geiselman[3]

[1]Department of Psychology
Arizona State University
Tempe, Arizona

[2]Department of Preventive Medicine
University of Southern California
Alhambra, California

[3]Department of Psychology
University of California, Los Angeles
Los Angeles, California

ABSTRACT

The experiment examined: (1) the effects of different types of processing of the alcohol beverage warning label on memory for the label content, (2) potential measures of memory for the alcohol warning label, and (3) whether cues to the alcohol warning label increase memory for the content of the label. We hypothesized that the warning label may be processed in three ways: (1) persons may read the label, (2) persons may read the label and describe its content to others, and (3) persons may see the label but not cognitively process the label. Processing effects were operationalized as three orienting tasks to the label (read, paraphrase, and count) which were compared to a control condition (no experimental exposure to the warning label). Four tests (free recall, recognition, word-stem completion, and controlled association) were compared. In one additional condition, subjects were cued to the warning label without prior experimental exposure. The free recall test was the most sensitive measure to different levels of processing. Average memory scores for the paraphrase and read conditions were higher than the count and control conditions. Average memory performance in the cued condition was superior to the control condition, suggesting that subjects remember the content of the warning from exposure to the label outside this experiment.

INTRODUCTION

On November 18, 1989 warning labels were required to appear on all alcoholic beverage containers sold in the United States. The warning label reads, "GOVERNMENT WARNING: (1) According to the Surgeon General, women should not drink alcoholic beverages during pregnancy because of the risk of birth defects. (2) Consumption of alcoholic beverages impairs your ability to drive a car or operate machinery, and may cause health problems." The legislation (Alcohol Beverage Labeling Act, 1988) was included in the Omnibus Anti-Drug Abuse Act of 1988, with the intent to inform and remind the public about the negative consequences of alcohol use.

The purpose of the present experiment was threefold: (1) to study the effects of different types of processing of the alcohol beverage warning label on memory for the content of the label, (2) to compare tests of memory for the content of the alcohol warning label, and (3) to determine whether cues to the alcohol warning label increase memory performance for the content of the label. The extent to which different memory tests are sensitive to different types of processing suggests which measures may be most effective for evaluating warning labels. In addition, we hypothesized that memory for the warning label can be measured by assessing memory performance in cued versus uncued conditions, revealing previous exposure to the warning label.

Type of Processing

We hypothesized that the warning label may be processed in three ways: (1) Persons may read the label, (2) persons may read the label and describe its content to others, and (3) persons may see the label but not cognitively process the label. We operationalized these scenarios by having subjects either read the label, paraphrase the label, or count the number of vowels in the label, respectively. The three conditions were compared to a control condition where there was no experimental exposure to the warning label.

The levels of processing framework (Craik & Lockhart, 1972; Lockhart & Craik, 1990) provides a theoretical basis for predicting the effects of different types of processing on memory. Shallow processing consists of encoding only the visual components of the label, such as the number of vowels, without semantic processing or elaboration. Deeper processing occurs when persons read and process the content of the label, thereby increasing elaboration of the label. Orienting tasks inducing deeper levels of processing lead to more elaborate memory traces than orienting tasks inducing shallow processing.

Type of Memory Test

Subjects completed one of four different tests. We were interested in whether the tests may access different information stored in memory. Free recall and recognition may access explicit memory, or "conscious recollection" (Schacter, 1987) of learned information. This reflects an deliberate retrieval of information presented or learned within a specific episode. In contrast, indirect tests of memory may access implicit memory, or memory without conscious recollection of a prior learning episode. Word-stem completion and controlled association tests are examples of indirect memory tests which have the potential of eliciting the unintentional retrieval of information (Schacter, Bowers, & Booker, 1989). However, the indirect tests (word-stem completion and controlled association) examined here may not strictly access implicit memory, as some subjects may have been aware that the tests were related to previous experimental exposure to the warning label. The use of direct and indirect tests of memory have been discussed and reviewed elsewhere (see Richardson-Klavehn & Bjork, 1988).

Effects of a Cue

In one additional orienting task, subjects were given cues to the warning label. If the alcohol warning label is already retained in subjects memory, then a retrieval cue or prime should activate memory for the other risks on the warning label. Thus the condition where subjects were cued to the warning label during the manipulation stage of the experiment was expected to improve retrieval of the warning label from memory relative to the control condition.

Summary

In summary, subjects were randomly assigned to one of five orienting tasks that reflected different levels of processing of the alcohol warning label. Subjects in the (1) control condition did not process any aspect of the warning label. In the four other conditions, subjects were either (2) cued to the label by reinstating the context surrounding the label and receiving a partial presentation of the label, (3) counted the number of vowels in the label, (4) read the label many times, or (5) paraphrased the content of the label. Subjects completed one of four tests reflecting direct (recall and recognition) and indirect (word-stem completion and controlled association) measures of memory for the warning label.

Orienting tasks inducing deeper-levels of processing (paraphrase or read) were expected to improve memory scores to a greater extent than the orienting task inducing a shallow level of processing (count). All four orienting tasks were expected to elicit better memory performance relative to the control condition, with the possible exception of the condition where subjects merely counted the number of vowels.

METHOD

Subjects

The participants were 288 students, with an average age of 19, enrolled in Arizona State University's introductory psychology course during the fall of 1990. Non-white subjects comprised 15 percent of the population, and 62 percent were male. Ninety-one percent of the subjects reported having one drink in the last month, while 49 percent had more than 21 drinks in the last month.

Design and Materials

Five levels of label exposure (i.e., orienting tasks) and four levels of test were between subjects conditions. Subjects were randomly assigned to receive one of the 20 (5 X 4) possible combinations of the orienting task and test conditions.

There were five orienting tasks. Two of the groups had litter or no exposure to the label: (1) a control group which read an unrelated paragraph (2) a group cued to the label by reinstating the context surrounding inclusion of the warning label on alcoholic beverages, but only saw a small segment of the actual label (the risk of impaired driving). In the last three conditions subjects were instructed to process the warning label at different levels by (3) counting the vowels in the label to increase data driven processing (4) reading the label many times over, and (5) paraphrasing the label for a scientist, family member, and a child to increase elaborative rehearsal.

Following the orienting task, all subjects completed a word-stem completion distractor task containing names of famous people within the movie and television industry.

The orienting tasks were crossed with each of the four tests: (1) free recall for the content of the label, (2) recognition of the four specific risks listed on the label from four distractors, (3) a word-stem completion test in which the first two letters of each of the four risks and each of the four distractors were shown with the rest of the word to be filled in, for example, consumption of alcoholic beverages impairs your ability to dr_____, and (4) a controlled association for the risks of alcohol use (Cramer, 1968).

Procedure

Subjects were administered the procedure in groups, with experimental condition determined by the particular test packet received. The procedures were timed, with the experimenter giving verbal feedback to "stop, and turn the page". Subjects were timed to equate the amount of experimental exposure to the label among the conditions. During the first three minutes, subjects conducted one of the five orienting tasks described above. Between the orienting task and the test, subjects completed a word-stem completion distractor task for two minutes. Three minutes were allotted to complete one of the four tests. Following the experiment, respondents completed a questionnaire assessing alcohol use, exposure to and knowledge of the alcohol warning label and other product warnings.

Scoring

Three different memory scores were computed: (1) the number correct out of the four risks displayed on the warning label, (2) the number correct out of the four risks displayed on the warning label minus the number of risks stated that were not on the warning label, (3) the number correct out of three of the four risks displayed on the alcohol beverage warning label. The risk of impaired driving was not included in the last comparison because subjects in the cued condition were given this risk as a cue. The first two dependent variables represent results unadjusted and adjusted for guessing. The unadjusted measure is presented as well as the adjusted measure due to the difficulty of determining false alarms across the tests. The last dependent variable was used to compare the cued condition to the other conditions. The covariates of age, gender, and monthly alcohol use changed the results of the analysis very little.

RESULTS

Unadjusted Memory Scores

The means of each group for the number correct out of the four label risks are shown in Table 1. There were significant main effects of orienting task (F (3, 211) = 7.18, $p<$ .001), and test (F (3, 211) = 15.48 $p<$ .001) for the number correct out of the four risks displayed on the warning label. A significant interaction of orienting task by test was found (F (9, 211) = 1.99, $p<$ .05), suggesting that the effects of processing differed across the tests.

Because there was a significant interaction between the type of orienting task and the type of test, each separate test was used as the dependent measure and specific orienting tasks were compared. The only significant simple effect was for the free recall test (F (3, 54) = 9.42, $p<$ .001). Comparisons of the orienting tasks indicated significant differences between the paraphrase versus count (F (1, 54) = 8.03, $p<$ .01), paraphrase versus control (F (1, 54) =

18.10, $p<$ .001), read versus count (F (1, 54) = 8.91, $p<$ .01), and read versus control (F (1, 54) = 19.47, $p<$ .001) conditions.

Table 1.
Means and Standard Deviations for Each Group.

Condition	n	Mean	SD
Recognition			
Paraphrase	15	2.67	1.35
Read	17	3.00	1.11
Count	11	2.45	1.13
Control	14	2.71	1.27
Word-stem completion			
Paraphrase	15	2.93	0.80
Read	16	2.94	1.12
Count	13	2.69	0.95
Control	12	2.08	1.08
Free recall			
Paraphrase	16	2.25	1.13
Read	16	2.31	1.14
Count	12	1.08	1.31
Control	14	0.57	0.65
Controlled association			
Paraphrase	16	2.31	0.60
Read	16	2.13	0.96
Count	12	2.17	0.58
Control	12	1.92	0.90

Note. The dependent measure is the number correct out of the four risks displayed on the alcohol warning label. The number of subjects per group varies as a result of the randomization process.

Memory Scores Adjusted for Guessing

For the number correct adjusted for guessing there were significant main effects of orienting task (F (3, 211) = 7.32, $p<$ .001), and test (F(3, 211) = 36.50, $p<$ .001). The interaction was not significant. Average memory scores for the paraphrase and read conditions were higher than the count and control conditions.

Orienting task comparisons indicated the paraphrase condition was not significantly different from the read condition. Paraphrase versus control (F (1, 211) = 12.74, $p<$ .001) was significantly different, while paraphrase versus count (F (1, 211) = 3.47, $p<$ .10) was marginally significant. The read versus count and read versus control conditions were significant: (F (1, 211) = 6.38, $p<$ .05) and (F (1, 211) = 18.20, $p<$ .001) respectively. There was not a significant difference between the count and control conditions, indicating the subjects in the count condition did not process the label at

a level deep enough to improve their memory for the risks. These results are generally consistent with the levels of processing framework, where the subjects who received the paraphrase and read conditions encoded the label to a greater extent than the subjects who counted the number of vowels in the label.

The test score means and standard deviations collapsed across orienting task indicated that the highest mean score was achieved in the recognition test (X = 2.59, SD = 1.24), the next highest score was for the word-stem completion (X = 1.84, SD = 1.09), followed by the free recall test (X = 1.29, SD = 1.50) and finally, the controlled association (X = 0.13, SD = 1.17).

Table 2.
Means and Standard Deviations for the Cued and Control Conditions.

Condition	n	Mean	SD
Recognition			
Cued	14	2.50	0.52
Control	14	2.07	0.92
Word-stem completion			
Cued	15	1.73	1.16
Control	12	1.17	0.94
Free recall			
Cued	17	0.65	0.79
Control	14	0.36	0.50
Controlled association			
Cued	15	1.20	0.68
Control	12	1.08	0.67

Note. The dependent variable is the number correct out of three of the four risks listed on the alcohol warning label, becuase subjects in the cued condition saw the risk of impaired driving.

Effects of a Cue

The dependent measure consisting of the number correct out of three risks compared the cued condition to the control condition. Table 2 displays the cued and control orienting task means for each test. Subjects in the cued condition performed significantly better than the control condition across all tests (F (1, 268) = 4.93, $p< .05$), suggesting that just cuing subjects to the label improves memory

performance. When adjusted for guessing, the effect is smaller (F (1, 268) = 2.91, $p< .05$, one-tailed).

DISCUSSION

It appears that the warning label may have an effect on memory for the risks displayed on the label, at least for the total number of risks remembered. Retrieval of the specific risks is enhanced by cues to the label (e.g., the history surrounding the law to include the warning on alcohol beverage containers) when the actual label is not seen. The risks appear to be stored in memory, and receiving a cue to the label facilitates subsequent retrieval of these risks, perhaps through a redintegration or activation of previously acquired associations. If these risks were not stored in memory prior to experiment participation, then no facilitative effect of a cue would have been found. Cuing retrieval of the label may be an effective technique for measuring the "real world" exposure to the label, without actually showing subjects the label. An alternative interpretation of these results is that the cued condition activated more alcohol-related risks in general. The latter interpretation would predict an increase in distractor risks as much as target risks, which was not found. The possibility that just cueing subjects to part of the label improves memory performance may be a fruitful topic for future research.

Generally, orienting tasks which induce deeper levels of processing of the alcohol warning label were associated with memory for the specific risks written on the warning label. The most significant and reliable effect was for the free recall test suggesting that deeper levels of processing lead to better performance generating the risks on the label. The effects of different levels of processing on free recall memory is one of the most robust effects in cognitive psychology. The lack of similar effects on recognition is not surprising given that recognition is generally perceived as less affected by the levels of processing manipulation. Recognition does not require the additional process of retrieval required by free recall.

Recent studies of tobacco (MacKinnon & Fenaughty, in press) and alcohol (MacKinnon, Pentz, & Stacy, 1991) warning labels suggest that the recognition test is sensitive to exposure to warning labels. The recognition test thus may be the more sensitive measure of memory while free recall may measure the depth of encoding more accurately. The word-stem completion and controlled association tests have not received much attention in a levels-of-processing framework. These tests may have functioned more like the recognition test in this experiment. Nevertheless, when adjusted for guessing the effects of the orienting tasks appeared to be the same across these tests.

In summary, deeper levels of processing are associated with greater memory performance for the content of the warning label. This effect may be stronger for free recall, which appears to be most sensitive to the processing manipulations in this laboratory experiment. In addition, the provision of a cue for one of the risks on the warning label appears to increase memory performance for the other warning label risks, revealing previous exposure to the warning label. Memory tests of this nature deserve increased attention in the understanding and evaluation of the effects warning labels have on memory and behavior.

ACKNOWLEDGMENTS

This work was supported in part by Public Health Service grant #AA8547.

REFERENCES

Alcohol Beverage Labeling Act (1988). H.R. 5409.

Craik, F.I.M., & Lockhart, R.S. (1972). Levels of processing: A framework for memory research. Journal of Verbal Learning and Verbal Behavior, 11, 671-684.

Cramer, P. (1968). Word Association. New York: Academic Press.

Lockhart, R.S., & Craik, F.I.M. (1990). Levels of processing: A retrospective commentary on a framework for memory research. Canadian Journal of Psychology, 44(1), 87-112.

MacKinnon, D.P., & Fenaughty, A.M. (in press). Substance use and memory for health warning labels. Health Psychology.

MacKinnon, D.P., Pentz, M.A., & Stacy, A. (1991). First-year effects of the alcohol warning label on adolescents. Manuscript submitted for publication.

Omnibus Anti-Drug Abuse Act (1988). H.R. 5210 or S. 2852.

Richardson-Klavehn, A. & Bjork, R.A. (1988). Measures of memory. Annual Review of Psychology, 39, 475-543.

Schacter, D.L. (1987). Implicit memory: History and current status. Journal of Experimental Psychology: Learning, Memory, and Cognition, 13(3), 501-518.

Schacter, D.L., Bowers, J., & Booker, J. (1989). Intention, awareness, and implicit memory: The retrieval intentionality criterion. In S. Lewandowsky, J.C. Dunn, & K. Kirshner (Eds.) Implicit Memory: Theoretical Issues. Hillsdale, New Jersey: Lawrence Earlbaum.

PRODUCT INFORMATION PRESENTATION, USER BEHAVIOR, AND SAFETY

Roger L. McCarthy, James P. Finnegan, Susan Krumm-Scott, and Gail E. McCarthy

Failure Analysis Associates
Palo Alto, California

ABSTRACT

A review of approximately 400 published articles, in addition to the authors' own research in the area of on-product warning label design and effectiveness, is summarized. Findings are examined for implications in the design and use of on-product warning labels for improved product safety through modification of user behavior. No scientific evidence was found to support the contention that on-product warning labels measurably increase the safety of any product. There was evidence that on-product warnings have no measurable impact on user behavior and product safety.

INTRODUCTION

As a nation makes the transition to an industrialized society with almost universal literacy, the society's tolerance of unexpected or accidental injury or death declines markedly. One manifestation of this increased civilization is an increased societal demand for safer man-made products and work environments. Risks that would have been accepted and even expected a century before become unacceptable. Shields, guards, check values, and the like are becoming increasingly common. Many of these safety-related design features would be unnecessary if the product user used the product with a reasonable regard for personal safety. It is the potentially unsafe acts of users that many modern safety features are designed to address. In addition to designing a product which will "do the job," it has become the designer's challenge to design the product to prevent the unsafe users and their bystanders from getting hurt, in spite of careless use or deliberate misuse.

Unfortunately, for most products it is just physically and/or economically impossible to design out all the different ways they can be misused to cause injury. Many products are limited in the extent to which safety features can reasonably be included. Often inclusion of additional "safety features" would render the product either less useful or reliable, or complicated beyond a point which the user will accept, or more dangerous. In these and other situations, some have recommended the use of on-product warnings as a safety measure.

The advocates of on-product warnings argue that, if a warning is provided on the product, there will be fewer (or no) injuries because the product user will comply with the warning. Implicit in this argument is the assumption that the user lacked knowledge of the hazard or the potential consequences of some action and that the imparting of this knowledge would result in modified behavior. This argument for the

inclusion of on-product warnings has indeed become quite popular, as evidenced by government regulations mandating certain warnings, legal decisions rendered based on the existence or non-existence of an on-product warning, professional workshops which address warning label design and application, numerous articles in technical publications extolling certain appropriate features of warnings, ANSI committees working to provide standards for on-product warning label designs, and at least several standardized industry warning label design programs. In essence, on-product warnings are becoming ubiquitous.

On-product warnings are formulated as information transfer devices, intended to communicate information to product users and to modify behavior. Thus, effectiveness of warnings in communicating information, in modifying behavior, and ultimately in reducing injuries, would appear to be extremely important. An effective warning would provide an efficient mechanism by which great strides in public safety might be achieved. It is with this perspective that Failure Analysis Associates (FaAA) has reviewed all the literature published in English related to consumer product warning label effectiveness. Incredibly, to date, there appears to be no solid evidence that on-product warnings have measurably improved the safety of any product. There is, however, evidence to indicate that on-product warnings do not improve product safety.

WARNINGS: EXISTING LITERATURE

After reviewing approximately 400 articles dealing with warnings, we find that this literature can be broadly sorted into categories based on the manner in which the warning issue was addressed.

Qualitative - editorial. Most of the articles which directly discuss warning labels relate to the potential utility of such warnings, the way in which warnings should be presented, and discussions of a perceived legal and social duty to provide warnings. Among the 91 such articles considered, several embody the common features of this group. Among these are articles by Peters (1984), Schwartz and Driver (1983), Sommese and Knopp (1978), Rheinstein and Baum (1980), Etzioni (1976), Riley, Cochran, and Deary (1981), Wilcox (1979), Kolb and Ross (1980), and Stephens and Barrett (1979).

These and numerous similar papers attempt to set the philosophical basis which gives rise to a "theory of warning." The general theme of these works appears to be based on the expectation that providing safety information is related to an increase in safety behavior. The articles discuss history of different forms of safety information presentation, qualitative guidelines for the inclusion of safety warnings, suggestions for wording and formatting warning labels, and contemporary issues relating hazard labeling and legal considerations.

Recognition - recall. The quantitative works most often represented in the literature dealing with warnings are those addressing recognition of the warning message and ability to recall that message at a later time. Ancillary to recognition and recall are articles dealing with visibility, contrast, readability, etc. Limiting the review to the topics of recognition, recall, and ancillary papers with direct relationship to signs and warnings produced 58 articles. This group consists of approximately one-half addressing highway warning signs and other transporation applications, and one-half more directly related to products.

Representative of the product-related warning research are articles by McGuiness (1977), Godfrey and Allender (1983), Riley, Cochran, and Ballard (1982) Bresnahan and Bryk (1975), Easterby and Hakiel (1977a, 1977b), Christ (1975), Collins (1983), and Collins and Lerner (1982). Among those articles dealing with readability are Dall and Chall (1948), Freimuth (1979), Kreindler and Luchsinger (1978), and Morris and Kanouse (1981).

These types of articles form the largest part of the existing body of applied quantitative research from which guidelines for design of warning labels, signs, and other safety literature may be inferred. The research addresses consumer preference for label design, preferred label shapes, graphic symbology and its interpretation, and word choice as a function of readability. Again, a premise in these papers is the assumption that information, provided in a manner which is comprehended, is useful for modification of safety-related behavior.

Standards and label systems. Not typically discussed in the technical literature, but relevant to warning labels and labeling issues, are existing standards which specify warning label design and use. Most well known of the organizations dealing with labeling standards is the American National Standards Institute. The current ANSI standard (ANSI, 1972) is now undergoing review.

Industries have also developed individual labeling systems. Among these systems are the Product Safety Sign and Label System (FMC, 1980), and Product Safety Label Handbook (Westinghouse, 1981). These systems are characterized by pre-prepared pictorials, color plates, and other graphic aids to facilitate the design of warning labels.

Relying in part on the ANSI standard and in part on opinion testimony, both federal and state governments have mandated specific warnings for various consumer products. Among the most active federal organizations in this regulatory arena are the Consumer Product Safety Commission, the Food and Drug Administration, the Department of Transportation, and the Occupational Safety and Health Administration. There are currently hundreds of regulations mandating warning labels.

Quantification of effectiveness. Among the publications reviewed by FaAA, the category most arduously sought and least represented in the literature is that dealing with quantitative effectiveness of warnings. Only a few studies are reported. One of the earliest is by Laner and Sell (1960). This work was performed in a real-world employment situation and addressed warning posters rather than on-product warnings. During a 20-week observation period, the observed hazardous behavior decreased approximately 11%. The results are somewhat confounded by the varying architectural designs of the test sites and might have been influenced by concurrent intervention of supervisory personnel. The relationship between observations made in this poster campaign and on-product warning label design or effectiveness is unclear. The results of this research stand in marked contrast to the safety campaign research and warning label research done subsequently.

The often-cited study directly dealing with the warning label issue is reported by Dorris and Purswell (1977). High school and college students were invited to drive nails with a hammer, the hammer contained a warning not to use the hammer. All students drove the nails, and in subsequent interviews none could report any knowledge of the existence of the warning label.

On a national scale, attempts to enhance safety through labeling have been notably ineffective. Nationwide, two of the most important public health and safety issues are the health risks of cigarette smoking and motor vehicle safety.

According to a report by the Federal Trade Commisssion (Myers, 1981), "the current health warning is rarely noticed and is not effective in alerting consumers to the health hazards of smoking" (over 300,000 smoking-related deaths per year).

In the area of motor vehicle safety, it has been widely reported that if everyone always wore seat belts, the national motor vehicle fatality figure (approximately 50,000 per year) could be decreased by at least 50%. In 1968, seat belts were mandated in American automobiles (FMVSS 208, 1967). Robertson, O'Neill, and Wixom (1972), using visual observation, reported 77% of metropolitan drivers and 90% of small town drivers wore no passenger restraint.

Shortly after the mandate, efforts began to evaluate and to increase seat belt use rates. These efforts included various types of warnings. In 1972, "buzzer and light" reminder systems were placed in all new cars. Later that year, Robertson and Haddon (1972) observed driver restraint use rates among drivers of vehicles with restraint systems, and with and without reminder system. Findings over 66,785 observations include an increase in use rate of not more than 2% (from approximately 15% to 17%). The authors conclude that "the buzzer-light system, can only be described as a public health failure."

In 1973, Bragg investigated seat belt use among persons previously involved in serious automobile accidents. The author states, "we conclude that a 'traumatic' event like a personal injury accident is not sufficient to induce or maintain seat belt use."

In the United States today, the seat belt use rate is approximately 10%, despite warnings, buzzers, lights, public information campaigns, and the often encountered "traumatic" event.

A review of data from the Fatal Accident Reporting System (FARS) showed that seat belt usage has not had a significant impact on the national fatality rate. This has been observed in other countries as well (McCarthy, 1984). The data also show that drivers of vehicles which impact something (accident initiators) are less likely to be wearing seat belts than drivers of vehicles which happen to be struck by someone else. In other words, those most likely to be involved in an accident (accident-initiators) and most in need of seat belts are less likely to comply with the seat belt warning. Further, the data suggest that seat belt usage may have undergone a slow but steady decline since 1979. This raises an important concern regarding potential decline of compliance with warnings over a period of time.

Another area of nationwide experience with hazard labeling involves the famous "Mr. Yuk" poisonous product label, designed to reduce children's attraction to hazardous household chemicals. The history of this symbol, originated in 1971, is outlined by the National Poison Center Network (1981). The original research involved providing children with various labels on representative containers. The containers that proved least interesting to the children were those with the Mr. Yuk symbol affixed. Use of the Mr. Yuk symbol grew nationwide. However, in 1982 Culver-Dickinson, Vernberg, and Spyker of the University of Virginia Medical Center reported a controlled study involving toddlers exposed to common chemical containers with and without the Mr. Yuk symbol. The authors comment, "we found no statistical difference in any of the measures of the deterrent value of the Mr. Yuk sticker." Fergusson, Horwood, and Beautrais (1982) report similar negative findings. And Schneider (1977), following research into safety labeling on household chemicals, offers the following: "Public regulations, for the most part, have contributed to the amount of verbiage placed on containers . . . the regulations may well have increased children's attraction toward hazardous substances."

A study of child poisonings is relevant to the role that lack of knowledge about hazards plays in certain accidents. Baltimore and Meyer (1969) investigated storage of toxic substances in 52 households where there had been a poison incident prior to the study (and in which knowledge of the consequences of improper storage could no longer be questioned), and in 52 randomly selected households with a young child, and "found no difference in the number of potentially toxic agents accessible to a 2 1/2-year-old in the homes of the control group and of the poisoned group."

Another sampling relating to quantitative understanding of warning effectiveness is the national experience with extremely flammable contact adhesives. In May 1970, cautionary labeling was required on all such adhesive containers of more than one-half pint volume, (Federal Register, 1970). The warning label addressed the flammable nature of the product and appropriate user behavior. In 1976 Nelson reported that at least 130 persons had been injured using the adhesives since 1970. These persons were largely adult males who had prior experience with the product and were using it as intended. As stated, "the resulting damage . . . . has led to an examination of the efficacy of the existing labeling of this product." In response to this study, the Consumer Product Safety Commission declared that "the Commission finds that this cautionary labeling is inadequate to protect the public." Concluding that there was not a labeling scheme which would achieve the desired outcome, the CPSC banned this product. (Code of Federal Regulations, 1978).

The last consumer product we will discuss is power lawn mowers. The number of injuries reported associated with gasoline power lawn mowers has been widely reported. In 1977 the Consumer Product Safety Commission conducted an intensive, locally-based information program to evaluate whether such programs would positively impact safety. Kerpelman (1978) reports the results of this intensive effort. Two control and two experimental sites, each site a city in Georgia, were involved in the experiment. Among the communications techniques employed were detailed fact sheets to be given to users, posters, radio and television spots, and intensive interpersonal interaction. Only at one site, that with the intensive interpersonal community outreach program, was it felt that the safety information did get through to the intended audience. This conclusion was drawn from survey data following the campaign. However, at this site an increase in power mower injuries was documented during the period of the campaign. The authors comment that the apparent rise may have been within the tolerance band of normal variation. The campaign failed to decrease the frequency of lawn mower injuries.

RESULTS

The findings from this literature review can be viewed in two sections:

Non-quantitative findings. A tremendous body of material exists discussing the warning label concept, warning message styles, recognition and recall of written and pictorial messages, and standards and regulations describing warning label use. Although future research may result in more "finely tuned" label graphics, the amalgamation of materials available to date appears adequate to guide label designers in creating state-of-the-art displays in label form. Unfortunately, none of the design variables is related in any known way to the actual effectiveness of warnings in changing behavior and reducing injuries.

Quantitative findings. In spite of the widespread use of warning labels, searches for scientific evidence have yielded virtually no reason to anticipate that warning labels on consumer products serve as effective mechanisms to increase safety. We have yet to identify a product that, when evaluated in an unbiased manner, clearly demonstrates the utility of any warning label which was placed on the product. Furthermore, the combination of warnings with intensive safety campaigns and multi-media presentations has typically failed to demonstrate a significant positive impact on safety. The reasons which would explain this finding are yet to be uncovered. However, for whatever underlying reasons, the expectation that labeling of consumer products to effect a positive safety outcome is unreliable. In the face of evidence that warning labels do not positively impact safety, use of on-product warning labels must be judged at best an ineffective safety measure and potentially a misallocation of safety resources.

REFERENCES

ANSI. Specifications for accident prevention signs (ANSI Z35.1). New York, NY: American National Standards Institute, 1972.

Baltimore, C. and Meyer, R.J. A Study of Storage, Child Behavioral Traits, and Mother's Knowledge of Toxicology in 52 Poisoned Families and 52 Comparison Families. Pediatrics 1969, 44, 816-820.

Bragg, B.W. Seat Belts - A good idea but are they too much bother - An analysis of the relationship between attitudes toward seat belts and reported seat belt use. Department of Transport, Road and Motor Vehicle Traffic Safety Branch, Ottowa, Canada, December, 1973.

Bresnahan, T.F., and Bryk, J. The hazard association values of accident prevention signs. Professional Safety, January, 1975, 17-25.

Christ, R.E. Review and analysis of color coding research for visual displays. Human Factors, 1975, 17, 542-570.

Code of Federal Regulations, Title 16, Part 1302. Ban of extremely flammable contact adhesives. Effective January 18, 1978.

Collins, B.L. Evaluation of mine-safety symbols. Proceedings of the Human Factors Society, Norfolk, VA, 1983, 947-949.

Collins, B.L., and Lerner, N.D. Assessment of fire-safety symbols. Human Factors, 1982, 24 (1), 75-84.

Culver-Dickinson, P., Vernberg, D.D., and Spyker, D.A. The deterrent value of "Mr. Yuk" stickers. 1982 International Congress of Clinical Toxicology. Snowmass, Colorado, 1982.

Dale, E., and Chall, J.S. A formula for predicting readability. Educational Research Bulletin, January, 1948, 27, 11-20.

Dorris, A.L., and Purswell, J.L. Warnings and human behavior: Implications for the design of product warnings. Journal of Products Liability, 1977, 1, 255-264.

Easterby, R.S., and Hakiel, S.R. Safety labeling of consumer products: Shape and color code stereotypes in the design of signs. College House, Costa Green, Birmingham, England: University of Aston in Birmingham, Applied Psychology Department, Report No. 75, December, 1977. (a)

Easterby, R.S., and Hakiel, S.R. Safety labeling of consumer products: Field studies of sign recognition. College House, Costa Green, Birmingham, England: University of Aston in Birmingham, Applied Psychology Department, Report No. 76, December, 1977. (b)

Etzioni, A. Caution: Too many health warnings could be counterproductive. *Psychology Today*, December, 1976, 20-21.

Federal Register, 35, No. 104, May 28, 1970, 8359.

FMC. *Products Safety Sign and Label System.* Santa Clara, CA: FMC Corporation, 1980.

FMVSS Federal Register Standard Number 208. Occupant crash protection 32.2415, 1967.

Freimuth, V.S. Assessing the readability of health education messages. *Public Health Reports*, November/December, 1979, 94 (6), 568-570.

Fergusson, D.M., Horwood, L.J., Beautrais, A.L. et al. A controlled field trial of a poisoning prevention method. *Pediatrics*, 1982, 69, 515-520.

Godfrey, S.S., and Allender, L. Warning messages: Will the consumer bother to look? *Proceedings of the Human Factors Society*, Norfolk, VA, 1983, 950-954.

Kerpelman, L.C. Evaluation of the effectiveness of outdoor power equipment information and education programs. Cambridge, MA: ABT Associates, Inc., AAI No. 78-27, March, 1978.

Kolb, J., and Ross, S.S. The responsibility to warn. In Kolb, J. and Ross, S.S. (Eds.). *Product Safety and Liability. A Desk Reference.* New York: McGraw-Hill, 1980.

Kreindler, B.J., and Luchsinger, V.P. How readable are your safety publications? *Professional Safety*, September, 1978, 40-42.

Laner, S., and Sell, R.G. An experiment on the effect of specially designed safety posters. *Occupation Psychology*, July 1960, 34 (3).

McCarthy, R.L., Taylor, R.K., Sanford, S.B., and Lange, R.C. Seat Belts: Effectiveness of Mandatory Use Requirements. Society of Automotive Engineers, SAE 840329, 1984.

McGuinness, J. Human factors in consumer product safety. *Proceedings of the Human Factors Society*, San Francisco, CA, 1977, 292-294.

Morris, L.A., and Kanouse, D.E. Consumer reactions to the tone of written drug information. *American Journal of Hospital Pharmacy*, 1981, 38, 667-671.

Myers, M.L. Staff report on the cigarette advertising investigation. Washington, D.C. Federal Trade Commission, 1981.

National Poison Center Network. *How Mr. Yuk Was Developed.* Pittsburgh, PA: National Poison Center Network, April, 1981.

Nelson, T.M. Hazard analysis on contact adhesive fires. U.S. Consumer Product Safety Commission, Bureau of Epidemiology, October, 1976.

Peters, C.A. Fifteen cardinal principles to ensure effectiveness of warning system. *Occupational Safety and Health.* May, 1984, 76-79.

Rheinstein, P.H., and Baum, C.S. Labeling effectiveness and the health environment. In Morris, L.A., Mazis, M.B. and Barofsky, I., (Eds.). *Product Labeling and Health Risk. Banbury Report 6.* Cold Spring Harbor Laboratory: Cold Spring Harbor, NY, 1980, 275-287.

Riley, M.W., Cochran, D.J., and Ballard, J.C. An investigation of preferred shapes for warning labels. *Human Factors*, 1982, 24 (6), 737-742.

Riley, M.W., Cochran, D.J. and Deary, J.E. Warning label design. *Professional Safety*, October, 1981, 44-46.

Robertson, L.S., O'Neill, B., and Wixom, C.W. Factors associated with observed safety belts. *Journal of Health and Social Behavior*, 1970, 13, 18-24.

Robertson, L.S., and Haddon, W. The buzzer-light reminder system and safety belt use. Insurance Institute for Highway Safety, Report No. DOT-HS-012 202, 1972.

Schneider, K.C. Prevention of accidental poisoning through package and label design. *Journal of Consumer Research*, September, 1977, 4.

Schwartz, V.E., and Driver, R.W. Warnings in the workplace: The need for a synthesis of law and communication theory. *University of Cincinnati Law Review*, 1983, 52 (1), 1-47.

Stephens, L.D., and Barrett, R. A brief history of a 20th century danger sign. *Health Physics*, 1979, 36 (5), 565-571.

Sommese, L.B. and Knopp, S.A. Packaging for safety. *National Safety News*, January, 1978, 67-71.

Westinghouse. *Product Safety Label Handbook.* Trafford, PA: Westinghouse Printing Division, 1981.

Wilcox, A.L. Have you seen any good danger signs? *Hazard Prevention*, 1979, 15 (6), 14.

WARNINGS ON CONSUMER PRODUCTS: OBJECTIVE CRITERIA FOR THEIR USE

Roger L. McCarthy, J. Neil Robinson, James P. Finnegan, and Robert K. Taylor

Failure Analysis Associates
Palo Alto, California

ABSTRACT

Consumer product warnings, often placards, buzzers, etc., are information displays that attempt to influence user behavior through the information presented. A review and background of warnings is presented. Assumptions underlying their employment and the lack of scientific validation of their effectiveness are discussed. Quantitative criteria are proposed for the use of warnings based on risk analysis. Examples of such analysis are presented. The limited information processing capability of man dictates that warnings be reserved for significant risks in the context of the products use, environment, and risks from other products. Contraindications for use of warnings are discussed.

INTRODUCTION

Consumer product warnings are an attempt to modify behavior to decrease risk of consumer product-related injuries. Many papers have been written on this subject. Aspects discussed include determination of whether users notice or read warning labels (Dorris and Purswell, 1977), investigations of whether reading instructions reduces injury rates (Tokuhata et al, 1976), discussion of influence of warning label design on effectiveness (Schneider, 1977), and relationship between warning labels and product liability litigation (B. Ross, 1974; K. Ross, 1981). However, as best we know, no one proposes objective criteria to determine if warning labels should be considered for consumer products. The main object of this paper is to first approach setting such criteria. These criteria are based on risk analysis ("heirarchy of risks") and propositions that warning labels should be reserved for significant risks in the heirarchy in the context of environment in which products are used and of other risks from the product. This paper also discusses background and underlying assumptions to use of warning labels, and contraindications for such use.

Risk is the product of frequency and severity of injury. All frequency and severity data in this paper are for injuries leading to emergency room admissions based on CPSC National Electronic Injury Surveillance System (NEISS) data. NEISS data are obtained from a statistical sample of hospital emergency rooms and are used by CPSC to obtain "national estimates" for total number of product-related injuries treated by hospital emergency rooms. The measure of severity is the CPSC severity scale. Severity values run from 10 for mild injury, through e.g., 81 for concussion to 2516 for death.

BACKGROUND TO THE USE OF WARNING LABELS

Use of warning labels to reduce risk is based on two fundamental assumptions:

1. Human behavior is important in controlling frequency and severity of consumer product-related accidents.

2. Such behavior can be modified in the direction of reducing frequency and severity of accidents by the presence of warning labels.

Our experience investigating numerous accidents leads us to believe that the first is valid; the overwhelming majority of accidents could have been prevented if the product user behaved differently. The second assumption is more doubtful. It is based on the assumptions that:

a) Users will notice and read the label.

b) Users will understand the label.

c) Information in the label is useful in preventing the accident or mitigating severity.

d) Users will act appropriately on information contained in the warning label.

There have been investigations aimed at determining the validity of assumption 2. Dorris and Purswell requested subjects use hammers with one of three warning labels. Two labels directed users to halt the task. Of 100 participants, no one even noticed the presence of the labels. Tokuhata studied injuries in a random selection of over three thousand households, concluding that "reading or not reading instructions about products apparently was not related to the propensity for accidental injuries, nor was there any clear association between cautioning children about dangerous products and the experience of accidental injuries." Dorris and Purswell (1978) note the "number of well documented cases where the public received specific warnings regarding floods, tornadoes or tidal waves and yet substantial numbers of people lost their lives because they chose to take no evasive or mitigating action." It is common experience that few people use seat belts in automobiles in spite of warning lights and buzzers. Robertson and Haddon (1972) compared belt usage between vehicles equipped with buzzers and lights and those not so equipped. They found no reliable difference in belt use.

These results throw serious doubt on the validity of assumption 2. People commonly fail to take action in response to warnings, even when they read or hear them, and it seems they often fail to notice the warnings. The authors are unaware of any empirical research or observations that show the validity of assumption 2, that warning labels can modify behavior to reduce consumer product accidents.

In view of this, why are warning labels used? There appear to be two, interconnected reasons: 1) intuitive reasoning suggests warning labels should reduce accidents, and 2) legal obligation mandates use of warning labels in some cases.

A great deal more research is necessary to resolve the contradiction between empirical observations and intuitive reasoning and legal obligation. In absence of such research, this paper proposes quantitative criteria as a guide as to when warning labels might be used on consumer products. We make no assumptions about their overall effectiveness and do not consider the design of warning labels here.

PROPOSED CRITERIA FOR USE OF WARNING LABELS

We propose two criteria for when warning labels may be considered for use on consumer products. We do not propose warning labels necessarily be used if they meet these criteria; other factors may dictate against their employment. These contraindications are discussed in the next section.

The criteria have been developed on the basis of heirarchy of risks; i.e., that there are numerous risks associated with all environments and consumer products. These risks generally range in importance from significant risks to risks whose frequency and/or severity is so low as to render them negligible. We propose that warning labels should be reserved for significant risks. We also propose that significance of risks be judged in context of the environment in which the item will be used and risk from other accident modes associated with the particular product. If both criteria are met, use of warning labels should be considered. The criteria are:

A. Warning labels should only be considered for use on consumer products when the total risk from the product is of some significance compared to the total risk of home activities; and

B. Employing warning labels that address a particular accident mode for a product should only be considered when the risk of that particular accident mode is significant compared to the total risk associated with the product.

The criteria are based on comparisons of risk. In comparing risk of one product with another or with the risk presented by the environment, it is necessary to know the number and severity of injuries. In addition, it is usually necessary to have a measure of "exposure," e.g., number of products in use and average time which a consumer uses the product. Using exposure allows comparison between common items and rare items, e.g., by comparing the risk per exposure unit for two products. Unfortunately, defining suitable measures of exposure applicable to such disparate products as stairs, circuit breakers, pencils and laundry detergent, for which the magnitude can be determined, is difficult. To facilitate discussion, this paper is limited to consideration of "common products." "Common products" are those consumer products which are commonly encountered in the home. Examples are numerous, including pens, stairs, TVs and soda bottles. Most people are exposed to common products daily. Exposures to these products are approximately similar. Excluded are products such as band saws, which are not common in homes. It also excludes products such as circuit breakers which, while being common in the home, are not frequently encountered by occupants. Risk can then be expressed per million people per year. We anticipate that the criteria could be extended to non-common products provided a suitable measure of exposure is used.

Tentatively, we propose quantitative interpretations of the two criteria, given below. Use of warning labels on common home products should be considered when:

A. The product contributes at least one percent of total risk associated with home activities; and

B. The risk from the particular accident mode considered for a warning contributes at least one tenth of the total risk for the product.

An appropriate modification should be made to criterion A for other environments.

Figure 1 illustrates schematically the heirarchy of risks and the proposition that warning labels should be reserved for significant risks. There are three lines of argument underlying this proposition. First, warning about events with a low level of risk might, if anything, distract attention from higher risks. An uncontrolled torrent of information could result in incorrect identification of information most critical to safety, resulting in concentration on relatively minor risks. Using warning labels for low level risks may have a negative effect on safety.

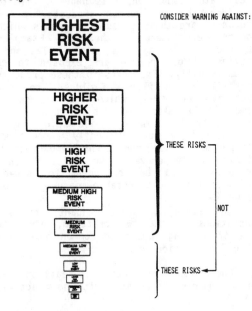

FIGURE 1 – RESERVING WARNING LABELS FOR SIGNIFICANT RISKS IN THE HIERARCHY.

Second, warning about low level risks would lead to very large numbers of warnings in the home, at least one on almost every common item. This point is illustrated in Tables 1 and 2. Table 1 shows the large number of injuries from some common consumer products each year. Table 2 shows the variety of different possible accident modes from just one common consumer product. With multiple warnings on common products, it is unlikely that anyone would pay attention to any particular warning. The purpose of warnings would therefore be defeated.

Third, for rare and not very obvious events, a warning label is unlikely to be heeded. People will rarely see such an event, may not particularly dread it, and may ignore warning labels. This factor may also operate with less rare events; e.g., automobile accidents may be sufficiently rare to fall partially in this category, partly accounting for why few people use seat belts. Slovic (1978) has speculated that repeated benign experience leads to neglecting the belts, in much the same way that subjects in his research on insurance decisions failed to insure against rare hazards.

TABLE 1

NUMBER OF INJURIES PER YEAR ASSOCIATED WITH SOME COMMON ITEMS

Product	Injuries/Year
Bicycles and Accessories	530,700
Beds	171,600
Pencils, Wooden and Unspecified	25,470
First Aid equipment	11,860
Toothpicks or hors d'oeuvres picks	8,440
Toy balls	5,290
Pens	4,040
Combs or hairbrushes, unpowered	3,490

Notes: Data from NEISS for 1979 and 1980 (data for toy balls are for 1973 and 1974)

TABLE 2

INJURY MODES FOR GLASS SOFT DRINK BOTTLES

Injury Mode	Number of Injuries (National Estimate)	Average Severity (CPSC Scale)	Risk Per Million People per year
Swallow glass	1,068	98.27	477
Accidental Contact with Glass	7,192	13.84	452
Fall on Glass	6,267	15.61	445
Drink Poison from bottle	712	110.40	357
Struck by glass	2,137	31.17	303
Bottle explosion	1,923	16.59	145
Step on glass	2,635	12.00	144
Drop Bottle (Break)	2,421	12.56	138
Handling glass	1,567	12.77	91
Cap Propulsion	427	35.83	70
Step on, trip over fall on (unbroken)	356	24.60	39
Swallow cap	71	81.00	26
Struck by bottle (unbroken)	214	14.67	14
Lifting bottle(s)	214	13.67	13
Fireworks in bottle	142	12.00	8
Air or soda in eye	142	12.00	8
Fall on cap	72	17.00	5
TOTAL	27,559	21.84	2735

Note: Data from NEISS data base for injuries leading to emergency room admission in 1980.

The reasons for judging the significance of risks in the context of the total risks associated with the environment and the product are similar to those given above. In particular, warning of low level risks may distract attention from higher level risks in the particular environment or associated with the particular product. Furthermore, people reasonably expect different risk levels in different environments. Thus, a risk level which is not sufficient to justify a warning label in the mining industry may be sufficient in the home, where lower risk levels are expected.

These arguments form the basis for the proposed quantitative levels in the criteria. If warning labels are to be reserved for significant risks, they should be restricted to products which make some significant contribution to the total risk in the environment. We have tentatively proposed a conservative, low cut-off where all products which contribute more than only 1% of total risk are considered for warnings. This means that up to one hundred common products may be considered. It is difficult to imagine that a lower cut-off level, encompassing more than this number of common home products, could be justified.

Similar arguments apply to choosing those accident modes which are to be considered for warning labels. Criterion B includes all accident modes which contribute at least one tenth of the total risk for the product. Thus, up to ten warning labels might be considered for a product. Again, it is difficult to imagine that a lower cut-off level could be justified. A lower cut-off would certainly not aid consumers in concentrating on those risks which significantly affect their safety.

The application of these criteria is illustrated by an example: the injury risk from a pressure-propelled cap from a glass soft drink bottle. Under some rare circumstances, usually during opening, the cap can come off suddenly without prior release of bottle pressure. In very rare cases, the cap may then cause injury.

National estimate for injuries involving cap propulsion leading to emergency room admissions in 1980 was 427*. In this year, there were approximately fourteen billion fillings of carbonated soft drinks in glass bottles. Injury frequency resulting in emergency room treatment is approximately 3 per hundred million bottles, an extremely low unit accident rate.

Table 3 shows risk per million people for some common home items. Note that stairs, etc., bathtubs and showers, ovens, etc., all contribute 1% or more of the total risk for home

* This figure most probably includes some cap propulsion incidents from plastic soft drink bottles. Therefore, it overestimates the number of injuries of this type involving glass soft drink bottles.

living. Thus, from criterion A, they should all be considered for warning labels. (However, as discussed below, labels may not be indicated for these products since the major accident modes are generally well known). Glass soft drink bottles do not meet criterion A, and therefore should not be considered for warning labels.

TABLE 3

COMPARISON OF RISK FOR HOME LIVING WITH SOME COMMON ITEMS

	Injuries/ Year	Average Severity	Risk/Million People/Year
Overall Home Living	5,610,000	48	1,220,000
Stairs, Steps, Ramps & Landings	709,400	29	93,500
Cooking Ranges, Ovens & Related Equipment	38,500	118	20,700
Bathtubs & Showers (Non-glass)	73,400	38	12,700
Cookware, Pots and Pans	28,000	75	9,550
Sinks & Toilets	28,600	29	3,770
Glass Carbonated Soft Drink Bottles	28,000	22	2,800

Notes: Data from NEISS for 1979 and 1980. Figures have been rounded subsequent to calculation.

With regard to criterion B, Table 2 shows the proportion of injuries resulting from each accident mode for glass soft drink bottles. It can be seen that cap propulsion risk is much less than a tenth of the total risk. Thus, both criteria indicate that a warning label should not be considered for this accident mode.

CONTRAINDICATIONS FOR WARNING LABELS

The criteria discussed in this paper refer to when warning labels should be considered. Even when considered, perhaps labels are inappropriate. Major factors which contraindicate using warning labels are:

1. Where the danger is obvious and well-known, or

2. Where the danger results from unreasonable misuse, or

3. Where the danger is not reasonably foreseeable by the manufacturer, or

4. Where no precautions can be advised in the warning to enable the user to anticipate or avoid the danger, or

5. Where the use of warning labels is impractical.

The first three factors are broadly similar to those discussed in the U.S. Department of Commerce Model Uniform Product Liability Act (Dept. of Commerce, 1979).

An example of the application of factor 4 is the CPSC response to a petition requesting glass coffee decanters carry an additional warning that the decanters may fail without prior warning or apparent cause. CPSC commented (CPSC, 1981) that such a warning label "is inappropriate because there are no additional precautions that can be recommended to avoid a potential "spontaneous failure."

Factor 5 includes circumstances where product size or conditions of use preclude use of labels. Size of the product limits area available for placards. Minimum useful placard size is limited by ability to see and read the placard. In some products these two limitations cannot be reconciled. One example is the surgeon's laser scalpel. The hand-held portion must be made as light-weight and pencil-size as possible, precluding meaningful warning labels. Some environments are so dirty, abrasive or chemically active that any label would rapidly be unreadable. Examples include the underside of automobiles and the digging mechanisms on heavy machinery.

Generally, factors 2, 3 or 4 will not be relevant to accident modes which pass criteria A and B. Dangers from unreasonable misuse, which are not reasonably foreseeable, or which cannot be anticipated or avoided will normally be sufficiently uncommon to have very low risk levels. Thus, if the criteria proposed above are used, only two factors will normally need to be considered. These are factors 1 and 5, the extent to which the danger is obvious and the extent to which the use of labels is impractical. The examples mentioned in the previous section, such as falling down stairs, are sufficiently known and obvious that warning labels would impart no further information. Other circumstances may not be so clear, however, and deciding the question of whether a particular hazard is sufficiently obvious and well-known can be difficult. There is presently little useful information in the literature to aid in such decision making.

SUMMARY

The background to the use of warning labels has been reviewed. A contradiction exists between empirical evidence, showing warning labels to have little or no value in reducing risk, and intuitive reasoning and legal constraints which may favor using warning labels.

Quantitative criteria for using warning labels are proposed. These criteria are based on heirarchy of risks and propositions that warning labels should be reserved for significant risks in the context of the environment and of other risks from the product. The criteria

state that use of warning labels on consumer products should only be considered when:

A. Overall risk from the product is significant compared to overall risk of home activities, and

B. Risk from a particular accident mode in question is significant compared to overall risk associated with the product.

We have tentatively proposed quantitative interpretations of these criteria. The reasons behind the criteria and propositions have been presented and discussed. The central argument is that a product user should be aware of the accident modes most critical to his/her safety and not be distracted by a host of warnings against minor risks. Contraindications for using warning labels are discussed.

REFERENCES

Consumer Product Safety Commission, "Glass Coffee Decanters: Denial of Petition," *Federal Register*, 7/15/81.

Dorris, A.L. and Purswell, J.L., "Warnings and Human Behavior; Implications for the Design of Product Warnings," *Journal of Products Liability*, 1(1977):255-264.

Dorris, A.L. and Purswell, J.L., "Human Factors in the Design of Effective Product Warnings," *Proceedings of the Human Factors Society*, 1978.

Ross, B., "Failure to Warn - A New Game for Lawyers, a New Challenge for Engineers," *Proceedings of Annual Reliability and Maintainability Symposium*, 1974.

Ross, K., "Legal and Practical Considerations for the Creation of Warning Labels and Instruction Books," *Journal of Products Liability*, 4(1981):29-45.

Schneider, K.C., "Prevention of Accidental Poisoning Through Package and Label Design," *Journal of Consumer Research*, 4(1977):67-74.

Slovic, P., "The Psychology of Protective Behavior," *Journal of Safety Research*, 10(2):58-68.

Tokuhata, G., Colflesh, V., Smith, M., Ramaswamy, K. and Digon, E., "Consumer Behavior and Product Injuries," *Journal of Safety Research*, 8(3).

U.S. Department of Commerce, Model Uniform Product Liability Act, 1979.

A BEHAVIORAL STUDY OF WARNING LABELS
FOR CONSUMER PRODUCTS:
PERCEIVED DANGER AND USE OF PICTOGRAPHS

Shirley M.Otsubo
California State University, Northridge
Northridge, California

Abstract

This study focused on the effectiveness of warning labels placed on consumer products differing in perceived "danger" or "hazard." A 2x4 between-subject design (N=131) was performed, incorporating two levels of product danger (circular saw=high level of danger; jigsaw=low level of danger) and four levels of warning label (words only, pictograph only, words+pictograph, and no warning). Effectiveness was investigated by studying the behavior of product users to determine who noticed, read, complied and recalled the warning message. Overall results indicated that subjects noticed, read and complied with warnings placed on the product perceived to be more dangerous than on the product perceived to be less dangerous. Additional data suggest that people more familiar with use of the product will tend to read, comply and recall the warning less than those less familiar. Also people more confident with the use of the product will tend to read and comply less than those less confident. Type of warning label showed no effect. However, in all conditions with a warning label, an average of 25.5% complied with the warning (range 12.5 - 50%), and without a warning label no one took precautionary action consistent with the warning message. The findings support the contention that the use of conspicuously designed and placed warning labels on products will influence people to behave cautiously.

INTRODUCTION

The use of warning signs and labels on consumer products are common in today's consumer market. We see them on ladders, household products, typewriters, and even stationery correction fluids. The number of products with warning labels seems almost endless, and yet there is limited data to support their effectiveness. Two important areas of research that have addressed warning effective include (1) the influence of user perceptions, and (2) the design of the warning signs or labels themselves.

One area of warning research has addressed users' perceptions of consumer products. Warning effectiveness may be influenced by the perception of "hazard" or "danger" of the product: the more dangerous a product is perceived, the more cautious an individual will be. For instance, Godfrey, Allender, Laughery, and Smith (1983) found the more hazardous a subject perceived a product, the greater chance the subject will look for a warning. Another study conducted by Wogalter, Desaulniers and Brelsford (1986) also found subjects would be more willing to read a warning on a product perceived to be hazardous. From these studies, the more individuals perceived the product to be hazardous, the more cautious they may be when using the product. Unfortunately most of the data from these studies have been collected from surveys and questionnaires, and have not been validated or verified through task performance. With the exception of a few studies (for example, Strawbridge, 1986; Wogalter, Godfrey, Fontenelle, Desaulniers, Rothstein, and Laughery, 1987) behavioral research involving observations of people actually using products are scarce.

Another area of warning research has investigated the design of the warning signs themselves. Recommendations and suggestions on warning sign readability have centered on the use of pictographs and graphics to symbolize warning hazards (Peters, 1983; FMC, Corp., 1985). Unfortunately empirical research has shown mixed results. Pictorial signs are not always easy to understand (Collins, Lerner & Pierman, 1982), and added to written warning labels, have not been shown to increase compliance (Friedman, 1987). However, pictures have been suggested to serve as "instant reminders" of the hazard (Peters, 1984) and basic research indicate that people recognize and recall pictures far better than words (Paivio, Rogers & Smythe, 1968; Standing, Conezio & Haber, 1970).

The current study focuses on some of the effects of warning design and user perceptions on warning effectiveness by observing users' behavior with actual products. The effects of words and graphics and the perceived differences in potential "danger" or "hazard" associated with products are investigated.

METHOD

Subjects

A total of 131 undergraduate psychology students from the California State University at Northridge participated individually in the experiment. The subject pool comprised of approximately half males and half females.

Materials

Products. Previous studies have found that likelihood of injury, severity of injury, familiarity with the product and complexity of the product may all contribute to the perception of "hazard" or "danger" of a product (Wogalter, Desaulniers, & Brelsford, 1987). In a preliminary survey, subjects were given a consumer product, and were asked to rate the product using a seven-point Likert-type scale. In this survey, two functionally similar products were found to be comparable in familiarity, recency of use, ease, safety, and confidence of use but not with respect to the frequency of use, likelihood of injury, and the multiplicative combination of likelihood of injury and severity of injury. These products were an electric jigsaw and an electric circular saw. Subjects had used the circular saw less frequently, felt more likely to be injured using the circular saw, and the combined score of likelihood times seriousness of injury was greater for the circular saw than the jigsaw.

The combined score of likelihood of injury and severity of injury was included because the combination has been suggested as a predictive measure of perceived hazardousness (Hammer, 1972; Slovic, Fischhoff, & Lichtenstein, 1980; Wogalter, et al., 1987). Although Wogalter et al.'s (1987) multiple correlation analyses study suggested severity alone provides good predictability of product hazardousness, it is possible their question regarding severity pooled perceptions of both severity and likelihood by questioning the severity of injury to him or herself instead of the perceptions of severity of injury to other users. Thus in this current study it was concluded that the circular saw would be perceived as more dangerous or hazardous than the jigsaw due to the different perceptions of likelihood of injury and the likelihood times severity factor.

Warning Sign Design. Three warning signs, shown in Figure 1, were used in this study. One warning was designed with "words only," another warning was designed with a "pictograph only," and the third warning was designed with both "pictograph and words." Pilot studies were run to optimize size, design, location and comprehension of warnings on the two products.

Figure 1. *Warning Labels*

The warning message was designed to convey four message elements: the level of hazard (CAUTION), the nature of the hazard (SHARP BLADE), the consequence of the hazard (CAN CUT), and the avoidance of the hazard (WEAR GLOVES) (Wogalter, Desaulniers, & Godfrey, 1985; FMC Corp., 1985).

The pictograph was designed to pictorially represent the same warning message as the "words only" sign. This was confirmed in a pilot study. The same warning message with both pictograph and words as specified above were also incorporated into one warning sign. The placement of the pictograph above the words follow guidelines recommended by FMC, Corp. (1985).

The final placement and size of the warning signs were determined by:

1. physical shape limitations of the tools,
2. consistent positioning of warning signs on both tools, by placing the warning on the handle of the saws,
3. legibility requirements for alphanumeric characters in the warning message, such as stroke width-to-height ratio, and
4. minimizing the possibility of obscuring and hiding the warning from natural hand movements by subjects.

Experimental Design

A 2x4 between-subject experimental design was employed. Two conditions of perceived product danger (high and low) and four conditions of warning sign design ("words only," "pictograph only," "pictograph+words," and no warning) were used.

A minimum of 16 subjects were assigned to each experimental condition with approximately equal number of males and females assigned to each condition.

Setting

The setting represented a real-world worktable for storing and using hand tools. Various tools were accessible to the subject, such as screwdrivers, hammer, various wrenches and pliers, nails, measuring tape, ruler, and pencil. Protective equipment were also available, such as a face mask, eye goggles, and hand gloves.

Procedure

Subjects were told that they would be expected to use an electric saw. If they felt uncomfortable with using the saw, they were given the opportunity to decline participation in the experiment. Six people declined. Those who participated were told to imagine that they were at home alone, and wished to repair a small bookcase. The subjects were directed to the worktable where various tools were located. A piece of wood was clamped down on the table with two C-clamps, and the subjects were instructed to repair the bookcase by first cutting 12 inches off the end of the wood, and then connecting the two wood pieces together with braces located on the table. The subjects were told to use any tools and equipment on the worktable and to perform the task the way they would normally approach it. Records of subjects' actions were noted, including whether gloves were used.

When subjects were observed plugging the tool in the extension cord (which was not plugged into an electrical outlet) and pressing the switch to turn on the power, they were stopped from continuing with the remainder of the task. Thus the subjects never actually used the tool. The tool was then removed from their sight.

An interview was conducted immediately thereafter to elicit the subject's perception and recall of the warning message. The subjects were initially asked whether they noticed a warning. If their response was yes, they were asked where the sign was located. Subjects were further probed whether they read and understood the warning. If they did, they were asked to interpret its general content. The subjects were further asked to recall the specific warning statements: the danger, the cause of the danger, and how the danger could be avoided. These responses on recall were recorded as incorrect (with a score of "0"), partially correct (with a score of "1"), and fully correct (with a score of "2"). To confirm their recall responses, the subjects were given a sheet of paper to draw the warning sign as accurately as possible. Comments and explanations for their actions were recorded.

Subjects then completed a questionnaire. A seven-point Likert-type rating scale was used to determine subject's level of perceived likelihood and severity of injury, the recency and frequency of use with the tool, their perception of the ease of use, level of safety and their confidence with use of the tool. On a dichotomous rating scale subjects were also asked whether they had used a similar tool, had been personally injured or knew of others who had been injured using tools. Subjects were also questioned as to the realism and general perception of the experimental setting and situation to assess face validity and fidelity.

Seven dependent variables were measured. These variables were:

1. whether the subject <u>saw</u> the warning;
2. whether the subject <u>read</u> the warning;
3. whether the subject recalled the <u>cause</u> of the hazard;
4. whether the subject recalled the <u>consequence</u> of the hazard;
5. whether the subject recalled the <u>avoidance</u> of the hazard;
6. how confident the subject was regarding the <u>meaning</u> of the warning sign; and
7. whether the subject <u>complied</u> with the warning.

Data on the first six variables were gathered through the post-experimental interview. Occurrence of the seventh variable was observed during task performance. Further information was collected in the follow-up questionnaire.

RESULTS

The use of a warning label over no warning was clearly apparent. Within the control group which had no warning, no one was observed using gloves. However, with the addition of a warning label, the overall results, across all warning conditions, showed that 64.3% noticed the warning, 38.8% read the warning and 25.5% complied with the warning.

Perceived "Danger" Between Products

As hypothesized, and shown in Table 1, more people noticed ($x2(1, \underline{N}=98)=4.20, \underline{p}=.04$), read ($x2(1, \underline{N}=98)=4.52 \underline{p}=.01$), and complied ($x2(1, \underline{N}=98)=8.38 \underline{p}=.004$) with the warning placed on the product perceived to be more dangerous (circular saw) than on the product perceived less dangerous (jigsaw). No significant differences were found between the products and recall of the warning messages.

TABLE 1

Subjects who noticed, read and complied with warning as a function of product type (based on total subjects)

	Noticed	Read	Complied
Circular	74%	52%	38%
Jigsaw	54%	25%	13%

To determine what may have contributed to these differences between products, questionnaire data were analyzed. Two-way analysis of variance tests revealed those who used the jigsaw perceived it to be easier to use ($\underline{F}(1,92)=6.81$, $\underline{p}=.01$), safer to use ($\underline{F}(1,92)=5.33$, $\underline{p}=.02$), felt less likely to be injured ($\underline{F}(1,92)=7.09$, $\underline{p}=.01$) and felt more confident ($\underline{F}(1,92=4.7$, $\underline{p}=.03$) using the jigsaw than those who used the circular saw. Also the combined score of likelihood times seriousness was significantly higher for the circular saw than for the jigsaw ($\underline{F}(1,92)=5.5$, $\underline{p}=.02$), and more subjects knew others injured using the circular saw than the jigsaw ($x2(1, \underline{N}=98)=6.63$, $\underline{p}=.01$).

Warning Label

Chi-square tests showed no significant differences between warning signs in noticing, reading, complying, comprehending or recalling the warning. However, questionnaire data revealed a difference between level of confidence ($\underline{F}(2,92)=3.55$, $\underline{p}=.03$). Subjects were more confident using the tool when the label with words-only was placed on the tool than when the label with pictograph+words was used ($\underline{C.diff.}=1.0$, $\underline{N}=32$, $\underline{p}<.05$).

Figure 2 shows overall percentages of those who noticed, read and complied with each type of warning for each product. As can be seen, compliance was as high as 50% when the words+pictograph warning was placed on the circular saw.

To test possible interactions between the product, warning label and dependent measures, all possible two-factor log linear models were constructed with product, warning label, and the measures of noticing, reading, complying, comprehending and recalling the warning. No interactions were found.

Differences Between Noticing, Reading, Complying and Recalling the Warning

Further detailed analyses were conducted on answers obtained from the follow-up questionnaire. These results are reported below.

Results revealed that those who noticed the warning felt that it was more likely that an injury would occur with the product than those who failed to notice the warning ($\underline{t}(96)=2.04$, $\underline{p}=.04$).

Subjects who read the warning were less likely to have had prior experience with the tool ($x2(1, \underline{N}=63)4.91$, $\underline{p}=.03$). Subjects who did not read the warning reported having used the tool more recently than those who did read

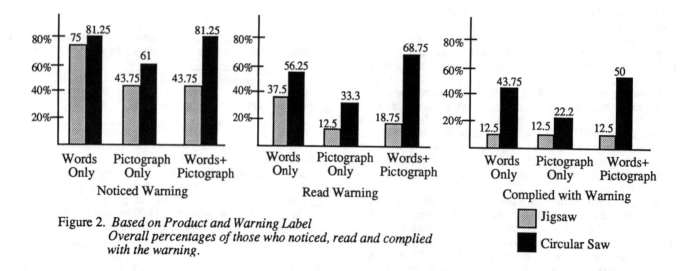

Figure 2. *Based on Product and Warning Label*
Overall percentages of those who noticed, read and complied with the warning.

the warning ($\underline{t}(30)=2.11$, $\underline{p}=.04$). Also those who read the warning reported less confidence in using the tool than those who did not read the warning ($\underline{t}(61)=2.31$, $\underline{p}=.02$).

Those who complied with the warning message as compared to those who did not comply: (1) had less experience with tools in general ($\chi 2(1,\underline{N}=40)=5.54$, $\underline{p}=.02$); (2) had less experience with a similar type of saw ($\chi 2(1, \underline{N}=40)=5.44$, $\underline{p}=.02$); (3) were less confident in using the saw ($\underline{t}(40)=2.04$, $\underline{p}=.05$); and (4) were more likely to have been personally injured using a similar tool ($\chi 2(1, \underline{N}=40)=5.06$, $\underline{p}=.02$). An unexpected result revealed those who felt a more severe injury would occur actually complied with the warning less than those who felt a less severe injury would occur ($\underline{t}(38)=-2.05$, $\underline{p}=.047$).

Differences in recall revealed those who could not recall the danger ("can cut") ($\chi 2(1, \underline{N}=38)=4.6$, $\underline{p}=.03$) and avoidance ("wear gloves") ($\chi 2(1, \underline{N}=38)=5.29$, $\underline{p}=.02$) of the warning message, had previously used a similar tool before.

DISCUSSION

The results indicate that the perceived differences between products will influence people to notice, read, and comply with warnings. This difference may be due to the perception of "hazard" or "danger" of the product. We can conclude that these products were perceived differently, and it is likely that this perceived difference in "danger" or "hazard" affected warning effectiveness. Detailed analysis of the data revealed of those who used the circular saw, the number who read the warning was two-thirds the number who noticed the warning, and the number of subjects who complied with the warning was two-thirds the number who read the warning. For those who used the jigsaw, the number who read the warning was one-half the number of those who noticed the warning, and those who complied with the warning was one-half the number who read the warning.

Surprisingly, for all independent variables, there were no significant differences found between any of the warning signs. Nevertheless, the warnings were effective in altering behavior. Across all warning conditions, an average of 25.5% of the people complied, with the highest rate of compliance (50%) occurring with the redundant (words+pictograph) warning on the product perceived as most hazardous or dangerous.

The gloves available to use were standard leather gloves instead of metal protected gloves. It can be argued that the gloves would not offer adequate protection when used with a circular or jigsaw. However, out of the 14 subjects who failed to comply with the warning and could recall its message, only three indicated they felt the gloves would not help. The remaining subjects explained that they were normally careful, and felt no need for protection. Further, if subjects did not feel adequately protected by the leather gloves, then the compliance percentage reported would represent an underestimation of the effectiveness of well designed labels. We must conclude that most likely few subjects considered the protection offered by the gloves during the experiment, and that the compliance rates are a fair reflection of the effectiveness of warning labels for products such as those used here, by subjects like those who participated.

Interestingly enough, contradicting Wogalter et al.'s (1987) study, severity of injury alone was not an important factor in determining whether subjects noticed, read or recalled the warning. Results in fact unexpectedly showed that those who perceived greater severity of injury actually complied less than those who felt less severity of injury would occur. What did seem important, with respect to compliance with the warning, were familiarity and personal injury in using the tool.

The purpose of the study was to show that products which varied in level of "danger" or "hazard" influenced warning effectiveness. The results from this study support this contention. Previous research have supported the use of severity of injury, likelihood of injury, complexity and familiarity as predictors of hazardousness. However, this current study also supports the notion of confidence of use. Perceived severity alone also was not found to influence product differences. Unfortunately the specific determination of what "hazardousness" or "dangerousness" entails still need to be determined through further research.

In summary, perceived differences between the products contributed to warning effective. An average of 38% complied with the warning using the circular saw (more dangerous), and 13% complied with the warning using the jigsaw (less dangerous). This difference may be due to varied levels of confidence, and/or perceived likelihood of injury. Differing levels of safety and ease of use did not seem to directly influence warning effectiveness, but may still play a part in determining differences in perception between the products. Familiarity and prior experience were also important factors in determining warning effectiveness, with those more familiar failing to read, comply and recall the warning.

REFERENCES

Collins, B., Lerner, N., & Pierman, B. (1982). Symbols for industrial safety. (Report No. NBSIR82-2485). Washington, DC: National Institute of Occupational Safety and Health.

FMC Corp. (1985). Product Safety Sign and Label System. Santa Clara, CA: FMC, Corp.

Friedman, K. (1987)., The effects of adding symbols to written warning labels on user behavior and recall. Unpublished master's thesis, California State University, Northridge, Northridge, CA.

Godfrey, S.S., Allender, L., Laughery, K.R., & Smith, V. (1983). Warning messages: will the consumer bother to look? In Proceedings of the Human Factors Society 27th Annual Meeting. Santa Monica, CA: The Human Factors Society.

Hammer, W. (1972). Handbook of System and Product Safety. Englewood, NJ: Prentice Hall, Inc.

Paivio, A., Rogers, T.B., and Smythe, P.C. (1968). Why are pictures easier to recall than words? Psychonomic Science. 11(4), 137-138.

Peters, G.A. (November, 1983). Toward effective warning for automobiles: a challenge to the trial bar. Trial Magazine. 19(11), 1214-119.

Peters, G.A. (May, 1984). 15 cardinal principles to ensure effectiveness of warning system. Occupational Health and Safety. 76-79.

Slovic, P., Fischhoff, B., & Lichtenstein, S. (1980). Facts and fears: understanding perceived risk. In R.C. Schwing and W.A. Albers, Jr. (Eds.), Societal Risk Assessment. New York: Plenum Press.

Standing, L., Conezio, J., & Haber, N. (1970). Perception and memory of pictures: single trial learning of 2500 visual stimuli. Psychonomic Sci. 19, 73-74.

Strawbridge, J.A. (1986). The influence of position, highlighting, and imbedding on warning effectiveness. In Proceedings of the Human Factors Society 30th Annual Meeting. Santa Monica, CA: The Human Factors Society.

Wogalter, M.W., Desaulniers, D.R., & Godfrey, S.S. (1985). Perceived effectiveness of environmental warnings. In Proceedings of the Human Factors Society 29th Annual Meeting. Santa Monica, CA: The Human Factors Society.

Wogalter, M.S., Desaulniers, D.R., & Brelsford, J.W. (1986). Perceptions of consumer products: hazardousness and warning expectations. In Proceedings of the Human Factors Society 30th Annual Meeting. Santa Monica, CA: The Human Factors Society.

Wogalter, M.S., Desaulniers, D.R., & Brelsford, J.W. (1987). Consumer products: how are the hazards perceived? In Proceedings of the Human Factors Society 31th Annual Meeting. Santa Monica, CA: The Human Factors Society.

Wogalter, M.S., Godfrey, S.S., Fontenelle, G.A., Desaulniers, D.R., Rothstein, P.R., & Laughery, K.R. (1987). Effectiveness of Warnings. Human Factors. 29(5), 599-612.

WARNING EFFECTIVENESS: WHAT DO WE NEED TO KNOW

Jerry L. Purswell, Ph.D.,P.E.
University of Oklahoma
Norman, Oklahoma

Richard F. Krenek, Ph.D.,P.E.
Krenek and Associates
Norman, Oklahoma

Alan Dorris, Ph.D.
Dorris and Associates
Peachtree City, Georgia

ABSTRACT

The forensic area of practice for human factors engineers has brought into sharp focus the differences of opinion which exist regarding the effectiveness of warnings in bringing about safe behavior on the part of the user of a product. This paper addresses the major issues which the authors believe must be researched further to provide the definitive answers needed regarding the effectiveness of warnings in a variety of possible applications. A review of the literature will demonstrate that there are few studies of warning effectiveness per se, while there are many studies that address such issues as the need for warnings and presumed criteria for preparing effective warnings. It is suggested that further research is needed which addresses warning effectiveness in actual use situations, and in turn identifies the importance of such variables as stimulus energy level, information overload, risk perception, cost of compliance and the interaction of warnings, instructions and training.

INTRODUCTION

The issue of the effectiveness of warnings in bringing about safe behavior is of significant interest to the following persons or organizations:

1. The designer/manufacturer of a product
2. The plaintiff and defense bar in tort litigation
3. The persons who serve as experts in tort litigation
4. The academicians, scientists and students in various fields who peform research in the area

This paper will highlight the need for more studies to identify the significant variables related to warning effectiveness from the perspectives of an expert in tort litigation and research in an academic community. There are other applied research issues of warning effectiveness from the perspective of the designer/manufacturer of a product which are beyond the scope of this paper which are also important in the overall question of warnings effectiveness.

RESEARCH ISSUES

Background

It has been 10 years since Dorris and Purswell (1977) published one of the first studies where warning effectiveness was empirically evaluated. In a second paper, (1978) a list of needed research was presented, including the following issues:

1. Optimum amount of information to be presented
2. Symbolic versus verbal warning effectiveness
3. Need for an appropriate methodology for studying behavior
4. Need to understand the factors that influence responses to warnings.

The recent two-volume work of Miller and Lehto (1986) provides an updated discussion of these and other research issues which confront one when the question of warning effectiveness is considered. However, of the 388 reference sources in their annotated bibliography on the topic of warnings, only 10 sources are listed as related to an analysis of warnings effectiveness, and of these, only 6 actually cite any experimental results. The literature is therefore still not very complete in identifying the variables which are related to the design of effective warnings, and the information which does exist is not very enlightening regarding the design of effective warnings because most of the warnings investigated were not effective in bringing about safe behavior.

The paucity of actual studies of warning effectiveness in the literature is perhaps not too surprising. These studies are difficult to perform for many products due to the logistics of collecting experimental observations in general, and the problem of inadvertantly introducing an experimental bias, i.e., the subject is influenced to read the warning and/or behave safely if he perceives that the purpose of the study is to evaluate warning effectiveness.

Need for a Conceptual Model

While it is possible to suggest goals to be achieved in warnings design, and to provide some guidance for designers (Dorris and Purswell, 1978; Peters, 1984; Rosenberg, 1981; Cunitz, 1981) it is now becoming clear that additional guidance based on sound research data is needed if more effective warnings are to be designed. In order to develop this data, our conceptual model of the warnings process must be refined to highlight the variables to be studied. Miller and Lehto (1986) have suggested a conceptual model based on the following sequential steps for a warning to be effective:

1. The subject must be exposed to the warning stimulus
2. The subject must attend to the stimulus
3. There must be active processing of the warning message
4. The subject must comprehend and agree with the warning message
5. The subject may be required to store the warning message as well perform search and retrieval functions.
6. An appropriate response must be selected
7. The subject must perform the response
8. The response must be adequate to avoid the injury

Note that it is possible to have a reasonably high success rate in the population for each of these sequential steps and still have a low overall effectiveness rate for the warning. The next sections of this paper will present some of the important research needs as related to one or more of these steps in the warning process.

Stimulus: Energy Level and Contact

Many human factors/ergonomics texts (McCormick, 1976; for example) present guidelines for designing the warning stimulus so that it has sufficient energy to be perceived under a given level of illumination at some distance. Similarly, information is presented regarding the location of the warning in the visual field for optimum contact. If a person is inclined to seek warning information, then the stimulus energy levels specified in these texts for various conditions of use are probably adequate for warnings design. However, there are many possible variables which can intervene to prevent warning information from being sensed. Miller and Lehto (1986) have used the term "filtering" to describe the effects of some of these variables on the sensing process. The net effect of these filtering variables is that most users of a product will not read the warning information. There is a definite need to perform research to better understand the following filtering variables:

1. **Information overload** can occur in at least four ways:

   a. Warning lists frequently include numerous items, thus raising questions about a user's ability to perceive/recall items in the middle of the list.

   b. The contents of a single warning may to too extensive, resulting in the perception that the warning is less effective (Wogalter et al., 1985).

   c. There may be too many individual warnings placed in the field of view.

   d. There may be other non-warning stimuli which are given priority over the warning stimuli.

The need exists for more research to understand the points at which information overload is likely to occur for each of the types of overload listed above.

A related research problem is to determine a satisfactory methodology for prioritization of individual warnings where space is limited and there are more warnings than can be accomodated in the space available.

2. <u>Faulty risk assessment</u> can result in an <u>individual failing</u> to look for a warning or to ignore a warning if one is perceived to be present. Dorris and Tabrizi (1978), Slovic, et al. (1980), Godfrey et al. (1983) have all noted the problems which exist in persons performing adequate risk assessments for products. More recently, Purswell, et al.(1986a) found that the amount of risk information provided did not significantly influence the subjective rating of hazard perceived. There is thus a need for more research to develop information concerning the way individuals use perceived risk information. In a sense, it is a "chicken and egg" type problem, i.e., a warning will not be read because a hazard is not perceived, and a hazard cannot be perceived without the warning information.

3. <u>Benign experience versus a warning</u> is a concept that has been suggested by Karnes et al. (1986) as one reason that warnings are filtered. The hypothesis is that if one is regularly exposed to a warning about a hazard while at the same time exposing themselves to the hazard the warning addresses without being injured, the warning will likely be filtered and even changes to improve the conspicuity of the warning will not likely prove to be effective.

Comprehension of Warnings

There are at least four types of problems in the area of warning comprehension where more research is needed:

1. <u>The meaningfulness of "signal" words</u> in calling attention to the severity of injury which can result if the warning is ignored. While it has been suggested by the FMC labeling system that the words "danger", "warning" and "caution" should be used to represent a hierarchy of decreasing potential for harm in designing warnings, this suggested format is not clearly supported by the research reported to date (Bresnahan and Bryk, 1975; Nikmorad, 1985). Miller and Lehto (1986) suggest that a better system might be extreme-danger, serious-danger and moderate-danger.

2.<u>The reading comprehension level required</u> to understand the warning. If warning messages are evaluated using one of the several tests developed for readability, it will be found that there is a wide range of values, starting with grade four or five and continuing through grade twelve or higher. A related problem is the design of warning messages where a chemical compound is involved. It is usually necessary to include a realtively large number of words to explain the health and safety consequences of exposure, the proper protective measures, and first aid measures when exposure does occur. In each case, there appears to be a definite tradeoff between the use of a smaller number of words with a more exact meaning versus a larger number of smaller words with less exact meanings.

3. <u>The meaningfulness of symbol</u> in lieu of words to communicate warning information. Ideally, warnings should be designed to be language independent where there is a significant probability that the intended recipient does not read English, or whatever language is used in preparing the warning. There is a need for more research information concerning such things as the culturally derived meaning of various symbols, and the correct approach for designing pictorials to communicate different concepts.

4. <u>The meaningfulness of warnings</u> as a <u>function of the task being performed</u>, or stated another way, the effectiveness of warnings when presented in the context of instructions as compared to presenting the warnings in a separate list without the context of the task being performed. It is possible to find warnings that are presented in the form of a list at the beginning of the instructions versus being presented at the point where the warning is needed in the context of performing some operation with a product. Some proponents of placing a warning list at the front of the instructions argue that the user may not notice the warning if it is imbedded in the instructions, while others argue that the warning will not be meaningful unless it is placed near the instructions to which it is related. One of the authors has a research project underway at the present time to provide some insight into this area of warnings design.

Warnings and Memory

For persons who deal with warnings design, it is a common experience to find that few warnings are stored in long term memory if they are more than six or seven lines long, or address more than this number of hazards in using a product. Surveys done by the authors of long term recall of the warnings on such products as spray paint cans, drain cleaners, electric power tools, or complex equipment such as cranes have demonstrated that most people cannot recall more than four or five items of information from the warnings. There is, of course, a distinction between having safety knowledge and remembering that the source of that knowledge was originally a warning. There is a need to have more research done to better understand the reasons for this lack of long term recall, i.e., is it related to the general problem of lack of active processing of warning information as described by Miller and Lehto (1986). Wright (1980) has described this problem for a warning displayed next to an antacid product, noting that less than 10% of the purchasers of the product could remember even a portion of the warning when asked upon leaving the store.

Given that most warnings are not generally committed to long term memory, then there arises the question of short term memory of warnings, and in particular the question of how our short term memory behaves in the presence of different stressors or distractors which may be present in the job task environment. More information is needed regarding the best process for committing warning information to long term memory and then recalling it when it is needed. Of course, it is possible that most people do not remember warnings because they filter the information and it never actully reaches long term memory (McCormick, 1976).

The Decision Making Process

Of all the areas where more research is needed, not just in the area of warnings, but in other areas of safety as well, the area of decision making seems to be among the most important. Slovic (1977, 1978) notes that people do not use risk information very objectively and consider that accidents are rare events which will not happen to them. The authors have noted this phenomenon often in performing safety research. It might be hypothesized that there is a threshold of perceived probability of an injury which must be reached before a person's behavior will be influenced by risk information such as contained in a warning. This perceived probability threshold may be relatively high, i.e., 1/100 before most persons will respond

to knowledge about hazards as presented in a warning. Fortunately, most products do not have this high a probability of injury per use, and therefore warning messages are either not perceived or not heeded. It is very important to obtain a better understanding of how our risk perception/risk acceptance interacts with the warning process.

Godfrey et al. (1985) noted that there is another factor operating in our decision process when we are confronted with a warning. The term "cost of compliance" was used to suggest why the warnings may not be heeded. If an individual complies with a warning, some cost in terms of money, time, effort or perceived enjoyment is extracted from the individual, and the perceived benefit must outweigh these costs. There may also be a benefit of non-compliance that is of significant importance to the individual. It may take the form of maintaining a macho image, more money for increased production, etc. Perhaps the costs and benefits of both compliance and non-compliance play a significant role in warning effectiveness. Since there is frequently a difference in the dimensions of cost and benefit, it appears, implicitly at least, that the individual constructs some type of utility function for making the tradeoff. Because there are likely many such transient functions employed by an individual, it may be difficult to describe such functions in a manner that renders them useful to perform safety analyses. The most promising descriptor found to date for such behavior is a questionnaire developed by Purswell, et al., (1986b) to measure attitudes about risk taking. Further research using this concept should add to our understanding of why a person behaves safely or not when presented with a warning.

RESEARCH STRATEGY

As noted in the beginning of this paper, it is difficult to perform research in the area of warnings design, and yet it is very important to complete some of the research suggested if we are to avoid the present controversies among human factors engineers and reduce the legal rhetoric which exists today in lieu of sound information. Some possible approaches are as follows:

1. To the extent possible, future accident investigation efforts should focus on such issues as hazard aware-

ness, perception of risk, and accident avoidance information which was obtained from a warning as compared to other sources.

2. Experimental approaches utilizing discriminant analysis should be used to better understand the relative influence of a variety of personal, product (including warnings) and environmental factors on safe behavior.

3. Carefully controlled studies should be done to determine the relative influence of human and environmental variables on the major factors discussed in this paper, and in turn the relative influence and importance of those factors on the success of the overall warnings/instruction/training process.

REFERENCES

Bresnhan, T. & Bryk, J. (1975). The Hazard Association Values of Accident Prevention. Professional Safety, 17-25.

Cunitz, R.J. (1981). Psychologically Effective Warnings. Hazard Prevention, 17:3, 5-7.

Dorris, A.L. & Purswell, J.L. (1977). Warnings and Human Behavior: Implications for the Design of Product Warnings. Journal of Products Liability, 1, 255-263.

Dorris, A.L. & Purswell, J.L. (1978). Human Factors in the Design of Effective Product Warnings. Proceedings of the Human Factors Society, 22nd Annual Meeting, 343-263.

Dorris, A.L. & Tabrizi, M.F. (1978) An Empirical Investigation of Consumer Perception of Product Safety. Journal of Products Liability, 2, 155-163.

Godfrey, S.S., et al. Warning Messages: Will the Consumer Bother to Look? Proceedings of the Human Factors Society, 27th Annual Meeting, 950-954.

Godfry, S.S., Rothstein, P.R. & Laughery, K.R. (1985). Warnings: Do They Make a Difference. Proceedings of the Human Factors Society 29th Annual Meeting, 669-673.

Karnes, E.W. & Rachwal, G. Effects of Benign Experiences on the Perception of Risk. Proceedings of the Human Factors Society 30th Annual Meeting, 121-125.

Lehto, M.R. & Miller J.M. Warnings, Volume I: Fundamentals, Design, & Evaluation Methodologies. (1986) Volume II: Annotated Bibliography. (1987) Ann Arbor, Michigan: Fuller Technical Publications.

McCormick, E.J. & Sanders, M.S. (1976). Human Factors in Engineering and Design (2nd ed.). New York : McGraw-Hill.

Nikmorad, H. (1985). A Study of Behavioral Responses In Regard to the Warning Labels on Consumer Products. Unpublished Master's thesis, University of Oklahoma, Norman, Ok.

Peters, G.A. (1984). 15 Cardinal Principles to Ensure Effectiveness of Warning System. Occupational Health and Safety, 76-79.

Purswell, J.L., Schlegel, R.E. & Kejriwal, S.K. (1986a). A Prediction Model for Consumer Behavior Regarding Product Safety. Proceedings of the Human Factors Society 30th Annual Meeting, 1202-1205.

Purswell, J.L. et. al. (1986b). Percieved Hazard Versus Risk Information. Unpublished research paper, University of Oklahoma, Norman, Ok.

Slovic, P. (1978). The Psychology of Protective Behavior. Journal of Safety Research, 10:2, 58-68.

Slovic, P., Fischhoff B., & Lichtenstein, S. (1977). Behavioral Decision Theory. Annual Review of Psychology, 28, 1-39.

Slovic, P., Fischhoff B., & Lichtenstein, S. (1980). Facts And Fears: Understanding Percieved Risk. in Societal Risk Assessment. New York: Plenum Press.

Rosenberg, S. (1981). FMC'S Systematic Approach to Product Safety Warning Labels. Agricultural Engineering, 62:10, 22-24

Wogalter, M.S., Desaulniers, D.R. & Godfrey, S.S. (1985) Percieved Effectiveness of Environmental Warnings. Proceedings of the Human Factors Society 29th Annual Meeting, 664-68.

Wright. P. (1979). Concrete Action Plans in TV Messages to Increase Reading of Drug Warnings. Journal of Consumer Research, 6, 256-269.

A PREDICTION MODEL FOR CONSUMER BEHAVIOR REGARDING PRODUCT SAFETY

Jerry L. Purswell, Ph.D.
Robert E. Schlegel, Ph.D.
Sashi K. Kejriwal
School of Industrial Engineering
University of Oklahoma
Norman, Oklahoma 73019

ABSTRACT

The objective of this study was the development of a model to predict whether a consumer would use a product safely as a function of sixteen different individual variables. Subjects were presented with four consumer products to use in an experimental setting where the true purpose of the study was concealed. Discriminant analysis was used to develop a prediction model to classify subjects into categories of safe or unsafe behavior. Prediction accuracy ranged from 68-86 percent for different types of behavior. The research illustrated which variables are important in determining whether a product will be used safely and has implications for product design, warnings, instructions for use and training.

INTRODUCTION

Anyone familar with the field of product liability litigation is aware of the problems of predicting how the user of a product will behave if presented with a situation where they must choose to take some specific action to use the product safely. In an effort to understand how different personal variables affect the behavior of a user when faced with a choice of safe or unsafe behavior, this study was undertaken.

Schwartz et al. (1978) studied the impact of objectively predetermined hazard information on consumer buying decisions, concluding that such information does have a significant impact on the decision to buy a product. Dorris and Tabrizi (1978) found little correlation between the perception of hazardousness of certain products and the hazard index of the Consumer Products Safety Commission. Slovic et al. (1980) found that safety experts could make good judgements about how hazardous a product was to use, while lay subjects were not able to make such judgements very well. Godfrey et al. (1983) found that the more hazardous a product is perceived to be, the more likely the user is to look for a warning label. Familiarity with a product caused it to be rated as less hazardous. Wright (1982) found that people reported they were less likely to read instructions on products used frequently. Dorris and Purswell (1977) found that none of 100 subjects read the warning label before using a hammer, thus suggesting that familiarity in using a product is related to the perceived hazard.

METHODOLOGY

Experimental Variables

If one compiles a candidate list of personal variables which could influence the safety behavior of a person when asked to use a product, there are a large number of possible candidates. Foremost on such a list is some measure of risk-taking by the person. There have been surprisingly few attempts to develop a useful measure of risk-taking propensity based on some type of survey instrument. Measures of risk-taking behavior were therefore chosen as experimental variables to be evaluated. These included the following:

1. Percentage of time that the subject wore seatbelts while driving in town, and on the highway.

2. Use of a life-jacket or not while boating on a lake.

3. Crossing the street while the "Don't Walk" is displayed.

4. Score on a special questionnaire instrument developed for this research.

The special questionnaire was developed and tested for subject pools of 15-20 subjects in a stepwise process, refining the questionnaire at each step until the mean score was approximateley the mid point of the scale used for a random group of subjects. The questionnaire was based on a five point scale from safe to very dangerous, covering the subject's attitudes toward areas such as nuclear power, household products, sports activities, work place hazards, etc.

Other variables evaluated as predictors of safety behavior were as follows:

1. Age of subject in years
2. Sex of subject
3. Hazard rating of the product by the subject
4. Familiarity of the subject with the product
5. Recency of use of the product
6. Injury experience with the product
7. Score from the Adventure-seeking scale in the Zuckerman test
8. Score from the Boredom-susceptibility scale in the Zuckerman test
9. Score from the Disinhibition scale in the Zuckerman test
10. Score from the Experience-seeking scale in the Zuckerman test
11. Total score from the Zuckerman test.

Experimental Design

The multivariate statistical method of analysis selected was discriminant analysis, which involves deriving the linear combination of two or more independent variables which will best discriminate between pre-defined groups, i.e., subjects who behaved safely and those who behaved unsafely when presented with the experimental task. The research question therefore was the determination of those variables having the best utility to predict safe or unsafe behavior from among the candidate set proposed.

Experimental Task

A group of products was selected to present a range of responses across the experimental variables chosen for study. A chemical drain opener and an electrical carving knife were chosen because of the likely familiarity of most subjects with these products. A sabre-saw was chosen because it was expected to be less familiar to most of the subjects than the first two items. Finally, a router was chosen for study because it was expected that it would be the least familiar to most of the subjects.

Because of the need to protect the subjects from injury, the type of tasks selected for evaluating safety behavior had to be restricted. Also, it was necessary to conceal the real purpose of the study from the subjects in order to obtain as true a behavioral response as possible. The subjects were asked to evaluate certain "ergonomic" features of the tools such as the size of the handle, the weight, or the balance. The "cleaning power" of the drain opener was to be evaluated.

For the drain opener, the safety behavior evaluated was whether the person read the warning label before starting to use the product to open a drain in a sink located in the experimental area. The safety behavior evaluated for the sabre-saw was whether the user unplugged the power cord while changing the blade, which they were asked to do at the start of the task. The instruction booklet with this instruction was placed next to the saw. Similiarly, the label on the electric knife warned users to unplug the knife before inserting the blades. The instructions for the router warned against eye hazards from wooden chips thrown during operation, and goggles were placed beside the router.

Subjects

A total of 50 subjects participated in this research. Subjects were obtained from the employee and student population of the University of Oklahoma, and from adults in a church-affiliated fitness and recreational center in Norman, Oklahoma. The age of the subjects age ranged from 21 to 80 years, with 25 in the 21-30 group, 14 in the 31-50 group, and 11 in the 51-80 group. There were 25 males and 25 females. Occupations included students, secretaries, nurses, medical doctors, carpenters, technicians, engineers, lawyers and housewives.

Procedure

All subjects were told that the purpose of the experiment was to determine preferences in product design. They were assured that all their responses would be confidential. Each subject was asked to use each product to perform a specific task as described earlier. The experimenter was prepared to interrupt any subject if there was danger of injury, and point out the safe way of using the product. This was done in such a way that the purpose of the experiment was concealed until all products had been used.

After the products had been used, each subject was was asked to complete the risk-assessment questionnaire and the Zuckerman tests. The experimenter then obtained the remainder of the information for the other experimental variables.

Of the sixteen independent variables, ten were continuously scaled, and six were discrete. The discrete variables were converted to rank order as follows:

1. male=1; female=2
2. product use: once/week=5; once/month=4; once/3 months=3; once/6 months=2; once/year or less=1
3. recency of use: last week=5; within the last 3 months=4; 6 months ago=3; 1 year ago=2; 1-5 years ago=1
4. injury experience: yes=1; no=0
5. wears life jacket: yes=1; no=0
6. crosses at pedestrian crossing: yes=0; no=1

RESULTS

The behavior of the subjects when presented with the experimental situation was recorded using one of the following five categories:

1. Subject did not look for any instructions or warnings before using the product in an unsafe manner.

2. Subject viewed instructions or warnings, but did not follow safe procedures in using the product.

3. Subject did not view warnings or instructions, but used the product safely.

4. Subject viewed instructions only and used the product in a safe manner.

5. Subject viewed instructions and warnings and used the product in a safe manner.

An attempt to fit a satisfactory discriminant function for the data showed that it was not possible to fit a func- tion for the five categories of behavior with satisfactory prediction accuracy. The five categories were then collapsed into the following two groups:

"Unsafe" Group: Original groups 1 & 2

"Safe" Group: Original groups 3, 4, & 5.

With this change, it was possible to predict the behavior of subjects with the following accuracies:

Electric knife: 68%
Sabre-saw: 73%
Drain cleaner: 79%
Router: 86%

The variables which proved to be most useful for predicting behavior for each product are shown below, with a comment following each about the nature of the relationship:

Sabre-saw

1. Score from questionnaire for measuring risk-taking attitude. Subjects with a higher score, i.e., less willing to take risks, were more likely to behave safely.

2. Score from the Zuckerman experience seeking scale. The more experience-seeking a subject claimed to be, the safer their behavior, which is the opposite of the expected result.

3. Crossing behavior at a pedestrian crossing. The behavior was as expected, i.e., subjects who didn't cross on a "Don't Walk" sign were more likely to behave safely.

Electric Knife

1. Score from questionnaire for measuring risk-taking attitude. Same comment as for sabre-saw.

2. Age of the subject. The lower the age, the more likely the subject was to behave safely.

3. Recency of use. The more recent the use of the knife, the safer the behavior.

Router

1. Score from questionnaire for measuring risk-taking attitude. Same comment as for the sabre-saw.

2 Age of the subject. The higher the age, the safer the behavior of the subject.

3. Familiarity with the product. The more familiar the subject with the router, the safer the behavior.

4. Seat belt usage in town. A subject using a seat belt in town was more likely to use the router safely.

5. Crossing behavior at pedestrian crossings. Same comment as for the sabre-saw.

Drain Cleaner

1. Score from the questionnaire for measuring risk-taking attitude. Same comment as for the sabre-saw.

2. Score from the Zuckerman experience-seeking scale. Same comment as for sabre-saw.

3. Subjective rating of the hazard of the product. The higher the subjective rating, the more likely the subject was the behave safely.

It was found that few of the subjects had any injury experience with the products, thus it is not surprising that this variable did not have any significant predictive value.

CONCLUSIONS

1. It is possible to measure risk-taking attitude with a questionnaire which has significant value in predicting the safe or unsafe behavior of persons when asked to use a product.

2. Discriminant analysis is a useful tool for dealing with the experimental variables which must be studied as a group when performing this type of safety research in a "real world" setting.

3. There is a need for much more research to help define the critical variables which determine whether someone will behave safely when confronted with a choice in using a variety of common products found around the household.

REFERENCES

Dorris, A. and Purswell, J., "Warnings and Human Behavior: Implications for the Design of Product Warnings", Journal of Products Liability, Vol. 1, 1977.

Dorris, A. and Tabrizi, M. F., "Consumer Perception of Product Safety: An Empirical Evaluation", Journal of Products Liability, Vol. 2, 1978.

Godfrey, S. et al., "Warning Messages: Will the Consumer Bother to Look", Proceedings of the Human Factors Society 27th Annual Meeting, 1983.

Schwartz, D., et al., "The Impact of Product Hazard Information on Consumer Buying Decisions: A Policy Capturing Approach", Proceedings of the Human Factors Society 22nd Annual Meeting, 1978.

Slovic, P., et al., "Perceived Risk: Psychlogical Factors and Social Implications", The Assessment and Perception of Risk, Royal Society of London, 1980.

Wright, P. et al. "Some Factors Determining when Instructions will be Read", Ergonomics, Vol. 25, No. 3, 1982.

Zuckerman, M., "Interest and Preference Test", Sensation Seeking: Beyond the Optimal Level of Arousal, Halstead Press Division of Wiley, New York, 1979.

Warning Compliance: Effects of a
Video Warning Sign and Modeling on Behavior

Bernadette M. Racicot
Department of Psychology
Rensselaer Polytechnic Institute
Troy, NY 12180

Michael S. Wogalter
Department of Psychology
North Carolina State University
Raleigh, NC 27695

ABSTRACT

The effectiveness of warnings and social influence (modeling) for improving safety behavior was examined in a laboratory setting. Although training programs aimed at improving safety behavior in the workplace frequently use videotapes with models portraying safe and unsafe behaviors, the effectiveness of training interventions of this type are rarely evaluated nor have results been published in the research literature. Training to increase safety behaviors can translate into large savings to an organization in terms of reductions in equipment damage, cost of liability litigation, and decreases in injury to both consumers and employees. The present research examined the effects of a posted (video) warning, video role-modeling, and a voice warning on compliance with safety behaviors. Participants were randomly assigned to one of three conditions, warning alone, warning and exposure to a video model performing the appropriate safety behaviors, or warning, video modeling, and a voice warning. The results showed that behavioral modeling presented through a video display significantly enhanced behavioral compliance compared to a video sign warning alone. The addition of a voice warning did not further increase compliance due to ceiling effects produced by the powerful influence of the modeling. Implications of this research for safety training programs and forensic human factors as well as suggestions for future research are discussed.

INTRODUCTION

Providing safer conditions for consumers and employees is a central goal and a major challenge for accident prevention programs. One common method used in accident prevention programs is the use of warnings. The purpose of warnings is to prevent people from performing unsafe behaviors that may be performed if warnings are not provided. Previous warning research has identified a number of factors that influence the behavioral effectiveness of warnings including: warning placement (Wogalter, Godfrey, Fontenelle, Desaulniers, Rothstein, and Laughery, 1987) embedding the warning within other text (Strawbridge, 1986) social influence of others (Wogalter, Allison, and McKenna, 1989) severity of consequences (Wogalter and Barlow, 1990) inclusion of pictorials (Jaynes and Boles, 1990) voice (Wogalter and Young, 1991) and cost of compliance in terms of effort required to comply (Wogalter et al., 1989). In addition, research in personnel psychology suggests that training programs that instruct individuals on how to use safe behaviors and motivate them to engage in these behaviors are useful for enhancing compliance with safety behaviors (Komacki, Barwick, and Scott, 1978; Reber, Wallin, and Chhokar, 1984). Furthermore, the use of safe behaviors by both employees and consumers is of interest to most organizations because of the potential for costly lawsuits resulting from injuries caused by the improper use of safety equipment or misinterpretation of instructions.

While warnings stress the avoidance of unsafe behaviors, behavioral modeling techniques focus on providing guidelines for the use of safe behaviors (e.g., Wogalter et al., 1989). Observational learning, the acquisition and subsequent enactment of behaviors exhibited by others, is affected by several processes. First, the individual must attend to the behavior of the model. Second, the individual must retain the information presented by the model. Third, the person must have the ability to perform the observed action. Finally, motivation to perform the modeled behavior must be present. When these four conditions are met, there is an increased likelihood that the observer will imitate the behavior of the model (Baron, 1992).

The concept of observational learning has been examined in many contexts. Wogalter et al. (1989) conducted two studies to examine the effects of a confederate performing safety behaviors on behavioral compliance. Participants in this study performed a laboratory chemistry experiment while exposed to a live model who either used or failed to use safety equipment (i.e., donning mask and gloves). Results indicated that participants were more likely to use safety equipment when the confederate also used the protective equipment. In addition, results of a field study in which a confederate used either an elevator or the stairs when a warning concerning potential malfunction of an elevator was posted confirmed the effects of social influence on compliance with warnings. Specifically, participants were more likely to use the stairs when the confederate heeded the warning than when the confederate did not.

Although research on behavioral modeling has supported the effect of social influence on behavioral compliance with safety measures, both studies discussed above utilized live models, thus it is unknown whether the use of other media such as videos would enhance behavioral compliance. In the training context, videotapes are often used to teach individuals the importance of safety behavior and to provide examples of safe and unsafe behaviors. However, the effectiveness of such safety training programs is rarely evaluated, and to date, studies of effectiveness have not appeared in the research literature. Thus, a purpose of the present study was to examine the effects of behavior modeling using a videotape that simulates the type of behaviors often used in safety training interventions. Validation of video-training programs could aid forensic human factors specialists in providing advice to organizations and the court on effective accident prevention methods.

Providing information through the use of both warning

signs and modeling may strengthen behavioral compliance. That is, an additive effect may occur. In order to maximize the effects of modeling, Wexley and Latham (1991) suggested that behaviors must be presented in a clear and detailed manner. Also, before observing a model, individuals should be cued to attend to the specific, relevant behaviors being modeled. Posted warnings may serve as an initial cue which focuses attention on appropriate behavior. Once attention is focused, the individual may be more likely to attend to the behavior of the model. The purpose of the present study was to examine the effects of both a warning and behavioral modeling on compliance with safety instructions.

In addition to posted warnings, the effect of a voice warning on behavioral compliance was also examined. Recent research has shown that voice warnings have a powerful effect on compliance (Wogalter and Young, 1991; Wogalter et al., 1991) especially when they are redundant with information in print warnings. For example, Wogalter and Young (1991) found that combining a voice warning with a printed warning resulted in greater compliance with the use of safety equipment than either a voice or print warning alone. Thus, another purpose of this research was to examine the effects of redundant messages by combining a posted warning and a voice warning along with the presentation of a video model exhibiting the intended safe behaviors.

In summary, three conditions were utilized to examine behavioral compliance. In the first condition, individuals were exposed to a posted (video) sign only. In the second condition, individuals were first presented with the sign and then the videotaped model. The third condition included the sign, the videotaped model and a voice warning. Compliance with the use of safety equipment (mask and gloves) during a chemistry task was assessed for all three conditions.

METHOD

Participants

Thirty-six undergraduate students from Rensselaer Polytechnic Institute participated for credit towards their introductory course or were paid $5.00 for their participation. Individuals were randomly signed to one of three conditions.

Design

The experiment consisted of three between-subjects conditions: (1) videotape of a warning sign, (2) videotape of the warning sign followed by a video shot of the mask and gloves, and a male model donning them, and (3) videotape identical to the second condition plus presentation of a voice warning. The wearing of protective gear by participants was recorded.

Materials

The basic task that participants performed is similar to that employed in Wogalter et al. (1987, 1989). Participants used a triple-beam balance, beakers, flasks, and graduated cylinders to weigh, measure and mix several substances. The substances were disguised to appear potentially hazardous but were actually safe (e.g., (powdered sugar

with green food coloring). A large supply of plastic gloves and face masks were also available on a laboratory table next to the equipment.

Two videotapes were constructed. In the no role-model video, only a full screen shot of the warning sign was presented for 30 seconds. The warning sign used was identical to one of the signs used in a study conducted by Wogalter, Rashid, Clarke, and Kalsher (1991) and contained the message: "CAUTION. Skin and Lung Irritant. Improper mixing may result in a compound that can burn skin and lungs. Wear rubber gloves and mask." The warning was in bold black print on a 31 x 31 cm bright yellow background. In the role-model videos, the warning sign was displayed for 10 seconds, followed by a full screen shot of several gloves and mask for 8 seconds, and then followed by a 12 second clip showing a 20-30 year old male approaching a table and putting on a mask and a pair of gloves. Two of the conditions lacked sound. In the third condition, the same role-model video was used except that during a 10 second shot of the sign, a male voice could be heard presenting the same warning message. Participants viewed the video before entering the laboratory room. There were no other warning messages except the videos. Participants watched the video on a 48 cm colored monitor at a distance of 2 m.

Procedure

Participants were asked to read and sign a consent form which described the study as investigating the procedures and equipment involved in a chemistry laboratory task and were then shown one of the three videotapes. They were asked to wear a white lab coat and then were shown how to use a triple-beam balance. The experimenter told the participant to perform the instructed tasks quickly and accurately, and then escorted them to the doorway, pointed to the laboratory table, and instructed the participant to enter the room and begin. The experimenter recorded whether the participant wore the protective gear.

Upon completion of the task, participants were asked to complete a questionnaire which asked whether or not they noticed the gloves, the masks, and whether they heard or saw a warning.

RESULTS

All subjects who wore one piece of safety equipment also wore the second piece (i.e., gloves and mask). In the video warning sign condition, 50% of the participants used the safety equipment provided. Ninety-two percent of the participants complied with the use of the safety equipment when provided with both the warning sign and the video role-model. When the voice warning was added to the warning sign and model condition, 100% compliance with safety procedures was obtained. The overall Chi-square test for the compliance data was significant, χ^2 (2, $N = 36$) = 10.99, $p < .01$. Subsequent Chi-square tests indicated that the two video role-model conditions produced nearly perfect compliance and both were higher than the video sign alone. Specific contrasts indicated that compliance was higher in the video sign/model condition as compared to the video sign alone condition, χ^2 (1, $N = 36$) = 5.04, $p < .05$. The contrast between the video sign alone condition and the video sign, model, and voice condition was also significant, χ^2 (1, $N = 36$) = 8.00, $p < .01$, indicating higher compliance in the latter condition. The contrast between the two modeling conditions was not significant.

The questionnaire data indicated that participants who reported seeing the safety equipment (i.e., gloves, masks) or reported hearing or seeing a warning, were more likely to comply with the warning. The following variables were significantly correlated with compliance: seeing the gloves, seeing the masks, and seeing or hearing the warning, ϕs ($\underline{N}$ = 36) = .34, .34 and .49, respectively, ps < .05.

DISCUSSION

Almost all of the participants in the role-model conditions performed the precautionary actions illustrated in the video. This result confirms the substantial social influence effect previously reported (Wogalter et al., 1989) but also extends this work. The earlier study used live models who simultaneously performed the task along with the participants. In the current study, the effect was accomplished by a video presented before the task and outside the context of the laboratory room. The voice warning did not further enhance the effect of the role-model video. This null finding was most likely due to a ceiling effect as the role-model had already pushed performance near complete compliance. The high rate of compliance in the video model conditions indicates how powerful training videos can be in encouraging the use proper use of safety procedures.

Results of the questionnaire data suggest that when individuals notice safety equipment and warnings, they are more likely to engage in safe behaviors. The major implications of these findings are that safety equipment should be placed in close proximity to where potentially dangerous tasks are being performed and that warnings and equipment should be salient to individuals required to perform such tasks.

The effects of the current study together with the findings of Wogalter et al. (1989) lends support for the potential effectiveness of training videos used to encourage and teach the use of safe behaviors in the workplace. With the advent of relatively inexpensive hand-held camcorders and video equipment, it is possible to produce videos that not only show dangers one should look out for but also the appropriate ways to avoid them. The cost of producing and implementing safety videos would be substantially lower in terms of employee injury, staff reduction, and any subsequent liability litigation that might occur as a result of a preventable injury. The present research also provides useful information to forensic human factors specialists on more effective methods of communicating hazard information. The utility of a safety video is not limited to employee safety programs. Many households now contain a video player, and therefore, inexpensive videos might be enclosed with certain consumer products that could better communicate its operation and potential hazards than an instruction manual.

Although the present study lends support for the use of videotaped training films for use in accident reduction, further research is needed to examine the effects of such interventions over time. Additional research is currently being conducted in our laboratory aimed at examining the effects of a delay between the observation of the role-model film and performance of appropriate behaviors. In this situation, it is possible that redundant warnings which include a voice warning may enhance the long-term retention of safety information and thus behavioral compliance.

REFERENCES

Baron, R. A. (1992). *Psychology* (2nd ed.). Boston: Allyn and Bacon.

Jaynes, L. S., and Boles, D. B. (1990). The effects of symbols on warning compliance. In *Proceedings of the Human Factors Society 34th Annual Meeting* (pp. 984-987). Santa Monica, CA: Human Factors Society.

Komacki, J., Barwick, K. D., and Scott, L. R. (1978). A behavioral approach to occupational safety: Pinpointing and reinforcing safe performance in a food manufacturing plant. *Journal of Applied Psychology, 63*, 434-445.

Reber, R. A., Wallin, J. A., and Chhokar, J. S. (1984). Reducing industrial accidents: A behavioral experiment. *Industrial Relations, 23*, 119-125.

Strawbridge, J. A. (1986). The influence of position, highlighting, and embedding on warning effectiveness. In *Proceedings of the Human Factors Society 30th Annual Meeting* (pp. 716-720). Santa Monica, CA: Human Factors Society.

Wexley, K. N., and Latham, G. P. (1991). *Developing and training human resources in organizations* (2nd ed.). New York: Harper Collins Publishers.

Wogalter, M. S., Allison, S. T., and McKenna, N. A. (1989). The effects of cost and social influence on warning compliance. *Human Factors, 31*, 133-140.

Wogalter, M. S., and Barlow, T. (1990). Injury likelihood and severity in warnings. In *Proceedings of the Human Factors Society 34th Annual Meeting* (pp. 580-583). Santa Monica, CA: Human Factors Society.

Wogalter, M. S., Godfrey, S. S., Fontenelle, G. A., Desaulniers, D. R., Rothstein, P. R., and Laughery, K. R. (1987). Effectiveness of warnings. *Human Factors, 29*, 599-612.

Wogalter, M. S., Rashid, R., Clarke, S. W., and Kalsher, M. J. (1991). Evaluating the behavioral effectiveness of a multi-modal voice warning sign in a visually cluttered environment. In *Proceedings of the Human Factors Society 35th Annual Meeting* (pp. 718-722). Santa Monica, CA: Human Factors Society.

Wogalter M. S., and Young, S. L. (1991). Behavioural compliance to voice and print warnings. *Ergonomics, 34*, 78-89.

BROADENING THE RANGE OF SIGNAL WORDS

N. Clayton Silver
Psychology Department
Appalachian State University
Boone, NC 28608

Michael S. Wogalter
Psychology Department
Rensselaer Polytechnic Institute
Troy, NY 12180

ABSTRACT

Most guidelines on warning design recommend using an appropriate signal word that connotes the degree of hazard involved. Usually three levels of signal words, DANGER, WARNING, and CAUTION are suggested for warnings that convey high to low degrees of hazard. The purposes of the present research were threefold. The first goal was to examine whether these terms differed in implied hazard level. The second goal was to determine whether an additional group of five words recommended in guidelines or used in previous research differed in connoted hazard level. The third goal was to explore the possibility of increasing the number and range of words that connote different levels of hazard. Subjects rated a list of 84 potential signal words on six questions assessing strength, severity of implied injury, likelihood of implied injury, attention-gettingness, carefulness, and understandability. The results indicated that DANGER connoted greater strength (arousal) than WARNING and CAUTION, but the results failed to show a difference between WARNING and CAUTION. Among other words tested, DEADLY was seen as having strongest arousal connotation, and NOTE the least. From the long list of 84 terms, a "short" list of 20 signal words was developed based on understandability, low variability, shortness of word, and frequency of use. It is suggested that an expanded list of signal words might alleviate potential problems of habituation from overuse of the currently recommended terms.

INTRODUCTION

Most standards and guidelines on warning design recommend the use of signal words on warnings for the purpose of calling attention to the safety sign and to convey the degree of seriousness of the hazard. Guidelines suggest that two to four levels of hazard be communicated by signal words. The American National Standards Institute guidelines (ANSI, 1972), *Z35.1*, recommends that the word DANGER be used to indicate hazards of immediate and grave peril and those capable of producing irreversible damage or injury. ANSI recommends the word CAUTION be used on signs to call attention to potential hazards that could result in severe but not irreversible injury or damage. Thus, DANGER is reserved for use on warnings of greater hazard level than the word CAUTION. Other guidelines advocate more than just two levels of hazard. The *Product Safety Sign and Label System* (FMC, 1985) recommends using DANGER, WARNING, and CAUTION with the selection based on the probability and degree of severity. The term DANGER is retained for immediate hazards which *will* result in severe personal injury or death. WARNING is retained for hazards or unsafe practices which *could* result in severe personal injury or death. CAUTION is retained for hazards or unsafe practices which *could* result in minor personal injury or product/property damage. A more recent draft of the ANSI (1988) guidelines, *Z535.4*, makes similar recommendations. The *Westinghouse Product Safety Label Handbook* (Westinghouse, 1981) extends the list by adding a fourth term, NOTICE, to indicate important but not hazard-related information.

In spite of these recommendations, only a few studies have investigated whether people actually perceive differential strength (arousal) from these signal words. That is, do people know that DANGER means a greater hazard level than WARNING and CAUTION, and that WARNING means a greater hazard level than CAUTION? The research literature is equivocal on this. Bresnahan and Bryk (1975)

found that DANGER expressed a greater level of hazard than CAUTION. However, Leonard, Matthews, and Karnes (1986) found no significant differences between DANGER, WARNING, and CAUTION on perceptions of risk. In addition, other research has also failed to find differences between experimental conditions in which signal words were manipulated (e.g., DANGER vs. CAUTION vs. no signal word in Ursic, 1985; WARNING vs. NOTE in Wogalter, Godfrey, Fontenelle, Desaulniers, Rothstein, & Laughery, 1987). In recent research, Leonard, Karnes, and Schneider (1988) used a set of symbols and the words DEADLY, DANGER, WARNING, CAUTION, BE CAREFUL, and ATTENTION. They found strong positive linear relationships between ratings in the symbol and word conditions. From this report, however, it was not clear whether there were significant differences among the words.

Because three levels of signal words, DANGER, WARNING, and CAUTION, are recommended in warning guidelines for the purpose of conveying high to low degrees of hazard, one goal of the present research was to determine whether these three terms differed in implied or connoted strength. Because other words have been either recommended or used in research, the second goal was to determine whether they also differed in implied hazard level.

Because the guidelines limit the number of words to signal hazards, overuse is possible. That is, the terms might appear so often that people habituate to them. Thus, with continued exposure, the signal words may no longer attract attention or signal anything (Cowan, 1988). For example, consider the industrial worker who is frequently exposed to the term DANGER in the course of using job-related equipment. Suppose that new, more hazardous equipment is introduced into the workplace. According to the standards, the term DANGER should be used as the signal word to convey maximal hazard. This term, because of prior overexposure, may no longer attract attention or adequately communicate the dangerousness of the new equipment. Accordingly, another purpose of the present research was to explore the possibility of enlarging the set of signal words. The goal was to develop a list of words that semantically connote a range of hazard. An objective, criterion-based selection procedure was planned a priori. Using ratings from a large set of potential words, a shorter list of words would be retained using criteria taken from guidelines on warning design including measures of comprehensibility, interpretability, and salience.

METHOD

Subjects

Twenty-eight University of Richmond undergraduates from an introductory psychology course participated to satisfy a research requirement. Another group of 34 undergraduates participated in a subsequent study for the purpose of obtaining rating reliabilities.

Materials and Stimuli

A list of potential signal words were selected from *Roget's Thesaurus* (Morehead, 1982) and a synonym dictionary (Devlin, 1982). From this initial selection, 111 terms representing a wide range of implied strength were obtained. Only single terms were included in the first list (e.g., the term CAREFUL was used instead of BE CAREFUL, cf. Leonard et al.,1988). At this point, some of the words were deleted from further consideration because they appeared to be inappropriate signal words for warnings (e.g., the terms, WOUND, CALAMITOUS, IMPAIR). This determination was made by three judges (the two authors and an undergraduate research assistant). Words could only be deleted at this stage if all three judges agreed to its unsuitability as a signal word. The retained list of 84 terms, shown in Table 1, were arranged into four randomly-determined orders. Subjects rated the terms on six questions on 9-point Likert-type scales anchored with 0 denoting absence of quantity to 8 indicating maximum quantity. The questions and anchors were:

1. "What is the *STRENGTH* of this term?" The numerical and verbal anchors for this questions were: (0) not at all strong, (2) slightly strong, (4) strong, (6) very strong, and (8) extremely strong.
2. "What is the *SEVERITY* of injury implied by this term?" The numerical and verbal anchors for this questions were: (0) not severe, (2) slightly severe, (4) severe, (6) very severe, and (8) extremely severe.
3. "What is the *LIKELIHOOD* of injury implied by this term?" The numerical and verbal anchors for this questions were: (0) never, (2) unlikely, (4) likely, (6) very likely, and (8) extremely likely.
4. "How *ATTENTION-GETTING* is this term?" The numerical and verbal anchors for this questions were: (0) not at all attention-getting, (2) slightly attention-getting, (4) attention-getting, (6) very attention-getting, and (8) extremely attention-getting.
5. "How *CAREFUL* would you be after seeing this term?" The numerical and verbal anchors for this questions were: (0) not at all careful, (2) slightly careful, (4) careful, (6) very careful, and (8) extremely careful.
6. "How *UNDERSTANDABLE* is this term? In making your rating please consider whether the term would be understood by ALL people in the general population (including young children, visiting foreigners, etc.)?" The numerical and verbal anchors for this questions were: (0) not at all understandable, (2) somewhat understandable, (4) understandable, (6) very understandable, and (8) extremely understandable.

Procedure

Each subject received a different random order of the six questions and one of the four random orders of the terms. Subjects were first told to read the entire list of terms to familiarize themselves with the variety of words listed. They were told to work on one question at a time and to rate all of the words on that particular question before beginning the next question. Subjects were told that even though some of the values on the scales had verbal anchors, they could use any whole number from 0 to 8.

RESULTS

Intercorrelations

The first set of analyses examined the intercorrelations of signal words means (collapsed across subjects) for the six questions. Table 2 shows that the responses to five of the six questions are highly related (*r*'s ranged from .90 to .96), except understandability. Clearly, these questions are measuring the same thing--what might be termed the arousal quality of the words. Correlations with understandability, while positive, were considerably lower.

To check the reliability of these data, another group of 34 subjects rated the same list of words on the questions of understandability, strength, and carefulness. The reliability of the ratings with the first group of subjects were .933, .904, and .930, respectively.

Table 1. *Eighty-Four Words Rated by Subjects.*

ACIDIC	FORBIDDEN	POISON
ADMONITION	HALT	POISONOUS
ALARM	HARMFUL	PRECARIOUS
ALERT	HAZARD	PRECAUTION
ATTENTION	HAZARDOUS	PREVENT
BEWARE	HEED	PROHIBIT
CAREFUL	HOT	PROHIBITED
CAUSTIC	IMPERATIVE	QUARANTINED
CAUTION	IMPORTANT	REFRAIN
CEASE	INFECTIOUS	RELEVANT
COMPULSORY	INFORMATION	REMINDER
CONSEQUENTIAL	INJURIOUS	REQUIRED
CONTAMINATION	JEOPARDIZE	REQUISITE
CORRODE	LETHAL	RISKY
CORROSIVE	MANDATORY	SERIOUS
CRITICAL	MEMORANDUM	SEVERE
CRUCIAL	NECESSARY	SIGNIFICANT
DANGER	NEEDED	STOP
DANGEROUS	NEVER	SUGGESTION
DEADLY	NO	SUSPEND
DESTRUCTIVE	NOTE	TOXIC
DIRECTIONS	NOTICE	UNPREDICTABLE
DISASTROUS	NOTIFICATION	UNPROTECTED
DISCONTINUE	NOXIOUS	UNSAFE
DON'T	OBLIGATORY	UNSOUND
ESSENTIAL	PARAMOUNT	URGENT
EXPLOSIVE	PERILOUS	VITAL
FATAL	PERTINENT	WARNING

Table 2. *Intercorrelations among questions.*

	Strength	Severity	Likelihood	Attention	Careful
Severity	.934				
Likelihood	.915	.961			
Attention	.961	.934	.904		
Careful	.940	.963	.964	.932	
Understand	.342	.249	.318	.385	.321

The word rating data were also examined with respect to objective characteristics of the words: frequency of use in the English language (Thorndike & Lorge, 1944; Francis & Kucera, 1982) and the number of letters and syllables in the words. Understandability was positively correlated with frequency of use ($r = .517$, $p < .0001$ with the Thorndike-Lorge count; $r = .429$, $p < .0001$ with the Francis-Kucera count) and negatively related to the number of letters ($r = -.491$, $p < .0001$) and syllables ($r = -.464$, $p < .0001$). Thus, the words rated more understandable, are used more frequently and have fewer letters and syllables. However, the correlations of these variables with the other five questions were much smaller: with the Thorndike-Lorge count, the r's ranged from -.044 to .026; with the Francis-Kucera count, the r's ranged from -.021 to .053; with the number of letters, the r's ranged from -.300 to -.176; and with the number of syllables, the r's ranged from -.265 to -.176.

Analysis of three signal words

The correlations indicated that five of the questions (strength, severity of injury, likelihood of injury, attention-getting, and carefulness) were measuring the same thing, which we have termed *arousal* (however, any of the five question labels could be substituted). To further examine the overall arousal quality, a repeated measures analysis of variance (ANOVA) using these five questions (collapsed over 84 words) indicated that there was no significant difference among the mean ratings of these questions, $F(4,108) = 1.84$, $p > .05$. With this evidence, and in order to gain a more powerful, general, or overall measure of arousal, the data was collapsed across the five questions creating arousal mean scores. The arousal scores were used in some of the following analyses to simplify the presentation of results.

One of our primary interests was to determine whether DANGER, WARNING, and CAUTION connoted a differential range of hazard. The top row of Table 3 shows that the term DANGER had a higher arousal mean than WARNING and CAUTION. A one-way repeated-measures ANOVA indicated a significant effect of signal word, $F(2,54) = 11.94$, $p < .0001$. Subsequent Newman-Keuls range tests showed that DANGER produced significantly higher arousal than either WARNING or CAUTION (p's < .05). WARNING and CAUTION did not differ ($p > .05$). Table 3 also shows the means each of the five arousal questions considered separately. The pattern of question means were similar to the overall arousal mean. The only

Table 3. *Mean ratings for Overall Arousal and for each Question as a Function of Signal Word.*

	DANGER	WARNING	CAUTION
Arousal mean	6.09	5.31	5.26
Strength	5.89	5.39	5.32
Severity of Injury	6.14	5.18	4.79
Likelihood of Injury	6.04	5.07	5.50
Attention-getting	6.00	5.39	5.32
Carefulness	6.36	5.50	5.39
Understanding	6.86	6.46	6.14

exception to this was CAUTION receiving greater ratings for likelihood of injury than WARNING. The ANOVAs were significant for severity of injury, $F(2,54) = 13.01$, $p < .0001$, likelihood of injury, $F(2,54) = 6.59$, $p < .003$, and carefulness, $F(2,54) = 5.89$, $p < .005$. Subsequent Newman-Keuls range tests for these effects showed that the only significant differences were between DANGER and WARNING or CAUTION (p's < .05). The reversal of the CAUTION and WARNING means for likelihood of injury was not significant.

The understandability means are shown on the bottom row of Table 3. The repeated-measures ANOVA indicated a significant effect of word, $F(2,54) = 5.78$, $p < .006$. Subsequent Newman-Keuls range tests showed only one reliable difference: DANGER received significantly greater understandability ratings than CAUTION ($p < .05$).

Analysis of other potential words

Another interest of the present research was whether other terms recommended or used in previous research would differ in their arousal quality. In these analyses, the words ATTENTION, CAREFUL, DEADLY, NOTE, and NOTICE were added to the data set that included DANGER, WARNING, and CAUTION. The overall arousal level means are shown in the first column of Table 4. The repeated measures ANOVA indicated a significant effect of word, $F(7,189) = 83.02$, $p < .0001$. Subsequent Newman-Keuls range tests showed that all differences among the overall arousal means were significant (p's < .05) except between ATTENTION and CAREFUL, and as shown earlier, between WARNING and CAUTION.

The understandability of the eight words were also examined and the means are shown in the second column of Table 4. The ANOVA showed a significant effect, $F(7,189)$

188

= 5.84, *p* < .0001. Subsequent Newman-Keuls range tests showed that NOTICE was significantly less understandable than all of the other words except for NOTE. NOTE was also significantly less understandable than WARNING, CAREFUL, and DANGER (*p*'s < .05). There were no other reliable differences between words on the dimension of understandability.

Table 4. *Overall Arousal and Understandability Means for 8 Words.*

	Arousal	Understandability
DEADLY	7.34	6.07
DANGER	6.09	6.86
WARNING	5.31	6.46
CAUTION	5.26	6.14
CAREFUL	3.81	6.50
ATTENTION	3.45	6.29
NOTICE	2.80	5.25
NOTE	2.12	5.50

Selection of signal words

Efforts were also directed at the development of a "short" list of signal words that covered a range of implied strength. An objective set of criteria was used in the selection process that first began with the list of 84 words. Because most guidelines emphasize comprehensibility, we deleted terms that received mean understandability ratings in the bottom one-third (33%) of the list. Another aspect of comprehensibility is interpretation. It is desirable to have terms that have a consistent meaning; that is, words that people interpret in the same way. Therefore, terms were deleted for which the summed variance of the five individual arousal questions exceeded an apparent breakpoint in the data (sumvar = 20.0). Also, deleted were terms for which Thorndike and Lorge (1944) and Francis and Kucera (1982) showed no occurrence or very infrequent occurrence (less than 2 per million words) in the English language. Lastly, word size was considered in the selection process. Because the size of a signal word affects its salience (i.e., larger type is more discriminable) and label or sign space is often limited, terms were deleted having greater than seven letters. Using these criteria, a "short" list of 20 signal words was formed from the original list of 84. This list is shown in Table 5 ordered on arousal-quality. This table also shows the individual question means and standard deviations.

DISCUSSION

The results showed that DANGER implied a more serious hazard than the word CAUTION, confirming Bresnahan and Bryk's (1975) finding. DANGER also implied greater hazard than WARNING. However, the present results failed to show that WARNING implied greater hazard than CAUTION. These two words basically mean the same thing; that is, people do not distinguish the terms with regard to hazard level. This result suggests that people do not discriminate between these two terms in the the way they are purported in current standards and guidelines. One possible reason for this finding is that lay people process the meaning of the terms WARNING and CAUTION using similar lexical information. By lexical

definition, warning means "something serving to warn, caution, or admonish" and caution means "a warning or admonition" (New Webster's Dictionary of the English Language, 1975). Apparently, people have acquired a similar connotation for these two words from personal experiences rather than from information received directly from warning signs.

The present research also examined the arousal quality of an additional set of signal words that were chosen for analysis because they had been used in previous research or recommended in guidelines. It was also shown that the word DEADLY possessed a significantly greater arousal quality than the other signal words. NOTE and NOTICE implied the least hazard. , All of the words showed a range of significantly different hazard levels, except for between ATTENTION and CAREFUL and between WARNING and CAUTION. The ordering of words corroborate the rankings of Leonard et al. (1988), although the rank order of ATTENTION and CAREFUL (or BE CAREFUL, cf. Leonard et al., 1988) was reversed.

Because the guidelines recommend a limited number of words to signal many hazards, their overuse is a problem. The arousal quality of the words might be reduced with continued exposure: They may no longer attract attention when reexposed in the same and other situations. For example, the term DANGER may not communicate extreme levels of dangerousness. One way to alleviate possible habituation effects might be to use a word with greater novelty but having similar or appropriate arousal properties, thus augmenting the signal word's attention-gettingness. A list of 20 words that semantically connote a range of hazard was developed based on measures of comprehension, interpretation, and salience. This list might be used as a starting point for subsequent warnings research and development, and might find use in assisting in the determination of the appropriate signal word for a given hazard. It should be emphasized, however, that several other important factors must be kept in mind when selecting the appropriate signal word: the hazard involved (the severity of injury and likelihood of injury), the suitability of the word (POISON makes no sense on an electrical hazard), person factors (target group population, knowlege and familiarity), and environmental factors (circumstances and surroundings).

There are a number of limitations to consider when interpreting the results of the present study. First, the signal words were presented out of context. Subjects just rated a series of words, making it difficult to know how the arousal quality of the words would be affected when placed in actual warnings in real-world settings. For example, is arousal enhanced or diminished when placed in warnings with appropriate or inappropriate levels of hazard? That is, do the words interact with other variables (e.g., symbols, different types of hazards)? Second, college freshmen and sophomores rated the words. Thus, it is difficult to know whether other groups of people interpret the words in the same way. The results did concur with the differential hazard interpretation of DANGER and CAUTION found by Bresnahan and Bryk (1975) who used industrial workers. The words, however, need to be evaluated using other target populations to determine their interpretation and understandability. For example, how would persons who do not have strong command of the English language interpret these words? Third, the list of 20 words that we

Table 5. Twenty Objectively-Selected Words Sorted on Arousal.

	Arousal	Strength		Severity		Likelihood		Attention		Carefulness		Understand	
	mean	mean	STD	mean	STD	mean	STD	mean	STD	mean	STD	mean	STD
NOTE	2.12	2.46	2.03	1.61	1.97	1.64	1.45	2.57	1.93	2.32	2.07	5.50	2.12
NOTICE	2.80	2.89	1.59	2.39	1.99	2.75	1.90	2.96	2.03	3.00	1.80	5.25	1.65
NEEDED	3.16	3.29	2.03	2.86	1.69	2.82	1.79	3.25	1.55	3.57	2.40	5.86	1.74
PREVENT	3.67	4.21	1.59	3.25	1.97	3.36	2.38	3.71	1.70	3.82	1.89	4.86	1.92
CAREFUL	3.81	3.96	2.19	3.32	1.96	3.54	1.99	3.57	1.79	4.68	1.96	6.50	1.26
ALERT	4.47	4.89	1.97	3.93	1.65	4.36	1.97	4.82	1.98	4.36	2.13	5.61	1.55
ALARM	5.19	5.61	1.71	4.64	1.99	5.04	1.69	5.32	1.59	5.36	1.75	5.96	1.64
CAUTION	5.26	5.32	1.85	4.79	1.75	5.50	1.67	5.32	1.76	5.39	2.06	6.14	1.43
HARMFUL	5.26	4.86	1.82	5.50	1.75	5.68	1.66	5.07	1.74	5.21	1.83	5.93	1.58
WARNING	5.31	5.39	1.99	5.18	1.83	5.07	1.58	5.39	1.83	5.50	1.35	6.46	1.67
BEWARE	5.41	5.32	1.95	5.46	1.43	5.36	1.70	5.50	1.75	5.39	2.01	6.57	1.91
URGENT	5.41	6.00	1.83	4.93	1.82	4.21	2.35	5.86	1.63	6.04	1.43	5.43	1.55
SERIOUS	5.51	5.46	1.44	6.04	1.62	5.50	1.75	4.79	1.81	5.79	1.93	6.07	1.58
SEVERE	5.55	5.89	1.59	5.68	1.39	5.75	1.92	4.93	1.74	5.50	1.79	4.25	1.69
VITAL	5.80	6.36	1.39	5.68	1.76	5.43	2.28	5.86	1.82	5.68	1.81	4.18	1.59
HAZARD	5.84	6.04	1.60	5.54	1.86	5.68	1.83	5.79	1.66	6.18	1.39	5.21	2.02
DANGER	6.09	5.89	2.02	6.14	1.69	6.04	1.83	6.00	2.09	6.36	1.61	6.86	1.56
POISON	6.74	6.54	1.37	6.79	1.87	6.75	1.69	6.64	1.81	7.00	1.63	6.93	1.46
FATAL	7.20	7.54	0.69	7.39	1.57	7.07	1.30	7.04	1.35	6.96	1.97	5.75	2.01
DEADLY	7.34	7.11	1.59	7.68	0.86	7.29	1.46	7.11	1.47	7.54	1.07	6.07	1.98

present is just that -- a list having certain criteria. Using other criteria, other lists could be formed. It is noted, however, that in lists using different criteria (e.g., number of syllables and different cut-off points), we arrived at lists that were similar to the one presented here.

ACKNOWLEDGEMENTS

The authors would like to thank Megan E. McGuire for her assistance in this research and Stephen L. Young for help on the final copy.

REFERENCES

ANSI (1972). *American National Standard Specification for Accident Prevention Signs: Z35.1.* New York: American National Standards Institute.

ANSI (1988). *American National Standard on Product Safety Signs: Z535.4 - Draft.* New York: American National Standards Institute.

Bresnahan, T. F., & Bryk, J. (1975). The hazard association values of accident-prevention signs. *Professional Safety*, January, 17-25.

Cowan, N. (1988). Evolving conceptions of memory storage, selective attention, and their mutual constraints within the human information-processing system. *Psychological Bulletin, 104,* 163-191.

Devlin, J. (1982). *A Dictionary of Synonyms and Antonyms.* New York: Warner Books.

FMC (1985). *Product Safety Sign and Label System.* Santa Clara, CA: FMC Corportation.

Francis, W. N., & Kucera, M. (1982). *Frequency Analysis of English Usage.* Boston: Houghton Mifflin.

Leonard, S. D., Karnes, E. W., & Schneider, T. (1988). Scale values for warning symbols and words. In F. Aghazadeh (Ed.) *Trends in Ergonomics/Human Factors V.* Amsterdam: Elsevier. 669-674.

Leonard, S. D., Matthews, D., & Karnes, E. W. (1986). How does the population interpret warning signals? *Proceedings of the 30th Annual Meeting of the Human Factors Society,* Santa Monica, CA: Human Factors Society, 116-120.

Morehead, A. H. (1982). *Roget's College Thesaurus.* New York: World Publishing.

New Webster's Dictionary of the English Language. (1975). New York: Consolidated Book Publishers.

Thorndike, E. L., & Lorge, I. (1944). *The Teacher's Word Book of 30,000 Words.* New York: Teachers College Press, Columbia University.

Ursic, M. (1984). The impact of safety warnings on perception and memory. *Human Factors, 26,* 677-682.

Westinghouse (1981). *Westinghouse Product Safety Label Handbook.* Trafford, PA: Westinghouse Printing Division.

Wogalter, M. S., Godfrey, S. S., Fontenelle, G. A., Desaulniers, D. R., Rothstein, P. R., & Laughery, K. R. (1987). Effectiveness of warnings. *Human Factors, 29,* 599-612.

THE INFLUENCE OF POSITION, HIGHLIGHTING, AND IMBEDDING ON WARNING EFFECTIVENESS

Jill Annette Strawbridge

Department of Psychology
California State University, Northridge*

An experiment utilizing 195 subjects investigated the behavoral influence of varying warning position, highlighting and imbeddedness on warning detection, recall and compliance. Subjects were given an unfamiliar consumer product to actually use, and direct behavioral observation and follow-up questions were utilized to measure the percentage of subjects who noticed, read and complied with the warning, plus the amount of information subjects could recall about the specific cause, nature and prevention of the danger. There was a steady decline in the number of subjects who first noticed, then read, and finally followed the warning across all measures. Imbedding information critical to warning compliance within the warning section was the only variable found to influence warning compliance. Imbedding the critical warning information significantly reducing warning compliance as compared to the beginning the warning section with the critical information (i.e., the unimbedded condition). Warnings were shown to be effective (47% when unimbedded). Clearly, however, consumer warnings could be improved further, by utilizing fail safe designs.

INTRODUCTION

Consumer product warnings are utilized to modify users' behavior by reducing, and ideally, eliminating product-related accidents. Such warnings are cautionary statements used to alert users to potential dangers. The effectiveness of warnings is based on three assumptions: 1) That human behavior is a critical factor in determining safe product use and misuse (McCarthy, Robinson, Finnegan & Taylor, 1982); 2) That human behavior can be altered to increase safe product use; and 3) That warning messages are an effective means of intervention to modify product-use behavior.

Manufacturers have a legal duty to warn of any reasonably forseeable product dangers, resulting from inherent properties of the product or from missuse. Warnings on consumer products are typically the only devices used to elicit safe product use. An Interagency Task Force on Products Liability (1977) reported that 18% of all product libilty cases involved warning defects; either a lack of, or inadequate warnings. A key issue in product libility cases is the "but for" test: But for the presence of the warning would the accident have occurred? This addresses the effectiveness of the warning in preventing the injury, had it been included.

Currently, the legal system places heavy emphasis on the importance of such written product warnings in determining product liability issues. The legal system's reliance on such warnings rests on the assumption that warnings are effective in influencing user behavior. Indeed, the critical issue in court often is, "would a warning have been effective?" Therefore the effectiveness of warnings is an important research issue.

Much of the literature availble on the effectiveness of warnings is composed of intuitive guidelines and surveys of hypothetical user behavior. Little behavioral data on warning effectiveness exists utilizing actual task performance. Indeed, the results of the limited studies utilizing task performace differ in their conclusions of warning effectiveness. Godfrey, Rothstein and Laughery (1985) found warnings to be effective in the various environmental situations in which they placed the warnings. Zlotnik (1982) concluded that the presence of warning messages shortened task completion times and reduced error rates within a proceduralized task.

Tokuhata, Colflesh, Smith, Ramaswamy, and Digon (1976), however, reported no significant differences in injury rates between subjects who did or did not read the instructions on product labels. McCarthy, Finnegan, Krumm-Scott and McCarthy (1984) concluded, on the basis of their literature review, that "there is not enough scientific evidence found to suppoort the contention that on-product warning labels measurably increase the safety of any product."

The purpose of the following research was to provide further behavioral data utilizing actual task performance in assessing product warning effectiveness. Warning position, highlighting and imbeddedness were manipulated and the effects on warning detection, recall and compliance were measured.

METHOD

Design

The experiment was a 2X2X3 between-subjects design. The independent variables tested were typographical highlighting, imbed- dedness, and the position of the warning. Each subject was tested on only one warning highlighting/ imbeddedness/position combination. Figure 1 shows an experimental warning condition, and the additional information provided on the stimulus bottle used.

*Currently at the Department of Industrial & Systems Engineering, The Ohio State University

Titan Super-Bonding Liquid Adhesive instantly bonds most materials for an ever-lasting hold. It's ideal for industrial or personal use, wherever a super-strength bond is required.
Directions: Use only on dry, clean surfaces. Position the spout over the areas to be permanently bonded, and apply a thin stream of the liquid adhesive. Let the bond dry for 60 seconds.
Non-harmful and non-flammable if product is used as directed. DANGER: Contains Acid To avoid severe burns, shake well before opening.
Titan Super-Bonding Liquid Adhesive may be used to bond a variety of substances. Use it on plastics, synthetics, leathers, nonporous materials, metals, fabrics, glass and any woods.
Ingredients: petrolium distillates, pure polyvinyl acetate resin, hydrochloric acid, dichloromethane, magnesium aluminum silicate, hydrolyzed animal protein, D & C yellow number 9.

Figure 1. Unhighlighted/Imbedded/Middle position Cell

The two levels of typographical highlighting consisted of an inverted message/background condition and a non-inverted condition. The imbeddedness variable refered to the placement of the critical warning information within the Warning section. The "critical" warning information was specified to include information about the cause, nature, and prevention of the danger. This information either proceeded or followed a non-critical warning statement. Hence, the warning information critical to safe product use was either imbedded or non-imbedded within the Warning section. The three levels of warning position were top, center, or bottom in relationship to the other constant features of the product label.

An additional control group was also included. In this condition the information critical to safe product use was incorporated within the Directions section of the product label. No separate warning section was included. The directions read as follows:

Directions: Use only on dry, clean surfaces. Shake well before opening. Position the spout over the areas to be permanently bonded, and apply a thin stream of the liquid adhesive. Let the bond dry for 60 seconds.

The study was designed to investigate the effects of the independent variables with respect to warning detection, warning recall, and warning compliance. To test these, the following six dependent variables were measured: the percentages of subjects who noticed the warning, read the warning, and complied with the warning, plus the amount of information subjects could recall pertaining specifically to the cause of the danger, the nature of the danger, and the prevention of the danger.

Subjects

A total of 195 subjects were run in the experiment, based on 15 subjects per each of the 12 experimental cells, plus an additional 15 subjects used in the control condition cell. Approximately 1/4 of the subjects in each experimental cell were male. The subjects were undergraduate psychology students from California State University, Northridge, who received class credits for participating in psychological experiments.

Procedure

Subjects were tested individually in the experiment. The experimental paradigm consisted of the following: each subject was presented with two items that needed to be adhered together. The only substance availible to a subject was a bottle of Liquid Adhesive. To determine if the specific bonding capabilities of this liquid adhesive would apply to the two materials in question, subjects had to read the back informational panel prior to use. The specific information pertaining to the bonding capabilities was listed in the Uses section of the label. Once subjects determined that the liquid adhesive was appropriate, they were instructed to actually glue the two items together.

To the extent that using the product was the ultimate goal, it was hypothesized that subjects should also read the Warning section, eventhough it was not what they were primarily looking for on the label. Depending on the experimental condition, the warning would precede or follow the Uses section.

The critical warning information warned subjects that the product contained acid, and to avoid severe burns, the bottle must be shaken prior to opening. Warning compliance consisted of product manipulation (i.e., shaking the bottle) prior to using the product. Therefore, direct user observation was easily employed to determine the influence of the warning on user product behavior. Follow-up questions were asked to assess what aspects of the warning message subjects could recall. Further questions were asked to provide insights into the underlying factors involved. These follow-up questions were specifically focused to determine if the user 1) noticed the warning, 2) read, and 3) followed the warning. The purpose was to determine where people dropped out of this three step process (if at all) and more importantly, if they did drop out, why.

Stimulus Materials

A plastic 12 ounce bottle of "Liquid Adhesive" and two substances to be hypothetically glued together were used. The back panel of the bottle contained five sections of equal length and format; a warning message, a promotional paragraph, a paragraph containing directions for use, a paragraph denoting the uses of the liquid adhesive, and finally a paragraph listing the ingredients.

The warning was designed to include four key informational features: 1) The nature of the danger; 2) The severity of the danger; 3) The cause of the danger; and 4) Information/instructions on how to avoid the danger.

The Warning section was developed after extensive pilot study testing for clairty and comprehension. The warning message was designed to present an easily identifiable and immediately harmful substance (i.e., acid), an easily defined and immediately forthcoming injury (i.e., burns), and an easy to perform solution to the potential hazard (i.e., shaking the bottle).

The two items used as gluing props were both substances listed on the label as being appropriate for use with the liquid adhesive. One item was a piece of fabric, the other item a piece of plastic. Both items were readily identifiable, in terms of their composition, by all of the subjects run in the experiment.

Object familiarity has been shown to be inversely proportional to the reading of warnings (Wright, Creighton, & Threlfall, 1982). Therefore, a non-gluelike shaped containter, in additional to calling the product a "liquid adhesive" (as opposed to "glue"), were used to reduce the familiarity aspect involved in normal glue use.

RESULTS

Collapsing across the three independent measures, the results show a consistent decline, beginning with the number of people who first noticed (91%), read (77%), and then complied with the warning (37%). The control group showed a similar dramatic drop in terms of the number of people who noticed the warning (100%) as compared to the number who followed the warning (33%). The overall percentages of subjects in the experimental and control groups across these dependent measures are given in Table 1.

Table 1

Overall Experimental Group Percentages and Control Group Percentages Across the Dependent Measures of Noticing, Reading, and Complying with the Warning

Dependent Variables	Experimental Group	
	Experimental Conditions	Control Group
Notice	91%	100%
Read	77%	100%
Shake	37%	33%

Therefore, the percentages of subjects who noticed and subsequently followed the warning directive were effectively the same regardless of where the statement was located. Placing the warning directive in the Directions, however, did significantly increase the number of subjects who read it (100%) compared to the experimental group data ($\underline{z}$ = 2.11, $\underline{N}$ = 195).

The effects of the three independent variables on the percentage of people who noticed, read, and followed the warning yielded dichotomous data. Each of the three recall items (recall that the danger was beinig burned, caused by acid, and could be averted by shaking the bottle prior to opening) were rated according to a 3-point scale; 0=incorrect recall, 1=partially correct, and 3=totally correct recall. This recall

data is intially reported utilizing a dichotomous analysis (by grouping partially and totally correct answers together). Separate recall analyses will be discussed at the end of this section, which take advantage of the continuous nature of the three-point scale data in its entirety.

Dichotomous Data: The following analyses reflect the influence of the three independent varibles in relationship to the amount of subjects who noticed, read, and followed the warning, plus the percentage of subjects who could specifically recall the nature of the danger indicated in the warning (i.e., severe burns), its cause (i.e., acid), and its remedy (i.e., shaking the bottle). Chi squared statistical analyses were used to test for the main effects of the dichotomous data. Interactions among the independent variables, as well as their main effects were assessed using Chi squared analyses in which the marginal proportions (as oppossed to theoretical proportions) were used to compute the Chi squared expected values (Winer, 1962). No interactions were found to exist among the independent variables.

Table 2 gives the subject percentages for the three independent variables across the dependent measures of noticing, read, and complying with the warning.

Table 2

Subject Percentages for the Independent Variables of Highlighting, Imbedding, and Position across across the Dependent Measures of Noticing, Reading, and Shaking the Product (i.e., Warning Compliance)

Dependent Measures	Independent Variables						
	Highlighting		Imbedding		Position		
	Yes	No	Yes	No	Top	Mid.	Bot.
Notice	92%	90%	88%	94%	93%	95%	85%
Read	83%	71%	73%	81%	77%	85%	70%
Shake	33%	40%	27%	47%	35%	40%	35%

A significant relationship was found between the imbedded dimension and the specific recall of Shaking the bottle as the desired action, χ^2(1, $\underline{N}$ = 180) = 9.12, $\underline{p}$<.01, ϕ = 0.22. A significant relationship was found between imbeddedness and correctly following the warning directive (i.e., shaking the product), χ^2(1, $\underline{N}$ = 180) = 4.58, $\underline{p}$<.05, ϕ = 0.16. Additionally, a significant relationship was found between imbeddedness and Acid (as the causal agent) recall, χ^2(1, $\underline{N}$ = 180) = 4.36, $\underline{p}$<.05, ϕ = 0.16. No other significant relationships were found.

The imbedded/unimbedded dimension appears, therefore, to be an important factor in influencing not only the recall of the specific dangerous agent involved, and the specific action required to avoid the danger, but is also critical in affecting whether the warning is actually followed. If the critical warning information is imbedded within the warning section, subjects are significantly less likely to remember what is causing the danger (i.e., acid), how to avoid the danger (i.e., shaking the bottle), and subsequently less likely to follow the warning than if this information was presented at the beginning of the warning section.

The only differential effect attributed to highlighting pertained to reading the warning, $X^2(1, \underline{N} = 180) = 3.82$, $\underline{p} < .05$, $\phi = 0.15$. Highlighting the warning significantly increased the number of subjects who read the warning, compared to the unhighlighted warning condition.

Position was found to have an effect on the subjects' ability to recall what the specific danger was (i.e., being burned), $X^2(2, \underline{N} = 180) = 6.19$, $\underline{p} < .05$, $\underline{C} = 0.18$. Simple Chi square analyses revealed that a significant difference exists between the middle and bottom positions in terms of burn recall, $X^2(1, \underline{N} = 180) = 5.83$, $\underline{p} < .025$, $\phi = 0.22$. The only effect of warning position was to significantly increase recall of the specific danger (i.e., burns) in the middle position relative to the bottom position.

The overall recall measures showed that 68% of the subjects who read the warning could recall that the dangerous agent was acid, 55% recalled shaking the bottle would avoid the danger, and 51% recalled that the specific danger was severe burns.

Recall Data: Analyzing the recall data independently, utilizing the 3-point scale data, revealed consistencies with the collapsed recall data results. Imbedding the critical warning information significantly reduced overall warning recall (M=2.89) compared to the unimbedded condition (M=3.68), $\underline{t}(137) = 2.02$, $\underline{p} < .05$ This result is consistant with the Chi squares findings that imbedding the warning significantly reduced recall of the agent causing the danger and how to avoid the danger.

Highlighting the warning (M=3.09) was not found to significantly improve warning recall compared to no highlighting (M=3.56). These results are consistent with the Chi square results indicating no significant differential recall due to highlighting. Similarly, no significant difference in recall was found based on position. The middle position yielded the highest recall (M=3.75), followed by the top position (M=3.24), with the bottom position yielding the lowest recall score (M=2.86).

Eighty-seven percent of the subjects in the control group condition were able to correctly recall that the message of "shake well before opening" was included within the Directions section.

DISCUSSION

Noticing, reading, and complying with a consumer product warning, in addition to recall of the cause of the danger, the nature of the danger, and the prevention of the danger were examined as a function of the highlighting, imbeddedness, and position of the warning.

Surprisingly, imbedding was the only variable shown to affect warning compliance and was therefore found to be the most critical variable in actually influencing user behavior. Imbedding the critical warning information significantly reduced warning compliance (47% compared to 27% when imbedded), as subjects stopped reading the warning prior to reaching the critical safety information. It was surprising to find that highlighting had no differential effect on compliance with the warning, considering that it significantly increased the number of subjects who read the warning. Similarly, although placing the warning information within the Directions significantly increased the number of subjects who read it (100% compared to 77% when placed within a Warning section), there was no significant difference due to this placement in terms of the number of users who actually followed the warning (33% compared to 37% within a Warning section).

A noteworthy finding was that some subjects were able to fully recall the warning yet failed to carry it out. Indeed, more than half a dozen subjects in the experimental conditions, and an overwhelming 77% of subjects in the control group, correctly recalled all three major elements of the warning (i.e., the cause, the danger, and the prevention), yet failed to follow the warning. These subjects reported that they simply "forgot" to comply with the warning. This occurred eventhough they had meant to do so, knew the cost involved personal injury (i.e., severe burns), and eventhough it was literally only a matter of seconds between reading the warning and using the product. Placing the critical safety information within a separate Warning section, as opposed to placing it within the Directions, dramatically reduced the number of these subjects who read and fully recalled the warning, yet failed to comply with the warning due to forgetting. This suggests that the utility of a Warning section may be that if the material is read, it becomes more salient and less forgettable to the user. Further research should examine the compliance rate when the critical prevention information is placed within a separate Warning section and within the Directions.

The best experimental conditons in terms optimizing warning compliance were the highlighted/unimbedded/middle position and the unhighlighted/unimbedded/bottom position cells, each yielding a 60% compliance rate. The worst experimental conditions in terms of warning compliance were the highlighted/imbedded/bottom position and the highlighted/imbedded/top position cells, each yielding a 20% compliance rate. Clearly, imbeddedness of the critical warning information is the key determinant of whether or not a warning is followed. Subject responses may help explain the paradoxical findings regarding the influence of highlighting.

Many subjects reported that they perceived their primary task to be one of finding the Uses section. The dramatic highlighting technique used (i.e., inverting the figure/ground contrast) made it easy to isolate and discount the warning section in their search for the Uses. Approximately 35% of the subjects reported that once they had read far enough into the Warning section to realize what it was, they stopped reading and continued on. This occurred despite the fact that the ultimate task was that of actually using the product; these subjects did not perceive that reading the warning was necessary. This finding is especially interesting, in as much as the experimental paradigm used represented a realistic user situation. It seems reasonable to conclude that how the user approaches the problem at hand will influence the nature of the product label search carried out, and the nature of the information extracted.

CONCLUSIONS

The steady decline in the number of subjects who first noticed, then read, and finally followed the warning was shown for each of the three independent variables. This indicates that even if people notice a warning, it does not necessarily follow that they will read it, or execute it. Clearly, the conspicuity of a warning is not singularly sufficient in persuading users to comply with warnings. Furthermore, even if users notice, read and recall the warning, there is no guarantee that users will follow the warning. These results suggest that even though users may be willing to follow product label warnings, this in and of itself may not be sufficient to induce the desired behavior.

The results of this experiment suggest that a well designed warning can be effective in increasing warning compliance: when the warning information critical to safe product use was not imbedded within the Warning section, almost half of the subjects complied (47%). To further increase warning compliance, system designers need to take steps beyond simply warning users. Fail safe designs need to be implemented to design potentially dangerous aspects out of the system.

ACKNOWLEDGEMENTS

This research was conducted to partially satisfy the requirements for the degree of Master of Arts in Psychology (Human Factors/Applied Experimental), at California State University, Northridge. I would like to express my sincere thanks to Dr. Mark S. Sanders for his help throughout this research endeavor.

REFERENCES

Godfrey, S.S., Rothstein, P. R., & Laughery, K. R. (1985). Warnings: Do they make a difference? Proceedings of the Human Factors Society-29th Annual Meeting, 1985, 669-673.

Interagency Task Force on Products Liability (1977). (Final Report II-54). Washington, D.C.: Department of Commerce.

McCarthy, R. L., Finnegan, J. P., Krumm-Scott, S., & McCarthy, G. E. (1984). Product information presentation, user behavior, and safety. Proceedings of the Human Factors Society-28th Annual Meeting, 1984, 81-85.

McCarthy, R. L., Robinson, J.N., Finnegan, J.P., & Taylor, R. K. (1982). Warnings on consumer products: objective criterial for their use. Proceedings of the Human Factors Society-26th Annual Meeting, 1982, 389-391.

Tokuhata, G., Colflesh, V., Smith, M., Ramaswamy, K., & Digon, E. (1976). Consumer behavior and product injuries. Journal of Safety Research, 8 (3).

Winer, B. J. (1971). General partition of degrees of freedom in a contingency table. In N. Garmezy, R. L. Solomon, L. V. Jones, & H. W. Stevenson (Eds.), Statistical Principles in Experimental Design (2nd ed.) (pp. 855-859), New York: McGraw-Hill.

Wright, P., Creighton, P., & Threlfall, S. M. (1982). Some factors determining when instructions will be read. Irgonomics, 25, 225-237.

Zlotnik, M. A. (1982). The effects of warning message highlighting on novel assembly task performance. Unpublished master's thesis, California State University at Northridge, Northridge, CA.

COMPONENTS OF PERCEIVED RISK FOR CONSUMER PRODUCTS

Kent P. Vaubel and Stephen L. Young

Rice University
Houston, Texas 77005

ABSTRACT

The present study examined the underlying dimensions associated with perceived risk for consumer products. Eighty undergraduate students evaluated 40 products using seventeen rating questions. Principal components analysis was then performed on the ratings. Results indicated the presence of three underlying components or dimensions along which the products varied. The first component dealt with qualitative aspects of the risks associated with a product, such as the degree to which potential hazards were known (or knowable) and the immediacy of their onset. The second component concerned subjects' familiarity with the product. The third component was associated with quantitative aspects of the risks and reflected notions about the magnitude of the potential harm (in terms of the number of potential victims) that might be incurred as a result of using the product. Subsequent regression analyses revealed that each dimension was significantly related to subjects' rated intent to act cautiously with a product. Overall, these results suggest that people do not perceive consumer products unidimensionally. Rather, such perceptions are best conceptualized as reflecting multiple underlying facets.

INTRODUCTION

The degree of caution that people are willing to take for a given product is determined largely by their perceptions of the risks associated with that product (e.g., Wogalter, Desaulniers & Brelsford, 1986, 1987; Young, Brelsford & Wogalter, 1990; Young, Martin & Wogalter, 1989). Risk is defined generally as "the chance of injury, damage, or loss" (Webster's New Universal Unabridged Dictionary, 1983). This definition suggests two facets of risk, both of which have been examined in previous literature: (1) the probability of injury ("the chance") and (2) the subjective/qualitative evaluation of the potential "injury, damage, or loss". The first aspect has often been termed "objective-" or "quantitative-" risk because it deals with a given injury event in terms of statistical probabilities or frequencies (i.e., estimated *likelihood* of injury). The second element is often described as "subjective-" or "qualitative-" risk because it deals with people's evaluations of the potential injury (i.e., *perceived* severity of injury). While these two dimensions of risk are not without overlap (probability estimations are subject to bias, and perceptions of injury severity may have quantitative dimensions such as monetary cost, etc.), they have served as valuable guides in the research on risk.

While both aspects of risk have been recognized in the literature, the probability or "chance" of a negative consequence has been seen as the primary component of risk perceptions (i.e., Winterfeldt, John & Borcherding,

1981). For example, early research by Paul Slovic and his colleagues demonstrated that this quantitative or objective aspect of risk played the principal role in determining people's perceptions about the hazards associated with various products and activities (e.g., Slovic, Fischoff & Lichtenstein, 1979). Slovic also recognized that there was a small but measurable *subjective* component of risk. However, quite a different pattern of results was observed by Wogalter, Desaulniers and Brelsford (1986). In this study, it was revealed that the qualitative or subjective component (more specifically, the *severity* of injury) played the primary role in shaping subjects' perceptions of risk. Furthermore, it was found that the objective aspect of risk (i.e., *likelihood* of injury) played no role in determining risk perceptions. This finding seemed to make sense in light of more basic research demonstrating severe biases in people's use of likelihood information (e.g., Desaulniers, 1991).

As a result, previous studies have produced inconsistent findings. Some research suggests that likelihood of injury is the primary determinant of risk perceptions, whereas other results indicate that the severity of potential injury is the sole determinant of peoples' perceptions of risk. To date, however, almost all of the research on risk has employed regression (or stepwise regression) procedures in an attempt to determine the relative contribution of different perceptions to the concept of risk. Such procedures, while statistically correct, are limited because of their inability to deal with shared variance between different variables (i.e., perceptions). While the intercorrelations of perceptions in these studies are usually *very* large, it is not uncommon for the regression procedure to extract one variable which accounts for as much as 98% of the variance of perceived risk (see Young, Brelsford & Wogalter, 1990). For explanatory purposes, these procedures are simply too limited.

The high intercorrelations among predictors of risk perceptions suggest the presence of components or dimensions which underlie judgements about risk. It is assumed that these latent dimensions *produce* the observed relationships among perceptions. Thus, the focus of the present study was to explore perceived risk by partitioning product perceptions into homogeneous and independent groups. To do so, principal components analysis (PCA) was employed to describe and explain the underlying characteristics or facets of products which evoke perceptions of risk.

METHOD

Subjects

Eighty Rice University undergraduates participated in exchange for credit in an introductory psychology course.

Materials

Seventeen rating questions, each with 9-point Likert-type scales, were obtained from previous research (*e.g.,* Slovic et al., 1979, Wogalter et al., 1986, 1987; Young, Martin & Wogalter, 1989; see Table 1). These questions could be divided conceptually into two distinct categories: 1) attributes or characteristics of the product (Questions 1 through 12) and 2) attributes or characteristics of the product user (Questions 13 through 17). This distinction was made to differentiate between product attributes which determine cautionary intent, as opposed to user characteristics which might elicit this type of behavior. The seventeen questions were each printed on a separate page and the order of the pages was randomized for each subject.

A list of 40 generic consumer products was randomly selected from a pool of over 950 products monitored by the National Electronic Injury Surveillance System (NEISS) database (U.S. Consumer Product Safety Commission, 1989; see Table 2). The products were listed on a response sheet and 17 blank spaces appeared to the right of each product name. Subjects indicated their ratings using these blank spaces. Four different orders of the products were employed.

Table 1. Questions about products (top panel) and users (bottom panel).

Q1. How <u>risky</u> is this product? - from (0) "Not at all risky" to (8) "Extremely risky.

Q2. How <u>severely</u> (i.e., degree, extent, or magnitude) might you be injured by this product? - from (0) "Not at all severe" to (8) "Extremely severe"

Q3. How <u>familiar</u> are you with this product? - from (0) "Not at all familiar" to (8) "Extremely familiar"

Q4. Are the risks associated with this product the kind that injure and/or kill people one at a time or large numbers of people at once? - from (0) "Injures/Kills one at a time" to (8) "Injures/Kills large numbers at a time"

Q5. To what extent do people encounter the risks associated with these products voluntarily? That is, to what extent are the risks associated with these products forced onto people (involuntary) or are consciously accepted (voluntary)? - from (0) "Extremely involuntary" to (8) "Extremely voluntary"

Q6. To what extent is the risk of death or injury immediate - or are the effects of the risk likely to appear at some later time? - from (0) "Immediate" to (8) "Delayed"

Q7. To what extent are the risks associated with this product known precisely to the persons who are exposed to the risk? - from (0) "Completely unknown" to (8) "Known precisely"

Q8. To what extent are the risks associated with this product known precisely to science? - from (0) "Completely unknown" to (8) "Known precisely"

Q9. Are the risks associated with these products new, novel ones or are they old, familiar ones? - from (0) "Completely old/familiar" to (8) "Completely new/novel"

Q10. Are the risks associated with this product the kind that people have learned to live with and can think about calmly or are the risks ones that people have great dread for (on a gut level reaction)? - from (0) "Completely common" to (8) "Extremely dreadful"

Q11. How often do you use this product? - from (0) "Not at all" to (8) "Very frequently"

Q12. How masculine or feminine is this product? - from (0) "Very masculine" to (8) "Very feminine"

Q13. How <u>likely</u> are you to receive <u>any</u> injury (major and/or minor) with this product? - from (0) "Never" to (8) "Extremely likely"

Q14. How <u>cautious</u> would you be when using this product? - from (0) "Not at all cautious" to (8) "Extremely cautious"

Q15. If you <u>saw</u> a warning on this product, how <u>likely</u> would you be to read it? - from (0) "Not at all likely" to (8) "Extremely likely"

Q16. To what extent can you, by personal skill or diligence, avoid the hazards associated with this product? That is, how much control do you have over being injured by this product? - from (0) "No control at all" to (8) "Total control"

Q17. Do you think that there should be a warning on this product? - from (0) "Definitely not" to (8) "Definitely so"

Table 2. Forty products selected from the NEISS database.

abrasive cleaner	aerosol containers
baby bathinetts	bench/table saw
benches	bicycles
blankets	bottles/jars
bubble baths	can opener
clotheslines	darts
diapers	drinking straws
dune buggies	food processors
footlockers	furniture polishes
gas cans	hair clippers
hair coloring	hair dryer
kerosene/oil heater	laundry baskets
laundry soap/detergent	lawn mowers
lighter fluid	log splitters
luggage	padlocks
pens/pencils	pogo sticks
rope/string	scissors
seeds	tables
upholstered chairs	water heater
whirlpool/hot tub	workshop staples

Table 3. The 12 predictors variables and their loadings on the three dimensions.

Variable & #		Component 1	Component 2	Component 3
8.	**KnownSci**	**0.9213**	-0.1110	0.2018
7.	**KnownPers**	**0.9064**	-0.0894	0.0559
2.	Severity	0.6979	-0.3674	0.5798
1.	Risk	0.6395	-0.4648	0.5860
5.	Voluntary	0.5995	-0.4732	-0.2736
12.	Masc/Fem	-0.7344	0.0282	-0.3342
6.	**Immediacy**	**-0.8720**	-0.1037	0.1454
11.	**Freq of Use**	-0.0930	**0.9125**	-0.0887
3.	**Familiarity**	-0.1009	**0.8856**	-0.1792
9.	Novelty	-0.4523	-0.5956	0.4281
4.	**Catastrophe**	0.0002	-0.0937	**0.9139**
10.	Dread	0.5539	-0.5396	0.6106

Note: The dimensions are separated by a blank row and the anchors for each dimension are in bold.

Procedure

Subjects rated each product on the 17 different questions using the scale which appeared beneath it. Subjects were instructed to rate each product on a given question before proceeding to the next question.

RESULTS

Ratings were initially collapsed across subjects and then the 17 variables were correlated with each other. Similar to previous research using these scales, the intercorrelations among the ratings were very high (r's = .76 to .98) suggesting the presence of components which underlie these manifest variables. In order identify these underlying dimensions, the rating data were collapsed across products and submitted to a principal components analysis (PCA) with Varimax rotation. It should be noted that ratings on the five questions which concerned the user (Questions 13 through 17 in Table 1) were withheld from the PCA since they were associated with user characteristics and not product characteristics. Some of the excluded questions were used in subsequent regression analyses to test the predictive validity of the dimensions generated by the principal components analysis.

Principal Components Analysis

Based on the scree plot and eigen values, results of the PCA suggested the presence of three components. The loadings for each variable are presented in Table 3. Inspection of the variables indicates that the first component deals with the degree to which product risks are known and the latency with which any adverse consequences might occur. This dimension was interpreted as *Uncertainty* about product risks (*eigenvalue* = 6.03). The second component, indexed primarily by the frequency-of-use and familiarity variables, suggested a dimension which related to the product itself. As such, it was simply labeled *Familiarity* with the product (*eigenvalue* = 2.69). Based on the finding that the catastrophe variable loaded highly on component 3 (*eigenvalue* = 1.27), this dimension was interpreted as relating to the magnitude of the potential harm (in terms of the *number* of potential victims) that might occur when using the product (*Catastrophe*).

Once the dimensions were labeled according to the pattern of variable loadings, an attempt was then made to test the validity of the interpretations by plotting each product in dimensional space. Overall, the distribution of products suggests that the dimensional interpretations were reasonable. For example, the plot of Uncertainty (component 1) by Familiarity (component 2) shows that "scissors", "bottles/jars" and "pens/pencils" fall at the upper extreme of Familiarity and that products such as "log splitter", "bench/table saw", and "lawn mower" were considered to have risks that were known and adverse consequences that were immediate in onset (see Figure 1). Space limitations prohibit the display of the other two plots, but they were similar in quality to the plot in Figure 1. The plot of components 1 (Uncertainty) and 3 (Catastrophe) revealed that products such as "gas cans", "kerosene/oil heaters" and "water heater" were viewed as having risks which were known and immediate in onset, and which had the potential for injuring/killing many. Products such as "hair coloring" and "bubble bath" had risks which were relatively unknown or delayed, and which did not have the potential to injure or kill many. The plot of Familiarity (component 2) and Catastrophe (component 3) also demonstrated the quality of the dimensional interpretations. Products such as "dune buggies" and "bench/table saws" were relatively unfamiliar items, with the potential to injure or kill many people at a time. At the other end of the spectrum, products like "drinking straw" and "pens/pencils" were very familiar products, with the potential to injure or kill very few people.

Regression Analysis

The final set of analyses attempted to compare results which would have been obtained using regression procedures with those of the principal components analysis. Toward this, two regression models were developed in which ratings of intention to act cautiously (Question 14) served as the dependent measure.

In the first model, stepwise regression was employed using ratings on the 12 product-related questions (those which were used in the PCA) as predictors. In keeping with previous findings using a similar methodology, the risk variable accounted for the most variance in subjects' ratings of intent to act cautiously ($R^2 = .948$). Based on this analysis alone, one might conclude that perceived risk is the primary determinant of whether an individual will act (or fail to act) in a cautious manner when using a product. However, two other predictors (severity, $r = .944$; dread, $r = .969$) had extremely high correlations with ratings of cautious intent and were highly correlated with ratings of risk (severity, $r = .976$; dread, $r = .984$). The fact that severity and dread were not chosen in the regression analysis suggests that this procedure uses a rather arbitrary method of variable selection and that it is not well suited for explanation.

The PCA presented in this study suggests that perceptions of risk are composed of three dimensions. A second regression analysis was performed on ratings of

Figure 1. Plot of the 40 products in the PCA factor space for components 1 and 2.

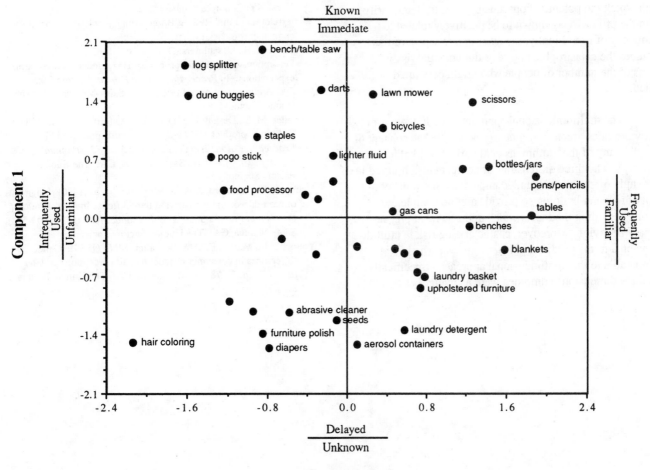

intent to act cautiously using the component scores for each product as predictors. Combined, the three dimensions accounted for 96.1% of the variance of cautious intent, which was slightly better than that of the single risk variable ($R^2 = .948$). Uncertainty (*beta* = .48, $p < .001$), Familiarity (*b* = -.39, $p < .001$) and Catastrophe (*b* = .37, $p < .001$) each contributed significant unique variance to the prediction of cautious intent. Conceptually, the direction of the standardized weights for each component suggests that unfamiliar or infrequently used products which are associated with unknown risks and which are characterized as having delayed and catastrophic consequences are products for which users will act cautiously.

DISCUSSION

Unlike previous research which has conceptualized risk as a unidimensional construct (primarily because of the limitations of the regression approach), the results of the present study suggest that judgments about product risks are multidimensional. These results indicate that people consider both the qualitative and quantitative aspects of the *risks* as well as the familiarity with the *product*. The qualitative component of risk includes the degree to which product hazards are known (or knowable) and the latency with which the potential consequences occur. Familiarity with the product was shown to be positively related to frequency of use. Finally, the quantitative aspect of risk includes the catastrophic nature of the potential risk in terms of the number of people who might be injured or killed.

The multidimensional approach used in the present study provides greater *explanatory* power for the concept of risk than any of the unidimensional variables (likelihood or severity). The three dimensions or components observed in this study offer a more detailed understanding of the concept of risk and in doing so provide a more complete picture regarding the facets which underlie rated precautionary behavior. Moreover, characterizing risk in multidimensional terms produces *predictive* power which is comparable to the unidimensional approach. Specifically, the three dimensions combined were a slightly better

predictor of cautious intent ($R^2 = .961$) than was the single risk variable selected in the stepwise regression ($R^2 = .948$). Moreover, *each* of the three components significantly influenced subjects' rated intent to act cautiously when using a product.

These results also offer a means of reconciliation for previous findings in the risk literature (i.e., Slovic et al., 1979; Wogalter et al., 1986, 1987). Rather than being an either-or proposition (i.e., *either* likelihood *or* severity of injury), results of the PCA provide an interpretation which accounts for both quantitative and qualitative aspects of risk. Future research might examine additional product lists as well as different subject populations to determine whether the dimensions suggested here are reliable.

REFERENCES

Desaulniers, D. (1991). An examination of consequence probability as a determinant of precautionary intent. Unpublished doctoral dissertation. Rice University, Houston, TX.

Slovic, P., Fischoff, B.& Lichtenstein, S. (1979). Rating the risks. *Environment, 21,* 14-39.

U. S. Consumer Product Safety Commission (1989). *NEISS Data Highlights.* Washington, DC: Author.

Webster's New Universal Unabridged Dictionary (1983). New York, NY: Simon & Schuster, Inc.

Winterfeldt, D., John, R. S. & Borcherding, K. (1981). Cognitive components of risk ratings. *Risk Analysis, 1,* 277-287.

Wogalter, M. S., Desaulniers, D. R. & Brelsford, J. W., Jr. (1986). Perceptions of consumer products: Hazardousness and warning expectations. In *Proceedings of the Human Factors Society-30th Annual Meeting.* (1197-1201). Santa Monica, CA: The Human Factors Society.

Wogalter, M. S., Desaulniers, D. R. & Brelsford, J. W., Jr. (1987). Consumer products: How are the hazards perceived. In *Proceedings of the Human Factors Society-31st Annual Meeting.* (p. 615-619). Santa Monica, CA: The Human Factors Society.

Young, S. L., Brelsford, J. W. & Wogalter, M. S. (1990). Judgments of hazard, risk and danger: Do they differ? In *Proceedings of the Human Factors Society-34th Annual Meeting.* (p. 503-507). Santa Monica, CA: The Human Factors Society.

Young, S. L., Martin, E. G. & Wogalter, M. S. (1989). Gender differences in consumer product hazard perception. In *Interface '89.* (p. 73-78). Santa Monica, CA: The Human Factors Society.

INJURY SEVERITY AND LIKELIHOOD IN WARNINGS

Michael S. Wogalter and Todd Barlow
Department of Psychology
Rensselaer Polytechnic Institute
Troy, New York 12180

ABSTRACT

Two experiments examined the influence of injury likelihood and severity in warnings on product hazard perceptions (Experiment 1) and behavioral compliance (Experiment 2). In Experiment 1, participants were given a set of front panel labels for 10 household consumer products. Warnings on the labels were constructed by manipulating the likelihood (low vs. high) and severity (low vs. high) of injury. Labels lacking a warning served as controls. Participants rated the product labels under the guise of a marketing study in which most of the questions concerned product familiarity, cost, and label attractiveness. Only one question was of interest which probed the level of hazard posed by the products. The results showed that (1) the presence of a warning increased the products' judged level of hazard, (2) products with high severity warnings were viewed to be more hazardous than products with low severity warnings, and (3) likelihood of injury in the warnings had no influence on hazard perceptions.

Experiment 2 used a chemistry laboratory demonstration task to test the effects of injury likelihood and severity in a warning on compliance behavior (i.e., wearing gloves as directed by the warning). Greater compliance was shown when warned of a more severe injury, but only when the injury was of lower likelihood.

In general, both experiments showed that injury severity influences warning effectiveness to a greater extent than injury likelihood. The results suggest that to inform people of a hazard and to motivate them to comply with a directed behavior, product warnings should communicate the severity of consequences.

INTRODUCTION

What information do people use to determine the level of hazard posed by consumer products? This question is important because research suggests that hazard perception is closely related to people's willingness to read product warnings (Godfrey, Allender, Laughery, & Smith, 1983; Wogalter, Desaulniers, & Brelsford, 1986; Young, Brelsford, & Wogalter, 1990).

Research also indicates that people's hazard perceptions are largely determined by the extent or severity of injury that might occur with virtually no contribution of how likely the injury might occur (Wogalter, Desaulniers, & Brelsford, 1987; Young et al., 1990). However, research on a related concept "risk" indicates that people's perceptions are determined by combining both severity *and* likelihood information (e.g., Lowrence, 1980; Slovic, Fischhoff, & Lichtenstein, 1979, 1980).

The methodology employed in previous work examined the relative effectiveness of likelihood and severity information by asking people to judge the hazard of generic names of products (e.g., Wogalter et al. 1986, 1987a; Young et al., 1990) or estimate the frequency or relative likelihood of accident events (e.g., Slovic et al. 1979, 1980). However, no study to date has investigated this issue using a more direct approach in which likelihood and severity information is manipulated in warnings. The present studies examine the effect of injury likelihood (low versus high) and severity (low versus high) information in warnings on hazard perceptions for commercially-available consumer products (Experiment 1) and measures their effect on behavioral compliance (Experiment 2).

EXPERIMENT 1

Experiment 1 investigated whether injury likelihood and severity information in warnings influences perceptions of hazard. The study was conducted under the guise of "marketing research" concerned with factors affecting people's decisions to purchase certain consumer products. Participants answered a variety of questions for each of a set of products. One question, which asked how hazardous they perceived the product to be, was of primary interest.

Method

Participants. Forty-six undergraduates from Rensselaer Polytechnic Institute participated for course credit in introductory psychology courses. Prior to this experiment, a different set of 30 students from the same population participated in a preliminary word rating study.

Stimuli and materials. Ten consumer products were chosen to represent a range of potentially hazardous household items (Alcon Optizyme Enzymatic contact lens cleaner, Dow bathroom cleaner, Excedrin extra-strength aspirin, Fresh Start laundry detergent, Klean-Strip paint thinner, Krylon fixative spray coating, Raid roach and flea fogger, Red Devil lye drain opener, Textra hair mousse, and Trugarde fabric stain protector). Labels from the products' front panels were duplicated using an optical scanner/digitizer (Thunderware Thunderscan), stored and manipulated using a computer and software (Apple Macintosh and Silicon Beach Superpaint), and reproduced using a 300 dot per inch printer (Apple Laserwriter).

Warnings on the front labels of the products were manipulated to differ with respect to conveyed injury likelihood (low versus high) and severity (low versus high) of injury that they conveyed. These two independent variables were orthogonally crossed to form four warning labels for each product: (1) Low likelihood, Low severity, (2) Low likelihood, High severity, (3) High likelihood, Low severity, (4) High likelihood, High severity. This manipulation was accomplished by changing some of the words in the warnings' verbal statements to convey different levels of likelihood and severity. Likelihood and severity terms were selected for inclusion in this experiment according to their distance on the respective dimensions which were based on results from a preliminary word rating study, which is described below.

Earlier, 30 Rensselaer Polytechnic Institute undergraduates rated a set of terms representing a range of likelihood and severity. Eleven likelihood terms (can, likely, may, might, occasionally, possibility, probable, seldom, a slight chance of, unlikely, and will) were rated on a 9-point Likert-type scale given the question: "What is the *likelihood* of injury implied by this term?" The following numerical and verbal anchors were provided: (0) never, (2) unlikely, (4) likely, (6) very likely, and (8) extremely likely. Ten severity terms (extensive, intense, irreversible, major, mild, minimal, minor, severe, slight, and superficial) were rated using the question: "What is the *severity* of injury implied by this term?" The following the numerical and verbal anchors were given: (0) not severe, (2) slightly severe, (4) severe, (6) very severe, and (8) extremely severe.

For low and high likelihood, the terms "can" (likelihood rating: $M = 3.40$, $s = 1.5$) and "will" (likelihood rating: $M = 7.73$, $s = 0.52$) were used, respectively. According to the earlier rating study, these two terms were significantly different in their conveyed likelihood, $t(29) = 17.3$, $p < .0001$. For low and high severity, "mild" (severity rating: $M = 1.43$, $s = .77$) and "intense" (severity rating: $M = 6.53$, $s = 1.07$) were used, respectively. These two terms were significantly different in their conveyed severity, $t(29) = 21.1$, $p < .0001$. Using the hair mousse product as an example, the warning statements for the four conditions were: "*Can* cause *mild* eye irritation" (Low likelihood, Low severity), "*Can* cause *intense* eye irritation" (Low likelihood, High severity), "*Will* cause *mild* eye irritation" (High likelihood, Low severity warning), and "*Will* cause *intense* eye irritation" (High likelihood, High severity) [italics added]. A fifth condition in which no warning was present on the product labels served as a control.

Some of the original product label warnings described more than one hazard (e.g., both consumption and skin contact). For purposes of control, all warnings in the current study warned of a single hazard, usually the first hazard mentioned on the original label. The specific kind of injury described in the warning statements was allowed to vary for compatibility with particular products. For example, the bathroom cleaner warned of consumption problems and the fogger warned of potential respiratory problems.

The warnings were placed in the same location as the original label warning. They were preceded by the signal word CAUTION, and were printed in font sizes and styles that best matched the fonts on the original label. Five booklets were formed having labels for all ten products with each booklet containing two product labels representing each of the five conditions. Labels for each product were balanced across booklets and label order in each booklet was randomized.

Fourteen questions were asked of each product, addressing such items as product familiarity, cost, and label attractiveness. The primary question of interest asked, "How hazardous is it to use this product?" Participants responded using a 9-point rating scale having the following numerical and verbal anchors: (0) not hazardous, (2) slightly hazardous, (4) hazardous, (6) very hazardous, and (8) extremely hazardous. The other 13 questions were included to disguise the purpose of the study and were not analyzed.

Procedure. Participants were initially told that the purpose of the questionnaire was to examine factors that might affect people's decision to purchase certain consumer products that they might see on a store shelf. Participants were given the questionnaire, response sheets, and one of the five booklets of product labels. Participants were told: (1) to move briskly through the questions, (2) to give their first impressions, and (3) to complete all questions for each product before moving to the next product. Approximately equal numbers of participants were given each of the five booklets (nine or 10 students per booklet). After completing the questionnaire, the students were debriefed on the true nature of the study and were thanked for their participation.

Results

Hazard ratings for the 10 products were collapsed to form mean scores for each condition composed of two product ratings. Thus, each participant contributed five scores to the repeated-measures analyses described below.

The first analysis examined whether hazard perceptions differed due to the simple presence of a warning on the label. A contrast comparing the warning conditions and the no warning condition was significant, $t(45) = 2.04$, $p < .05$, showing that products with warnings ($M = 2.28$) were perceived to be significantly more hazardous than products without warnings ($M = 1.79$).

The second analysis examined differences among the warning conditions. A 2 (high versus low likelihood) X 2 (high versus low severity) repeated-measures analysis of variance (ANOVA) showed a significant main effect of severity, $F(1, 45) = 6.33$, $p < .02$. Products with warnings conveying higher injury severity were judged to be more hazardous ($M = 2.50$) than products with warnings conveying lower injury severity ($M = 2.05$). No significant effect of the injury likelihood nor a significant likelihood X severity interaction was found ($ps > .05$).

Discussion

The presence of warnings on the front front label increased participants' perceptions of product hazard. Products lacking warnings were perceived to be less hazardous than product with warnings. The results also showed that the content of the warning message is important in affecting perceptions of hazard. Product labels with warnings conveying greater injury severity were perceived to be more hazardous than warnings conveying lower injury severity. The implication of these results is that failure to include a warning message on a potentially hazardous product might lead people to believe that the product is less hazardous than it really is. Even if a warning is present, it needs to give an accurate portrayal of the extent of possible injury. Apparently people use the magnitude of injury as a cue in determining their perceptions of product hazard. Thus, products capable of inflicting substantial injury should describe how badly a person might get hurt; otherwise, people may believe that the level of hazard is lower than it really is.

While the severity manipulation influenced perceptions of hazard, the results failed to show any influence of injury likelihood. This null result fails to support the suggestion in the risk literature that people's perceptions of risk is influenced by a combination of likelihood and severity information (Slovic et al., 1979, 1980). However, the failure to find an effect of likelihood on perceptions of hazard is in accord with Wogalter et al.'s (1987a) and Young et al.'s (1990) findings that injury severity is the primary determinant of perceptions of hazard.

This experiment, as well as Wogalter et al. (1987a) and Young et al. (1990), examined the influence of likelihood and severity information on perceptions of product hazard. All three of these studies examined their influence using ratings. The assumption has been that perceptions of hazard translates into cautionary behavior. However, this assumption has yet to be directly examined. The ultimate test is whether the warning's content influences people's precautiounary behavior. Experiment 2 examines the effect of injury likelihood and severity information in a warning on compliance behavior.

EXPERIMENT 2

The purpose of Experiment 2 was to determine the effect of injury likelihood and severity information in a warning on compliance behavior. Participants were placed in a chemistry lab and given a set of instructions containing one of four kinds of warnings or instructions lacking a warning. Compliance was measured by recording whether or not they engaged in safety behavior.

Method

Participants. Seventy-nine Rensselaer Polytechnic Institute undergraduates participated for course credit in introductory psychology courses. They were randomly assigned to conditions, each having 16 students except for the control condition which had 15. None had participated in Experiment 1.

Materials and procedure. The basic procedure is similar to the laboratory demonstration task described in detail in Wogalter, Godfrey, Fontennelle, Desaulniers, Rothstein, and Laughery (1987) and Wogalter, Allison, and McKenna (1989) with the exception that the warning in the current study directed participants to wear gloves rather than both mask and gloves. Participants were given instructions directing them to measure and mix various "chemicals." These "chemicals" were actually safe substances and solutions (flour, sugar, water, etc.) that were disguised with food coloring to set the appearance that the participants were working with potentially dangerous materials (i.e., that some risk was involved). A large number of disposable plastic gloves were located on the table containing the chemistry equipment.

Four groups of participants received a set of printed instructions. The instructions contained: 1) a short introductory paragraph, which provides a general description of the laboratory task, 2) a warning following the paragraph, and 3) the specific mixing directions. As in Experiment 1,

the four warning conditions were: (1) Low likelihood, Low severity, (2) Low likelihood, High severity, (3) High likelihood, Low severity, (4) High likelihood, High severity. The warning statements used in these conditions were:

(1) "Contact with skin *can* cause *mild* skin irritation. Wear gloves." (Low likelihood, Low severity);
(2) "Contact with skin *can* cause *intense* skin irritation. Wear gloves." (Low likelihood, High severity);
(3) "Contact with skin *will* cause *mild* skin irritation. Wear gloves." (High likelihood, Low severity);
(4) "Contact with skin *will* cause *intense* skin irritation. Wear gloves." (High likelihood, High severity).

All warning statements were preceded by the signal word WARNING. A fifth group received instructions in which the warning was absent (i.e., the space where the warnings were placed in the other conditions was left blank). Whether the participant put on the gloves before starting to mix the substances was recorded.

Results

Participants were given a score of "1" if they complied and a score of "0" if they did not. The compliance data were examined using Chi Square analyses. The overall analysis for the experiment was significant, $X^2(4, N = 79) = 18.28$, $p < .01$. This was followed by specific contrasts among conditions. A contrast comparing compliance in the no warning condition with the conditions in which a warning present was significant, $X^2(1, N = 79) = 13.47$, $p < .001$. There was greater compliance when a warning was present (42 of 64 participants or 66%) than when it was absent (2 of 15 participants or 13%). The only significant comparison among the four warning conditions occurred between the Low Likelihood, High Severity warning and the Low Likelihood, Low Severity warning conditions, $X^2(1, N = 32) = 4.80$, $p < .05$. Under lower likelihood, there was greater compliance with the higher severity warning (13 of 16 or 81%) than the lower severity warning (7 of 16 or 44%).

Discussion

Participants in the chemistry laboratory task more often engaged in precautionary behavior (wearing gloves) when a warning was present than when it was absent. This result supports earlier work (Wogalter et al. 1987b) and indicates that safety-related behavior can be enhanced by information communicated by a warning. Without the warning present, the frequency of precautionary behavior was much lower. While this result is not particularly surprising, it was unexpected to find that two participants put on gloves *without* a warning present directing them to do so. This may be due to the fact that many of the participants had or were currently taking chemistry classes at the university in which similar safety behavior is required.

The results also showed greater compliance when the warning conveyed information of a more severe injury than of a less severe injury. However, this difference was only shown for warnings describing an injury of lower likelihood. The difference between high and low severity was not shown for warnings expressing higher injury likelihood. The reason for the failure to find a difference for the higher likelihood is not clear. One possibility is that participants in the high likelihood conditions did not believe that harm would *definitely* occur if they mishandled the substances (perhaps from similar previous experience), and thus the warning message was less believable to them. Further investigation would have to be undertaken to test whether likelihood interacts with experiential, situational and/or product factors.

GENERAL DISCUSSION

Both experiments showed that the presence of a warning increases perceptions of product hazardousness (Experiment 1) and compliance behavior (Experiment 2) compared to its absence. The implication of these findings is that failure to include a warning for a potential hazard might lead people to underestimate the dangerousness involved. A particularly serious error would occur if people make the assumption that no warning means that the product (or situation) is safe. This belief might then translate into behavior that is less cautious than appropriate and possibly leading to injury. Moreover, it underscores the finding by Wogalter et al. (1986) which indicated warnings should be located in close proximity because this is where people expect them to be. If a warning is not located on or near the product people may not see the warning and assume that there is no hazard (Wogalter, Brelsford, Desaulniers, & Laughery, 1990).

Both experiments also showed that warning effectiveness was enhanced by information expressing greater than lesser injury severity. Experiment 1 showed a clear severity effect on product hazard perceptions. Experiment 2 confirmed this, in part, using a behavioral compliance measure. The results showed that a warning expressing higher injury severity produced greater behavioral compliance than a warning expressing lower injury severity, but only when it was accompanied by information imparting lower likelihood of injury. No effect of severity on compliance was found for warnings expressing higher likelihood of injury.

While the two experiments used very different procedures they, nevertheless, showed reasonably consistent findings. They support Wogalter et al.'s (1987a) and Young et al.'s (1990) finding which showed in multiple regression analyses that severity was a more important cue than likelihood in people's judgments of product hazard. It also supports Martin and Wogalter's (1989) suggestion that injury probabilities and frequencies may not be involved in people's decisions to behave cautiously.

Why would injury likelihood play such a minor role in perceptions of hazard and behavioral compliance, yet appear to play a role in other research concerned with perceptions of risk? One possibility concerns the different kinds of tasks involved in the respective research. In studies of perception of risk, Slovic et al. (1979, 1980) asked participants to estimate mortality rates or make comparative judgments of accident frequencies. This kind of judgment *demands* consideration of likelihoods which might be the reason why a contribution of this factor was found and the present results did not. Apparently, the effects of injury severity on perceptions are so pervasive that they affect judgments of likelihood. For example, Slovic et al. (1979, 1980) found that mortality rates for agents capable of producing severe consequences were overestimated, indicating that there is a

contribution of severity even for judgments strictly concerned with frequency of events. A similar result was noted by Martin and Wogalter (1989).

A second possible reason for the failure to find strong evidence for the influence of likelihood information is that the likelihood of consumer product injury is extremely low. While people are capable of making distinctions between products based upon the frequency of injury (Brems, 1986), the differences between relatively unlikely accident events are probably not considered in everyday judgments of hazard. That is, accidents are so infrequent that people may consider the likelihood of injury to be too small to be of concern. Thus, the most persuasive and vivid cue for judgments of hazard is the potential severity of injury that might occur.

These results indicate that the extent of injury is an important indicator that people use to make judgments about product hazard and to make warning compliance decisions. They also point to the need for warnings to inform consumers about the seriousness of the consequences to motivate them to comply with the directed safety behavior and thus avoid accidents and injury. An implication of these findings is that warning communications should focus more on how badly a person can get hurt than on how likely one will be hurt. In sum, it appears that to increase compliance with precautionary directives and to enhance perceptions of hazards, warnings should emphasize realistic consequences of product use.

REFERENCES

Brems, D. J. (1986). *Risk Perception for Common Consumer Products*. Unpublished Doctoral Dissertation, Rice University, Houston, Texas.

Godfrey, S. S., Allender, L., Laughery, K. R., & Smith, V. L. (1983). Warning messages: Will the consumer bother to look? In *Proceedings of the Human Factors Society 27th Annual Meeting* (pp. 950-954). Santa Monica, CA: Human Factors Society.

Martin, E. G., & Wogalter, M. S. (1989). Risk perception and precautionary intent for common consumer products. In *Proceedings of the 33rd Annual Human Factors Society Meeting* (pp. 931-935). Santa Monica: Human Factors Society.

Slovic, P., Fischhoff, B., & Lichtenstein, S. (1979). Rating the risks. *Environment, 21*, 14-39.

Slovic, P., Fischhoff, B., & Lichtenstein, S. (1980). Facts and fears: Understanding perceived risk. In R. C. Schwing & W. A. Albers Jr. (Eds.), *Societal Risk Assessment* (pp. 181-216). New York: Plenum Press.

Wogalter, M. S., Brelsford, J. W., Desaulniers, D. R., & Laughery, K. R. (1990). *Consumer product warnings: The role of hazard perception*. Manuscript submitted for publication.

Wogalter, M. S., Allison, S. T., & McKenna, N. A. (1989). The effects of cost and social influence on warning compliance. *Human Factors, 31*, 133-140.

Wogalter, M. S., Desaulniers, D. R., & Brelsford, J. W. (1986). Perceptions of consumer product hazards: Implications for the need to warn. In *Proceedings of the 30th Annual Human Factors Society Meeting* (pp. 1197-1201). Santa Monica: Human Factors Society.

Wogalter, M. S., Desaulniers, D. R., & Brelsford, J. W. (1987a). Consumer products: How are the hazards perceived? In *Proceedings of the 31st Annual Human Factors Society Meeting* (pp. 615-619). Santa Monica: Human Factors Society.

Wogalter, M. S., Godfrey, S. S., Fontenelle, G. A., Desaulniers, D. R., Rothstein, P., & Laughery, K. R. (1987b). Effectiveness of warnings. *Human Factors, 29*, 599-612.

Young, S. L., Brelsford, J. W., & Wogalter, M. S. (1990). Judgments of hazard, risk, and danger: Do they differ? In *Proceedings of the 34th Annual Human Factors Society Meeting*. Santa Monica: Human Factors Society.

CONSUMER PRODUCTS: HOW ARE THE HAZARDS PERCEIVED?

Michael S. Wogalter
Psychology Department
University of Richmond
Richmond, Virginia 23173

David R. Desaulniers
Psychology Department
Rice University
Houston, Texas 77251

John W. Brelsford Jr.
Psychology Department
Rice University
Houston, Texas 77251

ABSTRACT

Two questionnaire studies were conducted examining potential components of perceptions of consumer product hazardousness. In Study 1 subjects rated 72 consumer products on perceived hazardousness, expected severity of injuries, and perceived likelihood of injury. The results indicate that severity relates more strongly than injury likelihood with perceived hazardousness. Several product knowledge variables were also examined; these results indicate that technological complexity and confidence in knowing the product's hazards add unique variance beyond severity in the prediction of hazard perception. In Study 2 subjects generated accident scenarios for each of 18 consumer products. Subjects rated each scenario according to the severity of the accident and the probability of its occurrence and also provided ratings of overall product hazardousness. Results supported the findings of Study 1. The severity of product injury scenarios were strongly and positively correlated with hazardousness. Probability of injury ratings added negligible hazard predictiveness beyond severity. Product hazardousness was highly correlated with the level of precaution subjects would reportedly take when using the product. For high hazard products the first scenario generated was most severe compared to the other two scenarios. For low hazard products, the first scenario was most probable and the least severe of the scenarios generated. Practical and theoretical implications of the results are discussed.

INTRODUCTION

How do people distinguish between products that are hazardous and those that are not? The answer to this question has important implications for the prevention of consumer product accidents and the development of effective interventions. Such interventions may involve product redesign and protective barriers (e.g., safety caps). When these are not possible then warnings can be used to promote accident prevention.

In order for warnings to effectively prevent accidents, the warnings must be read. Wogalter, Desaulniers, and Brelsford (1986) report that subjects are more willing to read warnings on more hazardous products and expect such products to have warnings. This suggests that perceptions of hazardousness are important in determining precautionary intentions.

The possibility that consumers may incorrectly perceive the level of hazard is another reason why it is important to study perceptions of product hazardousness. For example, research suggests that people may misperceive the number of deaths associated with a variety of consumer products by overestimating infrequent causes and underestimating frequent causes (Slovic, Fischhoff, & Lichtenstein, 1979; Brems, 1986). An underestimation might lead an individual to be less inclined to engage in precautionary behaviors such as reading warnings and responding appropriately.

The purpose of the present research is to examine components involved in the formation of perceptions of hazardousness of consumer products. There are several possible sources of information that might combine to form such perceptions. For example, it is reasonable to assume that products which potentially inflict *severe* injuries or death are judged more hazardous than those capable of inflicting only minor injuries or discomfort.

Another possible component of hazardousness is the *likelihood* or *probability* of being injured by the product. Indeed, research by Slovic, Fischhoff, and Lichtenstein (1980a) suggests that perceptions of product hazardousness are determined by some *combination* of information about the severity and the probability of accidents involving a product. The possible contributions of perceived severity and likelihood of injury as predictors of hazardousness are examined in

the present research. Moreover, several combinatorial models involving severity and likelihood of injure are explored.

A further component possibly involved in the perception of product hazardousness is product knowledge. It is not unreasonable to assume that more familiar products are perceived to be less hazardous. Previous research suggests that there is a relationship between familiarity and hazardousness, though the research suggests that the relationship is more complex than intuition might suggest (e.g., Godfrey, Allender, Laughery, & Smith, 1983; Godfrey & Laughery, 1984; Wogalter et al., 1986). In addition to familiarity and its relationship to hazardousness, several other knowledge related variables were explored: frequency and time of contact, technological complexity of the product, and perceived confidence in knowing all of the product's hazards.

STUDY 1

Method

Subjects. Twenty-eight University of Richmond undergraduates participated for extra credit in introductory psychology courses.

Materials. The seventy-two generic product names used in the Wogalter et al. (1986) study were used. Each subject was presented with one of four randomly determined product orders. Subjects responded to eight questions for each product. Nine-point Likert-type scales ranging from zero to eight were used for each questions. All even scale values had verbal anchors. Each subject received a unique random ordering of the eight questions. The questions and anchors were as follows:

1) "How *hazardous* is this product?" The anchors for this question were: (0) not at all hazardous, (2) slightly hazardous, (4) hazardous, (6) very hazardous, and (8) extremely hazardous.
2) "How *severely* might you be injured with this product?" The anchors for this question were: (0) not severe, (2) slightly severe, (4) severe, (6) very severe, and (8) extremely severe.
3) "How *likely* are you to be injured by this product?" The anchors for this question were: (0) never, (2) unlikely, (4) likely, (6) very

likely, and (8) extremely likely.

4) "How *frequently* do you use this product?" The anchors for this question were: (0) never, (2) infrequent, (4) frequent, (6) very frequent, and (8) extremely frequent.

5) "How much *time* do you spend with this product each time you use it?" The anchors for this question were: (0) never, (2) short time, (4) medium time, (6) long time, and (8) very long time.

6) "How *familiar* are you with this product?" The anchors for this question were: (0) not at all familiar, (2) slightly familiar, (4) familiar, (6) very familiar, and (8) extremely familiar.

7) "Do you consider this product *technologically complex* ?" The anchors for this question were: (0) not at all complex, (2) slightly complex, (4) complex, (6) very complex, and (8) extremely complex.

8) "How *confident* do you feel you are in *knowing all the hazards* related to this product?" The anchors for this question were: (0) not at all confident, (2) slightly confident, (4) confident, (6) very confident, and (8) extremely confident.

Procedure. Subjects were given one of the four random orders of products. They were told to read the entire list of products to familiarize themselves with the range of products and were given three minutes to examine the list. In order to orient subjects to respond to the products generically rather than to specific brand names, subjects were told to assume that the products were from a new manufacturer or had a new brand name. Subjects rated the entire list of products before moving to the next question.

Results

Several analyses were performed on these data. In the first set of analyses, subject ratings for each of the eight scales were collapsed into mean ratings for each of the 72 products. Of particular interest was the prediction of hazardousness. The bivariate correlations of hazardousness with severity and likelihood were computed. A strong positive relationship between ratings of hazardousness and the expected severity of injury ($r = .89$, $p < .0001$) was found. The likelihood of injury yields a somewhat smaller correlation with ratings of perceived hazardousness ($r = .75$, $p < .0001$). The difference between these correlations is significant ($p < .01$).

Slovic et al. (1980a) have suggested that perceptions of product hazardousness are determined by some *combination* of information about the severity and the probability of accidents involving a product. Several multiple regression models involving severity and likelihood of injury as predictors of hazardousness were examined. The first analysis used an additive model. This analysis showed that once severity is used as a predictor of hazardousness ($r^2 = .79$), likelihood of injury does not increase predictiveness, producing an identical R^2 of .79 when both predictors are present.

A second model involved a multiplicative regression where the predictor was the product of severity and likelihood. This analysis produced an R^2 of .67. The variance accounted for is smaller than the variance accounted by severity alone.

A third model involved the variables severity, likelihood, and their interaction as predictors in a linear multiple regression on hazardousness. This analysis produced an R^2 of .83. The relative increment in variance accounted for compared to the simple linear regression using only severity as the predictor and an additive model using severity and likelihood as predictors is small (.04) but significant (p 's $< .05$).

Several other knowledge variables were examined in regard to their relationship with perceived hazardousness: 1) familiarity, 2) frequency of contact, 3) time of contact, 4) technological complexity, and 5)

perceived confidence in knowing all of the product's hazards. The simple correlations of these variables with hazardousness were initially explored. The results show product familiarity is significantly and negatively related to hazardousness ($r = -.36$, $p < .002$). Frequency of contact is negatively correlated with perceived hazardousness ($r = -.27$, $p < .02$). The amount time spent with the products is negatively, but not significantly, related to perceived hazardousness ($r = -.15$, $p > .05$).

In examining the relationship between perceived technological complexity and hazardousness, the results show that products perceived as more technologically complex are also perceived as more hazardous ($r = .35$, $p < .003$). Subjects were also asked how confident they were in knowing all the hazards related to each product. A correlational analysis shows a significant negative relationship to perceived hazardousness ($r = -.40$, $p < .0005$).

Overall, these correlations suggest a negative relationship between people's knowledge of products and perceptions of product hazardousness. Using multiple regression analyses, each variable's relative contribution to the prediction of hazard perception beyond the variance accounted for by a model involving the variables severity, likelihood, and their crossproduct was explored. The analyses indicate no additional predictiveness from the variables familiarity, frequency of contact, and quantity of contact. Only the variables technological complexity and confidence in knowing the hazards add statistically significant variance to the prediction of perceived hazardousness, 2% and 3%, respectively. Simultaneously adding both variables into the prediction equation adds 4%.

Discussion

The results indicate the best single predictor of hazard perception is the severity of injury. Although the simple correlation between hazardousness and likelihood was significant, subsequent multiple regression analyses indicated that the addition of likelihood to severity does not enhance the prediction of hazardousness. However, the further addition of the severity-likelihood crossproduct produces a small but significant increment in predictiveness. That severity, likelihood, and their interaction predicts the greatest amount of variance in perceptions of product hazardousness supports the suggestion of Slovic, Fischhoff, and Lichtenstein (1980a) that perceptions of product hazardousness are determined by some *combination* of information about the severity and the probability of accidents. However, the model involving severity, likelihood, and their interaction provides only slightly greater predictiveness (4%) than a much simpler model involving only severity. Despite the fact that this difference is significant, the importance of this difference is arguable. In terms of applications, severity might be the only important predictor of hazardousness.

The present results also suggest that products that are less frequently used and less familiar are perceived to be more hazardous. On the other hand, these two variable do not enhance the three-factor multiple regression model discussed above. It is interesting to note that a similar result was found by Wogalter et al. (1986). Though familiarity was negatively and significantly related to willingness to read product warnings, when hazardousness was already present in a regression equation, no significant increment in predictiveness due to familiarity was found. However, two other knowledge related variables did contribute significant variance to the prediction of hazard perceptions, ratings of confidence in knowing all the hazards related to the products and the technological complexity of the products. This latter result supports Slovic, Fischhoff, and Lichtenstein (1980a) who report results that suggest that more technologically complex situations are perceived to be more hazardous. Technological advances have produced complex products which might have hidden dangers. Apparently the lack of knowledge about such products' hazards is used in the cognitive formulation of overall product hazardousness.

Speculation might be made with regard to the evolutionary significance of these results. Survival may depend upon precautionary behavior when engaging in things unknown. The perception of hazardousness might well be involved in the determination of such precautionary behavior in humans.

STUDY 2

In Study 1 subjects made overall, abstract judgements of products. Study 2 used a somewhat different technique to examine perceptions of product hazard. In Study 2 subjects generated specific accident scenarios for each product and then rated the scenarios with regard to their severity and probability of injury. The data were examined in regard to perceptions of overall product hazardousness.

There was a further purpose of the second study. Wogalter et al. (1986) reported that, with products of greater hazard, subjects indicate a greater willingness to read product warnings. Reading warnings is one mode of precautionary behavior. The present study further examines the relationship between hazardousness and reported intent to behave in a precautionary manner.

A third purpose was to examine characteristics of the scenarios generated by subjects. Estimated severity and likelihood of potential outcomes are examined as a function of hazard level and scenario order.

Method

Subjects. Seventy Rice University and University of Houston undergraduates participated for extra credit in psychology courses.

Materials. The list of 18 products used in this study are shown in Table 1. Products were selected to represent a broad range of perceptions with regard to both severity and probability of potential accidents. A random order of these product names was arranged on the response sheet with spaces for subjects' scenario descriptions and ratings. The materials also included a question sheet which contained a set of instructions and the rating scales. The instructions and rating scales are described in the following section.

Procedure. Subjects were initially given a copy of the response sheet which contained the list of products and were asked to read over the list. Subjects were then given the question sheet which asked the subjects to carry out the following tasks.

The instructions for the first task asked subjects to assume that it was necessary for them to use each of the 18 products listed on the answer sheet. Subjects were asked to "Rate the *degree of precautions* you would take when using each product." Precaution was explicitly defined as "action to ensure safety." A 5-point rating scale was provided. The numerical and verbal anchors were as follows: (1) use with no precautions, (2) use with minor precautions, (3) use with moderate precautions, (4) use with substantial precautions, and (5) use with extreme precautions.

In the second task subjects were asked to "Imagine using each product. What *accidents* involving each product would you fear occurring?" Subjects were asked to report the first three accident scenarios that come to mind-- in the order that they come to mind. In doing this they were to describe each accident briefly stating both *how* each imagined accident occurs and the *kind of injury* received. To reinforce this instruction, the response sheet contained two columns labeled HOW and INJURY and three rows for the three accident scenarios. There was no time pressure to complete this task.

In the third task subjects were asked to "Rate the *severity* of each accidental injury" that they reported in the scenario generation task.

Space for the ratings were available next to the space available for the scenario descriptions. The rating scale was a 7-point scale containing the following numerical and verbal anchors: (1) no injury, (2) minor injury--remedied by first aid, (3) requires outpatient treatment, (4) short-term disability--under two weeks, (5) long-term disability, (6) permanent disability, and (7) death.

In the fourth task subjects were asked to indicate *how likely* it would be, during their next use of the product, that they would experience the types of accidents and injuries that they had generated in the scenario task. The rating scale was a 8-point scale containing the following numerical and verbal anchors: (1) extremely remote, (2) highly remote, (3) remote, (4) unlikely, (5) possible, (6) probable, (7) highly probable, and (8) almost certain.

In the fifth task, subjects were asked to provide an overall rating of perceived hazardousness of each product. Specifically, subjects were asked, "How *hazardous* do you feel each product is?" The rating scale was a 7-point scale containing the following numerical and verbal anchors: (1) not at all, (2) a little, (3) some, (4) moderately, (5) fairly, (6) very, and (7) extremely.

Results

In spite of the instructions directing subjects to report three accident scenarios for each product, many subjects failed or were unable to report more than one scenario. A total of 1260 observations (70 subjects X 18 products) were possible for each of the three scenarios. For the first scenario, 3% of the observations lacked either (or both) severity and probability ratings. For the second and third scenarios, the number of missing values was much higher, 25% and 54%, respectively.

These data were analyzed in three ways. As in Study 1 one set of analyses used data points that were product means averaged across subjects. The second set of analyses averaged across products to obtain subject means. The third set of analyses used non-averaged data involving the raw responses from all subjects and all products. Where data for an observation was incomplete, the observation was deleted from analysis.

The data used in the first set of analyses were derived from the raw data by collapsing across subjects; product means were entered into the analyses as the random variable. As in Study 1, several models were examined using correlational and regression analyses to predict perceived hazardousness. The correlation between hazardousness and the severity of the first scenario generated is large and significant ($r = .90, p < .0001$). The pattern of the correlations between hazardousness and the severity ratings of the second and third scenario is similar but smaller ($r = .82, p < .0001$, and $r = .72, p < .0001$, respectively). For the first and second scenario the correlations between hazardousness and probability of injury were not significant (p's $> .05$). However, the injury probability of the third scenario and hazardousness yields a positive correlation ($r = .67, p < .003$).

Table 1. Products used in Study 2.

aerosol insecticide/pesticide	gas powered lawnmower
aluminum extension ladder	liquid lacquer stripper
antacid	metal detector
apple sauce	outdoor gas grill
bathtub/shower	semi-automatic rifle
capsule diet aid	shampoo
chainsaw	steam iron
drip coffee maker	three-speed bicycle
electric hedge trimmer	toaster oven

Using predictions of hazardousness made from the severity rating of the first scenario as a base, several models of hazardousness prediction were examined in an effort to increase the proportion of variance accounted for. Neither the addition of the probability rating of the first scenario nor the further addition of a crossproduct term to the equation significantly enhanced predictability. Moreover, the severity and probability ratings of the second and third scenario failed to significantly increase the proportion of variance accounted for beyond that accounted for by the first scenario severity rating.

The second set of analyses used subject means (averaged across products) as the random variable. Simple correlations of hazardousness and the scenario ratings shows a reliable relationship between hazardousness and the severity ratings of the three scenarios (r = .34, p < .004; r = .42, p < .0004; r = .34, p < .006) and the probability of injury of the second scenario (r = .27, p < .03). The correlations of the other probability ratings were not significant (p 's > .05).

Using the subject means data, several models of hazardousness prediction were examined to see whether or not additional variance, beyond that predicted by the severity rating of the first scenario, might be accounted for. The addition of the first scenario's probability of injury rating significantly increases the prediction of hazardousness (from r^2 = .12 to R^2 = .17). Also, the addition of the second scenario severity rating to the first scenario severity rating significantly increments hazard prediction (to R^2 = .18). Moreover, a model including the linear addition of severity and probability ratings of the first two scenarios significantly increases hazard prediction beyond that provided by the severity rating of the first scenario alone (to R^2 = .24). No other regression model significantly enhanced prediction (including analyses with crossproduct terms).

The third data set used the non-averaged raw data, i.e., all subjects and products. Simple correlations between hazardousness and the scenario ratings shows reliable relationships between hazardousness and the severity ratings of the three scenarios generated by each subject (r = .50, p < .0001; r = .38, p < .0001; r = .33, p < .0001). The relationships of hazardousness to the probability of injury ratings for the three scenarios are also significant but these relationships are very small (r = .06, p < .04; r = .08, p < .02; r = .14, p < .001).

As in the earlier analyses, several hazardousness prediction models were examined with regard to the addition of significant variance beyond that attributable to the severity rating of the first scenario. The addition of the first scenario's probability of injury rating produces a small, but significant, increase in hazard prediction (from r^2 = .255 to R^2 = .28). Also, a model which includes the severity ratings of the first two scenarios and a model with all three severity ratings both significantly increments hazard variance accounted for beyond that accounted for by the first scenario's severity rating alone (to R^2 = .27, and to R^2 = .30, respectively). The further addition of the probability ratings (as well as more complex terms) to these latter two models containing the first two or three scenario severity ratings did not further enhance hazard prediction.

Another purpose of the present study was to examine the relationship between hazardousness and the degree of precaution subjects would reportedly take when using various products. Using the product means data (averaged across subjects), the correlation is extremely high, r = .98, p < .0001. A highly positive relationship is also seen using the subject means data (averaged across products), r = .74, p < .001 and using the non-averaged data, r = .79, p < .001. Obviously with the large amount of variance in common, it would be expected that both variables (hazardousness and degree of precaution) would have similar predictive models. Regression analyses using the product means data with the severity and probability ratings as

predictors of precaution provided a set of virtually identical results to those already reported for the prediction of hazardousness. The pattern was also similar using the other two sets of data.

Interest was also directed to the issue of whether the severity and probability of the generated accident scenarios differ as a function of hazardousness. Hazardousness ratings in each data set were split at the median and recoded to form two groups of high or low hazardousness. A mixed-model ANOVA with a between factor of high vs. low hazardousness and a within factor of the three scenarios was used on the severity and probability ratings for the three sets of data. The probability of injury analysis is discussed first. The probability means are presented in Table 2. The 2 X 3 ANOVA using the product means (averaged across subjects) yields an effect of scenario order, F (2, 32) = 13.13, p < .0001. The means on the bottom row of Table 2 show that the earlier generated scenarios are rated as more likely to produce injury than the accident scenarios generated later (Fisher's L.S.D. = .19). However, a significant interaction was also noted, F (2, 32) = 4.12, p < .03. For low hazard, the probability of injury for the sequentially generated accident scenarios decreases from the first to the second to the third scenario (Fisher's L.S.D. = .26). For high hazard, there are no significant differences among the scenarios. A similar pattern of results was found using the non-averaged data. The subject means data failed to show significant effects.

The scenario severity data were examined in the same manner as the probability data. Hazard scores in each data set were split at the median to form two groups of high and low hazardousness. A mixed-model ANOVA with a between factor of high vs. low hazardousness and a within factor of the three scenarios was used on the three sets of data. The expected effect of hazard level on severity was shown using the subject means data (averaged across products), F (1, 65) = 7.50, p < .008. Analysis of the other two sets of data produced this same effect as well other interesting results. The product severity means as a function of hazard level and scenarios are shown in Table 4. The ANOVA using the product means (averaged across subjects) yielded a main effect of scenario order, F (2, 32) = 5.90, p < .007. Examination of the bottom row of Table 4 shows a small, but significant, increase in the severity for the third scenario compared to the first and second (Fisher's L.S.D. = .14). However, the ANOVA also revealed a significant interaction, F (2, 32) = 34.82, p < .0001. For high hazard, the first scenario is more severe than the other two scenarios (Fisher's L.S.D. = .20). For low hazard, a different pattern is shown: one of increasing severity from the first to the third scenario. With low hazard, the first scenario is significantly less severe than the second scenario, and the second is significantly less severe than the third. A similar interaction pattern was shown for the non-averaged data, F (2, 1142) = 8.82, p < .0002, though there is no significant main effect of scenario order (F < 1.0).

Table 2. Mean *probability* of injury as a function of high vs. low hazard level and scenario order.

	Scenario 1	Scenario 2	Scenario 3
High Hazard	3.53	3.38	3.33
Low Hazard	3.68	3.30	2.95
mean	3.605	3.34	3.14

Table 3. Mean *severity* of injury as a function of high vs. low hazard level and scenario order.

	Scenario 1	Scenario 2	Scenario 3
High Hazard	4.70	4.345	4.35
Low Hazard	2.99	3.41	3.79
mean	3.845	3.88	4.07

Discussion

The results of Study 2 show that severity of injury is the primary determinant of the perception of hazardousness for common consumer products. The analyses using product means (averaged across subjects), subject means (averaged across products), and the non-averaged raw data show that in general probability of injury does not play a major role in the perception of hazardousness. Although some of the regression models showed significant increments in prediction beyond that predicted by severity, the increments are very small.

The results also show that perceived hazardousness is highly correlated with the degree of precaution reported by subjects when using the products. Precaution is a broad description of behavior representative of a number of specific behaviors designed to prevent injury when using a product. In addition to many precautionary behaviors that seem to be product specific, another type of precautionary behavior is the reading of warnings. The finding that hazardousness and precaution are highly related provides support for Wogalter et al.'s (1986) finding of greater reported willingness to read warnings on products that are perceived to be more hazardous.

The results also provide information related to the characteristics of accident scenarios generated by subjects. Accident scenarios that subjects generate first are the most probable, particularly for low hazard products. This result is in accord with the predictions of the availability heuristic (Tversky & Kahneman, 1973; Kahneman & Tversky, 1982). This heuristic posits that, when events are more easily recalled, they are judged to be more frequent. Whether the particular accidents recalled first are indeed more frequent can not be answered here. Other evidence (Slovic et al., 1979; Brems, 1986) indicates that subjects tend to overestimate infrequent accidents and underestimate frequent accidents.

The results also indicate that, for high hazard products, the first scenario is more severe than the other two scenarios. This result may also be explained by the availability heuristic (i.e., severe accidents are given greater media attention and are more vivid). For products of low hazard, the earlier scenarios were less severe than the latter scenarios. This result also seems reasonable, since the most probable accidents involving low hazard consumer products tend to be less severe.

GENERAL DISCUSSION

The combined results of Studies 1 and 2 indicate that severity of injury is the primary determinant of perceptions of product hazardousness. In most of the analyses, likelihood or probability contributed little or no additional unique variance to the prediction of hazardousness beyond that accounted for by severity. Likelihood of potential injuries may serve a more indirect role in the perceptions of

hazards; probability appears to influence the order in which injury scenarios are generated.

The results have implications for understanding the consumer's perception of product hazards and provide insights into information that might be useful in warning communications. The results indicate that product hazardousness and intent to use precautionary behavior is strongly related. This is fortunate and expected. However, the situation is problematic when a product is perceived to be less hazardous than it really is. For this product, less precautionary behavior might be used than is appropriate to prevent injury. One possible way to communicate the level hazardousness (i.e., the severity of injury) is through warnings. However, subjects in the Wogalter et al. (1986) study report that they would be less willing to read warnings on products they perceive to be less hazardous. This lack of willingness to read warnings on particular products might be countered by the conspicuous placement of salient warnings that attract and capture attention and which convey the seriousness of accidental injury. Recent research on warnings is beginning to illuminate the characteristics that comprise effective warnings which would aid in this regard (e.g., using appropriate signal words, pictorials, etc.).

REFERENCES

Brems, D. J. (1986). *Risk Perception for Common Consumer Products.* Unpublished Doctoral Dissertation, Rice University, Houston, Texas.

Godfrey, S. S., Allender, L., Laughery, K. R., & Smith, V. L. (1983). Warning messages: Will the consumer bother to look. *Proceedings of the Human Factors Society of the 27th Annual Meeting.* Santa Monica, CA: The Human Factors Society.

Godfrey, S. S., & Laughery, K. R. (1984). The biasing effects of product familiarity on consumers' awareness of hazard. *Proceedings of the Human Factors Society of the 28th Annual Meeting.* Santa Monica, CA: The Human Factors Society.

Kahneman, D., & Tversky, A. (1982). On the study of statistical intuitions. In D. Kahneman, P. Slovic, & A. Tversky (Eds.), *Judgements under uncertainty: Heuristics and biases* (pp. 493-508). Cambridge: Cambridge University Press.

Slovic, P., Fischhoff, B., & Lichtenstein, S. (1979). Rating the risks. *Environment, 21*, 14-39.

Slovic, P., Fischhoff, B., & Lichtenstein, S. (1980a). Facts and fears: Understanding perceived risk (pp. 181-216). In Schwing, R. C., & Albers, W. A. Jr. (Eds.), *Societal Risk Assessment.* New York: Plenum Press.

Slovic, P., Fischhoff, B., & Lichtenstein, S. (1980b). Informing people about risk. (pp. 165-180) In L. A. Morris, M. B. Mazis, & I. Barofsky (Eds.), *Product Labeling and Health Risks, Banbury Report 6.* Cold Spring Harbor, NY: Cold Spring Harbor Laboratory.

Tversky, A., & Kahneman, D. (1973). Availability: A heuristic for judging frequency and probability. *Cognitive Psychology, 5*, 207-232.

Wogalter, M. S., Desaulniers, D. R., & Brelsford, J. W. (1986). Perceptions of consumer products: Hazardousness and warning expectations. *Proceedings of the Human Factors Society 30th Annual Meeting.* Santa Monica, CA: The Human Factors Society, 1197-1201.

PERCEPTIONS OF CONSUMER PRODUCTS: HAZARDOUSNESS AND WARNING EXPECTATIONS

Michael S. Wogalter, David R. Desaulniers, John W. Brelsford, Jr.

Department of Psychology, Rice University
Houston, TX 77251

ABSTRACT

This research examines several characteristics of consumer products that influence warning communication. Seventy-two generically-named products were rated according to perceived hazardousness, familiarity, and several other measures: 1) willingness to read warnings, 2) need for warnings, 3) location of warnings, and 4) appearance of products with warnings. The results indicate that reported willingness to read warnings is strongly and positively related to the perceived hazardousness of the product. Though product familiarity is significantly related to willingness to read warnings, it provides little predictive value beyond hazardousness. Additional analyses showed, the more hazardous the product: 1) the greater the need for warnings, 2) the closer to the product one expects to find a warning, and 3) the less warnings detract from the appearance of such products. Implications of these results are discussed with regard to applications for warning design.

INTRODUCTION

In recent years human factors specialists have become increasingly concerned with the efficacy of consumer product warnings. Despite efforts to present warnings on products, it is apparent that in many instances warning information fails to reach the consumer. Thus, it is of interest to explore factors which contribute to failures in the warning communication process.

Why would product warnings fail to reach the consumer? There are several possible reasons. First, the consumer may not see the warnings. For example, Wogalter, Fontenelle, & Laughery (1985) have shown that warnings located following a set of instructions may not be seen. A second possible reason is that consumers may not comprehend warnings. For example, warning communication may be compromised when the reading level required by a warning is too high for the target audience (e.g., Pyrczak & Roth, 1976; Morris, Meyers, and Thilman, 1980). A third reason warnings fail to be communicated is that the consumer does not read a warning even when it is visible and comprehensible. Why might a consumer not read a product warning? Two fairly intuitive reasons come to mind. Either the consumer perceives the product to be nonhazardous, or believes he or she is already familiar with the product. There is some evidence to support these ideas. For example, Godfrey, Allender, Laughery, and Smith (1983) found that perceptions of product hazardousness are positively related, while familiarity is negatively related, to likelihood of looking for a warning. If people look for warnings, they probably have intentions of reading them.

In related research, Wright, Creighton, and Threfall (1982) examined factors determining when instructions for consumer products would be read. They report that simplicity of operation is the major determinant of this variable. However, they also report the unexpected finding that familiarity and safety do not relate to claims of reading instructions. In a practical sense, it is difficult to distinguish between consumer product instructions and warnings. Indeed, warnings are a special type of instructions describing what to do for purposes of personal safety and product reliability.

It thus appears that there are discrepant conclusions in the warnings literature: Godfrey et al.(1983) found that familiarity and hazardousness relate to the tendency to look for warnings. However, Wright et al.(1982) found that familiarity and safety do not relate to claims about reading consumer product instructions. It should be noted that there are numerous methodological differences between these studies. Godfrey et al. asked subjects whether they would look for warnings, whereas, Wright et al. asked whether they would read instructions. These studies also differed in terms of the number of products used (8 in the former vs. 60 in the latter study). It is not clear what effects these differences had.

The present research examines whether the perceptions of hazardousness and familiarity relate to willingness to read warnings. In addition we were interested in exploring several other kinds of warning expectations. These include: 1) need to warn, 2) expected location of warnings, and 3) whether warnings detract from the appearance of products. Such perceptions and expectations will likely influence warning communication and thus have implications for warning design.

METHOD

Materials and Design. A large sample of consumer products was selected from several major department store catalogs (e.g., Montgomery Ward, J C Penny, Best Products). These were combined with additional samples of common food and over-the-counter pharmacy items. Inspection of this sample revealed that most of these products could be placed into one of three general categories: 1) Electrical, 2) Chemical, and 3) Non-electrical Tools. A subset of 72 products was selected from our large sample. Several selection criteria were used: 1) products must conform to one of the above three categories, 2) products must represent a wide range of hazardousness under each category, and 3) products must be representative of common household items. Only the generic names of products were used. Table 1 lists the 72 products according to the three product-type categories.

Products were rated along several dimensions. The specific questions and rating scales are described as follows: (1) If you saw a warning on this product would you read it? The response to this question was made on a 6-point scale labeled from 1 to 6 and anchored from the low end to the high end with definitely no, probably no, possibly no, possibly yes, probably yes, and definitely yes, respectively. (2) How hazardous is the product? (3) How familiar is the

Table 1. Products categorized by product type.

ELECTRICAL

battery alarm clock	microwave oven
curling iron	photoflash unit
desk lamp	pocket calculator
digital watch	quartz/space heater
drip coffee maker	sewing machine
electric blanket	sunlamp
electric carving knife	steam iron
electric food slicer	toaster/oven
electric hedge trimmer	transistor radio
flashlight	oscillating fan
metal detector	vacuum cleaner

CHEMICAL

antacid	kerosene
apple sauce	lacquer stripper
artificial sweetener	milk
aspirin	nonprescription diet aid
baby powder	oven cleaner
cake mix	roasted peanuts
cough medicine	roll-on deodorant
drain cleaner	shampoo
dried cereal	skin moisturizer
eggs	soap
household bleach	suntan lotion
insecticide/pesticide	whiskey

NON-ELECTRICAL TOOLS

binoculars	hunting knife
chain saw	inflatable boat
clothesline	ladder
dart game	life vest
football helmet	ping pong table
garden shears	rake
garden sprinkler	screwdriver
gas outdoor grill	scuba gear
gas powered lawn mower	semi-automatic rifle
golf club	three-speed bicycle
hammer	wheel barrow
hiking boot	wood splitter

product? Questions 2 and 3 were worded to fit a 7-point scale labeled from 1 to 7 and anchored respectively with semantic labels of quantity : not at all, a little, some, moderately, fairly, very, and extremely. (4) Do you think there should be a warning on this product? This question used the same response scale as the first question. (5) Where would you most expect to find a warnings on this product? Several alternative choices were provided: on the product, on the package, at the beginning of an instruction booklet, at the end of an instruction booklet, on a piece of paper separate from the instructions, and the last alternative was "I would not expect a warning on this product." These alternatives were assumed to reflect an underlying distance metric indicating expected proximity between product and warning. These alternatives were subsequently coded from 1 to 6 with lower numbers indicating a shorter warning to product distance. (6) Do you think a warning that is visible when the product is in use would make the product less attractive? Subjects responded on the same 6-point scale used for questions 1 and 4 ranging from definitely no to definitely yes.

All subjects rated the 72 products on all six questions. The product names were listed along the left column of two rating sheets. Four random orders of products were used in order to control for possible order effects. To the right of the product names were six columns of blank spaces where subjects recorded their ratings.

Procedure. Initially, the experimenter read instructions to subjects stating that they would be rating a variety of consumer products on several dimensions. Subjects were then given the set of two sheets containing the product listing. They were told to read over these sheets to familiarize themselves with the type and variety of products. Two minutes were provided for subjects to examine the list. They were then given two pages of questions dealing with the products. It was emphasized that they should read each question in turn, and rate *all* 72 products on Question 1 before proceeding to Question 2, and so on. Subjects were told they were to assume that the generically-named products would soon be introduced under a new brand name. In a subsequent phase, an independent group of subjects rated the same set of 72 products on the hazardousness question.

Subjects. One hundred twenty-five Rice University undergraduates participated in this study. Subjects were run in groups of 5 to 20. Subjects were given psychology course extra credit. At a later time, an additional set of 20 psychology graduate students participated voluntarily in a replication of the product hazardousness ratings.

RESULTS

Several analyses were carried out using these data. Individual subject ratings were combined into mean ratings for each of the 72 products, and intercorrelations for all six questions were computed and can be seen in Table 2. Scatter plots of these data indicated linearity.

We initially focused on factors related to willingness to read warnings. Subjects report that they are more likely to read warnings on products

Table 2. Pearson-product moment intercorrelations for product warning perceptions and expectations.

	Read	Hazard	Familiar	Warn	Location
Hazard	.892				
Familiar	-.640	-.632			
Warn	.943	.953	-.623		
Location	-.885	-.807	.486	-.917	
Appear	-.448	-.538	.354*	-.510	.501

*$p < .002$, all other p's $< .0001$

perceived to be more hazardous ($r = .89$). Subjects also report that they are more likely to read warnings on less familiar products ($r = -.64$). It is interesting to note that the more hazardous products tended to be the least familiar ($r = -.63$). Hazardousness and familiarity were statistically controlled using partial correlations. The partial correlation between willingness to read and hazardousness -- controlling for familiarity -- reduces this relationship from .89 to .82. This decreases the common variance by about 15%, however, the remaining correlation is still highly significant ($p < .0001$). The partial correlation between willingness to read and familiarity -- controlling for hazardousness -- reduces this relationship from -.64 to -.22. This decreases the common variance by about 36%, and the remaining correlation is only marginally significant ($p < .06$). Perceived hazardousness accounts for 80% of the variance of willingness to read. Thus, there is only marginal effects of familiarity, over and above the effect of hazardousness.

We were also interested in examining whether familiarity would moderate the relationship between willingness to read and perceived hazardousness. Using regression analysis to predict willingness to read warnings with hazardousness and familiarity as predictors yields an overall R^2 of .81 ($n = 72$, $p < .0001$). With hazardousness as the first predictor, familiarity and its interaction with hazardousness contribute unimportant increments in predictiveness--less than 1.0% in each case ($p = .07$ and $p > .30$, respectively).

The present results clearly show that perceived product hazardousness is the primary determinant of reported willingness to read warnings. It is thus of interest to examine perceptions of product hazardousness in more detail. Specifically, we would like to know how other kinds of warning expectations relate to this variable. One such expectation is whether or not the product needs a warning. The need for warnings is highly related to willingness to read warnings ($r = .94$). Of course, given our earlier results, it would be expected that product hazardousness should also relate to whether or not a product needs warnings, and indeed, this is the case ($r = .95$).

Another topic of interest is the expected location of warnings. Certainly one reason a warning may not be read is because of its location. It is likely that the probability of noticing (or finding) a warning increases as the distance between the product and its warning decreases. We addressed this point by deriving a distance metric where the ordering of a set of multiple choice responses reflected expectations concerning proximity of the product to its warning. People report that they are more likely to read a warning the closer it is to the product ($r = -.89$). Further, the results show that with greater hazardousness people expect warnings to be located closer to the product ($r = -.81$).

These results suggest that proximity of the warning to the product is important for highly hazardous products. However, one might be concerned that such warnings would detract from the appearance of the product. Subjects were asked, "Do you think a warning that is visible when the product is in use would make the product less attractive?" The results indicate that, as products are perceived to be more hazardous, warnings are considered to detract less from the products appearance ($r = -.51$). For products rated greater than moderately hazardous, subjects reported a mean rating of 2.6 (in the "no" region of the scale).

Finally, the reliability of the hazardousness ratings in this study was tested. Independant hazardousness ratings were obtained from a second group of subjects. Hazardousness ratings exhibited a high degree of test-retest reliability ($r = .95, n = 72, p < .0001$).

DISCUSSION

The present results show that the primary determinant of the likelihood that warnings will be read is the products' perceived level of hazard. Though product familiarity is significantly related to willingness to read warnings, it provides little predictive power beyond hazardousness.

As noted in the introduction, two previous studies addressing related issues yielded contradictory results. Godfrey et al. (1983) found both hazardousness and familiarity to be related to the likelihood of looking for warnings. However, Wright et al.(1982) failed to find relationships between familiarity or product safety and willingness to read instructions.

It is not entirely clear why Wright et al. failed to find relationships between reading instructions and familiarity or safety. As previously mentioned, it is difficult to distinguish between product instructions and product warnings. It is possible that Wright et al.'s subjects were responding to general start-up directions--that is, how to make the product operate--rather than considering other aspects of the instructions like safety warnings. This explanation has some support, given Wright et al.'s results. People in this study report that they are more likely to read instructions that pertain to complex products than to simple ones. This suggests that their subjects primarily responded to concerns of making the product operational, rather than to questions of safety. Why Wright et al. (1982) failed to find a relationship between familiarity and the tendency to read instructions is not particularly obvious. One possibility is that the products were biased toward high levels of familiarity.

The present results show that more hazardous products are less familiar than less hazardous ones. We would suggest that this finding reflects perceptions of products in the real world and is not an artifact of our sample.

Our results showed several other interesting relationships. People expect products of greater hazard to have a greater need for warnings. In addition, with greater hazardousness, people expect warnings to be located closer to a product. Moreover, the results indicate that, as products are perceived to be more hazardous, warnings detract less from the products' appearance.

These results have several implications for

warnings on consumer products. Manufacturers of hazardous products should locate warnings in close proximity to their products, because this is where people expect them to be. Failure to locate warnings properly may lead people to assume the product is less hazardous than it actually is, and thus could lead to incorrect handling of the product. In addition, the present results suggest that manufacturers of hazardous products should not be overly concerned about detracting from the appearance of their products when locating warnings so they are clearly seen.

Another implication of these results is that people may fail to read warnings because they missjudge the hazardousness of the product. This result highlights the need for signal words (i.e., danger, warning, and caution) to indicate the degree of hazard. Additionally, the results of this study extend the findings of Wogalter, Desaulniers, & Godfrey (1985) that warnings involving more hazardous situations are perceived to be more effective than warnings for less hazardous situations. The present results suggests a reason--people are more likely to read warnings in hazardous situations and thus such warnings are more effective.

The present research deals with reported perceptions and expectations, rather than actual behavior. This research is an early step in the direction of determining factors that influence the reading of product warnings. Certainly, a more conclusive step should involve behavioral measures of reading warnings. For example, one question that should be examined in the laboratory or in the the field is: for what kinds of products will warnings not be read? Our results suggest that hazardousness is a critical variable related to the reading of warnings.

REFERENCES

Godfrey, S. S., Allender, L., Laughery, K. R., & Smith, V. L. (1983). Warning messages: Wil the consumer bother to look? In A. T. Pope and L. D. Haugh (Eds.), *Proceedings of the Human Factors Society 27th Annual Meeting* (pp. 950-954). Santa Monica, CA: The Human Factors Society.

Pryczak, F., & Roth, D. H. (1976). The readability of directions on non-prescription drugs. *Journal of the American Pharmaceutical Association, 16,* 242-267.

Morris, L. A., Meyers, A.. & Thillman, D. G. (1980). Application of the readability concept to patient-oriented drug information. *American Journal of Hospital Pharmacy, 37,* 1504-1509.

Wogalter, M. S., Desaulniers, D. R., & Godfrey, S. S. (1985). Perceived effectiveness of environmental warnings. In Swezey, R. W., Strother, L. B., Post, T. J., & Knowles, M. G. (Eds.). *Proceedings of the 29th Annual Human Factors Society Meeting* (pp. 664-668). Santa Monica: The Human Factors Society.

Wogalter, M. S., Fontenelle, G. A., & Laughery, K. R. (1985). Behavioral effectiveness of warnings. In Swezey, R. W., Strother, L. B., Post, T. J., & Knowles, M. G. (Eds.). *Proceedings of the 29th Annual Human Factors Society Meeting* (pp. 679-683). Santa Monica: The Human Factors Society.

Wright, P. Creighton, P., & Threlfall, S. M. (1982). Some factors determining when instructions will be read. *Ergonomics, 25,* 225-227.

PERCEIVED EFFECTIVENESS OF ENVIRONMENTAL WARNINGS

Michael S. Wogalter, David R. Desaulniers, Sandra S. Godfrey

Department of Psychology, Rice University, Houston, TX 77001

ABSTRACT

This study examined perceived effectiveness of warning signs for various hazard situations. Four-statement signs contained a signal word, a hazard statement, a consequence statement, and an instruction statement. Four additional three-statement signs, each with a different statement systematically removed from the four-statement sign, were used, for a total of 5 signs for each hazard situation. The results of Experiments 1 and 2 indicated that removing content statements reduced perceived effectiveness. Hazard and instruction statements were the most important statements, showing the greatest decrease in effectiveness when deleted. Signs for the most hazardous situations were perceived as the most effective warnings. Experiment 3 examined redundancy of statements in a sign. The results suggested that the deletion of redundant statements, particularly signal words, had less influence on effectiveness. The hazard statement showed the lowest redundancy consistant with it producing the greatest effectiveness decrement when deleted.

INTRODUCTION

As our society becomes more technologically advanced we must deal with increasingly more complex systems. Used appropriately these systems are capable of dramatically improving the quality of our lives. However, misuse of these systems has the potential to produce bodily injury or death.

The first line of defense against injury from hazardous situations is to "design out" the hazard and the second is to provide the necessary safety barriers. However, technology and/or costs may preclude designing out hazards, and adequate barriers are not always possible. Furthermore, proliferation in the variety and complexity of new technological systems decreases the likelihood that users will recognize the potential hazards. Even if users recognize that a hazard exists, they may misjudge the probablity of sustaining injury (Slovic, Fischhoff, and Lichtenstein, 1979) or the severity of the consequences. Hence the user must be directly informed of the exact nature and magnitude of the hazard, its potential consequences, and the appropriate and prohibited behavior in the hazard area. Warnings, although considered a last line of defense in the effort to protect the user from potential hazards, have become increasingly important. In recent years, personal injury and product liability litigation has presented issues relevant to the Human Factors professional. One issue of increasing concern has been the effectiveness of warnings.

It is important to note regarding effectiveness is that "the ultimate criterion is whether the warning has actually modified human behavior" (Peters, 1984). In essence behavioral effectiveness asks, has there been a reduction of undesirable and unsafe acts that would otherwise have occurred without the warning? A serious obstacle to conducting behavioral investigations is the absence of an appropriate methodology. One difficulty is the construction of a realistic and believable scenario. Obtaining behavioral measures through observation is also difficult due to the relatively low frequency of critical incidents. Controlled experimentation on effectiveness generates the problem of maintaining ecological validity without presenting the subject with a truly hazardous situation. Also there are problems of ethics in conducting studies concerning hazardous situations. Thus, although the ultimate criterion in measuring warning effectiveness is appropriate safety behavior, such research is very difficult to do in many situations.

In recent years, there has been increased use of rating measures to assess warnings. Subjective suitability should be considered in the choice of warnings (Smith & Weir, 1978). Rating studies have opened up the evaulation of warnings at costs considerably less than the construction of behavioral effectiveness studies. For example, Collins, Lerner, and Pierman (1982) examined understandability and preference of safety symbols for various referent situations. Understandability was assessed with respect to correct identification of meaning and confusions. Preference was assessed for potential symbols of referent hazards. This report contains a variety of useable pictorial warnings. Of particular interest in the present context is the finding that preferences generally corresponded to understandability.

The present experiments involved the ratings of effectiveness of verbal environmental warning signs. This contrasts with recent research on warnings that examine pictorial/symbolic modes of communicating warnings. Potentionally, these symbols can provide safety messages to foreign speakers, illiterates, and children. However, symbols may not adequately indicate the details of a safety message; for example, a symbol indicating a respiratory protection device might also need to indicate specific kind to be used. Word signs may thus be a necessary part of complex warning messages. In the present research, no abstract pictorial messages were used. We assumed adequate comprehension since the verbal messages were written in their simplest terms. Beliefs about sign effectiveness, rather than understandablility, were of prime interest.

The present research has been directed toward the identification of the features of the warning message which influence the perception of warning effectiveness. There are numerous publications which provide guidelines for the development of warning signs. Two of these are the *Product Safety Sign and Label System* (FMC, 1980) and the *Westinghouse Product Safety Label Handbook* (Westinghouse, 1981). There are published guidelines for the development of psychologically effective warnings (e.g. Cunitz, 1981; Peters, 1984). Although these publications differ in a number of details, they agree for the most part on the fundamental elements necessary for an effective warning. The most frequently noted characteristics are that warnings should attract attention, provide information about the level of the hazard, provide a direct statement of the hazard, motivate behavior by stating the consequences, tell people how to avoid being hurt, and provide this information in a clear and concise fashion.

These basic guidelines served as a basis for developing warnings in this research effort. Our warnings concerned environmental hazards as opposed to product warnings. Each warning consisted of four statements: a signal word appropriate to the referent hazard, a statement of the hazard, a statement of the consequences, and an instruction ast to appropriate behavior within the hazard area. The following signs are examples.

Signal word:	DANGER	WARNING
Hazard:	HIGH VOLTAGE WIRES	WATER CONTAMINATED
Consequence:	CAN KILL	ILLNESS MAY RESULT
Instruction:	STAY AWAY	DO NOT DRINK

Three experiments involved the manipulation of amount and type of information available in the warning sign. The complete four-statement signs were systematically compared to signs with some of the content removed. This was accomplished by 4 three-statement variations of each sign. Each of the 4 was the original sign without one of the component statements.

As the focus concerns those aspects of warnings that influence <u>perception</u> of effectiveness, this research does not involve direct behavioral measures of warning effectiveness. In Experiments 1 and 2, subjects rated a series of systematically manipulated warnings on effectiveness. Specifically, they were asked to imagine warnings placed in appropriate environments and to give a ratings indicating whether people would obey the signs. Experiment 3 examined redundancy of statements in warnings.

EXPERIMENT 1

Method

<u>Materials and Design</u>. Seventeen warning signs depicting various hazard situations were used. There were five variations of each sign. One variation was a complete sign consisting of the following four statements: a signal word, a hazard statement, a consequence statement, and an instruction statement.. The other four variations each had one statement missing. The four "incomplete signs" were constructed by systematically removing each statement contained in the four-statement signs.

Subjects rated the warnings an eight-point Likert-type scale indicating that a rating of zero should mean that the warning would have no effect on people seeing the sign and a rating of seven should indicate that the presence of the warning would ensure that most people would obey. This warning effectiveness rating was the dependent measure. Each subject rated all 85 signs. Warnings were made using the Apple Macintosh 24-pt. Monoco bold font, and they were presented subjects on an overhead projector. The content of the sign (five levels: one four-statement and four three-statement variations) was one independent variable; the hazard situation addressed by the seventeen different signs was the second independent variable.

<u>Subjects and Procedure</u>. One hundred-seven University of Houston undergraduate students participated for extra credit in psychology courses. Subjects were run in groups in four sessions. A different random order of signs was presented in each session. Stimuli were presented at the rate of one every 10 seconds. Subjects were specifically told not to make their ratings according to the level of hazard involved. Rather, it was emphasized that they should make their ratings on the basis of sign effectiveness given the signs were placed in appropriate locations. Prior to the experimental trials, subjects examined five sample signs.

Results

The mean effectiveness scores reported in Table 1 indicate that removal of any of the statements from the signs reliably reduces perceived effectiveness. Removal of either the hazard statement or the instruction statement results in the greatest drop in effectiveness. This result is not surprising given the fact that these two statements provide specific information about the hazard and how to avoid it. A somewhat smaller drop in perceived effectiveness occurs with the removal of the consequence statement or the signal word.

TABLE 1
Perceived Effectiveness as a Function of Warning Signs and their Content (Exp. 1).

	CONTENT			
<u>ALL</u>	MINUS <u>SIGNAL</u>	MINUS <u>HAZARD</u>	MINUS <u>CONSEQ</u>	MINUS <u>INSTRU</u>
5.04	4.77	4.47	4.72	4.50

A two-way repeated measures analysis of variance shows the effect of the content variable (removal of statements) to be significant, $F(4,424)= 20.03$, $p < .001$. This effect is also significant using individual signs as the random variable (collapsing across subjects), $F(4,64)=$

11.83, $p < .001$. Comparisons of the three-statement content means against the four-statement mean (collapsing across subjects and signs) shows that removal of any of the statements leads to a significant decrease in perceived effectiveness (all p's $< .01$). There is a significant main effect of the different hazard situations (signs), $F(16,1696)=82.15$, $p < .001$. This is not surprising given the number of referent hazard situations used; further discussion of this effect is deferred until Experiment 2.

Although the means for the four-statement signs are, in general, rated higher than all of the three-statement versions, the significant sign by content interaction, $F(64, 6784)= 5.93$, $p < .001$, indicates that the content effect may not hold in all cases. For a few signs, deleting a statement results in an increased rating of perceived effectiveness. With the large number of cell means involved in this experiment, correction for experiment-wise error rate is essential. Comparisons adjusting for alpha using Bonferoni's multiple-comparison test (minimum signficant difference = .52) shows that in no instance are any of the three-statement signs perceived significantly more effective than their corresponding four-statement signs. Of the 68 three-statement signs, 23 were rated significantly lower in effectiveness than the respective four-statement versions (9 lacking the instruction statement, 8 lacking the hazard statement, 5 lacking the consequence statement, and 1 lacking the signal word). There are 45 three-statement signs that did not differ reliably from the four-statement version.

EXPERIMENT 2

This experiment was a replication of Experiment 1 with a larger sample of stimulus signs. Different experimental instructions and rating scale were used to specify in operational terms a definition of warning effectiveness.

Method

Materials and Design. Subjects were told to rate "what percentage of people would be likely to obey the sign" rather than "how effective you think the sign would be." The ratings utilized an 11-point scale with the labels 0% to 100%. Below each point were the numbers 0 to 10 which corresponded directly with the percentages (e.g., 3 corresponded to 30%). Prior to this experiment, twelve "expert" judges (psychology faculty and graduate students) ranked 48 (17 from Experiment 1 and 31 "new") four-statement signs according to level of hazard. Twenty-five signs that had low variablility and were distributed across a wide range of hazards were used in this experiment. As in the previous experiment, there were five variations of each sign: one four-statement warning sign and four three-statement signs.

Subjects and Procedure. Eighty-one subjects from University of Houston and Rice University psychology courses were told to assume that each warning sign was placed in an appropriate location. They were told to make ratings based on the percentage of people, who after seeing the warning sign, would obey it. Subjects were told, for

example, that if 100 people see a particular sign but only 20 obey it, then this sign should receive a rating of 2 for 20%. If on the other hand, they thought that 70 people out of 100 would obey a particular sign, then it should be given a rating of seven for 70%. Each subject rated 125 warnings.

Results

The results are shown in Table 2. In general, the removal of any statement from the signs reduces perceived effectiveness. These means show basically the same pattern as Experiment 1. Removal of either the hazard statement or the instruction statement leads to the greatest drop in effectiveness. A somewhat smaller drop occurs with the removal of the consequence statement or the signal word.

TABLE 2
Perceived Effectiveness as a Function of Warning Signs and their Content (Exp. 2 using an 11-point scale).

		CONTENT		
ALL	MINUS SIGNAL	MINUS HAZARD	MINUS CONSEQ	MINUS INSTRU
7.28	7.12	6.65	6.83	6.54

A two-way repeated measures ANOVA shows the effect of the content variable was significant, $F(4, 320)= 23.72$, $p < .001$. This effect is also significant using individual signs as the random variable (collapsing across subjects), $F(4,96)= 8.34$, $p < .001$. Comparisons of the three-statement means against the four-statement mean shows that the individual removal of any of the statements leads to a significant decrease in perceived effectness (all p's $<.001$). A significant sign content interaction, $F(96, 7680)=9.95$, $p < .001$) indicates that the general content effect does not hold in all cases. Comparisons adjusting for alpha using Bonferoni's multiple-comparison test (minimum signficant difference = .79) showed that there was only one three-statement sign significantly more effective than its corresponding four-statement version. Of the 100 three-statement signs, 30 were rated significantly lower in effectiveness than the respective four-statement versions (11 lacking the instructions statement, 9 lacking the hazard statement, 8 lacking the consequence statement, and 2 lacking the signal word).

Various hazard situations show different levels of perceived effectiveness, $F(24, 1920)=52.31$, $p < .001$. This effect is difficult to interpret partly because it interacts with the content variable. However, examination of the four-statement signs revealed that those dealing with high-level hazards such as severe electric shock were rated as more effective than warnings of mild hazards such as wet slippery floor. In order to explore this relationship further, signs were rank ordered by "expert" judges as to the degree of hazard and these rankings were then paired with the mean perceived effectiveness ratings for the four-statement signs from both Experiments 1 and 2. Correlations between the two measures were significant, *r* = .80, *p* < .001 and *r* = .62, *p* < .001 respectively. These results strongly indicate that the greater the hazard depicted by the sign, the greater the perceived effectiveness of the sign. Perhaps people look for warnings around greater hazards, and perhaps the greater the hazard level the more motivation to comply.

Those instances where three-statement signs were rated equal to (or in a very few cases, somewhat greater than) the corresponding four-statement signs appeared to be due to the removal of obvious, implied, and redundant information. In some cases, the four-statement sign sounds somewhat silly because the information is so obvious. For this reason, some of the four-statement signs might be perceived somewhat effectiveness.

EXPERIMENT 3

The question asked here is whether the change in perceived effectiveness reported in Experiments 1 & 2 can be attributed to redundancy of the "deleted" statement in comparing three-statement to four-statement signs. It is predicted that the more unique or nonredundant the information provided by a statement, the greater the effect of that statement's removal will be.

Method

Materials and Design. The stimuli for this experiment were taken from the signs used in Experiment 1. The earlier set of signs was used because this experiment was started prior to Experiment 2. Specifically, sixty-eight three-statement signs (all four versions of each sign) were paired with the statements that were deleted from the original four-statement versions. Three-statement signs were presented simultaneously with related "deleted" statements. Subjects rated the degree to which the information in the single statement was already included in the information given in the three-statement sign, providing a measure of the degree to which subjects perceived the "missing" statement to be redundant. The term "redundancy" was not used in the instructions.

An 8-point Likert-type scale (with endpoints of zero and seven) was used to rate each sign/statement. Below each point on the scale were anchors describing degrees of amount (Bass, Cascio, and O'Conner, 1974). Each point of the scale was numbered and defined so that at the extremes zero represented NONE and seven represented ALL.

Subjects and Procedure. Sixty-six undergraduates from introductory psychology classes at the University of Houston, participated for extra credit. Seven sessions were run with each session using a different sign order. Subjects were told that they would be viewing several variations of a warning sign and that they should read each sign and the accompanying statement carefully and not confuse similar variations of signs. They were instructed to make their ratings on the basis of their world knowledge as well as the information being presented to them at that moment. Stimuli were presented at rate of one every 10 seconds. Three practice trials were given to acquaint subjects with the stimuli.

Results

Mean ratings of redundancy for each elemental statement with respect to the remaining three-statement warnings are shown along the first row in Table 3. These scores were obtained by collapsing across hazard situations to obtain the mean redundancy for content. Reordering the redundancy means shows the following descending order: signal word, consequence statement, instruction statement, and hazard statement. The signal word is the most redundant statement (relative to the other three statements of a sign), and the hazard statement is the least redundant. A within-subjects analysis of variance showed a significant main effect of redundancy for content type, $F(3,195)= 94.91$, $p < .005$). Tukey's Honestly Significant Difference test showed mean redundancy for the hazard statement was significantly lower than all other statement types (HSD=.37).

TABLE 3
Perceived redundancy of statement (in bold print from Exp. 3) and effectiveness differences without statement (in reg. print from Exp.1) as a function of content.

	CONTENT			
	Signal	Hazard	Conseq	Instruc
Redundancy	**5.85**	**3.70**	**5.56**	**5.46**
Exp 1 differences	-0.26	-0.57	-0.33	-0.53

Using the perceived effectivenesss data from Experiment 1, a measure of the change in perceived effectiveness due to the deletion of a statement was obtained by subtracting effectiveness ratings of the four-statement signs from the effectiveness rating of each of its four related three-statement signs. These effectiveness decrement scores (collapsing across hazard situations) are shown in the bottom row of Table 3. The pattern of mean redundancy ratings is the same but in the opposite order of the perceived effectiveness decrements. The deletion of more redundant information is associated with smaller decrements in perceived effectiveness. In other words, the greater the relative amount of information in a statement, the greater the negative effect of deleting that statement. The mean ratings for the hazard statement shows the lowest redundancy consistant with it producing a large effectiveness decrement when deleted.

A correlation of the 68 redundancy ratings with the corresponding perceived effectiveness decrement scores (from Experiment 1) yields a small but significant relationship, $r = .332$, $p < .005$. This indicates that deleting more redundant statement produces smaller decrements in perceived effectiveness. Separate correlations were calculated for signs of each of the four content statements in order to examine relationships across types of content deletions. A significant correlation was found between signal word difference scores and the redundancy ratings of signal words, $r = .520$, $p < .05$. This result is somewhat surprising given the special nature of signal words. Signal words were expected to receive consistently high redundancy ratings because their purpose is to attract attention rather than to transmit specific information. Since signal words reflect the degree of hazard in warning situations, it was expected that restriction of range would reduce the likelihood of obtaining significant results. The correlation indicates that as redundancy of signal words increase, there is a smaller decrement in perceived effectiveness when the signal word is deleted. Correlations for the three other types of content were not significant.

DISCUSSION

The results of these experiments recommend that environmental warnings, in general, contain four types of content statements: signal word, hazard statement, consequence statement, and instruction statement. The hazard and instruction statements are the most important in environmental warnings; deletion of these statements leads to the greatest reduction of effectiveness. The consequence statement and signal word were judged somewhat less important, but only by degree; the removal of any one of the four contents produces a decrement in perceived effectiveness. Although the deletion of statements did not, in general, increase perceived effectiveness, there are many instances with no significant decrement for three-statement signs. Hence, one may be able to delete some information without a substantial loss of effectiveness; this could be useful when brevity is necessary. Examples include cases such as highway signs, where there is insufficient time to read a long message, or where there are constraints on available display space. The procedures used in the present research allowed plenty of time and close scrutiny of the warning. In the real world this frequently is not the case.

The results suggested that redundancy is related to effectiveness, but redundancy does not describe the whole story--it does not explain much effectiveness variance. A more specific examination of redundancy in future may yield positive factors related to the improvement of warnings under degraded conditions.

Ratings are only a first step in evaluating effectiveness of warning signs. Ultimately, if the conditions allow, the sign should be tested in real-world settings to obtain measures of behavioral compliance (e.g.

studying accident rates). New methodologies need to be developed to test behavioral effectiveness. We should not, however, wait and do nothing to improve warning signs. Warnings should be tested by the methodologies available. Armchair philosophizing and theorizing, even by "experts," may be inappropriate despite the economy of designing warnings in the office (Miller, 1978). We need to go beyond the general impressions and demand controlled testing of warning elements and formats.

References

Bass, B. M., Cascio, W. F., & O'Conner, E. J. (1974). Magnitude estimations of expressions of frequency & amount. *Journal of Applied Psychology, 59*, 313-320.

Collins, B. L., Lerner, N. D., & Pierman, B. C. (1982). Symbols for industrial safety. Technical Report NBSIR 82-2485.

Cunitz, R. J. (1981). Psychologically effective warnings. *Hazard Prevention, 17*, 5-7.

FMC (1980)., *Product Safety Signs and Label System*, FMC: Santa Clara, California, 3rd Ed.

Laner, S. & Sell, R. G. (1960). An experiment on the effect of specially designed safety posters. *Occupational Psychology, 34*, 153-169.

Miller, J. A. (1978). *Labeling-The state of the art*. Cambridge, Massachusetts: Marketing Science Institute.

Peters, G. A. (1984). A challenge to the safety profession. *Professional Safety, 29*, 46-50.

Slovic, P., Fishoff, B. & Lichtenstein, S. (1979). Rating the risks, *Environment, 21*, 14-39.

Smith, G. and Weir, R. (1978). Laboratory visibility studies of directional symbols used for traffic control signal. *Ergonomics, 21*, 247-252.

Westinghouse (1981). *Westinghouse Product safety label Handbook*. Trafford, PA: Westinghouse Printing Division.

BEHAVIORAL EFFECTIVENESS OF WARNINGS

Michael S. Wogalter, Gail A. Fontenelle, Kenneth R. Laughery

Department of Psychology, Rice University, Houston, Tx 77001

ABSTRACT

A paradigm was developed to examine the effectiveness of warnings in a laboratory task. A task was presented to subjects as one examining how people perform a basic chemistry demonstration. Experiment 1 examined the effects of two locations of the warning (before and after instructions) and two different signal word presentations (WARNING and Note). An additional condition with no warning or signal word served as a control. No effects were found on time or accuracy. However, compliance (use of mask and gloves) was affected by the inclusion of the warning as well as by its location. Greatest compliance occurred when the warning was placed prior to the instructions. Experiment 2 replicated the effect of location. The addition of a printed statement placed before the instructions (with warning at the end) to read through the instructions before beginning produced intermediate compliance that was not significantly different from the warning beginning and end conditions. Observation revealed that when the warning message was at the end of the instructions subjects complied only when they saw the warning message before starting the task. These results indicate that if warnings are placed in front of instructions the consumer is more likely to read and comply.

Introduction

An increasingly important issue to Human Factors specialists concerns the effectiveness of warning messages. Do warnings influence the behavior of the people to whom they are directed? Unfortuantely there is little empirical evidence to indicate the circumstances in which warnings are or are not effective in this regard. McCarthy, Finnegan, Krumm-Scott and McCarthy (1984) concluded from a review of the literature that warnings are not effective. While we would agree that there is little evidence to support the contention that warnings are effective, we disagree with the conclusion that the evidence shows they are not. No doubt there are situations where warnings have little or no effect; however, finding no effect of warnings in a particular situation does not permit the general conclusion that warnings are not effective. Indeed, whether or not warnings are effective is not the question. Rather, research in this area should focus on determining the factors that influence effectiveness.

It is widely agreed that if one is to address the issue of warning effectiveness the ultimate criterion is whether the warning has actually modified human behavior. There is only one published report known to the authors that presents evidence that behavior can be affected by a warning, in this case, safety posters in the workplace. Laner and Sell (1960) posted signs illustrating the hooking back of chain slings onto a crane hook as a safety precaution when they are not in use. Behavior of workers was measured before (as baseline) and after poster placement in 6 steelworks. A seventh steelworks acted as an additional control. They found that, in general, the

posters increased the positive behavior depicted in the signs. They also found that this precautionary behavior was maintained for at least several weeks following sign placement. Further, the increase in safe behavior was greatest in those shops with low ceilings where the unsafe practice constituted the greatest hazard. Laner and Sell (1960) concluded that safety posters may be more effective if the warning messsage is directly relevant to the situation.

There are difficulties in carrying out research on effectiveness of warnings. Studies that directly observe behavior in the context of warnings have problems of detecting infrequent events as well as controlling numerous variables. The latter problem makes it particularly difficult to draw inferences about causal relationships. Laboratory studies may permit adequate control over extraneous variables, but often have the problem of generalizing the results to real-world settings. Such studies, particularly in dealing with warnings, may lack situational credibility. Creating situations that are within the boundaries of ethical considerations, while at the same time are believed to be hazardous by experimental subjects, is difficult.

The research reported in this paper consisted of a laboratory study (two related experiments) in which a paradigm was developed to examine the effects of two variables on the effectiveness of warnings. A critical point is that the laboratory task was one in which the warnings had face validity to the participants. The task was presented to the subjects as one examining how people perform a basic chemistry demonstration. The low-level hazards associated with the demonstration task were believable and realistic. The task was constructed so that several aspects of behavior could be assessed as dependent measures. The two experiments focused on the influence of the signal word and the location of the warning on effectiveness.

EXPERIMENT 1

Method

Subjects and Design. Fifty-one students from Rice University participated for extra-credit in an introductory psychology course. One subject in the warning at the beginning condition withdrew from the experiment soon after receiving the demonstration instructions. An additional subject was substituted to make the cell sizes equal (n=10). The design of the first study investigated the effects of two locations of the warning statement (before and after instructions) and two different signal words (WARNING and Note). These two factors were crossed in a between-subjects design. An additional condition that was identical to the others but lacked the warning statements served as a control.

Materials and Apparatus. Much of the laboratory equipment (glassware, etc.) was borrowed from the Rice Chemistry and Chemical Engineering departments. The equipment included a 500 gram analog scale, two graduated cylinders (80 ml. and 250 ml.), one large beaker (300 ml.), three large lockable Mason-type canisters, one volumetric flask (250 ml.), one measuring teaspoon, a glass stirring stick, and measuring paper. There was an ample supply of paper towels, several pairs of plastic gloves, and molded-paper masks located on the laboratory work table. Other laboratory glassware was available to the subject on the table, even though their use was not explicitly specified by the instructions. These items included one flask (100 ml.), two beakers (50 ml.), and one measuring tablespoon. A Mettler analytical scale was used by the experimenters to measure pre- and post-weights of the substances in the containers.

The instructions called for the handling and mixing of several different substances. The instructions did not name the actual substances except to refer to them by the number or letter label attached to the containers. The actual substances used were: water, bleached white flour, corn oil, table sugar, and yellow corn flower. An attempt was made to disguise some of these substances: green food coloring was added to the water, and red coloring was added to the sugar. These substance were selected for two reasons. First, they would not be truly hazardous; no actual harm would come to the subjects in the experiment. Second, these substances had a somewhat varied consistency and coloring.

Task and Procedure. Subjects entered a small room containing a table with the laboratory equipment. Subjects were told they could use the materials to do the demonstration task. They were handed the instructions, told to read them and begin. All subjects were given the following set of written instructions:

Demonstration Instructions

Before you are two graduated cylinders, several beakers, canisters, volumetric flasks and a scale. With these materials you will be asked to measure and combine specified amounts of five substances. The chemical identity of the substances are not revealed in order to avoid any effects of prior knowledge. Instead, they are identified by numbers and letters on the labels. The method for measuring the five substances and the order in which they are to be combined is given below. This demonstration can be performed without any previous laboratory experience. However, these materials and substances are expensive. Please treat them with care.

The five substances before you are to be combined in the order specified below.
(1) Using the scale, place 100 grams of substance A on measuring paper and then add directly to the large composition beaker.
(2) Pour 150 ml. of liquid #1 from the flask into the large graduated cylinder. Then pour liquid into the composition beaker.
(3) Mix the composition thoroughly.
(4) Pour liquid #2 directly from the small graduated cylinder into the composition beaker.
(5) Measure 4 level teaspoonfuls of substance B. Add to the composition beaker.
(6) Carefully mix these substances to form an even solution.
(7) Finally, using measuring paper and the scale, add 20 grams of substance C to composition beaker. Mix to complete the composition.
Please call the experimenter when you have completed these instructions.

The warning contained in the warning and note instructions is shown below:

(1) Skin contact may result in discoloration or irritation.
(2) Inaccurate measurement or improper mixing order may result in (a) an unusable product, (b) a foul-smelling gas or (c) a noxious gas.
Avoid skin contact with all substances.
Perform accurate measurements.
Mix substances in proper order.
Wear rubber gloves and mask.

The warning and note conditions differed by the signal word as well as the way it was presented. The signal word was always placed immediately prior to the warning statements. The warning was on the first or second page depending if it was at the beginning or end. The presentation format for the two signal words are shown below (as well as the first line of the warning statements).

WARNING

(1) Skin contact may result in discoloration or irritation.

or

Note: (1) Skin contact may result in discoloration or irritation.

Before and after each session, the experimenter measured weights of the containers specified directly and indirectly by the instructions using a highly accurate analytical Mettler balance. Subtracting the post-weights from the pre-weights provided an accuracy measure for the subjects performance on the task. Pre- and post-weights were gathered for the composition beaker, the canisters, the volumetric flasks, and the large and small graduated cylinders. In addition, while subjects performed the task the experimenter recorded elapsed times for several events. These included: time to put on the mask, time to put on the gloves, time to pick up the first laboratory object, and time to complete the task.

The task took an average of ten minutes to complete. After subjects completed the task they were debriefed and questioned concerning their hypotheses and beliefs about the purpose of the experiment.

Results

Accuracy measurements were not influenced by warning location or signal word (all p's > .10). Similarly, none of the time measurements showed signficant effects (all p's > .10). The use of protective equipment (gloves and mask), however, was clearly influenced by the location and presence of the warning. Table 1 shows the percentage of subjects who complied with the warning to use protective equipment for the different conditions. A one-way between subjects ANOVA indicated a significant effect of conditions, $F(4,45)=4.45$, $p <$ .01. Planned comparisons showed that the location (beginning vs. end) effect was statistically significant as was presence (warning vs. no warning). A significantly higher percentage of subjects used the mask or gloves when the hazard statment was present as compared to the no warning control group, $t(45)= 3.49$, $p < .001$. In addition, placement of the hazard message before the task instructions led to significantly higher percentage of subjects using the protective equipment, $t(45)= 2.13$, $p < .05$. There was no effect of the signal word manipulation, $t(45) < 1.0$.

Observation of the subjects in those conditions

where the warning message was at the end of the instructions suggested that if they turned the page before starting the task and read the warning, they tended to comply with it. If they did not turn the page they did not comply. Notes were taken by the experimenters on 18 of the 20 subjects in the "end" conditions. These observations indicated 10 of 18 in the end conditions did not turn the page. Of these 10 subjects, 9 did not put on the mask and gloves, while the 7 of the 8 subjects who turned the page complied by using the protective equipment.

EXPERIMENT 2

Subjects in Experiment 1 who did not turn the page may have been unaware that the instructions continued onto a second page. Alternatively, subjects may have simply decided after reading the instructions not to read further but rather to begin carrying out the task immediately. The second study was an attempt to examine the possibility that subjects were not aware of the second page and thus did not have the opportunity to comply with the warning. This experiment was also an attempt to replicate the basic findings of Experiment 1. In Experiment 2, two subject groups received the warning after the instructions. One group received a statement printed on the top of the first instruction sheet which told subjects to read through the entire set of instructions before beginning. The other group did not receive this printed statement. Experiment 1 suggested that if subjects turned the page before beginning the task, they generally complied with the warning. It was proposed that the presence of the "read through" statement would increase the number of subjects who turned the page and attended to the warning, and thus would increase the number who complied. If the presence of the statement increases compliance and compliance depends on turning to the second page of the instructions, then this would indicate that failure to comply was primarily caused by a failure to see the warning.

Method

Subjects and Design. Forty-six subjects from Rice University participated for extra credit in a course. Two groups of subjects received the warning after the instructions but differed as to whether they received (n=15) or did not receive (n=16) written instructions to read through the entire set of instructions before starting the task. A third group received the warning before the instructions (n=15).

Apparatus and Materials. The apparatus and materials were identical to those used in the first experiment with a few exceptions. First, there were only three sets of demonstration and warnings instructions. The materials for the warning at the beginning and warning at the end conditions were identical to those used in Experiment 1. An additional condition had the same instructions and warning as the warning at the end condition except that it had on the top of the first page the statement:

Please read through the entire instructions before beginning.

Procedure. The procedures and instructions were identical to those used in Experiment 1 with a few exceptions. No pre- and post- weights of the materials were obtained, because none of the accuracy measures in the first experiment approached significance. Although none of the time measures in Experiment 1 were signficant, they were relatively easy to record, so they were again recorded in this experiment. In addition, the experimenters took note of whether or not subjects turned the page before starting the task. Experiment 2 drops the signal word manipulation and adds a condition, warning at the end with "read through" instructions.

Results

Table 2 shows the percentage of subjects who complied with warning instructions to put on the mask and gloves before beginning the task. A one-way between-subjects ANOVA indicated a significant effect of conditions, $F_{(2,43)}=3.42$, $p <.05$. Planned comparisons replicated the location effect found in Experiment 1. Subjects who received the warning at the beginning of the instructions were more likely to comply than subjects who received the warning at the end without read through instructions, $t_{(29)}= 2.70$, $p <.05$. Compliance for subjects who received the warning at the end with "read through" instructions was intermediate between the other two conditions, but did not differ significantly from either the warning at the beginning, $t_{(28)}= 1.29$, $p >.20$ or the warning at the end groups, $t_{(29)}=1.27$, $p >.20$.

In the condition with the warning message at the end (without the "read through" instructions), 8 of 16 subjects turned to the second page before beginning. Every subject who turned the page complied with one exception. This subject reported reading the warning but chose not to comply. The remaining subjects did not turn the page and did not comply. These results were similar to those found in Experiment 1 for the warning at the end condition. In the warning at the end condition with "read through" instructions, 3 of 15 subjects did not turn the page and did not comply. Of the other subjects who turned the page, 10 complied with the warning. The remaining 2 subjects who turned the page did not comply, reporting that they did not read the warning. In general, if subjects turned the page they put on the mask and gloves ($r = .82$, $n=31$).

The "read through" instructions produced an increase in the number of people who turned the page (80% as compared with 50%), however, this difference was only marginally significant, $t_{(29)}= 1.78$, $p <.08$. The "read through" statement also tended to increase compliance (66.7% compared to 43.8% without the statement), though again this difference was not significant. However, it is important to note that the "read through" condition was not statistically different in percentage of compliance from the warning at the beginning condition. This result suggests a lack of power due to small sample size, or a weak manipulation. Though the "read through" condition was not statistically conclusive, the trend in the data shows that more people turned the page and complied with the printed statement than without the statement.

In general, these results indicate that the failure to attend to the warning before beginning the task was responsible for the differences in compliance. Experiment 2 firmly replicated the location effects of Experiment 1. No effect was found for the time measures (all p's >.10).

Discussion

The results of these two studies are encouraging. They indicate it is possible to study warning effectiveness with a laboratory paradigm, and they provide a demonstration that there are circumstances in which a warning can be effective in influencing the behavior of people. Specifically, these experiments indicate that the location of the warning with respect to other instructions affect compliance with the warning. In short, warnings must be seen and read in order to be effective. One cannot simply assume that because a warning is on a label or included in a set of instructions it will be encountered. Factors such as its location on the label are crucial to its effectiveness. Warnings labels frequently follow instructions on many products or are located opposite the instructions on a side panel. They may even be "buried" inside owners' manuals. Even when consumers are specifically told to read all instructions before using a product, it is highly probable that a significant percentage will simply read the information necessary to perform the task and ignore any additional information which might warn against possible hazards or provide instructions as how to avoid these hazards.

If the warning is placed in front of instructions the consumer is more likely to read and comply. The effectivenesss of a warning seems to depend on the ability of the warning to attract the consumers attention before contact with a hazard. The consumer can not comply unless he reads the warning and is made aware of the hazards and the means by which to protect himself against them.

The question of general effectiveness can not be definitively answered until the conditions which increase or decrease warning message effectiveness are clearly delineated. One such condition appears to be the placement or location of the warning message.

The paradigm developed for this study or others like it can be useful for establishing conditions under which behavior may be influenced by warnings. Clearly there is a need to develop an empirical basis on which human factors specialists can base warning design decisions and evaluations.

REFERENCES

Laner, S. and Sell, R. G. (1960). An experiment on the effect of specially designed safety posters, *Occupational Psychology, 34*, 153-169.

McCarthy, R. L., Finnegan, J. P., Krumm-Scott, S., & McCarthy, G. E. (1984). Product information presentation, user behavior, and safety. In M. J. Alluisi, S. De Groot, & E. A. Alluisi (Eds.), *Proceedings of the Human Factors Society, 28th Annual Meeting*, San Antonio, Texas, 81-85.

Table 1

Percentage of behavioral compliance (use of mask and gloves) to warning message as a function of conditions (Experiment I).

Warning at Beginning	Note at Beginning	Warning at End	Note at End	Control (no warning)
90	70	50	50	10

Table 2

Percentage of behavioral compliance (use of mask and gloves) to warning message as a function of conditions (Experiment 2).

Warning at Beginning	Warnining at End with "read through" instructions	Warning at End
86.7	66.7	43.75

Effects of Warning Signal Words on Consumer-Product Hazard Perceptions

Michael S. Wogalter
Department of Psychology
North Carolina State University
Raleigh, NC 27695

Stephen W. Jarrard
Department of Behavioral Sciences
U. S. Military Academy
West Point, NY 10996

S. Noel Simpson
Department of Psychology
Rensselaer Polytechnic Institute
Troy, NY 12180

ABSTRACT

This experiment investigated the influence of warning signal words and a signal icon on perceptions of hazard for consumer products. Under the pretext of a marketing research study, 90 high school and college students rated product labels on variables such as product familiarity, frequency of use, and perceived hazard. Sixteen labels from actual household products were used and stored on a computer. Nine of the products labels were used to carry the nine signal word conditions. Five conditions presented the signal words NOTE, CAUTION, WARNING, DANGER, and LETHAL together with a brief warning message. In two other conditions a signal icon (exclamation point surrounded by a triangle) was presented together with the terms DANGER and LETHAL. The final two conditions were controls, one had a warning message but had no signal word, and the other had no warning message or signal word. Seven product labels were "fillers" that never contained a warning. Results showed that the presence of a signal word increased perceived hazard compared to its absence. Between extreme terms (e.g., NOTE and DANGER), significant differences were noted, but not between terms usually recommended in warning design guidelines. The presence of the signal icon had no significant effect on hazard perception. Implications of the results and the value of the research methodology for future warnings' investigations are discussed.

INTRODUCTION

Most standards and guidelines on warning design recommend the inclusion of signal words in labels and signs to alert people that a hazard is present, and to indicate the degree of danger involved (e.g., ANSI, 1988; FMC Corporation, 1985; Westinghouse Printing Division, 1981). The standards usually recommend the terms DANGER, WARNING, and CAUTION to connote the highest to lowest levels of hazard, respectively. In recent years, research has begun to examine the validity of these guidelines. Do people actually interpret differences between warning terms? The answer to this question is equivocal. Some research has found no significant differences between terms. Leonard, Matthews, and Karnes (1986) found no differences in ratings of risk for the signal words (i.e., CAUTION, WARNING, and DANGER). Wogalter, Godfrey, Fontenelle, Desaulniers, Rothstein, and Laughery (1987) found no difference between the terms WARNING and NOTE in a behavioral effectiveness study. However, other studies (Bresnahan and Bryk, 1975; Dunlap, Granda, and Kustas, 1986) have shown reliable differences of connoted urgency between terms such as DANGER and CAUTION.

In a recent study, Wogalter and Silver (1990) examined 84 potential signal words. They specifically examined the level of hazard communicated by the three most common signal words (DANGER, WARNING, and CAUTION) plus five other terms that had been evaluated in earlier research. The results showed that DEADLY, DANGER, WARNING, CAUTION, CAREFUL, ATTENTION, NOTICE, and NOTE) signified greatest to least strength, respectively. All differences were significant except between ATTENTION and CAREFUL and between WARNING and CAUTION. Silver and Wogalter (1991) found similar results using elementary school and junior high school students.

All of the above studies used procedures that had participants evaluate the terms in the absence of any relevant context (i.e., either alone or as part of a list). While these studies used internally valid methodologies, their testing procedures lack the realism and ecological validity of an appropriate context. When tested in isolation, signal words could show effects that do not transfer to situations when they are presented with other information such as accompanying a warning message and other product label information.

The current study presents signal words in the context of warnings on consumer product labels—a more realistic method to assess their influence than heretofore employed. Participants performed the experiment under the guise of a marketing research study in which they were asked to examine the labels of several products and answer a series of questions about each product. One question was of primary interest. This question requested a judgment of the level of hazard posed by the product. In part, the other questions were included to help disguise the purpose of the study.

The five signal words compared in the present study were LETHAL,[1] DANGER, WARNING, CAUTION, and NOTE. These particular terms were included because of their use in previous signal word research (e.g., Leonard et al., 1986; Wogalter and Silver, 1990), or their inclusion in safety guidelines (ANSI, 1988; FMC Corporation, 1985; Westinghouse, 1985).

Several warnings' standards and guidelines also recommend that a signal icon (exclamation point surrounded by a triangle) be included with the signal word to help gain attention and communicate the existence of a hazard.

---

[1] The term LETHAL was used instead of DEADLY because pilot research suggested that the term DEADLY would not realistically appear on some of the less hazardous consumer products that we employed. Wogalter and Silver (1990; Silver and Wogalter, 1991) found LETHAL to connote significantly lower hazard than DEADLY, but significantly higher hazard than DANGER.

However, the influence of the signal icon has not been studied, except for recent research by Young (1991). Young (1991) found lower search times to find a warning on a simulated alcohol beverage warning when it included the signal icon. However, the influence of the signal icon on perceived hazard has not yet been investigated. It is possible that the signal icon will serve to attract attention to the signal word and warning, and as a consequence, increase perceptions of hazard. In the present study, this symbol was paired with two signal words, DANGER and LETHAL, and its influence was examined by comparing them to the words without the signal icon.

Lastly, two other conditions served as controls to establish the base line hazard perception of the products. One condition lacked a signal word and the other lacked both the signal word and its associated warning message. In the latter condition, no danger was described on the label.

Given the results of previous research, it was expected that product labels with: (1) LETHAL would connote the greatest level of hazard of the set of terms, (2) DANGER would connote greater hazard than both WARNING and CAUTION which may not differ between themselves, (3) the signal icon paired with LETHAL and DANGER would convey higher levels of hazard than the same terms without the signal icon, (4) NOTE would connote the least hazard of the set of signal words, (5) no signal word would connote less hazard than conditions with the signal word terms present, and (6) the no signal word and warning message condition would connote the least hazard.

METHOD

Participants

A total of 90 individuals participated. Forty-five were Rensselaer Polytechnic Institute undergraduates and 45 were students from a public high school in Troy, New York.

Materials and Stimuli

Sixteen brand-name consumer products were chosen to represent a range of hazard. The front labels were digitized using an optical scanner and stored in a computer with high-resolution graphics capability. Using paint and draw software, defects from the scanning process were corrected. Signal words and accompanying warning messages used font sizes and styles that most closely matched the print on the original label. Black and white versions of the product labels were reproduced using a 300 dpi laser printer.

Nine of the 16 product labels were used in the experimental conditions (aspirin, contact lens cleaner, drain opener, fabric protector, hair-styling mousse, paint thinner, pest-control fogger, plant food, and spray adhesive). Seven "filler" labels were also used (bandages, bath soap, facial tissue, index cards, shampoo, toothpaste, and towelettes). The fillers were relatively safe products that contained no signal word or warning of any kind on the front label. The purpose of including the fillers was to help maintain belief in the marketing study by reducing the likelihood that participants would notice that the study was studying warnings.

Most of the experimental product labels contained a preexisting warning message on the front label. When possible, this message was retained on the product label. However, for some products a different warning message was used in place of the original warning. These were adapted from a back-label warning or were constructed to describe a possible danger.

The nine experimental product labels acted as carriers for the signal word conditions. Five conditions involved only the signal words: NOTE, CAUTION, WARNING, DANGER, and LETHAL. In two other conditions, the signal icon was displayed accompanying the DANGER and LETHAL signal words, and was located above or to the left of the signal word. In addition, there were two control conditions: (a) the No Warning and Signal Word condition which lacked both the signal word and the associated warning message, and (b) the No Signal Word condition which had a warning message but no signal word. Example representations of four of the nine experimental conditions are shown in Figure 1.

Nine booklets were formed, each containing one label from all 16 products. The signal word conditions were rotated through all of the experimental product labels according to a balanced Latin square so that all experimental products appeared in every signal word/warning condition. The seven filler products were randomly inserted into the booklets. A second balanced Latin Square was used to order the product labels in the booklets.

Participants were given a questionnaire requesting responses based on nine-point Likert-type scales. The questions together the numerical and verbal anchors are shown below:

(a) *Frequency of Use:* "How frequently do you use this product?" The anchors were: (0) not at all, (2) infrequently, (4) frequently, (6) very frequently, (8) extremely frequently.

(b) *Attention:* "How likely is it that this product label would capture your attention if it were on a supermarket shelf?" The anchors were: (0) not at all likely to capture attention, (2) unlikely to capture attention, (4) likely to capture attention, (6) very likely to capture attention, (8) extremely likely to capture attention.

(c) *Familiarity:* "How familiar are you with this product (or a product of the same type)?" The anchors were: (0) not at all familiar, (2) slightly familiar, (4) familiar, (6) very familiar, (8) extremely familiar.

(d) *Hazard:* "How hazardous is this product?" The anchors were: (0) not at all hazardous, (2) slightly hazardous, (4) hazardous, (6) very hazardous, (8) extremely hazardous.

(e) *Likelihood of Purchase:* "How likely are you to buy this product?" The anchors were: (0) not at all likely to buy, (2) unlikely to buy, (4) likely to buy, (6) very likely to buy, (8) extremely likely to buy.

(f) *Expected Cost:* "How much do you think this product would cost." For this question, participants were asked to write the best estimate of the price in the space provided on the answer sheet.

Procedure

Participants were first given a consent form to sign. Participants were told that the study was a marketing

Figure 1

Example Images of Four Label Conditions Differing on the Presence of a Signal Word, Signal Icon, and Warning Message.

Signal Word plus Signal Icon

Signal Word Present

No Signal Word

No Signal Word or Warning

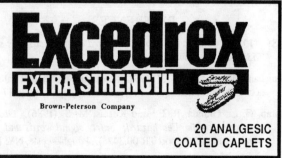

research survey dealing with people's perceptions of consumer products. Participants were given one of the nine product booklets and they were asked to examine all of the labels before beginning their ratings. After this initial examination, participants were given the questionnaire that asked them to rate the products on the six dimensions described above. They were told to rate the products in the order shown in their booklet. After completing the set of ratings, participants were debriefed and thanked for their time.

RESULTS

Mean hazard ratings (and standard deviations) of the signal word/warning conditions for both participant groups are shown in Table 1. A correlation of the mean hazard ratings between the two groups of participants (high school students and college undergraduates) in this table showed a strong positive relation, $r = .95$, $N = 9$, $p < .0001$.

A 2 (participant group) X 9 (signal word condition) mixed-model analysis of variance (ANOVA) showed a significant main effect of participant group, $F(1, 88) = 4.97$, $p < .05$. In general, the high school students ($M = 5.29$) gave higher ratings than the college students ($M = 4.77$). The ANOVA also showed a significant main effect of signal word condition, $F(8, 704) = 9.41$, $p < .0001$. Comparisons among the means showed that the No Warning or Signal Word condition produced significantly lower hazard ratings than all of the other conditions except the No Signal Word or NOTE conditions ($ps < .05$). The No Signal Word condition produced significantly lower hazard ratings than all of the conditions with signal words. NOTE produced significantly lower hazard ratings than DANGER and LETHAL—with or without the signal icon. Both CAUTION and WARNING produced significantly lower

TABLE 1

Mean Hazard Ratings of Signal Words for High School and College Students

Condition	High School Mean SD	College Mean SD	Overall Mean SD
No Warning or Signal Word	4.49 (2.88)	3.82 (2.44)	4.16 (2.68)
No Signal Word	4.42 (2.54)	3.53 (2.13)	3.98 (2.37)
NOTE	5.11 (2.46)	4.27 (2.22)	4.69 (2.37)
CAUTION	5.16 (2.52)	4.58 (2.15)	4.87 (2.35)
WARNING	5.36 (2.41)	4.62 (2.01)	4.99 (2.24)
DANGER	5.71 (2.34)	5.02 (1.73)	5.37 (2.07)
LETHAL	5.76 (2.48)	5.73 (2.25)	5.74 (2.35)
DANGER with Icon	5.69 (2.62)	5.13 (1.88)	5.41 (2.28)
LETHAL with Icon	5.96 (2.34)	6.18 (2.00)	6.07 (2.17)
mean	5.29	4.77	

hazard ratings than LETHAL—with or without the icon. Finally, DANGER was significantly lower than LETHAL with the icon. There was no significant interaction of participant group and signal word condition, $F(8, 704) < 1.0$, $p > .05$.

Specific examination of the signal icon involved a 2 (participant group) X 2 (presence vs. absence of icon) X 2 (DANGER vs. LETHAL) mixed-model ANOVA. This analysis produced only a main effect of signal word, $F(1, 88) = 4.14$, $p < .05$, showing that LETHAL ($M = 5.91$) was perceived more hazardous than DANGER ($M = 5.39$). No other effects were noted in this analysis, including none involving the signal icon. There was no main effect of signal icon or an interaction.

A series of 2 X 9 ANOVAs on the ratings for the other five questions showed only main effects: for capturing attention, $F(1, 88) = 18.74$, $p < .0001$, where the college students ($M = 3.02$) reported that the labels were more likely to capture their attention than the high school student ($M = 2.04$); and for familiarity, $F(1, 88) = 5.86$, $p < .05$ where the college students ($M = 3.43$) reported that they were more familiar with the products than the high school students ($M = 2.88$). None of the ANOVAs showed a significant involvement of the signal word factor (main effect or interaction) for the five non-hazard questions ($ps > .05$).

DISCUSSION

In general, the presence of a signal word raised hazard perceptions compared to its absence. Though there were differences between extreme terms, there were no significant differences between the intermediate terms CAUTION, WARNING, and DANGER—the signal words recommended by most standards and guidelines. This is consistent with results by Leonard et al. (1986). Nevertheless, the ordering of the means concurs with the ordering of the terms as defined by standards and the results of other research (Wogalter and Silver, 1990; Silver and Wogalter, 1991). Perhaps significant differences between the intermediate terms would be found with more participants and greater statistical power.

No effect of signal icon was shown. However, a positive trend was apparent when it was added to the term LETHAL, which produced the highest mean in the experiment. The signal icon's greatest utility is probably in attracting people's attention to the warning (Young, 1991), and may not have any additional influence beyond this (such as affecting hazard perception).

Results showed that the high school and college students produced consistently ordered hazard ratings to the signal word conditions, although they were significantly higher for the high school than the college students. This result concurs with the findings of Silver and Wogalter (1991) that younger individuals (elementary and middle school children) give higher hazard ratings to signal words than older individuals (college students). The age difference might be the result of more frequent exposure to hazard labels and signs by older individuals and the consequent habituation to the words arising from benign experiences. Frequent exposure probably reduces people's wariness. This explanation is similar to the familiarity effect shown in other research (Godfrey, Allender, Laughery, and Smith,

1983; Godfrey and Laughery, 1984; Wogalter, Brelsford, Desaulniers, and Laughery, 1991). With greater familiarity, people perceive a product to be less hazardous, are less likely to look for and read a warning, and are less willing to comply with a warning.

It had been expected that the two control conditions would produce different effects, and in particular, that labels with no warning or signal word would be perceived less hazardous than those lacking a signal word. This expectation arises from the fact that there is no hazard described on labels with no warning or signal word. However, no significant difference was found between the two control conditions, and interestingly, a trend in the opposite direction is apparent. At this point, the reason for this unexpected trend is unclear, and further investigation is needed to determine its reliability. The result might be related to an effect suggested by Ursic (1984) and extended in other research (Laughery and Stanush, 1989; Leonard, Ponsi, Silver, and Wogalter, 1989; Silver, Leonard, Ponsi, and Wogalter, 1991). That is, having no warning produces some uncertainty in the minds of consumers as to the safeness of a product. As a consequence of having some doubt, hazard perception is increased compared to labels that provide at least some information on hazards.

A comment on sampling is noteworthy. While the experiment did include a sample of students from a public high school representing a cross section of ethnic socioeconomic categories, the sample may not reflect all consumers. Currently, data are being collected at various public locales (e.g., shopping centers and libraries) to determine the present finding's generality. However, given that earlier work using other populations (e.g., Dunlap et al. 1986; Silver and Wogalter, 1991) has found relatively consistent results, we expect few differences from the present study with the data currently being collected

The present research adds to our knowledge of signal words, showing that signal words are capable of changing people's perceptions of product hazard. But in addition to the study's basic findings, the research methodology makes other advances. First, the research employed procedures to disguise the true purpose of the research (under the guise of a marketing research study), so that indirect and more realistic influences of the signal words could be measured. Second, the signal words were exposed to participants in the context of warning messages on product labels, providing greater external and face validity than previous research in this area. Third, the method of constructing the stimuli (e.g., computer digitization and manipulation of labels) holds promise for other investigations on the effects of warnings and label variables (e.g., on message content and format).

REFERENCES

ANSI (1988). *American national standard on product safety signs: Z535.4-Draft*. New York: Author.

Bresnahan, T. F., and Bryk, J. (1975). The hazard association values of accident-prevention signs. *Professional Safety*, January, 17-25.

Dunlap, G. L., Granda, R. E., and Kustas, M. S. (1986). *Observer perceptions of implied hazard: Safety signal words and color words* (Research Report TR 00.3428). Poughkeepsie, NY: IBM.

FMC Corporation. (1985). *Product safety sign and label system.* Santa Clara, CA: Author.

Godfrey, S. S., Allender, L., Laughery, K. R., and Smith, V. L. (1983). Warning messages: Will the consumer bother to look? In *Proceedings of the Human Factors Society 27th Annual Meeting* (pp. 950-954). Santa Monica, CA: Human Factors Society.

Godfrey, S. S., and Laughery, K. R. (1984). The biasing effects of product familiarity on consumers' awareness of hazard. In *Proceedings of the Human Factors Society 28th Annual Meeting* (pp. 388-392). Santa Monica, CA: Human Factors Society.

Laughery, K. R., and Stanush, J.A. (1989). Effects of warning explicitness on product perceptions. In *Proceedings of the Human Factors Society 33rd Annual Meeting.* Santa Monica, CA: Human Factors Society.

Leonard, D. C., Ponsi, K. A., Silver, N. C., and Wogalter, M. S. (1989). Pest-control products: Reading warnings and purchasing intentions. In *Proceedings of the Human Factors Society 33rd Annual Meeting* (pp. 436-440). Santa Monica, CA: Human Factors Society.

Leonard, S. D., Matthews, D., and Karnes, E. W. (1986). How does the population interpret warning signals? In *Proceedings of the Human Factors Society 30th Annual Meeting* (pp. 116-120). Santa Monica, CA: Human Factors Society.

Silver, N. C., Leonard, D. C., Ponsi, K. A., & Wogalter, M. S. (1991). Warnings and purchase intentions for pest-control products. *Forensic Reports, 4,* 17-33.

Silver, N. C., and Wogalter, M. S. (1991). Strength and understanding of signal words by elementary and middle school students. In *Proceedings of the Human Factors Society 35th Annual Meeting* (pp. 580-584). Santa Monica, CA: Human Factors Society.

Ursic, M. (1984). The impact of safety warnings on perception and memory. *Human Factors, 26,* 677-682.

Westinghouse. (1981). *Westinghouse product safety label handbook.* Trafford, PA: Westinghouse Printing Division.

Wogalter, M. S., Brelsford, J. W., Desaulniers, D. R., and Laughery, K. R. (1991). Consumer product warnings: The role of hazard perception. *Journal of Safety Research, 22,* 71-82.

Wogalter, M. S., Godfrey, S. S., Fontenelle, G. A., Desaulniers, D. R., Rothstein, P. R., and Laughery, K. R. (1987). Effectiveness of warnings. *Human Factors, 29,* 599-612.

Wogalter, M. S., and Silver, N. C. (1990). Arousal strength of signal words. *Forensic Reports, 3,* 407-420.

Young, S. L. (1991). Increasing the noticeability of warnings: Effects of pictorial, color, signal icon, and border. In *Proceedings of the Human Factors Society 35th Annual Meeting* (pp. 580-584). Santa Monica, CA: Human Factors Society.

The Influence of Location and Pictorials on Behavioral Compliance to Warnings

Michael S. Wogalter
Department of Psychology
North Carolina State University
Raleigh, NC 27695

Michael J. Kalsher
Department of Psychology
Rensselaer Polytechnic Institute
Troy, NY 12180

Bernadette M. Racicot
Department of Psychology
Rensselaer Polytechnic Institute
Troy, NY 12180

ABSTRACT

The efficacy of two warning-related factors to produce cautionary behavior in a chemistry laboratory task was examined. Experiment 1 compared the effects of a posted-sign warning and a within-instruction warning on behavioral compliance. The results showed that a warning embedded in a set of task instructions produced significantly greater compliance (the wearing of protective gear) than a similar, larger warning posted as a sign nearby. Experiment 2 reexamined the effect of location and also examined the influence of the presence versus absence of pictorials. The results of Experiment 2 confirmed the location effect of Experiment 1. No influence of pictorials was noted, although there was a nonsignificant increase in compliance when pictorials were added to the within-instruction warning. The results indicate that warning placement is important for eliciting behavioral compliance to safety messages. Explanations such as differences in field of view and perceived relevance are discussed.

INTRODUCTION

Warnings are an increasingly common component of workplace accident prevention programs. Their purpose is to prevent injury to people, equipment, and environment. Since the mid-1980s, behavioral compliance research has begun to identify variables that affect warning effectiveness. Some of these factors include: placement in a set of instructions (Strawbridge, 1986; Wogalter, Godfrey, Fontenelle, Desaulniers, Rothstein, and Laughery, 1987), social influence (Wogalter, Allison, and McKenna, 1989), severity of the consequences (Wogalter and Barlow, 1990), inclusion of pictorials (Jaynes and Boles, 1990), voice presentation (Wogalter and Young, 1991), and effort needed to comply (Wogalter et al., 1989).

Most research investigating behavioral compliance has been conducted in laboratory settings in which warnings are placed within a set of task instructions (e.g., Jaynes and Boles, 1990; Wogalter et al., 1987, 1989). In contrast, only a few studies have examined the effects of posted-sign warnings, and until recently, all of this research has been done in field settings (Laner and Sell, 1960; Saarela, 1989; Wogalter et al., 1987; Wogalter and Young, 1991). Recently, Wogalter, Rashid, Clarke and Kalsher (1991) evaluated a posted-sign warning in a controlled laboratory setting and they noted that the level of compliance was much lower than the levels reported in earlier research in which the warnings appeared in a set of task instructions (Jaynes and Boles, 1990; Wogalter et al., 1987, 1989). No research has directly compared the effects of a posted-sign warning and a within-instruction warning in a single experiment. One purpose of the present research was to determine the relative efficacy of these two types of warnings in producing behavioral compliance.

A second purpose was to examine whether adding pictorials to a warning influences compliance. Jaynes and Boles (1990) reported greater compliance when pictorials were added to a warning in a set of task instructions. However, Wogalter et al. (1991) reported no beneficial effect of pictorials when added to a posted sign. Therefore, Experiment 2 explores the possibility that the effects of pictorials differ when they are included within a set of printed instructions versus on a posted sign.

EXPERIMENT 1

This experiment examined the effectiveness of a warning placed in two locations (on a posted-sign versus within a set of task instructions). Compliance to the warning (the wearing of protective gear), as well as several other warning-related variables, was measured.

Method

Design and participants. This experiment consisted of four between-subjects conditions: (1) no warning (control), (2) posted-sign warning, (3) warning inserted within a set of task instructions, and (4) both posted-sign and within-instruction warnings. Forty-eight Rensselaer Polytechnic Institute (RPI) undergraduate students participated and were assigned randomly to each of four conditions in equal proportions (12 per condition).

Apparatus and materials. Participants used a triple-beam balance, beakers, flasks, and graduated cylinders to weigh, measure, and mix several substances and solutions as directed by a set of chemistry laboratory task instructions. This procedure is described in more detail in Wogalter et al. (1987, 1989, 1991). The substances and solutions were disguised to appear potentially hazardous but were actually safe (e.g., flour, colored water). A large supply of plastic gloves and face masks were available next to the equipment.

The warning is shown in Figure 1. The posted warning sign was in black print on a 31 x 31 cm yellow background and was identical to the no-pictorial warning sign used by Wogalter et al. (1991). The within-instruction warning, when present, was located in the middle of the task instruction sheet and was approximately 4% the size (6 x 6 cm) of the posted sign. It was otherwise identical to the sign except it had a white rather than a yellow background. The posted warning, when present, was located so it could be seen from the doorway upon entering the laboratory room and was positioned facing the participants 1.0 m away.

Procedure. Participants were asked to read and sign a consent form which described the study as investigating the procedures and equipment involved in a chemistry laboratory task. They were told that a set of specific instructions would be available on a table in the next room. After showing

Figure 1. *The Within-Instruction and Posted-Sign Warning in Experiment 1.*

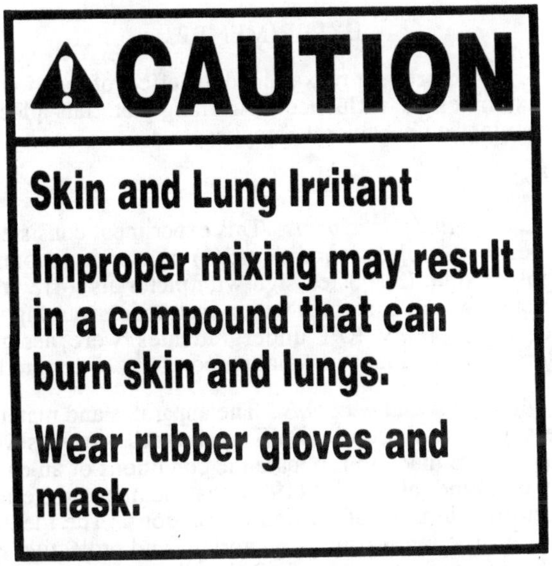

participants how to use a triple-beam balance, the experimenter told the participants to perform the chemistry task quickly and accurately, and then escorted them to the doorway of the adjoining room. The experimenter pointed to the laboratory table, and told the participant to enter and begin the task. Whether the participant wore the protective gear was recorded. If the participant had not completed the task within five minutes, they were told to stop. After the chemistry task, participants returned to the first room and completed a short questionnaire asking whether they saw the protective gear (mask and gloves), saw a warning of any type, and if so, what specifically did the warning say. Later, participants were debriefed and thanked for their time.

Results

Behavioral compliance. Preliminary analysis showed that if participants in the three warning-present conditions wore one piece of protective gear, they were very likely to wear the other piece, $\phi = .88$ ($N = 36$), $p < .0001$. Given this result, the first analysis of compliance used a score that counted participants as complying only if they wore *both* the mask and gloves. These compliance frequencies (and percentages) are shown in Table 1. The overall Chi-square test for these data was significant, $\chi^2(3, N = 48) = 24.67$, $p < .0001$. Greatest compliance occurred when the within-instruction warning was present. Comparisons among the individual conditions showed that all differences between

conditions were significant ($ps < .05$), except between the two within-instruction warning conditions.

Another measure of compliance was formed by summing the number of pieces of protective gear that each participant wore. This score ranged from 0 to 2. A 2 (Posted-Sign Warning: present vs. absent) X 2 (Within-Instruction Warning: present vs. absent) between-subjects analysis of variance (ANOVA) showed a significant main effect of Within-Instruction Warning, $F(1, 44) = 36.67$, $p < .0001$. The presence of the within-instruction warning ($M = 1.71$) produced significantly greater compliance than its absence ($M = 0.46$). There was no main effect of Posted-Sign Warning, but there was a significant interaction, $F(1, 44) = 4.08$, $p < .05$. Comparisons among the means using Fisher's Least Significant Difference test (LSD = 0.58 at $p = .05$) showed that the posted sign (only) condition produced significantly greater compliance compared to the no-warning control condition, but the posted sign produced no additional compliance when added to a within-instruction warning.

Questionnaire responses. Additional analyses examined the questionnaire responses. Table 1 shows the frequencies and percentages for the items asking participants whether they saw both pieces of protective gear and whether they saw a warning. Most participants saw the protective gear, and as a result, the Chi-square test showed no significant differences among conditions (in analyses counting both or either piece of gear). However, a significant effect was found for seeing the warning, $\chi^2(3, N = 48) = 28.70$, $p < .0001$. Paired comparisons indicated that all differences between conditions were significant, except between the two within-instruction warning conditions.

Analyses also examined whether memory of the warning differed between the conditions. On the questionnaire, participants were asked to give a specific description of the warning message. Responses were scored in two ways, by a lenient criterion and by a strict criterion. When scored according to the lenient criterion, a response was counted as correct if there was some mention about a hazard being present. Using the strict criterion, the components of the warning were broken down into 11 idea elements. The total number of elements included in each participant's response was divided by 11 to form proportion-correct scores. The memory scores are shown on the last two columns of Table 1. A 2 X 2 ANOVA on the lenient data showed a significant main effect of within-instruction warning, $F(1, 44) = 20.43$, $p < .0001$. Participants had greater lenient memory of the warning if the within-instruction warning was present ($M = .71$) than absent ($M = .17$). There were no other significant effects for the lenient

TABLE 1. *Dependent Measures as a Function of Warning Condition in Experiment 1.*

Condition	Compliance freq	Compliance %	Compliance Score (0-2)	See Protective Gear freq	See Protective Gear %	See Warning freq	See Warning %	Memory Lenient	Memory Strict
No warning (control)	0	0	.17	8	67	0	0	0	0
Posted-sign warning	4	33	.75	8	67	5	42	.33	.20
Within-instructions warning	11	92	1.83	12	100	11	92	.67	.32
Posted-sign and within-instructions warning	9	75	1.58	10	83	11	92	.75	.28

Note. n = 12 for all conditions (N = 48).

scores. The strict memory scores also showed a significant main effect of within-instruction warning, $F(1, 44) = 12.45$, $p < .001$. Participants had greater strict memory of the warning if the within-instruction warning was present ($M = .30$) than absent ($M = .10$). There was no main effect of posted sign, but there was a reliable interaction, $F(1, 44) = 4.69$, $p < .05$. Paired comparisons (Fisher's LSD = 0.16) showed that strict memory was significantly higher when the posted sign was present than when it was absent, but this was only true when the within-instruction warning was absent; there was no effect of the posted sign when the within-instruction warning was present.

Relation of compliance to the questionnaire responses. Lastly, the questionnaire responses were related to compliance using data from the three warning-present conditions ($N = 36$). There were substantial positive correlations between compliance and whether participants reported seeing the protective gear ($r = .70$), reported seeing the warning ($r = .90$), and remembering the warning ($rs = .69$ and $.60$ for the lenient and strict criteria, respectively), all $ps < .0001$. Additional correlations showed that participants who saw the warning also saw the protective gear ($r = .60$) and remembered the warning ($rs = .68$ and $.58$ for lenient and strict memory, respectively), $ps < .001$.

Discussion

Though all warning conditions produced greater compliance than the control condition, the within-instruction warning produced greater compliance than the posted-sign warning. This difference was found despite the fact that the within-instruction warning was much smaller and lacked the bright yellow background of the sign. These findings are consistent with the informal observation by Wogalter et al. (1991) of lower compliance to a posted-sign than to a within-instruction warning.

The questionnaire measures showed similar results. Participants were more likely to see the protective gear, see the warning, and remember it, if they were exposed to a within-instruction warning. These measures were strongly related to compliance.

EXPERIMENT 2

This experiment reexamined the effect of location and also examined the influence of warning pictorials added to the warnings on behavioral compliance.

Method

Design and participants. This experiment consisted of five between-subjects conditions: (1) no warning (control), (2) posted sign, (3) posted sign with pictorials, (4) within-instruction warning, and (5) within-instruction warning with pictorials. Eighty RPI undergraduates were assigned randomly to conditions in equal proportions (16 per group).

Apparatus and materials. The apparatus and materials were similar to those used in Experiment 1 except several changes were made to replicate the conditions of an earlier study by Jaynes and Boles (1990) that examined the effects of pictorials in a set of written instructions. The identical within-instruction warnings, pictorials, and protective gear employed by Jaynes and Boles (1990) were used. Depictions of the warning with and without pictorials are shown in Figure 2.

The within-instruction warnings measured 0.80 x 14.9 cm (with pictorials) and 3.5 x 14.9 cm (without pictorials). The three pictorials were previously evaluated and shown to be adequately understood by lay persons (Collins, Lerner and Pierman, 1982). The posted-sign warning was identical to the within-instruction warning except its area was approximately 7.5 times larger, measuring 2.1 x 41.75 cm (without pictorials) and 9.5 x 41.75 cm (with pictorials). When present, the posted-sign warning was located 68 cm away from the rim of the laboratory table with the bottom edge 13 cm above the table directly in front of participants' standing position at the table. Both the within-instruction and posted-sign warnings were black print on a white background.

Figure 2. *The Pictorial and Nonpictorial Warning used in the Within-Instruction and Posted-Sign Warnings of Experiment 2.*

WARNING: wear goggles, mask and gloves while performing the task to avoid irritating fumes and possible irritation of skin.

WARNING: wear goggles, mask and gloves while performing the task to avoid irritating fumes and possible irritation of skin.

Procedure. The procedure was similar to Experiment 1 except minor changes were made to replicate the method of Jaynes and Boles (1990). One notable change was that compliance to the warning included the wearing of goggles, in addition to the mask and gloves.

Results

The same compliance measures and questionnaire response that were analyzed in Experiment 1 were examined in this experiment. Three pieces of protective gear were present and required by the warning (instead of two in the first experiment). As a result, participants had to wear all three pieces of protective gear to be counted as having complied. The compliance score now ranged from 0 to 3, and the measures of seeing the protective gear and strict memory took the goggles into account.

Behavioral compliance. Compliance frequencies and percentages are shown in Table 2. The overall Chi-square test was significant, $\chi^2(4, N = 80) = 30.76, p < .0001$. As can be seen in the table, the within-instruction warning conditions produced the highest levels of compliance. Paired comparisons among conditions showed that all differences were significant ($ps < .05$) except between the control and the two posted-sign conditions, and between the two within-instruction conditions. If participants wore one piece of protective gear, they also tended to wear the other two pieces (rs ranged from .83 to 1.0, $ps < .0001$).

The other measure of compliance was the sum of the number of pieces of protective gear that each participant wore. In this experiment, the compliance score ranged from 0 to 3. Means for this measure are shown in Table 2. A 2 (Warning Location: posted-sign vs. within-instruction) X 2 (Pictorials: presence vs. absence) between-subjects ANOVA showed a significant main effect of Warning Location, $F(1, 60) = 30.73, p < .0001$. Within-instruction warnings ($M = 2.41$) produced significantly greater compliance than posted-sign warnings ($M = 0.75$). No other effects were noted in the analysis. Additional analyses compared the experimental (warning-present) conditions to the no-warning control condition. Results showed that the no-warning control produced significantly lower compliance than the two within-instruction warning conditions, but there was no difference between the control and the two posted-sign conditions.

Questionnaire responses. Table 2 shows the frequencies and percentages of the responses to the questionnaire items asking participants whether they saw the protective gear and a warning. For seeing the protective gear, the Chi-square test showed a significant effect of condition, $\chi^2(4, N = 80) = 21.92, p < .001$. More participants saw the protective gear in the two within-instruction conditions than the two posted-sign and no-warning conditions. The only exception was that the within-instruction warning without pictorials did not statistically differ from the posted-sign warning without pictorials. The two within-instruction conditions did not differ, and there was also no difference between the two posted-sign conditions.

The see-warning item showed a significant effect of condition, $\chi^2(4, N = 80) = 30.47, p < .0001$. Table 2 shows that participants most often noticed the warning in the within-instruction conditions. Paired comparisons indicated that all conditions were different from each other except between the two within-instruction warning conditions and between the two-posted sign conditions.

As in Experiment 1, memory of the warning was scored using a lenient and a strict criterion. In this experiment, however, to form the strict score the components of the warning were broken into eight idea units. Means of these two measures are shown in the last two columns of Table 2. A 2 X 2 ANOVA on the lenient data showed no significant effects. However, as expected, additional comparisons showed that all four warning-present conditions had significantly higher lenient memory scores than the no-warning control condition. A 2 X 2 ANOVA on the strict memory date showed a significant main effect of Warning Location, $F(1, 60) = 13.29, p < .001$. Participants in the within-instruction warning conditions ($M = .43$) had greater strict memory of the warning than participants in the posted-sign conditions ($M = .20$). There was no significant effect of Pictorials or interaction. All four warning-present conditions showed significantly greater strict memory scores than the no-warning control condition.

Relation of compliance to the questionnaire responses. Compliance in the four warning-present conditions ($N = 64$) was examined in relation to the questionnaire responses. Analyses indicated substantial positive correlations between compliance and whether participants reported seeing all three pieces of protective gear ($r = .74$), seeing the warning ($r = .80$), and remembering the warning ($rs = .59$ and .79 for lenient and strict memory, respectively), all $ps < .0001$. Additional correlations showed that participants who saw the warning also saw the protective gear ($r = .66$) and remembered the warning ($rs = .58$ and .81 for lenient and strict memory, respectively), all $ps < .0001$.

TABLE 2. *Dependent Measures as a Function of Warning Condition in Experiment 2.*

Condition	Compliance freq	Compliance %	Compliance Score (0-3)	See Protective Gear freq	See Protective Gear %	See Warning freq	See Warning %	Memory Lenient	Memory Strict
No warning (control)	1	6	.19	2	12	1	6	0	0
Posted-sign warning	3	19	.75	6	38	7	44	.31	.20
Posted-sign and pictorial warning	3	19	.75	5	31	7	44	.31	.20
Within-instructions warning	11	69	2.38	10	62	14	88	.56	.48
Within-instructions and pictorial warning	13	81%	2.44	14	88	14	88	.38	.38

Note. $n = 16$ for all conditions ($N = 80$).

Discussion

This experiment confirmed Experiment 1's finding that a posted sign produces a lower rate of behavioral compliance compared to the same warning appearing in a set of task instructions. The responses to the questionnaire items corroborated this conclusion. More participants in the within-instruction warning conditions saw the protective gear, saw the warning, and remembered the warning in the within-instruction warning conditions than in the posted-sign warning conditions. The posted-sign produced relatively small effects. Some of the analyses indicated that the posted signs were not significantly better than no warning.

The study failed to find a significant benefit of pictorials, although there was a positive trend of greater compliance when pictorials were present in the within-instruction warning. However, this trend was nonexistent for the questionnaire measures, and for all measures comparing the two posted-sign warning conditions.

GENERAL DISCUSSION

This research showed that a warning appearing in a set of task instructions is more effective in producing behavioral compliance than a warning on a nearby posted sign. Two explanations can be offered. First, although the sign was near the participant, it was outside of their primary field of vision. Participants were probably focusing on the chemistry materials and task directions, and not on the surrounding environment. Therefore, it is possible that the posted-sign warning was less accessible to participants because it was not contained within their main attentional focus. Second, it is possible that all participants saw the warning when it was present, but those in the within-instruction conditions might have believed that the warning was more relevant to them and to the task at hand than participants in the posted-sign conditions. In other words, participants in the within-instruction conditions might have perceived the warning to be an important component of the task because the it was included in the directions relative to participants in the posted-sign conditions whose warning was separated from the task instructions.

Interestingly, no effect of pictorials was seen in Experiment 2. Though it does not confirm Jaynes and Boles' (1990) finding, it does support a failure to find pictorial effects in other behavioral compliance research (Wogalter et al., 1991). Nevertheless, there was a slight trend of higher compliance when the pictorials were included in the task instructions in this study and in Wogalter et al. (1991). A pictorial effect might have been found had a larger sample of participants been included. Nevertheless, the failure to find an effect of pictorials should not be taken as evidence that pictorials are not a potentially important component of warnings. For example, pictorials have an important function for populations unable to read verbal commands (e.g., the illiterate, children).

An implication of this research is that printed instructions and work sheets given to employees should include warnings relevant to the task and environment in which the work is performed. Within-instruction warnings might be particularly useful for less experienced employees—whose attention is likely to be focused on the instructions and tasks, and not on other aspects of the surroundings. Signs, however, could act as occasional reminders for experienced workers who no longer need written task instructions. Additionally, there may be no other available way to inform visitors of work-area hazards other than through signage.

Future research in this area should continue to investigate ways to improve signage to facilitate capturing workers' attention and to increase the perceived relevance of the information to workers and their tasks. Moreover, greater emphasis should be given to target-audience variables, such as familiarity and experience, that may have important implications on whether warnings will have their intended effect.

REFERENCES

Collins, B. L., Lerner, N. D., and Pierman, B. C. (1982). *Symbols for industrial safety*. (Technical Report NBSIR 82-2485). Washington, DC: U.S. Department of Commerce.

Jaynes, L.S., and Boles, D. B. (1990). The effects of symbols on warning compliance. In *Proceedings of the Human Factors Society 34th Annual Meeting* (pp. 984-987). Santa Monica, CA: Human Factors Society.

Laner, S., and Sell, R. G. (1960). An experiment on the effect of specially designed safety posters. *Occupational Psychology, 34,* 153-169.

Saarela, K. L. (1989). A poster campaign for improving safety on shipyard scaffolds. *Journal of Safety Research, 20,* 177-185.

Strawbridge, J. A. (1986). The influence of position, highlighting, and embedding on warning effectiveness. In *Proceedings of the Human Factors Society 30th Annual Meeting* (pp. 716-720). Santa Monica, CA: Human Factors Society.

Wogalter, M. S., Allison, S. T., and McKenna, N. A. (1989). The effects of cost and social influence on warning compliance. *Human Factors, 31,* 133-140.

Wogalter, M. S., and Barlow, T. (1990). Injury likelihood and severity in warnings. In *Proceedings of the Human Factors Society 34th Annual Meeting* (pp. 580-583). Santa Monica, CA: Human Factors Society.

Wogalter, M. S., Godfrey, S. S., Fontenelle, G. A., Desaulniers, D. R., Rothstein, P. R., and Laughery, K. R. (1987). Effectiveness of warnings. *Human Factors, 29,* 599-612.

Wogalter, M. S., Rashid, R., Clarke, S. W., and Kalsher, M. J. (1991). Evaluating the behavioral effectiveness of a multi-modal voice warning sign in a visually cluttered environment. In *Proceedings of the Human Factors Society 35th Annual Meeting* (pp. 718-722). Santa Monica, CA: Human Factors Society.

Wogalter, M. S., and Young, S. L. (1991). Behavioural compliance to voice and print warnings. *Ergonomics, 34,* 79-89.

WARNING COMPLIANCE: BEHAVIORAL EFFECTS OF COST AND CONSENSUS

Michael S. Wogalter, Nancy A. McKenna, and Scott T. Allison
Psychology Department, University of Richmond
Richmond, Virginia 23173

ABSTRACT

Two laboratory experiments were conducted to examine the behavioral effects of cost and consensus on warning compliance. Subjects performed a chemistry demonstration task using a set of instructions that contained a warning directing them to wear a safety mask and gloves. In Experiment 1, cost was manipulated by locating the masks and gloves in either an accessible location (low cost) or a less accessible location (high cost). In Experiment 2, consensus was manipulated by the additional presence of a confederate subject who either did or did not comply with the warning. The results showed reduced compliance to the warning when the cost was high, and that the compliance rate was biased up or down depending on the behavior of the confederate. Implications of this research for facilitating warning effectiveness and safety are discussed.

INTRODUCTION

In their review of the literature on warnings, McCarthy, Finnegan, Krumm-Scott, & McCarthy (1984) concluded that research has failed to demonstrate that warnings are effective. This review produced considerable interest and research on the effectiveness of warnings (e.g., Wogalter, Godfrey, Fontenelle, Desaulniers, Rothstein, & Laughery, 1987). Research has begun to examine the kinds of conditions that facilitate and inhibit warning effectiveness. For example, Wogalter et al. (1987) have shown that warning placement can affect warning compliance. In addition, the factors of imbeddedness in text (Strawbridge, 1986), and salience (Wogalter et al., 1987) have been shown to affect compliance rates.

According to Cunitz (1981) and Peters (1984), product warning labels serve several functions. Warnings inform consumers about the possible dangers associated with the use of a product. Warnings also serve to persuade the consumer to comply behaviorally to the warning's instructions.

The present research begins with the assumption that product warnings represent an attempt to behaviorally influence consumers. Current social psychological theory distinguishes between two kinds of influence attempts. One assumes the target individuals systematically processes persuasive messages, and the other assumes the target individual uses heuristic processing of persuasive messages (Chaiken, 1980; Eagly & Chaiken, 1984). Systematic processors focus on the quality (content) of the persuasive arguments are persuaded more by the high quality arguments than low quality arguments (Petty, Cacioppo, & Goldman, 1981). In contrast, heuristic processors rely upon simple rules of thumb, or heuristics, to guide their thinking about the quality of a persuasive message. These individuals comply to an influence attempt only if the preconditions of one or more compliance heuristics are satisfied. Because people are exposed to more than 3,000 influence attempts daily (primarily from advertising), even systematic processors, to some extent, must rely on heuristics to guide their judgments about compliance (Cialdini, 1984).

Eagly and Chaiken (1984) have identified five major compliance heuristics, each of which may employed by the recipient of an influence attempt when deciding whether to be influenced. First, individuals who are confronted with a persuasive message may rely upon the expertness of the source of that message. For example, a physician's advice to change one's diet habits carries more weight than an admonishment from a casual friend. Second, we tend to be susceptible to greater influence from people whom we like than by people with whom we associate little positive affect. This is why advertising using the services of famous, likeable actors are successful in selling products. Third, a target of a persuasive message may evaluate the quality of that message by the sheer number of arguments contained in the message. The target uses the number of arguments as a heuristic to infer their quality, judging that argument quantity is diagnostic of soundness. Fourth, people are influenced by the presence of statistics in support of an argument. As a result, people buy more sugar-free gum when they hear that four out of five doctors recommend it than when they are simply told that chewing sugar-free gum has certain benefits.

The fifth compliance heuristic, consensus (also referred to as, social influence or conformity), is one of the focuses of the present research. People often use the behavior of others to infer the appropriate action for a given situation (Asch, 1955). As a result of consensus, targets observe the behavior of others to judge whether to comply. It implies that individuals will be more likely to comply to a warning when others are doing so. This heuristic also implies the reverse, namely, that individuals will be less likely to obey a warning when they see others ignoring it. The present research examines whether people are likely to be influenced by others when deciding to obey or not to obey warning instructions.

Another factor believed to affect the degree to which an individual is influenced is the perceived cost, in terms of time and effort, associated with the behavior desired by the source of influence. The role of cost has been investigated by previous researchers interested in the determinants of helping behavior (Piliavin, Piliavin, & Rodin, 1976).

These investigators varied the cost associated with engaging in a helping act and found that the higher the cost, the less likely subjects were to offer assistance to a stranger. Cost has also been shown to influence compliance to warning instructions. In a field study (Wogalter et al., 1987), subjects were more likely to disobey a warning on a set of doors when the warning requested that they take a more effortful diversion, and were more apt to comply when the warning requested less effortful behavior. The present research further examines cost on warning compliance, but in this case in a laboratory setting.

The following two laboratory experiments use a chemistry demonstration paradigm (Wogalter et al., 1987) in which subjects followed instructions to mix chemicals under varied conditions. The first experiment examines the effect of cost on warning compliance. The second experiment examines the effect of consensus.

EXPERIMENT 1

The purpose of the first experiment was to examine whether cost would affect warning compliance in a controlled laboratory situation. It is expected that subjects will be more likely to comply to a warning that instructs a low effort activity than a high effort activity.

Method

Subjects. Twenty-three University of Richmond students from an introductory psychology course voluntarily participated to fulfill a course requirement.

Materials. The equipment used to perform the demonstration task included: a triple beam balance, beakers, flasks, a graduated cylinder, a stirring rod, measuring spoons, aluminum foil measuring cups, disposable vinyl gloves and paper surgical masks. Purple and green water (made using food coloring) was contained in two wash bottles labeled Solution A and Solution B. Cannisters labeled Substance A, Substance B and Substance C contained green sugar, corn meal, and yellow powdered sugar. The solutions and substances were disguised to help set an illusion that subjects were mixing potentially hazardous chemicals.

Subjects used set of printed demonstration instructions that included a short description of performance expectations followed by a warning stating: "WARNING: Wear gloves and masks while performing the task to avoid irritating fumes and possible irritation of skin." Under the warning was the specific chemical mixing instructions. There were six steps describing how to measure and mix certain quantities of substances and solutions.

Procedure. Subjects signed consent forms in a small room where, for all subjects, there were many sets of gloves and masks on the only table present. Next, each subject was taken to a nearby room approximately 25 ft (7.6 m) away. This second room had a table containing the chemistry materials. The experimenter told the subjects that they should work as quickly and accurately as possible, that the quality of performance and time to perform the task was being measured. They were also told that if they encountered any problems, to do the best they could. An earlier pilot study yielded no significant effect for high vs.

low cost when subjects were given an unlimited amount of time to perform the task and were allowed to ask the experimenter questions. In the present experiment, subjects were told they would have a time limit of 5 min to complete the task and were asked not to ask questions during this time. Before subjects were given the written instructions, they were asked if they were familiar with a triple beam balance and if not, shown how to use it.

In the low cost condition, masks and gloves were not only in the consent forms, but also in the laboratory demonstration table as well. In the high cost condition, the masks and gloves were in the consent form room only. Subjects were later debriefed.

Results

The independent variable was high vs. low cost. The dependent variable was frequency of subject compliance (i.e., use of mask and gloves). Table 1 shows the observed frequencies and percentages. It is apparent from this table that subjects in the high cost condition complied less often than subjects in the low cost condition. A Chi-Square analysis of frequency showed the effect is significant, X^2 (1, N = 23) = 7.34, $p < .01$.

TABLE 1. Frequencies and Percentages of Warning Compliance as a Function of Cost

	Cost			
	Low		High	
Compliance	8	73%	2	17%
Noncompliance	3	27%	10	83%

Discussion

The results of Experiment 1 indicate that a cost of as little as walking 25 ft (7.6 m) to another location can produce lowered warning compliance. These findings are consistent with the Wogalter et al. (1987) field study that showed subjects were more likely to obey a warning when the cost is low than when the cost is high. The results also support the social psychological research on the effects of cost (Piliavin et al., 1976).

EXPERIMENT 2

The goal of Experiment 2 was to examine the effects of social influence on warning compliance. As mentioned in the introduction, social psychological research suggests that persons will be more apt to comply when other persons comply; conversely, people will be less likely to comply when other persons do not comply. In the present research, we investigated the influence of the behavior of one other person, a confederate. It is expected that subjects will be more likely to comply with a warning when the confederate complies than when the confederate does not comply.

Method

Subjects. Seventeen University of Richmond students from an introductory psychology course participated.

Materials and Procedure. The materials and procedure were identical to Experiment 1 except: 1) the equipment needed to perform the task was doubled, 2) only the low cost condition of Experiment 1 was used, and 3) a confederate, acting as another student, participated simultaneously with the subject. The confederate subject either complied or did not comply to the warning.

Results

Table 2 shows the observed frequencies and percentages of subject compliance. It is apparent from the table that subjects more often wore masks and gloves when the confederate complied with the warning than when the confederate did not comply. The Chi-Square analysis for these data is significant, X^2 (1, N = 17) = 8.24, $p < .01$.

TABLE 2. *Frequencies and Percentages of Warning Compliance as a Function of Confederate Compliance*

	Confederate Behavior			
	Compliance		Noncompliance	
Compliance	8	100%	3	33%
Noncompliance	0	0%	6	67%

Discussion

Warning compliance was reduced or enhanced depending on the behavior of the other person. Most of the subjects failed to comply when the confederate failed to comply. Although the means to comply were readily available in both conditions (i.e., masks and gloves), subjects tended to model the actions of the other person.

GENERAL DISCUSSION

The results of these studies show that subjects are more likely to comply with a warning: 1) in conditions of low cost than high cost, and 2) when they see another person complying than when they see another person ignoring the warning.

It is possible that subjects did not perceive any risk involved in the laboratory task. However, comments from subjects (e.g., questions about safety, trying to guess the chemical terms for the substances they used) suggests that we validly measured subjects' unwillingness to comply under conditions of some perceived risk.

Our results have several implications. First, it is preferable to have warnings that direct people to behave in

ways that are not effortful. Effort, instead, should be directed in the product design stage to remove the hazard. In cases where the hazard can not be removed, a warning is necessary. As we have seen, the simple presence of a warning does not mean that people will comply with its instructions. The warning should minimize behavioral effort to maximize compliance. Warnings should to be tested to determine whether the warning and/or product needs redesign. One way to reduce the behavioral cost is to provide the means to perform the correct behavior. For example, if protective equipment should be used in conjunction with a product (e.g., gloves with oven cleaners), one way to reduce the effort to comply would be to include the required protective equipment. The point is that product manufacturers should not expect that users will put forth effort to obtain the proper safety equipment except when it is convenient to do so.

Our results also show that the behavior of another person has a powerful influence on warning compliance. Compliance is higher when only one other person is seen to comply, and lower when only one other person is seen not complying. Therefore, all persons in potentially hazardous work environments should be encouraged to comply to warnings. For example, in workplace environments where a mask or respirator device is required by warnings, no worker should be seen working without the appropriate protective equipment.

We believe that social influence will have powerful effects in other warning domains and that compliance will be facilitated when others model the appropriate behavior. For example, the present results suggest that the introduction of persons to model the appropriate behavior might increase warning compliance. In short, seeing others do actions promotes similar actions in others. Safe behavior promotes safe behavior.

A comment should be made in regard to the generality of the consensus effect. Our study involved a situation where only one other person produced a powerful influence on warning compliance behavior. Subsequent research is needed to examine the effects of more than one other person on compliance. We would expect that the greater the number of social models present, the greater the consensus effect. However, it is unclear what pattern of effects would be found in cases when some persons are seen to comply to a warning and others are seen to ignore it. We speculate that behavior will be influenced in the direction of the majority and that when there is no clear majority, compliance judgments become increasingly dependent on other cues, possibly involving, the four compliance heuristics mentioned in the introduction. The effects of these and other variables, and their possible interactions, are left for subsequent investigations.

The present studies show that there are ways to influence the effectiveness of warnings (e.g., cost and consensus). Both effects are taken from social psychology. We have taken this approach to enhance our understanding of the factors that mediate the effectiveness of warning instructions. It is our belief that social psychological theory and research provides a useful source of ideas for this important area of research.

REFERENCES

Asch, S. E. (1955). Opinions and social pressure. *Scientific American, 193*, 31-35.

Chaiken, S. (1980). Heuristic versus systematic information processing and the use of source versus message cues in persuasion. *Journal of Personality and Social Psychology, 39*, 752-766.

Cialdini, R. (1984). *Influence*. New York: Harcourt Brace Jovanovich.

Cunitz, R. J. (1981). Psychologically effective warnings. *Hazard Prevention, 17*, 5-7.

Eagly, A. H., & Chaiken, S. (1984). Cognitive theories of persuasion. In L. Berkowitz (ed.) *Advances in Experimental Social Psychology* (Vol. 17), New York: Academic Press.

McCarthy, R. L., Finnegan, J. P., Krumm-Scott, S., & McCarthy, G. E. (1984). Product information presentation, user behavior, and safety. In *Proceedings of the Human Factors Society 28th Annual Meeting* (pp. 81-85). Santa Monica, CA: The Human Factors Society.

Peters, G. A. (1984). A challenge to the safety profession. *Professional Safety, 29*, 46-50.

Petty, R. E., Cacioppo, J. T., & Goldman, R. (1981). Personal involvement as a determinant of argument-based persuasion. *Journal of Personality and Social Psychology, 41*, 847-855.

Piliavin, I. M., Piliavin, J. A., & Rodin, J. (1976). Costs, diffusion, and the stigmatized victim. *Journal of Personality and Social Psychology, 32*, 429-438.

Strawbridge, J. A. (1986). The influence of position, highlighting and imbedding on warning effectiveness. In *Proceedings of the Human Factors Society 30th Annual Meeting* (pp. 716-720). Santa Monica, CA: The Human Factors Society, 716-720.

Wogalter, M. S., Godfrey, S. S., Fontenelle, G. A., Desaulniers, D. R., Rothstein, P. R., & Laughery, K. R. (1987). Effectiveness of warnings. *Human Factors, 29*, 599-612.

Behavioral Compliance to Personalized Warning Signs and the Role of Perceived Relevance

Michael S. Wogalter
Department of Psychology
North Carolina State University
Raleigh, NC 27695

Bernadette M. Racicot
Department of Psychology
Rensselaer Polytechnic Institute
Troy, NY 12180

Michael J. Kalsher
Department of Psychology
Rensselaer Polytechnic Institute
Troy, NY 12180

S. Noel Simpson
Department of Psychology
Rensselaer Polytechnic Institute
Troy, NY 12180

ABSTRACT

Recent research has shown that compliance to a posted warning sign is much lower than the same warning located within a set of task instructions, even when the sign is highly visible. One possible reason for this finding is that participants' believe the sign to be less relevant to the task and to themselves than the within-instructions warning. One purpose of the present research was to examine whether a personalized sign (with the participant's name) is more effective than a more conventional impersonal sign (with the signal word CAUTION). A second purpose was to examine the influence of a dynamic display compared to a static display. A sign composed of programmable light-emitting diodes (LEDs) presented the warning message using special effects (apparent motion) or it was displayed continuously. A third purpose was to examine whether various sign placements in a cluttered laboratory environment influences compliance. The wearing of protective equipment by participants as directed by the warning was the measure of behavioral compliance in a chemistry laboratory task. More participants wore the protective equipment when a warning was present than when it was absent. The personalized sign increased compliance compared to the impersonal sign. No effect of dynamic presentation was found, and the only effect among sign placements was found for perceived accuracy. The effect of personalization is explained in terms of the special alerting feature of one's own name and increased perceived relevance that results when the message is directed to them. Implications for flexible control of personalized warning messages using available technology are discussed.

INTRODUCTION

Workplace accidents and injuries are a major concern of employers. These incidents can be a result of many factors: the work tasks themselves, employees' behavior (e.g., failure to use protective gear), unsafe work environments (e.g., the presence of noxious chemicals), and improperly maintained or poorly-designed equipment. According to statistical data, reported job-related injuries have increased over the last decade (e.g., Ansberry, 1989). This increase in recorded injuries has been attributed to a variety of factors including greater employee workloads caused by escalating competition in a tighter world-wide economy. Many companies are using fewer employees who are less-experienced and who must produce at a faster rate and work longer hours (Milkovich and Boudreau, 1991). Together these factors, along with better reporting procedures and increased availability of workman's compensation, have produced the conditions for the higher injury rates seen in recent years.

As a result of increased reporting of work-related injuries, the Occupational Safety and Health Administration (OSHA) has applied more rigorous enforcement of stricter safety standards. As a rule, OSHA has held employers responsible for workplace safety even if accidents result from employees' failure to follow company policy with regard to safety procedures. For example, if an employee refuses to wear OSHA-required safety gear, the company may be held responsible. In 1986, OSHA initiated a standard called the "Right to Know" which requires companies to inform employees of any hazardous substances they might use in the course of their work, as well as the danger of exposure and the proper action to take if exposed (Milkovich and Boudreau, 1991). Although OSHA has intervened to enhance workplace safety, and many companies have initiated training programs to improve employee compliance with safety procedures, these measures do not guarantee that employees will perform the appropriate safety behavior on the job. In recent years, empirical studies have been conducted by Human Factors researchers to address the problems of communicating hazards and persuading people to comply with safety messages.

Research indicates that the effectiveness of warnings can be improved by making the message components more conspicuous (i.e., noticeable or salient). For example, empirical studies have shown that the addition of conspicuous print (Young and Wogalter, 1990), pictorials and icons (Jaynes and Boles, 1990; Young and Wogalter, 1990), voice (Wogalter and Young, 1991), and other enhancements (Wogalter, Godfrey, Fontenelle, Desaulniers, Rothstein, and Laughery, 1987) facilitate measures of warning effectiveness such as seeing and remembering the warning, and most importantly, behavioral compliance. Enhancing the conspicuousness increases the probability that the warning will be noticed, thereby increasing the likelihood that it will be read and complied with.

While some warnings' research has focused on increasing the salience of the message, another factor that influences warning effectiveness is the medium or channel used to communicate the message (e.g., Barlow and Wogalter, 1993). While there is a growing body of research on compliance to product-label and task-instruction warnings, research on compliance to posted warning signs has been relatively limited except for studies on transportation-related warnings (e.g., traffic signs). Recently, Wogalter, Kalsher and Racicot (1992, in press) showed that a highly visible posted warning sign produced significantly lower compliance than the same (but smaller) warning embedded as part of set of task instructions. Moreover, adding features intended to enhance the salience of the sign, such as a strobe light and pictorials, failed to increase compliance compared to a sign without the enhancements. Wogalter et al. (1992, in press) speculated that the sign's lowered compliance was possibly due to participant's belief that the sign was not directed to them or relevant to the tasks that they were performing. One purpose of the present study was to examine whether relevance is a factor that could influence people's willingness to comply to posted signs.

However, even if an effect of personalization is found, there is still a need to address the applicability of such research for real-world work environments. That is, how practical or even feasible is it to have personalized warning signs in the workplace? Clearly, personalization is not easily accomplished with conventional signs. However, recent technological advancements have assisted in making personalization possible. In the present study, a newly developed sign apparatus is used that allows multiple messages to be shown over time and this capability includes personalization. Specifically, the sign is composed of a large array of programmable light-emitting diodes (LEDs) which can be controlled by an attached keypad or a remote computer. Besides the potential benefit of having the flexibility to personalize a message (or present any number of multiple messages) as described above, these signs are capable of presenting information showing apparent motion created by on-off sequences of the LED array (i.e., special effects). A dynamic display might make the sign more salient which could be useful in capturing people's attention to the message compared to a more static display of the information. However, the possible advantage of this kind of dynamic information display has not yet been tested in an empirical study. Thus, a second purpose of the present research was to examine whether a dynamic display of a warning message produces greater compliance than a more conventional static display of the warning message.

Finally, a third purpose of the experiment was to examine whether placement of the warning sign in a cluttered environment influences compliance. Wogalter et al. (1992, in press) found that visual noise in the surrounding area of a sign reduced compliance. The present experiment examined a somewhat different question than the earlier research: Given that an environment is highly cluttered, are there better locations than others? A warning surrounded by relatively less background clutter should be more noticeable, and therefore more likely to be read and complied with compared to more background clutter. The current study examined the effect of three sign placements in a highly cluttered room on warning compliance behavior.

In summary, the effects of a personalized message, display motion, and sign placement on behavioral compliance to a warning was examined. Compliance was measured by observing whether or not participants wore the required safety equipment (mask and gloves) while performing a laboratory chemistry task. In addition, several other dependent measures were collected in a post-task questionnaire including whether participants saw the warning and protective equipment, and whether they could recall the warning's content, as well as ratings of perceived hazard, carefulness, and task-performance accuracy.

METHOD

Participants and Design

One hundred fifty-six undergraduate students from Rensselaer Polytechnic Institute (RPI) participated for credit in their introductory psychology course. The experiment was a 2 Personalization (Impersonal: presence of the signal word CAUTION versus Personal: presence of the individual's own name) x 3 Placement (A, B, C) x 2 Display Motion (Static, Dynamic) between-subjects design. A thirteenth condition with No Warning served as the control

group. Twelve students were randomly assigned to each condition.

Materials and Apparatus

In the Impersonal Warning (signal word) condition, the following message was displayed on the sign:

CAUTION! IRRITANT
Use Mask & Gloves

In the Personalized Warning condition, the signal word (CAUTION) was removed and was replaced by the participant's first name. Names were obtained from the research board posted in the RPI Psychology Department where participants' sign up to participate in research projects. The names was programmed into the sign message before participants entered the laboratory facilities. If the name was longer than eight characters, then a shortened version of the name (usually a conventional nickname or the last name) was used. A representation of the personalized sign is shown below:

[participant's name]! IRRITANT
Use Mask & Gloves

A programmable sign (Adaptive Micro Systems Inc., Alpha ES-440A EZ Key II) was used to display the warning messages. This LED sign can be programmed to show different messages with the included keypad or can be connected to a computer. It can simultaneously display a maximum of two lines of 18 two-inch (5.1 cm) characters. The outside dimensions of the sign apparatus were 39.4 in (100.1 cm) x 8.0 in (20.3 cm) x 4.0 in (10.2 cm) in length, height, and depth, respectively.

In static mode, the text of the warning was displayed continuously. In the dynamic mode, the message was displayed in apparent motion with four preprogrammed special effects (scrolling, explosion, snowing, and flashing). The duration of each special effect was approximately 1 s followed by 4 s of continuous on-time. Every 5 s another special effect was shown resulting in a total cycle time of 20 s for all four special effects.

The experiment took place in a large room that was a former chemistry teaching laboratory. The room contained several laboratory sinks and counters, Bunsen-burner connections, storage cabinets, etc. Moreover, this room was highly cluttered with various kinds of electronic equipment, paper, various containers, and other materials on tables, metal carts, and shelves.

The warning sign apparatus was placed in one of three locations. In Position A, the sign was on the laboratory counter where the participant performed the chemistry task. In this position, the sign was at a distance of approximately 14.7 ft. (4.5 m) to the left and on the same counter top as the work table where the participant performed the chemistry task. In Position B, the sign was placed at a more distant 18 ft (5.5 m) location to the left of the participant on another counter top in the room at the same height. This position was somewhat less cluttered then the other two placements. In Position C, the sign was approximately 8.1 ft (2.5 m) in front (but slightly to the left) of the participant in an area of the room that was more cluttered than the other two locations. In the control (no warning) condition, the sign was present in one of the three positions but the apparatus was turned off so that no message was shown.

Procedure

The laboratory materials were similar to those described in Wogalter et al. (1987, 1989). Actual chemistry laboratory equipment was used including triple-beam balances, beakers, flasks, and graduated cylinders. A large supply of plastic gloves and face masks were available on a laboratory table along with the other materials and equipment. Also present was a set of written instructions that directed participants to weigh, measure, and mix several chemical substances and solutions in a particular order. The substances and solutions were available in large glass containers which were labeled with an alphanumeric character to disguise their true nature. The chemicals were actually harmless: water, cooking oil, and powdered soap combined with food coloring.

At first, individual participants entered a room adjacent to the laboratory room described above. They were seated and given a consent form to read and sign. The contents of the form described the study as investigating the procedures involved in a chemistry laboratory demonstration task. After signing the form, participants were told that they would be performing a set of chemistry procedures in the next room and then were led to another area of the room where they were shown how to use a triple-beam balance to measure small quantities of material. Next, participants were told that in the adjacent room they would be receiving a set of instructions directing them to measure and mix various chemicals in a specified order. Participants were told that they should try to complete the set of steps as quickly and as accurately as possible. They were also told that once they began the task they should not ask the experimenter any questions and that if any problems arose they should recheck the instructions and do the best that they could.

Participants accompanied the experimenter to the doorway of a second room which contained the chemistry materials, equipment, and task instructions. The experimenter told participants to enter the room and begin. The experimenter stood in the doorway with a clipboard and stopwatch, and appeared to be recording the time required by the participant to complete each step of the instructions. In fact, the only real data recorded was whether participants complied with the warning (wore mask and gloves) before they began to mix the substances and solutions. After 5 min had elapsed, the participants were told to stop doing the task and were brought to the first room where they were asked to complete a questionnaire.

Among the various items on the questionnaire, participants were asked whether they saw: (a) any masks, (b) any gloves, and (c) a warning of any kind. For these questions, "yes" answers were given a score of "1" and "no" answers were given a score of "0." If they reported that they had seen a warning, they were requested to write the specific content of the warning message. Recall of the warning was scored using a lenient criterion. If the participant's answer stated something about an irritant, and/or the need to wear mask and gloves, the response was counted as correct (given a score of "1"; otherwise was given a score of "0").

The questionnaire also requested ratings on the three following items: (a) "How *hazardous* were the chemicals?" (b) "How *careful* were you in the task?" and (c) "How *accurate* were you in the task?" All three rating scales were Likert-type 8-point scales verbally anchored at the two ends with (0) "not at all" to (7) "very." After the completing the questionnaire, participants were given a debriefing on the actual purpose of the study and thanked for participating.

RESULTS

Behavioral Compliance

Behavioral compliance was defined as the donning of protective equipment (mask and gloves). Compliance was scored on a 3-point scale with "2" indicating the wearing of both kinds of protective equipment, "1" indicating the wearing of either the mask or gloves, and "0" indicating that neither the masks nor the gloves were worn.

An overall one-way between-subjects analysis of variance (ANOVA) on the compliance scores for all 13 conditions of the experiment showed a significant effect, $F(12, 143) = 2.25$, $p < .05$. A contrast between the No Warning (Control) condition and a composite of the 12 warning-present conditions was significant, $F(1, 154) = 5.13$, $p < .05$. Participants exposed to a warning were more likely to wear protective equipment ($M = .80$, $n = 144$) than participants not exposed to a warning ($M = .17$, $n = 12$).

The 12 warning conditions were analyzed using a 2 Personalization (Impersonal, Personal) x 3 Placement (A, B, C) x 2 Display motion (Static, Dynamic) between-subjects factorial ANOVA. The ANOVA showed a main effect of Personalization, $F(1, 132) = 7.88$ $p < .01$. Participants exposed to the personalized sign ($M = 1.01$) showed significantly greater compliance than participants exposed to the impersonal sign ($M = .58$).

The ANOVA also showed a small main effect of Placement, $F(2, 132) = 3.45$, $p < .05$. Although Placement A ($M = 1.08$) appeared to produce higher compliance than Placements B ($M = .65$) and C ($M = .67$), the Newman-Keuls multiple-range test showed none of the paired comparisons were significant ($ps > .05$). Furthermore, the ANOVA showed no main effect of Display Motion, or any significant interactions.

Post-Task Questionnaire

Analysis of the questionnaire data showed statistically significant effects for three items. First, reports of seeing a warning showed a significant effect in a chi square test among the 13 conditions, $\chi^2(12, N=156) = 25.18$, $p < .05$. The only reliable contrast among the experimental conditions was the expected finding that more participants reported seeing a warning when it was present ($M = .61$) than when it was absent ($M = .00$), $\chi^2(1, N=156) = 16.82$, $p < .001$.

Second, the recall scores showed a significant effect among conditions, $\chi^2(12, N=156) = 22.82$, $p < .05$. As expected, participants exposed to a warning ($M = .52$) more often recalled its content than participants not exposed to a warning ($M = .00$), $\chi^2(1, N=156) = 11.88$, $p < .001$. Also, the recall scores showed a significant effect of Personalization. A contrast between the personal and impersonal sign conditions, $\chi^2(1, N=144) = 10.03$, $p < .01$, showed that participants exposed to the personalized sign

(M = .61) more often recalled the warning than participants exposed to the impersonal (signal word) sign (M = .36).

Third, a one-way ANOVA (with all 13 conditions) on the accuracy ratings yielded a significant effect, $F(12, 143)$ = 2.59, $p < .01$. Participants exposed to a warning (M = 5.12) rated themselves as being significantly more accurate in performing the chemistry task than participants not exposed to a warning (M = 5.12), $F(1, 154)$ = 8.58, $p <$ .01. A 2 x 3 x 2 ANOVA (including only the 12 warning-present conditions) on the accuracy ratings showed two significant main effects. One was Personalization, $F(12, 132)$ = 10.74, $p < .01$. Participants in the personalized sign conditions (M = 5.65) rated themselves as more accurate than participants in the impersonal sign conditions (M = 4.60). The other main effect was for Placement, $F(12, 132)$ = 3.12, $p < .05$. Subsequent comparisons using the Newman-Keuls test showed that participants with the sign in Position B (M = 5.65) gave significantly higher accuracy ratings than participants with the sign in Position C (M = 4.67). Position A (M = 5.06) was intermediate, but did not significantly differ from the other two placements.

Of those participants who reported seeing a warning, 84.1% recalled its content and 58.0% complied with it by donning both masks and gloves. Also, participants who reported seeing a warning were more likely to report seeing both pieces of protective equipment than participants who did not report seeing a warning (80.7% versus 35.3%), $\chi^2(1, N=156)$ = 33.19, $p < .0001$.

Finally, the questionnaire data showed no significant differences among conditions using the ratings of perceived hazard, carefulness, and reports of seeing the masks and gloves ($ps > .05$).

DISCUSSION

The results indicated that a personalized sign (with the participant's name) increased compliance compared to an impersonal sign. Personalization presumably increased the directive's relevance to the participant and to the task they were performing. This result supports the suggestion by Wogalter et al. (1992, in press) that one reason for the relatively low level of compliance of a highly-visible posted sign (with and without the visual enhancements of a strobe and pictorials) is that people tend to believe that a sign is not relevant to them or the task that they are performing. By adding the individual's name to personalize the warning (as opposed to the impersonal sign with a signal word), participants would have difficulty concluding that the warning is not directed to them and that it is not important to perform the safety behaviors.

Further support for the notion of perceived relevance is provided by Racicot and Wogalter (1992). In this study, the use of videotaped models was effective in improving compliance compared to a posted sign. Since the model was in the same situation as the research participant, the warning was probably perceived as more relevant than a static (and impersonal) sign condition.

There is also another explanation for the personalization finding. Research in the auditory information processing literature (Moray, 1959) indicates that one's own name is a particularly good way to capture people's attention in the auditory modality. If the current results are viewed as

similar, then the name effect appears to be generalizable to the visual modality as well and potentially useful for alerting individuals to visual displays. Indeed, the results suggest that an individual's own name has greater alerting value than the signal word (whose intended purpose is, in part, to alert people that a hazard/warning is present). However, one potential benefit of signal words that is not provided by an individual's name is that these terms can also provide an indication of the level of hazard involved (Westinghouse, 1981; Wogalter and Silver, 1989). Nevertheless, the questionnaire data did not provide any support for this latter function of signal words as there were no differences between conditions for perceived hazard or carefulness.

The present research also supports another conclusion by Wogalter et al. (1992, in press). In their study, they showed that increasing the physical salience of certain features of the sign did not increase compliance. Specifically, no effect was found for the addition of a strobe light or pictorials to an otherwise visible sign without those features. In the present experiment, a feature that appeared to add salience—a dynamic LED display—produced no additional effect over a static LED display. In a review of the warning literature, DeJoy (1989) came to a similar conclusion: adding individual salient features to warnings do not always translate into increased compliance. Multiple methods of enhancement may be necessary before seeing substantial compliance gains.

In addition, sign placement in the cluttered room was also expected to show differences in compliance. While an ANOVA showed a small significant effect, none of the subsequent paired comparisons were significant (as sometimes happens). Warning location has been shown in several previous studies (e.g., Wogalter et al., 1987) to produce significant effects on compliance behavior. In this experiment, it was probably the case that none of the placements were sufficiently different from one another. The least cluttered location was still fairly cluttered. That is, the particular environment did not allow adequate power to evaluate the effects of location on compliance. Nevertheless, location did produce an effect using the accuracy ratings. The farthest, least cluttered, location produced the highest levels of reported accuracy. An explanation for this finding is not clear cut, particularly when no other dependent variable showed this effect, and no previous warning study has reported an accuracy effect. Further research is necessary to determine whether the effect is reliable and whether reports of accuracy reflect actual task accuracy.

Although the insertion of individuals' names into warning messages may seem difficult to implement, new and available technology has made its use feasible. In fact, systems could be developed in which the presentation could be done automatically, and thereby eliminate certain problems that have been cited at various times in the warnings literature. One of these problems is habituation. The use of electronic detectors embedded into encoded name tags could be used to detect individual employees and visitors entering safety-sensitive areas within a workplace. The detector could also be programmed to present a warning to particular individuals below some criterion level of experience each time they enter a safety sensitive area (e.g., new employees or visitors to a workplace) and to present a warning less frequently to others above some criterion level of experience/exposure to the warning. A procedure could also be implemented to track the number of times each individual has been warned, including the schedule of exposure, thus allowing for a more precise reinforcement-type schedule with intermittent and unpredictable subsequent presentations to serve as reminders.

REFERENCES

Ansberry, C. (1989, June 16). Workplace injuries proliferate as concerns push people to produce. *The Wall Street Journal*, pg. 1.

Barlow, T., and Wogalter, M.S. (1993). Alcoholic beverage warnings in magazine and television advertisements. *Journal of Consumer Research*.

DeJoy, D. M. (1989). Consumer product warnings: Review and analysis of effectiveness research. In *Proceedings of the Human Factors Society 33rd Annual Meeting* (pp. 936-940). Santa Monica, CA: Human Factors Society.

Jaynes, L. S., and Boles D. B. (1990). The effects of symbols on warning compliance. In *Proceedings of the Human Factors Society 34th Annual Meeting* (pp. 984-987). Santa Monica, CA: Human Factors Society.

Kalsher, M. J., Clarke, S. W., and Wogalter, M. S. (1993). Evaluation of a warning placard for communicating alcohol facts and hazards. *Journal of Public Policy and Marketing*, 12, 78-90.

Milkovich, G. T., and Boudreau, J. W. (1991). *Human resource management*. Boston, MA: Irwin.

Moray, N. (1959). Attention in dichotic listening: Affective cues and the influence of instructions. *Quarterly Journal of Experimental Psychology*, 11, 56-60.

Racicot, B. M., and Wogalter, M. S. (1992). Warning compliance: Effects of a video warning sign and modeling on behavior. In *Proceedings of the Human Factors Society 36th Annual Meeting* (pp. 608-610). Santa Monica, CA: Human Factors Society.

Westinghouse (1981). *Westinghouse product safety label handbook*. Trafford, PA: Westinghouse Printing Division.

Wogalter, M. S., Godfrey, S. S., Fontenelle, G. A., Desaulniers, D. R., Rothstein, P. R., and Laughery, K. R. (1987). Effectiveness of warnings. *Human Factors*, 29, 599-612.

Wogalter, M. S., Kalsher, M. J., and Racicot, B. M. (1992). The influence of location and pictorials on behavioral compliance to warnings. In *Proceedings of the Human Factors Society 36th Annual Meeting* (pp. 1029-1033). Santa Monica, CA: Human Factors Society.

Wogalter, M. S., Kalsher, M. J., and Racicot, B. M. (in press). Behavioral compliance to warnings: Effects of voice, context, and location. *Safety Science*.

Wogalter, M.S., and Silver, N.C. (1990). Arousal strength of signal words. *Forensic Reports*, 3, 407-420.

Wogalter, M. S., and Young, S. L. (1991). Behavioural compliance to voice and print warnings. *Ergonomics*, 34, 78-89.

Young, S. L., and Wogalter, M. S. (1990). Comprehension and memory of instruction manual warnings: Conspicuous print and pictorial icons. *Human Factors*, 32, 637-649.

Evaluating the Behavioral Effectiveness of a Multi-Modal Voice Warning Sign in a Visually Cluttered Environment

Michael S. Wogalter, Raheel Rashid,
Steven W. Clarke, and Michael J. Kalsher
Department of Psychology
Rensselaer Polytechnic Institute
Troy, NY 12180

ABSTRACT

This research examined the effects of a multi-modal warning sign on compliance behavior. Participants followed a set of printed instructions to perform a chemistry task that involved measuring and mixing disguised (nonhazardous) chemicals. Whether participants wore protective equipment as directed by the warning was measured. The environment around the sign was either visually cluttered or uncluttered. In some conditions, pictorials, a voice warning, and/or a flashing strobe light were added. The results showed that compliance was significantly greater when the warning was presented in an uncluttered environment compared to a cluttered environment. The results also showed that the presence of a voice warning produced a strong and reliable increase in compliance compared to conditions without a voice warning. No statistically reliable effects of pictorials or strobe were found though the results did show a trend of greater compliance when they were present. In addition, compliance was positively related to memory of the warning, perception of hazard, and reported carefulness. The results call attention to the importance of the context in which a warning is placed, and the potential benefits of voice warnings.

INTRODUCTION

In the past several years, issues of warning effectiveness have been a focus of human factors research. Because of the ethical constraints of exposing individuals to real dangers for experimental purposes, most of the early warning research used preference, legibility, memory, and comprehension tests as measures of effectiveness. Since the appearance of a review by McCarthy, Finnegan, Krumm-Scott, and McCarthy (1984) calling attention to the status of research at that time, new methodologies have been developed to assess warning effectiveness. One new methodology is the behavioral compliance paradigm.

The behavioral compliance paradigm places participants in settings that appear hazardous but are actually safe because precautions are taken in advance to ensure that the experimental situation is free from real danger. Compliance is assessed by observing the extent to which participants comply with a warning by performing some specific cautionary behavior (e.g., wearing of protective equipment). Since the mid 1980's, behavioral research has identified a number of factors that influence the effectiveness of warnings, including: warning placement (Wogalter, Godfrey, Fontenelle, Desaulniers, Rothstein, & Laughery 1987), embedding the warning in other text (Strawbridge, 1986), social influence of others (Wogalter, Allison, & McKenna 1989), severity of the consequences (Wogalter & Barlow, 1990), inclusion of pictorials (Jaynes & Boles, 1990), voice communication (Wogalter & Young, 1991), and effort needed to comply (Wogalter et al., 1989).

Most behavioral compliance research has been conducted in a laboratory situation in which a warning was embedded in a set of written task instructions (e.g., Jaynes & Boles, 1990; Wogalter et al., 1987, 1989). Only a few studies have examined the effects of a posted sign and all of this work has been done with field studies (Laner & Sell, 1960; Saarela, 1989; Wogalter et al., 1987; Wogalter & Young, 1991). No published research to date has examined the effect of a posted warning sign in a controlled laboratory situation. This was one purpose of the current study.

A second purpose was to examine the influence of the environmental context in which a warning is placed. In many real-world situations, warnings signs are located in cluttered environmental surroundings (e.g., amongst equipment and other printed materials). Although no previous study has examined the effects of visual clutter on warning compliance, related research indicates that irrelevant visual stimuli reduces detection of target stimuli (Cole & Hughes, 1984; Monk & Brown, 1975; Williams & Hoffmann, 1979). Because posted signs are often located outside the immediate field of view, a sign embedded in visual clutter increases the likelihood that it will be missed, and as a consequence, reducing compliance.

The current study also examined the effects of three other factors that might increase the salience of the sign in visual clutter. The variables were: pictorials, a voice warning, and a flashing strobe light. They were chosen because (a) previous research has shown increased compliance for pictorials and voice, and (b) related research suggests promising effects of a flashing strobe light. Jaynes and Boles (1990) showed greater compliance with pictorials present in a warning than when they were absent. Wogalter and Young (1991) showed greater compliance for a voice warning than a print warning inside a set of task instructions. No previous research has specifically examined the effect of a flashing light on warning compliance, but other research suggests that it might increase warning effectiveness. Guzy (1991) has recently shown that an amplitude-modulated stoplight increased the detection distance of a stoplight compared to a conventional continuous-on stop light. Moreover, human factors guidelines and general perceptual principles (e.g., Sanders & McCormick, 1987) suggest that a flashing light could be an effective means of gaining attention. Thus, it was expected that the presence of pictorials, a voice warning, and a flashing strobe light would increase the salience of a warning sign in visual clutter and thereby, reduce any camouflaging effect clutter might have.

These factors were not only studied individually but also

in combination (i.e., a multi-modal sign). Simultaneous investigation has certain advantages: (a) it allows the determination of each variable's strength in relation to other variables, and (b) it enables examination of any interaction effects. For example, it is possible that the presence of more than one method of enhancing salience produces a synergistic effect on compliance that is greater than would be predicted by their individual effects.

METHOD

Design

The experiment consisted of the 12 between-subjects conditions shown in Table 1. The primary dependent variable was whether participants complied with the warning by putting on the protective gear (wore mask and gloves).

Participants

Approximately half of the 198 participants were Rensselaer Polytechnic Institute (RPI) undergraduates and half were high school students taking undergraduate courses at RPI. They either received credit in their introductory psychology courses or remuneration of $5.00 for their participation. Participants were assigned randomly to conditions. All conditions had 18 participants except for the two control conditions which had nine each.

Materials and apparatus

The laboratory materials were similar to those described in Wogalter et al. (1987, 1989). Actual chemistry laboratory equipment was used such as a triple-beam balance, beakers, flasks, and graduated cylinders. A large supply of plastic gloves and face masks were also available on a laboratory table next to the equipment. A set of written instructions directed participants to weigh, measure, and mix several substances and solutions in a certain order. The substances and solutions were available in large glass containers and labeled by a letter to disguise their true nature. The chemicals were actually harmless: food coloring, colored water, cooking oil, and powdered soap.

The basic print warning sign (31 x 31 cm) appeared in black bold print on a bright, highly saturated yellow background. A signal icon (triangle-exclamation point) was located to the left of the signal word CAUTION on the top of the sign. Signal word letter height was 4 cm and the remaining message had letter height of 1.5 cm. In some conditions, this print sign: (1) was present or absent, (2) contained two pictorials illustrating the wearing of mask and gloves immediately below the printed statements, (3) had a strobe light attached to the sign that flashed for 8.25 s at a rate of 8 Hz with a duration of 2.2 ms per flash with a peak illuminance of 200,000 lux at 1.22 m, and/or (4) included a digitized male voice vocalizing the identical message as the printed sign. The 8.25 s vocal warning was stored on an EPROM chip and was presented at an average sound level of 83 dBA. The sign apparatus allowed the voice warning and strobe to be activated separately or together. The total dimensions of the sign apparatus were 53 cm high, 31 cm wide, and 16 cm deep. The printed sign was positioned on the front upper two-thirds of the apparatus. Below was the 15 cm diameter strobe light on the left and a speaker (for the voice) on the right. The entire apparatus was custom built by Accuform, Inc., Brooksville, Florida. The print warning

FIGURE 1. *Print Warning Sign with Pictorials.*

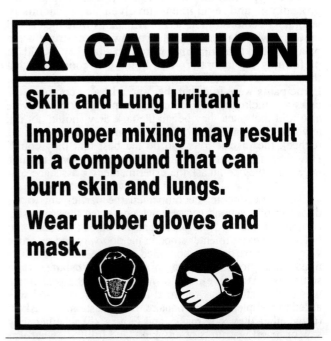

containing the two pictorials is shown in Figure 1. The sign lacking the pictorials was identical except that the line spacing of the verbal message was increased to fill the area taken by the pictorials in the sign shown in the figure.

The area immediately surrounding the laboratory table was either uncluttered (only the warning and the chemistry laboratory materials and equipment) or was cluttered with various kinds of extraneous tools and electronic equipment scattered in front of and on both sides of the laboratory demonstration table.

The strobe and voice were activated by the breaking of an infrared beam when participants crossed the area from the doorway entrance to the laboratory table. The warning sign (when present) was always positioned directly facing the doorway. Relative to the front of the laboratory table, the sign was at an angle of 35 degrees. The sign's placement was slightly offset to the right of the participants' forward position, approximately aimed at the participants' left shoulder, and was 1.0 m from the rim of the laboratory table. Table height was .95 m. The demonstration area was 1.7 m from the door.

In a preliminary study, the two pictorials were tested by placing them with nine other pictorials, and 12 RPI students were asked to write a description of what each represented. The responses were scored in two ways, using strict and lenient criteria. Correct responses with the strict criterion needed an indication that gloves or mask should be put on for protection against hazards (i.e., skin and hand for gloves, or lung and respiratory for mask), and with the lenient criterion, needed an indication that one should put on the gloves or mask. The test showed the gloves pictorial received 100% correct for both the strict and liberal criterions. The mask pictorial received 83% and 100% correct for the strict and liberal criterions, respectively.

Procedure

Initially, participants were asked to read and sign a consent form which described the study as investigating the procedures and equipment involved in a chemistry laboratory demonstration task. Participants were then asked to wear a white lab coat and shown how to use a triple-beam balance. Next, participants were told that they would be performing the laboratory task in the next room, and that they would be receiving a set of task instructions. Participants were told that they should try to complete the tasks as quickly and as accurately as possible. They were also told that once they began the task they should not ask any questions, and that if any problems arose they should recheck the instructions and do the best that they could. However, they were also informed that if it ever became necessary, they could ask the experimenter for assistance.

The experimenter accompanied the participant to the doorway of a second room which contained the chemistry equipment and told the participant to enter the room and begin. The experimenter stood in the doorway and recorded whether the participant complied with the warning (wore mask and gloves) before mixing the substances and solutions. After five minutes had elapsed, the participant was told to stop, was returned to the first room, and was asked to complete a questionnaire. The questionnaire asked: (a) whether they saw masks and gloves, (b) whether they saw or heard warnings of any kind, and (c) if so, what was the specific content of the warning. The questionnaire also requested ratings on the following items: (a) "How *hazardous* were the chemicals?" (b) "How *careful* were you in the task?" and (c) "How *accurate* were you in the task?" All three rating scales were Likert-type 8-point scales verbally anchored at the two ends with (0) "not at all" to (7) "very." After the questionnaire was completed, participants were debriefed and thanked for their participation.

RESULTS

Behavioral compliance

The primary dependent variable was whether participants put on and wore protective equipment (mask and gloves) during the demonstration procedure. Participants that put on one piece of protective gear also tended to put on the other piece ($\Phi = .91$). In the analyses presented below, participants were considered to have complied if they wore at least one piece of protective gear. Analyses considering masks and gloves separately, as well as compliance defined as having put on both pieces of equipment, showed essentially the same pattern of results although the scores were somewhat lower.

Compliance proportion means for the 12 conditions are shown in Table 1. Because there were no differences between the two control conditions ($p > .05$), in most of the remaining analyses, these two conditions were collapsed into a single No-Warning control condition.

A one-way between-subjects analysis of variance (ANOVA) showed a significant effect of conditions, $F(10, 187) = 7.12$, $p < .0001$. As can be seen in Table 2, the structure of the conditions allowed several 2 X 2 analyses. For example, using conditions 3, 4, 5, and 6 enables one to examine the effects of presence vs. absence of pictorials and clutter and their possible interaction (with the other variables

TABLE 1

Mean Proportion Compliance as a Function of Warning Conditions

Condition Number	Condition Description	Mean Compliance
(1)	Control-No Warning-No Clutter	.111
(2)	Control-No Warning-Clutter	.000
(3)	Print warning-No Clutter	.278
(4)	Print warning-Clutter	.111
(5)	Print warning-Pictorials-No Clutter	.444
(6)	Print warning-Pictorials-Clutter	.167
(7)	Voice warning only-Clutter	.611
(8)	Print warning-Voice warning-Clutter	.667
(9)	Print warning-Voice warning-Pictorials-Clutter	.722
(10)	Print warning-Strobe-Clutter	.222
(11)	Print warning-Pictorials-Strobe-Clutter	.278
(12)	Print warning-Voice warning-Pictorials-Strobe-Clutter	.833

Note. Control conditions 1 and 2 each had 9 participants. All other conditions had 18 participants.

held constant). In this particular analysis, a main effect of visual clutter was found, $F(1, 68) = 4.90$, $p < .05$. The presence of a cluttered environment ($M = .14$) significantly lowered compliance compared to the absence of clutter ($M = .36$). There was no effect of pictorials, nor was the interaction significant ($ps > .05$).

Every analysis involving the the voice warning showed significant effects ($ps < .0001$). As can be seen in Table 1, compliance in conditions with the voice warning present was substantially (and significantly) greater than comparable conditions with the voice warning absent. Voice did not interact with the other variables ($ps > .05$). In addition, no other significant effects were found in the analyses shown in Table 2 ($ps > .05$). Although the presence of pictorials and strobe appeared to show greater compliance compared to

TABLE 2

Planned 2 X 2 Tests

Independent Variables	Conditions
Print X Clutter	1, 2, 3, 4
Pictorials X Clutter	3, 4, 5, 6
Print X Voice	2, 4, 7, 8
Pictorials X Voice	4, 6, 8, 9
Pictorials X Strobe	4, 6, 10, 11
Voice X Strobe	6, 10, 9, 12

Note. All 2 X 2 analyses involved the manipulation of presence vs. absence of the independent variables. Condition numbers refer to the list in Table 1.

their absence, they never showed a significant effect. Analyses with greater statistical power were also performed. For the pictorials, a contrast compared conditions 5, 6, 9, and 11 (pictorials present) to conditions 3, 4, 8, 10 (pictorials absent). For the strobe, conditions 10, 11, and 12 (strobe present) were contrasted with conditions 4, 6, and 9 (strobe absent). However, neither contrast showed a significant effect (ps > .05).

Questionnaire analysis

Analysis of the questionnaire considered only the data for participants who were in the warning-present conditions (n = 180). The results showed that if participants complied with the warning, they also reported: (a) seeing the protective equipment (Φ = .45, p < .0001), (b) seeing or hearing a warning (Φ = .57, p < .0001), (c) believing the situation to be more hazardous (Φ = .36, p < .0001), and (d) being more careful (Φ = .28, p < .0001). There was no relation between accuracy and compliance (Φ = .004, p > .05).

For the questionnaire item asking what the warning said, memory for the content of the warning was scored in two ways, strictly and leniently. For the strict criterion, the warning message was divided into idea elements and one point was awarded for each element that was present in an answer. The accumulated points for each participant were then converted to proportion scores. For the lenient criterion, the entire response was scored as correct if there was some indication that a hazard was present or that there was some potential for harm. Both memory measures showed strong positive relations to compliance (r = .59 and Φ = .55, ps < .0001, for the strict and lenient criteria, respectively). The reliability of the scores was assessed by having another person who was unaware of conditions re-score a random sample of 30% of the responses (n = 59). Inter-rater agreement was calculated by dividing the number of agreements by the number of agreements plus disagreements and then multiplying by 100. Reliability was 94.1% and 98.3% for the strict and lenient scoring, respectively.

A similar pattern was found when comparing participants who complied or did not comply to the warning. Table 3 shows the means as a function of participant compliance. All comparisons between compliers and non-compliers were significant (ps < .0001) except for accuracy (p > .05).

A progressive drop was seen in the proportion of persons who reported seeing the protective equipment (M = .79), who reported seeing/hearing a warning (M = .59), and who actually complied with the warning (M = .43).

TABLE 3

Mean Proportions for Questionnaire Items as a Function of Participant Compliance

	see mask/ gloves	see/hear warning	hazard rating	careful rating	accuracy rating	strict memory	lenient memory
compliers	1.00	.91	2.86	4.66	3.91	.25	.71
non-compliers	.64	.34	1.39	3.20	3.90	.04	.17

DISCUSSION

The results showed that a warning sign placed in surrounding visual clutter is complied with less often than the same sign in a less cluttered surrounding. The implication is that the effectiveness of a warning depends on the context in which it is placed. This result supports a previously untested guideline that warning signs should stand out from the environment in order to attract attention (e.g., Cunitz, 1981; Peters, 1984, 1989; Wogalter et al., 1987). It also supports related research indicating that irrelevant visual stimuli reduces target detection (e.g., Cole & Hughes, 1984; Monk & Brown, 1975; Williams & Hoffmann, 1979).

The effect of visual clutter was probably enhanced by the sign's location relative to the participants' field of view. Although the warning could be clearly seen at the table and was within 1 m of the chemistry materials, it was not directly in front of them while standing at the table. Previous research indicates that warning location (Wogalter et al., 1987) and displacement of target stimuli away from the line of sight (outside the visual field) are important determinants of attention and search conspicuity (e.g., Monk & Brown, 1975). Additionally, an unpublished study in the first author's laboratory indicates that a warning placed in a set of written instructions is more often complied with than a similar warning placed on a nearby sign. Lowered compliance is probably due to the sign's separation from the participants' main field of view, reducing its noticeability.

The most striking finding was the large effect of the voice warning. Its power to influence compliance relative to the other variables indicates that voice warnings may be a very effective means of gaining behavioral compliance. This result supports the finding of Wogalter and Young (1991) showing greater compliance for voice warnings than comparable print warnings.

Although there was a tendency for greater compliance when the pictorials and strobe were present, no significant effects were found. The null finding for the pictorial is somewhat surprising given recent results by Jaynes and Boles (1990) who found that the presence of pictorials significantly increased compliance to a warning. One salient difference between the two studies is that Jaynes and Boles' warning (and pictorials) was placed in a set of printed instructions, whereas, it was on a sign in the current study. Pictorials may facilitate compliance only when the warning is placed in a visible location.

The failure to show an effect of the flashing light was also somewhat surprising because the flash rate (8 Hz) was within the acceptable range of most display guidelines (e.g., Mortimer & Kupec, 1983; Woodson & Conover, 1964). Two possible explanations can be offered. First, the strobe flashed for only a few seconds after being tripped by the participant entering the laboratory room. Second, the light was very intense. Although the on-duration of each flash cycle was very short, its illuminance was very high. Most participants looked in the direction of the sign when it started to flash, but almost immediately turned their head away (presumably because it was annoying and bright). Thus, while the strobe was able to attract attention, it did not hold attention. Had the flashing light been less luminous and the overall duration longer, it might have been an effective means of promoting compliance.

Compliance behavior was significantly related to memory of the warning, perception of hazard, and carefulness. These findings are not unexpected given that these are indications that the warning message was received. There was also a progressive drop in the proportion of participants who saw the protective equipment, who reported seeing/ hearing a warning, and who actually complied with the warning. Thus, there were more participants who were aware of the warning than who subsequently complied. A similar trend was noted by DeJoy (1989) in a review of other compliance research (Friedmann, 1988; Otsubo, 1988; Strawbridge 1986).

Finally, the potential advantages and disadvantages of voice warnings should be mentioned. The two foremost advantages are its attention-getting and omnidirectional qualities. Both are important considerations when visual attention is occupied and focused on other objects or tasks, as was case in the current study. In addition, reception of a voice warning does not necessarily require reorientation of attention away from a visual task as would be the case for a visually presented warning. In addition, voice warnings can provide, in a direct manner, specific hazard information (unlike simple nonverbal auditory warnings). Although complex *nonverbal* auditory warnings can inform, effective communication requires extensive training (Patterson & Milroy, 1980). Voice warnings do not require such training because they take advantage of people's verbal capabilities and their preexisting knowledge. Voice warnings can also benefit certain populations who have difficulty with printed language such as the blind and the illiterate.

However, there are some potential problems with the use of voice warnings. For example, voice warnings take time to be transmitted, and thus, very long messages should not be presented auditorily. In situations where many voice warnings could be activated, simultaneous presentation could make them virtually unintelligible. These disadvantages might be overcome by making the different messages and voices discriminable or by prioritizing the order of the messages. When large amounts of complex information must be communicated, the combination of a concise voice warning and a more complex print warning could be implemented. For example, a brief voice warning could be used to: (a) capture attention, (b) communicate the most important information concisely, and (c) cue the user to orient to a more detailed print warning. Where practical, redundant visual and voice warnings should be used so that when part of the voice message is missed, the full message can be reviewed visually.

Improvements in voice recognition and synthesis technology in recent years has made voice warnings more feasible by the development of voice generation chips and digitized sound processors. Together with the numerous kinds of tripping devices available to initiate a warning, voice warnings may be an effective means of gaining compliance in situations where a printed warning alone is inadequate.

REFERENCES

Cunitz, R. J. (1981). Psychologically effective warnings. *Hazard Prevention*, 17, 5-7.

DeJoy, D. M. (1989). Consumer product warnings: Review and analysis of effectiveness research. In *Proceedings of the Human Factors Society 33rd Annual Meeting* (pp. 936-940). Santa Monica, CA: Human Factors Society.

Friedmann, K. (1988). The effect of adding symbols to written warning labels on user behavior and recall. *Human Factors*, 30, 507-515.

Guzy (1991). Age and the perception of a modulating traffic signal light. In *Proceedings of the Human Factors Society 35th Annual Meeting*. Santa Monica, CA: Human Factors Society.

Jaynes, L.S., & Boles, D.B. (1990). The effects of symbols on warning compliance. In *Proceedings of the Human Factors Society 34th Annual Meeting* (pp. 984-987). Santa Monica, CA: Human Factors Society.

McCarthy, R. L., Finnegan, J. P., Krumm-Scott, S., & McCarthy, G. E. (1984). Product information presentation, user behavior, and safety. In *Proceedings of the Human Factors Society 28th Annual Meeting* (pp. 81-85). Santa Monica, CA: Human Factors Society.

Mortimer, R. G., & Kupec, J. D. (1983). Scaling of flash rate for a deceleration signal. *Human Factors*, 25, 313-218.

Otsubo, S. M. (1988). A behavioral study of warning labels for consumer products: Perceived danger and use of pictographs. In *Proceedings of the Human Factors Society 32nd Annual Meeting* (pp. 536-540). Santa Monica, CA: Human Factors Society.

Patterson, R. D., & Milroy, R. (1980). *Auditory warnings on civil aircraft: The learning and retention of warnings* (Civil Aviation Authority Contract 7D/S/0142). Cambridge, UK: MRC Applied Psychology Unit.

Peters, G. A. (1984). A challenge to the safety profession. *Professional Safety*, 29, 46-50.

Peters, G. A. (1989). Legal adequacy of warnings in risk information systems. *Products Liability Law Journal*, 1, 109-147.

Sanders, M. S., & McCormick, E J. (1987). *Human Factors in Engineering and Design* (6th Ed). New York: McGraw-Hill.

Saarela, K. L. (1989). A poster campaign for improving safety on shipyard scaffolds. *Journal of Safety Research*, 20, 177-185.

Strawbridge, J.A. (1986). The influence of position, highlighting, and imbedding on warning effectiveness. In *Proceedings of the Human Factors Society 30th Annual Meeting* (pp. 716-720). Santa Monica, CA: Human Factors Society.

Williams, M. J., & Hoffmann, E. R. (1979). Conspicuity of motorcycles. *Human Factors*, 21, 619-626.

Wogalter, M. S., Allison, S. T., & McKenna, N. A. (1989). The effects of cost and social influence on warning compliance. *Human Factors*, 31, 133-140.

Wogalter, M. S., & Barlow, T. (1990). Injury likelihood and severity in warnings. In *Proceedings of the Human Factors Society 34th Annual Meeting* (pp. 580-583). Santa Monica, CA: Human Factors Society.

Wogalter, M. S., Godfrey, S. S., Fontenelle, G. A., Desaulniers, D. R., Rothstein, P. R., & Laughery, K. R. (1987). Effectiveness of warnings. *Human Factors*, 29, 599-612.

Wogalter, M. S., & Young, S. L. (1991). Behavioural compliance to voice and print warnings. *Ergonomics* 34, 79-89.

INCREASING THE NOTICEABILITY OF WARNINGS: EFFECTS OF PICTORIAL, COLOR, SIGNAL ICON AND BORDER

Stephen L. Young

Rice University
Houston, Texas 77251

Because of the importance of noticeability on subsequent comprehension and compliance to warnings, guidelines suggest increasing the salience or conspicuity of warnings. Surprisingly, only a small amount of research has examined different methods of increasing the noticeability of warnings. Therefore, the current research orthogonally manipulated four salience variables (pictorial, color, signal icon and border) to determine their effect on noticeability of warning information. Subjects viewed 96 simulated alcohol labels on a computer, half with a warning and half without. Subjects indicated whether or not a warning was on the label and response latencies were recorded. The results showed that warnings containing a pictorial, color or an icon had significantly faster response times than warnings without them. However, the addition of a border did not improve response times. More detailed analyses showed interactions between the four salience manipulations. These results demonstrate that pictorials, color and icons can enhance the noticeability of warning information. Moreover, it is clear that these salience manipulations interact with each other and that they should not be used indiscriminately without adequate knowledge of these interactions.

To be effective warnings must be noticed, comprehended and followed. It is assumed that comprehension and compliance cannot occur until warnings are (at the very least) noticed. Based on this reasoning, guidelines for warning design suggest increasing the salience or conspicuity of warnings (Cunitz, 1981; Peters, 1984; Wogalter, Godfrey, Fontenelle, Desaulniers, Rothstein & Laughery, 1987). The present research examines four methods frequently recommended and commonly used to increase salience: pictorial, color, signal icon and border. Surprisingly, little research has been conducted examining the effect of these different methods on noticeability.

Pictorials have been suggested as a method of increasing the noticeability of warnings (FMC, 1985; Westinghouse Electric Corporation, 1981). Research demonstrates that pictorials do, in fact, increase the chance that a warning will be seen (Gill, Barbera & Precht, 1987; Laughery & Young, in press). Moreover, this increase in noticeability has been associated with an increase in comprehension and memory of a pictorial's associated warning message (Young & Wogalter, 1988; 1990). However, the enhanced noticeability afforded by pictorials has not always translated into increased behavioral compliance (Gill *et al*, 1987; Otsubo, 1988; Friedmann, 1988).

Color is another method commonly used to increase the noticeability of warnings. While there is more basic research supporting this suggestion than research directly related to warnings (e.g., Jones, 1962; Christ, 1975; Carter & Cahill, 1979), several warnings-related papers have shown beneficial effects of color on noticeability (Asper, 1972; Phillips & Noyes, 1980; Adams & Lien-tsang, 1981) and identification speed and accuracy (Ells, Dewar & Milloy, 1980). These findings support the notion that color can be used effectively to increase the chance that a warning will be seen.

Less research exists regarding the beneficial effect of signal icons. Only two papers could be found evaluating the effectiveness of signal icons relative to their absence. They found that the presence of an icon produced a significant decrease in task completion time and task errors (Zlotnik, 1982) and time to detect a warning (Laughery & Young, in press). In all of the other research dealing with signal icons, there is no experimental manipulation of icons. Rather, they are included simply because they are part of current standards put forth by ANSI (1987) and FMC (1985). While there is not an overwhelming amount of research regarding the role of signal icons in warning recognition, it is likely that the presence of icons will improve performance relative to their absence.

The final prominent method of increasing the salience of a warning message is the use of a surrounding border. As with signal icons, little research has examined the effect of borders on noticeability. Of the research that does exist, no effect (Zlotnik, 1982) or negative effects of border (Laughery & Young, in press) have been found.

Some of these methods of increasing noticeability have more empirical support than others. However, the prevalent use of these four methods in practice, as well as intuition, suggest that all of them *can* increase the noticeability of warnings. What is lacking, besides a consensus of experimental support for each method, is knowledge of the possible interactions between these methods. In order to accomplish both goals, the current research examines the orthogonal effect of these four salience manipulations (pictorial, color, signal icon and border) on noticeability of warnings for simulated alcohol labels.

METHOD

Subjects

Seventy-two subjects were recruited from the Houston community by Telesurveys, Inc., an independent telephone survey company. Selection was random with the stipulation that subjects be equally distributed across ethnic group (black, hispanic and white), gender and age (less than 25 years old, between 26 and 40 years old and over 40 years old). Subjects were paid twenty-five dollars for participating.

Materials

Ninety-six "alcohol labels" were constructed for fictitious beer, wine and liquor products. Half of the labels contained a warning and half did not. The only warning used was the Government Warning, which was mandated for alcohol containers in the U.S. as of November, 1989. Each label (17.5 cm x 23.5 cm) contained 5 "zones" or block-areas that could contain information (see Figure 1). Zone 1 always contained the brand logo and Zone 2 was always printed vertically from top to bottom. Only Zones 2, 3 and 4 could contain the warning. Figure 2 shows an example label with a warning in Zone 4. The non-warning information included material on the ingredients used, the importer, the brewery, nutritional content, and bar code information. The labels were presented with SuperCard (Silicon Beach Software) on an Apple MacIntosh IIcx with an Apple 12" RGB color monitor.

The warning was orthogonally manipulated in four ways. First, an associated pictorial was present to the left of the warning or it was absent. Second, the warning was printed in red (different color) or it was printed in black (same color). The color red was chosen because it has been shown to be very discriminable (Bloomfield, 1979) and is a "stereotype" color for hazards (Easterby & Hakiel, 1977). When color was used, the entire warning and everything associated with it was printed in red and nothing else on the label was red. Third, an icon was present above the warning or it was absent. Finally, a border was placed around the warning or the border was absent. The warning appeared in each of the three zones an equal number of times. This factorial combination (3x2x2x2x2) produced 48

Figure 1. Division of stimulus field into zones

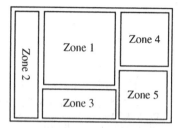

different warning configurations. The 48 labels without warnings were manipulated in the same way as the labels with warnings, except a different non-warning icon and pictorial were used.

Procedure

Subjects were administered a reading test to determine their ability to read and understand English. They were then given a questionnaire to gain demographic information, as well as information regarding their knowledge, attitudes and beliefs concerning alcohol and alcohol consumption. If a subject scored below 50% on the reading test, the experimenter read the questionnaire aloud and recorded subject's answers. After finishing the questionnaire, subjects viewed 96 simulated alcohol labels on the computer, one at a time. For each label, subjects indicated whether a warning was present by pressing a button labeled "Yes" (warning present) or a different button labeled "No" (warning absent). After pressing either button, the computer's internal timer stopped and the screen turned white (blank) for 4 seconds. After 4 seconds, an "X" appeared in the middle of the screen, alerting the subject that the next label would appear within one second. Subjects were instructed to focus on the "X" until the subsequent

Figure 2. Example label with warning in Zone 4

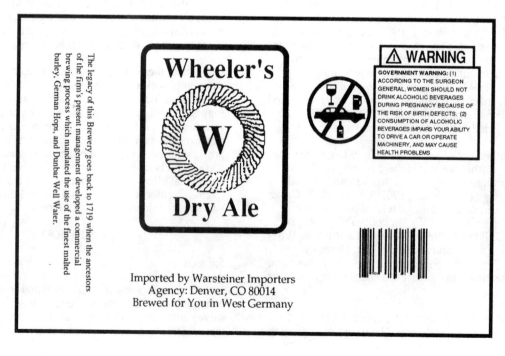

label appeared and then to start searching for the warning. Each subject was presented a different random order of the labels.

RESULTS

The first analysis examined subject differences (gender, age and ethnic group) in mean response times. A 2 (male vs. female) x 3 (younger vs. middle vs. older age) x 3 (black vs. hispanic vs. white) analysis of variance (ANOVA) was performed on mean time to find the warning (collapsed across all conditions with a warning). The only significant result obtained was a main effect of ethnic group, $F(2, 54) = 4.67, p < .02$. A Newman-Keuls post-hoc test showed that hispanics ($m = 3446$ ms) had significantly longer mean response times than either blacks ($m = 2198$ ms) or whites ($m = 1972$ ms). A 3 (ethnic group) x 2 (pictorial) x 2 (color) x 2 (signal icon) x 2 (border) ANOVA was performed to determine the nature of the ethnic differences. Ethnic group did not interact with any of the other manipulations, suggesting that the salience variables had the same effect on all three ethnic groups. It seems that the *overall* times for the hispanics were simply longer. One possible explanation for this finding is that these hispanic subjects had lower scores on the reading test administered prior to the experiment ($m = 51\%$ correct) than did the black ($m = 66\%$ correct, $p > .05$) or white subjects ($m = 89\%$ correct, $p < .01$). No other subject differences were found.

The next set of analyses examined differences between the orthogonally manipulated salience variables on response latencies (from the onset of the label to the response). Scores were collapsed across location and a 2 (pictorial present vs. absent) x 2 (color present vs. absent) x 2 (icon present vs. absent) x 2 (border present vs. absent) within-subjects ANOVA was performed on the labels containing warnings. Warnings with a pictorial ($m = 2475$ ms) produced significantly faster responses than warnings without a pictorial ($m = 2642$ ms), $F(1, 71) = 8.15, p < .01$. Warnings printed in red ($m = 2469$ ms) were located more quickly than warnings printed in black ($m = 2648$ ms), $F(1, 71) = 7.02, p < .01$. Warnings paired with an icon ($m = 2474$ ms) were located more quickly than warnings without an icon ($m = 2643$ ms), $F(1, 71) = 8.02, p < .01$. However, pairing a warning with a border ($m = 2517$ ms) produced a non-significant decrease in response latencies over warnings without a border ($m = 2601$ ms), $F(1, 71) = 1.75, p > .05$.

A more detailed examination showed only two interactions between the four manipulations. The first was between color and icon, $F(1, 71) = 5.94, p < .02$. The addition of an icon improved performance when the warning was printed in black (from 2805 ms to 2492 ms), but when the warning was printed in red, the addition of an icon produced a non-significant decrease in response latencies (from 2481 ms to 2457 ms). The only other interaction was pictorial x color x icon, $F(1, 71) = 10.87, p < .01$ (see Figures 3 and 4). When a pictorial was present, the addition of an icon facilitated performance regardless of the color of print (Figure 3). However, when no pictorial was present (Figure 4), the addition of an icon produced a significant improvement in performance, but only with black print. When color (red print) was used, there was a marginal *decrement* in response latencies with the addition of an icon, $F(1, 71) = 3.19, p = .08$.

Figure 3. Color by icon with pictorial.

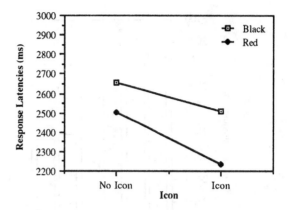

Figure 4. Color by icon with no pictorial.

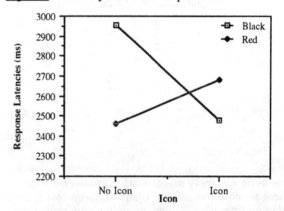

The final analysis compared the individual conditions with the baseline warning (the warning with none of the salience manipulations, see Figure 5). The baseline warning produced the second longest latency ($m = 2914$ ms). Non-significant improvements in response times over the baseline were observed with the singular addition of a pictorial ($m = 2795$ ms, $p > .05$), color ($m = 2580$ ms, $p = .08$) and an icon ($m = 2532$ ms, $p = .052$). The singular addition of a border to the baseline ($m = 2992$ ms) produced the longest latency of all the conditions. The combination of a pictorial, color and an icon ($m = 2217$ ms) produced the greatest improvement over the baseline, $F(1, 71) = 13.06, p < .001$. The addition of a border to this combination ($m = 2251$ ms) produced a non-significant decrement in response time ($m = 2292$ ms, $p > .05$).

DISCUSSION

These results demonstrate that pictorials, color and icons can enhance the noticeability of warning information. It has also been shown that a border does not affect time to find a warning in a visual field. However, when considering application of these findings to real-world labels, the limitations of the current research must be kept in mind. Limitations regarding the individual salience manipulations are presented under their respective heading, but two general ones may be presented here. First, these "labels" were presented by a computer and thus were not real labels at all. A label metaphor was used only to make the stimuli more "reasonable" or realistic. Therefore, it *could* be said that

<u>Figure 5</u>. Response latencies for the individual salience conditions.

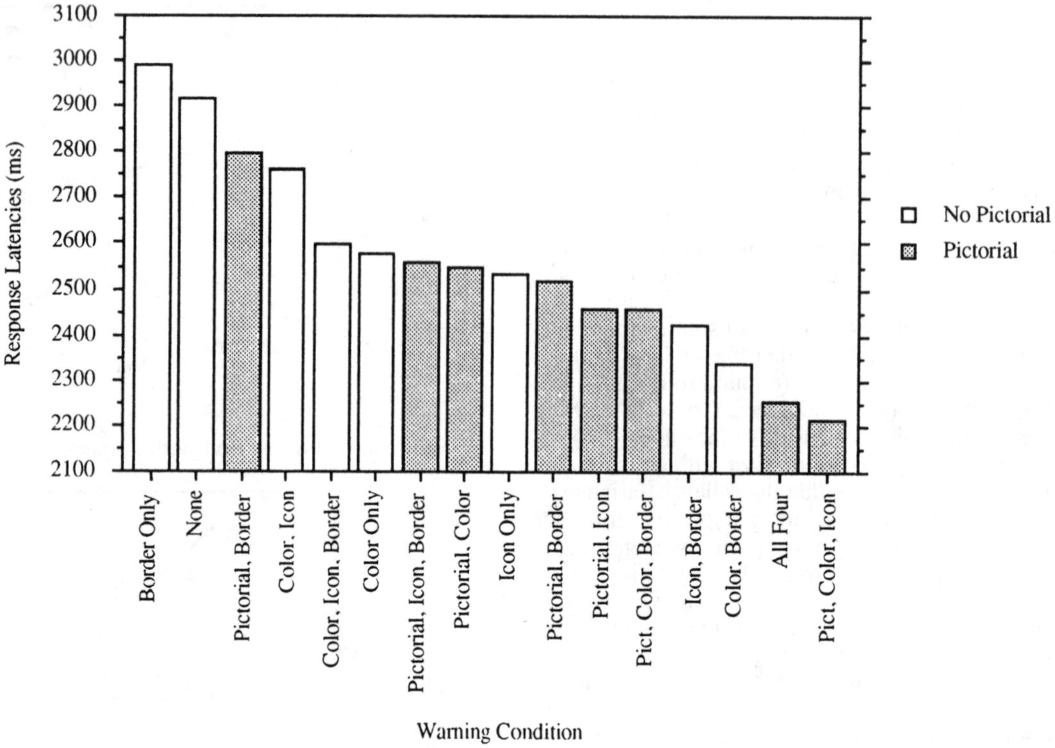

these results do not apply to real-world alcohol containers. Since there are no actual alcohol labels which employ these manipulations orthogonally, their effect for actual container labels must to be inferred from the existing research. Given that the present findings confirm previous research (which used different stimuli), it is expected that these results are valid and will apply to real-world labels.

Second, this research deals with recognition time as a measure of noticeability, which is merely one component of warning effectiveness. Other important considerations include readability, comprehension, etc. These kinds of issues are not addressed in the current research. Thus, it is suggested that noticeability should not be the only criterion by which a warning is selected for use.

Pictorials

The use of a pictorial was shown to have a beneficial effect on noticeability with these stimuli, supporting previous research (Laughery & Young, in press; Gill *et al*, 1987). However, it should be noted that one pictorial was used in this study and it represented only one of many possible content areas with regard to alcohol hazards. While the content of the pictorial may not have made as much (or any) difference in this study, it would most likely influence results if measures other than noticeability were examined.

It should also be noted that pictorials are different than the other salience manipulations. In addition to attracting attention, they convey information pictorially. Thus, they possess unique qualities which can benefit special user-groups, like illiterates or non-English speakers. These aspects of pictorials, while not addressed in this study,

should be considered when designing warnings. In light of the many different benefits associated with pictorials, it appears that their inclusion would be worth serious consideration in any system of warning design.

Color

Color also improved performance relative to its absence. The findings regarding color in this study should not be taken as a blanket-suggestion that warnings should be printed in red and not black. Although red has been shown to be a highly discriminable color that is often associated with warnings, the effect of color found here is probably due to the fact that the color warning was the only red item in the visual display. Previous research has shown that the total number of colors in a visual field, as well as the number of different colors, determines the effectiveness of color as a cue (Carter & Cahill, 1979). Thus, similar findings may be observed with other colors, given the same circumstances.

Signal Icon

The use of a signal icon improved performance compared to its absence. The signal word "Warning" was used in this study. Other signal words are frequently used in the warnings domain (Danger, Caution, Note, etc.), but it is not likely that the use of a different one would have affected these results.

Border

The inability of the border to improve response times in this study is in keeping with the previous research showing

252

no effect or even negative effects of border manipulations (Zlotnik, 1982; Laughery & Young, in press). The present border result can likely be explained by a psychological phenomenon known as *contour interaction*. This phenomenon states that closely adjacent contours can reduce the legibility of words (Anderton & Cole, 1982). Thus, the tight fit of the border around the warning text (in this case) may have interfered with discrimination of the text inside the border. It should not be concluded from the present study that borders are always detrimental to noticeability. These results merely suggest that, if borders are to (or can) have *any* beneficial effect, they must be used properly. If the contour of the border were farther away from the text, there is reason to suspect that borders would improve response times. However, because of the generally limited amount of space on alcohol labels, it seemed more valid to use the close-fitting border for the warnings in this study.

When it comes to recommending which of these salience manipulations to use, there are no simple answers. The fastest mean recognition time was found for the warning with a pictorial, color and an icon. However, the use of these three may not always be feasible because of space or economic considerations. Other combinations produce very similar times and may be just as adequate. If a pictorial, color and an icon cannot be used together, then care must be exercised when choosing a different combination of these variables. It has been demonstrated in this study that "more" is not necessarily better. For example, color was shown to be a generally effective method of increasing warning salience. However, this does not mean that color should be used indiscriminantly. The interaction of color with pictorial and icon demonstrated that, in some cases, color is harmful. The importance to designers of warnings and warning systems is clear: the noticeability of warnings can be increased, but the method by which this is carried out must be chosen carefully.

REFERENCES

Adams, A. S. & Lien-tsang, H. (1981). The coding of symbol signs. *Hazard Prevention*. 5-7.

American National Standards Institute (1987). ANSI Z535.2-Draft-1987: *American National Standard for Environmental and Facility Safety Signs*. New York.

Anderton, P. J. & Cole, B. L. (1982). Contour separation and sign legibility. *Australian Road Research, 12*, 103-109.

Asper, O. (1972). The detectability of two slow vehicle warning devices. *Journal of Safety Research, 4*, 85-89.

Bloomfield, J. R. (1979). Visual search with embedded targets: Color and texture differences. *Human Factors, 21*, 317-330.

Carter, R. C. & Cahill, M. C. (1979). Regression models for search time for color-coded information displays. *Human Factors, 21*, 293-302.

Christ, R. E. (1975). Review and analysis of color coding research for visual displays. *Human Factors, 17*, 542-570.

Cunitz, R. J. (1981). Psychologically effective warnings. *Hazard Prevention, 17*, 5-7.

Easterby, R. S. & Hakiel, S. R. (1977). *Safety Labelling of Consumer Products: Shape and Colour Code Stereotypes in the Design of Signs*. AP Report No. 75. College House, Gosta Green, Birmingham, B4 7ET, University of Aston, December 1977.

Ells, J. G., Dewar, R. E. & Milloy, D. G. (1980). An evaluation of six configurations of the railway crossbuck sign. *Ergonomics, 23*, 359-367.

FMC (1985). *Product Safety Sign and Label System*. Santa Clara, CA: FMC Corporation.

Friedmann, K. (1988). The effect of adding symbols to written warning labels on user behavior and recall. *Human Factors, 30*, 507-515.

Gill, R. T., Barbera, C. & Precht, T. (1987). A comparative evaluation of warning label designs. In *Proceedings of the Human Factors Society 31st Annual Meeting*. Santa Monica: The Human Factors Society, 476-478.

Jones, M. R. (1962). Color coding. *Human Factors, 4*, 355-365.

Laughery, K. R. & Young, S. L. (in press). Consumer product warnings: Design factors that influence noticeability. In *Proceeding of the 11th Congress International Ergonomics Association*.

Otsubo, S. M. (1988). A behavioral study of warning labels for consumer products: Perceived danger and use of pictographs. In *Proceedings of the Human Factors Society - 32nd Annual Meeting*. Santa Monica, CA: The Human Factors Society, 536-540.

Peters, G. A. (1984). 15 cardinal principles to ensure effectiveness of warning system. *Occupational Health and Safety*. 76-79.

Phillips, R. J. & Noyes, L. (1980). A comparison of colour and visual texture as codes for use as area symbols on thematic maps. *Ergonomics, 23*, 1117-1128.

Westinghouse Electric Corporation. (1981). *Product Safety Label Handbook*. Trafford, PA: Westinghouse Printing Division.

Wogalter, M. S., Godfrey, S. S., Fontenelle, G. A., Desaulniers, D. R., Rothstein, P. R. & Laughery, K. R. (1987). Effectiveness of warnings. *Human Factors, 29*, 599-612.

Young, S. L. & Wogalter, M. S. (1988). Memory of instruction manual warnings: Effects of pictorial icons and conspicuous print. In *Proceedings of the Human Factors Society - 32nd Annual Meeting*. Santa Monica, CA: The Human Factors Society, 905-909.

Young, S. L. & Wogalter, M. S. (1990). Effects of conspicuous print and pictorial icons on comprehension and memory of instruction manual warnings. *Human Factors, 32*, 637-649.

Zlotnik, M. A. (1982). The effects of warning message highlighting on novel assembly task performance. In *Proceedings of the Human Factors Society - 26th Annual Meeting*. Santa Monica: The Human Factors Society, 93-97.

MEMORY OF INSTRUCTION MANUAL WARNINGS:
EFFECTS OF PICTORIAL ICONS AND CONSPICUOUS PRINT

Stephen L. Young and Michael S. Wogalter
Psychology Department, University of Richmond
Richmond, Virginia 23173

ABSTRACT

The present research sought to determine whether the salience of warning messages would improve the memory of warnings in proceduralized instructions. Subjects studied one of four instruction manuals for a gas-powered electric generator under the guise that they would later operate the generator. In the manual, the appearance of eight different warning messages were altered in two ways: 1) The verbal messages were printed in either conspicuous print (larger with color highlighting) or in plain print (same as the other text). 2) The verbal warning messages were either accompanied by meaningfully-related icons or the icons were absent. Three kinds of memory tests were given to subjects. The results showed that subjects who received the manual containing Conspicuous Print, Icons Present warnings recalled the verbal warning content and the semantic meaning of the icons significantly better than subjects who received one of the other three manuals. Implications for the design of instruction manual warnings are discussed.

INTRODUCTION

Most electrical and gas powered devices are accompanied by an owner's instruction manual. In addition to a description of the correct operation of the device, the manuals often contain warnings. The warnings are intended to provide information on the nature of the potential hazards and ways to avoid injury to person and machine. Users may not read the manual and the accompanying warnings, but there is evidence that people are likely to read warnings for hazardous products (e.g., Godfrey, Allender, Laughery, & Smith, 1983; Wogalter, Desaulniers, & Brelsford, 1986).

Reading the manual and warnings does not, in and of itself, ensure that the warnings will be remembered at a later time. Since consumers may not always have the manual available when they use a hazardous product, it would seem important that instruction manual warnings be constructed in a manner most conducive for enhancing memory of the warnings. For this reason, research on user memory and recall of consumer product warnings is important. However, research on variables that affect memory of warnings is scarce (Lehto & Miller, 1986). Either no effect or very small effects of warning manipulations on memory has been reported (Desaulniers, 1987; Rothstein, 1985; Strawbridge, 1986; Zlotnik, 1982).

Intuitive reasoning suggests that if a warning is not noticed or seen, it cannot be remembered. Improving the chance that warnings will be noticed (i.e., through increased visibility or salience) should lead to more effective encoding and thus produce better memory and recall of warnings. Simply put, one possible way of enhancing memory is to make the warning more conspicuous.

Virtually every set of published guidelines on warnings emphasizes the characteristic of attention-getting (Cunitz, 1981; Peters, 1984; Wogalter, Godfrey, Fontenelle, Desaulniers, Rothstein, & Laughery, 1987). Warnings should stand out from a noisy background. Although several recent studies have shown that warning salience facilitates behavioral compliance, we have been unable to find any published research on the effects of warning conspicuity on memory. Zlotnik (1982), for example, embedded highlighted warnings which were blocked, cross-hatched, and multidimensionally printed (2-D vs. 3-D) in a set of procedural instructions. He was able to show that highlighting affected subjects' task behavior but the manipulation did not yield effects on memory. The present research reexamines the possibility that salient text facilitates memory. We expect readers will be more likely to notice and read conspicuously printed warnings, which in turn, should lead to better subsequent memory compared to the same warnings printed less conspicuously.

Another possible way of making warning messages more salient and more memorable is to include icons (symbols or pictograms). Dorris and Purswell (1978) conjectured that, in many situations, icons may be recognized more rapidly and may be more effective at conveying information about a potential hazard than a verbal message. However, Robinett and Hughes (1984) point out that, because of the complex nature of many hazards, icons cannot realistically exist by themselves as a method of communicating hazard information. In most situations, icons must be paired with written warning messages. So, in addition to the attention-getting characteristics of icons, the presence of icons might enhance memory in another way. By pairing icons and verbal warnings, they become associated in memory, and thus at reexposure, the icon might facilitate recall by cuing the warning message from memory.

The present research seeks to determine whether the salience of warning messages would improve the memory and recall of warnings in a set of operational instructions. Specifically, it is hypothesized that the inclusion of icons and the use of conspicuous print will enhance memory of warnings.

METHOD

Subjects

Sixty-four undergraduate students from the University of Richmond voluntarily participated in the experiment for credit in an introductory psychology course.

Materials

Four instruction manuals concerning the operation and maintenance of a gas-powered electric generator were prepared. This product was chosen for three reasons: 1) For most persons, it is an unfamiliar piece of equipment. 2) This product poses some risk of injury. 3) And since the generator is designed for use in a power outage, it will have to be safely operated in conditions in which it is impractical or impossible to reference an instruction manual (e.g., in rain or absence of light).

The basic ten-page manual was an adaption of several manufacturers' manuals and had the appearance of an actual owner's manual. The text of the manuals were printed in 12-point Helvetica font (except for the section headings which were in bold). It contained sections on the generator's operation and maintenance as well as detailed drawings of the generator. Each manual contained eight warnings. The warnings were either in plain or conspicuous print. Warnings printed in plain print had the same appearance as the other textual print in the manual. Conspicuous print warnings were printed in an 18-point Times font and were covered with transparent orange fluorescent highlighting. The warnings were accompanied by meaningfully-related icons or the icons were absent. The icons were obtained from an icon evaluation report by

Collins, Lerner, and Pierman (1982). Nine icons were used, one for each of the eight warnings, except for one warning about a potential gas explosion which had two icons paired with it. Thus, there were four manuals constructed to have have warnings in: 1) Conspicuous Print, Icons Present, 2) Conspicuous Print, Icons Absent, 3) Plain Print, Icons Present, and 4) Plain Print, Icons Absent. Figure 1 shows an example warning and the ways it was manipulated in the manuals.

Three tests were used to assess subject's memory of the warnings: a content question test, an icon recognition test, and an icon definition test. The content question test consisted of ten short answer questions. One question was created for each of the eight warnings. Each dealt with some aspect of the semantic content of the warning message (e.g., "What is the potential result of running the generator with the choke OPEN?"). The other two questions in the test dealt with operational aspects of the generator and were not analyzed. The icon recognition test consisted of 36 randomly placed icons and a numbered response sheet . Nine of the icons were actually used in the manuals; these were the target icons. (Note that two icons were used for one of the eight verbal warning messages). The test set also included nine icons which were similar in name and content to the target icons but were graphically different. The other 18 icons were 'pure' distractors. These were

---

Figure 1. Example of a Warning as a function of Conspicuous Print and Icons

Plain Print, Icons Absent

Warning: To prevent electric shock from faulty appliances, the generator should be grounded. Connect a length of heavy wire between the ground terminal and the ground source.

Plain Print, Icons Present

Warning: To prevent electric shock from faulty appliances, the generator should be grounded. Connect a length of heavy wire between the ground terminal and the ground source.

Conspicuous Print, Icons Absent

Warning: To prevent electric shock from faulty appliances, the generator should be grounded. Connect a length of heavy wire between the ground terminal and the ground source.

Conspicuous Print, Icons Present

Warning: To prevent electric shock from faulty appliances, the generator should be grounded. Connect a length of heavy wire between the ground terminal and the ground source.

Note: Shading represents orange highlighting.

icons that were not used in the manual. Nine of these 'pure' distractors had the same basic meaning as the other nine 'pure' distractors but were graphically different. In the icon definition test, the nine icons used in the manuals were placed on a blank sheet. Space was provided next to each for the subjects' responses.

Procedure

Subjects were given an instruction manual on the operation and maintenance of a gas-powered electric generator. Subjects read the manual under the expectation that they would later use the product. This was an attempt to have a more ecologically valid procedure than one using intentional memory instructions. Subjects were told that they were to learn about the generator so that they could operate it from memory later in the session. The premise that subjects would have to operate the generator was enhanced by their participation in another experiment just prior to the present study in which subjects solved a series of computer tasks using instructions. The impression given to the subjects was that the first experiment was a test of their ability to operate a complicated appliance with the instructions present, and that the generator manual task was a test of their ability to operate an appliance with the instructions absent (i.e., from memory).

At the end of a four minute study period, all subjects were told that they were in the "control" group and would not be operating the generator. They were instead given the three tests of their memory of the warnings in the following order: 1) content questions, 2) icon recognition, and 3) icon definition. In the content question test, subjects answered questions regarding each warning in the manual. In the icon recognition test, the subject's task was to recognize the nine icons used in the manuals with icons from a total of 36 randomly ordered icons. For each icon, subjects placed a "Y" (Yes, the icon was in the manual) or an "N" (No, the icon was not in the manual) at the corresponding number on the icon recognition sheet. Subjects also indicated their confidence in their answers by placing a "1" (guessed the answer), "2" (fairly sure of the answer), or "3" (very sure of the answer). The icon definition test required subjects to describe the verbal meaning of the icons used in the manuals. The subjects were instructed to write their response with specific reference to the instruction manual, but to guess if necessary. All tests sheets were graded without knowledge of which condition the subject participated.

A comment should be made regarding some of the peculiarities of the testing procedure. The three tests were given in a fixed order (i.e., not counterbalanced). The reason for this was, in part, because we were most interested in recall of semantic content as a function of format. To avoid possible carry-over effects, the content question test was always given first. The other two tests were constructed and given in an order that had the least potential for carry-over. All subjects were required to take the two icon tests regardless of whether or not they were exposed to a manual containing icons.

RESULTS

The data were initially analyzed using a set of planned comparisons between the Conspicuous Print, Icons Present

condition and the other three conditions. 2 X 2 between-subjects analyses of variance (ANOVAs) were used in addition to the planned comparisons because we were also interested in whether each of the modes of salience would, by itself, facilitate memory and whether together their influence changes.

Content Questions

The answers for the warning content questions were graded twice according to strict and liberal grading criteria. The strict grading criterion required that subjects include certain "key words" or specific details of the manual's warnings in their answer. The liberal grading criterion required that subjects convey the general meaning of the warning message. Correct answers for both criteria were scored as "1" and incorrect answers were scored as "0".

Table 1 shows the mean proportion correct scores for the warning message content questions using the strict and liberal criteria. The strict criteria scores are lower than the liberal criteria scores, but the pattern is similar for both measures. It is apparent from the table that the Conspicuous Print, Icons Present condition produced greater performance than the other three instruction manual conditions.

TABLE 1. Mean Proportion Correct as a Function of Warning Format for Verbal Content Questions

	Conspic Print Icons Pres	Conspic Print Icons Abs	Plain Print Icons Pres	Plain Print Icons Abs
STRICT	.47	.27	.32	.26
LIBERAL	.75	.56	.58	.53

Planned comparisons using the strict grading scores showed that subjects who read the manual with the Conspicuous Print, Icons Present warnings performed significantly better than subjects who read Conspicuous Print, Icons Absent, $t(30) = 3.34$, $p < .01$, and Plain Print, Icons Absent warning manuals, $t(30) = 3.38$, $p < .01$, and were marginally better than subjects who read the Plain Print, Icons Present warning manual, $t(30) = 1.95$, $p = .06$. For the liberal graded scores, the Conspicuous Print, Icons Present warning manual condition was significantly higher than the Conspicuous Print, Icons Absent, $t(30) = 3.03$, $p < .01$, the Plain Print, Icons Present, $t(30) = 2.26$, $p < .04$, and the Plain Print, Icons Absent conditions, $t(30) = 4.12$, $p < .001$.

An overall ANOVA on the strict data yielded a significant main effect of the icons, $F(1, 60) = 7.53$, $MSe = .038$, $p < .01$. Performance was higher when icons were present (.40) than when they were not present (.26). Neither the effect of conspicuous print alone nor the interaction was significant, $F(1, 60) = 2.67$, $p > .05$, and $F(1, 60) = 2.07$, $p > .05$, respectively.

The ANOVA on the liberal data yielded a significant main effect of the icons, $F(1, 60) = 6.28$, $MSe = .038$, $p <$

.02. Performance was higher when icons were present (.66) than when they were not present (.54). There was also a significant main effect of conspicuous print, F (1, 60) = 4.07, p < .05. Recall of the verbal content of the warning message was significantly greater with conspicuous print (.65) than with plain print (.55). The interaction was not significant, F (1, 60) = 1.92, p > .05.

Icon Recognition Test

Subjects' responses from the icon recognition test were examined a number of ways. Responses to the target icons (ones that appeared in the manual) were scored as hits (1's for "yes" responses) or misses (0's for "no" responses) to produce proportion hit scores. In addition, targets responses were converted to a confidence ratings which ranged from 1 to 6 ("N3" was assigned "1", "N2" assigned a "2", and so on, to "Y3" assigned "6"). A number of other recognition measures were also examined. The recognition test contained target-related distractors (similar in meaning to the target icons) and target-unrelated distractors. Scores on these sets of icons were examined separately and in combination. Moreover, a series of discrimination measures were derived for the purpose of eliminating response criteria effects from the target and distractor measures. The discrimination measures were target-distractor difference scores.

Planned comparisons were made between the Conspicuous Print, Icon Present condition and the Plain Print, Icon Present condition. We expected that between the two conditions containing icons, the conspicuous print version would yield greater recognition performance than the plain print manual. This was not found. None of the measures showed a significant effect of conspicuous print on icon recognition (all p's > .05). As expected, for all recognition measures, subjects who read manuals with icons present had significantly better recognition performance than subjects who saw no icons in the manual (all p's < .05). There were no other effects yielded by any of the ANOVAs on these data (p's > .05).

Icon Definition Test

The icon definition test was graded using both strict and liberal criteria. Under the strict grading criterion, subjects had to describe not only the inherent meaning of the icon, but also needed to be specific to the associated warning in the manual. Under the liberal grading criterion, subjects needed to convey only the general meaning of the icon. Correct answers were scored as "1" and incorrect answers were scored as "0".

Table 2 shows the mean proportion correct under the strict and liberal grading criteria. The table shows that greatest performance was produced by manuals containing Conspicuous Print, Icons Present warnings compared to the other three manuals. Planned comparisons using the strict scores showed that icon definitions were significantly more accurate for subjects reading the Conspicuous Print, Icons Present manual than the Conspicuous Print, Icons Absent, t (30) = 3.09, p < .01, the Plain Print, Icons Present, t (30) = 2.47, p < .02, and the Plain Print, Icons Absent manuals, t (30) = 5.52, p < .001. For the liberal graded data, the definitions produced by subjects reading the Conspicuous Print, Icons Present manuals were

significantly better than for subjects who read the Conspicuous Print, Icons Absent, t (30) = 3.25, p < .01, and the Plain Print, Icons Absent manuals, t (30) = 2.30, p < .03, but only marginally better than those who read the Plain Print, Icons Present manual, t (30) = 1.87, p < .08.

TABLE 2. Mean Proportion Correct as a Function of Warning Format for Icon Definitions

	Conspic Print Icons Pres	Conspic Print Icons Abs	Plain Print Icons Pres	Plain Print Icons Abs
STRICT	.48	.21	.26	.10
LIBERAL	.93	.81	.86	.85

Overall analyses using a 2 X 2 ANOVA on the strict data yielded a significant main effect of the icons, F (1, 60) = 15.10, MSe = .049, p < .001. Performance was higher when icons were present (.37) than when they were absent (.15). There was also a significant main effect of conspicuous print, F (1, 60) = 9.16, p < .004. Recall of the verbal content of the warning message was significantly greater with conspicuous print (.34) than with plain print (.18). The interaction was not significant, F (1, 60) = 1.01, p > .05.

The ANOVA on the liberal data yielded a significant main effect of the icons, F (1, 60) = 7.01, MSe = .011, p < .02. Performance was higher when icons were present (.40) than when they were absent (.26). Conspicuous print did not yield a main effect, F (1, 60) < 1.0, but it did enter into an interaction with icons, F (1, 60) = 4.49, p < .05. Performance was facilitated by the presence of icons when the warnings were printed conspicuously. The presence vs. absence of icons did not affect performance for warnings in plain print.

DISCUSSION

The present results show that increased salience of warnings enhances memory of their content. Presumably the reason for the facilitation is that salient warnings lead readers to notice and attend to the warnings. For both verbal warning messages and icon definitions, the presence of both icons and conspicuous print was found to produce memory performance that was higher than either method of salience alone or when both were absent.

In all three memory tests, the presence of icons improved performance over conditions with icons absent. Not only was facilitation seen for memory of the icons themselves but also for the icons' associated warning messages.

The effect of conspicuous print was smaller. The presence of conspicuous print showed a beneficial effect using the liberal graded warning content and strict graded icon definition measures. Conspicuous print also interacted with icons using the liberal icon definition measure. However, there was no effect of conspicuous print shown by the strict graded content measure, nor was there an additional benefit of conspicuous print for warnings containing icons using the recognition or liberal graded icon definition measures.

The icon recognition test produced results that were not particularly interesting. As expected, subjects who were exposed to icons had greater recognition performance than subjects who did not have icons in the manual. However, the possibility that the presence of conspicuous print with icons might facilitate icon recognition over the version with plain print and icons was not confirmed.

The icon definition test addressed the extent to which the icons cue memory of the verbal warning message. The strict criterion scores suggest that subjects were better able to recall the meaning of icons when they had previously viewed the icons paired with conspicuously printed warnings than subjects who had seen the icons paired with plain print warnings. This facilitated ability of the icon to cue hazard information when originally paired with salient text would be important in situations where the icon is seen very briefly or alone. Here the icon must cue the user to the kind of hazard present without reference to the written warning message. Our results suggest that an initial simultaneous presentation of the icon and saliently printed warning text enhances the icon's ability to cue recall of the warning message.

The present research has implications for writers of instruction manuals. Manuals should be designed in a way that readers will notice and attend to the warnings. The present results suggest that the way the warnings are presented in a manual affects memory of the warning's message. Memory of warning information is important because users of hazardous equipment may not have the manual present/available at the time of product use. Our results suggest that the inclusion of both icons and conspicuously printed warnings promote better memory of warnings. The implication for instruction manual design is clear: Warnings should be made salient.

Finally, a comment should be made regarding the generality of the present results. We examined the effect of warning salience using a manual for only one product. Future research should examine whether the effects shown here also hold for other products and manuals. For example, the effects of warning salience might be dependent on such factors as the type of product and consumer familiarity.

REFERENCES

Collins, B. L., Lerner, N. D., & Pierman, B. C. (1982). *Symbols for industrial safety.* (Tech. Report NBSIR 82-2485). Washington, DC: U.S. Department of Commerce.

Cunitz, R. J. (1981). Psychologically effective warnings. *Hazard Prevention, 17,* 5-7.

Desaulniers, D. R. (1987). Layout, organization, and the effectiveness of consumer product warnings. In *Proceedings of the Human Factors Society 31st Annual Meeting* (pp. 56-60). Santa Monica, CA: The Human Factors Society.

Dorris, A. L., & Purswell, J. L. (1978). Human factors in the design of effective product warnings. In *Proceedings of the Human Factors Society 22nd Annual Meeting* (pp. 343-346). Santa Monica, CA: The Human Factors Society.

Godfrey, S. S., Allender, L., Laughery, K. R., & Smith, V. L. (1983). Warning messages: will the consumer bother to look? In *Proceedings of the Human Factors Society 27th Annual Meeting* (pp. 950-954). Santa Monica, CA: The Human Factors Society.

Lehto, M. R. & Miller, J. M. (1986). *Warnings: Volume 1: Fundamentals, design, and evaluation methodologies,* Ann Arbor, MI: Fuller Technical Publications.

McCarthy, R. L., Robinson, J. N., Finnegan, J. P., & Taylor, R. K. (1982). Warnings on consumer products: Objective criteria for their use. In *Proceedings of the Human Factors Society 26th Annual Meeting* (pp. 98-99). Santa Monica, CA: The Human Factors Society.

Peters, G. A. (1984). A challenge to the safety profession. *Professional Safety, 29,* 46-50.

Robinett F., & Hughes, A. (1984). Visual alerts to machinery hazards: A design case study. In Easterby, R., & Zwaga, H. (Eds.), *Information Design: The Design and Evaluation of Signs and Printed Material* (pp. 405- 417). Chichester: John Wiley and Sons.

Rothstein, P. R. (1985). Designing warnings to be read and remembered. In *Proceedings of the Human Factors Society 29th Annual Meeting,* (pp. 684-688).

Strawbridge, J. A. (1986). The influence of position, highlighting, and imbedding on warning effectiveness. In *Proceedings of the Human Factors Society 30th Annual Meeting,* (pp. 716-720). Santa Monica, CA: The Human Factors Society.

Wogalter, M. S., Desaulniers, D. R., & Brelsford, J. W. (1986). Perceptions of consumer products: Hazardousness and warning expectations. In *Proceedings of the Human Factors Society 30th Annual Meeting* (pp. 1197-1201). Santa Monica, CA: The Human Factors Society.

Wogalter, M. S., Godfrey, S. S., Fontenelle, G. A., Desaulniers, D. R., Rothstein, P. R., & Laughery, K. R. (1987). Effectiveness of Warnings. *Human Factors, 29,* 599-612.

Zlotnik, M. A. (1982). The effects of warning message highlighting on novel assembly task performance. *In Proceedings of the Human Factors Society 26th Annual Meeting* (pp. 93-97). Santa Monica, CA: The Human Factors Society.

Relative Contribution of Likelihood and Severity of Injury to Risk Perceptions

Stephen L. Young
Dept. of Psychology
Rice University
Houston, TX 77005

Michael S. Wogalter
Dept. of Psychology
North Carolina State University
Raleigh, NC 27695

John W. Brelsford, Jr.
Dept. of Psychology
Rice University
Houston, TX 77005

ABSTRACT

The degree of caution that people are willing to take for a given product is largely determined by their perceptions of the risk associated with that product. Research suggests that risk perceptions are determined by the objective likelihood or probability of encountering potential hazards (Slovic, Fischhoff, and Lichtenstein, 1979). However, there is also research suggesting that objective likelihood plays little or no role in determining risk perceptions. Rather, risk is determined by the subjective dimension of the hazard or in other words, the severity of injury (Wogalter, Desaulniers and Brelsford, 1986, 1987). The present research examined aspects of these two studies in an attempt to reconcile the observed differences. Subjects evaluated either the Wogalter et al. (1986, 1987) products or the Slovic et al. (1979) items on eight rating questions. Results demonstrated that severity of injury was the foremost predictor of perceived risk for the Wogalter products, but that likelihood of injury was primarily responsible for ratings of risk for the Slovic items. The two lists differed substantially on all the dimensions evaluated, suggesting that the content of the lists is responsible for the contrary findings. In a second study, subjects rated another set of generic consumer products. These ratings showed a pattern of results similar to the Wogalter products. Overall, this research: (a) explains the basis for conflicting results in the risk perception literature, and (b) demonstrates that severity of injury, and not likelihood of injury, is the primary determinant of people's perceptions of risk for common consumer products.

INTRODUCTION

The degree of caution that people are willing to take for a given product is largely determined by their perceptions of the risk associated with that product. Risk is defined as "the chance of injury, damage, or loss" (Webster's New Universal Unabridged Dictionary, 1983) and this definition suggests that risk is an objective, probabilistic term: the *likelihood* ("chance") that a negative consequence will occur. Following this thinking, early research recommended that the proper way to motivate people to act with caution is to provide them with information that gives "an appreciation of the probabilistic nature of the world and the ability to think intelligently about rare (but consequential) events" (Slovic, Fischhoff, and Lichtenstein, 1980, p. 167). However, this has been very difficult to implement in research and in practice because of substantial and inevitable biases in the way people use likelihood information (Lichtenstein, Slovic, Fischhoff, Layman, and Combs, 1978). In addition to these biases, Desaulniers (1991) demonstrated that people cannot really differentiate between small probabilities (e.g., 1/10,000 and 1/100,000). These studies suggest that people do not (or are not able to) use likelihood information in a systematic manner.

If this is true, then how are perceptions of risk formed and used? The definition of risk given above suggests more subtly that there is a second, generally *subjective* component of risk: the dimensions of the "injury, damage, or loss" (i.e., *severity* of the injury). Wogalter, Desaulniers, and Brelsford (1986,

1987) and Wogalter, Brelsford, Desaulniers, and Laughery (1991) demonstrated that perceptions of risk were composed primarily of the severity of injury associated with a product and not the likelihood of that injury. These studies, as well as others (i.e., Young, Martin, and Wogalter, 1989; Young, Brelsford, and Wogalter, 1990), suggest that likelihood estimations do not contribute to people's judgments of risk. Rather, it is the perception of severity of injury that largely determines the degree of caution people are willing to exhibit.

Thus, some research suggests that likelihood of injury plays an important role in the determination of risk perceptions, whereas other research suggests that severity of injury is the principal component of risk. One potential reason for these differences is the nature of the words used to assess perceptions of risk. Specifically, the Wogalter studies used the term "hazard", while the Slovic studies used the term "risk". However, Young, Brelsford and Wogalter (1990) showed that there were *no* differences between these terms in the evaluation of risk perceptions. Thus, we are very confident that the Wogalter and Slovic studies were investigating the same construct and that the specific terms used to assess perceived risk is not responsible for the differences between the two studies. An additional difference between the Wogalter and Slovic studies is the content of the item lists that subjects evaluated. Wogalter et al. (1986, 1987) used a broad range of household consumer products; whereas Slovic et al. (1979) used some consumer products, but also included technologies and activities (e.g., nuclear power and mountain climbing). The differences in the nature of the item lists is the focus of the present paper.

STUDY 1

This study examines the nature of the two lists used by Wogalter et al. (1986, 1987) and Slovic et al. (1979) in order to assure that the respective findings are replicable and to determine whether they differ with respect to the relative contributions of injury likelihood and severity to risk perceptions.

Method

Subjects. Forty undergraduate students from the University of Houston participated in this experiment for credit in an introductory psychology class.

Materials. Table 1 shows the two lists of items that were used. Half of the subjects were exposed to the 72 products employed by Wogalter et al. (1986, 1987) and the other half were shown the 30 products, technologies and activities used by Slovic et al. (1979). The order of the products and items were randomized. Table 2 shows the 8 questions that subjects used to rate items. All scales employed 9-point Likert-type rating scales anchored from 0 (absence of a quantity) to 8 (maximum quantity). Five of the questions (Questions 1, 2, 4, 5, and 6) were taken from and are unique to Wogalter et al. (1986, 1987), whereas, the last two were unique to Slovic et al. (1979). Question 3 was common to both studies. The

questions were slightly reworded to accommodate products, technologies *and* activities, thus allowing the same questions to be used regardless of the item list that was presented to subjects. Also, it should be noted that Question 1 (Hazard) is used to assess risk perceptions, primarily because we have used this question many times before and because "hazard" has been shown to be equivalent to the term "risk" (Young et al. 1990). In the booklets, each question was printed on a separate page and the pages were randomly ordered.

Procedure. Subjects received one of the two lists and were told to rate the items for each question before going on to the next question. They were also instructed to make their ratings according to the order that the questions were presented in the booklet.

Results

Product differences on the 8 questions. Analyses initially compared the two item lists with respect to the mean ratings on the 8 questions. The lists differed significantly on all 8 rating questions ($ps < .05$, see the first two columns of Table 3). The 30 items were perceived to be more hazardous and less familiar than the 72 products. In general, subjects reported that they were more likely to be injured by the 30 items and that those injuries would be more severe and more catastrophic than with the 72 products. In addition, subjects reported greater intent to act cautiously and greater likelihood to read warnings for the 30 items than for the 72 products, at the same time believing that they had less control over being injured with the 30 items.

Table 1. A listing of the 72 Wogalter et al. (1986, 1987) products and the 30 Slovic et al. (1979) items.

Wogalter et al. (1986, 1987) products

Electrical

battery alarm clock	electric carving knife	oscillating fan	steam iron	curling iron	electric food slicer
photoflash unit	toaster oven	desk lamp	electric hedge trimmer	pocket calculator	transistor radio
digital watch	flashlight	quartz/space heater	trash compactor	drip coffee maker	metal detector
sewing machine	typewriter	electric blanket	microwave oven	sun lamp	vacuum cleaner

Chemical

antacid	cake mix	kerosene	roasted peanuts	alcoholic beverage	cough medicine
lacquer stripper	roll-on deodorant	apple sauce	drain cleaner	milk	shampoo
artificial sweetener	nonprescription diet aid	dried cereal	skin moisturizer	aspirin	eggs
oven cleaner	soap	baby powder	household bleach	pesticide	suntan lotion

Non-Electrical Tools

bicycle	garden shears	hunting knife	rake	binoculars	garden sprinkler
inflatable boat	screwdriver	chain saw	gas outdoor grill	ladder	scuba gear
clothesline	golf club	lawn mower	semi-automatic rifle	dart game	hammer
life vest	wheel barrow	football helmet	hiking boot	ping pong table	wood splitter

Slovic et al. (1979) items

bicycle	hunting	general (private) aviation	food preservatives	H.S. & college football
food coloring	railroads	skiing	handguns	pesticide
commercial aviation	X-rays	motorcycles	prescription antibiotics	spray can
motor vehicles	nuclear power	contraceptives	fire fighting	home appliances
mountain climbing	large construction	smoking	alcoholic beverage	lawn mower
swimming	vaccinations	surgery	electric power	police work

Table 2. A list of the 8 rating questions and their anchors.

1) **Hazard**: "How *hazardous* is this product, technology or activity?" The anchors for this question were: (0) not at all hazardous, (2) slightly hazardous, (4) hazardous, (6) very hazardous, and (8) extremely hazardous.

2) **Likelihood**: "How *likely* are you to receive *any* injury with this product, technology or activity, including all *minor* ones (requiring little or no first aid) and *major* ones (requiring emergency room treatment)?" The anchors for this question were: (0) never, (2) unlikely, (4) likely, (6) very likely, and (8) extremely likely.

3) **Severity**: "How *severely* (i.e., degree, extent or magnitude) might you be injured by this product, technology or activity?" The anchors for this question were: (0) not at all severe, (2) slightly severe, (4) severe, (6) very severe, and (8) extremely severe.

4) **Cautious Intent**: "How *cautious* would you be when using this product or technology or while doing this activity?" The anchors for this question were: (0) not at all cautious, (2) slightly cautious, (4) cautious, (6) very cautious, and (8) extremely cautious.

5) **Likelihood of Reading Warnings**: "If you *saw* a warning on this product or during this activity, how *likely* would you be to read it?" The anchors for this question were: (0) never, (2) unlikely, (4) likely, (6) very likely, and (8) extremely likely.

6) **Familiarity**: "How *familiar* are you with this product, technology or activity?" The anchors for this question were: (0) not at all familiar, (2) slightly familiar, (4) familiar, (6) very familiar, and (8) extremely familiar.

7) **Control**: "If exposed to the risks, to what extent can you, by personal skill or diligence, avoid the hazards associated with this product, technology or activity? That is, how much control do you have over being injured by this product, technology or activity?" The anchors for this question were: (0) no control at all, (2) some control, (4) control, (6) much control, and (8) total control.

8) **Catastrophe**: "Are the risks associated with this product, technology or activity the kind that injure or kill people one at a time or are they risks that injure or kill large numbers of people at a time?" The anchors for this question were: (0) injures/kill one at a time, (2) injures/kill a few at a time, (4) injures/kill several at a time, (6) injures/kill many at a time, and (8) injures/kill large numbers at a time.

Table 3. Means of the 30 items and 72 products (Study 1) and the 85 products (Study 2)

Questions	Mean Rating		
	30 Items (Study 1)	72 Products (Study 1)	85 Products (Study 2)
Hazardousness	3.74	2.66	2.89
Likelihood	3.42	2.41	2.51
Severity	5.03	3.08	3.39
Cautious Intent	4.81	2.80	2.87
Likelihood of Reading Warnings	5.11	3.64	3.72
Familiarity	3.89	3.96	4.57
Control	4.13	5.29	5.44
Catastrophe	2.38	0.64	0.95

Regression analysis with the 72 products. Regression analysis using hazard (risk) ratings as the criterion variable was performed on the 72 products. Scores for the analysis were means for items derived by collapsing across subjects within each scale. The greatest overall predictor of hazard was severity ($r = .973$), which accounted for 94.7% of the variance. Catastrophe contributed significant additional variance, increasing the total explained variance to 95.3%.

Regression analysis with the 30 items. Scores for the regression analysis on the 30 items was derived similar to the 72 product analysis. The 30-item regression analysis demonstrated that likelihood was the single best predictor of hazard, accounting for 86.6% of the variance. Familiarity made a significant contribution in addition to likelihood, augmenting the amount of explained variance to 88.9%.

Analysis of common products. Four products on the list used by Wogalter et al. (1986, 1987) were identical to product names used in the Slovic et al. (1979) list: bicycle, lawn mower, pesticide, and alcoholic beverage. These items were compared between lists to identify any contextual effects that might have influenced ratings. The results demonstrated that there were large and significant differences between ratings for the lawn mower and pesticide on the two lists (see Table 4). In general, potential injuries associated with the lawn mower and pesticide were considered less hazardous, less likely, and less severe when evaluated in the context of the Slovic products (compared to the Wogalter products). Also with these products, subjects reported that they would be less likely to read warnings or behave with caution when the items were presented in the Slovic list. The differences between product lists for alcoholic beverage and bicycle were smaller than with lawn mower or pesticide. These results suggest that, for some products, context influences perceptions.

Discussion

In previous research, severity of injury has been found to be the foremost predictor of risk perceptions. This finding has been reproduced again using the 72 products from Wogalter et al. (1986, 1987). Likelihood was not found to contribute significantly above and beyond severity. However, likelihood played a major role in determining perceived risk for the less familiar, more hazardous and more severe 30-item list of Slovic et al. (1979). It is possible that the effects found for each list are limited entirely to the stimuli employed in this study and that no generalization can be made beyond the content of these particular lists. However, the large and apparent qualitative differences between the two lists suggests that the 72 products may be more representative of consumer products in general than the 30 item list. These results also demonstrate that ratings for the common products in the lists were significantly influenced by the nature of the list in which it is included. For two of the common products (lawn mower and pesticide), perceptions varied considerably but consistently

261

between product on different lists. This suggests that perceptions of risk are subject to contrast effects with surrounding items.

STUDY 2

The Slovic et al. (1979) item list was shown to differ significantly with the list of products used by Wogalter, et al (1986). This is not entirely surprising considering that 57% of the Slovic et al. items are not consumer products at all. Based on this fact alone, it would seem reasonable to assume that the findings for the 72-product list would be more generalizable to consumer products than the 30-item list. While the 72-product list has been used in several previous studies, there has been no evaluation of whether the products on this list are representative of all common consumer products that people might use in their daily lives. Stronger conclusions could be made if similar effects were to be found using other products. Thus, Study 2 employed a different list of common consumer products to determine whether severity of injury is the foremost predictor of risk perceptions and whether likelihood is again relatively less important. The ratings on this newer list are compared to the ratings of the two lists used in Study 1.

Method

Subjects. Thirty-five undergraduates subjects from Rice University participated in this study for credit in an introductory psychology course.

Materials and procedure. Table 5 shows a list of 85 product names that were chosen at random from a list of over 950 products monitored by the National Electronic Injury Surveillance System (NEISS; U. S. Consumer Product Safety Commission, 1989). Four random orders of the list were created and the products were listed on two pages. The 85 products were rated on the same 8 questions used in Study 1. Other aspects of the method were identical to those employed in Study 1.

Results

Means on the 8 questions. The mean ratings of the eight questions for the 85 products were very similar to the pattern

Table 4. Means for the common products between Wogalter et al. (1986, 1987) and Slovic et al. (1979).

Questions	Alcoholic Beverage		Bicycle		Lawn Mower		Pesticide	
	Wogalter	Slovic	Wogalter	Slovic	Wogalter	Slovic	Wogalter	Slovic
Hazardousness	5.70	4.80	2.70	2.05	4.55	1.80*	5.95	3.65*
Likelihood	5.00	3.50*	3.70	3.25	3.60	2.20*	3.42	3.15
Severity	6.35	5.65	4.40	3.90	5.00	3.60*	5.74	4.30*
Cautious Intent	5.65	5.00	3.35	3.60	4.25	2.85*	5.32	3.80*
Likelihood of Reading Warnings	4.10	3.90	3.15	2.35	5.30	3.80*	6.58	5.25*
Familiarity	6.40	5.10*	7.35	7.15	5.90	6.00	4.42	3.60
Control	5.10	6.15	5.10	5.60	5.00	6.25*	4.47	3.15*
Catastrophe	5.40	3.35*	0.80	0.35	0.95	0.15	4.79	2.90*

* Indicates a significant difference between lists on this question (*p* < .05)

Table 5. A listing of the 85 products from the NEISS product list.

cribs	dune buggies	log splitters	toboggans	4 wheel ATV's
darts	diapers	lawn mowers	garage doors	benches
artificial Christmas tree	lighter fluid	baby bathinett	seeds	liniments
bleachers	bicycles	hot water	glass test tubes	pogo sticks
inflatable toys	hair clippers	pens and pencils	hair coloring	power sanders
power pruning equipment	padlocks	rope or string	toy weapons	pins and needles
toy cosmetics	snow blowers	toy sports equipment	children's play tents	saunas
clotheslines	luggage	electric toy cars	aerosol containers	ice crushers
food processors	orthopedic beds	manual lawn trimmers	laundry soaps/detergents	scissors
footlockers	chemistry set	tables	slow cookers	pressure cookers
gas water heater	bench/table saw	bubble baths	food warmers	workshop staples
wire	furniture polishes	swimming pool equipment	whirlpool/hot tubs	burglar alarms
built in swimming pools	laundry baskets	rust preventatives	sabre saws	blankets
hair dryers	pull down/folding stairs	glass bottles/jars	upholstered chairs	treehouse/playhouse
kerosene/oil heaters	can openers	drinking straws	rug shampooer	hay processing equipment
windshield wiper fluid	clothes dryer	beds	sheets or pillowcases	food grinders
gasoline cans	solid room deodorizer	household cleaners	abrasive cleaners	windows

of means observed for the 72 products (see Table 3). Comparisons between the means for the 85-product list in this study and the two lists from the first study showed that the 85-product list was statistically different from the 30-item list on every one of the 8 rating questions. In contrast, the 85-product list differed from the 72-product only on the familiarity dimension, where subjects reported being less familiar with the 85 than with the 72 products. Thus, it appears that the 85 products in this study are perceived to be (statistically) more similar to the 72 products used by Wogalter et al. (1986, 1987) than the 30 items used by Slovic et al. (1979).

Regression analyses

A regression analysis was performed on the 85 products using mean product scores collapsed across subjects. The single best predictor of hazard was severity ($r = .958$), accounting for 91.8% of the variance. The dimension of control contributed a small but significant amount of additional variance (0.8%).

Discussion

The results of Study 2 are very similar to the findings for the Wogalter products in Study 1. The means for the 8 rating questions were almost identical between the 85 and the 72 products. In addition, these two lists showed a similar pattern of results with regard to the substantial relationship between severity and risk perceptions.

GENERAL DISCUSSION

These results suggest that, for common consumer products, severity of injury is the single best predictor of risk perceptions. In two separate lists of products (the 85 and 72 product lists), severity of injury was shown to be the foremost predictor of hazard. Even though the two product lists were very different in terms of specific content, they exhibited a strikingly similar pattern of results. This suggests that severity of injury is probably the single best predictor of risk for many (if not most) common consumer products. We have no evidence to suggest that likelihood plays a part in people's perceptions of these products. The fact that severity was not a major predictor with Slovic et al.'s (1979) 30 items appears to result from the fact that they are substantially and qualitatively different from the kinds of items that most people encounter on a daily basis.

A tentative hypothesis can be made regarding why severity and likelihood are important in the different lists: People use severity information when forming perceptions of risk because severity is valuable and sufficient in most cases, involving greater use of heuristic processing than likelihood information (Desaulniers, 1991). However, when severity of the potential consequences reaches a certain level (i.e., *very*

severe injury or death), the only remaining uncertainty about the outcome is the probability of the dreadful event. For example, people's fear of plane crashes or nuclear disasters is based, not just on the severity of the potential consequences, but mostly on the probability of the event. Whether correct or incorrect, people generally perceive these events to be cataclysmic, with virtually no uncertainty about the severity of the disaster. In these cases, likelihood would be expected to play a role in risk assessments. It is possible that Slovic's list included many items which approached or surpassed this severity threshold (i.e., nuclear power, commercial aviation, fire fighting, surgery, X-rays, smoking, etc.) and thus produced an effect of likelihood.

The two studies presented here provide a basis for resolving discrepancies between the findings of Slovic and Wogalter. These results suggest that if one is rating items which are (on the whole) very hazardous, very likely to result in injury, very severe, very unfamiliar and very catastrophic, likelihood of injury will be an important variable in the formation of risk perceptions, and subsequently, people's intent to act cautiously. However, these attributes are not associated with the products that consumers generally use, and they may not play a role in people's risk perceptions in everyday situations.

REFERENCES

Desaulniers, D. R. (1991). An examination of consequence probability as a determinant of precautionary intent. *Unpublished Doctoral Dissertation.* Rice University, Houston Texas.

Lichtenstein, S., Slovic, P., Fischhoff, B., Layman, M. & Combs, B. (1978). Judged frequency of lethal events. *Journal of Experimental Psychology: Human Learning and Memory, 4,* 551-578.

Slovic, P. (1978). The psychology of protective behavior. *Journal of Safety Research, 10,* 58-68.

Slovic, P., Fischhoff, B., & Lichtenstein, S. (1979). Rating the risks. *Environment, 21,* 14-39.

Slovic, P., Fischhoff, B., & Lichtenstein, S. (1980). Informing people about risk. *Banbury Report 6.* Cold Springs Laboratory, p. 165-180.

U. S. Consumer Product Safety Commission (1989). *NEISS Data Highlights.* Washington, DC: Author.

Webster's New Universal Unabridged Dictionary. (1983). New York: Simon & Schuster.

Wogalter, M. S., Brelsford, J. W., Desaulniers, D. R., and Laughery, K. R. (1991). Consumer product warnings: The role of hazard perception. *Journal of Safety Research, 22,* 71-82.

Wogalter, M. S., Desaulniers, D. R. & Brelsford, J. W. (1986). Perceptions of consumer products: Hazardousness and warning expectations. In *Proceedings of the Human Factors Society - 30th Annual Meeting* (p. 1197-1201). Santa Monica: The Human Factors Society.

Wogalter, M. S., Desaulniers, D. R. & Brelsford, J. W. (1987). Consumer products: How are the hazards perceived. In *Proceedings of the Human Factors Society - 31st Annual Meeting* (p. 615-619). Santa Monica: Human Factors Society.

Young, S. L., Brelsford, J. W. & Wogalter, M. S. (1990). Judgements of Hazard, Risk & Danger: Do they differ? In *Proceedings of the Human Factors Society - 34th Annual Meeting* (p. 503-507). Santa Monica: Human Factors Society.

Young, S. L., Martin, E. & Wogalter, M. S. (1989). Gender differences in consumer product hazard perceptions. In *Proceedings of the Interface '89* (p. 73-78). Santa Monica: Human Factors Society.

Abstracts

*The year and page numbers following each abstract refer to the proceedings of the
Human Factors and Ergonomics Society annual meetings.*

A Methodological Taxonomy for Warning Research

Thomas J. Ayres, Madeleine M. Gross, Donald P. Horst, and J. Neil Robinson

Beginning with several empirical papers in the late 1970s, there has been considerable research concerned with assessing the effectiveness of such attempted safety interventions as on-product warnings and safety signs. The focus of research on warnings has shifted from a debate on whether warnings work, to systematic investigation of the factors that do or could influence safety-related product-user behavior. From the perspective of safety, the logical test of a warning must be reduction of the frequency and/or severity of accidents and injuries. A taxonomy of available research methods is described; strengths and problems associated with each method are discussed. Although research on topics related to warnings may legitimately address a wide variety of psychological issues, informed safety policymaking should rely primarily on well-controlled real-world studies. Within the restricted aim of making unambiguous contributions to generalizations that can inform safety policy, some methodological cautions are appropriate for both research and practitioners. (1992, pp. 499–503)

Selecting Comprehensible Warning Symbols for Swimming Pool Slides

Theo Boersema and Harm J. G. Zwaga

To reduce the hazardous behavior of swimming pool slide users, five warning messages were identified. For each warning nine symbols were developed. The comprehensibility of the symbols was tested using an evaluation procedure based to a large extent on the ISO testing procedure to determine the comprehensibility of public information symbols. Respondents were 202 swimming pool users between 7 and 19 years of age. Seven acceptable symbols were found referring to four of the five warnings. (1989, pp. 994–998)

Effect of Warnings in Advertising on Adolescents' Perceptions of Risk for Alcohol Consumption

N. Kimberly Bohannon and Stephen L. Young

The present study examined the effect of warning labels in alcohol advertising on the perception of risk for alcohol consumption. Under incidental conditions, subjects from two age groups, young ($M = 13.6$ years) and older ($M = 23.3$ years), examined a collection of magazine ads. Three of the ads in the booklet were for alcoholic beverages, and these were either accompanied by a warning or the warning was absent. When present, the warnings were manipulated by the orthogonal combination of text voice (2nd vs. 3rd person) and pictorial (presence vs. absence) in a between-subjects design. A fifth condition served as the no-warning control. After examining the magazine ads, subjects answered a questionnaire which assessed several dimensions related to the ads: number and type of ads, attractiveness of the ads, and number and type of warnings in the ads. Examination of the questions dealing with the risk of alcohol consumption indicated that adolescents rated their own risk lower than the risk to adolescents in general, but that this bias in risk ratings was not evident when warnings were present. There were also several other age and gender effects. While no individual warning manipulation was found to be consistently superior to another, the results suggest that warnings can be effective in producing proper estimations of risk in different age populations. (1993, pp. 974–978)

Likelihood of Reading Warnings: The Effect of Fonts and Font Sizes

Curt C. Braun, N. Clayton Silver, and Barry R. Stock

Legibility of a warning is a major issue in the labeling of various consumer products and over-the-counter and prescription drugs. The purpose of the present research was to examine certain variables that are associated with legibility, namely font type, font weight, point size, and point size contrast between the signal word and the main body of the warning. A sample of undergraduate students and elderly people rated 24 Ultra Tide detergent labels for their likelihood to read the warning, the saliency of the warning, and readability of the warning. The results indicated that participants were more likely to read the warning in Helvetica type than in Times or Goudy. Times was more likely to be read than Goudy. Bold type was more likely to be read than Roman type. There was a greater likelihood of reading the warning when the main body was in 10-point size as compared with 8-point size. A 2-point size difference between the signal word and the main body of the warning produced a greater likelihood of reading the warning over a 4-point size difference. One possibility for this result is that the 4-point size difference minimizes the importance of the main body of the warning, therefore making only the signal word salient. (1992, p. 926–930)

Risk Estimation for Common Consumer Products

Douglas J. Brems

This paper reports a study of risk estimation for common consumer products. Subjects estimated injury frequencies and recalled/identified accident scenarios. While performance on the frequency estimation task highlighted a surprising ability to assess relative levels of risk very quickly, the scenario recall task showed severe errors in judgment. In the frequency estimation task, estimates that were made within seconds of category presentation were just as accurate as those made after lengthy analysis. In the scenario recall task, subjects could recall or generate only about 40% of the common accident scenarios associated with each product category, and they overestimated their own ability to recall scenarios. When asked about specific scenarios that they had failed to identify, subjects cited both awareness and memory problems. These findings are discussed with reference to a model of risk perception in which the individual uses a readily accessible base of knowledge for assessing risks. (1986, pp. 556–560)

Evaluation of Mine-Safety Symbols

Belinda L. Collins

The effectiveness of safety symbols and hazard pictorials of mine-safety communication was determined in a multistage evaluation. The understandability of symbols for 40 messages and the perceived hazardousness of six different surround shapes were assessed. The effectiveness of a subset of 20 symbols was determined during an in-mine evaluation at two mines. (1983, pp. 947–949)

Consumers' Information-Processing Objectives and Effects of Product Warnings

Mark A. deTurck and Gerald M. Goldhaber

Based on human information-processing theory, it was hypothesized that consumers' information-processing objectives would influence the amount of time they devoted to examining product labels, their memory for product safety information, and, as a result, the likelihood that they would comply with safety recommendations. More specifically, it was expected that compared with consumers with an impression-set processing objective, consumers with a memory-set processing objective would: (1) devote more

time to examining product labels; (2) recall more safety-related information; and (3) be more likely to comply with safety recommendations. Results provided unequivocal support for the first two hypotheses and only partial support for the third hypothesis. (1988, pp. 445–449)

Cigarette Warnings: Recall of Content as a Function of Gender, Message Context, Smoking Habits, and Time

Daryle Jean Gardner-Bonneau, Fawzi Kabbara, Minjohn Hwang, Hans Bean, Marilyn Gantt, Kevin Hartshorn, Jennifer Howell, and Rahim Spence

The purpose of the present study was to assess the degree to which smokers and nonsmokers can recall warning information about the hazards of smoking, as a function of message context, time, and gender. Subjects were presented with printed messages, advertisements, or cigarette packs containing the four currently used warnings. Recall of the message content was measured immediately after viewing the message, as well as one week later. In general, recall of the informational content of the messages was poor. However, there were differences among the experimental conditions. Smokers recalled more information than nonsmokers, and more information was recalled from the printed messages and the cigarette packs than from the magazine advertisements. In addition, there were differences in the percentages of information recalled from the four messages. Suggestions for changes in the message content and design are offered, based on the currently available guidelines. (1989, pp. 928–930)

The Impact of Color on Warnings Research

Paul B. Kline, Curt C. Braun, Nancy Peterson, and N. Clayton Silver

Researchers have examined a variety of attributes that influence a warning's ability to communicate important product hazards. These attributes include font type, signal words, and the use of icons. One attribute that has been noticeably absent from the warnings literature is color. Therefore, the purpose of the present study was to determine the appropriateness of achromatic stimuli in product warning research. Thirty-three undergraduate students rated color and achromatic versions of 12 labels. These labels varied across four levels of product class and three levels of signal word. All labels were evaluated on six attributes: salience, readability, hazardousness, likelihood of injury, carefulness, and familiarity. A composite variable called "perceived hazard" was formed from the averaged ratings of hazardousness, carefulness, and likelihood of injury. Moreover, an additional variable, "perceived readability," was composed of the mean ratings of readability and salience. Results showed that color labels were perceived as more readable and hazardous than achromatic labels. Implications for warning research are discussed. (1993, pp. 940–944)

Warnings and Expert Opinions: An Evaluation Methodology Based on Fuzzy Probabilities

John G. Kreifeldt

A number of mandated and voluntary standards and guidelines expressed as good practice have been set out for the design of warnings. However, the question always arises as to whether or not a given warning will accomplish (or would have accomplished) its purpose of preventing injury whether or not it follows such guidelines. The answer to this question must be phrased in probabilities and sometimes only in qualitative form, such as "low probability," "high probability," "more probable than not," etc. In order to obtain such answers, experts are often consulted for their opinions. A methodology is presented which can be used as a basis for checking the consistency of the final conclusions or opinions using the concept of "fuzzy probabilities" and conceptually simple computations. The methodology is also of use to experts in formulating their opinions rationally and deducing their implications clearly. This methodology is presented here in the context of the opined probability of effectiveness of warnings and instructions, although it may be used in any context in which the total proposition can be phrased as a set of interrelated subpropositions, as is common in reliability theory, decision theory, and so on. (1992, p. 940–944)

Factors Affecting Consumers' Perceptions of Product Warnings: An Examination of the Differences between Male and Female Consumers

Cindy LaRue and H. Harvey Cohen

This study utilized a survey to investigate several factors that may influence consumers' perceptions of warnings. The purpose of this research was twofold: (1) to partially replicate a previous study of college undergraduates to see if similar results would be obtained in a random sample of consumers, and (2) to determine if these factors are significantly different depending on the sex of the consumer. Subjects rated 12 products according to: dangerousness, familiarity, their willingness to read a warning, need for a warning, and location of the warning. The results of this research are similar to those of the original study; therefore, the undergraduates

can be considered a good indicator of the general consumer population. Further analysis showed differences in the perception of warnings between male and female consumers. Females are more likely to feel a product should have a warning and are more likely to read a warning despite the perceived dangerousness of the product than are males. The likelihood of males reading warning labels depends on the perceived dangerousness and familiarity of the product. (1987, pp. 610–614)

Effects of Explicitness in Conveying Severity Information in Product Warnings

Kenneth R. Laughery, Anna L. Rowe-Hallbert, Stephen L. Young, Kent P. Vaubel, and Lila F. Laux

Manufacturers typically provide consumers with a warning message on the label of potentially hazardous products in order to encourage their safe use. Warnings often vary in explicitness and severity, where explicitness refers to the specificity of the stated injury consequences, and severity refers to the harshness of the consequences. This study examined the nature of the relationship between explicitness and severity and explored changes in people's perceptions of four common consumer products as a result of the exposure of warnings that varied on these two dimensions. The results show that explicitness and severity are related. The results also demonstrated that exposure to explicit warnings produced an increase in rated severity of injury and intent to act cautiously with a product. Overall this study suggests that, unless they are explicit, warnings on common consumer products may not change perceptions and subsequent intentions to act cautiously. (1991, pp. 481–485)

Adequacy of Responses to Warning Terms

S. David Leonard, Elisabeth Creel, and Edward W. Karnes

Previous research has indicated that many persons have difficulty in describing the seriousness of hazards that are associated with some terms frequently used in warnings. Alternative explanations for this failure could be lack of understanding or simply inability to express their knowledge. Two studies were conducted in an effort to get more definitive information about what the general public knows about these terms. The obtained evidence suggested that many terms commonly used alone in warnings are not adequate to inform users of the extent of the hazards associated with those warnings. These results are discussed in terms of the need for completeness in warnings. (1991, pp. 1024–1028)

Effect of Labels on Risk Perceptions of Consumer Products

S. David Leonard and G. William Hill

Previous studies have shown that many individuals do not know the meanings of terms often used as stand-alone descriptions of hazards. Leonard and Digby (1992) found subjects rated the danger associated with different products very differently despite being given the same hazard description. One possibility for the differences in ratings is that substances are experienced in very different quantities. While gasoline is usually seen in multigallon amounts, fingernail polish remover is seen in quantities of a few fluid ounces. An alternative explanation is that people's experiences (direct or vicarious) with the substances have given them different concepts of the characteristics of the substances. This study examined these alternatives by asking 88 subjects to rate the risk of a dangerous event occurring with the same specific quantity of each substance. Mean ratings over all subgroups indicated that they perceived less risk from certain substances than from others, although the substances are equally dangerous. Evidence for an experiential component of risk assessment was provided by differences between older and younger subjects on specific items. The importance of presenting information about the consequences of hazards in warnings was discussed. (1993, pp. 979–983)

Risk Perception and Use of Warnings

S. David Leonard, G. William Hill, and Edward W. Karnes

The purpose of the studies was to develop information about how the general public perceives the degree of danger represented by signal words in warnings. Although many organizations have guidelines for the determination of what signal words are to be used with a specific hazard, these are usually unknown to the public. For 15 items that had been rated for the seriousness of risk, 288 subjects were asked to indicate which signal word they would use to inform others of the hazard. Signal words that had been found to rate high in seriousness by Leonard, Karnes, and Schneider [1988; Scale values for warning symbols and words; In F. Aghazadeh, Ed., *Trends in ergonomics/human factors V*, pp. 669–674; Amsterdam: Elsevier] tended to be used more with items rated as higher risks. Differences were found among age groups with older subjects using signal words that carried more serious connotations. The possible warnings that might be used were discussed. (1989, pp. 550–554)

Development of Warnings Resulting from Forensic Activity

S. David Leonard and Edward W. Karnes

One of the arguments given for pursuing the rights of injured parties through the legal system in cases involving ergonomics principles is that it encourages corporations to modify their products or the warnings given about them to produce a safer environment. Unfortunately, this does not occur as often in practice as might be hoped. This report describes a case in which support for ergonomic research was provided by a corporation that wanted to ensure their warnings were adequate. The effectiveness of pictograms in aiding persons with a limited command of English was investigated. Pictograms were first tested on college students and modified in accordance with the feedback obtained from them. For the final test, subjects who were taking courses in English as a Second Language and courses for adults who were learning to read were selected. They were shown a letter printed in Greek symbols with a pictograph representing an individual calling to get more information about the letter, and they were asked to describe how they would go about determining what the letter said. Although not all subjects indicated that they would call the number listed, their responses indicated that they would use reasonable strategies for learning its contents. In addition to showing the feasibility of such research procedures, the experiment suggested that future research was needed on the development of symbols indicating the need "to do" certain activities. (1993, pp. 501–505)

Symbol Sign Understandability When Visibility Is Poor

Neil D. Lerner and Belinda L. Collins

Subjects viewed slides of symbol signs under difficult viewing conditions, simulating a building emergency situation. The subject indicated whether a symbol meant "exit" or not. Substantial differences in understandability were found among 18 exit symbols. Features that contributed to correct identification of exits and confusion from other messages were identified. (1983, pp. 944–946)

Risk Perception and Precautionary Intent for Common Consumer Products

Elaine G. Martin and Michael S. Wogalter

This study examined whether accident scenario analysis reduces accident frequency misestimations and leads to heightened precautionary intent for products. Subjects generated or were provided with accident scenarios and then made estimates. Other subjects made estimates at either a quick or slower pace without analysis. These and an additional group of subjects then rated precautionary intent for the products. Subjects gave ratings for confidence in their estimations and reported whether they had injury experience related to the products. No differences were found among group correlations with actual frequencies. The Hurried subjects reported lower precautionary intent ratings than other groups. Subjects with injury experience reported higher precautionary intent than subjects without such experience. No relationship was found between precautionary intent and frequency estimates. Personal knowledge of accidents rather than general knowledge of accidents or frequencies may be a better predictor of consumers' intended behaviors. (1989, pp. 931–935)

Recognizability and Effectiveness of Warning Symbols and Pictorials

David L. Mayer and Lila F. Laux

In this study we sought to determine the relative effectiveness of pictograms for a group of 139 subjects ranging in age from 17 to 83. We gave a pictogram identification task for 16 pictograms from the Westinghouse Product Safety Label Handbook (1981) to subjects. Pictogram identification ranged from 100% to completely unrecognizable. Generally, pictorials which depicted simply, clearly identifiable hazards or protective equipment were more identifiable than symbols. Pictograms which showed the injury occurring to a hand rather than the entire human figure were also more recognizable. Finally, to explore more than simple pictogram identification, we presented subjects with three pictograms: We asked half of the subjects to list all of the ways they could be hurt, injured or killed as well as any precautions they would take while using a product displaying one of the pictograms. The other half of the subjects endorsed precautions that they would observe on a checklist of possible precautions. In general, subjects were able to name at least one of the hazards associated with each graphic, but they generally did not name all of the hazards for a given pictogram. Sex and age effects are commented on in the paper. (1989, pp. 984–988)

Measured Impact of a Mandated Warning on User Behavior

G. E. McCarthy, D. P. Horst, R. R. Beyer, J. N. Robinson, and R. L. McCarthy

Two groups of expectant first-time mothers were asked to examine an automobile infant restraint and its instruction label, then to install the restraint in an automobile. The label for one group was presented in a warning format, as now required by federal regulation, while the label for the other group was not. Error rates were higher for the warning-label group, although the difference was not statistically significant. Most subjects rated the labels as "Good" or "Very Good," whether or not they installed the restraints correctly. Results illustrate that, in some situations, clear and direct instructions can be at least as effective as a warning in eliciting the desired behavior, and that subjective ratings of labels are not necessarily valid predictors of impact on behavior. (1987, pp. 479–483)

The Effect of Hazard and System Information on Estimated Risk

Janna L. Moore

Warning labels are used, in part, to increase risk estimates associated with hazardous equipment and products. Past research has demonstrated that exposure to warning labels is related to risk estimates; however, it is not known whether warning labels cause an increase in risk estimates, as is generally assumed, or whether individuals who appreciate the danger of a situation are more likely to notice, read, and comply with warning labels. The purpose of this research was to determine the impact of two types of information on estimated risk: hazard and basic system (nonhazard) information. Research participants (77 males and 89 females) were divided into one of four information groups: (1) hazard, (2) system, (3) control, and (4) both hazard and system. As expected, hazard information, presented in a warning label, increased risk estimates. Contrary to hypothesis, system information alone did not appear to increase risk estimates. Finally, risk estimates were highest for participants who received both hazard and system information. (1990, pp. 508–512)

Perceived Effectiveness of Danger Signs: A Multivariate Analysis

Donald J. Polzella, Michael D. Gravelle, and Ken M. Klauer

Fifty-eight subjects were shown randomly oriented facsimiles of 80 OSHA-standard danger signs and rated the signs on 13 dimensions related to perceived effectiveness. The data were analyzed by means of principal components analysis and a series of multivariate and univariate analyses of variance. Signs containing a hazard label and instructions (e.g., GASOLINE—NO SMOKING) were rated as least likely to be recalled at a later time; however, they were rated as easiest to understand, most informative, and most likely to be complied with. Signs containing a hazard label only (e.g., POISON) were rated as least informative and most difficult to understand; however, they were rated as most likely to be recalled, as depicting a high degree of danger, and likely to be complied with. Signs containing instructions only (DO NOT ENTER) were rated as generally less effective. (1992, pp. 931–934)

Emerging Methodologies for the Assessment of Safety-Related Product Communications

Timothy P. Rhoades, J. Paul Frantz, and James M. Miller

The analysis and prevention of accidents often addresses issues related to compliance with product usage and cautionary information found on the product and within its accompanying manual. The actual knowledge applied when using a product, however, likely comes from many other sources in addition to (or instead of) these sources. In cases where inappropriate knowledge is applied to the use of a product, an injury, property damage, or substandard output may occur. This being the case, the development of a product and its accompanying information should consider user knowledge and patterns of behavior in the absence or partial absence of printed product information. Contemporary guidelines for safety-related communications, however, emphasize the physical features and content of product information rather than formal analysis of user characteristics. To address these concerns, this paper suggests methods which may be further developed and validated to predict product usage behaviors and user interpretation of product information. The authors present applications of word association methods, semantic features analysis, and script analysis using a case study approach. In situations where undesired behavior is predicted, the authors suggest that user analysis may often indicate countermeasures other than the simple addition or alteration of written product information (1990, pp. 998–1002)

What Makes a Warning Label Salient?

Michael A. Rodriguez

Existing research indicates that warning labels are generally ineffective because users ignore them. One goal of the present experiment was to illustrate the importance that warning labels be as salient as possible. Features of salience examined in past research are size of the label, location, bold print, etc. The present study tests the effectiveness of warning label color

and shape in terms of subject compliance, retention of label details, and perception of danger level. Results indicated that a written label surrounded by a shape resulted in higher compliance than a label with no surrounding shape. Color had significant effects only in conjunction with shape. A red label elicited a higher rating of potential danger, with green next, and black and white the lowest. A red octagon was significantly more effective than other combinations in terms of invoking a greater retention of label detail and also drawing higher ratings of perceived danger. A neutral shape elicited both lower subject compliance and fewer compliance points. (1991, pp. 1029–1033)

Toward a General Theory of Risk Perception

Christopher W. Schacherer

Several risk perception studies employing univariate techniques have found very strong predictors of risk perceptions, but these results are of limited use in describing the cognitive process that results in perception of risk. Also, although a few multivariate investigations have been conducted, the validity of the obtained results is similarly limited due to concern over deriving easily interpretable solutions. The present study, therefore, attempts to derive a more valid model of the risk perception process through confirmatory factor analysis based on previously reported findings. (1993, pp. 984–988)

The Perceptual Determinants of Workplace Hazards

David Shinar and Oded M. Flascher

While there is a general agreement on what constitutes a safety hazard, the guidelines for assessing its risk or level of hazardousness are less clear. Ranking hazards according to their level of hazardousness is critical in setting safety improvement priorities and in addressing the more hazardous situations in the work environment. Interviews with safety experts and a literature review yielded 25 determinants of hazardousness. After narrowing the list to 11 variables, we empirically assessed the relationship between the overall assessment of a safety hazard's level of hazardousness and each of these variables. The results indicated that two variables were sufficient to account for 95% of the variance between hazards: likelihood of an injury and likelihood of slowing down work. This finding was cross-validated by using different groups for the assessment of the overall level of hazardousness and the assessment of the relevance of the different variables. Practical and theoretical implications are discussed. (1991, pp. 1095–1099)

Connoted Strength of Signal Words by Elderly and Non-Native English Speakers

N. Clayton Silver, Dana S. Gammella, Amy S. Barlow, and Michael S. Wogalter

A number of recent studies have examined the connoted strength of signal words used in sign and product label warnings. These words, such as danger, warning, and caution, are intended to differentiate various levels of hazard (high to low, respectively). Until recently, most studies have only used college students to evaluate signal words. Other populations who are at least equal to or possess greater risk of injury have not been studied. The main purpose of the present research was to determine whether other populations of persons, namely the elderly and non-native English speakers, derive similar meanings (i.e., connoted levels of hazard) from the signal words as have been shown in previous work for college students, as well as for a sample of grade-school children tested in Silver and Wogalter [1991; In *Proceedings of the Human Factors Society 35th Annual Meeting*, pp. 590–594]. A sample of 98 elderly persons and 135 non-native English speakers rated 43 potential signal words on how careful they would be after seeing each term. The results showed that the rank ordering of the words was consistent across both groups and this order corresponded with the ratings from earlier-studied populations. Moreover, there was a significant negative linear relationship between the number of words the non-native English speakers left blank and ratings of understandability by college students in previous research. The forensic implications and practical relevance of these results for hazard communication to diverse populations are discussed. (1993, pp. 516–520)

Strength and Understanding of Signal Words by Elementary and Middle School Students

N. Clayton Silver and Michael S. Wogalter

Several recent studies have examined the connoted meaning of signal words that are commonly used in product warning labels and signs. However, the tested population in almost all of these studies has used college students. One purpose of the present research was to determine if the hazard levels implied by signal words connote the same relative meaning to a different population of persons, namely elementary and middle-school students. A second purpose was to assess the understandability of signal words using an objective measure based on the number of missing ratings (i.e., ratings left blank). A third purpose was to develop a list of potential signal words that would be understandable to most younger persons. Elementary and middle-school students rated 43 potential signal words on carefulness

(i.e., "How careful would you be after seeing each term?"). A sample of 70 college students also rated the terms on carefulness, strength, and understandability. Although the younger students gave higher carefulness ratings to the words than did the college students, the rank order of the words was consistent across participant groups. In addition, ratings of understandability by college students were predictive of the terms that younger students left blank. Two shorter lists of potential signal words were derived that more than 95% or 99% of the youngest students (fourth and fifth graders) understood. The practical and forensic relevance of these results are discussed, including implications for hazard communication to persons of different populations. (1991, pp. 590–594)

The Development and Evaluation of Pictographic Symbols

Gary Sloan and Paul Eshelman

The premise adopted in this study is that representatives of the audience for whom a symbol is intended should be participants in its evolution as well as subjects in its evaluation. Several situations in need of product misuse warnings were supplied by a manufacturer of ovenware products. Symbol design possibilities were first generated for each message category and then design input was obtained from a sample of potential product users. New design candidates were developed on the basis of subject recommendations. Study generated symbols proved to be significantly more effective than designs used by the manufacturer for the same message categories as assessed by differences in reaction time and error rate. The relative effectiveness of different negation sign designs was also evaluated. Differences in both reaction time and subjective ranks of communicativeness suggest that a thin black cross is more effective in conveying negation than a thin black slash, a partial slash or cross, and a contour slash or cross. Significant differences were not found in the extent that the designs interfere with symbol recognition. (1981, pp. 198–202)

Effects of Warning Explicitness on Consumer Product Purchase Intentions

Kent P. Vaubel

Two studies examined the relationship between the explicitness of hazard consequences described by a warning label and purchase intentions. Subjects indicated buying preferences for consumer products displaying explicit and nonexplicit warning labels. Six common consumer products were used in Experiment 1. Subjects were shown a questionnaire containing information about products varying in price, quality, and warning label explicitness. Sixty-six subjects rated two products and ranked two products based on which they would be most likely to purchase. Results of the rating and ranking tasks suggest that products containing nonexplicit warnings were significantly more likely to be purchased. In Experiment 2, both explicit and nonexplicit warning labels were simultaneously presented for each of nine products, and subjects rated with which warning they would prefer to buy the product. Results of Experiment 2 indicate one product was rated significantly more likely to be purchased with an explicit warning label, whereas two products were rated more likely to be bought with nonexplicit warnings. There were no significant differences for the remaining six products. Overall, nonexplicit warnings were preferred to explicit warnings. However, this trend was reversed for one product, and for many products the detail with which a warning describes potential consequences had little effect on anticipated purchase decisions. (1990, pp. 513–517)

Product Evaluations and Injury Assessments as Related to Preferences for Explicitness in Warnings

Kent P. Vaubel and John W. Brelsford

Increasing concern about the impact that on-product safety information has on sales of a product has focused attention on consumer decision making as a new area within which to carry out warnings research. Examples of this new research domain include efforts aimed at exploring the relationships between anticipated purchase decisions and the level of detail with which a warning describes consequences of using a product. The level of detail with which consequences are described in a warning is referred to as the explicitness of the warning. In the research reported here, an attempt was made to examine purchase preferences for explicit warnings in the context of cost-benefit trade-offs made among fictitious products varying in societal value and potential harm. Seventy-three subjects were presented with brief written descriptions of seven products, each having associated with it a unique injury. Explicit and nonexplicit warnings accompanied each product description. Using a questionnaire, subjects evaluated each product in terms of its value to society and indicated whether it should be made available for sale in the United States. They then assessed the severity of the injury and the degree to which they felt it could be controlled by taking the proper precautions. Finally, subjects indicated which warning (explicit or nonexplicit) they would prefer on the product they were to buy. Overall, it was found that products having more detailed, or explicit, consequence information were overwhelmingly preferred. Other patterns indicated that greater purchase preferences for explicit warnings existed when products were considered high in societal value, ought

to be sold in the U.S., and when injuries were construed as being controllable. These findings suggest that explicit warnings do influence anticipated purchases of products about which there exists uncertainty concerning product-related danger. This influence appears to be contingent upon perceptions about the costs and benefits associated with the product. (1991, pp. 1048–1052)

Compliance with Warnings in High-Risk Recreational Activities: Skiing and Scuba

Alison G. Vredenburgh and H. Harvey Cohen

Warnings research generally has focused on identifying which factors influence people to read and remember the content of warnings. Additional research has determined that people tend to read warnings if they perceive an activity or product to be dangerous or if they are less familiar with it. However, for practical purposes, reading the label or warning does not go far enough. In addition to examining whether warnings have been read, the current study also addresses user compliance by surveying people immediately after they have completed a high-risk recreational activity (either skiing or scuba diving). The three areas examined in this study were whether the perception of danger affected the reading of, and compliance with, warnings; whether familiarity with an activity affected reading and compliance; and whether there was any difference in responses between men and women. Although there was no sex difference in whether subjects read warnings, women reported complying with the warnings significantly more than men. In accordance with stereotypes, men were more likely to participate in high-risk sports; claim to have a higher ability in the activity; and participated in the activity more often than the women (in the two years prior to this study). (1993, pp. 945–949)

The Effects of Context on the Comprehension of Graphic Symbols

Mark Vukelich and Leslie A. Whitaker

When graphic symbols are used to convey warning information, these symbols must be evaluated for effectiveness prior to their use. In general, the ability of these symbols to convey their intended meaning has been determined in tests which provide no contextual information surrounding the symbols. In the present study, 75 university students were tested to determine their comprehension of 20 different symbols using various context conditions. Verbal context was provided in two forms: full context and partial context. Full context consisted of a two-sentence description of the setting in which the symbol would be presented. Partial context consisted of a more general, two-word description of the use context. The control condition presented the symbols without contextual information. Comprehension was higher when full context was provided with the symbols than when the symbols were presented in isolation. For some symbols, the full context condition resulted in higher comprehension than the partial context condition and the partial context condition resulted in higher comprehension than the no context condition. Comprehension accuracy was also affected by the subject's familiarity with the symbols. Comprehension was higher for symbols rated high in familiarity than for symbols rated lower in familiarity. On the basis of these findings, a recommendation was made that evaluations should provide some form of contextual information along with the symbols to allow a more realistic test of symbol comprehension. (1993, pp. 511–515)

Judgments of Hazard, Risk, and Danger: Do They Differ?

Stephen L. Young, John W. Brelsford, and Michael S. Wogalter

There were three purposes of the present research. The first was to test whether some of the discrepancies found in the hazard and risk perception literature were due to differences between the connotations of the terms *hazard* and *risk*. The second purpose was to examine the relationship between willingness to read warnings and generalized cautious intent, as well as other relevant variables suggested by past literature. The third purpose was to examine the relation between objective measures of injury (e.g., frequencies of hospital emergency room admissions) and people's subjective perceptions. The results showed that the expressions of hazardous, risky, dangerous, and hazardous-to-use connote the same meaning to lay participants. Strong intercorrelations were found between overall unsafeness (a composite of the four hazard-risk expressions), injury severity, cautious intent, and willingness to read warnings. While injury likelihood played a small part in the prediction of willingness to read warnings, the results indicated that overall unsafeness (and severity of injury) play the foremost role in people's judgments of whether to read warnings and to act cautiously. No relationship was observed between objective measures of injury frequency and people's subjective perceptions of injury likelihood, which is taken as further indication that people do not readily use injury likelihood in their judgments of product safety. The implications are two-fold. First, the results suggest that lay persons do not interpret the term risk in the same way as do experts. These results suggest that other terminology and language may be needed to express probability to lay persons. Second, the results suggest that designers of warnings and educational materials should focus their attention on ways that appropriately communicate how badly a person can get hurt, rather than (or to a lesser extent) the likelihood of getting hurt. (1990, pp. 503–507)

The Effects of Warning Message Highlighting on Novel Assembly Task Performance

Morris A. Zlotnik

A review of examples and specifications relating to critical operating procedures revealed considerable variation in recommended standards for highlighting warning messages. An experiment was therefore conducted to examine the effectiveness of various methods of highlighting warning messages contained in the instructions for a novel assembly task. Findings indicated that the presence of warning messages shortened task completion times and reduced error rates between the experimental and control groups. (1982, pp. 93–97)

Comprehensibility Estimates of Public Information Symbols: Their Validity and Use

Harm J. G. Zwaga

Estimation scores of comprehensibility were obtained for 109 hospital symbols, divided over five different sets. These scores were compared with the results of a comprehension test of those symbols. It is shown that the estimation scores can be used in a reliable way to identify good and bad symbols at an early stage. It is further demonstrated that the number of symbols to be tested for the ISO testing procedure can be substantially reduced. (1989, pp. 979–983)

Bibliography

The following articles are from the proceedings of the Human Factors and Ergonomics Society annual meetings.

Adams, S. K., and Henderson, L. W. (1977). Analyzing the effectiveness of child-resistant closures by studying attempted entry behavior. (pp. 295–299).

Adams, S. K., and Trucks, L. B. (1976). A procedure for evaluating auditory warning signals. (pp. 166–172).

Albin, T. J. (1988). Relative contribution of behavior to slip and fall accidents in mining maintenance. (pp. 511–514).

Allen, R. W., and Schwartz, S. H. (1978). Alcohol effects on driver risk taking. (pp. 579–582).

Ayres, T. J., Gross, M. M., Fowler, G., McCarthy, R. L., Kaliknowski, A., and Lau, E. (1991). Evaluation of potential safety modifications by review of accident reports. (pp. 476–480).

Beringer, D. B. (1990). Perceived automobile safety as a function of body style, cosmetic design variation, and viewing distance. (pp. 1027–1031).

Bobick, T. G., Bell, C. A., Stanevich, R. L., Smith, D. L., and Stout, N. A. (1990). Analysis of selected scaffold-related fatal falls. (pp. 1072–1076).

Boydstun, L. E., Stobbe, T. J., and Chaffin, D. B. (1978). OSHA standards: Human factors research needs for fall warning systems. (pp. 5–11).

Brauer, M. M. (1979). Some product design review practices and procedures to assure lifecycle system safety. (pp. 220–221).

Campbell, T. F. (1978). A reflection on products liability— An insurer's viewpoint. (p. 670).*

Christ, R. E. (1974). Color research for visual displays. (pp. 542–546).

Christensen, J. M. (1979). Human factors engineering contributions to hazard analysis. (pp. 222–223).

Cochran, D. J., Riley, M. W., and Douglass, E. I. (1981). An investigation of shapes for warning labels. (pp. 395–399).

Cohen, D. M., and Cohen, H. H. (1991). What's on TV? Effects of televised advertising on consumer perceptions of products and product safety. (pp. 606–607).

Collins, B. L., Lerner, N. D., and Pierman, B. C. (1981). Assessment of workplace safety symbols. (p. 552).*

Czaja, S. J., Hammond, K., and Drury, C. G. (1983). Incidence and patterns of product-related accidents among the elderly. (p. 122).*

DeJoy, D. M. (1985). Use of written simulations in accident research and safety training. (pp. 531–535).

DeJoy, D. M. (1986). Behavioral-diagnostic analysis of worker compliance with hearing protectors. (pp. 1433–1437).

DeJoy, D. M. (1987). The optimism bias and traffic safety. (pp. 756–759).

DeJoy, D. M. (1988). Human factors model of workplace accident causation. (pp. 958–962).

DeJoy, D. M. (1990). Gender differences in traffic accident risk perception. (pp. 1032–1036).

Donner, K. A., and Brelsford, J. W. (1988). Cuing hazard information for consumer products. (pp. 532–535).

Dorris, A. L. (1991). Product warnings in theory and practice: Some questions answered and some answers questioned. (pp. 1073–1077).

Dorris, A. L., and Purswell, J. L. (1978). Human factors in the design of effective product warnings. (pp. 343–346).

Duchon, J. C., and Laage, L. W. (1986). The consideration of human factors in the design of a backing-up warning system. (pp. 261–264).

Elder, J. (1986). Hair dryer electrocutions—Can they be prevented? (pp. 908–910).

Evans, L., Wasielewski, P., and von Buseck, C. R. (1981). Compulsory seat belt usage and driver risk-taking behavior. (pp. 183–187).

Fechter, J. V., Jr. (1976). Product safety and product performance research at the National Bureau of Standards. (pp. 136–140).

Foley, J. P., and Lehto, M. R. (1990). The effect of law and training on all-terrain vehicle riders' safety-related behaviors. (pp. 966–970).

Fortenberry, J. C., and Smith, L. A. (1975). An analysis of human risk-taking in simulated occupational situations. (pp. 145–149).

Gamble, K. A., and Kalsher, M. J. (1990). Designing antecedent strategies for increasing safe driving: A pledgecard for encouraging belts and discouraging booze. (pp. 1091–1094).

Godfrey, S. S. (1987). A method for correcting biases in risk perception. (pp. 484–487).

Godfrey, S. S., Fontenelle, G. A., Brems, D. J., Brelsford, J. W., Jr., and Laughery, K. R. (1986). Scenario analysis of children's ingestion accidents. (pp. 566–569).

Griffith, D., and Actkinson, T. R. (1977). International road signs: Interpretability and training techniques. (pp. 392–395).

Grubbs, M. G. (1986). Driver behavior at intersections: An analysis of accident-related variables. (pp. 251–255).

Haas, E. C. (1992). A pilot study on the perceived urgency of multitone and frequency-modulated warning signals. (pp. 248–252).

Haber, S. B., Metlay, D. S., and Crouch, D. A. (1990). Influence of organizational factors on safety. (pp. 871–875).

Haga, S., Watanabe, K., and Kusukami, K. (1989). A new warning system for protected level crossings. (pp. 975–978).

Hakkinen, M. T., and Williges, B. H. (1982). Synthesized voice warning messages: Effects of alerting cues and message environment. (p. 204).*

Harris, K. S., Schutz, R. K., and Sadosky, T. L. (1975). The effects of target acuity, illumination level, distance, and age on eye focus time. (pp. 213–217).

Holt, R. W., Boehm-Davis, D. A., Fitzgerald, K. A., Matyuf, M. M., Baughman, W. A., and Littman, D.C. (1991). Behavioral validation of hazardous thought pattern instrument. (pp. 77–81).

*Abstract only.

Horowitz, A. D., and Dingus, T. A. (1992). Warning signal design: A key human factors issue in an in-vehicle front-to-rear-end collision warning system. (pp. 1011–1013).

Hoyos, C. G. (1983). Can we diagnose safety? (pp. 623–626).

Hudock, S. D., and Duchon, J. C. (1988). A safety risk evaluation of vigilance tasks in the U.S. surface mining industry. (pp. 990–994).

Irvine, C. H. (1978). A human factors approach to slippery floors, slippery shoes, and ladder design. (pp. 583–587).

Johnson, D. A. (1973). Effectiveness of video instructions on life jacket donning. (pp. 223–228).

Johnson, D. A., and Altman, H. B. (1973). Effects of briefing card information on passenger behavior during aircraft evacuation demonstrations. (pp. 215–221).

Johnson, D. A., Blom, D. I., and Altman, H. B. (1975). Videotape presentation of passenger safety information. (pp. 102–107).

Karnes, E. W., Leonard, S. D., and Newbold, H. C. (1988). Safety perceptions and information sources for ATV's. (pp. 938–942).

Knight, J. W., and Harju, D. J. (1982). Human factors implications of OSHA's impact on small manufacturers. (pp. 493–497).

Knowles, W. B. (1986). Children's safety knowledge. (pp. 721–724).

Kobas, G. V., and Drury, C. G. (1976). The bicyclists' exposure to risk. (pp. 484–487).

Kvålseth, T. O. (1983). Empirical studies of accident statistics and safety. (pp. 618–622).

LaRue, C. A., and Cohen, H. H. (1990). Consumer perception of light truck safety. (pp. 589–590).

Laughery, K. R., Sr., and Brems, D. J. (1985). An analysis of 4923 industrial accidents. (pp. 536–540).

Laughery, K. R., Mayer, D. L., and Vaubel, K. P. (1990). Tire-rim mismatch explosions: Human factors analyses of case studies data. (pp. 584–588).

Laughery, K. R., Young, S. L., and Rowe, A. L. (1992). Swimming pool diving accidents: Human factors analyses of case study data. (pp. 598–602).

Leighbody, G. P., Andrews, D., and Long, K. (1985). Patient falls and related variables: An examination of environmental design and safety. (pp. 702–705).

Leonard, S. D., and Hill, G. W. (1989). Risk perception is affected by experience. (pp. 1029–1033).

Leonard, S. D., Hill, G. W., and Otani, H. (1990). Emerging methodologies for the assessment of safety-related product communications. (pp. 1037–1041).

Leonard, S. D., and Karnes, E. W. (1991). Some uses of experimental techniques in forensic human factors. (pp. 595–599).

Lerner, N. D. (1981). Experimental evaluation of exit directional indicators. (pp. 193–197).

Lerner, N. D. (1985). Slope safety warning for riding-type lawn mowers. (pp. 674–678).

Lerner, N. D., and Huey, R. W., Jr. (1991). Residential fire safety needs of older adults. (pp. 172–176).

Lerner, N. D., Sedney, C. A., and Cannon-Bowers, J. (1988). Effectiveness of protective devices to prevent child drownings in home swimming pools. (pp. 915–918).

Levy, S. J. (1973). Legal aspects of product safety. (pp. 477–482).

Lin, R., and Kreifeldt, J. G. (1992). Understanding the image functions for icon design. (pp. 341–345).

Loewenthal, A., and Riley, M. W. (1980). The effectiveness of warning labels. (pp. 389–391).

Marinissen, A. H., Molenbrook, J. F. M., and Schoone-Harmsen, M. (1986). A secure way to safer products. (pp. 561–565).

Matthews, M. L. (1986). Aging and the perception of driving risk and ability. (pp. 1159–1163).

Matthews, M. L., and Boothby, R. D. (1980). Visibility of cyclists at night: Laboratory evaluation of three rear warning devices. (pp. 129–133).

Mayer, D. L., and Laux, L. F. (1989). Recognizability and effectiveness of warning symbols and pictorials. (pp. 984–988).

McDaniel, W. C. (1976). A measure of safety effectiveness. (pp. 222–225).

McGuinness, J. (1977). Human factors in consumer product safety. (pp. 292–294).

Menzer, G. W., and Curtin, J. G. (1978). Instructional system analysis applied to health and safety training in the coal industry. (pp. 649–653).

Middendorf, L. (1978). Judging clearance distance near overhead power lines. (pp. 664–668).

Miller, C. O. (1979). Human error and the legal process. (p. 25).

Miller, J. M., Frantz, J. P., and Rhoades, T. P. (1991). A model for designing and evaluating product information. (pp. 1063–1067).

Mortimer, R. G. (1991). Visual factors in rail-highway grade crossing accidents. (pp. 600–602).

Mortimer, R. G., and Sturgis, S. P. (1977). Evaluation of a high-deceleration braking signal in a driving simulator. (pp. 558–561).

Orr, M., and Hughes, S. T. (1988). Effectiveness of product safety warnings over time, and the generalization of warning signs. (pp. 897–900).

Pezoldt, V. J., Persensky, J. J., and Ramey-Smith, A. M. (1978). Lawn mower safety research. (pp. 659–663).

Philo, H. M., and Atkinson, L. M. (1978). The plaintiff's attorney. (p. 669).*

Philput, C. (1985). Driver perception of risk: Objective risk vs. subjective estimates. (pp. 270–272).

Plummer, R. W., Minarch, J. J., and King, E. L. (1974). Evaluation of driver comprehension of word versus symbol highway signs. (pp. 202–208).

Post, D. V. (1979). Are specifications of signaling systems for emergency, school bus, and service vehicles adequate? (pp. 282–284).

Ramsey, J. D. (1976). Product safety and liability considerations for home furnishings. (pp. 498–506).

Rasmussen, P. G., Chesterfield, B. P., and Lowry, D. L. (1980). Legibility of smoke-obscured emergency exit signs. (pp. 476–479).

Ratte, D. J., Lerner, N. D., and Huey, R. W., Jr. (1991). Development of child-resistant latches to prevent child access to home swimming pools. (pp. 1053–1057).

Ratte, D. J., Morrison, M. L., Lerner, N. D., and Bellegarde, M. (1990). Impact of age-related play and injury patterns on human factors criteria for playground equipment safety. (pp. 452–456).

Reising, J. M., and Hartsock, D. C. (1989). Advanced warning/caution/advisory displays for fighter aircraft. (pp. 66–70).

Rice, J. R. (1990). Human factors in the design of emergency communications systems. (pp. 239–243).

276

Robinson, G. H. (1986). Toward a methodology for the design of warnings. (pp. 106–110).

Robinson, G. H. (1991). Partial attention in warning failure: Observations from accidents. (pp. 603–605).

Robinson, G. H., and Jacobson, T. R. (1978). Human performance variability in accident causation. (pp. 517–521).

Rosinski, R. R. (1978). Perception of graphic displays of space. (pp. 78–80).

Rothstein, P. R. (1985). Designing warnings to be read and remembered. (pp. 684–688).

Rudov, M. H. (1973). Consumer health education: An analysis. (pp. 204–207).

Sanquist, T. F. (1985). Anticipatory adjustments during a warning interval: Cortical negativity and perceptual sensitivity. (pp. 958–961).

Saran, C. (1978). Agricultural safety and health—State of the art. (pp. 654–658).

Schmidt, J. K., and Kysor, K. P. (1987). Designing airline passenger safety cards. (pp. 51–55).

Schwartz, D. R., dePontbriand, R. J., and Laughery, K. R. (1983). The impact of product hazard information on consumer buying decisions: A policy-capturing approach. (pp. 955–957).

Shaw, B. W., and Sanders, M. S. (1989). Research to determine the frequency and cause of injury accidents in underground mining. (pp. 1004–1008).

Shealy, J. E. (1974). Risk-taking in skilled task performance. (pp. 78–84).

Shealy, J. E. (1979). Impact of theory of accident causation on intervention strategies. (pp. 225–229).

Shoptaugh, C. F. (1988). Risk-taking and driver behaviors: A laboratory study. (pp. 923–927).

Simonelli, N. M. (1978). An investigation of pictorial and symbolic aircraft displays for landing. (pp. 213–217).

Sloan, G. D. (1992). The application of an expanded accident sequence model to forensic human factors. (pp. 621–625).

Smith, D. B. D., and Watzke, J. R. (1990). Perception of safety hazards across the adult life span. (pp. 141–145).

Smith, J. C., and Weir, D. H. (1983). The design of motorcycle helmet headphones for emergency siren detection. (pp. 64–68).

Smith, K., and Hancock, P. A. (1992). Managing risk under time stress. (pp. 1019–1023).

Smith, L. L. (1992). Qualifying as an expert witness and a perspective on negligence. (pp. 616–620).

Stiehl, C. C., and Plauth, M. J. (1978). Human factors and safety in nuclear power plant control rooms. (pp. 644–648).

Stobbe, T. J., and Plummer, R. W. (1982). Case study: Ergonomic and hazard evaluation of a new consumer product. (pp. 515–519).

Strawbridge, J. A. (1988). An information-processing approach to the problem of medication noncompliance among older adults. (pp. 189–193).

Streff, F. M., and Kalsher, M. J. (1990). Response covariation as a design consideration in developing workplace safety interventions. (pp. 1067–1071).

Trucks, L. B., and Adams, S. K. (1975). Predicting the effectiveness of auditory warning signals in industrial environments. (pp. 368–374).

Turpin, J. A., and Constanza, E. B. (1980). A human factors evaluation of backhoe control designs and related safety issues. (pp. 49–53).

Vaubel, K. P., Donner, K. A., Parker, S. L., Laux, L. F., and Laughery, K. R. (1989). Public knowledge and understanding of overhead electrical power lines: A second look. (pp. 560–564).

Verhaegen, P. K., Toebat, K. L., and Delbeke, L. L. (1988). Safety of older drivers: A study of their over-involvement ratio. (pp. 185–188).

Waters, T. R., and Putz-Anderson, V. (1990). Promoting an ergonomic prevention program for reducing the risk of injury from manual lifting. (pp. 486–488).

Weaver, J. L., Kearns, J. D., and Urban, J. M. (1992). The expert witness. (pp. 566–567).

Weegels, M. F. (1992). Accidents with consumer products. (pp. 1024–1028).

Wiklund, M. E., and Loring, B. A. (1990). Human factors design of an AIDS prevention pamphlet. (pp. 988–992).

Wise, J. A., Anderson, M., and Jones, M. (1979). Assessing the safety and supportive features of home environments for the elderly. (pp. 242–246).

Woodson, W. E. (1979). Achieving safety objectives through household furnishings design. (pp. 247–251).

Woodward, J. L., and Adkins, G. E. (1981). Use of accident information in the development of mining industry training programs. (p. 553).*

Young, S. L., Laughery, K. R., and Bell, M. (1992). Effects of two type density characteristics on the legibility of print. (pp. 504–508).

Zwahlen, H. T. (1973). Risk-taking behavior and information-seeking behavior of drivers in a drive-through gap situation. (pp. 162–173).

Zwahlen, H. T. (1974). The effects of ethyl alcohol on a driver's driving skill, visual perception, risk acceptance, choice reaction times, and information-processing rates. (p. 116).*

Zwahlen, H. T. (1981). Driver eye scanning of warning signs on rural highways. (pp. 33–37).

Zwahlen, H. T., and DeBaid, D. P. (1986). Safety aspects of sophisticated in-vehicle information displays and controls. (pp. 256–260).

Proceedings Covered in This Book

Year	Title
1980	Proceedings of the Human Factors Society 24th Annual Meeting
1981	Proceedings of the Human Factors Society 25th Annual Meeting
1982	Proceedings of the Human Factors Society 26th Annual Meeting
1983	Proceedings of the Human Factors Society 27th Annual Meeting
1984	Proceedings of the Human Factors Society 28th Annual Meeting
1985	Proceedings of the Human Factors Society 29th Annual Meeting
1986	Proceedings of the Human Factors Society 30th Annual Meeting
1987	Proceedings of the Human Factors Society 31st Annual Meeting
1988	Proceedings of the Human Factors Society 32nd Annual Meeting
1989	Proceedings of the Human Factors Society 33rd Annual Meeting
1990	Proceedings of the Human Factors Society 34th Annual Meeting
1991	Proceedings of the Human Factors Society 35th Annual Meeting
1992	Proceedings of the Human Factors Society 36th Annual Meeting
1993	Proceedings of the Human Factors and Ergonomics Society 37th Annual Meeting

Note: The Society's name changed in 1993 to the Human Factors and Ergonomics Society.

Author Index

* Abstract only.

Subject Index

Human Factors and Ergonomics Society
Membership Benefits

What Is HFES?

The Human Factors and Ergonomics Society (formerly the Human Factors Society) is the principal professional association in the United States that is concerned with the study of human characteristics and capabilities and with the application of that knowledge to the design of the products, systems, and environments that people use.

Since its formation in 1957, HFES has promoted the discovery and exchange of human factors and ergonomics knowledge, as well as education and training for students and practitioners.

Members Have Diverse Backgrounds

HFES has more than 5000 members located throughout the United States and in 43 other countries. They are employed in industry, universities and colleges, government, consulting, military, public utilities, and other settings.

Members have academic specialties in psychology (39%), engineering (20%), human factors/ergonomics (7%), industrial design (2%), medicine (5%), and many other fields.

HFES Publications

All members receive four regular publications as a benefit of membership.

Human Factors. This quarterly peer-reviewed journal presents reports of basic and applied research, advances in methods and applications, and reviews of the state of the art. *Human Factors* is an invaluable source of information for those who work in the human factors and ergonomics field and a service to researchers who wish to disseminate their findings.

HFES Bulletin. This monthly newsletter covers news of Society events and committee activities, reviews of meetings and courses, job opportunities, ads for products and services, calls for papers, and issues of concern to human factors/ergonomics researchers and practitioners.

Ergonomics in Design. The Society's quarterly magazine contains articles, case studies, debates, commentary, and book and product reviews. The focus of *Ergonomics in Design* is the application of human factors/ergonomics research to the design, development, test, and maintenance of human-machine systems and environments.

Directory and Yearbook. Each year the Society updates its directory of members. Included are descriptions of the previous year's activities within HFES committees, chapters, and technical groups; alphabetical and geographical member listings; the HFES Code of Ethics; and the Society's Bylaws.

Members also receive discounts on other publications.

Standards Development Activities

Members represent the field in the development of national and international ergonomics standards on computer workstation and software design, medical devices, safety, and a number of other areas.

Technical Areas

There are 17 technical interest groups within HFES, each organized to promote information exchange: Aerospace Systems, Aging, Communications, Computer Systems, Consumer Products, Educators' Professional, Environmental Design, Forensics Professional, Industrial Ergonomics, Medical Systems and Rehabilitation, Organizational Design and Management, Personality and Individual Differences in Human Performance, Safety, System Development, Test and Evaluation, Training, and Visual Performance.

Technical groups contribute to the HFES annual meeting program, distribute newsletters, and conduct periodic meetings.

Local Chapters

Chapters offer events featuring noted speakers, tours of local facilities, symposia on developments in human factors, and social activities. For the location of a chapter in your area, call HFES at the number below.

Technical Meetings

The five-day annual meeting of the Human Factors and Ergonomics Society is held each fall and includes an extensive program featuring the latest research discoveries; methods for research, design, and training; panel discussions and debates on important issues in the field and in the practice of human factors; hands-on workshops by technical specialists; tours of technical and research facilities in the host city; and technical group meetings.

More than 100 lecture, panel, debate, symposium, demonstration, and special sessions are offered. Published proceedings are available at the meeting, representing the work of more than 300 member and nonmember contributors.

HFES members receive substantial discounts on meeting registration. The proceedings are included in the registration fee.

To receive information about joining HFES, contact the Society at:

Human Factors and Ergonomics Society
P.O. Box 1369
Santa Monica, CA 90406-1369 USA
310/394-1811
Fax 310/394-2410

Notes

Notes

Notes